W9-DIM-910

Fifth Edition

MENTAL RETARDATION
A Life Cycle Approach

CLIFFORD J. DREW, PH.D.
Associate Dean for Research, Graduate School of Education
Professor, Departments of Special Education and Educational Psychology
University of Utah, Salt Lake City, Utah

DONALD R. LOGAN, D.ED.
Professor and Chair, Exceptional Education Department
State University College of New York at Buffalo
Adjunct Professor, State University of New York at Buffalo

MICHAEL L. HARDMAN, PH.D.
Professor and Chair, Department of Special Education
University of Utah, Salt Lake City, Utah

Merrill, an imprint of
MACMILLAN PUBLISHING COMPANY
New York

MAXWELL MACMILLAN CANADA
Toronto

MAXWELL MACMILLAN INTERNATIONAL
New York Oxford Singapore Sydney

Cover art: Kathy Hickey, student at Southeast School, Columbus (Franklin County Board of Mental Retardation and Developmental Disabilities)
Editor: Ann Castel
Production Editor: Jan Mauer
Art Coordinator: Ruth A. Kimpel
Photo Editor: Gail L. Meese
Text Designer: Anne Flanagan
Production Buyer: Patricia A. Tonneman

This book was set in Clearface by Carlisle Communications, Ltd. and was printed and bound by Book Press, Inc., a Quebecor America Book Group Company. The cover was printed by Lehigh Press, Inc.

Macmillan Publishing Company
866 Third Avenue
New York, NY 10022

Macmillan Publishing Company is part of the Maxwell Communication Group of Companies.

Maxwell Macmillan Canada, Inc.
1200 Eglington Avenue East, Suite 200
Don Mills, Ontario M3C 3N1

Library of Congress Cataloging-in-Publication Data
Drew, Clifford J., 1943–
    Mental retardation, a life cycle approach / Clifford J. Drew, Donald R. Logan, Michael L. Hardman. — 5th ed.
        p.   cm.
    Includes bibliographical references.
    Includes index.
    ISBN 0-675-21357-6 : $35.95
    1. Mentally handicapped.   2. Mental retardation.
    3. Mentally handicapped—United States.
        I. Logan, Don R., 1931– . II. Hardman, Michael L.
        III. Title.
    [DNLM: 1. Mental Retardation.   WM 300 D776m]
HV3004.D73   1992
362.3—dc20
DNLM/DLC
for Library of Congress   91-7491
                                                               CIP

Printing: 1 2 3 4 5 6 7 8 9   Year: 2 3 4 5

Photo credits (all photographs are copyrighted by individuals or companies listed): 408, 424, AP/Wide World Photos; 373, Edgar Bernstein; 51, 64, 104, 275, 312, Andy Brunk/Macmillan; 390, Children's Hospital, Columbus, Ohio; 287 Cuyahoga County Board of Mental Retardation; 167, Mary Elenz-Tranter; 57, Rohn Engh/Sunrise Photos; 5, 99, Kevin Fitzsimmons; 154, Kevin Fitzsimmons/Macmillan; 397, Jo Hall/Macmillan; 71, Tom Hutchinson/Macmillan; 44, 185, 237, 428, Bruce Johnson/Macmillan; 33, Lloyd Lemmerman; 92, 291, 315, Lloyd Lemmerman/Macmillan; 25, 353, Macmillan; 244, Marjorie McEachron/Macmillan; 16, Gail Meese/Macmillan; 304, Ohio Department of Administrative Services; 119, Photo Researchers/Petit Format; 2, Michael Siluk; 136, John Telford; 385, Cathy Watterson; 213, 278, Randall Williams/Macmillan; 146, Allen Zak; 82, 172, 232, 270, 342, 362, Gale Zucker.

PREFACE

As you begin your reading of *Mental Retardation: A Life Cycle Approach,* we would like to give some perspective regarding what you will encounter. Our intent is to provide an introduction to mental retardation that is both readable and comprehensive. As suggested by the title, this volume is strongly based in human development. One of our reviewers termed it "womb to tomb." You will follow the development of individuals with mental retardation from conception through birth, infancy, and early childhood, then through the elementary-school, adolescent, and adult years. You will also examine these people as they become old. Mental retardation is a field in which this complete cycle of human life is important for a full understanding of the problems and issues involved.

Our intent is also to discuss the field of mental retardation from the perspective of many disciplines. A diagnosis of mental retardation and subsequent intervention may come from any of several disciplines and often requires their collaboration. Consequently, it is important to examine interdisciplinary effort and its impact on the person with mental retardation to see how society and its various agencies respond to, interact with, and assist these people and their families.

This text is designed primarily for students in the social and behavioral sciences who are at the upper division undergraduate or beginning graduate level. Students in psychology, educational psychology, special education, sociology, education, rehabilitation, and social work will find the book particularly relevant to their preparation. Pre-med students and individuals anticipating professional work in nursing, law, and administration will also find a great deal that facilitates their careers.

Changes in This Edition

This edition includes a new chapter on multicultural issues as they relate to mental retardation. Such factors as language differences, migrancy, diverse cultural mores, and poverty interact to make cultural diversity a difficult and complex matter for professionals working in the field of mental retardation. In addition to material in this chapter, other topics relevant to multicultural issues, such as assessment bias, are integrated throughout the text.

Viewing this book purely from the standpoint of volume of material, certain areas have achieved a maturity that permit a more complete attainment of our original goals for the text. For example, the text is, and always has been, focused on the full cycle of human development. Consequently, as the body of research on infants, toddlers, and adults with mental retardation has grown, our examination of these individuals has expanded. The commitment to analyzing mental retardation within the conceptual framework of human development remains and is much more complete in this edition than was possible when we wrote the first edition 17 years ago.

Our purpose for this version is largely the same as it was with the release of the first edition. As authors, we hope that we have refined our skills and come closer to achieving the dream we had from the outset. Additionally, the field has changed, and new topics have emerged as knowledge accumulated and societal emphases fluctuated. We have tried to reflect those changes while also retaining the fundamentals.

In addition to the basic information presented in the text, there are a number of pedagogical features to engage the reader actively, facilitate a more complete understanding of the material, and provide instructors with a wider variety of teaching options. Each chapter begins with core concepts to be found in the text. Each core concept is repeated where it is discussed and, finally, is related to core questions designed to promote student comprehension. At the end of each chapter is a round table discussion section that presents an issue or topic of interest in a format aimed at stimulating dialogue. All these features have been incorporated to encourage active participation and interaction with the material.

Acknowledgments

The changes in this edition were made based on suggestions from many sources and on our own observations of growth within the field. We are most appreciative for the guidance provided by our reviewers, colleagues, and students, who have contributed immensely to the development of this project. To those of you who gave so generously of your time reviewing earlier versions of this manuscript, we thank you. In particular we appreciate the assistance of Richard B. Denver, Indiana University; William L. Jones, Bloomsbury University; Susan Rosenkoetter, Associated Colleges of Central Kansas; Tes Mehring, Emporia State University; Peter R. Matthews, Lock Haven University; L. G. Hayes, William Patterson College. Their meticulous review of the manuscript and cogent comments helped greatly.

We are particularly grateful for the extraordinary help provided by Lisa Roosendaal in all phases of book preparation—Lisa, thank you! Finally, for the extra help in reading the manuscript when we couldn't find time, for accepting our frequent claims of fatigue, for providing encouragement, support, and generally putting up with us, we once again thank our families. The type of suffering they put up with may probably be found somewhere in our chapter on ethical concerns.

Clifford J. Drew
Donald R. Logan
Michael L. Hardman

CONTENTS

CHAPTER THREE
A Multidisciplinary Viewpoint   64

CHAPTER FOUR
Theories of Intelligence   82

CHAPTER FIVE
Assessment Issues and Procedures   104

PART TWO
Early Life and Preschool Years   145

CHAPTER SIX
Basic Principles of Early Development   146

PART FOUR
The Adult with Mental Retardation

CHAPTER ELEVEN
The Adult with Mental Retardation

PART ONE
Introduction

CHAPTER ONE

Concepts, Definitions, and Classifications

■ The concept of mental retardation is made more complex because the varying disciplines that deal with it hold widely divergent viewpoints.

■ Definitions of mental retardation have changed over the years as behavioral science has grown, become more complex, and included attention to broader aspects of the environment.

■ It is important to distinguish between incidence and prevalence and to consider other factors, such as SES, severity, and age, when determining how frequently mental retardation occurs.

■ Definitions and classifications of mental retardation have varied greatly over the years according to the factors receiving attention and the age groups of primary concern.

■ Parameters or bases of classification for mental retardation have differed a great deal over time.

■ Parameters of classification are often fluid and in some cases implicit, rather than explicit and well thought out.

■ Cross-categorical definition and classification models have emerged because conventional categories are not always effective and functional.

■ The purposes and uses of definition and classification schemes must be considered and related to assessment procedures employed and to the impact of labels.

■ New issues and future directions in the definition and classification of mental retardation may include a better balance between individual and environmental factors.

We are all aware that people differ greatly in many ways, yet for the most part we recognize a range of variability that we consider "normal." Behaviors and other characteristics in the normal range are not so extreme that they attract great attention. Outside this range the differences are extreme enough to attract attention. People have been interested in individuals with physical, mental, and behavioral differences that exceed normal variability at least since the beginning of recorded history. The perspectives that religion, psychology, education, and various branches of medicine offer on such phenomena have been prominent throughout history, and perceptions of abnormality have varied widely over time and from one discipline to another (Mahendra, 1985). Definitions and concepts of abnormality still differ and will probably continue to change as our knowledge expands and societal values shift. Like that of other disorders, the history of mental retardation has followed a changing path.

What is mental retardation? Such a question seems simple, yet it has plagued educators, psychologists, and other professionals for many years. Like questions in many areas of behavioral science, its simplicity is deceiving; any complete answer is highly complex. The literature about mental retardation shows that the response to this question has received much attention, particularly during the past 35 years. This chapter examines past and present concepts, definitions, and classification systems of mental retardation. By reviewing the material in this and the following chapters, the reader will have a good overview of mental retardation. Mental retardation is a multi-faceted phenomenon. It challenges education, medicine, psychology, law, society in general, and always the family involved. In this volume we have attempted to place mental retardation in its broadest perspective—squarely in the center of human existence—because above all, mental retardation is a human problem. It cannot be viewed from a narrow focus if one wishes to obtain an accurate and comprehensive perspective.

This chapter's primary emphasis is on the definition and classification concepts used in the United States. The chapter also provides students of mental retardation with

Beyond its implications for social institutions, mental retardation is a human problem that affects this child and all of us.

information on other approaches and a comparison of them. Appendix A (pp. 446–453) presents a brief overview of definitions and classifications used in other countries and a comparative picture of how they relate to those used in the United States.

MENTAL RETARDATION AS A CONCEPT

Core Concept	*The concept of mental retardation is made more complex because the varying disciplines that deal with it hold widely divergent viewpoints.*

The literature on mental retardation suggests strongly that conceptual issues are complex and somewhat unclear (Barnett, 1986; Tarjan, 1989). Professionals often respond to an initial request to define mental retardation by discussing what it is *not* and describing causes. Clarifying the concept of mental retardation has become increasingly complex as many previously unknown factors are taken into account.

Historical interest in mental retardation predates interest in many other handicapping conditions. Hippocrates and Confucius provided descriptions of mental retardation that date back to several hundred years B.C. Some believe that mental retardation was implicitly included in legal codes perhaps as long ago as 2500 B.C. (Scheerenberger, 1983). If people have been paying attention to it for so long, why do confusion and vagueness about the classification and definition of mental retardation still remain?

Many different factors contribute to this lack of precision and definition. Mental retardation always implies a reduced level of intelligence, and the concept of intelligence has played a central role in the definition of mental retardation. Every controversy about the nature of intelligence has a direct impact on the field of mental retardation, so part of the difficulty in defining mental retardation relates to the notion of permanence and measurement of intelligence.

Mental retardation has always been an area of interest and study for many disciplines, a fact that has contributed significantly to the problems of definitional and conceptual clarity. There has never been a legitimate science of mental retardation independent of other disciplines. Psychiatrists, sociologists, psychologists, educators, anthropologists, and many others—each with a different perspective and language—have all addressed the problem of mental retardation. The many different definitions and classification systems of these disciplines often tend to focus on the constructs of a particular profession rather than on the individual with the problem. Sociologists set out to study retardation as a social problem, psychologists examine it as a psychological problem, physicians treat it as a medical problem, and so on. There are even wide variations evident within professional areas, such as clinical, developmental, and experimental psychology (Kopp & Krakow, 1983). We do not intend to deny the value of a multidisciplinary approach to any problem; in fact we strongly subscribe to its worth. We do wish, however, to highlight the fact that the central conceptual focus, the individual with mental retardation, is in danger of being ignored. We intend to present mental retardation from a multidisciplinary perspective while maintaining a focus on the concept of the individual affected.

The absence of a single core conceptualization of mental retardation that is both logically and theoretically sound and still functional has seriously detracted from the preparation of professionals who work with those with retardation. Although a high degree of sophistication has been developed in certain technical aspects of programming for children (for example, diagnosis, behavioral control), the lack of an effective generic concept of mental retardation has impeded the overall progress of service delivery to these people. Professional expertise often consists of a great deal of technical skill in certain areas but a limited amount of knowledge about mentally retarded individuals in their total environment. Efforts are now under way to formulate conceptual frameworks that will facilitate more effective professional preparation. Individuals with mental retardation must be viewed as developing human beings with varying needs and characteristics, living in a society with fluid and complex performance standards.

From our viewpoint, there is a conceptual cornerstone that facilitates the exacting task of viewing mental retardation across disciplines, causes, and the full range of human life—*human development.* This book rests on this conceptual cornerstone, and its title—*A Life Cycle Approach*—derives from it. As you read this volume you will find that its overall structure is the life cycle, from conception through old age. Certain topics tend to stand somewhat alone, and in most cases, you will find mini-discussions of those topics in the context of development. We hope that the perspective of human development will be as useful and interesting to you as you examine the complex and fascinating study of mental retardation as it has been to us.

DEFINITION OF MENTAL RETARDATION

Core Concept	*Definitions of mental retardation have changed over the years as behavioral science has grown, become more complex, and included attention to broader aspects of the environment.*

Definitions of mental retardation have varied widely over the years and from discipline to discipline. Considerable agreement currently exists among the general definitions in use. The American Association on Mental Retardation (AAMR)* definition has basically been adopted by the American Psychiatric Association and is also nearly intact in the Federal Rules and Regulations for Public Law 94-142. The AAMR definition of mental retardation involves two main dimensions—adaptive behavior and measured intelligence. The most recent AAMR definition states that "mental retardation refers to

---

*The American Association on Mental Retardation (AAMR) was named the American Association on Mental Deficiency (AAMD) prior to 1987. For the sake of consistency we refer to the association as the AAMR throughout the text. Citations of publications by the association in reference lists vary depending on date of publication.

significantly subaverage general intellectual functioning existing concurrently with deficits in adaptive behavior and manifested during the developmental period" (Grossman, 1983, p. 1). The following statements illustrate the similarities in current definitions:

> "Mentally retarded" means having significantly subaverage general intellectual functioning existing concurrently with deficits in adaptive behavior and manifested during the developmental period. (Proposed Regulations, 1982, p. 33, 485)
>
> The essential features are: (1) significantly subaverage general intellectual functioning, accompanied by (2) significant deficits or impairments in adaptive behavior, with (3) onset before the age of 18. (American Psychiatric Association, 1987, p. 28)

The AAMR has attempted to enhance the clarity of concepts in its definition. Important terms have been specifically defined in the published manual. For convenience, these definitions have been excerpted and are presented in the box on page 9. Although subscription to the importance of adaptive behavior in mental retardation is long-standing, *measurement* of adaptive behavior has not achieved the desired precision in spite of great efforts in this area (Frankenberger & Harper, 1988; Kamphaus, 1987). Yet adaptive behavior remains a very important concept and point of consideration in the mental retardation field. Other areas of exceptionality (for example, learning disabilities) have also begun to consider adaptive behavior in attempting a more complete assessment of factors contributing to differences.

Including adaptive behavior in definitions during the early 1960s represented a rather dramatic broadening of formally stated criteria for mental retardation, as professionals had largely ignored adaptive behavior in framing definitions for many years. The adaptive behavior criterion does, however, raise certain issues that may be relevant as attributes of mental retardation. Individuals' behaviors are considered adaptive by the degree to which they manage their personal needs, display social competence, and avoid problem behaviors (Bruininks & McGrew, 1987). Others may view a person who is retarded as an individual who relies on some type of action on the part of the community for protection or support. Two factors usually enter into this perception: (1) the deficits or level of functioning of the individual with retardation, and (2) the threshold of community tolerance. The kind of action taken depends on the degree to which an individual deviates significantly from community norms—from those zones of behavior or performance society deems acceptable.

People who are mentally retarded often come to the attention of someone in their community because their behavior deviates (or is thought likely to deviate) enough from the norm to be noticeable. This is true regardless of the degree of retardation. Identification of the individual who is more severely retarded may occur at birth or very early in life. This usually happens because some anomaly, either physical or behavioral, is already observable at this stage of development. For those who deviate less obviously from the norm, identification may not occur until much later, as they begin to develop language or enter school. Initial suspicions may then be further investigated through formal diagnostic evaluation and clinical observation by professional personnel. Details about diagnosis and evaluation are given later in this volume.

DEFINITION TERMINOLOGY:
American Association on Mental Retardation

Mental retardation refers to significantly subaverage general intellectual functioning resulting in or associated with concurrent impairments in adaptive behavior and manifested during the developmental period.

General intellectual functioning is operationally defined as the results obtained by assessment with one or more of the individually administered standardized general intelligence tests developed for that purpose.

Significantly subaverage is defined as IQ of 70 or below on standardized measures of intelligence. This upper limit is intended as a guideline; it could be extended upward through IQ 75 or more, depending on the reliability of the intelligence test used. This particularly applies in schools and similar settings if behavior is impaired and clinically determined to be due to deficits in reasoning and judgment.

Impairments in adaptive behavior are defined as significant limitations in an individual's effectiveness in meeting the standards of maturation, learning, personal independence, and/or social responsibility that are expected for his or her age level and cultural group, as determined by clinical assessment and, usually, standardized scales.

Developmental period is defined as the period of time between conception and the 18th birthday. Developmental deficits may be manifested by slow, arrested, or incomplete development resulting from brain damage, degenerative processes in the central nervous system, or regression from previously normal states due to psychosocial factors.

The following chart illustrates possible combinations of measured intellectual functioning and adaptive behavior. Retardation may occur through physical trauma or central nervous system deterioration at any age beyond the developmental period. When manifestations occur later, the condition is more properly classified as **dementia** (see DSM-III—Organic Mental Disorders).

MEASURED
INTELLECTUAL FUNCTIONING

	Retarded	Not retarded
ADAPTIVE BEHAVIOR — Retarded	Mentally retarded	Not mentally retarded
Not retarded	Not mentally retarded	Not mentally retarded

From *Classification in Mental Retardation* (pp. 11–15) by H. S. Grossman, 1983, Washington, DC: American Association on Mental Deficiency. Copyright 1983 by the American Association on Mental Deficiency. Reprinted by permission.

INCIDENCE AND PREVALENCE

Core Concept	*It is important to distinguish between incidence and prevalence and to consider other factors, such as SES, severity, and age, when determining how frequently mental retardation occurs.*

Two terms have frequently been confused in the field of mental retardation—incidence and prevalence. **Incidence** refers to the number of new cases identified during a given time period (often a year). Tabulating incidence involves a count of all individuals newly identified as retarded during that period, whether newborns or youngsters diagnosed in school. **Prevalence** refers to all cases existing at a given time, including both newly identified cases and cases still labeled as retarded from some earlier diagnosis. Figure 1–1 illustrates how incidence and prevalence differ and how they relate to each other. Obviously these two kinds of counting do not result in the same number. But the terms have often been used rather loosely, sometimes interchangeably, in the literature. Wherever possible, examine incidence and prevalence separately.

How frequently do individuals evidence sufficient deviancy to be considered mentally retarded? A precise answer to this question is difficult to obtain. Accurate accounting is neither easy nor economically feasible. Inconsistent definition and classification schemes over the years have made the problems of determining frequency of retardation even more formidable, particularly from a cross-cultural perspective (Gallagher, 1985). Estimates of the prevalence of mental retardation in the United States generally range from about 1% to 3% of the general population, with the 3% figure being most consistently cited (Grossman, 1983). Rantakallio and von Wendt (1986) found similar figures for *both* incidence and prevalence in an actual census study over a 14-year period in Northern Finland. In its Eleventh Annual Report to Congress (1989), the U.S. Department of Education estimated that 15% of the handicapped children in U.S. public schools are mentally retarded.

Translating estimated U.S. percentages into numbers of individuals with retardation is interesting, albeit difficult. Although most estimates are dated, the epidemiology of mental retardation has not changed fundamentally in more than 30 years (Fryers, 1987). Scheerenberger (1964) estimated that in 1964 there were about 5.4 million people with mental retardation in the United States. He projected that by 1970 there would be 6.5 million such individuals. The President's Task Force on the Mentally Handicapped (1970) estimated that six million Americans were mentally retarded. Which figures are accurate? We cannot choose with any degree of confidence. Figures like these defy confirmation because of the astronomical cost of a complete census of those with retardation.

Those in the mildly retarded range represent by far the largest proportion of the retarded population. Grossman (1983) estimated that about 2.5% of the total population was mildly retarded. The moderate level of mental retardation, on the other hand, is generally thought to involve about 0.3% of the total population, and the severe and profound levels combined account for approximately 0.1%. These figures do not total exactly 3%, although they are close. Recent estimates suggest that about 90% of people with mental retardation function at the mild level (U.S. Department of Education, 1989).

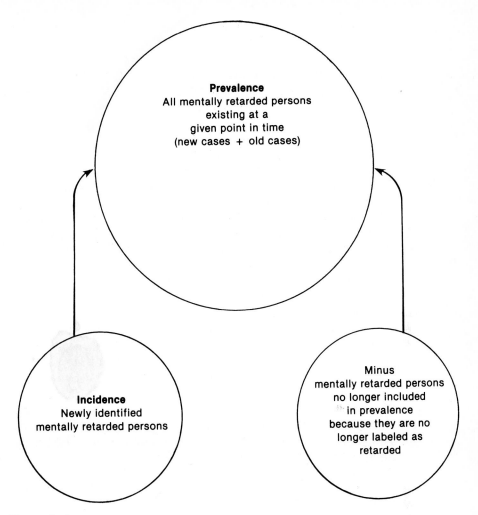

Figure 1–1
Incidence and prevalence of mentally retarded individuals

Some researchers have questioned the 3% prevalence figure. A hypothetical community of 100,000 was used by Tarjan, Wright, Eyman, and Keeran (1973) to generate estimates using both 1% and 3% levels. These authors found their 1% estimate to be quite similar to actual data collected by Mercer (1973a, 1973b) in a California community of 100,000. Interestingly, Mercer's data were collected during the mid-1960s, when the upper IQ limit for being classified as mentally retarded was 85. Tarjan et al. (1973) used an IQ of 70 as their upper limit. In other geographical settings some researchers have reported prevalence rates greater than 3%, while others have found less than 1% (e.g., Baird & Sandovnick, 1985; Cooper, Wilton, & Glynn, 1985). Many factors could contribute to the variations in rates of prevalence and incidence. Although estimates have been relatively stable recently, some controversy continues (Baird & Sandovnick, 1986; Richardson, Koller, & Katz, 1986).

Considerable variation is found in the incidence of mental retardation as one views different chronological age levels. Research has consistently indicated that the incidence of retardation is highest during the school years, approximately 5 to 18 years, with much lower numbers both at preschool and at postschool levels. This distribution relates both to the level of retardation and to the tasks presented to the individual at different ages. Before children enter the formal school environment, all but the more severely handicapped can perform as expected. Youngsters identified as being retarded before about age six are often moderately, severely, and profoundly retarded—levels of retardation that constitute only a small percentage of all retarded individuals. As children enter school, they encounter a concentrated emphasis on abstract learning, such as the acquisition of academic skills. In such an environment children with retardation become highly visible, since abstract skills are their area of greatest difficulty. The majority of youngsters identified as having retardation at this stage function in the mild range of intellectual deficit. The identification of cases of mental retardation decreases dramatically in people whose formal schooling has ended. The majority of individuals with mental retardation have been identified by the time they leave school. If no one has so identified an individual during the school years, when tasks emphasize abstraction, identification is unlikely to occur in the less demanding postschool environment.

The prevalence of mental retardation also varies a great deal as a function of age. Table 1–1 presents data based on the overall 1% estimates by Tarjan et al. (1973). Although estimated, these data agree with actual prevalence data collected by Mercer (1973a, 1973b). Estimated prevalence figures in Table 1–1 differ considerably as a function of both age and IQ. The total figures across all IQs reveals that by far the highest prevalence occurs in the six to 19 age range (68.8% of the population with mental retardation). The pattern of prevalence is similar for those who are retarded but have IQs of 50 and above, except that there is an even higher percentage falling in the six to 19 age range (80%) and smaller percentages in the preschool and postschool ranges. Several factors contribute to this pattern. The years of formal schooling are particularly taxing for those with mental retardation because the tasks require concep-

Table 1–1

Estimated prevalence of mental retardation in a community of 100,000 as a function of IQ and age (overall prevalence of 1%)

IQ	Age (years)				
	0 to 5	*6 to 19*	*20 to 24*	*25 +*	*Total*
0–19	8	18	4	20	50
20–49	36	70	20	74	200
50 +	25	600	25	100	750
TOTAL	69	688	49	194	1000

Adapted from "Natural History of Mental Retardation: Some Aspects of Epidemiology" by G. Tarjan, S. W. Wright, R. K. Eyman, and C. V. Keeran, 1973, *American Journal of Mental Deficiency, 77,* p. 370. Copyright 1973 by the American Association on Mental Deficiency. Reprinted by permission.

tual performance in areas in which they are most deficient. The drop in prevalence after school years is interesting and occurs for reasons related to but somewhat different from incidence influences. After formal education, many individuals with retardation (particularly those in the 50 + IQ range) are placed back in an environment where the demands focus less on their areas of greatest difficulty. They seem more able to adapt in the postschool environment. In addition to a lower incidence during postschool years, prevalence is also reduced because some individuals may no longer be functioning as retarded and are thus "declassified." This has often been referred to as the phenomenon of "disappearing" or "six-hour" retardation (referring to the time spent in school each day). This may indicate that the school curriculum is out of phase with later life and may not represent effective education, at least for these people.

The prevalence patterns in Table 1-1 also differ as a function of age for the lower IQ ranges. A much lower rate of prevalence occurs in children between the ages of six and 19. This pattern is influenced by a higher incidence during the early years of life and a higher mortality rate among more severely retarded individuals when they are young. (As you look at the data in Table 1-1, keep in mind that the age-range categories do not include the same intervals. This affects the percentages, but the data do reflect the general pattern of prevalence.)

Finally, mental retardation prevalence also varies across different levels of socioeconomic status (SES). Various estimates have suggested considerable prevalence differences as a function of SES and degree of impairment. Table 1-2 summarizes approximate prevalence rates of retardation per 1,000 school-age children by educational classification and community SES level. As indicated in Table 1-2, no difference appears in prevalence as a function of SES level at the dependent and trainable levels of impairment. The educable and slow-learner levels, however, show an increasing prevalence as SES decreases. These figures suggest that in the lower levels of retardation,

Table 1-2
Retardation prevalence per 1,000 school-age children by education classification and community SES level*

	Socioeconomic status		
Degree of impairment	*High*	*Middle*	*Low*
Totally dependent (IQ below 20)	1	1	1
Trainable (IQ 20 to 50)	4	4	4
Educable (IQ 50 to 75 or 80)	10	25	50
Slow learner (IQ 75 or 80 to 90)	50	170	300

*IQ ranges are given for the convenience of the reader. They represent approximate ranges that vary to some degree depending on the source of data.

where greater central nervous system damage pervades, different SES levels are equally vulnerable. The prevalence of milder impairments seems more sensitive to environmental influences. Since the majority of individuals with retardation are mildly impaired, the social dimensions of mental retardation stand out.

DEFINITION AND CLASSIFICATION: HISTORICAL BACKGROUND

Core Concept	*Definitions and classifications of mental retardation have varied greatly over the years according to the factors receiving attention and the age groups of primary concern.*

Over the years both definitions and classification systems of mental retardation have changed considerably. Definitions have been problematic from at least two standpoints. First, an historical examination of definitions indicates that early views focused on adults to the relative exclusion of other age groups. Second, it has been difficult to determine which factors should be included in a definition of mental retardation. Professional disagreement has abounded on this point, which also relates to classification. To classify any phenomenon, we must have some basis or bases for placing one individual in a certain category and another in a different one. These bases for identifying or grouping individuals have been termed **parameters** of definition and classification (Hardman, Drew, & Egan, 1984). Different parameters (bases) for viewing behavior as retarded have been employed over the years and have emerged in both definition and classification schemes.

Definitions

At least two factors have been prominent in the history of changes in mental retardation definitions. These are: (1) the ages involved, and (2) the definitional parameters included. Both warrant examination here.

For What Ages?

Early definitions of mental retardation varied to some degree with respect to age focus. Tredgold (1937) defined the condition of the adult with retardation in the following manner:

> A state of incomplete mental development of such a kind and degree that the individual is incapable of adapting himself to the normal environment of his fellows in such a way as to maintain existence independently of supervision, control or external support (p. 4).

Nearly 20 years later Benda (1954) gave the following definition of the mentally retarded adult:

> A mentally defective person is a person who is incapable of managing himself and his affairs, or being taught to do so, and who requires supervision, control, and care for his own welfare and the welfare of the community. (p. 115)

These types of approaches, with their emphasis on adult behavior, were particularly troublesome for professionals who were primarily inclined to work with children. Doll's (1941) perspective was in obvious contrast in that it highlighted the appearance of the handicap as a developmental phenomenon. Although other controversies revolved around Doll's work, it was an important forerunner of work on the chronological age dimension. Doll addressed the issue of mental retardation in childhood, but he also included the adult with retardation in his definition. He was specific in stating that retardation represented a mental subnormality that "has been developmentally arrested" and that "obtains at maturity." Consideration of the full range of chronological ages is essential to addressing the retardation problem, as is becoming increasingly important today.

In 1957 a project was begun under commission from the AAMR. The purpose of this activity (part of a larger project on technical planning in mental retardation) was to develop a manual of definition and classification terminology concerned with retardation. The resulting product was adopted as a formal definition by the AAMR (Heber, 1961). This definition has undergone refinement over the years (Grossman, 1973, 1977, 1983), and its current form appears on page 9. The AAMR statement (1961 and revisions) represented several significant changes in the definition and classification of mental retardation. It specifically addresses the problem of chronological age. It approaches mental retardation from a developmental framework but also attends to the adult who is retarded within the concept of adaptive behavior. Although it is similar to Doll's definition in including both children and adults, its terminology differs, and it avoids other definitional problems like incurability.

What Should Be Included?

A second problem area has been the inclusion or exclusion of particular definitional parameters. A number of these factors have changed over the years (either appearing or disappearing). Current literature still reflects strong differences of opinion about what should be included in the definition of mental retardation (see Barnett, 1986; Hodapp & Zigler, 1986; Zigler, Balla, & Hodapp, 1984).

Social Adaptation   Many efforts to define mental retardation have, in one fashion or another, included concepts of social adaptation or adjustment. These have reflected professional consensus that mental retardation is more than a low measured intelligence. But despite apparent conceptual agreement, professionals have begun to move toward formal functional measurement of social adaptation only in the last 25 years. Although sporadic attempts were made to assess other behavioral dimensions, measured intelligence long served as the primary criterion for mental retardation. Even after the inclusion of adaptive behavior in formal definitions, its measurement and use in diagnosis lagged. In some quarters, measured intelligence is still the preeminent, if not the sole, criterion. Questions about the relative roles of intelligence and social adaptation are of continuing interest (Barnett, 1986; Hodapp & Zigler, 1986; Zigler, Balla, & Hodapp, 1984).

Constitutional Origin   A number of definitional problems were caused by two factors that appeared periodically and repeatedly during the evolution of mental retardation definitions. These are best exemplified by Doll's (1941) definition, which specifically

Social adaptation is currently an important element in the definition of mental retardation.

stated that mental subnormality "is of constitutional origin" and "is essentially incurable." These two criteria generated considerable debate. Although not clearly defined, Doll's discussion of constitutional origin centered on the idea of pathology as the cause of mental deficiency. He specified that this could involve inherited biological problems or developmental alterations that biologically generate mental retardation.

A constitutional origin requirement posed particular difficulties for those with retardation who did not present identifiable etiology. With the group called *cultural-familial*, adherence to a criterion of constitutional origin required one of two decisions. Either this group, for which constitutional origin could not be identified, should not be considered retarded, or it must be assumed that an unidentifiable constitutional origin exists. Both alternatives present problems. The first tends to ignore the greater proportion of the population that functions at a retarded level. If taken literally, this approach could deter delivery of much-needed services to these persons. The second alternative sets a basic premise of the definition on extremely weak and vulnerable ground. In more recent thinking there is consensus that the constitutional origin criterion is too restrictive and cannot serve well in a functional conceptualization of mental retardation.

Incurability   Incurability as a definitional requirement for mental retardation has now met a fate similar to that of constitutional origin. In past years, however, this concept was all too often endorsed. One of the difficulties was that the idea of incurability contributed to a pessimistic attitude about the expenditure of effort and resources for work with the retarded population. Although a more optimistic attitude is spreading, some would still relegate allocation of resources for those with mental retardation to the lowest priority.

Incurability also presented logical difficulties in situations where an earlier evaluation caused a diagnosis of mental retardation, but a later evaluation did not support the diagnosis. This situation may exist because of a number of specific factors but generally involves two broad possibilities. First an error could have distorted either of the measurements. Second, the individual was mentally retarded at the time of the earlier evaluation, but because of changes between the measurements (for example, specific instruction or maturation), retardation no longer existed at the time of the second evaluation.

Regardless of the cause, individuals did seem to surface as mentally retarded at one point but not at another. Strict adherence to the concept of incurability was not possible because by definition, no reversal could occur. Consequently a complementary concept of pseudoretardation evolved (sometimes termed pseudofeeblemindedness in the early literature), an example of the need to explain or strengthen weak logic by the development of compensatory concepts. Often, as with pseudoretardation, these compensatory concepts were equally weak and lacking in sound logic. The concept of pseudofeeblemindedness required two offsetting inferences: errors in diagnosis and the difference between an existing condition and some "true" mental retardation. Pseudofeeblemindedness is not a relevant concept for use in cases of error in diagnosis. An error in measurement is just that—an error in measurement. It is much sounder logic to recognize it as such than to spend time searching for a clinical entity as an excuse.

Equally weak was the view that pseudofeeblemindedness represented a clinical condition different from some "true" mental retardation. The idea that there exists "true" mental retardation (and thus "false" or pseudoretardation) is cumbersome, to say the least. First, it implies that there are agreed-upon, identifiable causes. Such an implication relates to the criterion of constitutional origin, whose weakness has already been discussed. Second, the situation of retardation at an earlier point but not at a later point defies the incurability concept: The individual must not have been retarded at the first measurement, or retardation would have also been present at the second.

The complexity of these interrelated concepts was magnified by a controversy that was occurring simultaneously in the field of measured intelligence. The question at issue was a long-standing one and involved whether intelligence tests assess functioning or potential capacity. More recent trends in professional consensus favor functioning, although the issue is not completely dead. Interpretation of intelligence scores as measures of functioning dramatically clarifies the issues involved with incurability, pseudoretardation, and, more generally, the definition of mental retardation.

If intelligence is viewed as behavioral functioning, it is quite reasonable to expect situations in which an individual functions as mentally retarded at one time and not at another. Intervening experiences may have altered the level of functioning on the second measure so that the person does not exhibit a behavioral deficit. Such a viewpoint denies the incurability criterion and makes the concept of pseudoretardation unnecessary.

One of the important departures that the AAMR definition (Grossman, 1983) makes from the general trend of early definitional efforts is the formalization of a position concerning the framework from which intelligence measures are viewed. The definition specifically rejects the principle of potential intelligence and views mental status as representative of behavioral functioning level at the time of assessment. These changes in definitional position do not mean that professionals now uniformly view all mental retardation as curable. Such a position is unrealistic. But the requirement of incurability has been largely discarded from definitions because it is a nonfunctional perspective on the broad problem of mental retardation. The evolution of definition and philosophy has made two major advances. First, mental retardation is on much firmer conceptual ground than it was. Second, changes in the AAMR definition legitimate the conceptual framework by bringing it more in harmony with the realities of mental retardation as viewed in the community.

Comments   Despite advances, definitions of mental retardation still face philosophical problems that affect research, diagnosis, and decisions about services (Baumeister, 1987). Perhaps the most serious problem is simple and obvious. It does not seem efficacious to spend time and effort defining mental retardation without asking, "What is the purpose of this definition?" The purpose of definition, of course, was not completely ignored. Each of the early workers to define mental retardation was progressing in a given area of interest, probably with objectives clearly in mind. These purposes were, however, most likely in line with the definer's effort and not necessarily attentive to the broader problems of mental retardation. We believe that the confusion evident in the historical development of an encompassing definition of mental retardation is characteristic of an effort proceeding without overall purpose or direction. Absence of overall purpose is perhaps most obvious in educational programming. A definition should be useful, or there is little reason to have it. Yet we often find that the definition of mental retardation is of questionable use for educational programming, a facet of services that touches a major proportion of the population diagnosed as having retardation. This issue surfaces again as we consider classification schemes, and it is discussed at length in chapters 9 and 10.

Classification

Core Concept	*Parameters or bases of classification for mental retardation have differed a great deal over time.*

The historical evolution of classification schemes for mental retardation has shown confusion in concept and direction nearly parallel to that of efforts at definition. Perhaps the most serious difficulty with all classification schemes relates to the choice of parameters for classification. This problem has been particularly troublesome in the mental retardation field, once again partly because of the wide variety of disciplines interested in the phenomenon. The purpose or objective underlying the classification process in different disciplines has generated other difficulties. For example, a given difference in purpose between school administrators and physicians does not necessarily mean that their classification schemes are mutually exclusive or in conflict. But compatibility or joint focus is rare.

Problems also arise when a system's parameters of classification are unclear or incompletely described. Categorization frequently emphasizes one parameter while simultaneously employing one or two others that seem to be added informally and imprecisely. The difficulty does not arise from using multiple parameters for classification, for mental retardation is a multifaceted problem. However, it is important in using a given scheme to be explicit and precise about the parameters, noting which are primary, which secondary, and which of decreasing importance. As Hardman et al. (1984) have stated:

> A given classification . . . represents a single photograph of a condition. What is recorded only represents a given behavior at a particular time and in a particular set of circumstances. Parameters of classification provide us with a powerful tool for analyzing various category systems. Some parameters are present in one or two systems, whereas others are used to a certain degree in several. The parameters are important because they allow us to view exceptionality *across* differing classification perspectives. (p. 72; emphasis added)

Core Concept	*Parameters of classification are often fluid and in some cases implicit, rather than explicit and well thought out.*

Parameters for Classification

The literature reveals that a wide variety of parameters has been used in different classification schemes. Parameters represent the basis or bases for classifying a condition or behavior. Although used with varying frequency, six general parameters seem to persist: (1) symptom severity, (2) symptom etiology, (3) syndrome description, (4) adaptive behavior, (5) educability expectations, and (6) behavioral manifestations. These parameters are not necessarily mutually exclusive, but often intersect. For example, symptom severity is frequently associated with measured intelligence in the area of mental retardation. But one may also look at adaptive behavior and behavioral manifestations in terms of the severity of functional deficits. Parameters may also intersect when a person is diagnosed as being mentally retarded. The AAMR requires such an intersection between symptom severity (in terms of measured intelligence) and adaptive behavior. (The AAMR also employs a symptom etiology parameter that is discussed later.) Figure 1–2 presents parameters of classification and illustrates how they may converge in a particular case of mental retardation. This conceptualization is

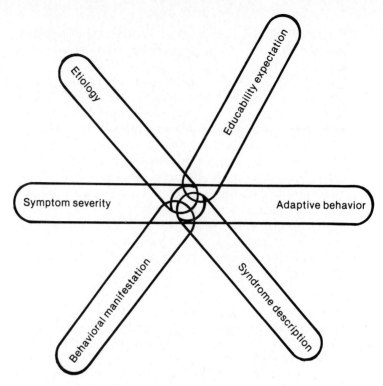

Figure 1–2
Parameters of classification

From *Human Exceptionality: Society, School, and Family* (p. 73) by M. L. Hardman, C. J. Drew, and M. W. Egan, 1984, Boston: Allyn & Bacon. Copyright 1984 by Allyn & Bacon, Inc. Reprinted by permission.

a flexible model; different parameters could be used in varying types of parameter intersections depending on the case and the system employed.

Symptom Severity   The most common criterion of symptom severity has been measured intelligence. Classification on this basis necessitates grouping individuals by IQ and then labeling the groups. For example, several early classifications used terms like *borderline retardate, moron, imbecile,* and *idiot.* Terman (1916) applied these labels to IQ unit groups of 70–79 for borderline, 50–69 for moron, 25–49 for imbecile, and 25 or below for idiot. Wechsler (1958) used the same terminology but with slightly different IQ units: 30–49 for imbecile and 29 or below for idiot. Use of the terms *moron, imbecile,* and *idiot* has been discontinued in the United States because of the words' negative connotations, but some of the literature from other countries continues to use these terms. Grouping by measured IQ remains pervasive, as is exemplified by the AAMR classification. Using the terms *mild, moderate, severe,* and *profound retardation,* the AAMR IQ units are based on the standard deviation of the test used. For example, on the revised Stanford-Binet test (standard deviation ± 15) these ranges are IQ 52 to 67, 36 to 51, 20 to 35, and below 20 for the four categories. Table 1–3 summarizes selected symptom severity classifications based on measured IQ for comparison purposes.

Symptom Etiology   Symptom etiology, the second general parameter, has primarily involved the biomedical aspects of mental retardation. It is most often viewed in a medical context and has often been called the medical classification. Three major systems have been instrumental in constructing the current view of etiological classi- fication in mental retardation: the World Health Organization's (WHO) *International Classification of Diseases* (ICD-9, 1978), the American Psychiatric Association's revised third edition of the *Diagnostic and Statistical Manual* (DSM-III-R, 1987), and the AAMR manual *Classification in Mental Retardation* (Grossman, 1983). Although not identical, the three systems are compatible with respect to etiology classification. The AAMR included the following 10 categories in its etiological classification:

1. Following infection and intoxication (e.g., congenital rubella, syphilis).
2. Following trauma or physical agent (e.g., mechanical injury at birth).
3. With disorders of metabolism or nutrition (e.g., phenylketonuria [PKU], galac- tosemia).
4. Associated with gross brain disease, postnatal (e.g., neurofibromatosis, intracranial neoplasm).
5. Associated with diseases and conditions resulting from unknown prenatal influence (e.g., hydrocephalus, microcephaly).
6. Associated with chromosomal abnormality (e.g., Down syndrome).
7. Associated with other perinatal (gestational) conditions (e.g., prematurity).
8. Following psychiatric disorder (e.g., autism).
9. Associated with environmental influences (e.g., cultural-familial retardation).
10. Associated with other conditions.

Approximately 75% to 85% of the total population of persons with mental retardation falls into categories 9 and 10. Categories 9 and 10 are miscellaneous groupings that specify the absence of verifiable structural characteristics. From this it is evident that the other categories, 1 through 8, often involve retardation associated with observable or at least verifiable existing characteristics. These eight etiological classifications ac- count for only 15% to 25% of all mental retardation. It is not surprising that earlier attempts at a definition based on visible characteristics encountered difficulty.

Syndrome Description   Another approach to classification involves the description of syndromes by symptom grouping. Like etiology, the syndrome description scheme is largely the province of medical workers. Observation of a pattern of both physical and behavioral characteristics usually results in identification of a syndrome, although physical descriptions have predominated.

The syndromes (for example, Down syndrome or mongolism, microcephaly, and hydrocephaly) are the stereotypes of mental retardation often held by people not work- ing in the field. Many people think of Down syndrome when mental retardation is

Table 1–3
Selected symptom severity classifications

Measured intelligence*

Source	90	80	70	60	50	40	30	20	10
Terman (1916)		Borderline—IQ 70 to 79		Moron—IQ 50 to 69		Imbecile—IQ 25 to 49		Idiot—IQ 24 or below	
Wechsler (1958)		Borderline—IQ 70 to 79		Moron—IQ 50 to 69		Imbecile—IQ 30 to 49		Idiot—IQ 29 or below	
American Association on Mental Deficiency (1961)		Borderline intelligence— −1 S.D., IQ 68 to 83		Mildly mentally retarded— −2 S.D., IQ 52 to 67		Moderately mentally retarded— −3 S.D., IQ 36 to 51		Severely mentally retarded— −4 S.D., IQ 20 to 35	Profoundly, mentally retarded— −5 S.D., IQ 19 or below
American Association on Mental Deficiency (1973, 1977, 1983)†				Mildly mentally retarded— −2 S.D., IQ 52 to 67		Moderately mentally retarded— −3 S.D., IQ 36 to 51		Severely mentally retarded— −4 S.D., IQ 20 to 35	Profoundly mentally retarded— −5 S.D., IQ 19 or below
American Psychiatric Association (1987)				Mildly mentally retarded— IQ 50 to 70		Moderately mentally retarded— IQ 35 to 49		Severely mentally retarded— IQ 20 to 34	Profoundly mentally retarded—IQ below 20

*IQ ranges from Stanford-Binet standard deviations (S.D.).

†The 1983 AAMR classifications placed a narrow band of IQ scores at each end of each level but are essentially the same as those in the table.

mentioned in a lay context. This may be because the defining characteristics for syndromes are often visible, or because the syndrome approach to classification has a long history. Syndrome names usually include either the name of the pioneering worker discovering the syndrome or the technical clinical terminology involved in diagnosis (for example, neurofibromatosis). Carter's (1978, 1979) volumes on medical aspects of mental retardation and the syndrome atlas by Gellis and Feingold (1968) contain detailed treatments of particular syndromes.

Adaptive Behavior   Adaptive behavior and concepts related to it have been involved in definition and classification for most of the history of effort in mental retardation. Only in about the past 35 years, however, have conceptualizations progressed far enough for adaptive behavior to be viewed by many as a parameter of classification, and even today there are a number of difficulties in using adaptive behavior to categorize individuals.

Much of the impetus for the current view of adaptive behavior came from the work of Sloan and Birch (1955). Their material was adapted for the AAMR *Manual on Terminology and Classification* in 1961 (Heber, 1961). Later revisions of this manual (Grossman, 1973, 1977, 1983) developed it further. One of the important factors in adaptive behavior as a classification parameter is that it attends to human development. Table 1–4 summarizes the illustrations of adaptive behavior levels by ages presented in Grossman (1983).

Adaptive behavior presents certain difficulties as a parameter of classification even today. If you refer to Table 1–4 you can see that adaptive behavior intersects with symptom severity at the mild, moderate, severe, and profound levels. This intersection led many to assume that deficits in adaptive behavior could be classified on the basis of standard deviation deficits, like measured intelligence. This assumption was corroborated by the fact that discussion of both parameters employed the same labels, and both appeared in the same document (the AAMR manual). Unfortunately, there were at least two problems with this reasoning: (1) adaptive behavior is only imperfectly correlated with intelligence (and evidence about the strength of the correlation is still inconclusive) and (2) the measurement of adaptive behavior is still under study. Its reliability, validity, standardization, cultural fairness, and scientifically established links to classification labels do not yet stand on firm ground (Coulter & Morrow, 1978; Iowa Task Force on Adaptive Behavior, 1981; Meyers, Nihira, & Zetlin, 1979). The importance of adaptive behavior is not in question. What has been and remains questionable is the establishment of an empirical base for assessment so that adaptive behavior can become more functional as a parameter of classification. It is clear that adaptive behavior must relate to various ages, environments, cultural milieus, and previous opportunities to learn, so that, even within this one parameter of classification, we find multiple elements for consideration.

Educability Expectations   Educability expectations have been viewed as a parameter of classification in the field of education for many years. This approach to classification is also known as the educational classification. Preference for including the term *expectation* is based on the form of this parameter, which is a statement or prediction of expected achievement. Generally there are three categories—educable, trainable, and custodial or severely

Table 1–4

Examples of adaptive behavior levels by age

Age and level indicated	Illustrations of highest level of adaptive behavior
Age 3 years and above: *profound* (NOTE: All behaviors at greater degree of impairment would also indicate *profound* deficit in adaptive behavior for persons 3 years of age or above.)	*Independent functioning:* Drinks from a cup with help; "cooperates" by opening mouth for feeding *Physical:* Sits unsupported or pulls self upright momentarily; reaches for objects; has good thumb-finger grasp; manipulates objects (plays with shoes or feet) *Communication:* Imitates sounds, laughs or smiles back (says "Da-da," "buh-buh" responsively); no effective speech; may communicate in sounds, gestures, or signs *Social:* Indicates knowing familiar persons and interacts non-verbally with them
Age 3 years: *severe* Age 6 years and above: *profound*	*Independent functioning:* Attempts finger feeding; "cooperates" with dressing, bathing, and toilet training; may remove clothing (socks) but not as an act of undressing as for bath or bed *Physical:* Stands alone or may walk unsteadily or with help; coordinates eye-hand movements *Communication:* One or two words (Mama, ball), but predominantly vocalization *Social:* May respond to others in predictable fashion; communicates needs by gestures and noises or pointing; plays "patty-cake"; plays imitatively with little interaction; occupies self alone with "toys" for a few minutes
Age 3 years: *moderate* Age 6 years: *severe* Age 9 years and above: *profound*	*Independent functioning:* Tries to feed self with a spoon with considerable spilling; removes socks, pants; "cooperates" in bathing, may indicate wet pants; "cooperates" at toilet *Physical:* Walks alone steadily; can pass ball or objects to others; may run and climb steps with help *Communication:* May use four to six words; may communicate many needs with gestures (pointing) *Social:* Plays with others for short periods, often as parallel play or under direction; recognizes others and may show preference for some persons over others
3 years: *mild* 6 years: *moderate* 9 years: *severe* 12 years and above: *profound*	*Independent functioning:* Feeds self with spoon (cereals, soft foods) with considerable spilling or messiness; drinks unassisted; can pull off clothing and put on some (socks, underclothes, boxer pants, dress); tries to help with bath or hand washing but still needs considerable help; indicates toilet accident and may indicate toilet need *Physical:* May climb up and down stairs but not alternating feet; may run and jump; may balance briefly on one foot; can pass a ball to others; transfers objects; may do simple formboard puzzles without aid *Communication:* May speak in two or three word sentences (Daddy go work); names simple common objects (boy, car, ice cream, hat); understands simple directions (put the shoe on your foot, sit

here, get your coat); knows people by name. If nonverbal, may use many gestures to convey needs or other information
Social: May interact with others in simple play activities, usually with only one or two others unless guided into group activity; has preference for some persons over others

6 years: *mild*
9 years: *moderate*
12 years and above: *severe*
15 years and above: *profound*

Independent functioning: Feeds self with spoon or fork, may spill some; puts on clothing but needs help with small buttons and jacket zippers; tries to bathe self but needs help; can wash and dry hands but not very efficiently; partially toilet trained but may have accidents
Physical: May hop or skip; may climb steps with alternating feet; rides tricycle (or bicycle over 8 years); may climb trees or jungle gym; plays dance games, may throw ball and hit target
Communication: May have speaking vocabulary of over 300 words and use grammatically correct sentences. If nonverbal, may use many gestures to communicate needs. Understands simple verbal communications including directions and questions ("Put it on the shelf," "Where do you live?") (Speech may be indistinct sometimes); may recognize advertising words and signs (ice cream, stop, exit, men, ladies); relates experiences in simple language
Social: Participates in group activities and simple group games; interacts with others in simple play ("store," "house") and expressive activities (art and dance)

9 years: *mild*
12 years: *moderate*
15 years and older: *severe*

Independent functioning: Feeds self adequately with spoon and fork; can butter bread; needs help with cutting meat; can put on clothes and can button and zipper clothes; may tie shoes; bathes self with supervision; is toilet trained; washes face and hands without help
Physical: Can run, skip, hop, dance; uses skates, sled, and jump rope; can go up and down stairs alternating feet; can throw ball to hit target
Communication: May communicate in complex sentences; speech is generally clear and distinct; understands complex verbal communication, including words such as "because" and "but." Recognizes signs, and words, but does not read prose material with comprehension
Social: May participate in group activities spontaneously; may engage in simple competitive exercise games (dodge ball, tag, races). May have friendship choices that are maintained over weeks or months
Economic activity: May be sent on simple errands and make simple purchases with notes; realizes money has value but does not know how to use it (except for coin machines)

Table 1–4, *continued*

Age and level indicated	Illustrations of highest level of adaptive behavior
	Occupation: May prepare simple foods (sandwiches); can help with simple household tasks (bedmaking, sweeping, vacuuming); can set and clear table *Self-direction:* May ask if there is "work" for him to do; may pay attention to task for 10 minutes or more; makes efforts to be dependable and carry out responsibility
12 years: *mild* 15 years and over: *moderate*	*Independent functioning:* Feeds, bathes, dresses self, may select daily clothing; may prepare easy foods (sandwiches) for self or others; combs and brushes hair; may shampoo and curl hair; may wash, iron, and store own clothes *Physical:* Good body control; good gross and fine motor coordination *Communication:* May carry on simple conversation; uses complex sentences. Recognizes words, may read sentences, ads, signs, and simple prose material with some comprehension *Social:* May interact cooperatively and competitively with others *Economic activity:* May be sent on shopping errands for several items without notes; makes minor purchases; adds coins to dollar with fair accuracy *Occupation:* May do simple routine household chores (dusting, garbage removal, dishwashing; preparing simple foods that require mixing) *Self-direction:* May initiate most of own activities; attends to task 15 to 20 minutes (or more); may be conscientious in assuming much responsibility
15 years and adult: *mild* (NOTE: Individuals who routinely perform at higher levels of competence in adaptive behavior than illustrated in this pattern should *not* be considered as deficient in adaptive behavior. Since by definition an individual is not retarded unless he shows significant deficit in *both* measured intelligence and in adaptive behavior, those individuals who function at higher levels than illustrated here cannot be considered to be retarded.)	*Independent functioning:* Exercises care for personal grooming, feeding, bathing, toilet; may need health or personal care reminders; may need help in selection and purchase of clothing *Physical:* Goes about home town (local neighborhood in city, campus at institution) with ease, but cannot go to other towns alone without aid; can use bicycle, skis, ice skates, trampoline, or other equipment requiring good coordination *Communication:* Communicates complex verbal concepts and understands them; carries on everyday conversation, but cannot discuss abstract or philosophical concepts; uses telephone and communicates in writing for simple letter writing or orders but does not write about abstractions or important current events *Social:* Interacts cooperatively or competitively with others and initiates some group activities, primarily for social or recreational purposes; may belong to a local recreational group or church group, but not to civic organizations or groups of

Age and level indicated	Illustrations of highest level of adaptive behavior
	skilled persons (photography club, great books club, or kennel club); enjoys recreation (bowling, dancing, TV, checkers, but either does not enjoy or is not competent at such activities as tennis, sailing, bridge, piano playing, or other hobbies requiring rapid, involved, or complex planning and implementation) *Economic activity:* Can be sent or can go to several shops to make purchases of several items without a note to shopkeepers; can make change correctly, but does not use banking facilities; may earn living but has difficulty handling money without guidance *Occupation:* Can cook simple foods, prepare simple meals, and perform everyday household tasks (cleaning, dusting, dishes, laundry); as adult can engage in semiskilled or simple skilled job *Self-direction:* Initiates most of own activity; will pay attention to task for at least 15 to 20 minutes; conscientious about work and assumes much responsibility but needs guidance for tasks with responsibility for major tasks (health care, care of others, complicated occupational activity)

Adapted from *Manual on Terminology and Classification in Mental Retardation* (pp. 25–33), edited by H. J. Grossman, 1977, Washington: American Association on Mental Deficiency. Copyright 1977 by the American Association on Mental Deficiency. Adapted by permission.

multiply handicapped (SMH)—although some professionals have included a fourth classification known as dull normal, which ranges just above educable in terms of measured IQ (approximately 75 or 80 to 90). Measured IQ ranges associated with the other categories include 50 to 75 or 80 for educable, 20 to 49 for trainable, and below 20 for SMH or custodial. Table 1–5 summarizes classifications by educational expectations.

Weaknesses are evident in most classification schemes, but educability expectations are vulnerable from a number of standpoints. These limitations are scrutinized and specifically addressed later in this chapter.

Behavioral Manifestations   The final classification parameter mentioned was for our purposes termed behavioral manifestations. This approach has been very popular in a number of areas of psychology as well as in several educational applications. It derives from applied behavior analysis and evaluates an individual based on observation of task performance. The behavioral description perspective differs conceptually from previously discussed classification schemes because it is not primarily concerned with grouping but focuses on the skills a person has or does not have (more precisely, to what

Table 1–5
Classification by educational expectation

Terminology	Approximate IQ range*	Educational expectation
Dull normal	IQ 75 or 80 to 90	Capable of competing in school in most areas, except in the strictly academic areas, in which performance is below average Social adjustment that is not noticeably different from the larger population's, although in the lower segment of adequate adjustment Occupational performance satisfactory in nontechnical areas, with total self-support highly probable
Educable	IQ 50 to 75 or 80	Second- to fifth-grade achievement in school academic areas Social adjustment that will permit some degree of independence in the community Occupational sufficiency that will permit partial or total self-support
Trainable	IQ 20 to 49	Learning primarily in the areas of self-help skills, very limited achievement in areas considered academic Social adjustment usually limited to home and closely surrounding area Occupational performance primarily in sheltered workshop or institutional setting
Custodial (SMH)	IQ below 20	Usually unable to achieve even sufficient skills to care for basic needs Will usually require nearly total care and supervision for duration of lifetime

*IQ ranges vary to some degree, depending on the source of data.

degree a task can be performed). Of greatest importance is individual skill level rather than placement in a category. This difference in approach deemphasizes norm-referenced or interindividual comparisons (one child's performance compared with others) and places assessment more in the context of an intraindividual or criterion-referenced framework (a child's performance compared with earlier performances).

Professionals who are strong proponents of behavioral analysis use behavioral manifestations as the only evaluation parameter. When this occurs, the behavioral manifestations parameter obviously does not intersect with other classification parameters. Traditional categories and labels are deemed unimportant in comparison to a precise description of behavioral status, which generates specific treatment intervention (instruction or behavior-shaping efforts aimed at enhancing skills). Many classification systems use behavioral descriptions of some type. In most systems, however, the behavioral description is a means by which one can determine a category and is secondary to the basic purpose of classification. As a single parameter, behavioral manifestation is a primary means of evaluation aimed at treating rather than categorizing.

The behavioral approach is particularly useful for educational programming, an area in which other frameworks have been weak. Yet it does not necessarily serve all purposes well. Administrative needs or determination and allocation of funds for programs make grouping and labeling necessary.

CROSS-CATEGORICAL ISSUES

Core Concept	*Cross-categorical definition and classification models have emerged because conventional categories are not always effective and functional.*

Mental retardation is one category among several that refer to atypical conditions involving ability or behavior. Others include such examples as learning disabilities and behavior disorders or emotional disturbance, among many more. The use of such categories has had a long history among professionals working in the various fields of disorders. Considerable interest has emerged in the literature regarding perspectives on disabilities that cross traditional categorical boundaries—often termed cross-categorical views (Hardman, Drew, Egan, & Wolf, 1990). Some authors contend that traditional categories do not adequately distinguish between different handicapping conditions and do not serve the needs of individuals from a service-delivery standpoint (Jenkins, Pious, & Peterson, 1988; Lilly, 1987; Reynolds & Birch, 1988). Unsurprisingly, some believe that cross-categorical views are not functional and see the traditional categories as being more appropriate (Braaten, Kauffman, Braaten, Polsgrove, & Nelson, 1988). The issues involved in categorical and cross-categorical approaches to defining disabilities have received substantial attention and continue to be controversial (Gartner & Lipsky, 1989; Lipsky & Gartner, 1989; Marston, 1987; Reynolds, Wang, & Walberg, 1987; Stainback, Stainback, & Forest, 1989).

Interest in cross-categorical definitions arose primarily because in certain circumstances the traditional categories did not clearly distinguish between people with disorders carrying different labels. In some instances those with disparate categorical labels did not appear all that different—they seemed to have a number of characteristics in common. Additionally, treatment or interventions for some individuals with different labels appeared to be quite similar, or at least to have a number of similar elements. What has become evident is that categorical terminology is functional for some purposes with some conditions, but that there are other circumstances where it does not serve well. It is important to give consideration to the purposes and uses of definition and classification schemes.

Hardman et al. (1990) developed a cross-categorical definition and classification model founded on the concept of symptom severity. These authors use the terms *mild learning and behavior disorders, moderate learning and behavior disorders,* and *severe and profound/multiple disorders.* Definitions for these broad categories include a range of ability and behavior deficits and a variety of assessment approaches; they address service delivery or intervention. While any framework of this nature is necessarily general, the focus of this scheme is on functional and behavioral specificity, articulated and evaluated for intervention purposes on an individualized basis. It is also clear that this particular cross-categorical model does not claim to supplant the conventional categories totally. The authors specify where disorders are distinctive and traditional categorical differentiation is relevant. But where categories do not serve well, the cross-categorical model diverges from such labels, emphasizing functional description of behavior and skill deficits and their prescriptive treatment.

Cross-categorical models appear most applicable to individuals who are mildly affected by a disability. People with mild mental retardation, mild behavior disorders, and mild learning disabilities have many shared characteristics (Hardman et. al., 1990). Youngsters at the mild disability level of functioning have a great deal of performance and skill overlap in the classroom, regardless of their specific labels (Jenkins et. al, 1988; Wang & Walburg, 1987). Service delivery from a cross-categorical model is most reasonable for these children (Forness & Kavale, 1984).

More severe disorders have greater distinctiveness, and conventional categories are more relevant. Individuals with moderate to severe disorders have fewer shared characteristics, although some remain, and these are typically acknowledged by cross-categorical models. Primary disabling conditions are more easily identified as impairment severity increases. People with more severe mental retardation are also more likely to be affected by multiple handicaps. This is particularly true for those at the lowest level of functioning. Those with profound mental retardation have a relatively high incidence of congenital heart disease, epilepsy, respiratory distress, sensory impairments, and poor muscle tone. From a definition or classification standpoint these are often viewed as associated conditions. From the perspective of intervention or treatment, each must be addressed on a case-by-case basis. Treatment is the ultimate outcome of any diagnosis and therefore of any definition or classification, irrespective of whether a conventional categorical or cross-categorical approach is used. An appropriate choice of classification scheme depends on the context of use.

PURPOSES AND USES OF DEFINITIONS AND CLASSIFICATIONS

Core Concept	*The purposes and uses of definition and classification schemes must be considered and related to assessment procedures employed and to the impact of labels.*

Definitions and classifications are developed for a variety of reasons. At times they provide a conceptual picture of the thing being defined or classified and facilitate communication between professionals. Beyond these roles, however, remains the vital reason for defining and classifying—the translation of statements into action.

The adequacy with which a classification scheme translates into practice is the acid test of the system. A number of factors influence the ease with which this translation can occur, of which two are particularly evident from the preceding discussion of definitions and classification. The first is how faithfully a scheme reflects reality; the second relates to how well the purposes or objectives of the group using a definition or classification are served.

If a classification or definition system is out of touch with actual circumstances, it is of questionable value and will probably fall into disuse. Perhaps the best example of such a situation in mental retardation involves the concepts of constitutional origin and incurability. Constitutional origin is out of phase with reality because it cannot be verified in many individuals who are functioning as retarded. This situation requires either that constitutional origin must be assumed or (if the definition is strictly adhered to) that services cannot legitimately be rendered. The idea of incurability is similarly out of harmony with reality, as is exemplified by the perceived necessity for a compensatory concept of pseudofeeblemindedness.

One must also consider the second factor: How well are the purposes or objectives of the group using a scheme served? Purposes and objectives have been nearly as numerous and diverse as the disciplines involved with mental retardation. Heber (1962) noted that mental retardation has historically been treated as "a social, administrative, and legal concept, rather than a scientific one." Current literature supports this statement, and the absence of discussions of mental retardation with clearly stated intervention purposes is striking.

Many past and present attempts at defining and classifying individuals with mental retardation have approached this process with grouping as a principal goal. Grouping, or placing like individuals together on some dimension, serves certain types of purposes well; yet others are addressed only minimally or not at all. For example, grouping may serve administrative convenience quite efficiently. It makes individuals easy to count, funds easy to allocate by type of individual, and services easy to justify to legislatures. Grouping also serves legal purposes well. Placing an individual in a particular category facilitates decisions about legal responsibility for action or guardianship. The reader should realize that we are writing from the perspective of a service professional or agency. In both cases a certain degree of impersonality is involved in decision making. Administrative personnel, legislators, and legal agencies are often working with numbersand names rather than with the individuals the numbers and names represent. We are not addressing the question of how well the individual is served by such decisions. For the individual, service or justice may be marginal or absent.

We do not intend to detract from the value of grouping or the progress that the field of mental retardation has made because of it. In fact, the impetus from legislation and administration of funds at local, state, and federal levels has permitted dramatic service improvements over the years. The issue is that one classification framework may be effective in one sector but serve another sector, whose purposes are different, poorly.

For the most part, educational classifications of retardation have followed the grouping approach. Unfortunately, such an approach may not be effective for purposes of instruction, particularly with problem learners. The evidence consistently indicates this, and educators of youngsters with mental retardation are recognizing the problems of group classification for instructional purposes.

Our earlier discussion of educational classification mentioned two approaches. The first, educability expectation, states anticipated educational achievement for educable and trainable individuals. But symptom severity expressed in IQ was also used, with ranges of approximately 75 to 80 or 90 for dull normal, 50 to 75 or 80 for educable, 20 to 49 for trainable, and below 20 for custodial (SMH). The IQ range approach serves a grouping function, whereas the statements of expectation seem to provide guidelines for prognosis. Problems arise when educational programs focus on grouping rather than specifying purposes, objectives, and resulting classificatory schemes more in harmony with the instructional process. The literature demonstrates a long-standing awareness of such problems. Concern has arisen when evaluation indicates that the curriculum for individuals with retardation reflects convenience in administrative arrangement as much as consideration for the student's needs.

An interesting phenomenon begins to emerge when one reviews a number of sources discussing mental retardation. Since classification and definition are related to diagnosis and evaluation, one serious deficit is evident with respect to both assessment and conceptualization. The conceptual weakness revolves around the relationship of evaluative assessment, classification, and ultimately, programming. We have evaluated; this is the classification; now what? Early approaches to this topic often suggested allowing nature to take its course, that we can "predict a typical course and outcome with a fair degree of confidence." This reflects quite closely the early educability approach. Diagnostic purposes are adequately served here if the only inclination is a passive response—no active education or instruction is implied. Current trends in instructional philosophy and technique do not support a passive predictive approach but dictate active intervention with specific behavioral objectives. There must be a logical and functional link between assessment and intervention (Shriner, Ysseldyke, & Christenson, 1989).

Criterion-Referenced versus Norm-Referenced Measurement

Definitions are not always precise; definitions of mental retardation have suffered difficulties compounded by the demand for measurement. This facet of the AAMR definition, one justifiably viewed as an important strength, has also created some difficulties. Because no goal for educational programming is stated, an apparent lack of purpose underlies the combination of definition, classification, and assessment techniques. The grouping approach predominating both in definition and classification and in the measurement technique involving evaluation has long been known as norm-referenced assessment. Norm-referenced evaluation has not historically been of much value for educational programming. More conceptually sound and pragmatically oriented evaluation approaches have been developed in areas other than mental retardation. It is necessary to explore these approaches' ideas about instruction for persons with retardation in order to make educational programming more effective.

Norm-referenced evaluation is the single type of psychological testing with which most people are familiar. Probably the best-known assessment of this nature is the intelligence test. The goal of norm-referenced evaluation is to measure an individual's functioning in comparison with some standard or group norm. A test score indicates whether the person stands above or below another student or some hypothetical average student. This type of evaluation is of value for purposes of grouping and, beyond that, has relevance for certain educational decisions. But the approach has limitations for overall instructional programming, and it cannot be expected to yield all the information necessary for the actual teaching process. Global acceptance of the norm measure

in the past has led to diminished educational effectiveness for those with mental retardation and much frustration with psychometric information in general.

During the past 15 years a counterpart evaluation concept has developed to meet
a variety of needs not addressed by norm-referenced assessment. This concept of
criterion-referenced evaluation does not place the individual's performance in comparative context with either other students or a normative standard. Criterion-referenced
assessment often focuses on specific skills and looks at absolute level of performance. It
attends to the actual level of mastery that an individual exhibits or, from a different
perspective, the level at which a student becomes unable to perform a given task. This
type of information is more useful to a teacher, because it indicates the level at which
to begin instruction. Criterion-referenced evaluation has become very popular in recent
years, but despite its obvious usefulness for instruction, it does not by itself provide all

Effective assessment must use a variety of types of measurement, often including direct
observation of specific skills, to develop a useful and accurate evaluation.

the information needed for a well-reasoned total educational effort. The development of effective total evaluation models related to learning has become a high priority. Such models are discussed in detail in Chapter 5.

Labeling

In examining classification it is important also to consider labeling. Labeling has been a source of controversy and concern for many years. For example, Maslow (1948) examined the potential problems of labeling, and interest in possible difficulties associated with such designations has continued (see Bromfield, Weisz, & Messer, 1986; Chassin, Stager, & Young, 1985; Hobbs, 1975a, 1975b, 1975c; Johnson, Sigelman, & Falkenberg, 1986; Macmillan, Jones, & Aloia, 1974). Classification and labeling are not necessarily synonymous. Hobbs (1975a) noted that "by *classifying* we mean the act of assigning a child or a condition to a general category or to a particular position in a classification system. . . . By *labeling* we mean to imply more than the assignment of a child to a category. We intend to include the notion of public communication of the way the child is categorized" (p. 43). This distinction is logical and important as we continue research on labeling. Under current classification schemes, however, it may have limited practical significance for those working as care providers. It is difficult to imagine a case in which an individual would be referred, evaluated, and classified without having some label attached. The nature of human communication involves giving names to phenomena we observe. To speak about something causes us to label it, whether by a given name, a type name, or an impression that the phenomenon gives to the speaker (and we typically have names or labels for such impressions). Labeling occurs more commonly than most of us consciously realize. There are many labels, types of labels, and sources of labeling (for example, societal, official, and unofficial labeling). What a label is intended to signify may differ from the meanings associated with the term. It is clear that terms evoke a variety of responses from different individuals (Bromfield et al., 1986; Chassin et al., 1985) and result in many types of services for those labeled. This is certainly the case for labels of deviance, illustrating the complexity of the relationship between labeling and other factors related to categorization and treatment, as well as part of the difficulty in determining the effects of labeling.

For many it has become fashionable to denounce labels and labeling with strong statements regarding their detrimental effects or lack of usefulness. Many have rallied to the cause of eliminating labels. The idea behind most of these efforts is that labeling has a negative impact on those labeled. This belief has great emotional appeal. But empirical evidence of the effects of labeling is difficult to obtain because of the complex interrelationship of labeling with other factors. Herein lies the importance of Hobbs' (1975a) statement. If we are to continue and progress in research on the effects of labeling, we must be able either to isolate the effects or to study the problem in the context of its complexities.

One of the most frequently discussed issues is that of the impact of a label on the individual who bears it, even though definitive evidence about this influence is much less available than folklore would suggest (Schuster & Butler, 1986). But the topic certainly warrants discussion, since it is so central to the controversy.

The idea of the self-fulfilling prophecy has played a prominent role in controversies related to labeling impact. This notion springs from an assumption that expectations and the treatment of the labeled individual resulting from those expectations largely determine the individual's behavior. The label, it is assumed, substantially influences expectations. This perspective came to popularity because of the widely cited work by Rosenthal and Jacobson (1966, 1968), although the idea had been presented long before (Merton, 1948). Despite its intuitive appeal, solid empirical evidence supporting the notion of the self-fulfilling prophecy has been limited. The Rosenthal and Jacobson (1966, 1968) work has been severely criticized for serious methodological flaws, and the controversy continues unresolved (Rosenthal, 1987; Wineburg, 1987). For example, Thorndike (1968) reviewed Rosenthal and Jacobson's work and described it in the following manner:

> In spite of anything I can say, I am sure it will become a classic—widely referred to and rarely examined critically. Alas, it is so defective technically that one can only regret that it ever got beyond the eyes of the original investigators! Though the volume may be an effective addition to education propagandizing, it does nothing to raise the standards of educational research. (p. 708)

Thorndike (1968) summarized by noting the following:

> The indications are that the basic data upon which this structure has been raised are so untrustworthy that any conclusions based upon them must be suspect. The conclusions may be correct, but if so it must be considered a fortunate coincidence. (p. 711)

Thorndike was certainly correct about the attention given to Rosenthal and Jacobson's work. He also appears to have been correct about its methodological flaws. Numerous studies have been unable to replicate Rosenthal and Jacobson's findings (Dusek & O'Connell, 1973; Fleming & Anttonen, 1971a, 1971b; Jose & Cody, 1971; Kester & Letchworth, 1972; Mendels & Flanders, 1973; Sorotzkin, Fleming, & Anttonen, 1974). Such evidence seems to deny the self-fulfilling prophecy notion. It is important to emphasize, however, that these studies were only unable to replicate the findings of Rosenthal and Jacobson and that even Thorndike admitted that "the conclusions may be correct" (1968, p. 711). It is most unfortunate that such an important problem was studied with such flawed methodology, particularly when it drew so much attention. There is little question that people like teachers form certain expectations of students with retardation. Evidence supports this assertion (Aloia & MacMillan, 1983; Ysseldyke & Foster, 1978). Yet it remains unclear what information teachers use in forming their expectations (Dusek, 1975), and the precise effect expectations (and labels) have is uncertain (Merton, 1987). Personal impressions that trigger biases may be formed on the basis of very little information (sometimes a single cue), even in the face of evidence to the contrary (Skowronski & Carlston, 1989). Attention to this topic, an important one in the field of mental retardation, continues (Brophy, 1983; Rosenthal, 1987; Wineburg, 1987).

NEW ISSUES AND FUTURE DIRECTIONS

Core Concept	*New issues and future directions in the definition and classification of mental retardation may include a better balance between individual and environmental factors.*

Mental retardation, like most other phenomena associated with human development and performance, is an enormously complex condition. It is not a unidimensional disorder; to capture the vital elements and contributors adequately in a single definition or classification system is far from simple. In this chapter we have examined some of the history of mental retardation definitions. Many changes have occurred over the years as theories have been discarded and weak logic strengthened. Although modifications have been evident, however, "The dominant systems of definition and classification have not changed radically over the past two decades. The focus continues to be on subaverage general intelligence and deficits in adaptive behavior . . ." (Baumeister, 1987, p. 799). The foundation remains a concept centered on individual people almost to the exclusion of the world around them.

We know that people do not function in a vacuum, and that environment significantly influences their performance. Throughout this volume there are references to the vital influence of environmental circumstances on the development of abilities, performance, and behavior. A weak link remains in our logic of definition involving mental retardation when the field admits the vast impact of environment on mental retardation and yet defines the phenomenon in relative isolation from this factor. Some believe that pressure will increase in the future to define and classify mental retardation with a more balanced view, focusing on "both the individual and the demands and constraints of specific environments" (Baumeister, 1987, p. 800). One of the major elements of mental retardation, intelligence, has been reformulated in such a manner (Sternberg, 1985) and this concept has also been placed in the context of mental retardation (Sternberg & Spear, 1985). Theoretical and empirical research must explore the extension of such thinking to issues of definition and classification.

Major challenges await us in reformulating the definition and classification of mental retardation to balance person and environment. One of the foremost questions confronting such an effort is utility in the field. Definition and classification must translate into practical applications of diagnosis and treatment. Such conceptions do little if they are no more than theories in the pages of scientific journals. Diagnosis and treatment, to be widely accepted, must not become so burdensome that they are not used. Experience with well-conceived assessment systems (Mercer & Lewis, 1977), which are comlplex and time-consuming, has suggested that lack of convenience is a deterrent to broad usage. Utility must receive attention in reconceptualization efforts that translate into field application. Additionally, some evidence suggests that an overwhelming number of minority children are classified as having mental retardation even under assessment systems designed to be pluralistic (Heflinger, Cook, & Thackery, 1987).

CORE QUESTIONS

1. How has the concept of mental retardation differed among disciplines, and how might this affect an individual with retardation?
2. How has consideration of adaptive behavior complicated the view of mental retardation, and how has it been a positive influence?
3. What is the difference between incidence and prevalence?
4. When considering the question of how frequently mental retardation occurs, how do SES, age, and severity affect the answer?
5. In what ways did the "constitutional origin" and "incurability" factors found in early definitions of mental retardation cause problems? How have they been addressed in more current definitions?
6. What ages were primarily addressed in early definitions of mental retardation? Why and how have definitions changed with respect to age?
7. How has the involvement of many disciplines studying mental retardation been both an advantage and a disadvantage?
8. What is a parameter of classification?
9. How are parameters of classification employed in an interactive fashion to identify an individual with mental retardation?
10. How do variations in classification specificity influence incidence and prevalence?
11. How might the use of unspecified parameters of classification cause difficulties in obtaining funding for services to mentally retarded individuals?
12. How can definition and classification systems serve some purposes well and yet be inappropriate for others?
13. Why is it important for there to be a relationship between definitions, classifications, assessment, and programming?
14. What difficulties may be encountered when using a grouping-oriented classification system and criterion-referenced assessment?
15. What difficulties may be encountered when using norm-referenced assessment in conjunction with a definition that does not focus on grouping, but instead emphasizes functional skill levels?

ROUND TABLE DISCUSSION

When discussing or otherwise considering any phenomenon, the definition of what is being addressed is the foundation upon which discussion is based. Communication between you and your student colleagues would be difficult indeed if some of you were talking about automobile transportation and others were considering air travel while you all were using the same term, say, "mustifig." You would encounter difficulty agreeing on cost per mile, miles easily traveled in an hour, and many other factors. This is an exaggerated illustration, but in some ways it is not all that different from mental retardation as it is defined, categorized, counted, and served.

In your study group or on your own, examine mental retardation from the perspective of sociology, medicine, psychology, education, and politics (for example).

Describe the phenomenon, discuss service, and address various aspects of how it should be conceptualized. Examine parameters of classification, labeling, assessment, and also consider worldwide input, as though you were receiving scientific information from all parts of the globe. After completing this exercise, determine how you will conceptualize the phenomenon of mental retardation in order best to learn all that must be known about it and how those affected can best be served. Reflect on the information in this chapter and consider the task facing early professionals working in mental retardation. They did (and do) not have a simple assignment. We hope you will do better.

REFERENCES

Aloia, G. F., & MacMillan, D. L. (1983). Influence of the EMR label on initial expectations of regular-classroom teachers. *American Journal of Mental Deficiency, 88,* 255–262.

American Psychiatric Association. (1987). *Diagnostic and statistical manual of mental disorders* (3rd rev. ed.) (DSM-III-R). Washington, DC: Author.

Anstey, T. J., & Gaskin, M. (1985). Service providers' understanding of the concept of normalization. *Australia and New Zealand Journal of Developmental Disabilities, 11,* 91–95.

Baird, P. A., & Sandovnick, A. D. (1985). Mental retardation in over half-a-million consecutive livebirths: An epidemiological study. *American Journal of Mental Deficiency, 89,* 323–330.

Baird, P. A., & Sandovnick, A. D. (1986). Reply to Richardson, Koller, and Katz. *American Journal of Mental Deficiency, 90,* 451–452.

Barnett, W. S. (1986). Definition and classification of mental retardation: A reply to Zigler, Balla, and Hodapp. *American Journal of Mental Deficiency, 91,* 111–116.

Baumeister, A. A. (1987). Mental retardation: Some conceptions and dilemmas. *American Psychologist, 42,* 796–800.

Benda, C. E. (1954). Psychopathology of childhood. In P. Mussen (Ed.), *Manual of child psychology* (2nd ed.) (pp. 1115–1116). New York: John Wiley & Sons.

Braaten, S., Kauffman, J. M., Braaten, B., Polsgrove, L., & Nelson, C. M. (1988). The regular education initiative: Patent medicine for behavioral disorders. *Exceptional Children, 55*(1), 21–29.

Bromfield, R., Weisz, J. R., & Messer, T. (1986). Children's judgments and attributions in response to the "mentally retarded" label: A developmental approach. *Journal of Abnormal Psychology, 95,* 81–87.

Brophy, J. E. (1983). Research on the self-fulfilling prophecy and teacher expectations. *Journal of Educational Psychology, 75,* 631–661.

Bruininks, R. H., & McGrew, K. (1987). *Exploring the structure of adaptive behavior.* Minneapolis: University Affiliated Program on Developmental Disabilities, University of Minnesota.

Carter, C. H. (1978). *Medical aspects of mental retardation* (2nd ed.). Springfield, IL: Charles C. Thomas.

Carter, C. H. (1979). *Handbook of mental retardation syndromes* (3rd rev. ed.). Springfield, IL: Charles C. Thomas.

Chassin, L., Stager, S., & Young, R. D. (1985). Self-labeling by EMR high school students in their mainstream and special education classes. *American Journal of Community Psychology, 13,* 449–465.

Cooper, T., Wilton, K., & Glynn, T. (1985). Prevalence, school progress and referral of mildly retarded children in regular classes. *Exceptional Child, 32,* 5–11.

Coulter, W. A., & Morrow, H. W. (Eds.) (1978). *Adaptive behavior: Concepts and measurements.* New York: Grune & Stratton.

Doll, E. A. (1941). The essentials of an inclusive concept of mental deficiency. *American Journal of Mental Deficiency, 46,* 214–219.

Dusek, J. B. (1975). Do teachers bias children's learning? *Review of Educational Research, 45,* 661–684.

Dusek, J. B., & O'Connell, E. J. (1973). Teacher expectancy effects on the achievement test performance of elementary school children. *Journal of Educational Psychology, 65,* 371–377.

Fleming, E. S., & Anttonen, R. G. (1971a). Teacher expectancy or my fair lady. *American Educational Research Journal, 8,* 241–252.

Fleming, E. S., & Anttonen, R. G. (1971b). Teacher expectancy as related to the academic and personal growth of primary-age children. *Monographs of the Society for Research in Child Development, 36,* (5).

Forness, S. R., & Kavale, K. A. (1984). Education of the mentally retarded: A note on policy. *Education and Training of the Mentally Retarded, 19*(4), 239–245.

Frankenberger, W., & Harper, J. (1988). States' definitions and procedures for identifying children with mental retardation: Comparison of 1981–1982 and 1985–1986 guidelines. *Mental Retardation, 26,* 133–136.

Fryers, T. (1987). Epidemiological issues in mental retardation. *Journal of Mental Deficiency Research, 31,* 365–384.

Gallagher, J. J. (1985). The prevalence of mental retardation: Cross-cultural considerations from Sweden and the United States. *Intelligence, 9,* 97–108.

Gartner, A., & Lipsky, D. (1987). Beyond special education: Toward a quality system for all students. *Harvard Educational Review, 57,* 367–395.

Gellis, S. S., & Feingold, M. (1968). *Atlas of mental retardation syndromes.* Washington, DC: U.S. Government Printing Office.

Grossman, H. J. (Ed.) (1973). *Manual on terminology and classification in mental retardation.* Washington, DC: American Association on Mental Deficiency.

Grossman, H. J. (Ed.) (1977). *Manual on terminology and classification in mental retardation.* Washington, DC: American Association on Mental Deficiency.

Grossman, H. J. (Ed.) (1983). *Classification in mental retardation.* Washington, DC: American Association on Mental Deficiency.

Hardman, M. L., Drew, C. J., & Egan, M. W. (1984). *Human exceptionality: Society, school, and family.* Newton, MA: Allyn & Bacon.

Hardman, M. L., Drew, C. J., Egan, M. W., & Wolf, B. (1990). *Human exceptionality: Society, school, and family* (3rd ed.). Newton, MA: Allyn & Bacon.

Heber, R. (1961). A manual on terminology and classification in mental retardation (2nd ed.). *American Journal of Mental Deficiency Monograph Supplement.*

Heber, R. (1962). Mental retardation: Concept and classification. In E. P. Trapp & P. Himelstein (Eds.), *Readings on the exceptional child: Research and theory* (pp. 69–81). New York: Appleton-Century-Crofts.

Heflinger, C. A., Cook, V. J., & Thackery, M. (1987). Identification of mental retardation by the System of Multicultural Pluralistic Assessment: Nondiscriminatory or nonexistent? *Journal of School Psychology, 25,* 177–183.

Hobbs, N. (1975a). *The futures of children.* San Francisco: Jossey-Bass.

Hobbs, N. (Ed.) (1975b). *Issues in the classification of children* (Vol. 1). San Francisco: Jossey-Bass.

Hobbs, N. (Ed.) (1975c). *Issues in the classification of children* (Vol. 2). San Francisco: Jossey-Bass.

Hodapp, R. M., & Zigler, E. (1986). Reply to Barnett's comments on the definition and classification of mental retardation. *American Journal of Mental Deficiency, 91,* 117–119.

Iowa Task Force on Adaptive Behavior. (1981). *Assessment, documentation and programming for adaptive behavior: An Iowa Task Force report.* Des Moines: Department of Public Instruction.

Jenkins, J. R., Pious, C. G., & Peterson, D. L. (1988). Categorical programs for remedial and handicapped students: Issues of validity. *Exceptional Children, 55*(2), 147–158.

Johnson, C. G., Sigelman, C. K., & Falkenberg, V. F. (1986). Impacts of labeling and competence on peers' perceptions: Mentally retarded versus nonretarded perceivers. *American Journal of Mental Deficiency, 90,* 663–668.

Jose, J., & Cody, J. J. (1971). Teacher-pupil interaction as it related to attempted changes in teacher expectancy of academic ability and achievement. *American Educational Research Journal, 8,* 39–49.

Kamphaus, R. W. (1987). Conceptual and psychometric issues in the assessment of adaptive behavior. *Journal of Special Education, 21,* 27–35.

Kester, S. W., & Letchworth, G. A. (1972). Communication of teacher expectations and their effects on achievement and attitudes of secondary school students. *Journal of Educational Research, 66,* 51–55.

Kopp, C. B., & Krakow, J. B. (1983). The developmentalist and the study of biological risk: A view of the past with an eye toward the future. *Child Development, 54,* 1086–1108.

Lilly, M. S. (1987). Lack of focus on special education in literature on educational reform. *Exceptional Children, 53*(4), 325–326.

Lipsky, D. K., & Gartner, A. (Eds.). (1989). *Beyond separate education: Quality education for all.* Baltimore: Paul H. Brookes.

MacMillan, D. L., Jones, R. L., & Aloia, G. F. (1974). The mentally retarded label: A theoretical analysis and review of research. *American Journal of Mental Deficiency, 79,* 241–261.

Mahendra, B. (1985). Subnormality revisited in early 19th century France. *Journal of Mental Deficiency Research, 29,* 391–401.

Marston, D. (1987). Does categorical teacher certification benefit the mildly handicapped child? *Exceptional Children, 53*(5), 423–431.

Maslow, A. (1948). Cognition of the particular and of the generic. *Psychological Review, 55,* 22–40.

Mendels, G. E., & Flanders, J. P. (1973). Teacher expectations and pupil performance. *American Educational Research Journal, 10,* 203–212.

Mercer, J. R. (1973a). *Labeling the mentally retarded.* Berkeley: University of California Press.

Mercer, J. R. (1973b). The myth of 3% prevalence. In R. K. Eyman, C. E. Meyers, & G. Tarjan (Eds.), *Sociobehavioral studies in mental retardation* (Monographs of the American Association on Mental Deficiency, No. 1).

Mercer, J. R., & Lewis, J. F. (1977). *System of multicultural pluralistic assessment.* New York: Psychological Corporation.

Merton, R. K. (1948) The self-fulfilling prophecy. *Antioch Review, 8,* 193–210.

Merton, R. K. (1987). Three fragments from a sociologist's notebooks: Establishing the phenomenon, specified ignorance, and strategic research materials. *Annual Review of Sociology, 13,* 1–28.

Meyers, C. E., Nihira, K., & Zetlin, A. (1979). The measurement of adaptive behavior. In N. R. Ellis (Ed.), *Handbook of mental deficiency, psychological theory and research* (2nd ed.) (pp. 431–481). Hillsdale, NJ: Lawrence Erlbaum.

President's Task Force on the Mentally Handicapped. (1970). *Action against mental disability.* Washington, DC: U.S. Government Printing Office.

Proposed Regulations. (1982). *Federal Register, 33,* 845.

Rantakallio, P., & von Wendt, L. (1986). Mental retardation and subnormality in a birth cohort of 12,000 children in Northern Finland. *American Journal of Mental Deficiency, 90,* 380–387.

Reynolds, M. C., & Birch, J. W. (1988). *Adaptive mainstreaming.* New York: Longman.

Reynolds, M. C., Wang, M. C., & Walberg, H. J. (1987). The necessary restructuring of special and regular education. *Exceptional Children, 53*(5), 391–398.

Richardson, S. A., Koller, H., & Katz, M. (1986). Comments on Baird and Sandovnick's "Mental retardation in over half-a-million consecutive livebirths: An epidemiological study." *American Journal of Mental Deficiency, 90,* 449–450.

Rosenthal, R. (1987). Pygmalion effects: Existence, magnitude, and social importance. *Educational Researcher, 16*(9), 37–41.

Rosenthal, R., & Jacobson, L. (1966). Teacher expectancies: Determinants of pupils' IQ gains. *Psychological Reports, 19,* 115–118.

Rosenthal, R., & Jacobson, L. (1968). *Pygmalion in the classroom.* New York: Holt, Rinehart & Winston.

Scheerenberger, R. C. (1964). Mental retardation: Definition, classification, and prevalence. *Mental Retardation Abstracts, 1,* 432–441.

Scheerenberger, R. C. (1983). *A history of mental retardation.* Baltimore: Paul H. Brookes.

Schuster, T. L., & Butler, E. W. (1986). Labeling, mild mental retardation, and long-range social adjustment. *Sociological Perspectives, 29,* 461–483.

Shriner, J. G., Ysseldyke, J. E., & Christenson, S. L. (1989). Assessment procedures for use in heterogeneous classrooms. In S. Stainback, W. Stainback, & M. Forest (Eds.), *Educating all students in the mainstream of regular education* (pp. 159–181). Baltimore: Paul H. Brookes.

Skowronski, J. J., & Carlston, D. E. (1989). Negativity and extremity biases in impression formation: A review of explanations. *Psychological Bulletin, 105,* 131–142.

Sloan, W., & Birch, J. (1955). A rationale for degrees of retardation. *American Journal of Mental Deficiency, 60,* 258–264.

Sorotzkin, F., Fleming, E. S., & Anttonen, R. G. (1974). Teacher knowledge of standardized test information and its effect on pupil IQ and achievement. *Journal of Experimental Education, 43,* 79–85.

Stainback, S., Stainback, W., & Forest, M. (Eds.). (1989). *Educating all students in the mainstream of regular education.* Baltimore: Paul H. Brookes.

Sternberg, R. J. (1985). *Beyond IQ: A triarchic theory of human intelligence.* London: Cambridge University Press.

Sternberg, R. J., & Spear, L. C. (1985). A triarchic theory of mental retardation. In N. R. Ellis and N. W. Bray (Eds.), *International review of research in mental retardation* (Vol. 13) (pp. 301–326). Orlando, FL: Academic.

Tarjan, G. (1989). Mental retardation revisited. *Psychiatric Annals, 19,* 176–178.

Tarjan, G., Wright, S. W., Eyman, R. K., & Keeran, C. V. (1973). Natural history of mental retardation: Some aspects of epidemiology. *American Journal of Mental Deficiency, 77,* 369–379.

Terman, L. (1916). *The measurement of intelligence.* Boston: Houghton-Mifflin.

Thorndike, R. L. (1968). Review of *Pygmalion in the classroom* by R. Rosenthal and L. Jacobson. *American Educational Research Journal, 5,* 708–711.

Tredgold, A. F. (1937). *A textbook of mental deficiency* (6th ed.). Baltimore: William Wood.

U.S. Department of Education. (1989). To assure the free appropriate public education of all handicapped children. *Eleventh Annual Report to Congress on the Implementation of the Education of The Handicapped Act.* Washington, DC: U.S. Government Printing Office.

Wang, M. C., & Walburg, H. J. (1987). Four fallacies of segregation. *Exceptional Children, 55,* 128–137.

Wechsler, D. (1958). *The measurement and appraisal of adult intelligence* (4th ed.). Baltimore: Williams & Wilkins.

Wineburg, S. S. (1987). The self-fulfillment of the self-fulfilling prophecy. *Educational Researcher, 16*(9), 28–37.

World Health Organization. (1978). *International classification of diseases.* (9th rev. ed.) (Vol. 1). Geneva: Author.

Ysseldyke, J. E., & Foster, G. G. (1978). Bias in teachers' observations of emotionally disturbed and learning disabled children. *Exceptional Children, 44,* 613–615.

Zigler, E., Balla, D., & Hodapp, R. (1984). On the definition and classification of mental retardation. *American Journal of Mental Deficiency, 89,* 215–230.

CHAPTER TWO

Multicultural Issues

Core
Concepts

- Cultural diversity results in important differences that require consideration as one examines mental retardation as a concept and in the context of individual diagnosis.
- Poverty exists among many culturally different groups and creates a number of environmental disadvantages that may impair a child's mental development.
- Social values that differ from culture to culture may result in behavioral or performance deviation from the cultural majority, which some might view as reflecting mental retardation.
- Language differences that create academic difficulties for some culturally different children may place them in jeopardy of being considered as having mental retardation.
- Personnel and procedures involved in the assessment, diagnosis, and intervention process may all contribute to a biased overrepresentation of culturally different children as mentally retarded.
- Cultural diversity may result in some influences that generate actual developmental disadvantages as well as differences.
- We must change basic models of research on mental retardation so that we can more fully understand the influences of cultural diversity on human development.

Differences from normal functioning are part of the nature of mental retardation. People with mental retardation exhibit lower intellectual performance, with concomitant reduced functioning in social skills. The perspective and expectations for both intellectual and social functioning derive from the context of our society. As we have seen in Chapter 1, the definition of mental retardation emerges from societal expectations. Standards of performance are broadly defined by the social majority. The source of these general performance standards gives rise to several concerns related to ethnic and cultural diversity that have existed for many years.

Core Concept	*Cultural diversity results in important differences that require consideration as one examines mental retardation as a concept and in the context of individual diagnosis.*

Countries with multiple cultures, like the United States, are always faced with circumstances where definitions of acceptable behavior differ between various groups. Yet broad and general standards that cross cultural boundaries also operate and are determined in some way. Typically such definitions emanate from sources and institutions that primarily represent the views of the cultural majority. Scientists, public officials, and others in positions of authority more often reflect the perspectives of the cultural majority than those of smaller groups or population segments.

Issues related to cultural diversity are integrated into topical discussions in this volume, where they play a major role. These issues pervade many aspects of mental retardation, such as causation, assessment, prevention, and placement and treatment. In this chapter, however, we examine certain subjects separately.

One serious problem is that of misdiagnosis and classification of individuals as having mental retardation when, in fact, their behavior or performance is related to cultural difference rather than significantly reduced functioning. The concept of the self-fulfilling prophecy (the idea that you become what you are labeled) is prominent in this area. The self-fulfilling prophecy suggests that, if a person is labeled as having mental retardation, over time he or she will begin to function as a person who has mental retardation—even if the initial diagnosis was inaccurate.

The self-fulfilling prophecy was first specifically discussed by Merton (1948) although it did not become well known until publication of the work of Rosenthal and Jacobson on teacher expectations (1968a, 1968b, 1968c). Rosenthal and Jacobson's results suggested that children's performance levels reflected their teachers' expectations to a substantial degree. This research generated a great deal of controversy (as indicated in Chapter 1), and the topic remains one of considerable interest (Merton, 1987; Rosenthal, 1987; Wineburg, 1987). We still have much to learn before the effects of expectation are fully understood. It is clear, however, that the self-fulfilling prophecy represents an area of concern, particularly for youngsters who may be identified as having mental retardation on the basis more of cultural background than of performance level.

ASSOCIATED INFLUENCES

Many factors contribute to what we are and how we function in the world around us. We inherited certain material from our parents that affects how we look and act. We also are greatly influenced by both our current environment and the one in which we grew up. All of these contributions come together in a complex, interactive manner to impact the person that each of us now is as an adult.

Certain influences that contribute to lowered intellectual functioning are related to culturally different populations in this country. They are associated with mental retardation by virtue of environmental conditions that are beyond the control of the people shaped by them, for example, poor health care and poverty. Other influences are inherent where there is cultural and ethnic diversity—cultural and social mores and language differences are two. These more purely cultural influences come into play with respect to a literal perspective of the term *differences* in the sense that behavior and performance that are predominant in one culture may not play the same role in another. All of these factors concern workers in the area of mental retardation.

Poverty

Core Concept	*Poverty exists among many culturally different groups and creates a number of environmental disadvantages that may impair a child's mental development.*

Poverty is one of the strongest influences on our sociocultural environment today, and impoverished economic circumstances are more often found among ethnic minorities than their white counterparts. The U.S. Bureau of the Census (1985) indicates that 11.5% of the Caucasian population live below the poverty level. The proportions of black and Hispanic populations in this economic condition, however, are much higher—33.8% and 28.4%, respectively. This situation places many members of ethnic minorities at a considerable disadvantage from several standpoints, including a greater probability of malnutrition and a greater risk from such toxic agents as lead and other harmful environmental substances (Brooks-Gunn & Furstenberg, 1986). Extreme poverty may also lead to homelessness, which contributes to irregular school attendance, chronic health problems, and a number of developmental delays (Landers, 1989).

Poverty affects the type and level of health care people receive as youngsters and the nutrition that builds their physical systems during important developmental periods, both before birth and during the first few years of life. Evidence suggests that during these periods ethnic minorities suffer from more health complications than their white counterparts do. Gelfand, Jenson, and Drew (1988) examined these issues and noted that "only 5 percent of white upper-class infants suffer complications at birth, compared with 15 percent of low-socioeconomic-status (low SES) whites and *51 percent* of all nonwhites (who have very low incomes as a group)" (p. 64). Children who begin their developmental years in such unfavorable circumstances have a substantial probability of continued slower or abnormal development and of being labeled as having mental retardation.

Cultural-Social Mores

Core Concept	*Social values that differ from culture to culture may result in behavioral or performance deviation from the cultural majority, which some might view as reflecting mental retardation.*

Certainly cultural and social mores do not contribute to a person's mental retardation in the same way as genetic abnormality. They do, however, play a significant role in how others view the person's performance in particular areas and in the person's demeanor. And these matters influence the overall view of a person's level of functioning, making a direct impact on whether that individual is seen as having mental retardation.

Different cultures view education and formal schooling quite differently. The U.S. educational system follows the value system of the white cultural majority. It does not equally reflect the beliefs of the members of various subcultures who spend time in our schools. Belief structures are very different in our subcultures, and sources of knowledge, wisdom, and attitudes toward achievement are diverse. Table 2–1 summarizes selected differences between our dominant culture and that of some Native Americans. The differences are almost overpowering, particularly when one considers that these ideas have permeated children's early developmental years and shaped their views of the world. This type of culture-specific value system can and often does substantially control how a youngster approaches, acts, and performs in school. It takes little imagination to see how a child with different cultural priorities might do poorly and be considered eligible for a diagnosis of mental retardation.

Table 2–1
Native American values versus dominant culture

Native American	Dominant Culture
Wisdom of age and experience is respected. Elders are revered by their people.	Older people are made to feel incompetent and rejected.
Excellence is related to a contribution to the group—not to personal glory.	Competition and striving to win or to gain status is emphasized.
Cooperation is necessary for group survival.	Competition is necessary for individual status and prestige.
Children participate in adult activities.	Adults participate in children's activities.
Family life includes the extended family.	Family life includes the nuclear family.
Time is present-oriented—this year, this week—NOW—a resistance to planning for the future.	Time is planning and saving for the future.
Clocktime is whenever people are ready—when everyone arrives.	Clocktime is exactly that.
Work is when necessary for the common good.	Work is from 9 to 5 (specified time) and to obtain material possessions and to save for the future.
Whatever Indian people have, they share. What is mine is ours.	What is mine stays mine.
Good relationships and mutual respect are emphasized.	Success, progress, possession of property, and rugged individualism are valued above mutual respect and maintaining good relationships.
People express their ideas and feelings through their actions.	People express themselves and attempt to impress others through speech.
People conform to nature.	People try to dominate and desecrate nature.
Early childhood and rearing practices are the responsibility of the kin group.	Early childhood and rearing practices are the responsibility of the nuclear family.
Native religion was never imposed, nor did it proselytize other groups.	Religious groups proselytize, coerce, and impose their beliefs on others.
Land gives the Indian his identity, his religion, and his life. It is not to be sold, not owned, but used by all.	Land is for speculation, for prestige, to be owned, sold, or torn up.
Going to school is necessary to gain knowledge. Excelling for fame is looked down upon by the Indian.	Going to school is necessary to gain knowledge and to compete for grades.
Indians have a shorter childhood, and the male is held to be a responsible person at the age of 16.	There is an extended childhood, and the male is held to be a responsible person at the age of 21.
People are usually judged by what they do.	People are usually judged by their credentials.

Adapted from "Teaching the American Indian Child in Mainstream Settings" by F. C. Pepper, 1976, in R. L. Jones, ed., *Mainstreaming and the Minority Child* (pp. 135–136), Reston, VA: Council for Exceptional Children.

Cultural and social mores may also significantly influence the treatment of individuals with disabilities and the services sought by their families. Mental retardation is a disorder that many different cultures recognize, but how it is conceptualized, how it is treated, and its social interpretation are as diverse as the cultures (Manion & Bersani, 1987). For some groups, accepting certain handicapping conditions is very difficult (Correa, 1987). Differing religious beliefs and superstitions often play a significant role in the way people view abnormality, and they have a considerable impact on acceptance (Smith, 1987). And for the different family structures of various cultural subgroups, this influences caregiving for family members with handicapping conditions. For example, the extended families common to black and Hispanic cultures affect beliefs about where care for such individuals should come from and may result in anxiety or even suspicion regarding special services from outside the family (Fishgrund, Cohen, & Clarkson, 1987; Turner, 1987; Yacobacci-Tam, 1987). Similarly, Asian parents of handicapped youngsters may feel great shame and be unwilling to seek or even accept outside assistance (Leung, 1987; Morrow, 1987).

Cultural and social mores clearly affect how individuals approach and interact with institutions that represent authority and reflect the belief systems of the cultural majority. Because of this diversity, different demeanors and behaviors have different meanings in various population subgroups. Behavior that is valued and seen as reflecting intelligence by one culture may be viewed as offensive, unwise, or even unintelligent in another. Including these complex cultural influences is vital when one considers the overall phenomenon of mental retardation. Cultural influences are of great practical impact as children from cultural minority groups are educated. They also challenge us to prove the conceptual soundness and utility of mental retardation definitions (Baumeister, 1987).

Language

Core Concept	*Language differences that create academic difficulties for some culturally different children may place them in jeopardy of being considered as having mental retardation.*

Cultural diversity also results in a number of language differences that often contribute to academic difficulties in a school system designed and operated by the cultural majority. Academic problems stemming from language differences may result in referral, assessment, and inappropriate labeling of a child as having mental retardation if consideration is not given to cultural factors. Language differences may be absolute, as when a youngster's family speaks a language other than English. Additional differences may be found when the youngster's linguistic patterns represent what is known as nonstandard language. **Nonstandard language** is particularly evident in the communication patterns of some cultural or racial subgroups. An illustration of this phenomenon is Black English. While nonstandard from the viewpoint of the cultural majority, Black English does represent a speaking pattern that has a regular grammatical style and pronunciation rules (Folb, 1980; White, 1984). Table 2–2 lists some of the linguistic characteristics of Black English.

Language patterns emerging from the speech configurations illustrated in Table 2–2 are sufficiently different from those of the cultural majority to cause considerable academic difficulty for a youngster in the school system. It is easy to see how a teacher from the dominant culture might find it hard to understand the child. It is also not difficult to see how teachers and others might think that the child had a language deficiency or disorder, and so might refer the child for testing for mental retardation. Once into the referral-assessment cycle the child using nonstandard language could be diagnosed and placed in special education service patterns that could label that individual for life. This is a particularly unfortunate outcome if the diagnosis of mental retardation is erroneous and due to a cultural difference rather than actual intellectual status.

Misdiagnosis based on language differences places assessment in a critical position. Language differences and inaccurate or biased diagnostic assessment for mental retardation has received considerable attention in the literature. There is a long history of blaming biased

Language differences present serious problems for this child who may be misdiagnosed as having mental retardation.

Table 2-2
Some linguistic characteristics of Black English

Linguistic Categories	Characteristics	Examples	
		Standard English	*Black English*
Phonological differences			
Initial position	Merging of /f/ with /th/	thigh	fie
	Merging of /v/ with /th/	Thou	vow
Medial position	Deletion of /r/	Carol	cal
	Merging of /i/ and /e/	pen	pin
	Merging of /v/ with /th/	mother	movver
	Merging of /f/ with /th/	birthday	birfday
Final position	Deletion of /r/	sore	saw
	Deletion of /l/	Saul	saw
	Simplification of consonant clusters:		
	/st/	past	pass
	/ft/	left	leff
	/nt/	went	wen
	/nd/	wind	wine
	/zd/	raised	raise*
	/md/	aimed	aim*
	/ks/	six	sick
	/ts/	it's	it*
	/lt/	salt	saught
Morphological differences			
Future	Loss of final /l/	you'll	you

*These items also are morphological differences.

From "Special Education and the Linguistically Different Child" by D. N. Bryen, 1974, *Exceptional Children, 40,* 593. Copyright 1974 by the Council for Exceptional Children. Reprinted by permission.

assessment for the overrepresentation of minority children in special education. It should be noted also, however, that there are those who believe assessment is a much-maligned excuse for this overrepresentation (Maheady, Towne, Algozzine, Mercer, & Ysseldyke, 1983).

ISSUES OF ASSESSMENT AND INTERVENTION

Core Concept	*Personnel and procedures involved in the assessment, diagnosis, and intervention process may all contribute to a biased overrepresentation of culturally different children as mentally retarded.*

Table 2-2, *continued*

Linguistic Categories	Characteristics	Examples	
		Standard English	*Black English*
Past tense	Simplification of final consonants such as:		
	/st/	passed	pass
	/nd/	loaned	loan
Plural	Deletion of final /s/ and /z/	50 cents	50 cent
		3 birds	3 bird
Syntactical differences			
Auxiliary verb	Deletion of auxiliary	He is gone.	He goin.
Subject expression	Repetition of subject	John lives in NY.	John, he live in NY.
Verb form	Substitution of past participle for simple past form	I drank the milk.	I drunk the milk.
Verb agreement	Deletion of /s/ for third person singular present tense	He runs home.	He run home.
Future form	Substitution of a variation of present progressive tense	I will go home.	I'ma go home.
Negation	Use of double negative	I don't have any.	I don't got none.
Indefinite article	Deletion of /n/	I want an apple.	I want a apple.
Pronoun form	Substitution of objective for nominative case	We have to do it.	Us got to do it.
Preposition	Difference in preposition	He is over at his friend's house.	He is over to his friend house.
Copula ("be")	Use of durative *be* for *is*	He is here all the time.	He be here.

The role of assessment has been central in dealing with culturally different people and mental retardation. Diagnostic testing for deficiencies or differences is at the core of the process by which we determine if an individual has mental retardation. If this process is unfavorably biased against cultural differences, then the likelihood increases that a child who actually reflects diversity rather than deficiency will be labeled mentally retarded. Youngsters from minority backgrounds do appear more frequently in disability categories than would be expected based on the proportion of culturally different people in the population. Ethnicity is also a predictor of placement in residential facilities, although there are other factors as well (Borthwick-Duffy, Eyman, & White, 1987; Meyers, Borthwick, & Eyman, 1985). This disproportionately high rate of identification frequently involves deficiencies diagnosed through psychoeducational assessment (Prasse & Reschly, 1986), which suggests that the evaluation process has a serious bias.

Measurement bias can occur in many fashions. Cultural bias in assessment leads to inaccurate results based on cultural background. Such results are testing artifacts— conclusions from an evaluation that reveal cultural background rather than actual mental abilities or skills (Reynolds, 1987). This type of error in psychological assessment has been of concern to professionals for many decades (e.g., Burt, 1921), and arguments about the causes of such bias, its effects, and resolutions of it continue in the scientific literature (Lopez, 1988; Malgady, Rogler, & Constantino, 1987; Miller-Jones, 1989).

Norm-referenced measurement procedures, which often employ norm data, language patterns, and knowledge or content based on the cultural majority, are highly vulnerable to assessment bias. Under the conditions presumed by norm-referenced tests, individuals from minority and culturally different backgrounds have a built-in performance disadvantage (Wood, Johnson, & Jenkins, 1986). This type of inequitable assessment has played a dominant role in widely publicized court cases involving Hispanic and black students (*Diana v. State Board of Education,* 1970; *Larry P. v. Riles,* 1972, 1979). Such cases have had a major impact on the manner in which testing is viewed.

Attempts to design culturally fair test instruments have been made for many years but have met with little success. Certain improvements were achieved with respect to minimizing conspicuous culture-specific components (Luftig, 1989) and developing complex systems of assessment that attempt to consider cultural background through multiple measures (Mercer & Lewis, 1977). Difficulties remain, however, and minority children still appear to have a distinct disadvantage even with procedures intended to account for diverse backgrounds (Heflinger, Cook, & Thackery, 1987).

Attention to the instruments of assessment *without concern for the people and processes involved in evaluation* leaves room for considerable cultural bias in psychological assessment. People often make diagnostic and classification decisions based on specific data and form impressions from scant information (Skowronski & Carlston, 1989). Efforts must be undertaken to minimize the personal bias of professionals involved in psychological assessment. This will probably require additional training or different preparation specifically aimed at incorporating information about cultural factors into the evaluation. Earlier we examined the influences associated with minority and culturally different status. Knowledge of such information about each individual child is extremely important in any assessment and often must be obtained through interviews with parents and other significant people in the youngster's environment. Professionals must obtain this background information in a manner sensitive to differences in cultural attitudes and mores, or it too has the potential for being inaccurate or biased. Table 2–3 lists some interview topics that are often important when evaluating the status of a culturally different child.

Psychological assessment plays a vital role in assessing mental retardation. It is an important component in the process of identifying and serving those who need specialized treatment. Assessment must not, however, become a mechanism for discrimination or an expression of cultural prejudice. To allow such misuse runs counter to the

Table 2–3
Guidelines for interviewing parents about cultural and environmental influences

After talking with community members about the general cultural characteristics of the community, it is still necessary to discover what experiences each child has had. The following set of questions can be used to find out about the direct cultural and environmental experiences of the child so that appropriate educational programs can be planned.

1. What language(s) do the parents speak to each other?
2. What language(s) do the parents speak to the child?
3. What language(s) do the children use with each other?
4. What language does the referred child prefer to use when playing with friends?
5. Who takes care of the child after school? What language is used?
6. Who lives in the home (parents, grandparents, etc.)?
7. How much time does each parent have to interact with the child?
8. With whom does the child play when at home?
9. What television programs are seen in each language?
10. Are stories read to the child? In what language is the reading material written?
11. What language is used in church services, if attended?
12. What does the child do after school and on weekends?
13. What responsibilities does the child have in the home?
14. How is the child expected to act toward parents, teachers, and other adults?
15. In what cultural activities does the family participate?
16. How do the parents expect adults to act toward the child?
17. Are there any specific prohibitions in the everyday interactions between adults and children, for example, do not look adults in the eye when talking to them, do not pat children on the top of the head, do not ask children questions?
18. How long has the family been in this country?
19. How long has the family been in the local community?
20. How much contact does the family have with the homeland? What kind of contact?

From *Speech and Language Assessment for the Bilingual Handicapped* (pp. 111–112) by L. J. Mattes and D. R. Omark, 1984, San Diego: College-Hill Press. Copyright 1984 by College-Hill Press. Reprinted by permission.

basic purpose of intervention to help those who need treatment. Chapter 5 is devoted solely to assessment. As you read and study Chapter 5 it is important to keep multicultural issues firmly in mind.

HUMAN DEVELOPMENT AND MULTICULTURAL ISSUES

| Core Concept | *Cultural diversity may result in some influences that generate actual developmental disadvantages as well as differences.* |

A wide variety of factors affects the course of human development, ranging from inherited genetic material to environmental influences such as nutrition, disease, and toxic substances. All of these may have favorable or unfavorable consequences on the rate and quality of a young person's developing abilities, depending on how they come in contact with the individual and when the contact occurs. Many are discussed in more detail in later chapters as we address the developmental abnormalities resulting in mental retardation. In this section we address how some of these influences are associated with cultural diversity and how they may, in this context, have an impact on the development of children and youth from minority cultures.

Earlier in this chapter we discussed impoverished economic circumstances as a condition often associated with ethnic minority status in this country. For example, poverty occurs much more frequently among the black and Hispanic populations than it does in those representing the cultural majority. Nearly three times as many members of these groups live in conditions below the poverty level as do members of the dominant culture (U.S. Bureau of the Census, 1985). Such circumstances severely limit accessibility to quality health care, adequate nutrition, early stimulation, and a variety of other environmental features that promote favorable growth and development in youngsters. These matters dramatically influence maturation both prenatally and during the important growth periods after birth. During these times in the life cycle crucial physical, neurological, and cognitive structures undergo their most rapid growth. The foundations of a person's development are laid at this point and play a very strong role in determining how later maturation proceeds. To the degree that inadequate health care, nutrition, and other circumstances exist in culturally diverse populations, children in these groups are placed at risk for delayed or otherwise abnormal development that may result in mental retardation. Chapters 7 and 8, in particular, discuss such unfavorable developmental circumstances and their potential outcomes.

The influences just mentioned may generate serious developmental disadvantages for culturally different youngsters, adversely affecting basic neurological and cognitive structures. In addition to these factors, what is learned during the formative years plays a pivotal role in later behavior. The content of what is learned may produce sociocultural differences that set minority youngsters apart from their peers in the cultural majority. Earlier we noted that cultural and social mores influence the view of education and formal schooling. Different cultures display divergent belief structures, with varying opinions about the sources of wisdom and knowledge and attitudes toward achievement. Certain Native American cultures view excelling in school unfavorably, whereas the dominant culture places a high value on such behavior (see Table 2–1). These and other types of social values are learned very early in the developmental life cycle and have a powerful influence on how children approach and engage the world about them. Their impact on how youngsters from culturally different populations perform in institutions that are designed and operated by the cultural majority should not be underestimated. Such early learning is extremely durable and often creates serious conflict as youngsters encounter varying belief systems in the world beyond their cultural background.

Society's role in changing the circumstances of human development is not clear. There is little argument that it is important to alter the contingencies that present

Severe malnutrition and poor health care resulting from impoverished living conditions occurs more frequently among culturally different populations and may lead to mental retardation.

developmental disadvantages to children. To do otherwise runs counter to the basic philosophy of a society that explicitly promotes the well-being of all its people. However, serious philosophical questions arise about the degree of conformity society should require. Most would not subscribe to a basic doctrine that requires culturally diverse belief systems to be brought into conformity with those of the cultural majority. The dimension of developmental differences presents a complicated challenge, one that is not easily solved.

NEW ISSUES AND FUTURE DIRECTIONS

Core Concept	*We must change basic models of research on mental retardation so that we can more fully understand the influences of cultural diversity on human development.*

The face of behavioral science is undergoing tremendous changes in its basic research models. Quantitatively oriented experimental and clinical psychology have formed the foundations of traditional research methodologies used in the study of mental retardation. These methodologies have usually had a quantitative, norm-referenced framework as their context. The largest body of research in mental retardation reflects investigation of the phenomenon as a concept of performance or ability deficit predominantly viewed in relation to normative abilities derived from the cultural majority. Historically only isolated researchers have pursued investigations of mental retardation emphasizing the study of individuals in the context of their environment (see Edgerton, 1967, 1975, 1976, 1980, 1984; Edgerton & Bercovici, 1976; Edgerton, Bollinger, & Herr, 1984).

Our understanding of mental retardation is only as adequate as our research models. It is important to realize that mental retardation does not occur in the laboratory but in the context of our broader society. While the laboratory has provided us with considerable information, that information must be placed in context to achieve understanding, which, from the perspective of this chapter, means consideration of cultural diversity issues. Social and cultural environments must become integral in our study of child development both generally and with regard to developmental deviations like mental retardation (LeVine, 1989).

The study of mental retardation as a part of the social and cultural environment is gaining considerable momentum. Qualitative research models, like those of ethnography, hold great promise for future understanding of this multidimensional problem. As Stainback and Stainback (1989) note, "There is growing interest in the potential contributions of qualitative research to scholarly inquiry, and what was a quiet and perhaps peripheral aspect of educational research has been moving rapidly toward center stage in recent years" (p. 271). Where once little was written about methodology, now there are volumes beginning to rival those available in quantitative research (Goetz & LeCompte, 1984; Lincoln & Guba, 1985; Miles & Huberman, 1984; Stainback & Stainback, 1988).

As these changes are occurring it is important to realize that our choice of methods is expanding (LeVine, 1989), not that one is supplanting another. There is little reason to think that the future will involve discarding the strengths of quantitative investigation. What will be needed is the strength of multiple methods studying the same questions with the same populations. Future research will require disciplined eclecticism (Shulman, 1986) to incorporate the necessary rigor while shedding the narrow perspective of a single model (Anderson, 1989). Such an approach holds great promise for improving our understanding of the complex interactions of cultural diversity and mental retardation (Lerner & Lerner, 1989).

CORE QUESTIONS

1. How does cultural diversity result in differences that one must address when considering mental retardation conceptually?
2. How does cultural diversity result in differences that one must consider when diagnosing an individual as having mental retardation?
3. How does poverty create environmental circumstances that might impair a child's mental development?
4. How might social values emerge in the behavior or performance of a culturally different individual and suggest a diagnosis of mental retardation?
5. How might language differences place a child in jeopardy of being diagnosed as having mental retardation?
6. How do assessment procedures potentially place a culturally different individual at an unfair disadvantage, with the possible result of a mental retardation label?
7. How might assessment personnel influence diagnostic evaluation in a manner that inaccurately identifies a culturally different individual as having mental retardation?
8. How might the environmental circumstances of cultural diversity have such an adverse influence on human development that they help to cause mental retardation?
9. How have traditional research models in mental retardation failed to account for the influences of cultural diversity in human development?

ROUND TABLE DISCUSSION

Mental retardation is a problem that, by definition involves differences from normal functioning. Individuals with mental retardation perform poorly from both intellectual and social perspectives. In examining mental retardation it is important to consider who sets the norms of behavior and performance. For the most part, society shapes these norms based on the views of the cultural majority, without much reflection of the belief structures of ethnic minority populations.

In your study or discussion group examine the potential effects of having one segment of the population set the standards for another group, focusing on a subgroup that does not share the belief systems of the majority. Remember that ethnic minorities represent a greater proportion of those labeled handicapped than would be expected. Does this represent discrimination? How do you separate discrimination from actual disadvantages associated with cultural diversity? Should performance or behavior reflecting cultural differences be considered in applying the label of mental retardation?

REFERENCES

Anderson, G. L. (1989). Critical ethnography in education: Origins, current status, and new directions. *Review of Educational Research, 59,* 249–270.

Baumeister, A. A. (1987). Mental retardation: Some conceptions and dilemmas. *American Psychologist, 42,* 796–800.

Borthwick-Duffy, S. A., Eyman, R. K., & White, J. F. (1987). Client characteristics and residential placement patterns. *American Journal of Mental Deficiency, 92,* 24–30.

Brooks-Gunn, J., & Furstenberg, F. F. (1986). The children of adolescent mothers: Physical, academic, and psychological outcomes. *Developmental Review, 6,* 224–251.

Burt, C. (1921). *Mental and scholastic tests.* London: King.

Correa, V. I. (1987). Working with Hispanic parents of visually impaired children: Cultural implications. *Journal of Visual Impairment and Blindness, 81,* 260–264.

Diana v. State Board of Education. C-70-37 R.F.P., (N.D. California, Jan. 7, 1970).

Edgerton, R. B. (1967). *The cloak of competence: Stigma in the lives of the mentally retarded.* Berkeley, CA: University of California Press.

Edgerton, R. B. (1975). Issues relating to the quality of life among mentally retarded persons. In M. J. Begab & S. A. Richardson (Eds.), *The mentally retarded and society: A social science perspective.* Baltimore: University Park Press.

Edgerton, R. B. (1976). *Deviance: A cross-cultural perspective.* Menlo Park, CA: Cummings.

Edgerton, R. B. (1980). The study of community adaptation: Toward an understanding of lives in process. In E. D. Schulman, *Focus on the retarded adult: Programs and services.* St. Louis: C.V. Mosby.

Edgerton, R. B. (1984). Anthropology and mental retardation: Research approaches and opportunities. *Culture, Medicine, & Psychiatry, 8,* 25–48.

Edgerton, R. B., & Bercovici, S. M. (1976). The cloak of competence: Years later. *American Journal of Mental Deficiency, 80,* 485–497.

Edgerton, R. B., Bollinger, M., & Herr, B. (1984). The cloak of competence: After two decades. *American Journal of Mental Deficiency, 88,* 345–351.

Fishgrund, J. E., Cohen, O. P., & Clarkson, R. L. (1987). Hearing impaired children in Black and Hispanic families. *Volta Review, 89*(5), 59–67.

Folb, E. A. (1980). *Runnin' down some lines: The language and culture of black teenagers.* Cambridge, MA: Harvard University Press.

Gelfand, D. M., Jenson, W. R., & Drew, C. J. (1988). *Understanding child behavior disorders* (2nd ed.). New York: Holt, Rinehart, & Winston.

Goetz, J. P., & LeCompte, M. D. (1984). *Ethnography and qualitative design in educational research.* San Diego: Academic.

Heflinger, C. A., Cook, V. J., & Thackery, M. (1987). Identification of mental retardation by the System of Multicultural Pluralistic Assessment: Nondiscriminatory or nonexistent? *Journal of School Psychology, 25,* 177–183.

Landers, S. (1989). Homeless children lose childhood. *The APA Monitor, 20*(12), 1, 33.

Larry P. v. Riles. 343 F. Supp. 1306 (N.D. California 1972); 343 F. Supp. 1306, 502 F. 2d 963 (N.D. California 1979).

Lerner, R. M., & Lerner, J. V. (1989). Organismic and social-contextual bases of development: The sample case of early adolescence. In W. Damon (Ed.), *Child development today and tomorrow* (pp. 69–85). San Francisco: Jossey-Bass.

LeVine, R. A. (1989). Cultural environments in child development. In W. Damon (Ed.), *Child development today and tomorrow* (pp. 52–68). San Francisco: Jossey-Bass.

Leung, B. (1987). *Cultural considerations in working with Asian parents.* Paper presented at the conference of the National Center for Clinical Infant Programs, Los Angeles.

Lincoln, Y. S., & Guba, E. G. (1985). *Naturalistic inquiry.* Beverly Hills, CA: Sage.

Lopez, S. (1988). The empirical basis of ethnocultural and linguistic bias in mental health evaluations of Hispanics. *American Psychologist, 43,* 1095–1096.

Luftig, R. L. (1989). *Assessment of learners with special needs.* Boston: Allyn & Bacon.

Maheady, L., Towne, R., Algozzine, B., Mercer, J., & Ysseldyke, J. (1983). Minority overrepresentation: A case for alternative practices prior to referral. *Learning Disability Quarterly, 6,* 448–456.

Malgady, R. G., Rogler, L. H., & Constantino, G. (1987). Ethnocultural and linguistic bias in mental health evaluation of Hispanics. *American Psychologist, 42,* 228–234.

Manion, M. L., & Bersani, H. A. (1987). Mental retardation as a Western sociological construct: A crosscultural analysis. *Disability, Handicap, and Society, 2,* 231–245.

Mercer, J. R., & Lewis, J. F. (1977). *System of multicultural pluralistic assessment.* New York: Psychological Corporation.

Merton, R. K. (1948). The self-fulfilling prophecy. *Antioch Review, 8,* 193–210.

Merton, R. K. (1987). Three fragments from a sociologist's notebooks: Establishing the phenomenon, specified ignorance, and strategic research materials. *Annual Review of Sociology, 13,* 1–28.

Meyers, C. E., Borthwick, S. A., & Eyman, R. K. (1985). Place of residence by age, ethnicity, and level of retardation of the mentally retarded/developmentally disabled population of California. *American Journal of Mental Deficiency, 90,* 266–270.

Miles, M. B., & Huberman, A. M. (1984). *Qualitative data analysis: A sourcebook of new methods.* Beverly Hills, CA: Sage.

Miller-Jones, D. (1989). Culture and testing. *American Psychologist, 44,* 360–366.

Morrow, R. D. (1987). Cultural differences—Be aware! *Academic Therapy, 23,* 143–149.

Prasse, D. P., & Reschly, D. J. (1986). Larry P.: A case of segregation, testing, or program efficacy? *Exceptional Children, 48,* 490–500.

Reynolds, C. R. (1987). Race bias in testing. In R. J. Corsini (Ed.), *Concise encyclopedia of psychology* (pp. 953–954). New York: John Wiley & Sons.

Rosenthal, R. (1987). Pygmalion effects: Existence, magnitude, and social importance. *Educational Researcher, 16*(9), 37–41.

Rosenthal, R., & Jacobson, L. (1968a). *Pygmalion in the classroom: Teacher expectation and pupils' intellectual development.* New York: Holt, Rinehart, & Winston.

Rosenthal, R., & Jacobson, L. (1968b). Self-fulfilling prophecies in the classroom: Teachers' expectations as unintended determinants of pupils' intellectual competence. In M. Deutsch, I. Katz, & A. R. Jensen (Eds.), *Social class, race, and psychological development* (pp. 219–253). New York: Holt, Rinehart, & Winston.

Rosenthal, R., & Jacobson, L. (1968c). Teacher expectations for the disadvantaged. *Scientific American, 218,* 19–23.

Shulman, L. S. (1986). Paradigms and research programs in the study of teaching: A contemporary perspective. In M. C. Wittrock (Ed.), *Handbook of research on teaching* (pp. 3–36). New York: Macmillan.

Skowronski, J. J., & Carlston, D. E. (1989). Negativity and extremity biases in impression formation: A review of explanations. *Psychological Bulletin, 105,* 131–142.

Smith, R. D. (1987). *Multicultural considerations: Working with families of developmentally disabled and high-risk children. The Hispanic perspective.* Paper presented at the conference of the National Center for Clinical Infant Programs, Los Angeles.

Stainback, S., & Stainback, W. (1988). *Understanding and conducting qualitative research.* Reston, VA: Council for Exceptional Children.

Stainback, W., & Stainback, S. (1989). Using qualitative data collection procedures to investigate supported education issues. *Journal of the Association for Persons with Severe Handicaps, 14,* 271–277.

Turner, A. (1987). *Multicultural considerations: Working with families of developmentally disabled and high-risk children. The Black perspective.* Paper presented at the conference of the National Center for Clinical Infant Programs, Los Angeles.

U.S. Bureau of the Census (1985). *Current population reports* (Series P-60, No. 149). Washington, DC: U.S. Government Printing Office.

White, J. (1984). *The psychology of Blacks: An Afro-American perspective.* Englewood Cliffs, NJ: Prentice-Hall.

Wineburg, S. S. (1987). The self-fulfillment of the self-fulfilling prophecy. *Educational Researcher, 16*(9), 28–37.

Wood, F. H., Johnson, J. L., & Jenkins, J. R. (1986). The *Lora* case: Nonbiased referral, assessment, and placement procedures. *Exceptional Children, 52,* 323–331.

Yacobacci-Tam, P. (1987). Interacting with the culturally different family. *Volta Review, 89*(5), 46–58.

CHAPTER THREE
A Multidisciplinary Viewpoint

Core Concepts

Historical Perspectives

Mental Retardation and the Disciplines

   Disciplinary Perspectives and Contributions / Terminology / Contributions of
   Biological and Medical Sciences / Contributions of the Behavioral Sciences /
   Contributions of Education / Disciplinary Factionalism

New Issues and Future Directions

Core Questions

Round Table Discussion

References

<table>
<tr><td>

Core Concepts

</td><td>

- The concept of mental retardation is continually influenced by economic, societal, and situational factors.
- People with mental retardation often need more interaction with many disciplines and professions than do those not considered to be retarded.
- No *single* discipline has the breadth and depth of expertise and resources necessary to provide for people who are mentally retarded.
- The term *mental retardation* encompasses a wide range of behaviors; it is both a label of fact and a label of conjecture.
- The medical profession has a long history of involvement in the field of mental retardation.
- Many behavioral sciences, particularly psychology, have been concerned with mental retardation.
- Education has probably been the most involved with the problems associated with mental retardation of any discipline or profession.
- In order to better serve and provide for individuals with mental retardation, we must continue to work toward overcoming friction between disciplines.

</td></tr>
</table>

The concept of mental retardation is one that has meaning in personal, social, and behavioral contexts. The various ways we have classified and defined mental retardation over the years (see Chapter 1) emphasize how the concept of mental retardation has changed. As our perceptions have changed, our understanding and acceptance have been profoundly affected. In this chapter we discuss some services and programs that have added to our knowledge about mental retardation and provided insights into the development of social and educational programs for those it primarily affects.

HISTORICAL PERSPECTIVES

A brief examination of the mental retardation field's past is important. Without some historical perspective we begin each decade in a state of amnesia about what has succeeded and what has failed; without an understanding of the past we are cognitively isolated and lack perspective on our present condition. Our present advances have been built on the courage of a few insightful and caring persons who could see beyond the everyday, dreaming and working for a better world for those with mental retardation. Such individuals had a compassionate desire to improve the condition of their fellow humans.

<table>
<tr><td>

Core Concept

</td><td>

The concept of mental retardation is continually influenced by economic, societal, and situational factors.

</td></tr>
</table>

Mental retardation has existed in all societies and in all ages, but this does not mean that the way we have viewed mentally retarded people has been unchanging. Many diverse conceptualizations and varying characteristics have figured in different descriptions of people with mental retardation, depending on societal and situational influences during a given period. In fact, as one looks at the history of mental retardation, the picture is chameleonlike; its appearance changes with the attitudes and convictions of the time. The concept of mental retardation has been elusive for a variety of reasons, not the least of which have been aspects of the economic, social, and political climates of various cultures throughout history.

The following historical synopsis is intended to provide a brief accounting of (1) attitudinal changes based on the needs, ideas, and temporal conditions to the nineteenth century, and (2) the developing interest in and concern about mental retardation since 1800. For more comprehensive information the reader is directed to Scheerenberger (1983).

Before 1800, with a few notable exceptions, mental retardation was not considered an overriding social problem in any society, because those who were more severely retarded were either killed or died of natural causes at an early age. Those whom we would term mildly retarded could function fairly well in an agrarian society.

Although the earliest written reference to mental retardation is dated 1552 B.C. (Scheerenberger, 1983), anthropological studies have generated evidence of mental retardation substantially predating that time. Severe head injuries were not uncommon during early times, and they most certainly resulted in aberrations. Human skulls dating to the Neolithic Age indicate that crude brain surgery had been performed. The surgical procedures were apparently intended to cure abnormal behavior. The methods used may have proceeded from the assumption that evil spirits caused abnormal behavior and that opening a hole in the skull permitted them to escape. Not all such operations were performed on mentally retarded persons, but regardless of the reason for it, the treatment at times may have produced quasi-retarded behavior.

Through the ages, socioeconomic conditions have influenced human understanding and treatment of people with mental retardation considerably. Primitive tribes often looked on mental and physical defects with fear or as signs of disgrace, largely because of the stigma associated with such conditions. Superstitions and myths also bolstered this view. In a more pragmatic sense the handicapped often represented an economic drain on the tribe. Nomadic tribes in particular could ill afford to be burdened by nonproductive members who consumed limited food and water supplies but did not tangibly contribute to the common welfare. Individuals with retardation were frequently viewed as superfluous even when tribal civilization progressed and a less nomadic existence began to prevail. The advent of farming and grazing could not dispel the threat of famine, which remained constantly on the horizon. The economic usefulness of handicapped people was similar to what it had been during more nomadic times. Neither the religious nor the economic perspective was conducive to the care and maintenance of people with retardation—nonproductive citizens were expendable.

Political authority also has been a potent force throughout history in determining the lot of those with mental retardation. Sometimes authority supported harsh treatment of handicapped individuals; at others, a much more humane approach was in vogue. In the sixth century, for example, Pope Gregory I issued a decree that instructed the faithful to assist those who were crippled. During this period various types and degrees of care were provided for handicapped people, including those with retardation, who were commonly referred to at that time as idiots. In a similar vein England, under the rule of King Henry II (twelfth century), enacted legislation known as *de praerogative regis* (of the king's prerogative). Individuals who were "natural fools" became wards of the king; for the first time the law distinguished those we would now view as mentally retarded from those we would call mentally ill. These were isolated efforts on behalf of retarded people. Unfortunately history is replete with examples of extremely discriminatory and repressive practices. Individuals with mental retardation, as well as those with other handicapping conditions, have long been at the mercy of the more able majority.

Although we look on the attitudes of earlier societies as being extremely primitive and uninformed, a serious examination of current thinking and practices results in a more balanced, less complacent, perspective. The battles of numerous advocacy groups in the courts and other arenas are public testimony that many problems in our handling of people with mental retardation remain. Future societies will probably think that our present efforts are nearly as primitive as we consider those of the past.

Any historical discussion of mental retardation must address the topic of reproductive sterilization, which has come to the fore periodically. The sterilization issue has been entangled with a number of other questions—the nature versus nurture dispute, political and economic issues, and moral and social debates. Some early genealogical studies were very influential in generating the sterilization controversy in the United States. One such study by Henry Goddard (1913) received particularly widespread attention. Goddard traced the descendants of a Revolutionary War soldier to whom he gave the pseudonym Martin Kallikak. At one time in his life, Kallikak had sexual relations with a barmaid and fathered an illegitimate child. The descendants of this union were reported to be primarily thieves, prostitutes, and other social undesirables. Kallikak later married a "normal" woman; their descendants were purportedly normal and, in some cases, superior. The resulting conclusion was that because of genetics, one group was doomed to a life of degeneracy, whereas the other was almost certainly destined to be successful. Such reports fostered a sterilization movement in the early part of this century. Fear of mental retardation lent widespread support for methods that would "control" it, among them sterilization and incarceration. The result was an almost immediate and complete destruction of special schools in some states. Institutions became custodial in order to "protect" society and prevent reproduction. This was a considerable philosophical backlash, since there had previously been at least guarded optimism that institutions would be able to provide education and training for those of their residents with mental retardation. Societal fears, therefore, have influenced the nature, role, and function of such institutions.

With the shift in purpose, mentally retarded people in institutions were viewed as permanent residents. They were not trained for any eventual return to society. Such actions represented the simplistic solution of preventing "problem" members of society from having children who might in turn also become "problem" citizens. With this solution, people could at once both deny responsibility for undesirable social conditions like retardation and allow expenditures for the care and well-being of those affected by it.

Although sterilization remains an issue, there has been a fortunate reevaluation of the situation, brought about by considerable expansion of our knowledge of heredity and advances in the social-skill training of those with mental retardation. Increased sophistication in research methodology has called studies like Goddard's into serious question. For example, we are much less inclined to discount the effect of environmental influences on human development than was once the case. The descendants of Martin Kallikak and the barmaid were probably victims, at least in part, of their social situation. The descendants of Kallikak and his "normal" wife no doubt benefited from better educational and social conditions. A rational perspective requires consideration of both heredity and environment to avoid decisions and practices based on inadequate evidence.

MENTAL RETARDATION AND THE DISCIPLINES

Disciplinary Perspectives and Contributions

Earlier we referred to the variety of disciplines concerned with mental retardation. We now turn our attention to interdisciplinary collaboration as it is related to the complex problem of mental retardation.

Core Concept	*People with mental retardation often need more interaction with many disciplines and professions than do those not considered to be retarded.*

In a very real sense, people with mental retardation are no different from the rest of the population. Their need for love, independence, support, and respect is the same as everyone else's. We all profit from the services and contributions of medicine, education, psychology, sociology, anthropology, social work, and religion, to name only a few areas. Individuals with mental retardation may also benefit from all of these disciplines, but perhaps to an even greater degree. Here our earlier claim that such people are no different from others becomes an obvious overstatement. During their lifetime, retarded citizens will probably receive services from a broader range of disciplines than their more mentally able counterparts. This dramatically highlights a need to consider the multiple professions involved in the field of mental retardation. The delivery of services and understanding of individuals with mental retardation are far beyond the scope of any single discipline. As a social phenomenon, mental retardation falls within the purview of a number of professions.

Core Concept	*No single discipline has the breadth and depth of expertise and resources necessary to provide for people who are mentally retarded.*

Disciplines are organized naturally around a circumscribed body of knowledge, but their boundaries are somewhat arbitrary and information tends to overlap across disciplines. Societal problems do not readily align themselves according to the convenience of individual disciplines. Still, the academic model of establishing a disciplinary focus has been an effective method for directing intellectual efforts in particular areas. Before addressing the problem of better interdisciplinary cooperation, we need to examine some linguistic considerations briefly and then explore the contributions of some broad areas of disciplines.

Terminology

Core Concept	*The term* mental retardation *encompasses a wide range of behaviors; it is both a label of fact and a label of conjecture.*

The term *mental retardation* has a ring of precision to many people. That is, one is either mentally retarded or one is not. This is in part due to the scientific orientation of the west, in which constancy, regularity, and predictability are assumed. Past definitions of mental retardation show that perceptions of the phenomenon have changed over time. From characterizing mental retardation as a genetically determined and incurable condition, we have moved toward a more fluid conceptualization that includes not only biomedical causes but also social factors in determining whether someone is retarded at a given time (Grossman, 1983). This change is the result of a number of factors, including advances in the natural and social sciences, economics, and the use of less pejorative terms (i.e., mildly, moderately, and severely/profoundly retarded rather than moron, idiot and imbecile).

As a concept, mental retardation shares with other phenomena the distinction of being linguistically influenced. "Since language meaning develops in a social context it is not surprising there have been many definitions of mental retardation; time and conditions have had an important impact on determining its nature, scope and importance within a society (Logan, 1981, p. 3). The label of mental retardation is an encompassing one that includes a wide range of behavior. It shares with other such "people-labeling terms" the attribute of being a convenient, generalized expression about persons or groups.

Mental retardation is both a label of fact and a label of conjecture (Cromwell, Blashfield, & Strauss, 1975). This linguistic separation is necessary to prevent the confusions of the past. A label of fact must be quantifiable and verifiable, whereas a label of conjecture may include concepts which are (as yet) only hypothesized. As a label of fact, mental retardation must demonstrate observed characteristics that are verifiable and quantifiable, perhaps determined by biomedical diagnosis. Down syndrome, Tay-Sachs disease, and anencephaly are examples of conditions that can be verified through observation and medical techniques, although existing tests can quantify only approximate intelligence levels. Only about 20% of mental retardation is caused by biomedical factors, however. For the remaining 80%, the actual cause is uncertain. Therefore, mental retardation is also a label of conjecture. The influence of environment has been a major source for speculation, as the incidence of milder forms of mental retardation is much higher in lower socioeconomic classes.

The framework within which a discipline views mental retardation affects societal perception of the nature and extent of the problem. A technologically oriented society like the United States responds to "breakthroughs," "cures," and "innovations" much more enthusiastically than it does to the social complexity and ambiguous nature of cultural problems. The so-called natural sciences tend to be more favored by people from such countries because the results seem more tangible and dramatic. Social sciences, on the other hand, are viewed with more suspicion because they work with the more fluid values, perceptions, and beliefs of society.

The orientation of a discipline affects its view of people with mental retardation. Differences in orientation result from the reasons individuals go into a particular

Professionals from different disciplines need to work as team members to provide appropriate services for people with mental retardation.

discipline and from the training philosophy inherent in each discipline. It is not surprising, therefore, that physicians look for medical causes, psychologists seek psychological factors, and sociologists are interested in group influences on the behavior of individuals. Each discipline, at least initially, sees a mentally retarded person from its own perspective. This should not, however, preclude different professions from at least being aware of and appreciating the contributions of their colleagues in related areas.

Contributions of Biological and Medical Sciences

Mental retardation is best exemplified as a label of fact where there is an identifiable condition, and identifiable conditions are most frequently caused by a biomedical reason that results in structural damage. Even in this area, however, the cause of retardation is not always clear. Some chromosomal abnormalities are not always inherited (Down syndrome, microcephaly), and environmental factors like lead poisoning and infection can help cause structural damage.

Core Concept	*The medical profession has a long history of involvement in the field of mental retardation.*

The medical profession has long been involved in mental retardation in a number of ways. A physician is frequently the first professional to identify, diagnose, and counsel parents of children with retardation. When mental retardation is evident at birth, as in the more severely handicapped either by birth trauma or by congenital condition, a physician is usually the first professional consulted. This is because most parents have a family physician or pediatrician with whom they have had previous contact. At this point, if something appears to be amiss, parents will most probably turn to the professional they are accustomed to consulting.

Physicians usually view retardation as a physiological problem. Although changes in this viewpoint are evident in the medical field, physicians frequently have not had sufficient background to understand the nonmedical ramifications of mental retardation. This may limit their effectiveness in working with the family as a unit. It certainly deters them from providing maximally effective parent counseling, which has often been one of their tasks. Changes in medical training, however, promise considerable improvement in the physician's knowledgeability.

Another important area of medicine that warrants mention is that of medical research. Advances in medical research have had a dramatic impact on certain types of mental retardation. Because of intense efforts in investigating some of the clinical syndromes, such as phenylketonuria (PKU) and hypoparathyroidism, it has become possible and even common to implement procedures that prevent some forms of mental retardation. To reach this point, however, interdisciplinary collaboration was required. Once medical research had located the causal factor, it became necessary to turn to those skilled in chemistry and nutrition to implement preventive measures. Thus, even in what appears to be a very limited area—preventing a few selected types of mental retardation—the importance of interdisciplinary effort is evident.

Advances in genetics have opened avenues that should allow us to prevent some forms of mental retardation. Present research in genetic engineering gives promise of the future elimination of many more extreme deviations. Both positive and negative outcomes of such progress must be considered, a process that calls for input from multiple disciplines. At present some forms of mental retardation are preventable before conception. Prospective parents who may be carriers of defective genes can undergo genetic screening and receive counseling regarding the likelihood of their having defective offspring. Parents at risk are then faced with the decision whether or not to have children. Similar options are currently available to parents who have conceived, but face the probability of giving birth to a defective infant. Many moral and social issues surrounding such decisions are currently being debated nationally in legal and ethical forums, as well as in the basic sciences.

Psychiatry has a very lengthy history of dealing with mental retardation. When the American Association on Mental Deficiency (now the American Association on Mental Retardation) was organized in 1876, it began with eight charter members, all psychiatrists. Psychiatrists, when they have dealt with mental retardation, have primarily focused on the more severely handicapped. This practice has resulted in an inaccurate view of the broad spectrum of mental retardation. Past approaches have also tended to operate from a curative, traditional medical model. In view of such a posture it is little wonder that the psychiatric profession in general has become somewhat discouraged and uninterested in mental retardation. Leaders and progressive thinkers in psychiatry, however, have advocated a shift away from the microscopic approaches of the past. Within the discipline there is considerable hope that territories will become less rigidly marked, which would be a potentially positive shift for more adequate delivery of services to those with mental retardation.

Contributions of the Behavioral Sciences

Core Concept	*Many behavioral sciences, particularly psychology, have been concerned with mental retardation.*

Since mental retardation is partially a social phenomenon, one would expect that the academic fields concerned with behavior would have expressed interest in it. But although behavioral sciences have made many important contributions, most have dealt with mental retardation in only a limited fashion. Each field has generally operated independently and within the confines of its own terminology and parameters. The consequent reduction in effective contributions to education about and treatment of mental retardation exemplifies the importance of interdisciplinary collaboration. Still, each of the behavioral fields has added to the store of knowledge about mental retardation.

Psychology has been the behavioral science most directly involved in studying mental retardation. Three important areas to which psychology has contributed are intelligence theory and testing, learning theory research, and interpersonal social aspects. Knowledge about mental retardation would not have progressed as far as it has without the data and knowledge generated by experimental psychology. Likewise, the testing and the evaluation provided by psychometric researchers and school psychologists have long been a part of the overall picture in providing programs for children with mental retardation. This discipline, however, like others, has frequently operated independently, within the confines of its own terminology and perspective.

Anthropology has focused very little attention on mental retardation, and yet it has offered some extremely important insights into the broader perspective of the problem. R. B. Edgerton (1968) described the anthropological study of mental retardation as nonexistent and made a plea for drastically expanded efforts. Edgerton's (1967) work represents an important contribution by an anthropologist and has added much information about the adaptation of people with retardation to their environments. Although the data provided by Edgerton (1967) and Edgerton and Bercovici (1976) are important in and of themselves, their research approach has far-reaching implications in other ways and for other disciplines.

From the standpoint of research methodology, anthropology offers some intriguing possibilities. The anthropological approach to research is basically one of observing and recording information about people in their natural environment. This is a substantially different approach from that normally used in the study of mental retardation. More often than not, mental retardation researchers have elected the research method of experimental psychology, which studies the person with mental retardation in terms of performance or reaction to some artificially imposed treatment or situation. Consequently, we know little about the performance or adaptation of the individual with retardation in a variety of natural environments. The anthropological method of investigation is providing useful information to complement our existing knowledge base. Educational planning in particular might profit substantially from knowledge about how people with retardation operate in a natural setting. Thus, anthropology is a discipline that has not been heavily involved in mental retardation to date, but one that may make substantial contributions in an interdisciplinary effort.

Sociology has been investigating mental retardation at least tangentially for a number of years (Farber, 1968, 1986). A recent series of articles (Carrier, 1986a, 1986b; Milofsky, 1986) has addressed the use of sociological models in placing special education in a historical framework. These authors discuss the need to view disabilities from a sociological perspective rather than from the traditional clinical model. Such issues should become increasingly important in the years to come as the United States and other countries continue to face the complex problems of mental retardation. But the potential contribution of sociology to our understanding of retardation in a larger societal framework remains largely untapped.

The law has periodically been an important force in the area of mental retardation. Unfortunately, the legal profession, as opposed to other disciplines, tends to operate in an adversarial role. The case of *Covarrubias v. San Diego United School District* (1971), which challenged special class placements, offers an example of the usual legal role. In it an injunction negated further placements until procedural changes had been made. Only recently have collaborative alliances been formed between the legal and other professions.

The preceding discussion of selected disciplines has both given examples of disciplinary perspectives and stressed the absence of interaction between disciplines. We could easily have selected other areas for inclusion because of their attention (or lack of it) to mental retardation.

Contributions of Education

Core Concept	*Education has probably been the most involved with the problems associated with mental retardation of any discipline or profession.*

Although many areas have contact with mentally retarded individuals as need or interest arises, education—specifically special education—is perhaps most comprehensively involved by virtue of its nature and delegated role in our society. Educators do not have the luxury of viewing the world from a restricted framework or retreating behind disciplinary fences when faced with the multidisciplinary needs of those with mental retardation. The role of education in mental retardation has been primarily one of instruction. In a comprehensive service-delivery model, however, the idea of instruction is an oversimplification. People do not exist in isolation or learn in a vacuum. The real contribution of education in aiding the understanding of mental retardation has been to (1) identify needs, (2) stimulate research and theory, and (3) coordinate a host of services.

Identifying children with mental retardation was one of the earliest efforts of education. The first intelligence test worthy of the name was developed by Alfred Binet at the behest of the French minister of public education. The task is to develop a way to determine which children were likely to fail in school programs and would need special help, and the measurement of intelligence has therefore been largely influenced by educational needs rather than the interests of the discipline. Over the years first educators and then theorists and test-makers recognized that personality factors were also important in determining a child's present and future performance levels. We have since been introduced to the concepts of adaptive behavior and social intelligence. The involvement of education in mental retardation greatly facilitated the development of these and other constructs. In other areas the great strides in differential diagnosis, individualization of instruction, task analysis, and contingency management techniques were all enhanced by educators and their interest in providing better services for youngsters with mental retardation. For example, the need to understand mild mental retardation has influenced research efforts to increase our knowledge about the importance of environmental influences on intelligence. The development of secondary school programs has created a need for appropriate curricula and has prompted research on the sociological factors that relate to community placement for adolescents and young adults with mental retardation.

Without proactive recognition by education of the needs of those with mental retardation, we would not be where we are today in either understanding or providing services for this group of people. We do not wish to disparage the academic disciplines and their contributions, but only to place their relative contributions into proper perspective. Education often has been a core stimulating the efforts of the disciplines and then using their findings for the betterment of society.

Disciplinary Factionalism

Core Concept	*In order to better serve and provide for individuals with mental retardation, we must continue to work toward overcoming friction between disciplines.*

The foregoing discussion outlined various disciplinary perspectives. As one reviews their contributions, it becomes evident that efforts within a profession, when isolated from substantive interdisciplinary collaboration, often result in less effective delivery of services to people with mental retardation. Although change has been slow, the different disciplines are making progress toward bridging the gaps between their perspectives and diminishing disciplinary friction. At least two factors have prompted this progress. First, experience has shown that the mentally retarded persons being served are the ultimate victims of inadequate cooperation. This has provided a considerable impetus toward increasing cooperation. A second factor promoting change is the realization that something can actually be done to promote interdisciplinary collaboration—and that it may not be so difficult to accomplish. When knowledge is limited to a single field, differences in perspective and disciplinary friction result. The acquisition of enough information to understand another perspective reduces friction. Occasionally a broader knowledge base may bring about the realization that apparent differences in perspective are actually not so divergent as first thought.

Beyond the problems resulting from different perspectives, professional jealousy and territorialism often generate additional differences to a point where openly antagonistic factionalism exists between people in different disciplines. Such factionalism manifests itself in many ways, from published criticism to daily interaction between practitioners working—in theory together—in the field of mental retardation. To some degree examination of roles and issues in the public forum, such as published articles, is healthier than other forms of factionalism; it may often be constructive.

Disciplines within an organization or agency frequently disagree. One has only to attend regional or national conventions to hear derogatory comments about "the medical contingent," "those educators," "this division," or "that psychology group." Such an atmosphere of dissension results more in political conflict than in constructive improvement and hinders interdisciplinary collaboration substantially. We have made these comments in all editions of this text. It is fortunate that collaborative advances have been made, but the problem still remains.

Beyond the professional organizational level similar factionalism exists openly in state service and political arenas. Agencies frequently compete for limited funds to operate their programs, and lobbying techniques may aim to improve the lot of one group by making another appear inadequate. When they use such tactics to preserve an agency or a discipline, people often lose sight of the real reason for cooperation: to serve those citizens with mental retardation.

Since factionalism exists at various levels, it is not surprising that some friction also occurs at the practitioner level—the contact point between the service-delivery system and the client. The same professional jealousies and perceived territorial rights are found in daily interactions between professionals in contact with clients who are mentally retarded. A teacher may become angry because the school psychologist does not provide information that is helpful for instruction. The psychologist may deride the teacher for being unable to understand a psychological report and make an intuitive leap from it to instructional activities. Beyond differences in the way an individual with retardation is viewed—whether from the standpoint of instruction or that of test performance— professional antagonism aggravates the problem of inadequate cooperation.

Factionalism becomes unacceptable when it interferes with the work of the practitioner. Here it becomes most obvious who suffers as a result of an inability to cooperate; fortunately improvement seems to be greatest at this level. Practitioners have more opportunities to see the unfortunate results of inadequate service than do professionals who work less closely with clients who are retarded. It is therefore much more difficult for them to ignore or remain unaware of the crucial necessity for interdisciplinary cooperation and mutual effort.

The advent of the idea of least restrictive placement for all handicapped children has led to the placing of a number of children in "regular" education classrooms. Special education personnel, it was promised, would support the regular education teacher. Although there are instances where this has been successful, frequently special education personnel have not been able to provide the degree of service needed. In today's schools many regular teachers have students with mental retardation mainstreamed in their classes. In some cases these teachers are only superficially or not at all familiar with the characteristics of mental retardation.

NEW ISSUES AND FUTURE DIRECTIONS

Two broad considerations about cooperation between disciplines must be examined. One is the knowledge base; the other is the service base. We can best approach the accumulation of data through both multidisciplinary and interdisciplinary models. Multidisciplinary efforts are those in which various disciplines approach a particular problem from their own focus (for example, psychological aspects of mental retardation or medical aspects of mental retardation). Each discipline's data base grows, but frequently little of the information is of help in crossing disciplinary boundaries. Unlike the multidisciplinary method, the interdisciplinary model attempts to develop "knowledge bridges" between disciplines. From these efforts subdisciplinary areas like social psychology, sociolinguistics, and neuropsychology have developed.

Recently there has been a serious movement in special education to refrain from labeling handicapping conditions. Such terms as *mental retardation, behavior disorders,* and *learning disabilities,* although convenient for communication, often tell little about a person's characteristics or skill level. Likewise, these terms, when used in social contexts, often create flawed perceptions, imprecise applications, and inaccurate generalizations. Tradition has also designated disciplines by labels—psychology, education, psychiatry—which are extremely convenient for communication. Contemporary society could not operate without terminology and classifications. Disciplinary labels do, however, generate certain difficulties. Although they may help communication in restricted settings, they also generate myriads of connotations for each discipline. As a result, the same type of stereotyping that handicapping labels produce also emerges from the use of disciplinary labels. The labels all too frequently serve primarily to specify and promote boundaries—to assert territorial rights. And territorialism is a strong deterrent to effective interdisciplinary collaboration.

We suggested earlier that a broader knowledge base appears to facilitate interdisciplinary collaboration. In retrospect this seems logical—perhaps simplistic. Without at least some information about another person's profession it is extremely difficult even to communicate, much less to collaborate.

We are all quite experienced at obtaining information by reading journals and books. In many cases, however, book learning alone is not enough to break down interdisciplinary barriers. Frequent personal contact with individuals from other professions is more valuable. In fact, some would maintain that such contact is not only helpful but prerequisite to facilitating interdisciplinary efforts.

When the topic of interdisciplinary collaboration is raised, people often indicate that attitudes must change before it can occur. Although most would agree with such a statement, few would be able to specify how to accomplish this. Attitude is an extremely elusive concept, and it is far from easy to tell how one knows when an attitude has changed. It is somewhat easier, however, to speak in terms of altering certain behaviors.

One important behavioral change for interdisciplinary collaboration involves reaction to terminological differences. Frequently there are dramatic differences in terminology between professions. A person's use of a different terminology often generates negative reactions, sometimes even openly derogatory remarks, from individuals with different disciplinary perspectives. It is easy to see how such reactions lend themselves to friction and antagonism rather than to cooperation. Individuals working in an interdisciplinary setting must minimize their negative reactions to differences in terms. This does not mean adopting another's terms, concepts, and approaches, but it does imply that value judgments about the approach of the other discipline should be set aside. For example, I may not choose to incorporate the term *ego strength* into my vocabulary or conceptualization. If that is an important term in your disciplinary perspective, however, I can understand its meaning and judge it as different—but not as inappropriate—terminology. Certainly the acceptance of "differentness" is a goal of people working for the benefit of individuals with mental retardation, and improvements in interactions among professions can reduce friction and ultimately promote greater effectiveness in terms of interdisciplinary collaboration.

A second major behavioral change has to do with the delivery of services to those with mental retardation. We have seen how the various disciplines, operating through their applied branches, work independently of one another. Educators have often been left with a series of tests and reports that are mostly meaningless for planning a given child's educational program. In an interdisciplinary service approach model, although assessments are independently derived, the program parameters are decided on in collaboration. This approach, however, also has some drawbacks. Hardman, Drew, Egan, and Wolf (1990) point out that too often professional cooperation diminishes after initial program development, and efforts at coordinating services are often limited.

A third method, called the *transdisciplinary approach,* has emerged as an effort to overcome some of the problems of the other two models. The approach emphasizes the role of a primary therapist, who acts as the contact person for service provisions, so that the number of professionals with direct child contact is minimal. In a transdisciplinary plan no discipline is dominant; all should support each other and make their own contributions. This approach requires a mature professional attitude that recognizes and allows for relevant disciplinary contributions. The emphasis is on the person with mental retardation and that person's needs rather than on the disciplines working independently or without coordination. The role of the teacher (whether regular or special) in this method becomes predominant, since the teacher sees the children on a daily basis and is most conversant with their skills, aptitudes, and needs. The teacher, then, would be the primary therapist and the focal point for diagnoses and direct service to the child.

One of the crucial points of a chapter on disciplinary collaboration involves the purpose of the professional effort. Often people in the various disciplines working in mental retardation lose sight of the reason for their effort—the citizen with retardation. Too much time and attention are devoted to professional self-preservation, sometimes to the detriment of the individuals being served. We in the fields frequently focus more on our professional image than on the needs of those with mental retardation. Whether the perspective is primarily medical, educational, psychological, or based on some other discipline, it is essential that we maintain our focus on serving the total individual.

CORE QUESTIONS

1. How did politics, economics, and basic life styles affect the lives of persons with mental retardation before 1900?
2. What were some of the factors that influenced the development of institutions in the United States for persons with mental retardation?
3. Why is the term *mental retardation* considered to be linguistically influenced?
4. Why is mental retardation both a label of fact and a label of conjecture?
5. What are three areas in which psychology has contributed to our understanding of those with mental retardation?
6. What are the primary contributions of education in helping to understand the phenomenon of mental retardation?
7. What are some of the reasons that disciplinary factionalism has arisen and continues to exist?
8. What can be done to reduce frictions between disciplines and professions involved with persons with mental retardation?

ROUND TABLE DISCUSSION

As a concept, mental retardation has been with us throughout recorded history. Our perception of what is and what is not deemed mental retardation has changed continually. With the development of scientific approaches to the study of human behavior, many disciplines and professions emerged and began to identify areas of primary investigation, concern, and service.

In a discussion group consider the societal influences on mental retardation and how present-day attitudes toward persons with mental retardation may or may not reflect them. What would be some realistic approaches to overcoming disciplinary and professional friction?

REFERENCES

Carrier, J. G. (1986a). Sociology and special education: Differentiation and allocation in mass education. *American Journal of Education, 94*, 281–312.

Carrier, J. G. (1986b). Reply to Milofsky's comments on "sociology and special education." *American Journal of Education, 94*, 322–327.

Covarrubias v. San Diego Unified School District 7-394, Tex. Rptr. 1971 (unpublished).

Cromwell, R. L., Blashfield, R. K., & Strauss, T. S. (1975). Criteria for classification systems. In N. Hobbs (Ed.), *Issues in the classification of children* (Vol. 1, pp. 4–25). San Francisco: Jossey-Bass.

Edgerton, R. B. (1967). *The cloak of competence: Stigma in the lives of the mentally retarded.* Berkeley: University of California Press.

Edgerton, R. B. (1968). Anthropology and mental retardation: A plea for the comparative study of incompetence. In H. J. Prehm, L. A. Hamerlynck, and J. E. Crosson (Eds.), *Behavioral research in mental retardation* (pp. 75–87). Eugene, OR: Rehabilitation Research and Training Center in Mental Retardation.

Edgerton, R. B., & Bercovici, S. M. (1976). The cloak of competence: Years later. *American Journal of Mental Deficiency, 80*, 485–497.

Farber, B. (1968). Sociological research in mental retardation. In H. J. Prehm, L. A. Hamerlynck, and J. E. Crosson (Eds.), *Behavioral research in mental retardation* (pp. 97–109). Eugene, OR: Rehabilitation Research and Training Center in Mental Retardation.

Farber, B. (1986). Families with mentally retarded members: An agenda for research, 1985–2000. In J. J. Gallagher and B. B. Weiner (Eds.), *Alternative futures in special education* (pp. 25–41). Reston, VA: Council for Exceptional Children.

Goddard, H. H. (1913). *The Kallikak family.* New York: Macmillan.

Grossman, H. J. (1983). *Classification in mental retardation.* Washington, DC: American Association on Mental Deficiency.

Hardman, M. L., Drew, C. J., Egan, M. W., & Wolf, B. (1990). *Human exceptionality: Society, school and family* (3rd ed.). Boston: Allyn & Bacon.

Logan, D. R. (1981). *Mental retardation and public policy.* Paper given at the Third Linguistic Institute on Language and Public Policy, Cancún, Mexico.

Milofsky, C. (1986). Is the growth of special education evolutionary or cyclic? A response to Carrier. *American Journal of Education, 94*, 313–321.

Scheerenberger, R. C. (1983). *A history of mental retardation.* Baltimore: Paul H. Brookes.

CHAPTER FOUR

Theories of Intelligence

- Of all the ways people differ, none has generated as much continuing interest and speculation as has intelligence.
- As people moved from primarily hunting and gathering and/or agrarian societies, interest in the development of intelligence became emphasized.
- The relationship between intelligence and mental retardation was stated soon after the application of the scientific approach to the study of human behavior.
- Because of the development of quantitative measures intelligence has too often been thought of as linear; because of societal influences its qualitative aspects also must be considered.
- Discussion about the causes of mental retardation stimulated the debate about whether intelligence is primarily genetically determined or environmentally influenced.
- The need to know about the influence of a person's expectations, motivations, and social intelligence has stimulated research on the relationship between sociopersonal factors and intelligence.
- Attempts to measure it have generated considerable controversy about definitions of intelligence.
- Guilford and Piaget present two different approaches to the complex task of understanding the nature of intelligence.
- The trend toward a reconceptualization of intelligence includes a renewed interest in affect, achievement, and qualitative factors.

*Core
Concept*

Of all the ways people differ, none has generated as much continuing interest and speculation as has intelligence.

Human differences are concretely manifested by height, weight, skin and hair coloring, physical coordination, sex, and many other distinctive attributes that make individuals recognizable. In much more subtle ways we are also able to differentiate people with regard to their creativity, personality, and intelligence, to name but a few of the more abstract human traits. All these traits are of interest, but none has been so controversial as intelligence. Intelligence has been an intriguing subject for philosophers, psychologists, and laypeople for a variety of reasons. In western culture few concepts have been as avidly pursued as that of intelligence, both in definition and in measurement. At times it seems we have been so caught up in quantifying intelligence that we have difficulty keeping the concept in focus.

Two contributors to the problem are (1) our too rapid development of tests that purport to reflect intelligence and (2) a simplistic notion that test performance is valid and reliable regardless of cultural or motivational influences. There certainly has been no lack of awareness about these influences. Investigators in all behavioral sciences have pointed out definitional problems and the influence of behaviors that do not lend themselves to quantification. Our "success" in developing tests is perhaps our greatest handicap, particularly if the tests neglect other relevant aspects of intelligent behavior such as the influence of social and cultural mores, language, early environmental influences, physical development, and sex-role expectations.

Core Concept	*As people moved from primarily hunting and gathering and/or agrarian societies, interest in the development of intelligence became emphasized.*

The phenomenon of intelligence has been of interest for centuries. When people first became aware of differences in mental abilities is of little consequence, but it surely predates recorded history. As the gregarious nature of humans became evident through social groupings, the need to specify skills and competencies of group members became necessary to facilitate the efficient division of labor. The need to prepare individuals for group membership came to the fore when people saw that some were more skilled in certain areas than others. As societies developed and became more complex, the need to explain individual differences also increased in importance. The development of theories of intelligence parallels society's progress from the hunting group through the agrarian community to the industrial metropolitan area and into the atomic and space-age megapolitan region. The rapid movement into information-oriented societies, with ever-expanding computerization of activities, has placed a renewed emphasis on the importance of intelligence.

The advent of the space and computer age and the development of world markets made the need to identify those with high intellectual ability more pronounced. Governments of industrial nations have undertaken searches and provided rewards for the intellectually capable through grants for higher education, merit scholarships, and the promise of exciting, well-paid positions in a variety of areas. Conversely, this emphasis has also brought about increased attention to those whose intellectual capabilities are limited. Such individuals constitute a concern in technologically advanced societies because they frequently become social liabilities. In less mechanized times individuals with limited intellectual ability could often make sufficient contributions to society. As technology has advanced and influenced the entire spectrum of society, the need for unskilled and semiskilled individuals has diminished. Machines now more efficiently perform the work formerly done by individuals with little formal education. This has not been a great problem for those who have the requisite intellectual ability, but simply lack the necessary training to undertake more skilled labor. But for those who cannot profit educationally to the same extent as their more intelligent peers, opportunities for high status and a fulfilling life have sharply decreased. Any humane society must explore ways to reduce the social and economic liability of all its less gifted citizens, including those with mental retardation, and at the same time provide educational opportunities commensurate with such individuals' intellectual abilities. Since individual self-respect often depends on developing resources through education, for a society to do less than it is able degrades and demeans both its citizens and the society itself.

In these circumstances the need to identify and isolate particular characteristics associated with limited mental ability, both from biological and environmental causes, becomes paramount. As we have implied, limited intellectual ability has been identified as the central problem. The term *intelligence,* connoting relative acuity, has been a popular abstraction for centuries. Most civilized cultures have recognized intelligence as an important factor in group survival, development, and progress. As with other abstractions, however, it has been an elusive concept to define. The need to understand, define, and measure this phenomenon remains an important task as we attempt to provide better care for those with mental retardation in our society.

Humanity's attempts to come to grips with intelligence are manifested in an almost infinite number of theories about its nature. Theories play a vital role in assisting us as we try to delineate the inherent nature or substance of intelligence. Intelligence is not a directly observable phenomenon. In many respects it is a fluid concept because social values, socioeconomic conditions, and technological advances tend to affect our perception of it both individually and collectively. Well-constructed theories can assist us in identifying the relevant attributes of intelligence for further empirical investigation. Theories serve the dual purpose of being both tools and goals. They assist us in developing researchable hypotheses for empirical investigations and provide scientists with a way of integrating and ordering existing empirical laws.

The following sections trace the development of theories about intelligence from early times through the present day. The intent is to provide the reader with a historical appreciation for the problems humanity has encountered in its attempts to investigate intellectual capabilities and to describe present ideas about intelligence.

EARLY SPECULATIONS ABOUT INTELLIGENCE

Concern about cognitive abilities and the recognition of individual differences can be traced to the Chinese, who used testing to determine the capabilities of applicants for civil service positions over 4,000 years ago. The earliest recorded mention of mental retardation is thought to be in the Therapeutic Papyrus of Thebes in 1552 B.C. (Doll, 1962). Plato, in *The Republic,* also recognized the importance of determining individual differences in intelligence. The Greek philosophers Anaxagoras (c. 528–500 B.C.), Diogenes (412–323 B.C.), and Aristotle (384–322 B.C.), among others, were interested in and concerned with the composition and nature of the mind. The Greek physicians Hippocrates (460–375 B.C.) and Galen (c. A.D. 139–200) attempted to provide a natural, in place of a supernatural, explanation of mental abilities and mental phenomena.

As societies evolved an early interest was the need to identify the mental ability of a person charged with a crime. Sir Anthony Fitzherbert (1470–1538) is credited with being the first to provide a working definition that was legally useful and that included developmental, intellectual, and social aspects—giving it a somewhat modern ring. Henry Swinburne (1560–1623) added tests of the ability to measure cloth or to repeat names of the days of the week to assist in determining a lawbreaker's mental ability and, consequently, that person's responsibility under the law. The seventeenth-century legal criterion for responsibility was that the person charged needed to have the understanding of a 14-year-old. In earlier times society had difficulty differentiating between retardation and mental illness. Doll (1962) quotes John Locke, who in 1690 provided what is purported to be the first usable distinction between idiocy and insanity: "Herein seems to lie the difference between idiots and madmen, that madmen put wrong ideas together and reason from them, but idiots make very few or no propositions and reason scarce at all" (p. 23).

Many questioned the feasibility of attempting to quantify mental abilities because of their intangible and elusive nature. Obviously we have made a great deal of progress in psychological assessment since the early times described above. Scientific research has contributed enormously to the development of procedures for quantifying psychological abilities. But current psychometric theories continue to be plagued by the complexities of measuring intelligence (Cronbach, 1990).

TOWARD A SCIENTIFIC APPROACH

Core Concept	*The relationship between intelligence and mental retardation was stated soon after the application of the scientific approach to the study of human behavior.*

For all intents and purposes, the application of the scientific approach to human behavior began with a group of researchers who, in the late eighteenth and early nineteenth centuries, began investigating individual differences. Their academic backgrounds represented a variety of scientific disciplines from astronomy to philosophy. They became interested in differences in individual observations, both among observers reacting to the same phenomenon and in a single person's repeated observations. Since observational variations influenced the scientific approach, which demanded accuracy and reliability, many scientists became interested in being able to control or account for the influence of individual differences.

During the late 1700s an attempt was made to move from theory to practice in studying intellectual development. In 1779 an 11- or 12-year-old boy was found wandering wild and naked in the woods of Aveyron in France. The boy, later named Victor, was brought to Jean Itard at the National Institute for the Deaf and Dumb in Paris. Itard, who had been forewarned that Victor might be an "imbecile," began working enthusiastically with the boy. It was not particularly uncommon at this time to find persons with apparent mental abnormalities who had wandered from their homes and been found again after a few days in a state like Victor's. There were, however, many who felt that these "wild souls" had been lost in infancy and reared by animals. Such individuals were viewed as lacking normal intelligence because they had been deprived of the sensory input needed for human intellectual development. Itard felt that if the wild boy of Aveyron were exposed to the right kind of sensory input, his intelligence would develop. Itard's goal was to provide him with sensory and motor training, and with the experiences Victor had presumably missed. Itard worked with Victor for five years in all, keeping detailed records of all of his activities. At the end of this time Itard confessed his failure, since (among other things) Victor never learned to speak, although he did learn to read simple words and to dress himself.

But Itard's supposed failure was really a victory. He had amply demonstrated that a rather seriously retarded boy could be greatly improved and brought to a higher level of functioning than anyone had previously imagined. His work gained him the recognition of the French Académie and opened a new field of education.

At about the same time Jean Etienne Esquirol, a French physician and a colleague of Itard, was studying the differences between mental retardation and mental illness. Esquirol pinpointed lack of language as a primary deficit of people with retardation and determined that such people could often learn unskilled tasks and do elementary reading and writing. Alfred Binet and Théophile Simon later capitalized on Esquirol's observations that the deficits of retarded people were mainly intellectual and not sensory. They also followed his thinking that linguistic ability was a useful diagnostic criterion in developing a standardized intelligence scale.

Edouard Seguin, a student of both Esquirol and Itard, believed that people with mental retardation could be helped. He spent many years demonstrating that, with patience and determination, mentally defective children could be educated. In 1837 Seguin began a school for youngsters who were mentally retarded. Professional people from all parts of the world came to observe his methods of working with those who were retarded. Seguin moved to the United States in 1850, where he was instrumental in developing programs for people with mental retardation. He also proposed the formation of a national association for a concerted attack on the problem of mental deficiency, a work presently carried on by the American Association on Mental Retardation (AAMR).

In France, the need to have objective measures to identify mentally subnormal persons became increasingly important not only to determine responsibility under the law, but also to place people in the special classes that were becoming prevalent in the late 1800s. Subjective appraisals for placement were inadequate, so a search for more objective measures to ascertain mental ability was undertaken. Many scientists interested in human behavior were investigating such measures. But it was Alfred Binet (1857–1911), a Frenchman trained in law and medicine who became interested in psychology who, with his student Théophile Simon (1873–1961), developed the first intelligence test. Because of Binet's interest in intelligence, the minister of public education commissioned Binet and Simon to investigate the development of a test to assist schools in placing mentally defective children in appropriate classes. In 1905 Binet and Simon published a 30-item scale, considered by its authors to be only a perfunctory approach to the problem. In 1908 they published a revised form, which grouped 59 subtests over age levels from three to 13 years.

Henry Goddard, the director of research at the Vineland Training School in New Jersey, was traveling in Europe in 1908 and came across the Binet-Simon scales; in 1910 he translated them into English. Although several psychologists modified the scales, it was Lewis Terman who, after a great deal of research using American populations, published a test in 1916 based on the original 1908 Binet-Simon Scale of Intelligence.

Despite considerable controversy, the Binet scales revolutionized diagnosis and treatment of people with mental retardation.

The Concept of Intelligence

Core Concept	*Because of the development of quantitative measures intelligence has too often been thought of as linear; because of societal influences its qualitative aspects also must be considered.*

There are about as many ways to define intelligence as there are people interested and motivated enough to try. Over 30 years ago, Abraham (1958) reported that 113 different definitions of "the gifted" were found by a student writing a term paper on the subject. Likewise, mental retardation, at the other end of the intellectual spectrum, has produced a plethora of definitions. The number of definitions for these two intellectual extremes has led many people to think of intelligence in a quantitative sense. Intelligence, however, cannot be considered solely as a simple linear phenomenon ranging from more to less or from bright to retarded. The complexity of human intelligence dictates that its qualitative aspects must also be considered. An appreciation of the many determinants affecting intelligence is necessary if we are ever fully to understand and appreciate the phenomenon. From genetic selection at conception through prenatal, natal, and postnatal stages, and on through early development, there exists an almost infinite number of variables that can affect the intellectual abilities of the developing human organism. As scientists have grappled with the concept of intelligence, two questions have consistently stood out: How is intelligence developed, and how can we gain some understanding of its composition in order to make predictions about future behavior? Neither question is completely answered yet.

DEVELOPMENT OF INTELLIGENCE

Core Concept	*Discussion about the causes of mental retardation stimulated the debate about whether intelligence is primarily genetically determined or environmentally influenced.*

The question of how intelligence develops has generated what is most commonly referred to as the nature versus nurture controversy, which was directly stimulated by the phenomenon of mental retardation. Is intelligence genetically determined with little or no contribution from later environmental conditions and influences, or is it primarily dependent on environmental factors, with only a limited genetic contribution? Advocates of both positions have at times been vociferous in championing their view and claiming the naïveté of their opponents. The controversy has gone on almost continuously in this country since the turn of the century, with many social and economic factors affecting the way society views and provides for people with mental retardation.

Out of this controversy has emerged a more reasoned approach that is attempting to establish the interrelatedness and interaction of heredity and environment. It would seem to be an indication of theoretical maturity to move from extremes toward a middle position that is able to recognize and draw on the facts established by both sides.

The dilemma that spurs such heated debates is not really whether hereditary factors or environmental conditions play the major role in mental retardation, but their presumed effect. It is well established that some conditions are caused by hereditary factors, for example, microcephaly, neurofibromatosis, and Tay-Sachs disease. Similarly, it has also been shown that environmental conditions can affect the level of mental functioning. It is therefore no longer a matter of debate whether genetics affects human intelligence or whether environmental factors play a part in the dynamics of intelligence. Both play a role in which each depends on the other for intelligence to be manifested. The contributions of heredity in setting the limits of intelligence are recognized, and the influence of environmental factors is accounted for in determining the range of intelligence. Figure 4-1 illustrates this interaction, showing that the inherited genetic material (genotype) of particular individuals or groups, when affected by environmental factors, produces an observable result (phenotype) that is directly proportional to how favorable the environment is.

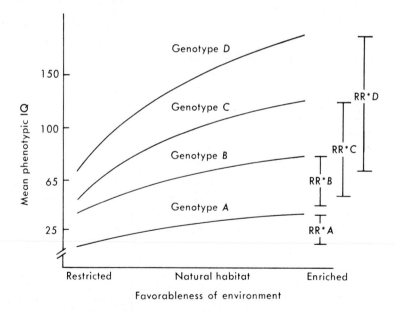

Figure 4-1

Scheme of the reaction range concept for four hypothesized genotypes   Note: Marked deviation from the natural habitat has a low probability of occurrence. RR signifies reaction range in phenotypic IQ.

From "Genetic aspects of intelligent behavior" by I. Gottesman. In *Handbook of Mental Deficiency*, ed. N. R. Ellis, 1963, New York: McGraw-Hill. Copyright 1963 by McGraw-Hill Co. Reprinted by permission of Norman R. Ellis.

Although the concept of interaction between heredity and environment is acceptable to almost all scientists, there remains a controversy about how much each aspect contributes. We are presently unable accurately to partition genetic and environmental contributions into percentages to indicate the precise amount that each contributes to individual performance. Attempts to ascertain the relative contributions of each continue, ranging from "best guesses" to stringently controlled research. Studies using twins have generally found that identical twins, whether raised together or apart, are more similar than random pairs of nonrelated persons. There are problems, however, even with this research methodology, because all variables cannot be controlled, and twins are often placed in similar environments when raised apart (Gelfand, Jenson, & Drew, 1988).

One example of the nature versus nurture debate was Arthur Jensen's (1969) controversial publication in the *Harvard Educational Review* and his subsequent book entitled *Straight Talk about Mental Tests* (1981). Jensen's thesis is that there are two types of learning tasks. His first type (type I) includes associative learning tasks, which depend on memorization and require little transformation of the material learned. His second type (type II) is conceptual learning, in which transformation of the learned material is requisite for success. In addition to defining these two types, Jensen has argued strongly that heredity may have a greater effect than environment on the development of intelligence.

Factors Influencing Intelligence

Core Concept	*The need to know about the influence of a person's expectations, motivations, and social intelligence has stimulated research on the relationship between sociopersonal factors and intelligence.*

Intelligent behavior is affected by a variety of factors that are only partially amenable to current measurement techniques. Most initial concerns about schoolchildren have to do with inappropriate behavior, not a perceived lack of intelligence. The AAMR definition of mental retardation (see Chapter 1) now includes a measure of adaptive behavior, which attempts to address these related and, in a practical sense, more important influences on personal and social success. A person's expectancy that something will occur, motivation, and ability to understand social situations form social intelligence.

Expectancies are attitudes that prompt a person to decide whether something may or may not occur. They are related to previous experiences. A person with an expectancy of failure in a certain situation, for example, cannot be expected to enter the same or similar situations with a positive expectation of success. Some research has suggested that those who are mildly mentally retarded tend to have lower expectancies for success than do those who are not, but that successful experiences raise their expectancy levels (Cromwell, 1976; Gruen, Ottinger, & Ollendick, 1974).

Motivation is related to expectancies as well as to competence and anxiety. A person who expects to fail and who does not feel competent generally has little motivation to

This adult's expectancies may have a significant influence on the youngster's performance.

engage in new or different tasks. Low motivation can influence test results by preventing the test-taker from trying.

Social intelligence reflects a person's ability to understand and engage effectively in social situations. Adaptive behavior is a corollary of social competence. Professionals have recognized for some time that social behavior is one of the primary factors in determining whether a person is mentally retarded or not. We are all familiar with people who, despite a low IQ, are sufficiently socially aware to function adequately in society. A number of attributes (subcomponents) of social intelligence have been identified. For a more complete description and conceptualization of social intelligence, see Ford (1986).

MEASUREMENT OF INTELLIGENCE

Core Concept	*Attempts to measure it have generated considerable controversy about definitions of intelligence.*

Questions about the measurement of intelligence elicit controversy over definition. How intelligence is defined influences the methods used to determine relative degrees of intelligence for prediction purposes. Basically, there are two extremes in how we think about intelligence. Some people take a factorial approach, attempting to isolate and identify the component parts of the intelligence concept. Others conceptualize intelligence as a holistic construct that is either hypothetical or is so intermingled with total personality that it cannot be conceived of as a separate and distinct entity. Most definitions fall between these two extremes.

It is one thing to theorize about the nature of intelligence and another to attempt to measure its parts. First one must make a decision about the components that the essentials of the phenomenon under consideration comprise. If, for example, prospective test-makers believe that intelligence cannot be understood apart from personality, then their test must necessarily include measures of such things as emotions, experiences, physical condition, age, and other factors involved in personality development. This would certainly provide a better measurement than we presently have, not only to predict behavior, but also to foster intellectual ability and capabilities. The obvious difficulty with this approach is that it is presently impossible to construct tests to include all the factors that would be required. Because of this, our intelligence tests can measure only limited samples of behavior at a given time in a given place.

The best tests of intelligence presently available cannot and should not be considered as the right way or the only way of measuring intellectual ability. Intelligence cannot be measured directly. As with any other concept, its primary components must be identified before any inferences can be made. The measurable attributes of a concept (in this case, intelligence) must be isolated, evaluated, and subjected to experimental analysis. This is what Binet did, for example, in deciding that judgment was involved in intellectual functioning. The degree to which a test-maker is successfully able to identify **measurable attributes** (often referred to as *subtests*), standardize them, and provide validity and reliability data is the essence of test development. Our current intelligence tests include attributes that test-makers believe are the best of the measurable aspects of intelligence now available. How well a person performs on the components of a test (examples: vocabulary, judgment, analogies) determines how much we can infer about the individual's relative intelligence.

The question of how far a test of intelligence is able to measure attributes of intelligence adequately is a source of continuing debate. In this regard Binet was aware of the shortcomings of his scale when he stressed the importance of qualitative variables that influence test results. Such matters as a child's persistence and attention definitely have an impact on test score.

As the use of intelligence tests with different groups increased over the years, it became clear that many factors militate against the indiscriminate use of tests and quick stereotyping of a person by IQ. We hope that a renewed call for consideration of the rights of others has raised a new consciousness. Many of the early psychologists and educators in the mental testing movement in the United States warned against indiscriminate use of intelligence and IQ tests and against belief in their sanctity.

At the end of the twentieth century we in the field of intelligence testing find ourselves in the position of having promised too much, of having neglected such important aspects of the intelligence puzzle as social and motivational aspects, and of having allowed practical considerations to outdistance sound theoretical development. In order to avoid getting ahead of ourselves, we now need to turn back and look at the development of theory and its relationship to the testing movement.

Most tests have emanated from the factorialists rather than from those who have taken the holistic approach toward intelligence. Charles Spearman (1863–1945) initiated the factorial approach and believed that intelligence could best be expressed through two factors: a general or "g" factor and a specific or "s" factor. Spearman (1904) assumed that the "g" factor represented "true intelligence" in that the various tests of intelligence were consistently interrelated. He then hypothesized that a "g" factor was present in all valid tests of intelligence, because it appeared to be a constantly recurring entity. But since the correlations were not perfect among tests, Spearman further hypothesized that an "s" factor was also present—though to a lesser degree than the "g" factor—and that the "s" factor resulted from those activities that could be associated with particular situations.

A contemporary of Spearman, Edward L. Thorndike (1874–1949), took a broader view in developing a multifactor theory. He believed that intellectual functioning could be divided into three overall factors: (1) abstract intelligence, in which a facility for dealing with verbal and mathematical symbols is manifested, (2) mechanical or concrete intelligence, in which the ability to use objects in a meaningful way is stressed, and (3) social intelligence, in which the capacity to deal with other persons is paramount. Thorndike took issue with Spearman's two-factor theory, maintaining that the correlations among tests, although demonstrably high, were not necessarily attributable only to a "g" factor. Further, Thorndike believed that neural interconnections in the brain influence intelligence and that whether the number of these interconnections is high or low can be inferred from a person's performance capabilities.

Core Concept	*Guilford and Piaget present two different approaches to the complex task of understanding the nature of intelligence.*

A considerable amount of debate arose as a result of the apparent disagreement between Spearman and Thorndike. Research over the next 40 years showed that much of the presumed difference between their data was due to divergent research techniques rather than to substantive differences between their theories. But the debate remains unresolved. Proponents of the multifactor versus the single-factor theory are still at odds; the issue is still important. The work of J. P. Guilford and Jean Piaget, two theorists who have approached the problem from different theoretical frameworks offers a perspective on the complex task of defining intelligence.

Guilford and his associates at the University of Southern California have continued research on the factorial approach to identifying the primary elements of intelligence. Guilford (1982) proposed a three-dimensional theoretical model that specifies parameters (content, products, and operations), incorporates previously identified primary factors, and assumes the existence of yet unidentified factors. This model (Figure 4–2) postulates the existence of 150 possible primary intellectual abilities. In Guilford's structure of intelligence the intent is to identify discrete factors and distinguish them from one another. Guilford (1982) has indicated that the model should not be seen as a collection of orthogonal factors, but as a model to stimulate thinking about intelligence.

Guilford and his associates believe that human thought processes involved in the **content** division can be subdivided into five major categories: (1) visual (having a visual or tactile form, as, for example, books, trees, houses, and clouds), (2) auditory (involving the processing of sounds into meaningful symbols), (3) symbolic (possessing a summarizing quality: numbers, musical notes, codes), (4) semantic (requiring that

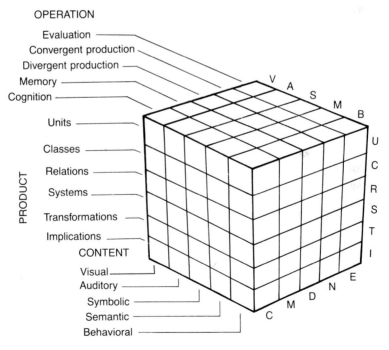

Figure 4–2
The structure-of-intellect model with three parameters
Adapted from *The Nature of Human Intelligence* by J. P. Guilford, 1967, New York: McGraw-Hill.
Copyright 1967 by McGraw-Hill Book Co. Adapted by permission.

meanings be attached to intangibles: the word *pencil* refers to object), and (5) behavioral (involving such nonverbal qualities as perceptions, desires, and moods).

The **product** aspect of Guilford's intelligence model currently includes six major types or categories that serve to organize figural, symbolic, and semantic content. The subdivisions are (1) units (the processing of a single item: a number, letter, a word), (2) classes (the classification of sets of items or information by common properties, as with figure symbols), (3) relations (the activity of developing relationships between a product subdivision and a content subdivision or even relationships between relations), (4) systems (an aggregate of interacting parts, as in sentence diagramming, numerical operations, or social situations), (5) transformations (the more abstract and creative activity of transforming material into results, conclusions, or physical configurations different from those anticipated), and (6) implications (the most abstract of the product subdivisions—one that involves anticipation and making predictions).

The third division of Guilford's model, **intellectual operation,** includes the mental processes involved in using the information or content with which it works. Guilford defines five types of operations: (1) cognition (the process of comprehension, knowing, understanding, familiarity; the comprehension of interesting material in a nonthreatening atmosphere, for example, games, television); (2) memory (the ability to recall specific information, such as arithmetical steps, telephone numbers, and others; both short- and long-term memory are included in this subdivision; (3) divergent production or thinking (the process of being able to generalize and produce alternatives based on information possessed or provided); (4) convergent production or thinking (the process of being able to produce an acceptable response derived, it is assumed, from a large quantity of material); and (5) evaluation (such mental activities as judging, comparing, contrasting, making decisions, and others).

Jean Piaget (1896–1980) is unique among theorists in that he approached the problem of understanding intellectual functioning from an entirely different framework. Instead of developing various tasks and then evaluating the correctness of the response, Piaget focused on the psychological process that led to the response. In addition, he was primarily concerned with interpreting the development of behavior.

Whereas Guilford was influenced by early work in factorial statistical analysis, Piaget's early preparation was in biology and zoology. His approaches have evolved over more than 50 years. During this time his work has gone through three distinct phases. In the first phase he investigated children's language and thought, judgment and reasoning, conception of the world, conception of physical causality, and moral judgments. During this phase Piaget questioned the view that child development resulted completely from either environmental or genetic influences. His investigations demonstrated that mental growth was influenced neither entirely by nature nor solely by nurture, but rather by the continuous interaction of both aspects. In the second phase he attempted to observe intelligence and development of the idea of reality in his three children by observing their behavior in situations involving objects and persons. Piaget demonstrated a genius for observation that was continually guided by his theoretical formulations, and in his observations he accumulated evidence to support his theories on the development of cognitive structures. In the third phase of Piaget's research he and his associates investigated a number of issues that had arisen in his early theories: concrete operations, conservation, relations, preconceptual symbolization, formal operations, sensorimotor stages, probability, perceptions, illusions, logical operations, and so on.

Piaget postulated a series of intellectual developments. The order of their appearance is important, but not the age at which they appear. He believed that intelligence is an **adaptive** process and is only one aspect of all biological functioning. The environment places an individual simultaneously in the position of adapting to it and modifying it. The term *accommodation* was used by Piaget to describe the adaptation of an individual to the environment; he used the term *assimilation* to describe an individual's modification of the environment to fit his or her perceptions. An organism is considered to have adapted when there is **equilibrium** (balance) between accommodation and assimilation. Piaget used this biological concept of equilibrium in describing learning activities. A child at play uses assimilation—the stick becomes a fishing pole, a rifle, or a baton; the shoe becomes a car or a boat. When the child is playacting, however, accommodation becomes predominant: the youngster becomes an astronaut, a rock or movie star, or a champion tennis player in an attempt to imitate the desired model through accommodating ephemeral perceptions. Assimilation and accommodation are complementary and antagonistic functions. Each creates alternate states of disequilibrium until the two are gradually resolved into a state of equilibrium.

Piaget postulated a sequence of developmental periods and substages that he believed to be generally the same for everyone. According to Piaget (1960), maturation and experience influence a child's rate of progress through the following sequences. The four main periods and their substages are as follows:

1. *Sensorimotor period.*   This period is from birth to about 1½ to two years of age. In this period the child is involved in a number of behavioral activities leading to a stable imagery.
2. *Preoperational period.*   The preoperational period is divided into two substages: preconceptual and intuitive.
   a. *Preconceptual substage:* This substage occurs from about 1½ to about four years of age. Symbolic thought and language manifest themselves, indicating the child's awareness of objects and realization of his or her relation to and interrelation with them. The child is now able to initiate actions.
   b. *Intuitive substage:* From about three to seven years of age the child's thought is restricted to what is directly perceived. The child enters this stage unable to understand constancy, believing that, for example, the amount of liquid is less and not the same in a bowl than in a narrow cylinder. By the end of this stage the child is able to recognize other points of view but is not able to transfer generalizations to other situations.
3. *Concrete operations period.*   This period falls roughly between seven and eleven years of age. During this stage the child moves toward the ability to understand the conservation of quantity, length, and number. The youngster now understands, for example, the constancy of the amount of liquid regardless of the size or shape of the container and is able to generalize about other situations.

4. *Formal operations period.*   From approximately 11 years of age onward, the child is involved in a continuous refinement of approaches to complex problems. The child engages in reasoning activities that are beyond a concrete operational approach. Children are now hypothesizing and making correct deductions. Words, which provide the developing human being with increasingly abstract concepts to manipulate, are now a primary tool used to solve problems.

Piaget posited a developmental theory of intelligence. He envisioned both qualitative and quantitative differences as the person develops. His orientation differed from that of other theorists engaged in studying intelligence and represented a different way of looking at children's intellectual growth.

NEW ISSUES AND FUTURE DIRECTIONS

The work of the theorists reviewed and discussed stands as a foundation for future developments in cognition and our understanding of intelligence. Guilford's structure-of-intellect (SOI) model, for example, is currently being seen as a possible guide to future thinking in the field (Tyler, 1986). Piaget's primary contribution may have been the way he examined the process of developing behavior (intelligence) rather than his actual theories. Flavell (1982, 1985) has questioned the value of Piaget's developmental stages for the future study of intellectual development, and Mann and Sabatino (1985) have pointed out that Piaget's influence on education, particularly on special education, has not had the impact that many had hoped for.

Core Concept	*The trend toward a reconceptualization of intelligence includes a renewed interest in affect, achievement, and qualitative factors.*

There appears to be a movement away from test development per se and toward a reconceptualization of what we know about intelligence and testing. Lohman (1989) has identified three emerging trends in the field. The first is a recognition of the importance of affect in any attempt to understand intelligence. The second is a move toward a better understanding of achievement in relation to intelligence rather than a view of them as distinct. The third trend is a renewed interest in the association between learning and development. This represents an attempt to make a connection between a quantitative, psychometric approach and a qualitative, developmental view in understanding learning and, consequently, intelligence.

Two theorists who have received considerable recognition in recent years are Robert J. Sternberg and Howard Gardner. Sternberg has developed what he terms a "triarchic" theory of human intelligence (Sternberg, 1985). There are three elements to his theory: contextual, experiential, and componential. The **contextual** element addresses the importance of culture and the behaviors that the culture considers intelligent. Sternberg maintains that intelligent behavior in contextual situations involves being able to adapt to the environment, selection of another environment, or shaping the present environment to meet personal attributes (skills, interests, values) better. The way a person goes about adapting, selecting, or shaping varies from one culture to the next. Each culture identifies what types of activities are acceptable, important, and valued. Therefore, being able to interact in a purposeful way with one's culture is an indication of contextual intelligence.

Sternberg's **experiential** element is related to the learning experiences a person faces. Intelligence is involved when the events a person engages in are either themselves novel or present new problems, or when people practice responses so that they can respond quickly and easily. Intelligence may be determined by the way in which individuals approach new or novel tasks, as long as they have some experiential background that prepares them to undertake the task. Sternberg maintains that a person's ability to

Experience with telephones helps children develop social skills.

learn needed material to an automatic level facilitates intelligence. At the automatic level the learned material becomes part of memory. Sternberg believes that this allows a person to devote more processing capabilities to learning new or novel tasks.

The **componential** element attempts to identify those internal cognitive factors that underlie intelligent behavior. This subtheory is related to the environments in which a person lives. Three aspects, or components, are involved. First are **metacomponents,** the processes people use in deciding how to solve a problem, in monitoring the process being used to solve it, and in evaluating the results. Second are **performance compo-nents,** which are the activities a person uses to carry out the strategy for solving the problem. **Knowledge-acquisition components** are the third part of the componential subtheory. These components selectively encode new information, combine this new information, and then make comparisons between the newly learned material and previously learned material.

Sternberg and Spear (1985) discuss the implications of the triarchic theory for mental retardation. They believe that the breadth of the triarchic theory is necessary in order to account adequately for the many causes and ramifications of individual per-formance. The theory forces a more comprehensive look at behavior, including mental retardation, than many past approaches have required. Sternberg and Spear (1985) further maintain that it is possible that mental retardation alone may not seriously impair a person from adapting to the environment. If the environment is related and supportive of a person's skills and abilities, then there is little reason to believe that that person cannot function at an acceptable level.

The triarchic theory is a much broader theory of intelligence than many previously proposed. The theory goes beyond intelligence—as exemplified by the ability to perform scholarly work—to extend the horizons of our concept of intelligence. We are, however, still faced with the same problems that have plagued previous theorists: How are the adaptive behaviors (social intelligence, creativity, compassion) to be measured? This may not be an insurmountable task given the progress that has been made and the fact that adaptive behavior is now identified as an essential ingredient of intelligence in a major theory.

Howard Gardner's theory of multiple intelligences is another recent broad-based theory. Gardner became dissatisfied with both Piagetian intelligence theory and the orientation of schools toward linguistic and logicomathematical symbolization (Gard-ner & Hatch, 1989). His research convinced him that the mind is modular and is capable of working with many symbolic systems (numerical, linguistic, spatial) inde-pendently. A person may be particularly adept at one symbolic system (say, music) without having concomitant skills in other systems. By measuring only one or two aspects of intelligence (linguistic and logical), existing tests define intelligent behavior very narrowly. Gardner has defined intelligence very broadly to include solving prob-lems and creating products that have value in at least one cultural setting. As a result of extensive research and analysis of the work of others, Gardner has developed a list of seven types of intelligence. He believes that everyone possesses all seven cognitive elements, but do not display them uniformly because of both hereditary and environ-mental influences. The types of skills people possess direct their future endeavors, as long as the culture accepts and is responsive to the importance of that skill. For example, a person with excellent linguistic aptitude may flourish in a society that values such abilities, but be frustrated in developing these skills in a culture that is more logicomathematically oriented.

Gardner and Hatch (1989) propose that there are seven intelligences. Each one is distinct from the others, but they are related and complementary. They are as follows:

1. *Logicomathematical.*   Relates to the ability to carry out numerical and reasoning tasks and is a critical skill for mathematicians and scientists.
2. *Linguistic.*   This ability focuses on language and its uses. Writers and poets have high skill levels in this domain.
3. *Musical.*   Associated with the composition and performance of music. Composers and performers exhibit a high degree of ability in this area.
4. *Spatial.*   Relates to the ability to see objects clearly in a visual-spatial sense and to manipulate them based on dimensional perceptions. Artists (particularly sculptors), astronauts, pilots, and others demonstrate a high degree of this type of intelligence.
5. *Bodily-kinesthetic.*   This type of ability is translated into bodily movement, both fine- and gross-motor ability. Examples of individuals with high levels of this skill are dancers, athletes, and surgeons.
6. *Interpersonal.*   Includes the ability to perceive the feelings and attitudes of others. Individuals who successfully interact with others are skilled in this area. Examples: politicians, therapists, salespeople.
7. *Intrapersonal.*   This component can be summarized as the ability to know oneself. Persons who are in touch with their feelings, strengths, and weaknesses demonstrate a high capacity in this area. Psychiatrists and clinical psychologists are expected to possess this skill to a high degree.

There is much movement in the areas of theory and testing at the present time. The recognition that affect is important and that there may be different intelligences is producing a renewed vigor in the area of cognition and learning. The next decade should see advances in the field of theory and testing. We must, however, proceed with caution in order not to embrace every new theory or test without thoughtful analysis. We should learn at least that much from past errors. The broadening of intelligence theory to include things like culture and experience follows closely on calls for reconceptualizing mental retardation (Baumeister, 1987). Rethinking the concepts of mental retardation was encountered in Chapter 2 on multicultural issues and emerges again in Chapter 5, where we examine assessment.

════ **CORE QUESTIONS** ════════════════════════════

1. How have societal changes affected our concepts of intelligence?
2. Why are theories both a tool and a goal?
3. What was the impetus behind the development of the first "intelligence" test?
4. Why is the work of Jean Itard important?
5. What is meant by the nature versus nurture controversy, and why is it important?

6. Why is social intelligence an important aspect of intelligence?
7. Why can't intelligence be measured directly?
8. What is the orientation of factorialists toward understanding intelligence?
9. What approach did Piaget take in his study of intellectual development? How does it differ from the factorial approach?
10. In what ways are the theories of Sternberg and Gardner similar to and different from earlier theories of intelligence?

ROUND TABLE DISCUSSION

Humankind's search for the critical aspects of and the keys to the development of intelligence has been rigorously carried out by many scientists. We have moved from simplistic views of what intelligence is to complex theories about its characteristics. In doing so we have identified both quantitative and qualitative aspects of intelligence. For those interested in the study of mental retardation, an understanding of past history, present formulations, and future considerations about intelligence is both important and necessary.

In a study group discuss the development of our knowledge about intelligence to the present day. As a part of the discussion members should relate what they feel were important developments and what they were surprised to learn. Further discussion should focus on what individuals feel about the different approaches and how their perception of persons with mental retardation has been influenced by using one or another approach.

REFERENCES

Abraham, W. (1958). *Common sense about gifted children.* New York: Harper & Row.

Baumeister, A. A. (1987). Mental retardation: Some conceptions and dilemmas. *American Psychologist, 42,* 796–800.

Cromwell, R. (1976). Ethics, umbrage, and the A B C Ds. *Minnesota Education, 2,* 42–47.

Cronbach, L. J. (1990). *Essentials of psychological testing* (5th ed.). New York: Harper & Row.

Doll, E. E. (1962). A historical survey of research and management of mental retardation in the United States. In E. P. Trapp & P. Himelstein (Eds.), *Readings on the exceptional child* (pp. 21–68). New York: Appleton-Century-Crofts.

Flavell, J. H. (1982). Structures, stages and sequences in cognitive development. In W. A. Collins (Ed.), *The concept of development: The Minnesota symposia on child psychology* (Vol. 15). Hillsdale, NJ: Lawrence Erlbaum.

Flavell, J. H. (1985). *Cognitive development.* Englewood Cliffs, NJ: Prentice-Hall.

Ford, M. E. (1986). A living systems conceptualization of social intelligence: Outcomes, processes and developmental change. In R. J. Sternberg (Ed.), *Advances in the psychology of human intelligence* (Vol. 3, pp. 119–171). Hillsdale, NJ: Lawrence Erlbaum.

Gardner, H., & Hatch, T. (1989). Multiple intelligences go to school: Educational implications of the theory of multiple intelligences. *Educational Researcher, 18*(8), 4–10.

Gelfand, D. M., Jenson, W. R., & Drew, C. J. (1988). *Understanding child behavior disorders* (2nd ed.). New York: Holt, Rinehart and Winston.

Gruen, G., Ottinger, D., & Ollendick, T. (1974). Probability of learning in retarded children with differing histories of success and failure in school. *American Journal of Mental Deficiency, 79,* 417–423.

Guilford, J. P. (1982). Cognitive psychology's ambiguities: Some suggested remedies. *Psychological Review, 89,* 48–59.

Jensen, A. (1969). How much can we boost IQ and scholastic achievement? *Harvard Educational Review, 39,* 1–123.

Jensen, A. (1981). *Straight talk about mental tests.* New York: Free Press.

Lohman, D. F. (1989). Human intelligence: An introduction to advances in theory and research. *Review of Educational Research, 59,* 333–373.

Mann, L., & Sabatino, D. A. (1985). *Foundations of cognitive process in remedial and special education.* Rockville, MD: Aspen.

Piaget, J. (1960). The general problems of the psychobiological development of the child. In J. M. Tanner & B. Inhelder (Eds.), *Discussions on child development* (pp. 3–27). London: Tavistock.

Spearman, C. E. (1904). General intelligence: Objectivity determined and measured. *American Journal of Psychology, 15,* 201–293.

Sternberg, R. J. (1985). Beyond IQ: A triarchic theory of human intelligence. London: Cambridge University Press.

Sternberg, R. J., & Spear, L. C. (1985). A triarchic theory of mental retardation. In N. R. Ellis and N. W. Bray (Eds.), *International review of research in mental retardation* (Vol. 13, pp. 301–326). New York: Academic.

Tyler, L. (1986). Back to Spearman? *Journal of Vocational Behavior, 29,* 445–450.

CHAPTER FIVE

Assessment Issues and Procedures

Core Concepts

Issues and Concepts

Assessment Utilization / Technical Soundness / Normative and Criterion Referencing / Formative and Summative Evaluation / Assessment Bias / Mental Age and Intelligence

Early Life

Screening Concepts / Early Life Assessment

Preschool Years

Intellectual Functioning / Language Functioning / Perceptual-Motor Functioning / Social/Adaptive Behavior

Elementary School Years

Intellectual Functioning / Achievement / Assessment Systems

Adolescent and Adult Years

Intellectual Functioning / Vocational Functioning

New Issues and Future Directions

Core Questions

Round Table Discussion

References

- Careful attention to the proper use of assessment instruments has a great impact on the results of measurement.
- The technical soundness of psychoeducational assessment involves three factors: norms, reliability, and validity. Each factor has not always been carefully considered in instrument development and utilization.
- The purpose of any assessment greatly influences the procedure(s) employed and the way data are interpreted. Recognition of this has led to the development of such important concepts as norm and criterion referencing and formative and summative evaluation.
- Mental age and IQ have historically been central in assessment of mental retardation, although many other factors are emerging as important for full evaluation.
- Assessment procedures are quite different depending on the age of the person and the performance area being evaluated.
- Screening assessment is very important throughout a person's life span, but it is crucial in early life.
- Prenatal evaluation can provide extremely important information about the fetus.
- Assessment of the newborn can identify problems and prompt immediate intervention to prevent mental retardation.
- Evaluation beyond the newborn stage includes many assessment areas not previously amenable to measurement.
- Functioning in intellectual, language, perceptual-motor, and social/adaptive behavior is important in evaluating the status of preschool youngsters. Proper assessment must employ procedures appropriate for this age range.
- Multiple areas of functioning must be evaluated during the elementary years. Proper evaluation uses technically and conceptually sound procedures appropriate for this age range.
- Assessment during adolescent and adult years involves utilization of age- or functioning level–appropriate procedures. Attention must also be given to the changing purposes of evaluation in these years.

Psychological assessment has a long and rich history when compared with other areas of behavioral science. Within psychological assessment what has received the most attention is intelligence measurement. Work in the measurement of intelligence has been a major force in all psychological assessment, and the roots of psychological assessment go deep into the field of mental retardation.

Serious efforts to measure intelligence began with the work of Alfred Binet in 1904. Binet was commissioned by school officials in Paris to develop a means by which those children who were "truly dull" could be identified. Although there had been interest in psychological measurement before this, Binet's assignment is generally viewed as an important beginning.

The influence of psychological assessment has long been felt far beyond the area of mental retardation, and its methodology has become increasingly complex, sophisticated, and, some would say, elegant. In certain areas, however, its sophistication may be no more than superficial. This chapter discusses assessment issues, frameworks, and procedures from the perspective of mental retardation and in terms of the various phases of the human life cycle.

ISSUES AND CONCEPTS

Work in the measurement of intelligence has a very long history. Efforts to evaluate other areas of functioning—personality, language, and social development—have also been under way for a long time. Although so much effort has gone into it, much of the work has not been undertaken in as thoughtful a manner as might be appropriate or desirable.

Assessment Utilization

Core Concept	*Careful attention to the proper use of assessment instruments has a great impact on the results of measurement.*

One difficulty plaguing behavioral evaluation over the years has been the misuse of assessment procedures. Instrument development has occurred at a very rapid rate, often at the expense of careful and deliberate thought about the purposes and uses of the tests. Assessment literature reflects serious concern about usage over many years (e.g., Anastasi, 1950, 1988; Fuchs & Fuchs, 1986; Gronlund & Linn, 1990; Haney, 1984). Drew (1973) stated that "evaluators and educators seem plagued with an *instrumentation fixation* to the near exclusion of attention to questions of 'Why are we testing' " (p. 324). He further noted that "technical precision in psychological assessment has nearly always been far in advance of conceptual precision" (p. 323). Technical precision in this context refers to instrument construction; conceptual precision has to do with considerations of the underlying purposes for assessment and the use of the resulting information. There are some serious arguments about how much technical precision has been generally achieved (e.g., Flynn, 1985; Ysseldyke & Algozzine, 1982). But the usage problem is fundamental and may be even more serious, since, logically speaking, concepts need to be in place before an evaluation can take place. Even evidence from current practice raises serious questions. Ysseldyke, Algozzine, Richey, and Graden (1982) found minimal relationships between assessment data and decisions made by placement teams (correlations ranging from −.13 to +.29). Schenck (1980) also reported limited relationships between assessment information and the instructional prescriptions of individualized education programs (IEPs) designed for 243 handicapped children. Subjects with mental retardation constituted a relatively small part of the sample (learning disabled [LD] = 186, emotionally disturbed [ED] = 28, educable mentally retarded [EMR] = 29). But assessment concerns are just as serious for those with mental retardation as for the other groups. Schenck concluded that "results of the investigation indicated that the long-term goals and short-term instructional objectives of the IEP have limited foundation in the psychological assessment" (p. 341). She further noted that "procurement of diagnostic data solely for purposes of differential diagnosis denies the need to address the unique learning requirements of the learner" (p. 341). Perhaps a more direct question is Why should we test if the information is not directly used for instruction or other intervention? The conceptual problems related to purpose and usage may also be reflected in the practical applications of assessment.

Psychoeducational instruments have proliferated over the past 20 years. There is probably an instrument available that purports to measure every facet of human behavior that one would want to evaluate. Further, new instrumentation is being developed and placed on the market continually (and at what seems to be an accelerating rate). Yet there are questions about the degree of technical precision of much psychoeducational assessment. This concern is an appropriate one. But the problems related to technical precision are not the result of insufficient knowledge or theory about instrument development and measurement. Measurement theory has become a rather highly developed area in behavioral science and has been studied for many years (e.g., Cronbach, 1990; Hopkins & Stanley, 1981). Unfortunately, many instruments on the market do not give adequate attention to sound measurement practices. The great demand from the field appears to have resulted in inadequate instruments.

Technical Soundness

Core Concept	*The technical soundness of psychoeducational assessment involves three factors: norms, reliability, and validity. Each factor has not always been carefully considered in instrument development and utilization.*

Norms
Normative data should be collected as the test is developed and refined. This part of the standardization process provides an estimate of typical performance with which to compare an individual's test scores. To obtain such data, a sample of subjects representative of the group for which the test is intended take the test instrument. The results from the sample define the norms for that test. Norm data adequacy is important in standardized instrumentation. The norm group should include a representative sample; the group must be large enough to constitute an adequate sample of performance; and data should be relatively current, with revisions at least once every 15 years (American Psychological Association, American Educational Research Association, & National Council on Measurement in Education, 1974). Additionally, the compilers must give an adequate description of normative data and the data collection process so that users can evaluate the test.

Reliability
Reliability, the second basic area of technical soundness, refers to the degree of consistency with which an instrument measures a behavior or performance level (i.e., to

what degree does similar performance under similar conditions result in similar assessment scores?). Evaluation is of little use if scores fluctuate widely even when behavior is stable. Reliability is expressed in terms of reliability coefficients (e.g., .50, .85, .90). Higher coefficients indicate more reliable measurement. Different reliability levels may be acceptable depending on the type of decision for which the data are to be used. Salvia and Ysseldyke (1987) suggested that test scores being reported for groups and used for administrative purposes should have a minimal reliability of .60. They further noted that for individual student decisions such as "tracking and placement in a special class," the minimum reliability should be .90 and that individual screening instruments should have at least a .80 reliability (p. 127). Test developers should adequately describe their reliability data and how the coefficients were derived.

Several methods may be used for determining test reliability. **Test-retest reliability** represents a measure of stability over time and is obtained by administering the instrument to a large group of subjects and retesting them after some time has passed. Scores from the two sessions are then correlated to obtain a reliability coefficient. **Alternate-form reliability** determines the degree to which two forms of a test measure the same trait. To obtain alternate-form reliability a large group of subjects takes two forms of the test, and the scores on these alternate forms are correlated. **Internal-consistency reliability,** also known as *split-half reliability,* is derived by testing a single group of subjects once. The test items are split, and scores on the two halves are correlated.

Validity

Generically **validity** represents the degree to which a test measures what it purports to measure. If the objective is to assess intellectual functioning, scores are of limited value if they mostly represent test anxiety, shyness, or socioeconomic status. Instrument developers should offer evidence about the validity of their test and about how the test was derived. This requirement is also part of the federal regulations (Public Law 94-142).

There are a number of methods for deriving validity. **Content validity** is determined by examining the content of the test to judge whether the instrument adequately assesses what is intended. **Criterion-related validity** is an assessment of how well an individual's performance on a task can be estimated by his or her test score. This can be evaluated in two ways, concurrent and predictive. **Concurrent** criterion-related validity involves administering test instrument and task nearly simultaneously. **Predictive** criterion-related validity involves administering the tests to predict task performance at some later time. In both types the test and performance scores are correlated.

Establishing the technical soundness of psychoeducational assessment is rather involved, as this brief discussion suggests, but professionals are not lacking in the necessary theoretical and technical knowledge. Perhaps for a variety of reasons, however, standardized tests that fall short in technical soundness have frequently been developed, marketed, and used. Salvia and Ysseldyke (1987) examined normative information on numerous standardized, norm-referenced instruments and found that nearly a quarter of them had inadequately constructed or described norms. The reliability of many commonly used tests may also be questionable (Ysseldyke & Algozzine, 1982), and the validity of a number of standardized instruments has been challenged (Salvia & Ysseldyke, 1987).

Instrumentation weaknesses are a serious concern to all behavioral scientists involved in assessment and treatment of disordered individuals. We discuss such weaknesses here because we believe that professionals should be conscious of them, guard against them, and make improvements. But we do not advocate discontinuing psychoeducational assessment or not using existing instruments when appropriate. Although some take such a position, even those who have studied instrumentation and found it lacking (e.g., Ysseldyke & Algozzine, 1982) do not support it. We would, however, encourage greater care and thoughtfulness in the use and development of instruments.

Normative and Criterion Referencing

<table>
<tr><td>*Core Concept*</td><td>*The purpose of any assessment greatly influences the procedure(s) employed and the way data are interpreted. Recognition of this has led to the development of such important concepts as norm and criterion referencing and formative and summative evaluation.*</td></tr>
</table>

Our earlier discussion mentioned norms and norm-referenced assessment. One important conceptual development in the field of assessment has been the distinction between norm-referenced and criterion-referenced evaluation.

Norm Referencing

Early assessment of intelligence focused on how an individual performed compared to others. A child's test score was viewed in relation to his or her age-mates or some standard norm. Research and repeated testing of individuals at various ages usually establish norms or bases for comparison. Similar procedures are used in assessment of factors other than intelligence. Personality measures usually compare one person's response to certain questions with those of other people who have particular personality descriptions. Educational achievement is often measured by the amount of information a child has accumulated, as demonstrated by correct responses on a variety of test questions. The child's performance is then compared with that of other children who are about the same age or grade level.

Assessment in which the performance of an individual is compared with that of others is known as **norm-referenced evaluation.** The phrase is self-explanatory. How well an individual performs is referenced in relation to the scores of others by using established norms. Mental age (MA) is a concept that is norm-referenced, and Binet and Simon (1908) intended it to be so when they first defined MA. Many other areas of assessment, particularly those using standardized tests, are also norm-referenced.

The norm-referenced approach has been predominant for many years. For the most part, professionals involved in all types of assessment (developmental status, intelligence, personality, and so on) have interpreted performance relative to norms. Norm referencing has served some purposes well. During the development of assessment as a science, it was the foundation for both researchers and practitioners working in all areas of human behavior. But gradually some serious problems have come to light.

As the science of human behavior progressed, measurement problems that obviously needed attention developed. Standardized tests provided information that was useful for some purposes but unhelpful for others. Educators, for example, frequently found that scores from norm-referenced evaluation did not translate easily into teaching plans. A single score was often used for decisions about educational placement, with little or no additional information about the child. Such single scores gave the teacher at best meager guidance concerning activities and specific areas to target in instruction (Galagan, 1985). A global score or a psychologist's report did not indicate where to begin in teaching specific mathematics or reading skills. This left teachers with many practical problems to solve in trying to teach the child. No logical link connected evaluation and instruction.

Similar problems emerged in working with individuals with mental retardation and other handicaps in social-vocational efforts and other aspects of the adult world (Felce, de Kock, Mansell, & Jenkins, 1984). Norm-referenced assessment information did little to facilitate placement, planning, and programming. Professionals working in such social agencies as welfare and employment departments and sheltered workshops soon found that they had to augment such information with their own more specific evaluations. Sheltered workshop directors, for example, had to determine what specific skills a client with retardation already had, and which needed to be taught for the individual to perform productively.

Criterion Referencing

Criterion-referenced evaluation has become nearly synonymous with what norm-referenced evaluation is not. Individual performance is not compared with some norm. Criterion-referenced evaluation assesses specific skill areas individually instead of generating a score based on a composite of several skills.

As noted, criterion-referenced evaluation does not compare the individual's performance with that of others. Tasks are usually arranged in a sequence of increasing difficulty, and a person's functioning is viewed in terms of absolute performance level, or the actual number of operations completed. If a child is being tested on counting skills and is able to progress successfully through counting by twos but no further, that is his or her absolute performance. The child counts by twos with 100% accuracy, but by threes with 0% accuracy. This level of performance may be referenced in one or both of two ways. First, the evaluator and the teacher (frequently the same person) would ask, "Is this level of proficiency adequate for this child at this time?" The level of proficiency necessary for the child is the criterion (hence the term *criterion-referenced evaluation*). If a child needs to be able to count by threes, the teacher knows exactly what instruction to give. As the child progresses he or she may need to perform at a more advanced skill level, depending on environmental requirements, and the criterion for this skill will change accordingly.

A second way that performance or skill level is referenced involves comparison of the individual's performance in one area with performance in others; for example, a child may perform well in letter recognition but poorly in sound blending. The evaluator examines performances in various skill areas, frequently constructs a profile of the child's strengths and weaknesses, and pinpoints instructional effort from the profile. The referent for evaluation data is still in one individual's performance, but now between skill areas. Usually the measurement involves performance on specific tasks. The evaluator draws no inferences about such abstract concepts as intelligence, instead relating measurement directly to instruction. Criterion-referenced evaluation has improved the relationship between evaluation and teaching, changing the way education is conceived and executed.

Past years have witnessed a theoretical difference of opinion in child assessment. Obviously norm- and criterion-referenced evaluations operate from different approaches. Proponents of each viewpoint have spent much time and effort defending their positions, often without careful examination of what the other approach has to offer. This is unfortunate; such professional wrangling has little positive result. While arguments continue, attention to basic measurement principles and reasoned applications have begun to replace rhetoric (see Haertel, 1985; Sewell, Hinnells, O'Connell, & Edwards, 1989).

The concepts of criterion-referenced evaluation have been applied in a wide variety of settings, one of the most pertinent applications being the direct linkage between assessment and classroom instruction. This use has grown and evolved into another application that has received a great deal of attention recently, curriculum-based assessment. **Curriculum-based assessment** uses the sequential objectives of the student's curriculum as the referent or criterion for evaluating progress (Blankenship, 1985). This approach emphasizes the link between instructional objectives and assessment, improving the potential for instructional decision making (Cundari & Suppa, 1988). Curriculum-based assessment also provides a natural and efficient process for screening assessment (Joyce & Wolking, 1987) a topic examined later in this chapter.

Scrutiny of both types of assessment has led many to conclude that neither approach in isolation results in a totally effective evaluation process. Criterion-referenced evaluation is useful for specific instructional programming, a need not served well by norm-referenced evaluation. Many children with mental retardation must, however, ultimately function in a larger world, perhaps in a regular educational setting on a partial basis. This broader world usually operates on a competitive basis, with children's performances compared to each other, so it is largely a norm-referenced world. To maximize a child's chances for success, information that will indicate how the child's performance compares with others in the larger world must be obtained. It would be disastrous to bring a child's skill level from point A to point B (criterion-referenced evaluation) and find that point C was necessary for success in a regular educational setting. Those working with individuals who are mentally retarded cannot afford to be rigid in using only some of the tools available to them. Since they serve different purposes, both norm- and criterion-referenced evaluation must be used.

Formative and Summative Evaluation

Other conceptual developments look directly to the purposes of evaluation. Bloom, Hastings, and Madaus (1971) presented one such notion that received widespread attention.

They viewed evaluation in terms of two broad categories: formative and summative. **Formative evaluation** in this framework is assessment that does not focus on a desired ultimate behavior, but rather on the next step in an instructional program. Formative evaluation is frequently an integral part of the instructional program, as ongoing assessment. **Summative evaluation** is quite different. It involves assessment of terminal behaviors and evaluates a child's performance at the end of a given program. These conceptualizations have also been combined with norm- and criterion-referenced evaluation and other measurement models to develop functional and comprehensive views of assessment (Laveault, 1987; Moore, Fifield, Spira, & Scarlato, 1989). Myopic views of evaluation and psychological assessment seem to be giving way to more thoughtful approaches to the broad field. This is promising, since it means that workers in the field are being more thorough and reasoned in their consideration of assessment.

Assessment Bias

Another concern of assessment is the awareness of discriminatory testing, a factor examined in the context of multicultural issues in Chapter 2. Questions about discriminatory assessment surface particularly often with respect to the standardized, norm-referenced testing of minority group children. Blacks, Hispanics, and Native Americans, as well as others, have legitimately claimed that evaluation instruments contain cultural bias and prejudice (Roberts & DeBlassie, 1983; Slate, 1983). Such bias generates inaccurate results that are at least partially due to cultural background rather than actual mental abilities or skills (Reynolds, 1987). Since psychoeducational assessment instruments are usually devised by individuals from the cultural majority, test items are probably more representative of that group than others. Likewise, norms are more frequently based on the performance of individuals from the cultural majority than on that of minority subgroups. When minority children's scores are compared with norms established on other populations, therefore, the children are often at a disadvantage because of cultural differences (Wood, Johnson, & Jenkins, 1986). Such bias in psychological assessment has been evident for many years, although only in recent decades have significant efforts begun to remedy the problem (Padilla, 1988; Taylor, 1990).

But the results of attempts to construct unbiased instruments have been very disappointing, leading some to contend that the conceptual foundations and uses of norm-referenced evaluation are more important issues and are more likely to be at fault than instrumentation (Drew, 1973). Some of the efforts undertaken are beginning to place the assessment of minority children on firmer ground. In part this has meant moving from norm-referenced to criterion-referenced procedures (Plata, 1985). There remains, however, much research to be done in this area, because a full understanding of bias, its effects on assessment outcomes, and a resolution of the problem remain elusive (Lopez, 1988; Malgady, Rogler, & Constantino, 1987; Miller-Jones, 1989).

Minority children still represent a disproportionately large segment of the population identified as mentally retarded (Prasse & Reschly, 1986). Some researchers claim that basic educational reform is needed in addition to work in assessment development (Taylor, 1990). The problem of cultural unfairness remains, whether the problem is one of assessment bias or one of prejudice in the educational system. The reader can find a more complete examination of the range of environmental and cultural factors associated with minority status in Chapter 2. From the discussion there it is clear that some factors, such as poverty, are broad societal problems far beyond the scope of psychoeducational assessment.

Although the issues in the preceding discussion have been articulated in the past, the reader should not assume that these problems have evaporated with the passage of time. The problems of educational uses and misuses of norm-referenced assessment have been addressed only in a limited fashion and, some believe, inappropriately (Taylor, 1990). Issues arising from the use of criterion-referenced assessment have yet to be broadly explored; they merit much more attention (Drew, 1973; Plata, 1985). Further, professional training in diagnostic assessment remains limited and needs to be reformed (Elbert, 1984). The need for reform has become crucial in view of recent evidence about how little information goes into forming impressions (Skowronski & Carlston, 1989). Ordinary human frailty leaves plenty of room for racial and cultural bias on the part of psychodiagnosticians. Our work is scarcely begun.

Mental Age and Intelligence

Core Concept	*Mental age and IQ have historically been central in assessment of mental retardation, although many other factors are emerging as important for full evaluation.*

Two additional concepts require brief attention. Neither is new to the field of psychological assessment. In fact, both have great historical significance and have been particularly prominent in the assessment of intelligence. These are the ideas of mental age and intelligence quotient (IQ). They serve as convenient summaries of an individual's performance on tasks that presumably tap behavior representing intelligence. Both, however, have caused difficulties, primarily from the ways people have used them.

Mental Age

The concept of **mental age** (MA) was developed by Binet and Simon (1908) as a means of expressing a child's intellectual development. An MA score represents the average performance of children with chronological age (CA) equal to that score. For example, a child who obtains an MA of 5 years 6 months has performed in a manner similar to the average performances of children whose CA is 5 years 6 months (norm-referenced concept). MA has been a useful concept, especially in mental retardation, since it is referenced to average intellectual development at various CA levels. The general idea of mental development expressed by MA is easy to grasp. MA provides a convenient means of communication with parents and others about children with mental retardation. Most parents and other laypeople have had opportunities to observe children at various ages, so they have behavioral reference points that help them generally understand the abilities of individuals with mental retardation.

The MA concept has been less useful in other contexts. Since it is a summary score derived from performance on various types of test items, it is a composite measure. The single score provides little information about specific skill levels, which is why the preceding discussion included qualifying statements about understanding mental development "generally." Two children may obtain the same MA and have very different patterns of skill strengths and deficits. For example, an MA of 7 years might be attained by a child who is chronologically age 5 years and by another who is chronologically age 9 years. These children might be labeled "bright," "retarded," or a number of other terms. The same MA may have been obtained from very different specific performances. The developmentally advanced child (CA 5) more frequently succeeds in verbal reasoning and abstract items. The slower child (CA 9) more frequently responds correctly on performance items or those for which previous learning was highly repetitive. Equivalent MAs do not indicate similar skill capabilities; the usefulness of the concept is limited in terms of teaching, particularly when instruction is pinpointed to skill deficits.

Intelligence Quotient

The **intelligence quotient** (IQ) came into use somewhat later than MA. Originally IQ was derived by dividing an individual's MA by the CA and multiplying the result by 100. Thus a child 6 years old who obtained an MA of 6 would have an IQ of 100 ($6/6 = 1 \times 100 = 100$). This approach to IQ calculation was known as *ratio IQ*. Certain difficulties developed in the use of the ratio IQ, prompting its decline beginning about the mid-1940s. Since that time, the deviation IQ has been used as an alternative to the ratio calculation. This approach uses a statistical computation known as the *standard deviation* to derive the IQ. The deviation approach to determining IQ offered several advantages. The ratio calculation was quite unstable from age level to age level, making IQ comparison between ages difficult. The deviation approach for deriving IQ is a standard score with much more stability along the age continuum. The ratio calculation also became problematic as the individual approached adulthood. As CA increases, there is an apparent leveling or even a decline in measured intelligence, even when more items are answered correctly. The ratio IQ thus was less viable for assessing individuals other than developing children. Because deviation IQ is referenced to a standard score, it circumvents these difficulties and is more consistent at all ages.

IQ, like MA, is a composite measure derived by performance in several skill areas. The problems noted for MA and IQ are similar in this regard. The global score, while providing an overall assessment of performance, does not indicate specific skill strengths and deficits, a problem that may have been more acute with IQ than with MA. Because of its single score and apparent simplicity, users of IQ have tended to forget the component performance of the score and have treated it instead as a unitary concept. Also, people began to look on the score as sacred and permanent rather than as a reflection of performance on a variety of tasks. This misconception led to considerable misuse and eventual disenchantment with the concept.

IQ remains in use today, and in many cases the abuses continue. We hope, however, that people using IQ now have a better perspective on what it actually assesses and less often see it as a permanent status marker resulting in labels that themselves become entities. Modification of the IQ concept, plus expansion of evaluation concepts in general, appear to have prompted movement in the direction of more realistic use of the IQ score.

One final point needs mention in this section. Earlier we discussed the important link between assessment and treatment. In some situations it has seemed that testing was being conducted with no very clear notion of possibilities for intervention. Such assessment is at best illogical. A second issue having to do with the assessment-treatment link is this: some practitioners claim that the amount of testing required significantly detracts from instructional time. This is a serious problem, particularly when the time available is limited (the school year). A balance is clearly needed, since assessment is ancillary to the primary goal of effective intervention. If assessment and intervention are not in balance, service-delivery needs are not being met.

Our discussion has explored certain issues and conceptual developments in psychological assessment. The examination was by no means exhaustive, but it does provide a backdrop for the study of assessment procedures.

EARLY LIFE

Core Concept	*Assessment procedures are quite different depending on the age of the person and the performance area being evaluated.*

Different assessment procedures are necessary at various stages in the life of a child. This section examines approaches to evaluation during the early years of life, from birth to about two years of age.

Evaluation at this point in the life of children is conducted for at least two related purposes: (1) identification of children who are already retarded in their development and (2) identification of children who have a high probability of becoming developmentally retarded later. The President's Committee on Mental Retardation (Meier, 1973) stated that these purposes were the two components of early screening assessment. In the discussion that follows, we first examine the idea of screening, then look at reasons for identification and explore potential results. Identification cannot stand alone, or it would be merely an exercise.

Screening Concepts

Core Concept	*Screening assessment is very important throughout a person's life span, but it is crucial in early life.*

Screening is somewhat like sorting sizes for things like fruit. For example, oranges might be rolled across a screen with certain sized holes. These holes would permit oranges of an acceptable size or smaller to fall through. Those that were larger than the acceptable marketable size would not fall through the screen and would be sorted out for other purposes (special gift packages). Those that fell through would include oranges of marketable size plus those that were much smaller. A second screening process might then be used. This second phase would involve a screen with holes that were much smaller than the first screen's. The only oranges that would fall through the second screen would be those that were unmarketable because they were too small (these could be used for frozen orange juice). This would leave only those oranges that were in the size range that the buying public prefers. Screening for retardation is somewhat like this. Only those who are now developmentally retarded or exhibit behaviors that suggest that they will later be retarded are sorted out by early screening.

Early identification of handicapping conditions is highly important. First of all, in certain cases the ultimate impact of a handicapping condition can be reduced substantially with early treatment or intervention. Certain handicaps may even be prevented if action is taken soon enough. The idea of prevention focuses particularly on children who are thought to be at risk for developmental retardation at a time other than infancy. Obviously, for some children neither of these possibilities for treatment really exists. These are the children who are severely retarded, frequently because of a birth defect or congenital malformation. Such conditions make identification easier, but because of the severity of the problems, positive action is more difficult. But even in these situations early identification plays a vital role in terms of planning for the future of the child and the family.

Certain problems persist in accomplishing early screening assessment for mental retardation. One serious difficulty in assessing young children is accuracy of prediction. The behavioral repertoire of the infant is much different from that of the child at age six or 10 years. The infant is primarily functioning in a motor-skill world. Grasping, rolling over, sitting, and crawling are a few of the baby's behaviors. Infant vocalizations are quite limited and frequently focus on physiological factors like hunger, pain, and fatigue. Early screening tries to predict later behaviors that are very different. Since the best predictor of performance on a given task is performance on a sample of that task or a similar one, in most cases impossible with an infant, prediction is not so accurate as one would like.

But this does not mean that no prediction is possible. If this were so, there would be little reason even to consider early screening. Fortunately for child-care workers, developmental status and progress in the psychomotor areas that dominate the world of the infant do predict, even though grossly, later levels of functioning. Accuracy of prediction is much greater with the severely impaired infant, who exhibits clearer signs of impairment earlier. The mildly handicapped present the greatest challenges to early screening.

Another concern in early screening assessment involves the factors evaluated. Recent research and thinking in this area have made some changes in the indicators that early screening assesses. Valuable predictive information may be obtained by evaluating environmental factors in addition to examining the child's developmental status directly. Professionals have traditionally used such indicators as socioeconomic status and parental education and occupation to differentiate between environments, but now other factors have been shown to be more important influences on a child's development. Some of these include parents' language style, their attitudes about achievement, and general involvement with the young child. Research is beginning to study these areas, which promise to become even more important in the future.

Early screening has generally been discussed in terms of its positive value for the child who is faced with the possibility of mental retardation and for the child's parents. In a broader societal context, certain ethical issues arise. One of the negative outcomes of early assessment is labeling. Labels and their impact on children have been a serious concern in special education for some time. The potential for harm is even greater when and if a label is attached to a youngster in infancy. To avoid labeling, child-care workers must move to behavior- and skill-oriented descriptions. And here we should say once more that assessment, evaluation, or early screening cannot be justified if its only purpose is identification. During the school years, evaluation and education must be linked. Purposive evaluation is even more crucial in the early years. The negative effect of assessing a young child, stigmatizing the child with a label, and doing nothing in the form of positive action beyond that is unimaginable. We do not support evaluation at any time in the life of an individual if it is only for categorization.

Earlier we mentioned the problems involved in evaluation of minority groups. These problems are of even greater concern in early assessment, for issues of poverty, race, and environment play an even larger role in early screening. As professionals gain skill in dealing with these issues, not only early childhood assessment but also early childhood education should become increasingly important in treating mental retardation.

Early Life Assessment

Prenatal

Core Concept	*Prenatal evaluation can provide extremely important information about the fetus.*

Advances in medical science and health-care techniques over the past decade have had a significant impact on the field of mental retardation. One area in which dramatic developments have occurred involves prenatal assessment and detection of mental retardation.

During pregnancy the most common assessment involves routine monitoring of the physical condition of mother and fetus by the obstetrician or other trained health-care personnel. Part of this assessment process includes a detailed record of the mother's family and medical history. In addition to the history, the mother's blood pressure, uterus size, urine status, and other indicators are monitored throughout the pregnancy to assure that no symptoms are present that would signal danger for the fetus as well as the mother. At this level of examination the mother's physical condition is the primary source of information for assessment. The obstetrician also examines the fetus by various means as the pregnancy proceeds. This ongoing monitoring is crucial to maximize the probability of a healthy baby's being born. The mother's diet is frequently altered, and occasionally medication is administered to correct minor deviations from the optimum situation for fetal development. Women who do not have access to good health care run a much higher risk of giving birth to a defective child. High-risk pregnancies are more frequent among women who cannot afford adequate health care or for some other reason do not have adequate medical resources available to them.

Routine ongoing prenatal assessment is generally adequate as long as a healthy mother and fetus are involved. Certain danger signs, however, prompt more extensive evaluation. If the family or medical history suggests that a particular problem may occur (for example, an inheritable disorder), routine monitoring is not sufficient. If the mother's or fetus's physical condition is deviant, more extensive evaluation and action are in order. In such cases evaluation becomes diagnosis aimed at the prenatal assessment of fetal status. Certain biological and chemical characteristics of the fetus can be measured. Diagnostic analyses of this type are not possible with every type of retardation, and work has focused on clinical syndromes that involve genetic metabolic disorders resulting in severe mental retardation.

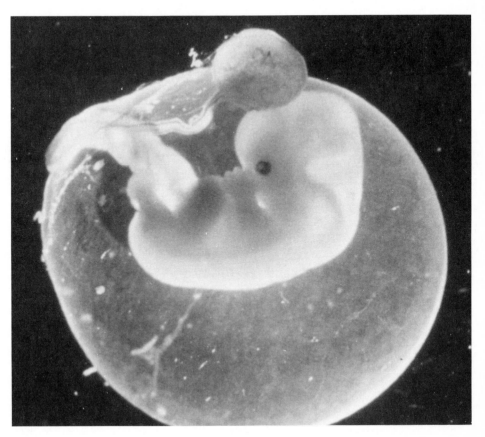

Prenatal assessment of this young fetus is important since this represents a vulnerable period.

Accurate diagnosis is possible for a variety of hereditary disorders, including galactosemia, Gaucher's disease, maple syrup urine disease, and Tay-Sachs disease. These disorders are rare, but in an entire society the ability to detect and take action is a major contribution to the field of mental retardation. Even more significant is the ability to prevent the personal tragedies resulting from the birth of children with such devastating disorders. In most cases parents of these children are forced to watch a progressive deterioration from what appeared to be a healthy normal baby to a child destined for a passive existence or premature death.

This kind of prenatal assessment is not yet routine. For the most part the general obstetric monitoring mentioned suffices for a first level of screening, like the first screening in our orange-sorting analogy. In certain cases, however, metabolic or genetic disorders have a higher probability of occurrence, and in these cases current thinking recommends routine diagnostic prenatal evaluation. Tay-Sachs disease, for example, is a disorder transmitted genetically and primarily found in individuals of Ashkenazi Jewish origin. When two individuals with this background plan to have children, it is wise always to evaluate fetal status from a prenatal diagnostic standpoint. There are also strong arguments for evaluation of all pregnant women over 40 years of age. Maternal age is important in the birth of children with Down syndrome. The detection process for prenatal identification of Down syndrome is still being refined. As this work progresses, it is quite possible that such diagnostic screening will be recommended even for others younger than 40 years.

Newborn

Core Concept	*Assessment of the newborn can identify problems and prompt immediate intervention to prevent mental retardation.*

A variety of assessment techniques are used with the newborn. Clinical assessment at this time is vital. Immediately following birth several factors are noted and rated using what is known as the Apgar score. This procedure is generally completed by delivery room staff at one and five minutes after birth and may be repeated, if needed, until the infant's condition has stabilized. Five factors are included in the Apgar scoring: heart rate, respiratory effort, muscle tone, reflex irritability, and color. Each is rated by giving a score of 0, 1, or 2 (0 indicating low or weak, 2 high or strong). The separate scores are added together. Extremely low Apgar scores at the five-minute measure suggest a potential problem. Newborns with a five-minute score of three or below have three times as many neurological problems at age one as babies of similar birth weights with Apgar scores of seven to 10. Apgar scores of six or lower are viewed with concern. Infants with such scores are usually monitored closely for the first several days, with interventions as necessary.

Medical laboratories can conduct other assessment procedures during the very early part of a child's life. Many of these procedures attempt to detect inherited or congenitally present abnormalities (they overlap with some of the procedures discussed under prenatal diagnosis). As with the prenatal evaluation process, biological-chemical analysis is frequently the means for newborn screening. Analysis of blood specimens alone allows for detection of a number of inherited abnormalities:

Phenylketonuria (PKU)*

Maple syrup urine disease*

Tyrosinemia*

Homocystinuria*

Histidinemia*

Valinemia*

Galactosemia transferase deficiency*

Argininosuccinic aciduria*

Orotic aciduria*

Hereditary angioneurotic edema

Galactosemia transferase or kinase deficiency*

Emphysema (adult)

Liver disease (infant)

Sickle cell anemia

Items marked with an asterisk are treatable conditions. Treatment can prevent or substantially diminish the developmental problem that would result if the condition were unknown or ignored. These treatable disorders make up most of those we have listed, a fact that seems to support neonatal screening. Yet such assessment is not necessarily routine. Diagnosis of these disorders can be made from analysis of a dried blood spot, and in each case completely or partially automated analysis is possible, streamlining the process and permitting cost-effective mass screening. It is to be hoped that in the future, health-care services will routinely include biological-chemical analysis.

Certain other abnormalities are detectable from clinical observation at the newborn stage. Medical examination of conditions like Down syndrome and cranial anomalies can indicate the existence of a problem with considerable accuracy. Such effective evaluation, however, involves only conditions that are present and observable either at birth or in the first few days of the infant's life.

Beyond the Newborn Stage

Core Concept	*Evaluation beyond the newborn stage includes many assessment areas not previously amenable to measurement.*

There is certainly no widespread agreement concerning when one stage of development ends and another begins. In fact, it is misleading even to suggest that a "stage" is an

identifiable and discrete entity. Even the theories of stages have been strongly challenged (Flavell, 1977). Usage of terms like *newborn, infant,* and *early childhood* is fluid
at best. In the previous section the term *newborn* meant the time shortly after birth.
The use of this term was not intended to suggest that the term covered a "stage"; it was
used for convenience. Henceforward we place evaluation in an age context instead of
using terms that connote stages.

Certain measurements are difficult to make from birth through the first few years
of life (Gaussen, 1984; Hanson, Smith, & Hume, 1984). This is particularly true when
attempting to predict later intelligence (Cohen & Parmelee, 1983). Before the child
acquires language, his or her sensorimotor development is necessarily the basis for
evaluation. Since later intelligence measures are heavily weighted according to verbal
performance, prediction difficulty is natural. There has, however, been progress in this
area of assessment.

Intellectual   Numerous instruments and evaluation procedures attempt to assess intellectual functioning in young children. The Cattell Infant Intelligence Scale is one of
the better-known instruments for evaluation of very young children. The Cattell scale,
which is heavily oriented toward sensorimotor assessment, is used on children from two
to about 30 months of age. This scale was designed as an extension of the revised
Stanford-Binet intelligence test to lower ages. Research has indicated that the Cattell
scale is useful for predicting the intellectual functioning of mentally retarded children
referred for examination by physicians. Its predictions are less accurate, however, for
broader samples of children. This suggests that the Cattell Infant Intelligence Scale may
be useful for screening purposes but is less helpful for general prediction in a population
that is not high-risk. Although well-known, the Cattell scale is somewhat dated; other
instruments are currently more useful (Atkinson, 1990a).

Similar to the Cattell scale in some respects are the revised Bayley Scales of Infant
Development. The Bayley scales, although they take longer to administer, have certain
strengths over the Cattell scale (Goldstein & Sheaffer, 1988; Atkinson, 1990a). The
Bayley scales include test items for the first two months after birth, which may be an
advantage for situations where assessment of the very young or of older individuals
functioning at a very low level is required (see Whiteley & Krenn, 1986). Further, there
are subscales for mental and motor performance, which have clinical appeal but may be
misleading. Like the Cattell scale, the Bayley scales rely heavily on the assessment of
sensorimotor performance, since there are few other means of performance evaluation
at this age. Also like the Cattell, the Bayley Scales are accurate for certain high-risk
populations like premature babies (Ross, 1985). The two instruments overlap so much
that they are sometimes described as interchangeable for diagnostic purposes.

Other techniques have been developed and are used by many professionals for early
assessment of a child's intellectual functioning. J. Meier, in the 1973 report of the
President's Committee on Mental Retardation, discussed several approaches in addition
to those mentioned above, including the Kuhlmann-Binet Scale (birth through 30
months), the Griffiths Scale (birth through four years), and the Revised Gesell Scale
(birth through five years). Our discussion of the Bayley and Cattell scales is presented
because they are more widely known.

Language   Although it is closely related to cognitive development, separate and distinct efforts have focused on early language assessment. The primary work in assessment of language before age three months has involved clinical analysis of certain factors in the infant's cry. This kind of assessment has not been widely used and thus far appears to be of limited practical value.

Language assessment after the three months has used several different procedures including the Playtest (Friedlander, 1971) and the Early Language Assessment Scale (Honig & Caldwell, 1966). The Playtest approach (three to 12 months) is aimed at assessment of children's receptive language ability, which Friedlander characterized as "the effectiveness of their listening to the fine-grained aspects of natural sound and language stimuli [and] their methods of using natural sound input in the integration of their sensory experiences." This evaluation goes beyond mere hearing acuity. It makes natural sound processing a central issue and also focuses on the young child's receptive abilities in terms of language.

Of particular interest in this area is research comparing children with substantial impairment in speech development to children without such disorders. During the Playtest, television storytelling sequences were shown to the two groups of children. Narration proceeded in a natural, clear fashion as well as in garbled form. The group of children with normal speech development exhibited a high level of interest and attention to the story with natural narration but not to the story with the incomprehensible narration. Those children with speech development problems watched both the natural and the incomprehensible narration sequences with equally high interest and attention. These results suggest that children with speech development disorders do not discriminate between garbled and clear narration. This line of work may make valuable contributions to the study of receptive language. Developmental retardation, at least in the language area, may be predictable from such assessment. Future research and development of these techniques could lead to important advances in the evaluation of young children. The sophisticated instrumentation of these techniques precludes mass screening.

The Early Language Assessment Scale developed by Honig and Caldwell (three months to four years) is designed to evaluate young children's receptive and expressive language abilities. This technique primarily focuses on the young child's response to certain stimuli provided by the examiner. The examiner presents commands, nonword auditory stimuli, and some visual stimuli and imitation items. The child's performance is scored on a rating sheet in terms of receptive and expressive language development. Very little training is necessary for administering this evaluation, and routine language development screening seems quite feasible with this test. Although it is not widely used at present, this approach is promising for routine health and well-baby evaluation. Since health-care personnel conduct the primary monitoring at this age ongoing assessment could easily be made during visits with the pediatrician and office staff.

Word production is another means of evaluating young children's early language development. Reznick and Goldsmith (1989) report that the language development of infants between one and two years of age can be effectively assessed in this manner. Parental reporting of the child's word production appears to be reliable and predictive. Further study of this approach is in order.

Evaluation of language development is an increasingly important area of interest in terms of early assessment, particularly with respect to developmental mental retardation (Rocissano & Yatchmink, 1983). As professionals continue to refine skill description, specific areas of performance level will become more important. Language assessment may represent only language skill rather than trying to measure the abstract concept of mental development. It is already clear that an area like language will be broken down more into component behaviors. As this occurs, efforts in evaluation, screening, and diagnosis will probably take on a very different description, increase professionals' predictive ability, and certainly lead more directly to intervention and modification.

Social/Adaptive Behavior   Evaluation of social-emotional development presents a challenge to those working with young children. All the instruments that try to assess this area of behavior have a common problem—the reliability of the assessment itself. Of the 10 listed in the 1973 report of the President's Committee on Mental Retardation (Meier, 1973), only three have "adequate" reliability and validity. Two of these include the time shortly after birth (Vineland Social Maturity Scale, birth to 18 years, and the functional analysis approach, birth to adult). The third (Quantitative Analysis of Tasks) covers the period from one to six years.

The Vineland Social Maturity Scale was constructed with sequentially ordered, age-graded items that cover several content areas. These areas include self-help skills, self-direction, locomotion, occupation, communication, and social relations. Its author designed the scale basically to assess a child's performance and ability in terms of progress toward independence. Two approaches to data collection are involved, an interview with the parent and observation of the child. When the child is not present or available, information is gathered solely from the interview. Although this scale has been judged adequate in terms of both reliability and validity, there have been a number of concerns about it over the years, including allegations of cultural bias (Slate, 1983). Such concerns led to revision of the original scale, resulting in the Vineland Adaptive Behavior Scale (Harrison, 1985; Sparrow, Balla, & Cicchetti, 1984a, 1984b). Standardization information about the revision is still coming in from field applications and research. Early results are promising, although caution appears warranted. Results should be used only to augment clinical decisions (Atkinson, 1990b).

Also applicable in the very early life of a child is assessment that, for want of a better term, has been labeled as the functional analysis approach. Although not designed as an instrument per se, this work rests on the basic principles of applied behavior analysis and is highly relevant to issues of early childhood assessment. The functional analysis approach to assessment requires direct observation of the child rather than reliance on behavioral description reported by an informant. Observation is conducted of children who are referred for behavioral or developmental problems; it takes place in the setting in which the problem occurs. Data are typically divided into three categories: behavioral deficits, behavioral excesses, and inappropriate stimulus control. Within these general categories the behavioral description of the child's functioning is very specific, permitting precise intervention rather than a broad-spectrum or "shotgun treatment" approach. Its specificity is a definite strength of the functional analysis assessment framework, but observation requires substantial training in applied behavior analysis. Either professional or paraprofessional staff members with the proper preparation can conduct the evaluation. A second strength of functional analysis assessment is its use of direct observation rather than such indirect methods as interviews. Interviews have long been viewed as problematic and have added substantially to the difficulties of reliability and validity of assessment.

The Quantitative Analysis of Tasks developed by White and Kaban (1971) also requires direct observation. Here the observer takes a very different approach from that of functional analysis. Like functional analysis, the White and Kaban technique involves careful observation of a child's behavior and the environmental stimulus conditions in a natural setting, but unlike functional analysis, the evaluator not only observes but also makes inferences about and describes the child's apparent purpose in terms of the recorded behavior. This interpretation of the child's purpose is then coded and scored with reference to several criteria. The coding of social tasks involves numerous purposes, including to gain attention, avoid attention, gain approval, annoy, maintain social contact, compete, and provide information. Although the manual is quite specific in its coding instructions, the quality of the observer's inferences is obviously crucial. The strength and reliability of the evaluation (or its weakness and unreliability) depend on this factor. This evaluation should be administered by trained paraprofessionals. Regardless of who the evaluator is, the soundness, accuracy, and reliability of assessment rest heavily on the judgment and, consequently, the training of the observer.

Multiple Domain Assessment   Discussion thus far has focused on instruments and techniques that assess a child's developmental status in a limited area. Although the boundaries of performance areas are far from distinct, many have attempted to assess intellectual development, language development, and social-emotional development discretely, as well as to consider the early health status and possible presence of inheritable disorders. Assessment from a somewhat broader framework, including infant-environment interactions, has attracted much attention in recent years (Gaussen & Stratton, 1985), and developmental screening techniques that evaluate several factors simultaneously while still providing specific information in each area have been designed. These techniques have become popular for several reasons, one certainly being the greater efficiency of using a single instrument to assess several performance areas. Over the years six different multifactor instruments have received substantial attention: the Rapid Developmental Screening Checklist (1972), designed by the Committee on Children with Handicaps, American Academy of Pediatrics (chaired by Margaret Giannini, 1972); Guide to Normal Milestones of Development (Haynes, 1967); the Developmental Screening Inventory (Knobloch, Pasamanick, & Sherard, 1967); the CCD Developmental Progress Scale (Boyd, 1969); the Revised Denver Developmental Screening Test (Frankenburg, Dodds, Fandal, Kazuk, & Cohrs, 1975); and the Program Assessment Chart (Gunzberg, 1963). Only selected techniques are discussed here. (For more comprehensive information about these instruments, see either the original sources or others focusing on this area exclusively, for example, Meier, 1973, and Salvia and Ysseldyke, 1987.)

One rather widely used multifactor instrument is the Revised Denver Developmental Screening Test. This instrument is useful from birth to six years of age and scores a child's status in four different areas of development: gross-motor, fine-motor, language, and personal-social. It is easily administered in about 20 minutes (including scoring and interpretation), requires no special training, and is available in Spanish. Considerable research has been conducted on the Denver scale's standardization and prescreening procedures (Prescreening Developmental Questionnaires [PDQ]) (Burgess, Asher, Doucet, Reardon, & Daste, 1984). Results generally report adequate reliability and validity for a screening instrument, although some have questioned the full Denver norms (Salvia & Ysseldyke, 1987). It appears that the Denver test is not always precise in identifying children who later develop poorly even though such youngsters generally have scores that are more likely to be abnormal (Greer, Bauchner, & Zuckerman, 1989). This instrument needs greater sensitivity.

Similar to the Denver scale in a number of ways is the CCD Developmental Progress Scale, used from birth to eight years of age. This instrument evaluates a child's developmental status in three areas: motor skills, communication-interpersonal skills, and self-sufficiency skills. The motor-skills area actually represents a combination of the two motor areas of the Denver scale. The CCD scale is preferable to the Denver scale for older children, whereas the Denver is more appropriate for younger children, a judgment based on the Denver scale's concentration of test items at the younger ages (birth to 18 months) with a substantial decrease in the number of items for ages four to six years. The CCD scale includes an equal number of items at all levels from birth to eight years, making this instrument far stronger than the Denver scale at the age levels above four years. Either instrument can be appropriately used between two and four years of age.

Both the Denver and CCD scales rely on parent reporting and direct observation of the child as sources for developmental status information. Parent reporting has been notoriously problematic throughout the history of measurement and evaluation. The basic difficulty in this area lies with the accuracy of the information provided and agreement between rating sources—parents, teachers, and others (Soyster & Ehly, 1986). Recognizing the possibility of faulty recall, Boyd (1969) addressed yet another point of vital importance in relation to parental reporting. It is Boyd's position that to obtain accurate reports of the child's typical behavior, the phrasing of the question is crucial. Questions must be posed in a manner that elicits behavioral descriptions and not in a fashion that suggests socially appropriate answers. Checklist interviews tend to result in inaccurately high ratings because of parents' defensive assumption that the question means the child should be able to perform the task. Phrasing is important in eliciting parental information. Although requiring a description of typical behavior does not solve all of the problems of parental reporting, it helps reduce one source of data contamination.

PRESCHOOL YEARS

Core Concept	*Functioning in intellectual, language, perceptual-motor, and social/adaptive behavior is important in evaluating the status of preschool youngsters. Proper assessment must employ procedures appropriate for this age range.*

There is no clear-cut age at which certain instruments stop being used altogether and others become appropriate. Some assessment techniques discussed in the preceding section can be used during the preschool years, whereas others are not. Likewise, certain evaluation procedures discussed in this section extend down to the early years. This section examines selected evaluation procedures used primarily during the years immediately preceding a child's school enrollment.

Intellectual Functioning

The type of assessment most frequently associated with developmental mental retardation is the measurement of intelligence. Although many think of intelligence as a concrete entity, it is really an abstraction, something that is inferred to exist to a greater or lesser degree depending on an individual's performance on selected tasks. With recent developments in evaluation has come the conceptual clarification that a particular score on an intelligence test is representative of various performances and that the concept of intelligence, as a general ability, is an inferred rather than a known, observable entity.

Part of the conceptualization of intelligence results from the framework of early instrumentation. Binet's early work was based on the idea that intelligence was a general ability factor. Consequently, his approach involved a mixture of items and aimed at an assessment that represented a composite measure, presumably including performances related to the notion of general intelligence. The revised version of Binet's earlier work, the Stanford-Binet test, still generates a composite measure. But some uses of this instrument in clinical and diagnostic settings have resulted in attempts to isolate various performances.

The Stanford-Binet test is recommended as appropriate for ages two years through adulthood. Frequently, however, other instruments are used for individuals over 12 years of age because of the longer administration time required for older people. The Stanford-Binet has frequently been viewed as the standard against which intelligence measurement is compared. Its 1972 edition (Terman & Merrill, 1973) has, however, been questioned on several bases. Salvia and Ysseldyke (1987) have raised serious reliability, validity, and normative concerns regarding this edition.

Another instrument frequently used with preschool children to assess intelligence is the Wechsler Preschool and Primary Scale of Intelligence (WPPSI). The WPPSI is recommended for use with children from ages four to 6½ years. Designed somewhat differently from the Binet test, the WPPSI organizes items into eleven subtests by content area. This encourages the use of the instrument as a measure of more specific skill areas. (The WPPSI, published in 1967, is a much more recently developed instrument than other Wechsler scales, although the others have been revised.) The WPPSI has been used increasingly with the preschool child for whom evaluation of intellectual performance is required. The WPPSI presents particular difficulties with the very capable child. There appears to be a ceiling on the items, which results in inaccurate assessment for these children. It does, however, provide a useful instrument for preschool children who are already suspected of functioning at a lower than average level.

Bush and Waugh (1982) discussed the Peabody Picture Vocabulary Test—Revised (PPVT-R) and its earlier forms (PPVT) as an instrument for assessing intelligence in preschool children. Its authors (Dunn & Dunn, 1981) describe it as assessing general intelligence only in terms of vocabulary. Dunn and Dunn characterized the instrument as primarily providing an index of achievement or scholastic aptitude. The PPVT-R is designed for quick administration (typically 10 to 15 minutes) and can be used with individuals from ages 2½ to 40 years. The examiner presents a printed page with four numbered pictures and reads a stimulus word. Children being tested then point to the picture they believe best represents the word that was read. Salvia and Ysseldyke (1987) noted that the data have adequate reliability for screening purposes, but data on the validity of the measure are lacking. When employed appropriately, with an awareness that it samples only receptive vocabulary, the PPVT-R is a very useful screening instrument.

Language Functioning

As the child grows older, the distinction between assessing language development and assessing intellectual functioning becomes increasingly blurred, to the point of imperceptibility. This results from several factors. First, at least in terms of normal language development, the child's language structure rapidly grows more sophisticated. Menyuk (1988) noted that by the time normal children reach three to four years of age they can use all the basic syntactic structures in language. A different response mode becomes possible from when the very young child was operating almost totally as a sensorimotor organism. Test developers who are working with children of this age range are quick to take advantage of this new response mode. The assessment of intellectual status includes a much heavier verbal component as the child gets older, so that the relationship between language and intellectual assessment grows closer.

As evidence of this situation, the PPVT-R warrants mention for its language assessment. Although the PPVT-R is occasionally described as an intelligence test, many professionals view it more as a receptive language measure. Some characterize it primarily as such a measure (Dunn & Dunn, 1981; Lerner, 1988). Because of the way the items are presented, the view of the PPVT-R as measuring receptive language is plausible, although some research suggests caution in interpreting results as receptive language (Altepeter, 1989).

The Illinois Test of Psycholinguistic Abilities (ITPA) is also frequently viewed as assessing language. Developed for use with children from about 2½ to 10 years of age, the ITPA is a highly complicated instrument that provides a profile of the child's performance in 12 different subtest areas. Initially the ITPA was primarily used with children who had learning disabilities. As concepts of prescriptive education have grown in popularity, however, application of the ITPA has spread to other populations, including those with developmental retardation. Although the ITPA is a useful instrument, it is not without problems. It is cumbersome to use (at least for some subjects) and requires considerable examiner training. Additionally, some of the subtests are far from pure in their measurement of a specific skill, and depending on the setting, they may or may not yield relevant instructional information. A third problem with the ITPA is its standardization population. Only children with IQ scores between 84 and 116 were included in the normative group, so a large data base does not exist for many children with mental retardation. This does not altogether preclude its use, but the existence of such data would offer a clearer picture of the ITPA's measurement properties when used with children who are mentally retarded. Salvia and Ysseldyke (1987) examined the instrument and suggested that the norms of the ITPA are inadequate, its reliability poor, and its validity questionable. These criticisms may surprise many who have used the ITPA extensively, but it emphasizes the importance of examining assessment devices before use.

The ITPA has perhaps been more useful as a conceptual framework than as an assessment instrument. It changed the way many professionals view the child, moving many toward the functional analysis of skill level as a way of thinking. This has long been the position of those skilled in applied behavior analysis, but a gap remains. Proponents of applied behavior analysis want much more precision in skill definition than the ITPA makes possible. The conceptual change is, however, significant when viewed from the broader perspective of the purposes of evaluation.

Various language assessment instruments with differing degrees of precision and standardization also exist (examples include the Houston Test of Language Development, the Mecham Verbal Language Development Scale, and the Utah Test of Language Development). But instead of describing all such instruments we wish to discuss the larger question of evaluation approach. Many professionals concerned with practical application have viewed assessment as important only in its relation to intervention or instruction. Such a perspective does not place much value on scores unless they represent performance precisely related to specific instructional activities—which will result in skill change. Such an approach tends to discount issues like cause (except in the rare cases that can be rectified by surgery). Evaluation in this framework often reflects ongoing monitoring built into the instructional program or designed specifically for a given instructional program (for example, the DISTAR Language Program). This kind of assessment is in line with the concepts of prescriptive education (in fact, it represents a potent force in the development of those concepts) and is precise in pinpointing where instructional effort is most needed.

Perceptual-Motor Functioning

Assessment of perceptual-motor skills is more commonly conducted with children suspected of having learning disabilities than with those thought to be developmentally retarded. Yet perceptual-motor functioning is a crucial skill area in instruction for children with mental retardation. Without the various visual-motor skills, the child can scarcely perform the tasks required in many instructional settings, and a child who has difficulty in these areas should be assessed for specific level of functioning and have instructional activities designed in relation to these skills.

One of the better-known assessment techniques in the perceptual-motor area is the Frostig Developmental Test of Visual Perception (Frostig & Horne, 1964). This instrument is designed for use with children from about four to eight years of age, but one can extend this age range for children who exhibit developmental retardation to a significant degree. The Frostig test can be administered either individually or to groups and assesses five different areas: (1) eye-motor (hand) coordination, (2) figure-ground perception, (3) form constancy, (4) position in space, and (5) spatial relations. Frostig has designed remediation activities that are coordinated with the evaluation instrument. From her viewpoint, identification of perceptual deficits is crucial for early remediation (kindergarten and first grade) to allow normal school progress.

Another device used for assessment in the perceptual-motor area is the Purdue Perceptual-Motor Survey (Roach & Kephart, 1966). Although the Purdue survey was not designed specifically for preschool assessment (norms are based on children between six and 10 years old), there is again some latitude in the age range. The developmental theory behind the Purdue survey portrays the child as moving through a sequence of learning stages much like those postulated by Piaget. The survey includes 22 items arranged in 11 different subtests. The Purdue survey homes in on three major perceptual-motor skill areas: laterality, directionality, and perceptual-motor matching.

The Developmental Test of Visual-Motor Integration (VMI) (Beery, 1967) also measures perceptual-motor skills. This instrument involves a paper-and-pencil performance by the child, to whom geometric forms are presented as stimuli to be copied. Although the VMI was designed primarily for use at the preschool and early primary levels, the manual notes that it can be administered to children from two to 15 years of age. The VMI was devised to assess how well motor behavior and visual perception are integrated. Like other perceptual-motor evaluations, it tries to identify fundamental skill deficits related to academic tasks. Such skills are pinpointed for remedial instruction.

The assessment devices we have just discussed focus on perceptual-motor skills from the viewpoint of the integration of perceptual functioning and motor performance. These two crucial skill areas operate in concert for many academic tasks. Sometimes, however, it is desirable to evaluate the status of one component without having the other influence the assessment. With many instruments this is not possible because, for example, a severe motor problem substantially reduces the overall performance score. Under these conditions an examiner could not evaluate a child's visual perception because the task combines visual and motor components. The Motor-Free Visual Perception Test (MVPT) (Colarusso & Hammill, 1972) tries to circumvent this problem. This test presents the child with a series of plates involving various visual images. The need for motor response is minimal because the child may be required to respond only with a nod or shake of the head as the examiner points to the drawing components. This approach holds promise for situations where physical disability impairs motor responses.

Social/Adaptive Behavior

Evaluation approaches for assessing social skills were discussed in the section on very young children. In many cases the upper age range of the measures extends far beyond the young child into preschool and elementary school years and even beyond. As the child progresses, judgments or ratings by others—caretakers, teachers, and parents—are often part of social skill assessment. It is important to remember that their ratings are not always reliable and in agreement (Soyster & Ehly, 1986). But such information sources are very important, and continued research is needed to solve these difficulties.

Adaptive behavior is a concept involving skills that may be generically viewed as part of social competence. As mentioned in Chapter 1, adaptive behavior is now included in the AAMR's formal definition of mental retardation. The Vineland Social Maturity Scale used to be the measure of choice for adaptive behavior. But now the AAMR has developed an instrument specifically geared to evaluation of adaptive and maladaptive behavior in individuals who are either suspected of or confirmed as being mentally retarded. This is the AAMR Adaptive Behavior Scale (ABS) (Nihira, Foster, Shellhaas, & Leland, 1974). The ABS is described as also being appropriate for individuals who are emotionally maladjusted. It measures the individual's effectiveness in adapting to the natural and social demands of the environment. Several factors, for example, self-abusive behavior, destructive behavior, sexually aberrant behavior, independent functioning, and time and number concepts are evaluated. Scales are available for young children through adults, although caution must be exercised in interpreting scores. A critical analysis of specific skill levels in particular areas forms a better basis for program planning. This is especially true because institutional subjects made up a large part of the standardization population, so that score interpretation for those who are mildly handicapped is difficult. Questions have been asked about the standardization data on both the original ABS and the Public School Version (Salvia & Ysseldyke, 1987) although revision research has been promising (see MacDonald & Barton, 1986).

The Cain-Levine Social Competency Scale (Cain, Levine, & Elzey, 1963), was developed for assessing trainable mentally retarded children from five years to 13 years and 11 months, but the clinician may find that its usefulness extends beyond the categorical boundaries of the trainable child. Designed as a behavior rating scale, this instrument involves 44 items divided into four subscales: self-help, initiative, social skills, and communication. Results include an overall score as well as performance scores in each of the four subscale areas. These scores can be useful for screening and initial planning of socially oriented training and also for evaluation of training effectiveness.

ELEMENTARY SCHOOL YEARS

Core Concept	*Multiple areas of functioning must be evaluated during the elementary years. Proper evaluation uses technically and conceptually sound procedures appropriate for this age range.*

The elementary school child who is developmentally retarded may be somewhat out of phase with the usual chronological age–formal education sequence. We use the phrase *elementary years* here only as a guideline. The overlap in age ranges for assessment approaches has already become obvious. Only techniques that become appropriate for this age range receive primary attention in this section. We devote separate attention to emerging systems of assessment. For example, one system, the System of Multicultural Pluralistic Assessment (SOMPA), evaluates across several attribute areas and cannot be appropriately discussed under a specific area subheading (such as intellectual or achievement).

Intellectual Functioning

Several previously mentioned intellectual assessment instruments reached into the five-to-12-year age range. In addition to these techniques, one of the best-known intelligence tests becomes age appropriate in this range, the Wechsler Intelligence Scale for Children—Revised (WISC-R). The WISC-R is recommended for use with children between the ages of five and 15 years. This instrument was designed in a somewhat similar fashion as the WPPSI for younger children. The WISC-R has 12 subtests divided into two general areas, verbal and performance. Ten of these subtests are used to generate scores for verbal and performance dimensions (digit span and maze subtests are not included in the scoring of this revised edition). Like most standardized instruments, the WISC-R is basically a norm-referenced instrument. Its score gives a composite IQ that indicates general ability. The revised edition, however, also provides for a profile of the child's performance in individual subtest areas, which generates more specific information than the composite IQ.

The WISC-R, developed in 1974, has a long history and a large data base behind it. Its predecessor, the WISC, was developed in 1949. Over the years it accumulated a vast data base and considerable research, which helped to define the measurement properties of the revised instrument. Questions have been raised regarding the comparability of the WISC and the WISC-R (Flynn, 1985) although other measurement properties, such as test-retest reliability, have appeared to be adequate (Whorton, 1985).

Although the recommended age range extends from about five to 15 years, the WISC-R is not always the preferred instrument in this range. For general assessment of mental retardation, some view the Stanford-Binet test as the stronger instrument up to age eight, mostly because of its standardization and clinical use. As data accumulate on the WISC-R, this preference may no longer hold. Certainly the WISC-R is more appropriate for children from about eight to 15 years of age.

Achievement

Many of the specific areas of assessment previously discussed for earlier age levels continue to be important during the elementary years. Determination of which areas require evaluation is based on a critical analysis of the areas in which the child has difficulty. One assessment area, however, becomes more important to evaluate than before—achievement. Many procedures assess academic achievement during the elementary years, including formal standardized instruments as well as techniques for daily monitoring. Each approach has its strengths and weaknesses depending on the purpose of the evaluation.

The Wide Range Achievement Test (WRAT) (Jastak & Jastak, 1978), which has two levels, is a general achievement test that assesses a child's performance in three areas: reading (pronunciation and word recognition), spelling, and arithmetic (computation).

The Level I WRAT is used with children from five years to 11 years and 11 months of age, the Level II version from 12 years of age to adulthood. The scores are in the form of global achievement scores expressed as grade equivalents and percentiles. This type of score reporting does not give enough detail about specific skills to be of much use in planning instruction, making the WRAT useful for screening, but dubious for anything else.

Another instrument used to measure achievement is the Peabody Individual Achievement Test (PIAT) (Dunn & Markwardt, 1970). The PIAT is designed for use from kindergarten through the twelfth grade. Although the PIAT is also a general achievement measure, it is more useful than the WRAT for instructional purposes. It comprises five subtests, including mathematics, reading recognition, reading comprehension, spelling, and general information. Easily administered, the PIAT results in a profile of the child's performance in the areas tested. The scores are presented in a variety of forms, including percentiles, age equivalents, grade equivalents, and both standard scores and raw scores. Depending on the specific evaluation purpose, the examiner may select any of these score forms as the appropriate method of reporting.

Another set of instruments that is useful for assessing academic achievement is the Metropolitan Achievement Test battery (Luftig, 1989). This is an example of how standardized instrumentation can be used in a meaningful fashion with individuals who are mentally retarded—but in a way the test developer may not have conceived. The Metropolitan test represents a comprehensive battery made up of several instruments with an extensive normed age range. Beyond the readiness scale, which provides a global evaluation (in specific skill levels), the primary and advanced batteries test several different areas, including word knowledge, word analysis (for the younger levels), reading, language, spelling (older levels), computation, mathematical concepts, and mathematical problem solving. The normed areas of evaluation are not as important as what can be done with them. When analyzed in terms of the skills required by each item, the Metropolitan test battery can provide a vast amount of information about a child's functioning. This information can then be coordinated for specific determination of discrete activities for the child's instructional program (Sparrow, Blachman, & Chauncy, 1983). This kind of analysis demands considerable information and teacher training in task analysis and precision teaching. When such educational expertise is brought to the teaching task, instruments like the Metropolitan test battery are highly relevant for the education of both children with mental retardation and others. More frequently, Metropolitan data are presented in score summary form, which may be used for administrative purposes but are certainly less useful from an instructional standpoint.

The achievement instruments discussed thus far have been general achievement measures, with some providing specific skill information. On certain occasions it is necessary to use an instrument that focuses specifically on one content area and provides an in-depth assessment of subskills in that area. Such an instrument is the Keymath Diagnostic Arithmetic Test (Luftig, 1989). Keymath was developed for use with children as young as the preschool level and ranging upward through grade seven. Both traditional and new mathematical skills are assessed, with 14 subtests divided into content, operations, and applications. Scores create a profile of specific skills, although

Keymath may also be scored on total test performance basis for use in placement or other administrative decisions.

Achievement assessment that results in only grade- or age-equivalency scores (as well as percentiles and standard scores) is norm-referenced information. These same tests may be used in ways that make them criterion-referenced, if the child's performance is not compared with other children's or with some norm. The more discrete and specific an assessment is, the greater its potential for drawing specific inferences for instruction. The highest relevance for instruction comes from assessment that is an integral part of the instructional program. Ideally, this type of achievement assessment continuously monitors a child's progress in specific skills. Instruction is aimed precisely at the child's level of functioning, permitting a highly efficient interface between evaluation and instruction. There is much in favor of such an approach for educating those who are developmentally retarded.

Assessment Systems

Measurement procedures examined thus far have had one area as their primary focus. Clinicians have often found it necessary to use several instruments to obtain a complete picture of an individual's capabilities. But some assessment development efforts evaluate a number of different attributes.

The System of Multicultural Pluralistic Assessment (SOMPA) (Mercer & Lewis, 1977) evaluates a variety of attribute areas and is an attempt to provide for comprehensive assessment. It is designed to be used with children from five to 11 years of age. Assessment is extremely comprehensive and views the individual in terms of three broad perspectives: (1) the medical model, (2) the social system model, and (3) the pluralistic model. The medical model portion includes five different areas: physical dexterity, weight by height, visual acuity, health history, and the Bender Visual-Motor Gestalt Test. The social system model assesses adaptive behavior and school functioning level (using primarily the WISC-R). The third broad area, the pluralistic model, views the child in terms of "estimated learning potential" and two sociocultural scales (one of the child's own ethnic group and a second based on the school culture). Scoring for all measures is converted to percentiles and placed in a profile. The SOMPA is revolutionary in approach and addresses child functioning in a manner that has not been undertaken previously on any widespread basis. Some professionals are skeptical about this potential use because of the massive nature of the evaluation and there are questions about its clinical usefulness because of problems with reliability (Oakland & Shermis, 1989). But many believe that it will be useful and will circumvent some common problems. Longitudinal research suggests that the SOMPA has some validity for predicting school achievement for ethnic minority students (Figueroa & Sassenrath, 1989).

A second larger evaluation system is the Woodcock-Johnson Psychoeducational Battery (Woodcock, 1978). This system covers an unusually wide age span (three to 80 years) and is designed to evaluate scholastic aptitude, cognitive ability, academic achievement, and interests. The Woodcock-Johnson battery is made up of 27 subtests divided into three parts: cognitive ability (assesses both cognitive ability and scholastic aptitudes), academic achievement, and interests (both academic and nonacademic).

Administration of the entire battery requires more than two hours, although it is shorter if only a portion of the subtests are employed to assess specific areas. Salvia and Ysseldyke (1987) considered the Woodcock-Johnson adequately standardized, although validity data are not available to support all the recommended uses. The usual cautions apply also to the Woodcock-Johnson.

ADOLESCENT AND ADULT YEARS

Core Concept	*Assessment during adolescent and adult years involves utilization of age- or functioning level–appropriate procedures. Attention must also be given to the changing purposes of evaluation in these years.*

The phrase *adolescent and adult years* is only a general reference, in this section used to mean 13 years of age and older. Many of the evaluation techniques previously examined extend well into this age range.

Intellectual Functioning

The instrument frequently used in the middle adolescent and older years is the Wechsler Adult Intelligence Scale—Revised (WAIS-R) (Wechsler, 1981). This is a slightly revised version of the earlier WAIS, which is still used periodically and remains the topic of some research (Coolidge, Rakoff, Schwellenbach, Bracken, & Walker, 1986). Nearly 80% of the WAIS content remained unchanged or was modified only slightly in the WAIS-R. The WISC-R, discussed earlier, extends into the early adolescent years (five to 15 years). The WAIS-R is appropriate for assessing the intellectual functioning of people older than 15. The WAIS-R subscales are the same as the WISC-R's, except that there are 11 rather than 12 subscales. Some questions have been raised about its comparability to the WAIS and other instruments (Flynn, 1985, Spitz, 1986).

Vocational Functioning

One area that becomes increasingly relevant as the person with mental retardation grows older is his or her skill level for vocational training and placement. During adolescence and adulthood the individual who is mentally retarded usually encounters vocational training as a part of formal education. The nature of this training (as well as later placement) varies considerably depending on the degree of impairment.

Evaluation in this area, like that previously discussed, must be considered in light of its purpose. One purpose of past research on evaluation has been the prediction of vocational success. A second purpose is the evaluation of training and placement success. Work samples seem to be best for evaluation in this area. Work-sample assessment is analogous to evaluation that uses applied behavior analysis techniques. Such precise analysis of skill level has provided the most practically oriented information in other areas, and thus its precision in vocational assessment is not surprising. Evaluation takes

Certain paper and pencil assessments are still used to evaluate functioning during the adolescent and adult years.

place in a setting that is as nearly natural as possible. The close link between the evaluative procedure and its purpose or referent setting provides the most useful and also the most accurate data. Perhaps the strongest deterrent to more widespread acceptance of this approach is convenience. Work samples as a test tend to be cumbersome in terms of development and administration, but the assessment techniques are not nearly so inconvenient when they are an integral part of a training program. The logistics of developing a convenient evaluation system rationally related to program activities and to job success remains the challenge of professionals who work in assessment generally and with handicapped individuals in particular.

NEW ISSUES AND FUTURE DIRECTIONS

Historically many of the issues raised in assessment have paralleled prevailing debates and issues in mental retardation. This was illustrated by the early nature versus nurture controversy on the source of intelligent behavior and continues today in more abstract questions about fundamental conceptions of mental retardation (e.g., Baumeister, 1987). Assessment in mental retardation is moving from its position as a somewhat isolated, almost laboratory-based activity into the center of culture, society, and environment. It is no longer acceptable merely to test people's ability in a "stimulus-free environment" to determine how they will adapt and function in the broader world where they live. Newer research methodology tries to study people in the context of their environment more than ever before (Stainback & Stainback, 1989). Social and cultural environments will become integral in our study and assessment of mental retardation (Levine, 1989).

The changes will serve some very important purposes in the field of psychoeducational measurement. From one standpoint, they should present a more accurate view of how an individual functions and what his or her ability is in the relevant environmental context. We hope that such an assessment will also have greater utility than previously has been the case (for example, ability testing that has little usefulness for instruction). From another perspective, assessment in context may also hold promise for alleviating some of the problems of evaluating individuals from minority subgroups. Integrating information about environmental circumstances, culture, language, and other pertinent factors into a child's evaluation has considerable potential for producing more appropriate assessment.

But better methods will not solve certain assessment difficulties. Designing environmentally contexted measurement will not do away with prejudice. Improvement will not be so great that assessment inaccuracies are solely the result of racial bias on the part of the examiner. This is a problem of professional ethics. Additionally, placing assessment in environmental context is not simple. It is likely to be both difficult and cumbersome. This must be of concern to those working in the area of measurement, for if assessment is not user friendly, it will not be used.

CORE QUESTIONS

1. Why are the uses of assessment procedures so important in the outcome of evaluation?
2. A number of difficulties were found with the calculation of intelligence quotient by the ratio method. What were some of them, and why was the deviation method found preferable?
3. Why is it essential to clarify the purposes involved in assessment before one embarks on a testing effort?
4. Many conceptual developments have been important in the field of assessment during the past years. Among them have been the notions of formative and summative evaluation and the distinctions between norm- and criterion-referenced assessment. How do these concepts fit into the evaluation picture, and why were they important?

5. Different reliability levels are required for different intervention decisions. Why is this, and how do our instruments stand with respect to measurement precision?
6. What are the advantages and limitations of the concepts of mental age and IQ? Why do these measures alone not provide adequate information for a full evaluation?
7. What are some difficulties encountered in predicting later functioning from infant assessment procedures?
8. Outline potential assessment instruments or procedures that you would find important during the prenatal period. Describe conditions that would prompt such assessment.
9. Describe assessment procedures you might employ for early life (neonatal) and preschool years. Discuss conditions that would prompt you to undertake such assessment.
10. How might you plan an appropriate evaluation plan for children during the elementary school years? What considerations would come into play in your assessment plan?
11. Outline relevant assessment considerations for the adolescent and adult years. How are these different from earlier considerations?
12. In reviewing the life-span perspective, how do purposes change and what considerations must be given to selection of an assessment approach?

ROUND TABLE DISCUSSION

Assessment is much more complex than merely picking up a test and administering it to a child. Careful consideration must be given from the outset to why one is evaluating and what is to be the result. Throughout the assessment process one must exercise care in the choice of techniques, in how to undertake procedures, and in how to interpret data. And proper assessment must also consider the age of the individual being evaluated, since different domains become relevant at different ages and techniques diverge widely.

In your study group or on your own, design an evaluation plan that will attend to the considerations raised in this chapter. If you are working with others, have each person be responsible for a different age level and one or two individuals attend to the conceptual issues related to assessment. Compare your final plan with an existing one that you are aware of, such as that used in a school district. Full consideration of the life span must extend beyond the school years to health and social service agencies.

REFERENCES

Altepeter, T. S. (1989). The PPVT-R as a measure of psycholinguistic functioning: A caution. *Journal of Clinical Psychology, 45,* 935–941.

American Psychological Association, American Educational Research Association, & National Council on Measurement in Education. (1974). *Standards for educational and psychological tests.* Washington, DC: American Psychological Association.

Anastasi, A. (1950). The concept of validity in the interpretation of test scores. *Educational and Psychological Measurement, 10,* 67–78.

Anastasi, A. (1988). *Psychological testing* (6th ed.). New York: Macmillan.

Atkinson, L. (1990a). Reliability and validity of ratio developmental quotients from the Cattell Infant Intelligence Scale. *American Journal on Mental Retardation, 95,* 215–219.

Atkinson, L. (1990b). Intellectual and adaptive functioning: Some tables for interpreting the Vineland in combination with intelligence tests. *American Journal on Mental Retardation, 95,* 198–205.

Baumeister, A. A. (1987). Mental retardation: Some conceptions and dilemmas. *American Psychologist, 42,* 796–800.

Berry, K. E. (1967). *Developmental test of visual-motor integration: Administration and scoring manual.* Chicago: Follett.

Binet, A., & Simon, T. (1908). Le développement de l'intelligence chez les enfants. *L'Année Psychologique, 14,* 1–94.

Blankenship, C. S. (1985). Using curriculum-based assessment data to make instructional decisions. *Exceptional Children, 52,* 233–238.

Bloom, B. S., Hastings, J. T., & Madaus, G. F. (1971). *Handbook on formative and summative evaluation of student learning.* New York: McGraw-Hill.

Boyd, R. D. (1969). *CCD developmental progress scale. Experimental form, manual and direction.* Portland: University of Oregon Medical Center, Department of Clinical Psychology.

Burgess, D. B., Asher, K. N., Doucet, H. J., Reardon, K., & Daste, M. R. (1984). Parent report as a means of administering the Prescreening Developmental Questionnaire: An evaluation study. *Journal of Developmental and Behavioral Pediatrics, 5*(4), 201–203.

Bush, W. J., & Waugh, K. W. (1982). *Diagnosing learning disabilities* (3rd ed.). Columbus: Charles E. Merrill.

Cain, L. F., Levine, S., & Elzey, F. F. (1963). *Manual for the Cain-Levine social competency scale.* Palo Alto, CA: Consulting Psychologists Press.

Cohen, S. E., & Parmelee, A. H. (1983). Prediction of five-year Stanford-Binet scores in preterm infants. *Child Development, 54,* 1242–1253.

Colarusso, R. P., & Hammill, D. D. (1972). *Motor-free visual perception test.* San Rafael, CA: Academic Therapy Publications.

Coolidge, F. L., Rakoff, R. A., Schwellenbach, L. D., Bracken, D. D., & Walker, S. H. (1986). WAIS profiles in mentally retarded adults. *Journal of Mental Deficiency Research, 30,* 15–17.

Cronbach, L. J. (1990). *Essentials of psychological testing* (5th ed.). New York: Harper & Row.

Cundari, L. A., & Suppa, R. J. (1988). The potential uses of curriculum-based assessment for decision making in special education. *Exceptional Children, 35,* 143–154.

Drew, C. J. (1973). Criterion-referenced and norm-referenced assessment of minority group children. *Journal of School Psychology, 11,* 323–329.

Dunn, L. M., & Dunn, L. M. (1981). *Peabody picture vocabulary test—Revised.* Circle Pines, MN: American Guidance Service.

Dunn, L. M., & Markwardt, F. C. (1970). *Peabody individual achievement test.* Circle Pines, MN: American Guidance Service.

Elbert, J. C. (1984). Training in child diagnostic assessment: A survey of clinical psychology graduate programs. *Journal of Clinical Child Psychology, 13,* 122–133.

Felce, D., de Kock, U., Mansell, J., & Jenkins, J. (1984). Assessing mentally handicapped adults. *British Journal of Mental Subnormality, 30,* 65–74.

Figueroa, R. A., & Sassenrath, J. M. (1989). A longitudinal study of the predictive validity of the System of Multicultural Pluralistic Assessment (SOMPA). *Psychology in the Schools, 26,* 5–19.

Flavell, J. H. (1977). *Cognitive development.* Englewood Cliffs, NJ: Prentice-Hall.

Flynn, J. R. (1985). Wechsler intelligence tests: Do we really have a criterion of mental retardation? *American Journal of Mental Deficiency, 90,* 236–244.

Frankenburg, W., Dodds, J., Fandal, A., Kazuk, E., & Cohrs, M. (1975). *Developmental screening test: Reference manual—Revised 1975 edition.* Denver: LA-DOCA Project and Publishing Foundation.

Friedlander, B. Z. (1971). Automated evaluation of selective listening in language-impaired and normal infants and young children. *Maternal and Child Health Exchange, 1,* 9–12.

Frostig, M., & Horne, D. (1964). *The Frostig program for the development of visual perception: Teacher's guide.* Chicago: Follett.

Fuchs, D., & Fuchs, L. S. (1986). Test procedure bias: A meta-analysis of examiner familiarity effects. *Review of Educational Research, 56,* 243–262.

Galagan, J. E. (1985). Psychoeducational testing: Turn out the lights, the party's over. *Exceptional Children, 52,* 288–299.

Gaussen, T. (1984). Developmental milestones or conceptual milestones? Some practical and theoretical limitations in infant assessment procedures. *Child Care, Health and Development, 10,* 99–115.

Gaussen, T., & Stratton, P. (1985). Beyond the milestone model: A systems framework for alternative infant assessment procedures. *Child Care, Health and Development, 11,* 131–150.

Goldstein, D. J., & Sheaffer, C. I. (1988). Ratio developmental quotients from the Bayley are comparable to later IQs from the Stanford-Binet. *American Journal on Mental Retardation, 92,* 379–380.

Greer, S., Bauchner, H., & Zuckerman, B. (1989). The Denver Developmental Screening Test: How good is its predictive validity? *Developmental Medicine and Child Neurology, 31,* 774–781.

Gronlund, N. E., & Linn, R. L. (1990). *Measurement and evaluation in teaching.* New York: Macmillan.

Gunzberg, H. C. (1963). *Progress assessment chart (P.A.C.) (form I, form II).* London: National Association on Mental Health.

Haertel, E. (1985). Construct validity and criterion-referenced testing. *Review of Educational Research, 55,* 23–46.

Haney, W. (1984). Testing reasoning and reasoning about testing. *Review of Educational Research, 54,* 597–654.

Hanson, R., Smith, J. A., & Hume, W. (1984). Some reasons for disagreement among scorers of infant intelligence test items. *Child Care, Health and Development, 10,* 17–30.

Harrison, P. L. (1985). *Vineland adaptive behavior scales classroom edition manual.* Circle Pines, MN: American Guidance Service.

Haynes, U. (1967). *A developmental approach to case-finding with special reference to cerebral palsy, mental retardation, and related disorders.* Washington, DC: U.S. Government Printing Office.

Honig, A. S., & Caldwell, B. M. (1966). *Early language assessment scale.* Syracuse: Syracuse University Press.

Hopkins, K. D., & Stanley, J. C. (1981). *Educational and psychological measurement and evaluation* (6th ed.). Englewood Cliffs, NJ: Prentice-Hall.

Jastak, J., & Jastak, S. (1978). *Wide range achievement test.* Wilmington, DE: Authors.

Joyce, B. G., & Wolking, W. D. (1987). Standardized tests and timed curriculum-based assessments: A comparison of two methods for screening high-risk students. *Journal of Psychoeducational Assessment, 5,* 185–193.

Knobloch, H., Pasamanick, B., & Sherard, E. S. (1967). A developmental screening inventory. In U. Haynes (Ed.), *A developmental approach to case-finding with special reference to cerebral palsy, mental retardation, and related disorders* (pp. 77–85). Washington, DC: U.S. Government Printing Office.

Laveault, D. (1987). Application of the measure of intellectual functioning and adaptability to the formative evaluation of abilities in adults. *Revue Canadienne de Psycho-Education, 16,* 11–21.

Lerner, J. W. (1988). *Learning disabilities: Theories, diagnosis, and teaching strategies* (5th ed.). New York: Houghton Mifflin.

LeVine, R. A. (1989). Cultural environments in child development. In W. Damon (Ed.), *Child development today and tomorrow* (pp. 52–68). San Francisco: Jossey-Bass.

Lopez, S. (1988). The empirical basis of ethnocultural and linguistic bias in mental health evaluations of Hispanics. *American Psychologist, 43,* 1095–1096.

Luftig, R. L. (1989). *Assessment of learners with special needs.* Boston: Allyn & Bacon.

MacDonald, L., & Barton, L. E. (1986). Measuring severity of behavior: A revision of Part II of the Adaptive Behavior Scale. *American Journal of Mental Deficiency, 90,* 418–424.

Malgady, R. G., Rogler, L. H., & Constantino, G. (1987). Ethnocultural and linguistic bias in mental health evaluation of Hispanics. *American Psychologist, 42,* 228–234.

Meier, J. (1973). *Screening and assessment of young children at developmental risk: Report of the President's Committee on Mental Retardation.* (DHEW Publication No. [OS] 73–90). Washington, DC: U.S. Government Printing Office.

Menyuk, P. (1988). *Language development and use.* Glenview, IL: Scott Foresman.

Mercer, J. R., & Lewis, J. F. (1977). *System of multicultural pluralistic assessment.* New York: Psychological Corporation.

Miller-Jones, D. (1989). Culture and testing. *American Psychologist, 44,* 360–366.

Moore, K. J., Fifield, M. B., Spira, D. A., & Scarlato, M. (1989). Child study team decision making in special education: Improving the process. *Remedial and Special Education, 10,* 50–58.

Nihira, K., Foster, R., Shellhaas, M., & Leland, H. (1974). *AAMD adaptive behavior scale, 1974 revision.* Washington, DC: American Association on Mental Deficiency.

Oakland, T., & Shermis, M. D. (1989). Factor structure of the sociocultural scales. *Journal of Psychoeducational Assessment, 7,* 335–342.

Padilla, A. M. (1988). Early psychological assessments of Mexican-American children. *Journal of the History of the Behavioral Sciences, 24,* 111–117.

Plata, M. (1985). The use of criterion-referenced assessment with bilingual handicapped students. *Journal of Instructional Psychology, 12,* 200–204.

Prasse, D. P., & Reschly, D. J. (1986). *Larry P.:* A case of segregation, testing, or program efficacy? *Exceptional Children, 52,* 333–346.

The rapid development screening checklist (1972). Committee on Children with Handicaps. New York: American Academy of Pediatrics.

Reynolds, C. R. (1987). Race bias in testing. In R. J. Corsini (Ed.), *Concise encyclopedia of psychology* (pp. 953–954). New York: John Wiley & Sons.

Reznick, J. S., & Goldsmith, L. (1989). A multiple form word production checklist for assessing early language. *Journal of Child Language, 16*, 91–100.

Roach, E. F., & Kephart, N. C. (1966). *The Purdue perceptual-motor survey.* Columbus: Charles E. Merrill.

Roberts, E., & DeBlassie, R. R. (1983). Test bias and the culturally different early adolescent. *Adolescence, 18*, 837–843.

Rocissano, L., & Yatchmink, Y. (1983). Language skill and interactive patterns in prematurely born toddlers. *Child Development, 54*, 1229–1241.

Ross, G. (1985). Use of the Bayley Scales to characterize abilities of premature infants. *Child Development, 56*, 835–842.

Salvia, J., & Ysseldyke, J. E. (1987). *Assessment in special and remedial education* (4th ed.). Boston: Houghton Mifflin.

Schenck, S. J. (1980). The diagnostic/instructional link in individualized education programs. *Journal of Special Education, 14*, 337–345.

Sewell, G., Hinnells, M., O'Connell, A., & Edwards, M. (1989). Support for assessment. *Support for Learning, 4*, 227–229.

Skowronski, J. J., & Carlston, D. E. (1989). Negativity and extremity biases in impression formation: A review of explanations. *Psychological Bulletin, 105*, 131–142.

Slate, N. M. (1983). Nonbiased assessment of adaptive behavior: Comparison of three instruments. *Exceptional Children, 50*, 67–70.

Soyster, H. D., & Ehly, S. W. (1986). Parent-rated adaptive behavior and in-school ratings of students referred for EMR evaluation. *American Journal of Mental Deficiency, 90*, 460–463.

Sparrow, S. S., Balla, D. A., & Cicchetti, D. V. (1984a). *Vineland adaptive behavior scales interview edition, survey form manual.* Circle Pines, MN: American Guidance Service.

Sparrow, S. S., Balla, D. A., & Cicchetti, D. V. (1984b). *Vineland adaptive behavior scales interview edition, expanded form manual.* Circle Pines, MN: American Guidance Service.

Sparrow, S. S., Blachman, B. A., & Chauncy, S. (1983). Diagnostic and prescriptive intervention in primary school education. *American Journal of Orthopsychiatry, 53*, 721–729.

Spitz, H. H. (1986). Disparities in mentally retarded persons' IQ derived from different intelligence tests. *American Journal of Mental Deficiency, 90*, 588–591.

Stainback, W., & Stainback, S. (1989). Using qualitative data collection procedures to investigate supported education issues. *Journal of the Association for Persons with Severe Handicaps, 14*, 271–277.

Taylor, R. L. (1990). The *Larry P.* decision a decade later: Problems and future directions. *Mental Retardation, 28*, iii–iv.

Terman, L., & Merrill, M. (1973). *Stanford-Binet intelligence scale: 1972 norms edition.* Boston: Houghton Mifflin.

Wechsler, D. (1981). *WAIS-R manual: Wechsler adult intelligence scale—Revised.* New York: Psychological Corporation.

White, B. L., & Kaban, B. (1971). *Manual for quantitative analysis of tasks of one- to six-year-old children.* Cambridge: Harvard University Press.

Whiteley, J. H., & Krenn, M. J. (1986). Uses of the Bayley mental scale with nonambulatory profoundly mentally retarded children. *American Journal of Mental Deficiency, 90,* 425–431.

Whorton, J. E. (1985). Test-retest Wechsler Intelligence Scale for Children—Revised scores for 310 educable mentally retarded and specific learning disabled students. *Psychological Reports, 56,* 857–858.

Wood, F. H., Johnson, J. L., & Jenkins, J. R. (1986). The *Lora* case: Nonbiased referral, assessment, and placement procedures. *Exceptional Children, 52,* 323–331.

Woodcock, R. (1978). *Woodcock-Johnson psychoeducational battery.* Boston: Teaching Resources.

Ysseldyke, J. E., & Algozzine, B. (1982). *Critical issues in special and remedial education.* Boston: Houghton Mifflin.

Ysseldyke, J. E., Algozzine, B., Richey, L. S., & Graden, J. (1982). Declaring students eligible for learning disability services: Why bother with the data? *Learning Disability Quarterly, 5,* 37–44.

PART TWO
Early Life and Preschool Years

CHAPTER SIX

Basic Principles of Early Development

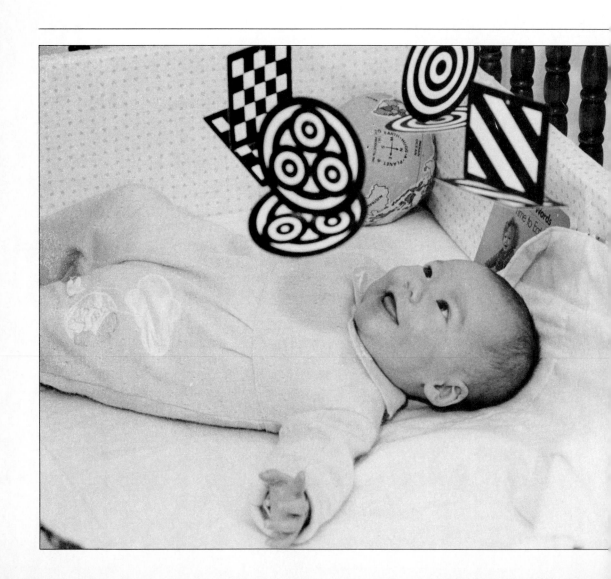

- Genotype, phenotype, growth matrix, and maturation are terms for important concepts in human development.

- Theories of human development have differed dramatically about the importance of influences ranging from prepotency of genetic material to total environmental shaping.

- The human developmental process has been characterized by some as one of continuous growth, while others have viewed it as a series of abrupt, discontinuous stages.

- Certain periods of development are critical both for growth and because of the organism's vulnerability to injury and developmental risk during them.

- Cephalocaudal and proximodistal growth trends begin very early in prenatal development and can also be observed during the first few years of life.

- Prenatal fetal development during weeks 10 through 12 is particularly important because of the tissues being formed at that time.

- The birth process represents another important time when potential risk to the child is high.

- Many consider the time immediately following birth as the most dangerous period of human life.

- The knowledge gained from scientific advances both holds great promise for improving the early developmental fortunes of children and raises serious social questions.

This chapter addresses some of the basic concepts of human development that are behind the organization for the volume as a whole. The developmental life cycle is our fundamental perspective, the glasses through which we examine mental retardation. We have already seen that mental retardation is a multidimensional condition. Myriads of factors contribute to its occurrence and have been studied and treated by many different disciplines, as recorded in Chapter 3. We believe that only a unifying conceptual framework can give coherence to any understanding of mental retardation. Further, it is our contention that human development is a better conceptual vehicle than any other. We examine the biological, psychological, and educational dimensions of mental retardation from a developmental perspective, and explore the complex interactions of these seemingly disparate topics from a developmental approach.

Achenbach described the first edition of his book on developmental psychopathology as "a book about a field that hardly exists yet" (Achenbach, 1982, p. 1). And yet, child development has traditionally held a very prominent position in psychology and education, even though it has undergone the rigors of the scientific method only during the last century (Berger, 1983). Above all, studying the course of human development is a quest for understanding human behavior, a conceptual organizer through which explanations are sought to comprehend why people behave as they do.

Developmental psychology is a way of looking at things and an extremely useful means of examining such abnormalities as mental retardation (Drew & Bukatko, 1990). To some degree Achenbach's statement remains valid, although perhaps it needs modification. Developmental psychopathology, the developmental study of psychological deviance, has become increasingly visible in recent years. But as a field of study it is still maturing with respect both to its knowledge base and to its research methodology.

This chapter, while no substitute for a basic course in human growth and development, introduces those principles of early development that have particular relevance to mental retardation. In addition to the points just made, there are other reasons for the central importance of basic concepts of child development to the study of mental retardation. For many subgroups of the population with mental retardation, developmental factors are central to intellectual, physical, and psychological status. From a basic biological standpoint, many of the clinical syndromes are integrally related to human development. Beyond biology, the broad psychological view of the cultural-familial retarded population has long spotlighted child development within the nature versus nurture controversy, and this group represents the largest proportion of people with retardation. Acquaintance with the concepts of child development is essential for the student of mental retardation.

HUMAN DEVELOPMENT: TERMINOLOGY, CONCEPTS, AND THEORY

Core Concept	*Genotype, phenotype, growth matrix, and maturation are terms for important concepts in human development.*

The field of human growth and development has become more complex as research and technology in all of its contributing sciences have advanced. The information base has dramatically expanded because of additions from biology, embryology, genetics, psychology, and many other areas—all of which have been molded into a body of highly technical knowledge with unique properties beyond those of the contributing areas. Background information about developmental terminology, concepts, and theoretical perspectives is important to an understanding of the human development field.

Concepts and Terms

Many forces come to bear on a person's life status at any given time. *Life status* as used here refers broadly to one's physical, psychological, and behavioral attributes as well as to talents and abilities. All these personal elements are influenced by genetic material inherited from parents plus environmental circumstances that have nourished or impeded development. These components combine and interact in a unique fashion to produce the person we see at a particular point. As we begin this discussion of early development it is important that you become acquainted with certain terms and concepts pertaining to the elements in this complex human equation.

Our parents pass on to us genetic material that strongly affects what we become. This genetic material can be likened to a computer chip that encodes a number of messages. These messages are activated to influence many aspects of our physical and psychological growth. Geneticists use the term **genotype** to refer to the genetic message makeup of an individual. Established at conception by the combining of sperm and ovum, the genotype is usually constant. Only rarely does this constancy fail, as when a mutation or other error in cell division alters subsequent cell divisions. The human genotype is not readily accessible for actual inspection, but the **phenotype,** a term that refers to observable physical traits, may be used to draw inferences about the genotype. The phenotype is the observable result of interaction between the genotype and the environment.

Growth matrix is another related term in child development. The growth matrix is also the result of interactions between heredity and environment. Although partially observable (because it includes the phenotype), the growth matrix also includes all of the internal aspects of a child that generate a given response in a particular situation. The growth matrix is more than a simple combination of phenotype and genotype, however. One distinction is that while genetic concepts are relatively constant, the growth matrix changes as interactions occur between the organism and its environment. The growth matrix is a product of that interaction and at the same time determines or regulates individual response patterns.

Child-development specialists also use maturation in a way that requires definition. Although some difference in usage exists, professionals employ the term **maturation** to signify any development or change in the status or underlying process of a behavioral trait that takes place in the demonstrable absence of specific practical experience. In the present context one additional restriction is added: the absence of specific instruction. Thus in this context maturation is distinguishable from learning, which refers to changes associated with specific practice or instruction. In many situations it is difficult to discriminate between changes resulting from maturation and changes resulting from learning. A history of maturation and of learning and a combination of the two are involved in any child's current developmental status. This developmental status and its components are very much related to the notion of readiness.

Readiness exists when the child is at a point in development (including previous maturation and learning) where he or she might be expected to profit from a particular situation. An example often spoken of is "reading readiness." From the present standpoint, reading readiness refers to the point in a child's development at which one could expect progress as a result of exposure to reading experience or instruction. Of course, if the status from either a maturational or previous learning standpoint were deficient (inadequate to establish readiness), the child is not expected to progress as a result of a given stimulation. There is no magic formula "X amount of maturation plus Y amount of previous learning equals readiness." Although developmental readiness includes both, widely varying amounts and types of each may exist in different children who have reached readiness for an experience.

Developmental Theories

Core Concept	*Theories of human development have differed dramatically about the importance of influences ranging from prepotency of genetic material to total environmental shaping.*

We know that human development and its complexities have been of interest since the beginning of recorded history. Some of the most common theoretical positions have an extremely long history. Certain prescientific explanations of human growth and development, although amusing in retrospect, used to be very popular.

Preformationist Perspective

The preformationist theory of human growth and development had a substantial following in the past. Preformationism assumed that the human organism is preformed before birth; it proposed that the foundation elements of human behavior are intact from the beginning and do not develop or change from a qualitative standpoint during life. The preformationist thus denied the importance of growth and development except in the sense of quantity, or growing larger. The early homuncular theory of human reproduction exemplified the preformationist position. This theory held that a completely formed, tiny person existed in the sperm. This tiny person, termed a *homunculus,* began to grow in size at conception but did not change in the sense that tissue changes occurred qualitatively, such as in the formation of various organs.

The preformationist position largely discounted the effects of environment on human development. As suggested by the homuncular theory, prenatal as well as postnatal environment was of little consequence as far as development went. Usually the concessions made to environmental effects involved only expansion of existing abilities, drives, and behaviors. Preformationists thought that neither new growth nor directional influence of development did much to change the preformed organism.

Predeterministic Perspective

At first glance the predeterministic theorists seem to have held assumptions similar to the preformationists'. Although their outcome is much the same, there were some significant differences between the two theoretical positions.

Predeterministic positions did not view human development as a simple accentuation of a preformed organism. Qualitative growth and tissue differentiation played a substantial role in most theories of predeterminism. An example of this is found in the doctrine of recapitulation, which was described in great detail by G. Stanley Hall (1904). Recapitulation hypothesized that the development of the child from conception to maturity progressed through all the evolutionary phases of the human race. Although quite popular for a period around the turn of the century, this theory fell into disfavor primarily because of the absence of objective or observable data to support its sweeping hypotheses (Gleitman, 1986).

As noted, the outcome of predeterministic theories was essentially the same as preformationism in that environmental influence was thought to be minimal, perhaps limited to restricting development. Growth patterns were viewed as innate or internally regulated. More recently, the disciplines of biology, genetics, and embryology have provided factual knowledge supporting the notion that certain development is primarily regulated internally (for example, prenatal growth and certain infantile behavioral development). Former predeterministic contentions of innate control, however, involved broad applications that have received no scientific support.

Tabula Rasa Perspective

Tabula rasa in the present context refers to approaches that emphasize the prepotency of environmental influences. The term means "blank slate" and was popularized by John Locke in the seventeenth century. For purposes of this discussion, *tabula rasa* is used generically to represent positions emphasizing extreme environmental impact.

Contrasting with the approaches of preformationism and predeterminism, tabula rasa positions minimized the influence of internal factors (such as heredity) on human development. Environment was seen as playing a predominant role in nearly all aspects of development. Tabula rasa theorists considered the human organism plastic and infinitely amenable to molding by external influences. Thus an individual's ability was dependent on what was "written" on the blank slate through experience. The weakness of this framework, like preformationism's and predeterminism's, was the extreme to which proponents of the position went.

Neither the tabula rasa nor the predeterministic approach to child development has been satisfactory. There is little logical or empirical support for a belief in preformed human functioning at birth. With the exception of very simple reflex responses, there seem to be few human behavioral dimensions that are not influenced by environment. The fundamental error of predeterministic proponents was their disregard for the impact of experience. Tabula rasa theorists caught the pendulum at the opposite end of its swing. The assumption that environmental impact is a significant contributor to human growth and development does represent reality, but tabula rasa theorists emphasized the impact of this factor far too strongly.

Interactional Perspectives

Current positions concerning the evolution of human development generally subscribe to the notion of an interaction between heredity and environment (Lerner, 1987; Shaffer, 1985). Both genetic and environmental factors set limits for growth as well as selectively influencing each other. Genetic material determines limits even under the most favorable environment conceivable. Likewise, environment limits the fulfillment of genetic potential. Genetic material determines which factors in the environment are more potent by rendering the organism more sensitive to some than to others. Similarly, environmental factors like cultural or ecological factors operate on genetic expression by providing selective influences on ability development.

The interactional approach to human growth and development emphasizes analysis of relationships between heredity and environment. This represents a substantial difference from earlier positions, which assumed the prepotence of one over the other.

Although other approaches may be conceptually simpler, the interactional position seems to represent reality better.

THE DEVELOPMENTAL PROCESS

Growing support for the interactional approach to human development generated a more intense focus on the developmental process. Researchers and theoreticians alike began to ask questions that were more amenable to study than were the philosophical positions exemplified by former views. This section presents an examination of various dimensions of the developmental process.

Continuity Versus Discontinuity of Growth

Core Concept	*The human developmental process has been characterized by some as one of continuous growth, while others have viewed it as a series of abrupt, discontinuous stages.*

The nature of the developmental process has raised a series of interesting questions. At times these questions have become controversial and have been the subject of much debate. One area that has generated substantial discussion involves the continuity or discontinuity of human growth. The question is Does development proceed by gradual continuous quantitative change or in stages typified by abrupt discontinuous changes in quality?

Theories emphasizing stages encouraged the discontinuity view of human development. Early developmental stage theories implied that there was little or no overlap of process from one stage to tne next. Each developmental stage was specifically and qualitatively different from the others. The first developmental theorist to dismiss the notion of discontinuity was Piaget (1926). With his background in biology and zoology, Piaget was able to formulate a theory of stages of cognitive development that incorporated the occurrence of immature and mature responses at all developmental levels. He conceived of intelligence as having three global developmental periods: (1) the period of sensorimotor intelligence, (2) the period of preparation for and organization of concrete operations, and (3) the period of formal operations. Sensorimotor intelligence development, he thought, began at birth and continued for about the first two years of life. In the second period, from about two to 11 years of age, Piaget viewed the development of intelligence as involving the essential formation of a conceptual framework that the child uses in interaction with the environment. The third period, from 11 years of age on, is the time when Piaget contended that an individual works with abstract thought. During this period (formal operations) the person begins to be able to think of hypothetical possibilities instead of relying exclusively on concrete operations, in which cognition depends on a concrete or real object as a basis. Piaget conceived the total developmental picture as one of a dynamic interaction, with the organism operating on the environment as well as being molded by it. His theory has come under heavy fire

The interaction of young children with others and their environment is very important to their early development.

(Flavell, 1982; Shultz, 1982). Flavell (1985), for example, does not believe that the stage concept will play an important role in future scientific work on cognitive growth.

The continuity position contends that growth is a gradual process rather than a series of abrupt changes followed by periods of less rapid change (plateaus). A variety of factors can be mentioned in support of the theory of growth continuity. First, it is well known that both mature and immature responses are made by children at all levels of development. Second, theories of continuity test hypotheses generated from general behavior theories more effectively than do discontinuous stage theories.

There have been strong proponents of both continuity and discontinuity of development. Growth and development specialists, however, have largely gone beyond the point where this kind of polarized thinking prevails. No on believes that theoretically formulated stages are precise definitions involving exact ages, behaviors, and response levels. They are convenient approximations based on averages and are useful in conceptualizing developmental processes and suggesting directions for research (Berger, 1983).

Critical Periods and Developmental Vulnerability

Core Concept	*Certain periods of development are critical both for growth and because of the organism's vulnerability to injury and developmental risk during them.*

Developmental deviancy is a central concern in the field of mental retardation, as it is in other disorder areas (Schwartz & Johnson, 1985). In view of this, of vital importance to those studying mental retardation is the concept of developmental vulnerability. Here we use *vulnerability* to refer to how susceptible the organism is to being injured or altered by a traumatic incident. *Traumatic incident* is defined broadly to include such occurrences as toxic agents (poisons) and cell division mutations, as well as other deviations from the usual sequence of development.

Research in biology and embryology has provided a great deal of information about how human growth occurs (Johnson, 1988). From the time of conception, a series of complex cell divisions occurs that ultimately results in the entity we call a human being. During the early part of this developmental process, the two original cells divide repeatedly from a mass no larger than the point of a sharp pencil (at about 14 days) to the size of a newborn child. Obviously this implies a very dramatic growth process. Cell division occurs extremely rapidly in the first few days after the ovum is fertilized by a sperm. The mass that is to become the fetus does not actually become implanted or attached to the mother's uterus until about two weeks after fertilization. In this short period cell division has progressed with considerable speed and has begun the process of tissue differentiation. Both the speed of cell division and the process of tissue differentiation are important with regard to the vulnerability to trauma.

As cell division begins, chemical reactions occur that generate new cells of different types (tissue differentiation). These cells multiply, forming three different layers of tissue: the ectoderm, the mesoderm, and the endoderm. Figure 6-1 pictorially represents the three cell tissue layers. Although the tissue layers are named because of their early developmental position (ectoderm, outer layer; mesoderm, middle layer; endoderm, inner layer), they eventually form different parts of the organism. Parts of the ectoderm become nervous tissue, various types of muscle come from the mesoderm, and so on. During the time that a particular organ or system is being formed, the cells generating that system divide very rapidly. There are specific periods when, for instance, the central nervous system is the primary part of the organism that is developing. During that time, the cells that constitute the central nervous system divide more rapidly than other types of cells, and at this time the central nervous system is most

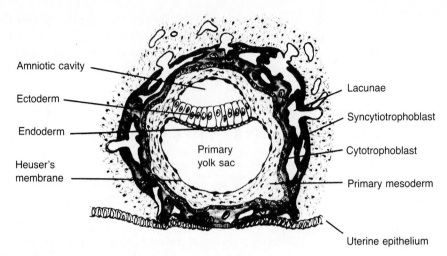

Figure 6–1
Conceptus at about 12 days, showing cell tissue layers
From *Synopsis of Anatomy* by L. J. A. Didio, 1970, St. Louis: C.V. Mosby. Copyright 1970 by C.V. Mosby Co. Reprinted by permission.

vulnerable to trauma. If a toxic agent or infection occurs in the mother at this time, the developing central nervous system (or some particular part of it) will probably be the most affected.

There are various other critical periods during prenatal development. These periods are biologically critical for the healthy growth of the fetus. Some professionals have long suspected that critical periods also exist after birth. Hypotheses of postnatal critical periods have varied considerably. In some cases the "critical periods" of early childhood have been viewed as those times that are optimal for the child to learn or experience certain things. Others have conceived the critical-period idea in terms of irreversibility, holding that, if a child does not acquire certain skills or does not experience certain stimuli at the appropriate time, development will be altered in some way that is not reversible. Under some circumstances the theoretical outcome of either viewpoint is the same. The child, if not taught at the critical time, may not learn given material as well as might be possible.

The critical-period concept has had considerable effect in both research about and education of very young children. Educational programs like Montessori have flourished because of the intuitive appeal of the critical-period concept. But firm research evidence supporting the importance/irreversibility view has been fragmentary in certain areas and vigorously challenged by some researchers (Flavell, 1985; Lerner, 1987).

PRENATAL DEVELOPMENT

The prenatal period of human development has long been recognized as highly important. As with any unknown or unexplored phenomenon, very early explanations of prenatal development tended to be more philosophical and metaphysical than scientific in orientation, for example, the prescientific notion of the homunculus. Contemporary advances in research methods have permitted at least limited glimpses of this previously unexplored region. Although much of our current information about prenatal development has come from studies with animals, direct knowledge about the human organism is continually increasing. This section surveys the sequence of prenatal development. Information about this subject facilitates a broader understanding of developmental deviations as they relate to mental retardation.

Core Concept	*Cephalocaudal and proximodistal growth trends begin very early in prenatal development and can also be observed during the first few years of life.*

Early cell division, as we know, occurs at different rates, depending on which portion of the organism is mainly being formed at that time. Beyond these variations in developmental rates are two important general growth trends that warrant mention. The first is known as the cephalocaudal developmental trend, or growth gradient. As the term suggests, the fetus develops more rapidly in the head area (*cephalo-*) first, with maturation in the lower extremities (*caudal*) or "tail" following. At almost all stages of a young child's development the upper regions (and behaviors associated with these regions) are more nearly complete than the lower regions. Dramatically evident prenatally, the cephalocaudal trend also is present after birth. A young child is skilled in a behavior involving the arms before developing a similar skill in the legs. The second general developmental trend is the proximodistal gradient. This term refers to the fact that more rapid growth and development occur near the center of the organism (*proximo-*), with extremities (*distal*) maturing later. This trend is also present both prenatally and during the first few years of infant life. Very soon after fertilization occurs, the cell division process commences that ultimately results in a fully formed human. As noted earlier, it takes about two weeks for the dividing cell mass to become attached to the uterus. Even before this implantation occurs, the cells begin to differentiate. As the ectoderm, mesoderm, and endoderm are initially formed, there remains considerable flexibility in what individual cells within those layers can become. Thus at the 14-day stage a given cell within the mesoderm could still grow into something besides the parts of the body usually formed from the mesoderm. Determination of resulting organs at this point is more a function of layer position than of the composition of the cell. Cell flexibility disappears, however, as growth proceeds. The layers themselves become increasingly differentiated, and as this occurs individual cells become more specialized (Johnson, 1988). Table 6–1 summarizes some of the types of structures associated with each tissue layer.

   At the time of implantation the embryo is still very small. Despite all that has gone on, the mass is little larger than a dot made by a sharp pencil. The estimated size is about that of a ball 2mm in diameter, and the weight cannot even be estimated. It is difficult for us even to conceive that such a tiny piece of matter is not only living but has already begun to differentiate in anticipation of forming such structures as eyes, a brain, and muscles.

Table 6–1
Cell tissue layers of the embryo

Endoderm	Mesoderm	Ectoderm
Epithelium of pharynx, tongue root, auditory tube, tonsils, thyroid	Muscles (all types)	Epidermis, including cutaneous glands, hair, nails, lens
Larynx, trachea, lungs	Cartilage, bone	Epithelium of sense organs, nasal cavity, sinuses
Digestive tube	Blood, bone marrow	Mouth, including oral glands, enamel
Bladder	Lymphoid tissue	Anal canal
Vagina	Epithelium of blood vessels, body cavities	Nervous tissue
Urethra	Kidney, ureter, gonads, genital ducts	
	Suprarenal cortex	
	Joint cavities	

Adapted from *Developmental Anatomy* (7th ed.) by L. B. Arey, 1974, Philadelphia. Copyright 1974 by W. B. Saunders Co. Reprinted by permission.

After implantation (14 days) activity continues at an extremely rapid pace. By about the 18-to-24-day point (from the time of fertilization = fertilization age) weight is still undeterminable; size, is portrayed in Figure 6–2. At this point blood cells have begun to form, much like those that will serve in later life (Little, 1990).

By the time the embryo has reached the four-week point (fertilization age) several developments have occurred. Weight is detectable, at about 0.4 grams. Figure 6–2 portrays the embryo's approximate size and shape at this point. A primitive circulatory system has developed, and the heart structure has begun pulsation (Johnson, 1988; Little, 1990). The fourth week also sees initial formative stages of other systems, such as trunk muscles and muscles necessary for respiratory and intestinal functions. Limb buds appear at this time, and the nervous system reaches a point that is crucial for development of both the sense organs and the area that will later become the spinal cord. Figure 6–2 illustrates that the tiny embryo has already assumed the curved shape of the unborn human. This shape is primarily generated at the four-week period by a very rapid lengthening of the neural tube (spinal area), which is not matched by growth on the front or ventral side.

At 6½ weeks fertilization age the embryo has grown and developed to a considerable extent. Figure 6–2 illustrates the approximate embryonic size and shape at this time. The circulatory system and heart are now more nearly complete. Figure 6–2 shows the positioning of the eyes on either side of the head area. Later these will assume the more frontal position characteristic of the human infant. Lungs and intestinal systems are more complete, and for the first time a primitive form of the gonad is observable. Differentiation of this tissue has not occurred yet with respect to sex (Johnson, 1988).

Figure 6–2 also portrays the embryo at about 7½ weeks fertilization age. At this point the embryo begins to develop openings for waste systems (both urethral and anal). The circulatory system reaches a stage at which heart valves develop, and sensory nerve tissue in the upper region progresses.

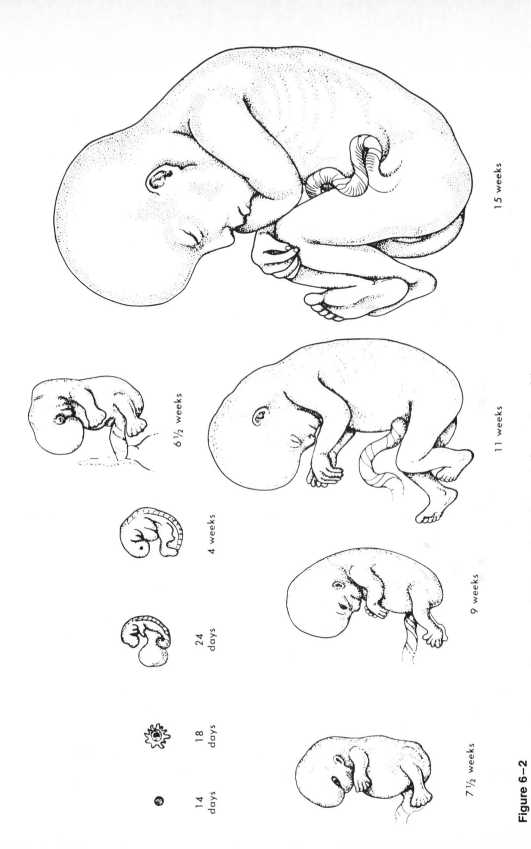

Figure 6–2

The actual size of human embryos at early stages of development. Comparison of the relative stages of external development is also indicated.

From *Child health maintenance: Concepts in family centered care* (2nd ed.), (p. 105) by P. L. Chinn, 1979, St. Louis: C.V. Mosby. Copyright 1979 by C.V. Mosby Co. Reprinted by permission.

14 days   18 days   24 days   4 weeks   6½ weeks   7½ weeks   9 weeks   11 weeks   15 weeks

As the fertilization age reaches the eighth week, the embryo is essentially complete. Beyond this point it is commonly referred to as a fetus. There is some difference with regard to when this term is applied. Although most use it in the ninth week (Johnson, 1988; Little, 1990), some consider the fetal period to begin in the eighth week (Freiberg, 1987), and others define it somewhat later. Figure 6–2 illustrates the size and shape of a fetus at about the ninth week. The eyes have begun to assume frontal position. The fetus has noticeably changed its posture. The head region at this point constitutes nearly half the total mass, and the cerebral cortex has formed.

Core Concept	*Prenatal fetal development during weeks 10 through 12 is particularly important because of the tissues being formed at that time.*

Particularly crucial growth occurs in the head region during weeks 10 through 12. From about this time through the thirteenth week the palate completes fusion. The forehead is somewhat outsized in comparison to the rest of the head (see Figure 6–2) and at this point contains a brain that is essentially complete in configuration. Inspection of the external organs permits determination of the sex of the fetus. The skeleton begins the process of becoming bone matter (ossification), and the vital structures of the eyes are nearly formed (Sarnat & Mueller, 1990).

A fetus at this point (12 weeks) has completed one of the most crucial periods in its developmental life span. By no means is the tiny fetus ready to take on the outside world, but the primary body structures are formed. In Chapter 7 we refer repeatedly to the first trimester of prenatal life. From our discussion of vulnerability and its relationship to tissue growth, it is very easy to see why this period is so vital. Trauma occurring during these first weeks is most likely to injure the essential body structure being formed at this time. The fetus at 12 weeks weighs about 19 grams. It has a long way to go, but has made a lot of progress since the mass was so tiny that it could not be weighed.

During the second trimester of prenatal life (weeks 12 through 24), the fetus reaches a weight of approximately 600 grams. Appearance leaves no doubt at this point that the fetus is a tiny human. The second trimester is also the time when the mother first experiences fetal movement. Fetal bodily proportions change as illustrated in Figure 6–2 (15 weeks). Several important internal developments occur during the second trimester. Various glands mature to the point that metabolic functions can begin. The lungs become complete, although not until the third trimester are they adequate to sustain life. An extremely important function called myelinization also begins during the second trimester. **Myelinization** refers to the development of a sheath-like material that covers and protects the nervous system. During the second trimester, development of the myelin covering begins in the spinal cord area. This process continues during the third trimester, when the myelinization of higher cortical matter begins. Completion of the myelin covering of the cerebral cortex is primarily accomplished after birth (Little, 1990; Sarnat & Mueller, 1990). The progression of the myelin covering also relates to the child's vulnerability to trauma (see Chapter 7).

The development that occurs during the final trimester of prenatal life is essential for sustaining life outside the mother's body. One vital change involves the final development of the lung structures. Changes continue right up to the last month of gestation. The fetus is also growing larger and stronger at a rapid rate. By the time term is reached, at about 40 weeks gestational age, the average fetus weighs somewhere around 3,200 grams. Sensory organs continue to develop, reaching functional stage at birth. Thus although the basic structural components have long since been formed, the third trimester of gestation involves developments that are crucial for survival.

BIRTH

At the end of the pregnancy, after about 280 days of gestation, the fetus leaves the intrauterine environment of the mother's body and begins its life in the outside world. Despite the vast improvements in delivery techniques that have occurred over the years, many facets of childbirth are still not well understood. This section presents a survey of the salient aspects of this dramatic event.

Core Concept	*The birth process represents another important time when potential risk to the child is high.*

Preparation for childbirth is not something that can occur at the last moment. Certain changes in the mother's anatomy have been under way since about midpregnancy; these changes are necessary for birth to proceed smoothly. The muscle structure of the uterus has been rearranged substantially in order to facilitate fetal expulsion. Another change that is essential to permit passage of the fetus through the birth canal has occurred in the cervical area. Figure 6–3 illustrates an advanced fetus in the uterine environment. In the latter days of pregnancy and during the onset of labor, expansion occurs in the upper part of the cervical area. By the time the fetus is moving down the birth canal, the cervical muscle structure has expanded to the point where the tubelike structure shown at the bottom of Figure 6–3 no longer exists. The loosening of the cervix, called effacement, is an important change in the muscle structure that must occur for the fetus to be expelled.

The exact mechanism that triggers labor remains mysterious. Many possibilities have been investigated, including both chemical (hormones) and mechanical (degree of uterine expansion) agents. The usual and desirable fetal position at the onset of labor is with the head toward the cervix, as illustrated in Figure 6–3. This position occurs in more than 80% of all childbirths. As the fetus begins to move downward into the birth canal, the pelvic girdle stretches more. The pressure of the pelvic girdle also molds the head of the fetus, so that newborns often have strangely shaped heads. Later the head returns to its natural shape.

All of this movement is generated by labor, the muscle contractions of the uterus. At the same time that the fetus moves downward, it turns counterclockwise from the

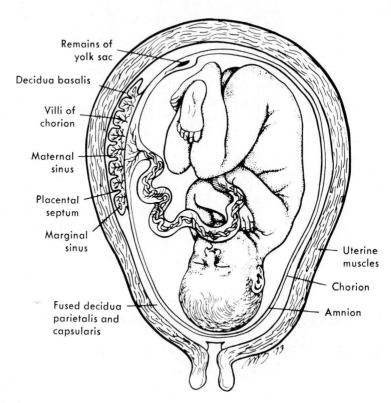

Remains of
yolk sac

Decidua basalis

Villi of
chorion

Maternal
sinus

Placental
septum

Marginal
sinus

Fused decidua
parietalis and
capsularis

Uterine
muscles

Chorion

Amnion

Figure 6–3
Advanced fetus in uterine environment
From *Child health maintenance: Concepts in family centered care* (2nd ed.), (p. 109) by P. L. Chinn,
1979, St. Louis: C.V. Mosby. Copyright 1979 by C.V. Mosby Co. Reprinted by permission.

effect of the uterine muscle action. Figure 6–4 shows a series of fetal positions during
the birth process.

Once expelled, the infant is usually followed a few minutes later by the placenta,
which has provided oxygen and nourishment and disposed of waste. Now the infant
must do these things. The respiratory tract is immediately cleared of the remaining
amniotic fluid and mucus, and the infant begins to breathe. This is the time that most
new mothers and fathers remember as the first cry of their newborn. This crying serves
an important function, and if the infant does not begin it spontaneously, the physician
must provide stimulation. Crying expands the infant's lungs with air for the first time,
causing the circulatory changes that accompany the use of the lungs and loss of the
placenta.

The birth process is very complex, and unfortunately, does not always proceed
smoothly. Difficulties can arise that result in mental retardation. Some of the possible
problems are discussed in Chapter 7.

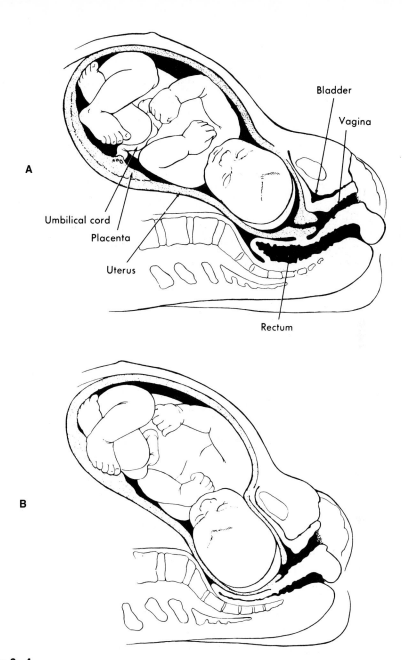

Figure 6–4

A, Engagement. B, Descent with flexion.

From *Childbirth: Family Centered Nursing* by J. Iorio, 1975, St. Louis: C.V. Mosby. Copyright 1975 by C.V. Mosby Co. Reprinted by permission.

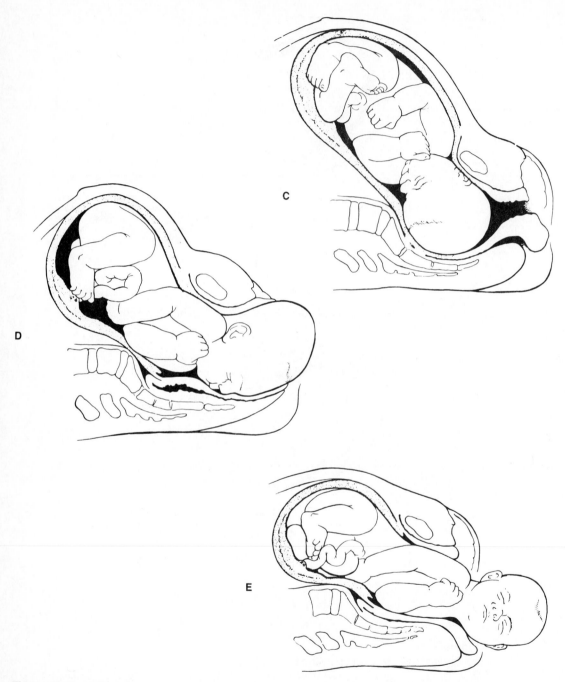

Figure 6–4, *continued*
C, Internal rotation. D, Extension. E, External rotation.

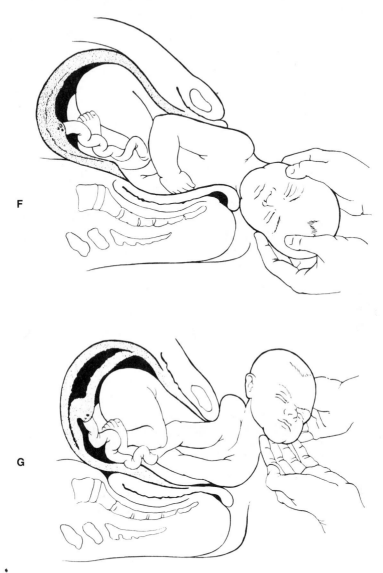

Figure 6–4, *concluded*
F, Delivery. G, Lateral flexion.

NEONATAL DEVELOPMENT

The term *neonate* is often applied to the baby during the first two months after birth. Beyond that period the terminology is varied and less specific. Here we examine early life, some of whose principles apply beyond the neonatal period. Later chapters treat development of the infant and the older child.

The first few weeks of extrauterine life are crucial. Most authorities view the first month as being among the most dangerous in the life span (Little, 1990). Many of the developmental functions begun in utero are continuing but without the protective agents they had before. In addition to physiological changes, a variety of forces initiate the neonate's rapid development in psychological and behavioral areas. As development proceeds, previous and ongoing physiological changes fuse with changes generated by environmental stimuli (such as learning) to form the integrated complex of responsiveness we call a human being.

From a behavioral standpoint the neonate seems to be little more than a mass of reflex actions, and at this age assessment of reflexes is the primary method of evaluation by health-care professionals. The infant's movements seem primarily nonpurposeful and nonspecific and more often than not involve nearly the entire body. This movement pattern usually involves gross motor movements often accompanied by verbal output (crying). The frequency and intensity of movements rises between feedings and tends to diminish as the hungry neonate becomes satisfied. Cephalocaudal and proximodistal developmental trends continue after birth. These are perhaps best observable in the behavior patterns of the first two years of life. More mature responses tend to appear earlier in areas closest to the brain (for example, eye movement) and progress downward and outward. The neonate's gross-motor movements precede any control of more distal movements like those of the fingers. Infants can also usually reach for and grasp objects accurately long before they can walk.

Certain physiological changes occur very rapidly during the first period of postnatal life. The central nervous system exhibits dramatic growth during the first four years, with acceleration leveling off in later childhood. For example, during this growth period brain weight increases nearly 400% over what it was at birth. In addition to quantitative changes, the brain matter is rapidly developing the convolutions or folds that are vital to later cognitive function (Sarnat & Mueller, 1990).

The progress of myelinization, which begins prenatally and continues during the first 12 months after birth, declines thereafter. The progression of the myelin sheath to some degree follows the course of central nervous system development. At birth the lower or subcortical portion of the central nervous system (spinal cord, brainstem) govern the neonate, and this part of the central nervous system is first to receive the myelin covering. Later, the higher cerebral matter is involved in myelinization and likewise begins to take charge of the child's behavior. The myelin sheath is essentially complete at age two, although fragmentary myelinization apparently continues through adolescence and perhaps even middle adult life (Sarnat & Mueller, 1990). In our consideration of mental retardation the myelinization process becomes important when considering possible injury to the central nervous system (see Chapter 7).

At birth the sensory organs, particularly the eyes and ears, are nearly complete in structure. Certain parts of the retina are yet to be completed, but basic sight exists at birth. For the first few weeks the infant's eyes tend to operate independently rather than together. By about six weeks, however, eye fixation is pretty well coordinated. Visual acuity appears to be imperfect during the neonatal and infant periods. Early images are blurred forms, patterns, and shapes, but visual acuity improves rather rapidly from about 20/300 at the neonate stage to approximately 20/100 by six months of age (Freiberg, 1987).

Hearing is apparently intact at birth. The neonate responds to a wide variety of auditory stimuli, suggesting that probably the full range of humanly detectable sound is available quite early. Additionally, the neonate seems able to identify where sounds come from. The development of auditory discrimination needs much more investigation. Part of the ability to discriminate sounds may be a learned or acquired skill.

The sense of taste is more difficult to study in a very young child than some of the other sensory avenues. Evidence indicates that even at the neonatal stage, the infant makes gross taste discriminations. Such discrimination, however, is primarily observable in different behavioral reactions to sweetness versus other tastes, such as sourness

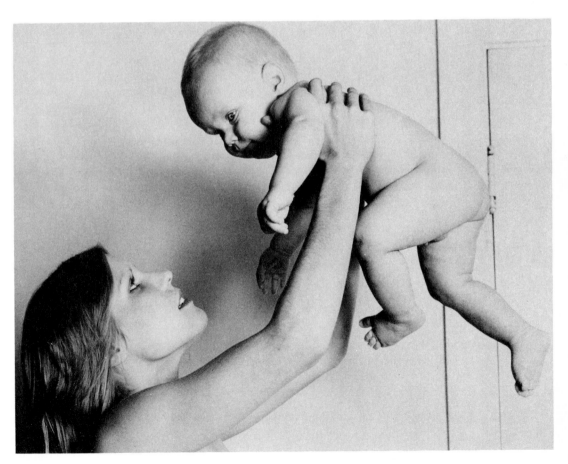

Many environmental stimuli operate in this youngster's world and affect development.

and bitterness. This sense improves with experience. The sense of smell is even more difficult to study than that of taste, so we have very little evidence about it in the neonatal period. It does, however, seem that the neonate is responsive to very dramatic or intense odors and that sensitivity increases during the infant stage.

We mentioned earlier that the behavioral repertoire of the newborn is limited. During the first few weeks of postnatal life, verbal output is primarily limited to crying. Crying seems mostly to be associated with discomfort of some sort, although at times the source of discomfort is not evident, as parents well know. From birth hunger is the standard stimulus for crying. Later the young child learns to use crying as a means of communicating in a wide variety of situations that are unpleasurable. Other verbal output (for example, gurgling, cooing, and general noise) seems to develop considerably later, often not becoming a significant part of the behavioral repertoire until the infant is several months old.

The sucking response is an important component of neonatal behavior. In addition to its obvious value to the child in terms of feeding, it remains an important early check of well-being. A weak sucking response is a signal for concern. The neonate tends to suck in response to a variety of stimuli, both in terms of the type of stimulus and of the body part stimulated (Rochat, 1983). Later responsivity diminishes and can be elicited primarily around the mouth.

NEW ISSUES AND FUTURE DIRECTIONS

Core Concept	*The knowledge gained from scientific advances both holds great promise for improving the early developmental fortunes of children and raises serious social questions.*

Most of this chapter has addressed matters pertaining to development from the prenatal period through birth, and influential factors impinging on the young human during this time. Perhaps nowhere in the developmental life cycle have the advances of technology and research information generated so many potential treatments for health and other problems as in this time frame. This progress has created both optimism and uncertainty.

The past 30 years have witnessed "revolutionary scientific progress in understanding genetic function" (Johnson, 1988, p. 395). Many of the findings have led to interventions that would have been unimaginable in the past. The level of detailed description of genetic material now possible holds enormous potential for a variety of treatments, many with implications for the field of mental retardation. As an example, Johnson (1988) suggests that it soon will be possible to predict and correct certain genetic lesions. Such a capability would permit removal of specific genes (for example, those causing sickle cell anemia or phenylketonuria) and replacement with synthetic genes able to function normally. While such suggestions seem like science fiction on one level, we should recall that it was not long ago that in vitro fertilization was front-page news. Now we have thousands of children who have been born as a result of in vitro fertilization (Johnson, 1988) and such events hardly warrant attention.

Advancements like those mentioned above create marvelous possibilities, but they also cause uncertainty and controversy. One constant concern is the ethics of such interventions, and further, the possibility that the science that creates opportunities also has the potential for social and moral abuse. We *can* perform many of these procedures, but *should* we? Genetic engineering may hold promise for eliminating certain diseases, which might mean that more people would survive and have a better quality of life. Is such improvement of the human gene pool appropriate when the world population as a whole cannot be properly nourished? Who will decide which genetic defects should be corrected, determining who lives and who dies? Our technological capability has outstripped our wisdom and the refinement of our ethical thinking. Certainly this is not the first time we have faced such ethical dilemmas (e.g., Hardman & Drew, 1978, 1980). These questions demand serious attention and examination of how such progress affects public policy (Gallagher, 1987; Vietze, 1987).

CORE QUESTIONS

1. Compare the concepts of genotype and phenotype and discuss how they relate to the growth matrix.
2. The tabula rasa approach to explain human growth and development differed significantly from both the preformationist and predeterministic positions. Compare and contrast these three approaches. How do you think their proponents would differ in their explanations of mental retardation, and why might the interactional view be more helpful for a major portion of those who are retarded?
3. How are the notions of discontinuous growth and critical stages related? Discuss the views of continuous and discontinuous human growth in terms of prenatal and neonatal development.
4. In what manner does the speed of cell reproduction influence vulnerability to trauma that might cause mental retardation? How does this relate to the often noted "first trimester" of pregnancy, particularly with respect to weeks 10 through 12?
5. Why would you expect a new baby's head and arm movements to be more mature than those of its legs? What other growth gradient is also typical of early development?
6. What important physical changes in the mother prepare her for giving birth? How is the baby physically influenced during birth?
7. Why is the neonatal period a time of risk for the baby, and what important physical developments are continuing at this time?
8. How do scientific advances present technical capabilities that contribute to moral or ethical dilemmas?

ROUND TABLE DISCUSSION

A basic understanding of early human development is important background for the study of mental retardation. There are many prenatal influences that have a substantial impact on a child's status. During this time many vital organs are being formed, and tissue growth occurs at a phenomenal rate. This is all occurring in the womb during a relatively short period of about nine months. Biological and embryological information suggests that such processes as myelinization are taking place, central nervous system tissue is being formed, and many other matters essential to the well-being of a young child are going on.

In your study group or on your own, examine these processes as if through the eyes of a preformationist, predeterminist, tabula rasa theorist, and interactionist. Using the material presented in this chapter, as well as other sources, explain the prenatal developments mentioned (myelinization, central nervous system development, brain development, and so on). Try to integrate the concepts of continuous/discontinuous growth and critical periods into your arguments from each theoretical perspective. Push your explanations and arguments to extremes, as early developmental theorists did. Do you find taking an extreme position the most difficult part of your tasks, or are the fundamental premises more problematic? After this examination of the basic principles of development, where do you stand theoretically as you prepare to push ahead with your study of mental retardation?

REFERENCES

Achenbach, T. M. (1982). *Developmental psychopathology* (2nd ed.). New York: John Wiley & Sons.

Berger, K. S. (1983). *The developing person through the life span.* New York: Worth.

Drew, C. J., & Bukatko, D. (1990). Developmental psychopathology. In M. Daehler & D. Bukatko (Eds.), *Child psychology.* Boston: Houghton Mifflin.

Flavell, J. H. (1982). Structures, stages, and sequences in cognitive development. In W. A. Collins (Ed.), *The concept of development: The Minnesota symposia on child psychology* (Vol. 15, pp. 1–28). Hillsdale, NJ: Lawrence Erlbaum.

Flavell, J. H. (1985). *Cognitive development.* Englewood Cliffs, NJ: Prentice-Hall.

Freiberg, K. L. (1987). *Human development: A life-span approach* (3rd ed.). Boston: Jones and Bartlett.

Gallagher, J. J. (1987). Public policy and the malleability of children. In J. J. Gallagher & C. T. Ramey (Eds.), *The malleability of children* (pp. 199–208). Baltimore: Paul H. Brookes.

Gleitman, H. (1986). *Psychology* (2nd ed.). New York: W.W. Norton.

Hall, G. S. (1904). *Adolescence: Its psychology and its relation to physiology, anthropology, sociology, sex, crime, religion and education.* New York: Appleton-Century-Crofts.

Hardman, M. L., & Drew, C. J. (1978). Life management practices with the profoundly retarded: Issues of abortion, euthanasia and withholding treatment. *Mental Retardation, 16,* 390–396.

Hardman, M. L., & Drew, C. J. (1980). Parent consent and the practice of withholding treatment from the severely defective newborn. *Mental Retardation, 18,* 165–169.

Johnson, K. E. (1988). *Human developmental anatomy.* New York: John Wiley & Sons.

Lerner, R. M. (1987). The concept of plasticity in development. In J. J. Gallagher & C. T. Ramey (Eds.), *The malleability of children* (pp. 3–14). Baltimore: Paul H. Brookes.

Little, G. A. (1990). Fetal growth and development. In R. D. Edent & F. H. Boehm (Eds.), *Assessment and care of the fetus: Psychological, clinical, and medicolegal principles* (pp. 3–15). Norwalk, CT: Appleton & Lange.

Piaget, J. (1926). *The language and thought of the child.* New York: Harcourt Brace.

Rochat, P. (1983). Oral touch in young infants: Response to variations of nipple characteristics in the first months of life. *International Journal of Behavioral Development, 6,* 123–133.

Sarnat, H. B., & Mueller, D. L. (1990). Fetal neurology. In R. D. Edent & F. H. Boehm (Eds.), *Assessment and care of the fetus: Psychological, clinical, and medicolegal principles* (pp. 43–67). Norwalk, CT: Appleton & Lange.

Schwartz, S., & Johnson, J. H. (1985). *Psychopathology of childhood: A clinical-experimental approach* (2nd ed.). New York: Pergamon.

Shaffer, D. R. (1985). *Developmental psychology: Theory, research, and applications.* Monterey, CA: Brooks-Cole.

Shultz, T. R. (1982). Rules of causal attribution. *Monographs of the Society for Research on Child Development* (Serial No. 194, *47*[1]).

Vietze, P. M. (1987). Science policy and the concept of plasticity. In J. J. Gallagher & C. T. Ramey (Eds.), *The malleability of children* (pp. 191–198). Baltimore: Paul H. Brookes.

CHAPTER SEVEN

Mental Retardation: Influences and Causation During the Prenatal and Neonatal Periods

Core Concepts

Early Causation

Professional Intervention

New Issues and Future Directions

Core Questions

Round Table Discussion

References

*Core
Concepts*

- Inadequate birth weight and gestational age are the problems that most commonly place an infant at developmental risk. They can be caused by a number of factors.

- Chromosomal abnormalities and genetic errors are causative agents in a number of mental retardation syndromes.

- Various types of interactions between the mother and unborn fetus can cause damage resulting in mental retardation.

- Fetal damage causing reduced mental functioning may occur from such factors as maternal infection and drug ingestion.

- A number of problems during the delivery of a baby may cause damage that results in mental retardation.

- Many different forms of professional intervention can prevent or minimize mental retardation during the prenatal and neonatal period.

Early life is a period of human growth and development that deserves much attention in the study of mental retardation, since it is such a crucial part of the life cycle. The organism is almost wholly at the mercy of the environment and is vulnerable to its impact both prenatally and after birth. Chapter 6 examined normal developmental processes during early life. This chapter considers influences and causes of mental retardation in the same period (conception through early infancy).

Discussion of influences and causation of mental retardation during the prenatal and neonatal periods requires attention to certain physiological conditions and, when possible, the treatment of these conditions. Frequently the medical profession primarily interacts with a child at risk for mental retardation during this early period. Instead of an in-depth examination of the medical aspects of mental retardation, however, we wish to make readers aware of influences on mental development during this period. We discuss more common conditions of retardation beginning during this period as well as those rarer ones for which intervention can prevent retardation or reduce its impact. A variety of developmental and ongoing life processes can go awry at this time and result in reduced intellectual functioning. In fact the beginning student occasionally wonders how any child ever manages to get through this period at all without deviation or abnormality. The vast majority of children, however, do develop to a level of functioning that is considered normal or average.

Maternal and fetal conditions play a central role in fetal development. A variety of maternal and fetal conditions may also help cause mental retardation during early life. These influences may result in mental retardation that ranges from profound or severe to only mild deviations from normal. Such varying degrees of disability can be conceived of as a **reproductive casualty continuum.** This notion views the mildly handicapped child at the less extreme end of the casualty range; individuals with more severe retardation and stillborn infants are at the more extreme end. Spontaneous abortion occurring early in pregnancy may represent one extreme of the continuum; mild retardation or slight disabilities in basically normal children represent the other.

EARLY CAUSATION

We have already seen that the first portion of the life cycle is extremely important. Many view development during the prenatal period and immediately after birth as the most critical in the entire life span. Fortunately, most infants enter extrauterine life after a full, successful gestational period, with no complications of labor and delivery, and no factors during the first month of life that lead to serious illness or disability. When a serious problem does occur in these early months, however, the family must often adjust to having a child with a permanent mental or physical handicap. Several conditions are known to place the fetus or infant at high risk for development of serious illness or permanent disability.

The Fetus and Infant at Risk: Birth Weight and Gestational Age

Core Concept	*Inadequate birth weight and gestational age are the problems that most commonly place an infant at developmental risk. They can be caused by a number of factors.*

Many different problems can occur during the prenatal and neonatal periods. Each of the difficulties discussed here is a condition that places the infant in one risk category or another. The most prevalent of these problems are inadequate birth weight and gestational age (Creasy, 1990). Although these problems do occasionally exist alone, there is more often an accompanying maternal, genetic, or traumatic condition.

Infants born before the thirty-eighth week of gestation are generally classified as **preterm,** those born between the thirty-eighth and forty-second weeks are referred to as **term,** and those delivered after the forty-second week are known as **postterm** infants. Great progress has been made in infant survival through improved obstetric care, even under difficult circumstances. Creasy (1990) notes that approximately 98% of infants born after the thirty-second week of gestation now survive. Survival rates diminish substantially, however, for infants born before that time (Creasy, 1988). Birth weight is a second important factor in infant mortality (Koops, Morgan, & Battaglia, 1982). Depending on the gestational age, an infant may be considered as "small for gestational age," "appropriate for gestational age," or "large for gestational age." Current medical care suggests that both gestational age and birth weight should be taken into account. Since it is now possible to estimate the maturity of a newborn by physical signs of maturation, care for the infant can be more adequately geared to the particular needs that occur according to gestational age. Such improved care has led to a dramatic decrease in neonatal mortality in the United States.

Predisposing Factors

Research has identified several factors related to low birth weight and inappropriate gestational age. Each of the problems discussed in later sections (infant chromosomal aberrations, maternal-infant interaction problems, early pregnancy trauma) can be associated with early termination of pregnancy. But several other conditions also appear to lead to early pregnancy termination and inadequate birth weight.

Maternal age and pregnancy history are significant factors in risks to the fetus. Mothers under the age of 20 or over 35 are more likely to suffer early pregnancy termination than are women between those ages (Creasy, 1990). Likewise, women who have a history of miscarriages, stillbirths, or premature deliveries tend to have as much as a 30% chance of recurrence (Carr-Hill & Hall, 1985). Socioeconomic factors are also related to the incidence of preterm and low gestational weight infants (Peterson, 1987). For example, research over a number of years has suggested that the father's occupation correlates to substantial differences in the incidence of prematurity and infant mortality, as indicated in Table 7–1. Such data should not be interpreted as indicating that the occupation of a child's father directly causes prematurity, but that factors associated with occupation (say, socioeconomic status) are related to health matters like nutrition and health care.

Premature birth rates have also been associated with ethnicity, although this factor is probably more closely aligned with extremes of socioeconomic status (wealth, poverty) than with ethnic differences per se. The percentage of infants born prematurely to white Americans is consistently about half the percentage born prematurely to nonwhite Americans. Viewing the extremes of socioeconomic status more specifically, 51% of all nonwhites (who have lower incomes as a group) have birth complications, whereas only 5% of white upper-class births are so affected (Gelfand, Jenson, & Drew, 1988).

Multiple pregnancies account for a high percentage of infants born with low gestational age and birth weight, and their concomitant problems. The reasons are complex and numerous, including primarily difficulties of placental insufficiency that lead to ineffective transfer of nutrients across the placenta late in pregnancy and hence to fetal malnutrition. Labor and delivery often commence before term, and the infant is usually small for gestational age. Placental problems are not clearly understood and, when no other cause can be identified, are often attributed to inadequate intrauterine growth. Placental insufficiency implies an impaired exchange between mother and fetus through the placenta. Several well-defined placental lesions are associated with fetal and

Table 7–1

Premature birthrate according to father's occupation

Occupation	Incidence per 1,000 Live births
Farmer	33.8
Professional	49.1
Laborer	71.8
Service worker	78.3
Farm laborer	88.1

From "Patterns of prematurity in Oregon" by C. Kernek, H. Osterud, and B. Anderson, 1966, *Northwest Medicine, 65*, p. 639. Copyright 1966 by the authors. Reprinted by permission.

infant disorders (examples: blockage of fetal vessels in the placenta, early placenta separation, a single umbilical artery).

Maternal smoking is another factor that has been associated with inadequate growth during fetal life (Hetherington & Parke, 1986). Mothers who smoke more than 20 cigarettes a day give birth to growth-retarded (but not necessarily preterm) infants two or three times as often as nonsmoking mothers. The precise reasons for this difference have not yet been completely delineated, although evidence suggests two probable factors: (1) smoking mothers tend to eat less, and (2) the vascular constriction caused by smoking restricts uterine blood flow (Spellacy, 1990). But other related factors may be as important as the actual problem of maternal smoking.

Maternal alcohol consumption can also seriously injure the fetus. In its most severe form, alcohol-induced fetal injury is known as fetal alcohol syndrome. Some problems linked to fetal alcohol syndrome are facial abnormalities, cardiac defects, defects in joints and limbs, neurological abnormalities, and mental retardation (Landing, Galvis, Wells, & Hardy, 1989; Sarnat & Mueller, 1990). Even moderate alcohol consumption by pregnant women can result in fetal problems, although the exact amounts and risk have not been well established (Brendt & Beckman, 1990; Sokol, Drugan, & Evans, 1990). It is clear, however, that alcohol consumption during pregnancy can cause decrements in measured intelligence (Streissguth, Barr, Sampson, & Darby, 1989). Cases where less severe damage results are now being recognized as fetal alcohol effect, and children who suffer from it exhibit milder but clearly evident forms of developmental problems. The effect of maternal alcohol consumption has been recognized for many years (e.g., Sullivan, 1899). For a long time, however, research on the problem was quite scarce, and fetal alcohol syndrome was described only in the early 1970s (see Jones, Smith, Ulleland, & Streissguth, 1973).

Maternal nutrition is another incompletely understood factor, although evidence thus far has indicated that it is very important to fetal health (Chez & Chervenak, 1990). Many families who eat poorly belong to a less than affluent socioeconomic stratum, and the dietary practices of a subculture often influence them. Thus it seems difficult to put a finger on the factors in this complex set of interacting variables that have primarily contributed to increased rates of low birth weight and gestational age problems. A pregnant woman has greater nutritional requirements than a woman who is not pregnant. For example, caloric requirements increase by about 300 kilocalories per day during the third trimester (Chez & Chervenak, 1990), which may result in about a 25-pound maternal weight gain. Additionally, both the protein and the calcium requirements of a pregnant mother increase. Maternal malnutrition, which often reflects a lifelong state of inadequacy, has been implicated in damaging the fetus, particularly the fetal central nervous system. Such findings are difficult to evaluate and substantiate, however, because we cannot examine the direct transfer of nutrients to the fetus or determine the fetus's exact nutritional requirements.

Finally, unwed and teenage mothers tend to have preterm infants and miscarriages more often than do married mothers (Hayes, 1987). In some cases these circumstances are related to lower socioeconomic status and even poverty, which increases the mother's potential for reduced physical well-being and greater psychological stress (Peterson, 1987). Regardless of precise causation, the developing youngster in such a situation is placed at greater risk. One early study reported a rate of premature births of 93.6% among one group of unwed mothers in Oregon in the mid-1960s (Kernek, Osterud, & Anderson, 1966). Although the startling rate of infant prematurity among unwed mothers found in this study has not been widely supported in more recent research, it is clear that such mothers more often deliver prematurely (Hayes, 1987; Peterson, 1987). Several socioeconomic factors may be responsible.

Associated Problems

Infants at risk, especially those with inadequate birth weight and gestational age, tend to be susceptible to serious stress after birth. Problems are primarily complications of respiratory and cardiac failure, infection, and nutritional disorders. They account for many of the sequelae associated with birth weight and gestational age inadequacies.

Complications of respiratory and cardiac failure lead to serious interference with the delivery of oxygen to the developing fetal tissues. The central nervous system is particularly vulnerable, for even though a newborn can tolerate longer periods of anoxia (low oxygen level) than can an adult, a continuing lower level of oxygen to the tissues interferes with critical development occurring during the preterm period. Central nervous system tissue cells are still developing until about the forty-fourth week after fertilization, and the tissue depends on oxygen for adequate development. An infant who is born at risk before term and who develops such oxygen delivery interference is particularly jeopardized with respect to developing adequate neural tissue, although we do not yet fully understand the relationship between such interference and future development. With continuing improvements in neonatal care, however, including prevention of respiratory and cardiac complications and improved care for the infant with these complications, medical personnel anticipate reducing the serious neurological sequelae of prematurity.

Infection is another serious complication for infants with low birth weight or gestational age problems. The fetus and preterm infant are extremely susceptible to infection from organisms that ordinarily do not cause illness for older individuals, and infants have few physiological mechanisms with which to combat infection. An infection that begins in the skin can rapidly progress to serious illness—pneumonia, septicemia (widespread infection of the blood), or meningitis (infection of the central nervous system). And because an infant does not exhibit the usual signs of infection, for example, fever, diagnosing an infection may be difficult or impossible until it has become serious. Infection of the central nervous system in particular leads to grave and permanent consequences, affecting the child's neurological capacity in later life.

Nutrition and oxygen intake are more big problems for infants of low birth weight and inadequate gestational age. Such infants miss the optimal nutritional source, the placenta, and suffer from inadequate intake of basic metabolic nutrients. Of particular importance during the last few months of gestation is acquisition of glucose, proteins, and oxygen through the placenta, for these materials nourish all growing tissues, particularly those of the central nervous system. Central nervous system tissue depends on each of these nutrients not only for growth and development but also for survival. When an infant is born with fetal malnutrition from placental insufficiency, nutrition to help the child recuperate must be incorporated into the routine care. Oxygen administration is most complicated for infants of low birth weight or inadequate gestational age, since transfer of the ambient oxygen across the lung-blood barrier cannot be directly measured. An infant may be underoxygenated while receiving large percentages of oxygen, or overoxygenated while receiving relatively low concentrations of oxygen. Excessive oxygenation causes damage to the retina of the eye and eventually blindness, a process known as retrolental fibroplasia.

Psychological and Educational Sequelae

It has been extremely difficult to determine precisely the psychological and educational sequelae of birth weight and gestational age inadequacies. Separating these difficulties from the confounding variables of low socioeconomic status and racial minority groups that consistently have more births in this category is part of the problem. Groups in which greater numbers of infants are born with gestational age and birth weight problems also have a higher percentage of educational and psychological problems among their young children (Gelfand et al., 1988; Hardman, Drew, Egan, & Wolf, 1990). Comparison of investigations is difficult because of varying definitions of prematurity, low birth weight, and gestational age. Findings of long-term studies, which are necessary in order to determine educational sequelae, are often outdated by the time the data can be collected. That is, by the time a child who was born prematurely reaches six years of age or older, medical and nursing care for preterm infants has progressed so much that the findings are not germane for infants born several years earlier. For example, 20 years ago little was known about the administration of oxygen to preterm infants for the treatment of lung disorders or prevention of anoxia. Today great advances have been made in these and other related areas, so that most infants cared for in a high-risk specialty center receive optimal oxygenation of body tissues throughout the critical period of instability. It is hoped, therefore, that we now are able to offset the seriously detrimental effects of anoxia, which may have caused many of the psychological and educational sequelae reported for children born in the previous two or three decades.

An older interesting investigation conducted by Rubin, Rosenblatt, and Balow (1973) studied psychological and educational sequelae of prematurity and outlined a number of areas of difficulty that have received further attention. Infants in this study were born at the University of Minnesota Hospital between 1960 and 1964, and socioeconomic status was a controlled factor. The investigation included only infants representing the urban population of the north central United States, with an almost exclusively Caucasian racial background. The infants were classified according to both gestational age and birth weight. The major findings reported by Rubin et al. (1973) suggested that preterm males of low birth weight and full-term infants of both sexes with low birth weight are at high risk of eventual impairment in school functioning. Other research has continued to support the conclusion that premature youngsters are a high-risk group in several ways (Cohen & Parmelee, 1983; Creasy, 1990; Silva, McGee, & Williams, 1984). Rubin et al. (1973) found that low birth weight was associated with a number of abnormal conditions, among them low Apgar scores and elevated bilirubin levels during the neonatal period, and that birth weight rather than gestational age was the major correlate of neurological, psychological, and educational impairment. Low birth weight males and low birth weight full-term children of both sexes show a significantly higher incidence of school problems calling for special school services than do full-term children. Low birth weight children also tend to score lower than full birth weight peers on measures of cognitive and language development (Crnic, Ragozin, Greenberg, Robinson, & Basham, 1983; Rocissano & Yatchmink, 1983; Rose, 1983; Silva et al., 1984; Ungerer & Sigman, 1983). It also appears that at later ages, low birth weight children were smaller in stature and had a higher incidence of diagnosed neurological abnormalities than normal birth weight children. Thus evidence has mounted over the years that low birth weight and gestational age present considerable difficulties and are related to mental retardation (Creasy, 1990).

Chromosomal Aberrations and Genetic Errors

Core Concept	*Chromosomal abnormalities and genetic errors are causative agents in a number of mental retardation syndromes.*

A number of problems occur, particularly during the prenatal period, as a result of chromosomal and genetic errors. In many cases mental retardation that results from these difficulties falls into well-known syndrome classes of retardation.

Chromosomal Aberrations

Chromosomal aberrations occur when some abnormality emerges in the number of chromosomes or in the configuration of the chromosomes in the body. Figure 7–1 illustrates a karyotype or classification of photographed human chromosomes obtained from a blood or skin sample. The karyotype is arranged in standard form, and determinations of the particular chromosomal anomaly causing an abnormal condition can be identified from it. The karyotype shown in Figure 7–1 is a normal chromosomal configuration with 44 autosomal and two sex chromosomes. One kind of abnormal condition involves extra chromosomes, such as three chromosomes in position 21 or two or more X or Y chromosomes. Another type of common aberration involves abnormally shaped chromosomes, for example, an excessively long "arm" on number 15.

When 45 chromosomes are present with only a single X sex chromosome, the child has the condition called Turner syndrome, or gonadal aplasia. The child is nearly always female, since the Y chromosome conveys maleness to the individual. Gonads are rudimentary, no secondary sex characteristics develop at puberty, and there may or may not be accompanying physical signs like bow-leggedness or webbed neck and abnormalities of the kidneys and heart (Blair, 1989; Carson & Simpson, 1990). A substantial number of individuals with this problem who survive the prenatal period and reach the newborn stage have developmental difficulties and mental retardation (Little, 1990).

Many aberrations occur on the chromosomes of groups A through G. These chromosomes are referred to as *autosomal* because they contain genetic material that does

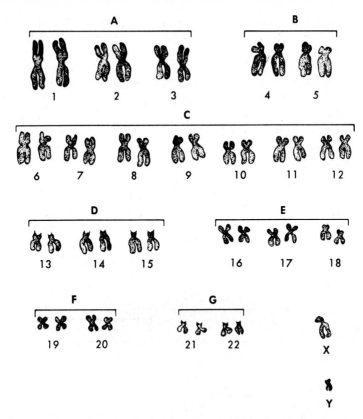

Figure 7–1

Karyotype classification of human chromosomes

From *Child Health Maintenance: Concepts in Family Centered Care* (2nd ed.) by P. L. Chinn, 1979, St. Louis: C.V. Mosby. Copyright 1979 by C.V. Mosby Co. Reprinted by permission.

not involve sexual characteristics. Down syndrome can occur from any one of three different aberrations of the autosomal chromosomes. The first type is trisomy, or nondisjunction, in which there is an extra chromosome in the G group. This is the most common cause of Down syndrome, and there is a definite correlation with maternal age. The risks increase from 0.69 per 1,000 births for mothers in their early 20s to over 18 per 1,000 in mothers 40 or older (Cahalane, 1989).

A second type of chromosomal difficulty resulting in Down syndrome is translocation, occurring in 9% of affected infants born to mothers under the age of 30 and in 2% of affected infants born to mothers over the age of 30. In translocation some of the chromosomal material of the twenty-first pair in the G group detaches and becomes attached to a chromosome of the fifteenth pair in the D group, causing an extra long chromosome in the karyotype. A parent is sometimes the carrier of this condition, as can be detected through genetic studies of both parents and child. When the aberration is not inherited it occurs as a result of a chance chromosomal error.

The third condition resulting in Down syndrome is mosaicism. In this case, the cells of the individual's body are identified as mixed. Some contain trisomies, and others are normal. This error occurs during the very early cell divisions after fertilization, with some cell groups forming normally before the error occurs. Such individuals tend to exhibit milder manifestations of the condition, which may reflect the stage of development at which the chromosomal error began.

The clinical characteristics of Down syndrome vary but are similar enough that most individuals with Down syndrome resemble one another more than they resemble their own family members. There is a lateral upward slope of the eyes, protruding tongue because of a small oral cavity, short nose with flat bondage caused by underdevelopment of the nasal bone, flattened head front and back, shortness of fingers, especially the fifth, wide space between the first and second toes, and short, stocky build. These children are more likely than the general population to have congenital heart defects and leukemia, and are more susceptible to respiratory infections. There is almost always mental deficiency, with IQ scores in the moderate to severely retarded ranges. A few individuals have IQs in the normal range, and the effect of early stimulation and education programs results in improved mental and neurological functioning for some with Down syndrome. Considerable research continues on Down syndrome including such topics as racial factors (Ershow, 1986) and chromosomal abnormalities involved (e.g., Cox & Epstein, 1985; Davidson, Rumsby, & Niswander, 1985). Some work in this area includes examination of the trisomy 21 condition by using such animal models as mouse trisomy 16 (Cox & Epstein, 1985; Epstein, Cox, & Epstein, 1985).

Genetic Errors

Genetic errors are conditions that result from inheritance factors involving specific genes. Such disorders are rather poorly understood, and investigation of these problems is somewhat restricted because of the limitations of studying human genetic material. Genetic disorders can be identified through study of family inheritance patterns, but examination and identification of these problems are difficult. Such conditions cannot be studied the way chromosomal disorders can, for it is not presently possible to obtain information about genetic material from study of the chromosomes. Most genetic errors are rare, but a few that result in mental retardation happen often enough that diagnostic and treatment approaches have been developed. One example of such a condition is phenylketonuria (PKU), which has become one of the most thoroughly studied genetic defects. It occurs about once in every 10,000 live births and accounts for about 0.5% of patients in institutions for individuals with mental retardation. It is transmitted by an autosomal recessive gene that appears with highest frequency in northern European ethnic groups; it is rare in black and Jewish groups. Affected individuals produce less of the enzyme necessary for metabolism of phenylalanine, leading to an accumulation of this product in the serum, cerebrospinal fluid, tissues, and urine. The effect of this metabolic malfunction on the central nervous system is grave; all untreated individuals become severely mentally retarded within the first few months of life. Elevated phenylalanine in the blood or urine can be detected within a few weeks after consumption of milk, which contains the substance. Many states have instituted mandatory screening procedures for all infants in order to institute early treatment measures and to minimize or prevent the serious effects of the untreated condition. It is now possible to diagnose PKU prenatally, although the technique is not widely employed (Cahalane, 1989). In addition to mental retardation, affected children develop some degree of microcephaly and have blond hair, blue eyes, and very sensitive skin.

A number of other disorders are due to specific recessive genes. In these cases the parents are carriers of a deficient gene but are phenotypically normal. When the recessive genetic material combines, however, the children may develop conditions that result in mental retardation. One such disorder is galactosemia, which occurs when an infant cannot properly metabolize galactose, a chemical generated during digestion of milk products. Newborns with this condition who are on milk diets rapidly develop symptoms that can become life-threatening—jaundice, vomiting, and a tremendously heightened vulnerability to infection. Intellectual development may also suffer. Early detection and treatment through strict dietary means can dramatically improve the infant's potential development, although some difficulties may persist. Longitudinal research on treatment effectiveness remains inexact because of the disorder's relative rarity, a common difficulty with such genetic problems.

Influences from Maternal-Fetal Interaction

Core Concept	*Various types of interactions between the mother and unborn fetus can cause damage resulting in mental retardation.*

Several abnormal maternal-fetal interactions have serious consequences for the infant. Infants of diabetic mothers, for example, are always high-risk babies because of their excessive birth weight for gestational age and their usually low gestational age. Physical anomalies are also more common among infants of diabetic mothers, and the infants are prone to several serious illnesses during the neonatal period, for example, lung disorders, seizures, hypoglycemia (low blood glucose), and hyperbilirubinemia (resulting in jaundice). The mother's diabetic condition places the child at serious risk from several standpoints. The incidence of neurological sequelae is largely dependent on the severity of the maternal diabetes and the neonatal course, including gestational age and complications during this period (Claireaux & Reed, 1989).

The problem of maternal-fetal Rh-factor incompatibility has a more direct effect on the infant's neurological capacity. In this instance the mother has a negative Rh blood factor and the infant a positive Rh factor. The mother reacts to the infant's positive factor by developing antibodies that destroy the infant's blood cells, leading to serious consequences during fetal life and the neonatal period. The infant's condition is known as *erythroblastosis fetalis*. The higher the level of antibodies in the mother's blood, the more serious the effect on the fetus. In the most severe form, known as fetal hydrops, the fetus begins to develop severe anemia, enlargement of the heart, liver, and spleen, and deterioration of the body tissues. In most cases the fetus dies during the late second or early third trimester and is stillborn. If the child is born alive, survival is unlikely. A moderate form of erythroblastosis fetalis, known as *icterus gravis,* occurs more frequently, since in many instances the infant's delivery is induced before term to prevent progression of the disease to the more severe form. When this occurs, an infant is placed in the disadvantageous position of being delivered preterm, but the hazards are less than those of a more severe form of erythroblastosis fetalis. Such an infant, in addition to low gestational age, may also be of low birth weight because of the condition's effect in utero. The infant is typically anemic, jaundiced, and has an enlarged spleen and liver. The high level of bilirubin, occurring from the metabolism of red blood cells, accounts for the jaundice and for any central nervous system damage. As the bilirubin level rises rapidly, adequate excretion cannot occur, and molecules enter the skin tissue with a toxic effect known as *kernicterus.* If the infant survives the first week of life, outlook for survival is good. The possibility of neurological sequelae, however, depends on the severity of the hyperbilirubinemia and accompanying illnesses occurring during the neonatal period. When the blood factor incompatibility effects are minimal, as is usual for the first or second infants of most Rh-negative mothers, neonatal problems are minimal, and there are no neurological sequelae (Mahnovski & Pavlova, 1989).

Trauma During Early Pregnancy

Core Concept	*Fetal damage causing reduced mental functioning may occur from such factors as maternal infection and drug ingestion.*

Trauma can occur to the fetus during the first trimester from a variety of causes, including drug or chemical ingestion and maternal infection. The teratogenic effects of such exposures are poorly understood, but it is known that, while the exact effect of most teratogens is not specified, the timing of exposure probably leads to specific kinds of anomalies. Thus when a mother contracts rubella during the first trimester of pregnancy, resulting anomalies are probably related more to the timing of fetal exposure than to the specific effects of the virus. Teratogenic effects on the fetus include intrauterine growth retardation, central nervous system infection, microcephaly, congenital heart disease, sensorineural deafness, cataracts and/or glaucoma, and anomalies of the skin. There is a wide range of severity and variability in the occurrence of each possible condition. Again, range of severity is probably related to the timing of the infection, as well as the possible individual susceptibility of a particular mother and fetus to the effects of the infection. The infant is likely to have a number of physical, behavioral, and intellectual handicaps (Brendt & Beckman, 1990).

The Birth Process

Core Concept	*A number of problems during the delivery of a baby may cause damage that results in mental retardation.*

Mental retardation may result from a variety of influences that produce many forms of physical trauma and developmental deviation. This section focuses on influences operative during the birth process.

The birth process has long been characterized as an extremely traumatic event in the life of the human organism. Birth trauma has been described as the basis for many psychological problems. Early proponents of the psychoanalytical school (e.g., Sigmund Freud) attributed all later life anxiety to the separation shock felt at birth. A variety of other phenomena, such as the content of adult dreams, have been thought at times to reflect birth trauma. Although there is little doubt that birth is a stressful occurrence, recent thinking places much more emphasis on its physical than its psychoanalytical aspects.

Chapter 6 outlined briefly the sequence of events that occurs during the birth of a baby. Although the birth process is a stressful time, there is minimal danger if the baby is positioned head first, facing downward, and if the mother's pelvic opening is adequate for the child. This, of course, assumes that fetal development has progressed without mishap to this point. Two general types of problems during birth can result in mental retardation: (1) physical trauma or mechanical injury and (2) anoxia or asphyxia. The first is almost self-explanatory. Physical trauma or mechanical injury refers to some occurrence during birth that injures or damages the baby so as to impair mental

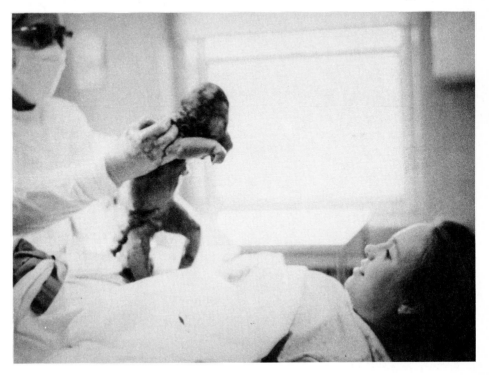

This mother and baby have just completed a rather traumatic process successfully.

functioning. In anoxia or asphyxia, the baby is deprived of an adequate oxygen supply for a period long enough to cause brain damage, thereby reducing mental functioning. Many conditions can be responsible. Although these problems are given different labels and appear to be quite dissimilar, they are frequently interrelated.

It has been mentioned that the danger of birth injury is relatively low if the fetus is positioned correctly. When labor begins, the most favorable position is head first and facing toward the mother's back. Other fetal positions are considered abnormal and can cause numerous problems, depending on the situation. Both mechanical injury and anoxia can result from abnormal fetal presentation.

One well-known abnormal position is breech presentation. Breech presentation occurs when the buttocks rather than the head present first. Figure 7–2 illustrates a breech presentation and can be compared with the more normal presentation illustrated earlier in Figure 6–3.

Physicians are becoming increasingly reluctant to deliver babies in breech position through the birth canal. Except when the delivery is conducted by extremely skilled personnel, the danger to the baby is substantial. More and more frequently a baby lying breech within the uterus is delivered by cesarean section, which involves abdominal surgery and extraction of the baby through the uterine wall.

Numerous difficulties are encountered in breech birth if delivery is executed through the birth canal. Since the head presents last, it reaches the pelvic girdle (the bony hip structure of the mother) during the later, more advanced stages of labor. Contractions are occurring rapidly at this point, and the head does not have an opportunity to proceed through the slower molding process possible earlier in labor. Additionally, the molding

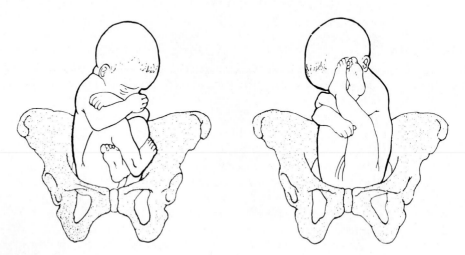

Figure 7–2

Examples of breech fetal position

From *Childbirth: Family Centered Nursing* (3rd ed.) by J. Iorio, 1975, St. Louis: C.V. Mosby. Copyright 1975 by the C.V. Mosby Co. Reprinted by permission.

may occur in an abnormal and damaging fashion since the skull is receiving pressure in an atypical manner.

Abnormal pressure in breech birth can result in mechanical injury to the brain matter in at least two general ways. Since the skull is still quite soft, rapid compression, which crushes a portion of the brain, can cause an injury. Such damage is less likely in normal presentation since the skull is molded more gently, permitting protective fluid to absorb the pressure. A second type of injury can also be viewed as mechanical. The rapid pressure and shifting of cranial bones may be severe enough to damage the circulatory system around the brain and lead to a hemorrhage in the skull, which in turn damages brain tissue.

Breech birth may also result in fetal anoxia. Since the skull is the last part of the body delivered, the baby must depend entirely on the umbilical cord as a source of oxygen until birth is complete. But the positioning can make the cord too short to remain attached while the head is expelled. In this case, the placenta can become partially or completely detached while the baby's head is still in the birth canal. This separation, of course, eliminates the oxygen supply, and oxygen deprivation can happen if delivery is not completed quickly. Severe tissue damage can result if the head is not expelled and oxygen supplied through the baby's lungs. This presents an extremely serious problem if the head becomes lodged in the pelvic girdle, preventing or substantially slowing progress down the birth canal. Anoxia may also occur even if the cord is long enough to remain attached throughout delivery. We have already noted that the head is the tightest fit for the baby moving through the pelvic girdle. At the beginning of delivery, a section of the umbilical cord is necessarily drawn through. Depending on how tightly the skull fits into the bony pelvic structure, the cord can become pinched and the oxygen supply shut off. If this state lasts long (as in the situation of the lodged skull noted earlier) an anoxic condition will result just as if the cord had been cut.

These descriptions are only a brief look at the difficulties of breech delivery and how they can cause damaged tissue and reduced mental functioning. Such problems, as well as numerous variations, are the reason why cesarean delivery is favored in breech presentations.

The transverse position, illustrated in Figure 7–3, is another abnormal fetal position presenting severe problems. In this presentation the fetus lies across the birth canal. All of the injury problems noted with the breech position are potential difficulties with this presentation, depending on how delivery proceeds, and a multitude of other problems face the attending physician. If it is possible to rotate the fetus safely, then delivery through the birth canal may be attempted. This is particularly true if the baby can be moved into a normal or nearly normal head-down position. If the fetus cannot be satisfactorily rotated, a cesarean section is performed.

Abnormalities of fetal presentation can cause many difficulties during birth. Such problems may result in reduced mental functioning because of mechanical injury or anoxia, or both. Abnormal presentation, however, is not the only type of problem to occur during the birth process. The initial stages of labor are important for several reasons. As the fetus proceeds into the birth canal, the pelvic girdle begins to stretch.

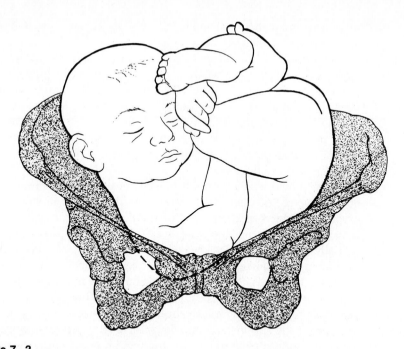

Figure 7–3
An example of transverse fetal position
From *Childbirth: Family Centered Nursing* (3rd ed.) by J. Iorio, 1975, St. Louis: C.V. Mosby. Copyright 1975 by the C.V. Mosby Co. Reprinted by permission.

With a normally positioned fetus, the head is also molded to permit passage through the bony pelvic structure. This process occurs during early labor, when uterine contractions are less intense and less frequent than they later become. Consequently normal molding and stretching occur without sufficient stress to cause injury to the baby. This takes time. Delivery of a baby after a labor of less than about two hours is known as *precipitous birth* and causes considerable concern about the adequacy of time for gentle skull molding. Precipitous birth increases the risk of tissue damage and increases the probability of mental retardation.

Time is also important at the other end of the continuum—when labor is unusually prolonged (24 hours or more). Most deliveries do not approach 24 hours in length; seven to 12 hours is average. A variety of conditions may accompany prolonged labor. Under certain circumstances the uterine conditions deprive a fetus of oxygen, which after a lengthy labor results in either anoxia or a stillborn baby. This is a particular problem if the membranes have ruptured early, and labor is prolonged without delivery. Additionally, in a long period of advanced labor, the fetal skull is under an unusual amount of pressure, which can lead to intracranial hemorrhage. In either case the probability of tissue damage and resulting mental retardation substantially increases.

This section has briefly reviewed influences and causes of mental retardation occurring at birth. Our examples of conditions are the ones that are most prevalent, better known, and more easily understood. But even this abbreviated presentation can make readers who have just begun to study mental retardation wonder how a normal birth ever happens, but perspective must be maintained. The vast majority of babies are born normally and are ready for the challenges of the postnatal world.

PROFESSIONAL INTERVENTION

Core Concept	*Many different forms of professional intervention can prevent or minimize mental retardation during the prenatal and neonatal period.*

We have examined a few conditions that can result in mental retardation. Through various types of professional intervention, mental retardation can be prevented or at least curtailed in many instances.

Children who are born at high risk because of inappropriate birth weight or gestational age are frequently predisposed to mental retardation. As we have seen, problems often arise when prenatal care is either inadequate or nonexistent. Inadequacy or lack of availability of prenatal care is often related to lack of financial resources, ignorance, a value system that does not include high regard for prenatal care, inefficient health-care plans, or a combination of these factors.

Limitations in financial resources may result in inadequate prenatal dietary intake, lack of necessary drugs and vitamins, and lack of supervision by health-care specialists. Many mothers are uneducated about the necessity for prenatal care. Others who are informed do not always incorporate good prenatal care into their value systems, ignoring advice from health-care specialists. Government-supported health-care programs are frequently overburdened and inadequately staffed. Expectant mothers, frustrated by long waits and impersonal care, may become too discouraged to continue seeking prenatal care. Generally speaking, enhancing the mother's health has positive influences on the unborn child's well-being (Albino, 1984).

Professional intervention can greatly reduce the incidence of high-risk children. Low-income families lacking the financial resources for adequate prenatal care need to be directed to the proper agencies of government-supported health care. In addition, these families should be directed to various sources to obtain supplemental foods, such as agencies that distribute food stamps, maintain surplus food programs, and provide other types of resources to improve the diet of the entire family and especially the expectant mother. Social workers, public health staff, and other individuals working directly with the families can offer this information. It is imperative that families be advised how and where to apply for aid. Supplemental nutrition and care programs significantly improve the chances of many high-risk infants, and benefits extend to other family members (Chez & Chervenak, 1990; Christiansen, 1984). Many agencies require extensive documentation to verify financial need. Families should be tutored in the skills necessary to complete application forms as well as in the ways to obtain documentation of financial need.

The heavy caseloads of physicians in government-supported programs could be much lightened by utilization of other health-care specialists, for example, certified nurses and midwives. The growing corps of pediatric nurse practitioners can help families achieve better postnatal care.

Some genetic conditions and chromosomal aberrations can be dealt with effectively through professional intervention. Since the majority of Down syndrome cases are of the nondisjunctive or trisomy variety, a high percentage tend to be related to advanced maternal age. Health-care specialists and social workers can encourage couples to have their children at an earlier age, preferably before the prospective mother is 35. Older couples might be urged to exercise birth control methods or at least be informed of the possible consequences of having children at more advanced ages. Young mothers who have children with Down syndrome should have a chromosomal analysis to determine if the condition is related to translocation. If a translocation exists, then the likelihood of a genetic or inherited etiology is high. These parents can be counseled and advised of the risks involved in having other children. Under such conditions sterilization or other forms of birth control may be considered. Amniocentesis can show the existence of a translocation in the fetus, giving the parents a chance to make an informed decision about terminating the pregnancy via therapeutic abortion. The issue of abortion is highly controversial; we discuss it at length in Chapter 14. Although abortion may or may not be acceptable to the counselor, the counselor should avoid imposing personal values on parents, who are entitled to know what their alternatives are and that the decision regarding the alternatives is rightfully theirs (Moroney, 1986).

Routine screening can diagnose certain disorders, such as PKU, early. Screening for PKU can be accomplished by a stick test that can determine abnormal levels of phenyl-alanine in the urine. The Guthrie test also determines abnormal presence of phenyl-alanine through the examination of the patient's blood.

Dietary restrictions can often prevent mental retardation caused by PKU. As early as possible, the child is placed on a diet that is essentially free of phenylalanine. Commercially prepared diets include Ketonil and Lofenalac. The earlier a child is placed on a restricted diet, the greater the chances of avoiding mental retardation. While evidence suggests that a child with PKU may eventually be removed from the restricted diet, the appropriate time is specific to the individual.

RH-factor incompatibility between mother and fetus can frequently lead to eryth-roblastosis fetalis and hyperbilirubinemia, which can cause brain damage and mental retardation. Bilirubin levels can be monitored effectively by periodic testing with a Coombs' test or through amniocentesis, which samples the bilirubin level in the am-niotic fluid (Mahnovski & Pavlova, 1989). When the fetus is affected by a high bilirubin content, professional intervention may take the form of induced labor so that the child is born before the bilirubin level reaches a critical point. There have also been some efforts toward exchange transfusion through a fetal leg extended by surgery, and ex-change transfusion immediately after birth has been effective in many instances. One of the most dramatic breakthroughs in medical intervention is the development of in-trauterine transfusions. Guided by X-ray films, the surgeon extends a long needle through the mother's abdomen into the peritoneal cavity in the abdomen of the fetus. Blood of the same type as the mother's is then transfused into the fetus. Thus the incompatibility factor is eliminated and the fetal blood is immune from the mother's antibodies.

Rh$_o$ immune globulin (RhoGAM), a desensitizing drug, was introduced to the general public in 1968. If RhoGAM is injected into the mother within 72 hours of her first child's birth, it desensitizes her body to the Rh-factor antibodies, and she can begin her next pregnancy without the antibodies in her bloodstream. The procedure can be performed after the birth of each child and will largely preclude the development of antibodies, provided it is done faithfully after each birth. Between intrauterine transfusions and desensitization through RhoGAM, there should be few incidents of death or mental retardation in the future resulting from Rh-factor incompatibility.

As indicated earlier, the first trimester of pregnancy is critical in any type of fetal insult or injury. During this period expectant mothers must exercise extreme caution to avoid any exposure to irradiation, which may affect the fetus, or to infectious diseases. Rubella immunization is now available that can and should eliminate the possibility of widespread rubella epidemics. Parents can greatly reduce the possibility of rubella in their homes by immunizing all children in the family. This also protects future mothers from contracting the disease while pregnant.

Prevention of trauma during delivery is the major concern of adequate obstetrical management. Primary concerns include maintaining adequate fetal oxygenation during labor and delivery, ensuring appropriate delivery if there is a fetus–pelvis size disproportion, and providing adequate observation and care of the infant during the first hour of life. Regional high-risk care centers for mothers provide an extremely high level of specialized care for both mothers and infants known to be in one of the risk categories described. These centers have significantly decreased maternal and infant mortality, and one of the most important contributions that can be made in prevention of mental retardation is early identification of mothers and infants at risk to allow their transfer to a specialized center.

NEW ISSUES AND FUTURE DIRECTIONS

As we approach the beginning of the twenty-first century, fetal and neonatal medicine offers both promise and challenge. On the favorable side, our knowledge has increased phenomenally during the past 20 years. Jonas (1990) reminds us that it was in the 1970s that we witnessed what were then called "miracles" that permitted prenatal diagnosis of in utero developmental problems. Now we have progressed to the point of actually performing surgery to correct serious defects while the fetus is in utero (Harrison et al., 1990).

In many cases our advances in knowledge have been driven by progress in technology, which permits actions scarcely imaginable before. Prenatal surgery (Harrison et al., 1990) is one illustration, but there have been other significant advances in the boundaries of knowledge that offer potential for preventing mental retardation while sometimes treading on unstable ethical ground. One such possibility is the prenatal diagnosis of PKU. Cahalane (1989) notes that this is "now feasible, using cloning and gene mapping techniques" (p. 610). While prevention is clearly desirable, societal questions always come up when techniques have potential for abuse. Genetic mapping and its related technological capability present social and ethical issues that have yet to be fully addressed, let alone resolved.

Also challenging are the ethics of what professionals can now do to maintain life. We are, through heroic efforts and applications of new technology, saving the lives of seriously endangered youngsters. One must ask—and many are asking—At what cost with respect to quality of life? In some cases children are kept alive who would have died in earlier times. But in some instances these youngsters, although alive, suffer severe mental or physical damage and may exist only in a vegetative state. This raises serious ethical questions about withholding treatment. The questions are not new (see Hardman & Drew, 1978, 1980) but are becoming increasingly important as we continue to employ our rapidly advancing knowledge and technology. Chapter 14 examines some of these difficult social and ethical issues in more detail.

Other challenges presented by society during the final decade of this century are also significant, and many of them affect the prenatal and neonatal development of our children. In some cases, even the widely heralded advances of technology will be sorely tried if we intercede and prevent developmental injury. It is well known that the use of certain substances during pregnancy creates risk for the unborn fetus. As indicated earlier, concern for fetal alcohol syndrome has expanded in recent years to include fetal alcohol effect, which causes less severe fetal damage but has observable detrimental effects as the youngster matures. Other substance use and abuse during pregnancy raise new questions almost daily as new drugs are developed and we learn more about diseases. The U.S. Department of Health and Human Services reports that more than 100,000 crack cocaine babies are born each year, a figure that is probably very conservative (National Council on Disability, 1990). The full range of sequelae is not yet known, but it is clear that developmental neurological problems, learning difficulties, and short attention spans are likely in such youngsters. Other drugs also present concern. Some estimates suggest that 375,000 babies born annually are exposed to illegal substances (Parrino, 1990). Many of these youngsters will have mental retardation.

Serious disease states continue to beset society and have significant implications for the health and development of young children. Perhaps the most publicized as we enter the 1990s is human immunodeficiency virus (HIV), which is linked to AIDS. There is much that we do not know about the effects of HIV on infants, but it appears to affect them differently than it does adults. The principal impact often seems to be on the central nervous system, which clearly relates to mental retardation. Approximately 50% of HIV-positive infants develop microcephaly, a serious condition associated with severe and profound mental deficits (Parrino, 1990). While infants born to mothers with HIV do not always have the condition, the Centers for Disease Control report a greater increase in the disease among newborns than any other group.

CORE QUESTIONS

1. What factors appear to contribute to inadequate birth weight and gestational age problems, and how do they place an infant at risk for mental retardation? Give examples.

2. How do different types of Down syndrome occur, and why might they relate to differing levels of intellectual functioning?

3. Why is maternal-fetal interaction important? How can it contribute to the proper development of a baby, and how to mental retardation? Give examples.

4. Why is the first trimester of pregnancy so important to the developing fetus, and how might maternal infection during this period influence the fetus?

5. Why is fetal positioning important in normal delivery of a baby, and how might abnormal presentation cause mental retardation?

6. How might professional intervention with respect to maternal nutrition during the first trimester of pregnancy be important in preventing mental retardation?

ROUND TABLE DISCUSSION

Prenatal development is a very important phase in the life cycle of an individual, and a number of processes can malfunction to cause mental retardation. There has been rising concern about drug and alcohol use, particularly among young people. Some claim that programs aimed at curtailing abuse of such substances represent moralistic "hype" and an intrusion on the individuals' rights to privacy. Others argue that, morals aside, such programs provide important knowledge related to the health of those involved as well as their future children.

In your study group or on your own, examine and reflect on the information this chapter contains about early development and mental retardation. Consider this material in light of substance abuse and discuss the pros and cons of educational and awareness programs like those you see on television.

REFERENCES

Albino, J. E. (1984). Prevention by acquiring health-enhancing habits. In M. C. Roberts & L. Peterson (Eds.), *Prevention of problems in childhood.* New York: John Wiley.

Blair, J. D. (1989). The reproductive systems. In G. B. Reed, A. E. Claireaux, & A. D. Bain (Eds.), *Diseases of the fetus and newborn: Pathology, radiology and genetics* (pp. 333–372). St. Louis: C.V. Mosby.

Brendt, R. L., & Beckman, D. A. (1990). Teratology. In R. D. Eden & F. H. Boehm (Eds.), *Assessment and care of the fetus: Physiological, clinical, and medicolegal principles* (pp. 223–244). Norwalk, CT: Appleton & Lange.

Cahalane, S. F. (1989). Screening for genetic disease. In G. B. Reed, A. E. Claireaux, & A. D. Bain (Eds.), *Diseases of the fetus and newborn: Pathology, radiology and genetics* (pp. 599–614). St. Louis: C.V. Mosby.

Carr-Hill, R. A., & Hall, M. H. (1985). The repetition of spontaneous preterm labour. *British Journal of Obstetrics and Gynaecology, 95,* 921–924.

Carson, S. A., & Simpson, J. L. (1990). Spontaneous abortion. In. R. D. Eden & F. H. Boehm (Eds.), *Assessment and care of the fetus: Physiological, clinical, and medicolegal principles* (pp. 559–574). Norwalk, CT: Appleton & Lange.

Chez, R. A., & Chervenak, J. L. (1990). Nutrition in pregnancy. In R. D. Eden & F. H. Boehm (Eds.), *Assessment and care of the fetus: Physiological, clinical, and medicolegal principles* (pp. 215–222). Norwalk, CT: Appleton & Lange.

Christiansen, N. (1984). Social effects of a family food supplementation and a home stimulation program. In J. Brozek & B. Schurch (Eds.), *Malnutrition and behavior: Critical assessment of key issues*. Lausanne: Nestlé Foundation.

Claireaux, A. E., & Reed, G. B. (1989). The pancreas. In G. B. Reed, A. E. Claireaux, & A. D. Bain (Eds.), *Diseases of the fetus and newborn: Pathology, radiology and genetics* (pp. 291–298). St. Louis: C.V. Mosby.

Cohen, S. E., & Parmelee, A. H. (1983). Prediction of five-year Stanford-Binet scores in preterm infants. *Child Development, 54,* 1242–1253.

Cox, D. R., & Epstein, C. J. (1985). Comparative gene mapping of human chromosome 21 and mouse chromosome 16. *Annals of the New York Academy of Sciences, 450,* 169–177.

Creasy, R. K. (1988). Preterm labor and delivery. In R. K. Creasy & R. Resnik (Eds.), *Maternal-fetal medicine: Principles and practice*. Philadelphia: W.B. Saunders.

Creasy, R. K. (1990). Preterm labor. In R. D. Eden & F. H. Boehm (Eds.), *Assessment and care of the fetus: Physiological, clinical, and medicolegal principles* (pp. 617–630). Norwalk, CT: Appleton & Lange.

Crnic, K. A., Ragozin, A. S., Greenberg, M. T., Robinson, N. M., & Basham, R. B. (1983). Social interaction and developmental competence of preterm and full-term infants during the first year of life. *Child Development, 54,* 1199–1210.

Davidson, J. N., Rumsby, G., & Niswander, L. A. (1985). Expression of genes on human chromosome 21. *Annals of the New York Academy of Sciences, 450,* 43–54.

Epstein, C. J., Cox, D. R., & Epstein, L. B. (1985). Mouse trisomy 16: An animal model of human trisomy 21 (Down syndrome). *Annals of the New York Academy of Sciences, 450,* 157–168.

Ershow, A. G. (1986). Growth in Black and White children with Down syndrome. *American Journal of Mental Deficiency, 90,* 507–512.

Gelfand, D. M., Jenson, W. R., & Drew, C. J. (1988). *Understanding child behavior disorders* (2nd ed.). New York: Holt, Rinehart and Winston.

Hardman, M. L., & Drew, C. J. (1978). Life management practices with the profoundly retarded: Issues of abortion, euthanasia and withholding treatment. *Mental Retardation, 16,* 390–396.

Hardman, M. L., & Drew, C. J. (1980). Parent consent and the practice of withholding treatment from the severely defective newborn. *Mental Retardation, 18,* 165–169.

Hardman, M. L., Drew, C. J., Egan, M. W., & Wolf, B. (1990). *Human exceptionality: Society, school, and family* (3rd ed.). Boston: Allyn & Bacon.

Harrison, M. R., Adzick, N. S., Longaker, M. T., Goldberg, J. D., Rosen, M. A., Filly, R. A., Evans, M. I., & Golbus, M. S. (1990). Successful repair in utero of a fetal diaphragmatic hernia after removal of herniated viscera from the left thorax. *New England Journal of Medicine, 322,* 1582–1584.

Hayes, E. (Ed.) (1987). *Risking the future: Adolescent sexuality, pregnancy, and childbearing* (Vol. 1). Washington, DC: National Academy Press.

Hetherington, E. M., & Parke, R. D. (1986). *Child psychology: A contemporary viewpoint* (3rd ed.). New York: McGraw-Hill.

Jonas, H. S. (1990). Foreword. In R. D. Eden & F. H. Boehm (Eds.), *Assessment and care of the fetus: Physiological, clinical, and medicolegal principles* (p. xv). Norwalk, CT: Appleton & Lange.

Jones, K. L., Smith, D. W., Ulleland, C. N., & Streissguth, A. P. (1973, June 9). Pattern of malformation in offspring of chronic alcoholic mothers. *The Lancet, 1* (7815), 1267–1271.

Kernek, C., Osterud, H., & Anderson, B. (1966). Patterns of prematurity in Oregon. *Northwest Medicine, 65,* 639.

Koops, B. L., Morgan, L. J., & Battaglia, F. C. (1982). Neonatal mortality risk in relation to birth weight and gestational age: Update. *Journal of Pediatrics, 101,* 969–977.

Landing, B. H., Galvis, D. A., Wells, T. R., & Hardy, B. E. (1989). Disorders of the kidneys and urinary tract of importance in the perinatal period. In G. B. Reed, A. E. Claireaux, and A. D. Bain (Eds.), *Diseases of the fetus and newborn: Pathology, radiology and genetics* (pp. 373–392). St. Louis: C.V. Mosby Co.

Little, G. A. (1990). Fetal growth and development. In R. D. Eden & F. H. Boehm (Eds.), *Assessment and care of the fetus: Physiological, clinical, and medicolegal principles* (pp. 3–15). Norwalk, CT: Appleton & Lange.

Mahnovski, V., & Pavlova, Z. (1989). Blood disorders. In G. B. Reed, A. E. Claireaux, and A. D. Bain (Eds.), *Diseases of the fetus and newborn: Pathology, radiology and genetics* (pp. 417–440). St. Louis: C.V. Mosby.

Moroney, R. M. (1986). Family care: Toward a responsive society. In P. R. Dokecki & R. M. Zaner (Eds.), *Ethics of dealing with persons with severe handicaps: Toward a research agenda* (pp. 217–232). Baltimore: Paul H. Brookes.

National Council on Disability. (1990). HHS releases report on crack babies. *Focus* (Spring, pp. 1, 8). Washington, DC: Author.

Parrino, S. S. (1990). NCD will consider infants at risk. *Focus* (Spring, pp. 2, 6). Washington, DC: National Council on Disabilities.

Peterson, N. L. (1987). *Early intervention for handicapped and at-risk children.* Denver: Love Publishing.

Rocissano, L., & Yatchmink, Y. (1983). Language skill and interactive patterns in prematurely born toddlers. *Child Development, 54,* 1229–1241.

Rose, S. A. (1983). Differential rates of visual information processing in full-term and preterm infants. *Child Development, 54,* 1189–1198.

Rubin, R. A., Rosenblatt, C., & Balow, B. (1973). Psychological and educational sequelae of prematurity. *Pediatrics, 52,* 352.

Sarnat, H. B., & Mueller, D. L. (1990). Fetal neurology. In R. D. Eden and F. H. Boehm (Eds.), *Assessment and care of the fetus: Physiological, clinical, and medicolegal principles* (pp. 43–67). Norwalk, CT: Appleton & Lange.

Silva, P. A., McGee, R., & Williams, S. (1984). A longitudinal study of the intelligence and behavior of preterm and small for gestational age children. *Journal of Developmental and Behavioral Pediatrics, 5,* 1–5.

Sokol, R., Drugan, A., & Evans, M. I. (1990). Substance abuse. In R. D. Eden and F. H. Boehm (Eds.), *Assessment and care of the fetus: Physiological, clinical, and medicolegal principles* (pp. 683–691). Norwalk, CT: Appleton & Lange.

Spellacy, W. N. (1990). Intrauterine growth retardation. In R. D. Eden and F. H. Boehm (Eds.), *Assessment and care of the fetus: Physiological, clinical, and medicolegal principles* (pp. 643–649). Norwalk, CT: Appleton & Lange.

Streissguth, A. P., Barr, H. M., Sampson, P. D., & Darby, B. L. (1989). IQ at age 4 in relation to maternal alcohol use and smoking during pregnancy. *Developmental Psychology, 25,* 3–11.

Sullivan, W. C. (1899). A note on the influence of maternal inebriety on the offspring. *Journal of Mental Science, 45,* 489–503.

Ungerer, J. A., & Sigman, M. (1983). Developmental lags in preterm infants from one to three years of age. *Child Development, 54,* 1217–1228.

CHAPTER EIGHT

The Mentally Retarded Child During Infancy and Early Childhood

<table>
<tr><td>

Core Concepts

</td><td>

- Physiological growth during infancy and early childhood plays a central role in the general development of an individual, laying the foundation for many skills and behaviors.
- Early intervention often demands partnership between professionals and parents.
- During the early childhood years mental retardation is likely to become evident in language development.
- Cognitive development during infancy and early childhood involves many complex processes including some in areas where children with mental retardation have great difficulty.
- Developmental problems in social and emotional functioning can have a serious impact on a young child's ability to adapt and chances to succeed.

</td></tr>
</table>

Development during infancy and early childhood is vital to the continued growth and well-being of an individual. The importance of this period can hardly be overemphasized, because these years are critical for all children. Experiences during infancy and early childhood can promote the attainment of optimal development potential, or they can deter the fulfillment of this potential. In the first situation, intellectual functioning may be enhanced so much that the child operates in the upper ranges of capability. In the second, experiences may detract from the developmental process so much that permanently lowered functioning results. The effects of environmental influences during infancy and early childhood are often more lasting and pervasive than during any later phase of the life cycle. It is not surprising that this period causes stress and a variety of emotional responses in the families of mentally retarded youngsters (Affleck, Tennen, & Gershman, 1985; Goldberg, Marcovitch, MacGregor, & Lojkasek, 1986).

This chapter focuses on development during infancy and the preschool years and on environmental influences that promote or detract from the fulfillment of potential. We examine four broad areas of development: (1) physical, (2) language, (3) cognitive, and (4) psychosocial. Although these are interrelated, they also represent distinct areas of development that have been the subject of much research. Each of the four areas is critical in one fashion or another to a child's ability to learn. In what follows we review pertinent research with regard to expected traits of development, traits evident in children with mental retardation, and environmental influences.

PHYSICAL DEVELOPMENT

<table>
<tr><td>

Core Concept

</td><td>

Physiological growth during infancy and early childhood plays a central role in the general development of an individual, laying the foundation for many skills and behaviors.

</td></tr>
</table>

Several major body systems are involved in a discussion of physical development. Those most often considered include the gastrointestinal, renal, endocrine, skeletal, reproductive, neurological, and muscular systems. Each has an important function, although those most closely related to the learning process are the neurological and musculoskeletal systems. These two systems are integrally related from a functional standpoint and are occasionally thought of as one—the neuromotor system. Neurological and motor functions are also influenced by important stimuli, and responses are provided by the endocrine system. For the purposes of this text, we examine neuromotor development to become familiar with the physical dimensions of learning and the influences of the environment on this aspect of development.

Neuromotor Development

An examination of physical development must consider a number of components of the neurological system. This system is composed of the brain, spinal cord, and peripheral neurons, including the autonomic system, which is functionally related to the endocrine system. Neurological pathways extend to the muscle and skin tissues and provide for the transmission of neurological sensations from the environment to the central nervous system. These pathways also serve as the means for neurological control and response between the central nervous system and the muscles that permit movement and vocalization appropriate to various environmental stimuli. The processes involved in stimulus reception and neurological functioning cannot usually be studied directly. They may, however, be investigated indirectly by observing a variety of performance areas and comparing a given child's functioning with age-appropriate levels. Neurological maturation is a critical dimension of the child's overall development and plays a particular role in cognitive, language, and psychosocial development. More complete attention is given to these areas in later portions of this chapter. Here we focus directly on the development of the neuromotor system and examine certain conditions of physical development that can be detected in children with mental retardation.

Head and Brain Characteristics

A child's neurological development and capacity are known to be related to head and brain size. As noted earlier, the brain grows very rapidly during the prenatal period. This rapid growth continues after birth; a two-year-old's brain is approximately 90 percent of adult brain size. Although this growth cannot be directly observed, it can be assessed indirectly by measuring the head circumference. Normal circumference ranges have been established for each sex at each developmental stage. For example, the mean head circumference for male infants at birth is 34.5 cm and reaches 49 cm by the age of two. Female infants, on the other hand, have a mean head circumference of 34 cm at birth and reach 48 cm by the age of two. A deviation of ± 2 standard deviations from the expected mean head circumference at any age is a sufficient variation to warrant concern. If such a condition occurs, the child must undergo extensive medical testing to determine if there is a serious pathological condition present that threatens physical health and that may threaten intellectual functioning. An example of such a condition is microcephaly, in which the head circumference is below the norm by two standard deviations or more. (Children with microcephaly also are characterized by several other physical abnormalities and are typically rather severely retarded.) The child's brain size is limited, and abnormalities of brain tissue formation may also be present. Limited brain size, tissue abnormalities, or both may result from a genetic condition or from a condition affecting the skeletal tissue surrounding the brain that arrests the growth of brain tissue. In either case the neurological system is seriously impaired, and mental retardation results.

Other conditions produce a head circumference that is significantly larger than expected and may indicate a situation that is of serious concern. Hydrocephalus, for example, is a syndrome characterized by exceptionally large head size even though the brain may be inadequately developed or normal, depending on the precise cause of the condition. This condition is related to an increase in the amount of cerebrospinal fluid that circulates in the brain cavity and spinal column area. The excess fluid puts increased pressure on surrounding structures and leads to damage of brain tissue and ultimate mental retardation, regardless of initial capacity.

Other brain developments also occur at a rapid rate during the early years. Sulci, or convolutions, in the lobes of the brain deepen and become more prominent and numerous during this period. These continue to develop throughout life but more gradually than during the early years. The development of sulci, it is thought, reflects processes of learning, memory, and the ability to reason and form conceptualizations. A child who has inadequate neuromotor control and function or shows a developmental delay may suffer from some abnormality of form or function of the brain, although the defect is not typically detectable directly. Some information concerning the size and shape of the brain can be obtained using X-ray procedures, but the primary cause of the child's lack of coordination, speaking difficulty, and limited ability to learn usually cannot be identified with certainty as a defect of the brain tissue. Frequently, direct evidence of brain abnormality must await autopsy, and even this type of examination can provide only limited information in most cases, such as evidence of identifiable lesions in brain tissue. There may, however, be indications that the neurological tissue of the nervous system has not been adequately stimulated at an ideal period of development—a process that is imperative for development of adequate neuromotor function (Levine & Jordan, 1987).

Myelinization

Myelinization, discussed in Chapter 6, is commonly accepted as an important developmental process, although the precise nature of its growth and function remains unknown. Myelinization involves the development of a protective insulating sheath that surrounds the brain and neurological pathways. This sheath presumably operates somewhat like the insulation on an electrical wire and allows nerve impulses to travel along the nerve pathway rapidly and without diffusion. The newborn has an incomplete myelin sheath, which accounts for nonspecific reactions to stimuli and a lack of motor coordination. Consequently, the infant exhibits generalized body movement and crying in response to a painful stimulus to the foot rather than specific withdrawal of the foot and attention to the source of the stimulus with specific vocalizations indicating pain.

As with other growth patterns, myelinization proceeds in a cephalocaudal and proximodistal fashion, which provides for the pattern of acquisition of gross-motor control before fine-motor control. By the age of two, a major portion of the myelin sheath is formed, and the child's motor capacity is relatively mature.

Reflexes and Voluntary Behavior

Reflex behavior is a primitive human response in comparison to many that are now characteristic of general human functioning. Development of reflex behavior is thought to have evolved early in human history out of necessity for protection in a harsh environment. Later sophisticated cognitive skills developed that made voluntary action directed toward protection of the organism possible. Much of the reflexive behavior of early infancy gradually fades as voluntary control develops through association pathways of the nervous system. Some reflexes persist throughout life, such as the knee jerk, eye blink, and reaction of the eye pupil to light. During early childhood, voluntary movement becomes predominant for the child who is neurologically healthy, although involuntary movement on one side of the body may mirror voluntary movement on the opposite side. This involuntary mirroring action is pronounced in children who suffer damage to the central nervous system, but the phenomenon itself does not suggest damage unless it persists beyond the preschool years or is so pronounced that it interferes with the child's voluntary movements. Predominance of the one-sided voluntary function is generally established fully by the age of four, and a child typically demonstrates a preference for right or left hand use in performing motor tasks.

Emotions and the Central Nervous System

The brain limbic system is located in the central portion of the tissue and surrounds the hypothalamus. This system functions specifically to mediate emotional and temperamental dimensions of behavior. Sensations such as pleasure or discomfort and the individual meaning that such experiences develop originate and are stored in this system. Other behaviors known to be related to these areas of functioning include excitement, anger, fear, sleep, and wakefulness. Maturity in these response areas progresses as a young child begins to experience a wider range of environmental stimuli and is able to exercise more behavioral self-control as well as control over the behavior of others. The feeling response predominates in early childhood in terms of determining behavior, indicating that the limbic system is functioning and that associations with voluntary control areas are not fully accomplished. As growth continues and these associations mature, a child becomes more effective in disguising and voluntarily controlling emotional components of behavior.

Sensory Organs and Cranial Nerves

Development and integrity of cranial nerves and specialized sensory organs also play an important role in a young child's general functioning status. These maturational processes are essential to the child's ability to receive stimuli from the environment and integrate them into the perceptual and memory components of the central nervous system. Cranial nerves are distinct neural pathways that provide for the specialized sensory function and motor performance of the sensory and other essential organs and surrounding muscle structure. These nerves approach functional maturity by the age of three and can be tested by assessing sensory organ functions. Ears and eyes are particularly crucial for receiving stimuli related to learning. Other sensory functions, such as smell, taste, touch, and the sense of movement, however, are also important in providing essential neurological stimulation.

Optimal functioning levels for the capacities of taste and smell are attained during infancy. These senses also come under the influence of voluntary control and association with other sensory areas. A young child is able to, and often will, refuse to taste a food that looks unpleasant or about which others have made negative comments. The child is able to respond accurately to the sensation that a taste or smell arouses and begins to learn associations between certain tastes and smells and culturally accepted values. Preferred foods in a child's culture become palatable, and foods that are not acceptable become displeasing. The role of these sensory capacities in terms of learning problems is not currently understood, but it does appear that significant learning stimuli come through these channels.

Hearing is often thought to be the most critical sense for learning. Children with hearing deficits seem to have more interference with learning than children with other types of sensory disturbances. This effect obviously varies substantially depending on the child and the nature and severity of the deficit. The sense of hearing relies on intact tissue structures between the external ear and the brain cortex, including the important cranial nerves involved in hearing functions. Functional structures of the ear also are related to the sense of balance and movement.

An infant's hearing apparatus is mature at birth except in two areas: myelinization of the cortical auditory pathways beyond the midbrain and resorption of the connective tissue surrounding the ossicles of the middle ear. The infant obviously can hear and also can respond differently to loud noises (by crying) and to soft, soothing sounds (by relaxing and becoming calm). The child's reaction to sound at this stage is characteristic of reactions to most stimuli; it is generalized and involves movements of the entire body. Typically, these movements are of a gross-motor nature and are nonspecific; they tend to be characterized by a thrashing of the arms, body, and legs or by a generalized calming. As myelinization proceeds, the child begins to exhibit an ability to localize sound direction. By the age of two to three months the child can respond by turning the head toward the sound.

But an infant does not have fully developed hearing like an adult's. This is not present until about seven years of age and involves complex cortical functioning, including the ability to listen, to respond with discrimination, to imitate sounds accurately, and to integrate the meaning of sounds. Identification of hearing deficits during the first year of life is vital for maximally effective treatment and maintenance of optimal learning capacity. If a child's hearing deficiency can be identified at this time, and some means of providing auditory stimulation instituted, the child's ability to integrate the meaning of auditory stimuli later in life and to maintain and use these neurological pathways as an avenue for learning is substantially enhanced.

An infant has rather limited visual acuity at birth, although vision is fully developed by the age of six. At birth an infant is able to differentiate only generally between light and dark. Development of visual acuity progresses rather rapidly during the neonatal period, and by the age of six months an infant is generally able to recognize objects and people. The ability to follow movement in the environment also begins to develop during the first months of life, and completely coordinated eye movements should be evident by the sixth month. A preschool child who is unable to see a single object when looking at it with both eyes (binocularity) has a condition known as *amblyopia*. Amblyopia creates some unusual difficulties with regard to a child's perceptual behavior. Since the child sees two separate overlapping objects instead of a single unified perception, he or she begins to block the perception of one eye, in order to see a single object through the preferred eye. Lack of use and stimulation of the other eye leads to gradual deterioration of the neural pathways from the eye to the central nervous system. This can cause permanent loss of function of the eye if it continues to be unused. The effects of amblyopia illustrate the vital role of adequate stimulation in order for neurological tissue to develop and maintain adequate function.

Integration of incoming visual stimuli with existing neurological functions is an extremely important factor in early learning. By about two to three years of age the child begins to be able to remember and recall visual images. Along with an interest in pictures, the child also begins to enjoy producing geometric shapes and figures. These abilities create a readiness to recognize symbols, or to read, which typically appears by the time the child is four years old. A further visual discrimination that has important implications for early learning processes is color recognition. For the most part, color recognition is well established by the time the child is five.

Summary

Many complex factors contribute to neuromotor developmental advances during early childhood. Growing muscles, practice of motor skills, continuing organization of associations between established neural pathways, and the establishment of new pathways are only a portion of the developmental process that is under way. During this period the ability to maintain focal attention, a hallmark of early childhood, also emerges. Almost incredible gains are evident in cognitive and intellectual functioning, memory, consciousness, and thought. The role of each structure in the nervous system with regard to the various forms of mental retardation is not well understood. It is apparent, however, that an inadequacy in one dimension of the development of the nervous system is typically accompanied by inadequacies in the system generally. Thus the child who evidences developmental delays in motor performance during early childhood frequently also exhibits delays in emotional development, language development, and cognitive development (Smith & von Tetzchner, 1986), since each of these dimensions of performance depends on the general adequacy of the nervous system. Table 8–1 summarizes selected developmental landmarks during the first two years of life in terms of a few motor, psychosocial, and verbal developmental features. Remember that a child who is delayed in one area of development is likely also to exhibit signs of delay in others. Such a child's behavior may be generally more like that of children who are chronologically younger.

Table 8–1
Selected developmental landmarks

	Months							
	1	2	3	4	5	6	7	8
MOTOR								
Sitting				⟨		⟨	Supported	
Walking								
Sucking								
Standing								⟨
Crawling							⟨	
Creeping								
Bowel control						⟨		
Bladder control								
Head: prone		⟨	Lifts head	⟩				
sitting			⟨	Bobs	⟩			
PSYCHOSOCIAL								
Smiling				⟨ Spontaneous ⟩		Mirror image		
Reacting to others			⟨	Follows moving people		⟩ Discriminates		
Feeding					⟨ Solids ⟩		⟨ Holds	
Socialization	⟨							
VERBAL								
Crying								
Cooing			⟨			⟩		
Babbling, resembles one syllable						⟨	Tone	
Imitation of word sounds								
Some word understanding (dada, mamma)								
Word repertoire								

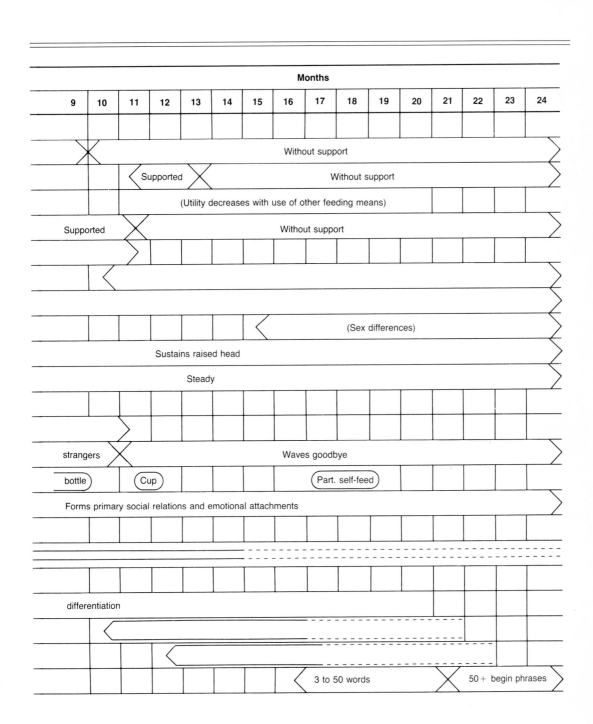

| Months | | | | | | | | | | | | | | | |
| 9 | 10 | 11 | 12 | 13 | 14 | 15 | 16 | 17 | 18 | 19 | 20 | 21 | 22 | 23 | 24 |

Without support

Supported   Without support

(Utility decreases with use of other feeding means)

Supported   Without support

(Sex differences)

Sustains raised head

Steady

strangers   Waves goodbye

bottle   Cup   Part. self-feed

Forms primary social relations and emotional attachments

differentiation

3 to 50 words   50 + begin phrases

Effects of the Environment

Each of the child's capabilities and neuromotor functions has an optimal time during the developmental cycle for appearance and integration into the system as a whole. The child's development of these specific capabilities during such periods is vulnerable to disruptions that can produce either temporary or permanent problems. Some of these disruptions result from environmental influences. There is general agreement that the effects of environmental conditions or stimuli on a young child are great, although the exact influences of specific environmental conditions remain poorly understood (Scarr & Arnett, 1987). An early theory developed by Hebb (1949) offers some interesting notions about possible effects of early deprivation or stimulation of the neurological system on later intellectual functioning.

Hebb postulated that the human brain comprises two interrelated types of tissue, sensorimotor and associative. It was his view that sensorimotor tissue is primarily determined genetically and provides for the reflexive, sensory, and motor functions of the body. Associative tissue, in contrast, is partially determined by genetic endowment but must be developed and established through environmental stimulation, mainly occurring during the first two years of life. Hebb believed that the nature of this development (of associative functions) determined the extent of future intellectual capacity of the individual. Hebb thought that the way stimulation and development happen underlies the higher cognitive functions of the brain. The major portion of the child's behavioral repertoire during the first two years is less complex than in later life and is largely supported by the sensorimotor functions of the brain. Consequently, sensorimotor experiences substantially contribute to the development of associative tissues and functions in the first two years. Hebb's theory has not been subjected to direct empirical testing, so we do not know whether it represents an accurate account of actual neurological development during early life. His theory however, stimulated investigation aimed at examining the influence of early environmental experiences. Investigations focusing on the effects of early environmental experience represent an important endeavor in the field of mental retardation and behavioral science in general. Studies that have supported the importance of early stimuli have not accumulated enough evidence for us to draw firm conclusions, although certain trends are beginning to emerge. For example, extreme environmental deprivation, particularly during early childhood, appears to be a potent unfavorable influence. Such extreme deprivation can result in pervasive developmental delays and potential mental retardation (Bryant & Ramey, 1987; Guralnick & Bricker, 1987). Perhaps the most dramatic evidence for this involved observations of children who, early in life, were subjected to conditions that resulted in extreme deprivation (Gesell, 1941; Mason, 1942).

There is much evidence about how sensory deprivation of visual stimuli during early life affects a child (Peterson, 1987). Some information comes from early studies of restoration of vision after an early developmental period during which the child was blind (Gregory & Wallace, 1963; London, 1960). This unique source of investigation has been made possible mostly by surgical removal of congenital cataracts and by corneal transplants. After surgery and a period of study to learn the meaning of visual stimuli, subjects continued to experience difficulty in pattern discrimination and ability to generalize. Although they were able to learn that a particular symbol was a triangle or a square, they had great difficulty perceiving the image as such without relying on ancillary aids to recognition (for example, counting the number of corners). Further, subjects might recognize a two-dimensional geometric shape as a square on paper, but could not recognize the same shape in another format (such as a box).

It is difficult to relate such extreme cases to less extreme instances of sensory deprivation that occur in poor environments. It seems reasonable to expect that a child who does not have an opportunity to experience and practice certain sensorimotor skills will not develop such specific motor capacities. The effects of deprivation on later development of intellectual functioning, however, remain uncertain. Hebb's (1949) position suggests that a wealth of sensory stimulation during the first two years, regardless of type, should promote favorable development of an individual's cognitive and intellectual skills. Some evidence suggests that variety in stimulation is also important in cognitive development (Peterson, 1987). Limited environmental stimulation, a lack of systematic or ordered interpretation and mediation, or limited motivation may bring about stimulus deprivation and, with it, limitations in the development of intelligence.

Several factors prevent a systematic accumulation of data on the effects of deprivation. The ethics of using human subjects clearly and appropriately prevents experimental manipulation of stimulus deprivation in a manner that may harm subjects. Occurrences of natural events that result in environmental deprivation are unsystematic and involve such situational variation that investigation of these instances provides data of only limited value. Studies like the one on early visual deprivation are few and have become even more so as a result of advances in medical technology. Because of these bars to the study of deprivation, many researchers have turned to the study of stimulus enrichment in an effort to gather evidence about the influence of environmental sensory stimuli on the development of intellectual functioning. One approach to this type of investigation compares the functioning of young children who, as infants, received a natural wealth of sensory stimulation with that of children who were relatively deprived of such environmental stimulation. Although the evidence suggests some differential effect, the data are too global for hard-and-fast conclusions. Even these investigations are not free of difficulties since, in many cases, it is unclear that presence or relative absence of environmental stimuli is the only influential variable.

Skeels and Dye (1939) reported on a classic study of early stimulation effects. These investigators, studying the influences of stimulation on children under three years of age, compared two groups of institutionalized infants placed in two different types of environments. Thirteen infants with IQ scores ranging from 35 to 89 were removed from an orphanage and placed in wards of an institution for children with retardation where attendants and older women who were retarded gave them a great deal of attention and stimulation. After a year and a half of this type of treatment, the IQ scores of the children had increased 27.5 points. The comparison group (12 infants with IQ scores ranging from 50 to 103) remained in the orphanage, where attention and stimulation were minimal. These children's IQs dropped 26.2 points during the same period. As noted, however, it is not clear in studies like this one whether differences between the two groups are caused by sensory stimulation alone or by other related factors in combination with the stimulation. Additionally, while it seems apparent that stimulation influences the rate of development, it is not clear whether stimulation is responsible for any lasting effect on the quality of functioning for normal children.

Over the years a number of investigators attempted to manipulate sensory stimulation experimentally during the first few years of life (Burns, Deddish, Burns, & Hatcher, 1983; Greenberg, Uzgiris, & Hunt, 1968; Ottinger, Blatchley, & Dennenberg, 1969; White, 1967). In large part these studies have focused on the influences of visual stimulation during the early months of life and have demonstrated that controlled stimulation has marked effects on the rate and quality of specific aspects of development. Once again, the question whether such effects are lasting or significant with respect to the quality of future intellectual functioning remains unanswered. And investigations that experimentally manipulate environmental stimuli are not without problems. Although sounder in their research design, such studies have raised ethical questions about experimental manipulation. Concern focuses on the ethical appropriateness of providing stimulation to one group while not providing (thus denying) such treatment to the comparison group(s). These are difficult questions without easy solutions, and they put stumbling-blocks in the way of accumulating a solid data base.

One notable long-range study, the Milwaukee Project, which focused on early and intensive stimulation, has received considerable attention (Garber & Heber, 1977; Heber, Dever, & Conry, 1968; Heber & Garber, 1971; Heber, Garber, Harrington, Hoffman, & Falender, 1972; Strickland, 1971). Data from this investigation present substantial evidence for the effectiveness of an early intensive stimulation program on the development of disadvantaged infants in Milwaukee, Wisconsin. The infants, born to mothers with IQ scores below 75, were placed randomly in experimental and control groups. The experimental program of sensory stimulation began in the home shortly after birth, and then the child was brought daily to a center for regular, planned stimulation continuing over a period of 5 years. At the study's conclusion, the experimental infants were estimated to have an average IQ score 33 points higher than the control group's.

As additional research takes place to discover the effects of stimulation of the nervous system during the first two years of life, it may become possible to draw more accurate conclusions about the relationship of the development of this system to later intellectual functioning and to determine the vulnerability of the nervous system to the environment during the first two years of life. At this time we can safely conclude that sensory stimulation is beneficial in affecting the rate and perhaps the quality of all traits that depend on development of the neuromotor system.

Professional and Parental Intervention

Core Concept	*Early intervention often demands partnership between professionals and parents.*

Concerns among professionals working with infants and young children include identification of children who begin to display developmental delays, prevention of the occurrence of delays when possible, and assistance to child and family when a developmental problem is present. Professionals who most often come in contact with children during infancy and the preschool years are health-care workers, particularly physicians and public-health nurses. These individuals frequently depend on the aid and cooperation of social workers, nutritionists, and dietitians to assist in providing comprehensive services to families with multiple problems and needs.

Screening is a very important process in the overall evaluation scheme (see Chapter 5), and is crucial for identifying children who may be exhibiting delays in rate and quality of development. The American Academy of Pediatrics (1971) has established standards for children's health care that recommend monthly screening for all infants during the first six months of life, with intervals increasing gradually until the child is seen annually. Health-care visits should include an assessment of the child's behavior at home since the last visit, health status, and eating patterns. Physical systems are also evaluated, including the neuromotor system, in order to determine whether development is adequate, and behavioral observations confirm the appearance of behavioral landmarks at each appropriate age. Each visit should also include discussion and guidance sessions with the child's parents on the subjects of developmental and health status. Finally, the child receives immunizations to prevent serious contagious disease, and blood and urine tests are made at regular intervals. The family should have developmental guidance to help prevent accidents and alleviate conditions that could lead to problems.

The routine health care just described is an important means of identifying unexpected developmental problems, but it becomes even more critical for the family of a child once a problem has been identified. Both the child with mental retardation and the family need a great deal of support and assistance to meet the challenges of daily care and health maintenance. The health-care team is well equipped to provide such assistance.

Prevention of mental retardation has always been something that professionals in the field have sought to achieve. It is not, however, a subject whose principles are easy to grasp, nor is it one that is free of controversy (see Chapter 14). One of the major difficulties in conceptualizing prevention lies with the field of mental retardation. Mental retardation, as a condition, is an extremely heterogeneous phenomenon. It varies greatly in terms of causation, severity, environmental circumstances, and professional disciplines concerned. By now the reader knows that mental retardation is a problem with many facets; it is sociocultural, psychological, biomedical, and much more. The complex nature of the problem makes conceptualizing prevention in any sort of global fashion most difficult. There have, however, been some notable if limited successes in prevention.

Screening and treatment for the enzyme-deficiency disease PKU (see Chapter 7) is a classic example of an instance in which a definite problem and subsequent treatment can result in preventing or reducing the effects of mental retardation (Cahalane, 1989; Pennington, van Doorninck, McCabe, & McCabe, 1985). Continued assistance from the health-care team is critical. The child must be placed on an extremely restricted and expensive diet in order to offset the enzyme deficiency. This puts certain pressures on the family, and maintenance of adequate and balanced nutrition for the child and the entire family can become a serious problem. The child's health can also be in jeopardy because of increased susceptibility to infection and other factors.

Well-defined prevention programs like that implemented with PKU are scarce. But theories like Hebb's and research results have stimulated considerable interest among health-care workers in identifying families and children who are at risk because of inadequate environmental stimulation. Health-care workers are often the only professional people who are in contact with such families on any systematic basis, so the task of identification of problems is most logically approached from a health-care standpoint. Nurses and child-development specialists have begun programs of environmental stimulation and enrichment in many communities. As the programs develop, research evidence will be forthcoming and will, it is hoped, add to our understanding of the effectiveness of this type of intervention.

The idea of enhanced stimulation is also generating increased interest in intervention beyond the prevention arena. When a child is identified as already mentally retarded and developmentally disabled, health-care workers and child-development specialists have often begun infant stimulation programs to make the most of the child's development. As research findings suggest, such intervention in field settings has resulted in notable progress (Casto & Mastropieri, 1986). Children whom one would normally expect to be significantly delayed in physical neuromotor development have shown impressive acceleration in physical development. For example, a child with Down syndrome is typically delayed by several weeks or months in all aspects of neuromotor development. These delays in young Down children and other retarded youngsters typically include sitting, crawling, walking, talking, eating, and even social behaviors like smiling and peer interaction (Berger & Cunningham, 1986; Strain, 1985).

Infant stimulation programs focus on systematic, planned stimulation of the infant in all sensory modalities. The desired result of such programming is acceleration of the child's development so that these skills appear at a time more nearly consistent with that of normal children of the same chronological age. All six perceptual systems must be stimulated, but multiple stimulation is not necessarily undertaken at any single session; one perceptual system at a time may be stimulated on a given occasion. This is often done to enhance clarity and specificity for parents, who are frequently involved heavily in program implementation and act as important interveners (Bruder, 1987; McConkey & Martin, 1983; Slater, 1986). At some point during the program, however, each of the senses is the focus of stimulation, including vision, hearing, touch, kinesthetic movement, smell, and taste. Thus the parent may be instructed to strike a particular kitchen pot with a spoon near the infant, to rattle a toy, and generally to present as many hearing stimuli as possible to attract the infant's attention. As the infant responds, other perceptual systems may be stimulated, and the same stimuli are repeated, but at different distances from the child. Frequently, the next step involves engaging the infant in active participation in the stimulation program. The child may be encouraged to hold the sound-producing spoon, move the rattle, manipulate soft cotton or a hard rock, and so on.

Most children born into families who are not living in poverty receive a wealth of stimulation in all sensory modalities. Such stimulation is a routine part of their environment and results from ordinary interactions and activities of the family. For the most part these infants are wanted and loved; they are held and carried, cuddled, talked to, placed near the activities of the other children and adults in the family, and taken in the car for trips into the community. These are all a natural part of each day's activities. But many infants are born into environments lacking some or all of the features often taken for granted by the average middle-class family. The world of such children may have substantially less stimulation than is characteristic of many middle-class environments (Allen, Affleck, McGrade, & McQueeney, 1984). During their early months, they may spend a great deal of time alone, in a room with little color, and with limited interaction with other people. When they are fed or changed, they may be handled only briefly, and the bottle often may be propped beside them instead of hand-held. Early experiences outside this meager environment may not exist at all.

Reduced stimulation can also be found in other situations. For example, a relative lack of stimulation may be offered to the child born with a significant physical handicap, even if the family is not of limited means. Such a child may be difficult for the family to look at or to interact with and, consequently, may to a considerable extent be excluded from the activities of the family. This child is not the beautiful baby the family anticipated, and they may not wish to carry him or her into the community to participate in routine activities.

Establishment of a planned sequence of stimulation programming for such infants is one type of effort to provide an environment that more closely resembles the rich experience children must have for normal development. The justification for such a

Programs of stimulation are important to the development of young children with mental retardation.

program does not rest on the valuation of a life style found in "middle" America. Instead it is based on the belief, reinforced by accumulating evidence, that such stimulation and early intervention is of benefit to the child's intellectual development (e.g., Casto & Mastropieri, 1986; Sharav & Shlomo, 1986). Stimulation programs draw heavily on the child's home environment regardless of socioeconomic level. A family of limited income in a home with modest furnishings can provide interaction patterns and sensory stimulation as beneficial as those found in a better-off family.

LANGUAGE DEVELOPMENT

Core Concept	*During the early childhood years mental retardation is likely to become evident in language development.*

Mental retardation may manifest itself in a variety of ways and in a variety of behavioral domains. Perhaps the most serious and obvious deficit involves delayed language development. Expressive language may even be completely absent. Parents and teachers commonly attribute most, if not all, of the child's learning problems to language deficiencies.

Normal Language Development

Table 8–2 provides some guidelines for normal developmental landmarks, including language and prelanguage behaviors. The normal progression of language development is an important indicator of general cognitive maturation. A newborn is usually expected to cry, make other generalized sounds, and to be cooing and babbling by three to six months. First words generally appear in the babbling from nine to 14 months, and simple sentences are formed by 18 to 24 months. Basic syntactical structures are usually in place by three to four years, and speech sounds are articulated correctly, in context, by four to eight years of age. This progression suggests that, for a normal child, the basic language structure is largely complete sometime between four and eight years of age. Certainly as maturation continues beyond this point, language facility also tends to grow and expand, but such growth is largely an embellishment of existing structures.

The process involved in language development has been the source of considerable theoretical debate. A substantial portion of this debate began in 1957 with the publication of B. F. Skinner's *Verbal Behavior*. It was Skinner's contention that verbal behavior is behavior reinforced through the mediation of other people who themselves have a prolonged history that has conditioned them in ways of "precisely" reinforcing the speaker (Skinner, 1957). The mediation of others and the reinforcing consequences continue to be important to maintenance of verbal behavior after initial acquisition. This view of language development is at variance with the beliefs of Chomsky (1957) and Lenneberg (1969), who maintain that language is an innate capacity that is specific to the human species and dependent on the maturation of the brain and nervous system.

Table 8-2
Normal language and prelanguage development

Age	Behavior
Birth	Crying and making other physiological sounds
1 to 2 months	Cooing as well as crying
3 to 6 months	Babbling as well as cooing
9 to 14 months	Speaking first words as well as babbling
18 to 24 months	Speaking first sentences as well as words
3 to 4 years	Using all basic syntactical structures
4 to 8 years	Articulating correctly all speech sounds in context

Lenneberg (1969) discarded learning theory as a relevant explanation for language development. His basis for this view (opposed to Skinner's) was that the onset of language occurs in children at a similar age in all cultures of the world despite enormous cultural differences. Lenneberg also noted that language can be impaired by specific brain lesions that leave other mental and motor functions intact. He asserted that teaching cannot result in language acquisition unless the individual has the innate biological propensity for language.

Chomsky's (1957) position is more of a theoretical compromise, for he recognized that reinforcement plays some role in language development. But reinforcement, according to Chomsky, accompanies natural inquisitiveness, casual observation, a strong tendency to imitate, and an extraordinary capacity to generalize, hypothesize, and process information. These other capacities operate in a very complex manner that may be largely innate or may develop through learning or maturation of the nervous system. From Chomsky's position, language results from rule-governed processes, and these processes account for the suddenness and complexity of the child's language development.

Theoretical debate concerning language development has enriched our considerations of how it occurs. Although it is unfortunate that so much energy has been expended in controversy and refutation, the value of different opinions should not be overlooked. Each of these theorists contributed substantially from his own position, and the various hypotheses will probably blend in some fashion in the future as we continue to unravel the process of normal language development.

Delayed Language Development

There is little question that language development is commonly delayed among those who are mentally retarded (see Cardoso-Martins, Mervis, & Mervis, 1985; Murdock & Hartmann, 1984). Scales to measure language development of the child with mental retardation specifically have not received widespread attention, although clinical assessment of language functioning has long been a concern (Snyder, 1988). Normative language development instrumentation is useful insofar as it helps to identify the extent of the delay or deficiency. Numerous language development scales have been constructed over the years (see Chapter 5). Some of these scales include the phonological (sound), semantic (meaning), morphological (word form), and syntactical (word order) skills acquired by normal children. All these areas of assessment are important in evaluating language development both for children who appear to be progressing normally and for those who exhibit delay. For the most part, language development scales focus on the period from birth to five or 10 years of age. Such instrumentation provides a useful armory for those concerned with language development and particularly delayed or deficient language development.

Delayed language development presents a difficult problem, particularly in our contemporary society. Exactly how delayed language relates to reduced intellectual functioning, or mental retardation, is unclear, although research continues (e.g., Smith & von Tetzchner, 1986). Delayed language development is not a simple characteristic. Hass and Hass (1972) drew some enlightening analogies. They suggested that the communicative plight of the severely retarded 10-year-old who has been institutionalized for several years might be likened to that of an English-speaking college student in France who finds that school-acquired French is not adequate for satisfactory communication. They further noted that such a 10-year-old child might be in somewhat the same position as an anthropologist in a newly discovered primitive culture who fails to communicate successfully with the inhabitants of this culture. Hass and Hass indicated that (1) all the college student must do is master some of the surface features of French, since the semantic representation and basic communication skills are already functional, and (2) the anthropologist may make significant progress based on theoretical background and experience. But the retarded child may well be faced with a very different problem. Such a child may have to construct the entire experiential organization and content on which linguistic and/or cognitive variations are based. The child's problem is infinitely more complex and difficult than that faced by the hypothetical college student or anthropologist.

Professionals have made efforts to counteract language delay in mentally retarded youngsters. Unfortunately, language rehabilitation efforts with this population in general lagged for many years because of the attitudes and perceptions of many speech and language specialists. A substantial number of such specialists have opposed working with the mentally retarded population on the grounds that speech and language rehabilitation is almost impossible for these individuals. Such attitudes, although regrettable, are somewhat understandable in view of some of the theories about language development. If one believes that language development is innate to humans, many children with mental retardation are inappropriate subjects for speech and language therapy, since language may not appear to be innate to them. Other theoretical schemes offer a more optimistic outlook for mentally retarded children. For example, B. F. Skinner's research provides a strong theoretical basis for working with children whose language skills fail to develop normally. Evidence is accumulating that language development during the early years is directly influenced by learning and social-experiential factors for children with mental retardation, just as it is for their normal peers. (Kaiser, Alpert, & Warren, 1987; Rondal, 1988).

A number of efforts at language rehabilitation for youngsters with mental retardation are based on Skinner's ideas. Several approaches have focused on the establishment of imitative repertoires in children with retardation in order to facilitate speech and language development. These procedures have often had promising results. Although details vary from technique to technique, major characteristics include the following:

1. Imitation apparently can be learned by children who initially did not have significant imitative behavioral repertoires.
2. Imitation combined with differential reinforcement can be used to train for both simple naming or labeling and generative repertoires of plurality, simple sentences, and verb tense usage.
3. Imitation can be regarded as a particular type of learning set that exemplifies the rule "Do as the model does."
4. Language development and consequent behavior that is rule-governed can be fairly directly related to the simple training procedures of differential reinforcement and fading, which teach a child to match a series of different behaviors that are modeled.
5. A child with a widely generalized imitative repertoire can be significantly influenced by language models in the environment. Such generalization is essential to the normal acquisition of speech and language.

Some of these results have prompted programming approaches to language development stimulation that may well alter the course of progress for the mentally retarded child (Guralnick & Bricker, 1987; Ramey & Campbell, 1987).

COGNITIVE DEVELOPMENT

Core Concept	*Cognitive development during infancy and early childhood involves many complex processes including some in areas where children with mental retardation have great difficulty.*

Cognitive development refers to an individual's developing capacity to formulate thoughts. Ordinarily, *perception* refers to sensory experiences received from the environment, whereas *cognition* is used for the meaning and thought patterns that emerge as a result of combinations of perceptions. The purposes of this book are well served by these definitions, although the explanations vary depending on the context and the authority consulted. In this section we discuss the work of selected theorists who have examined cognitive development and its implications for mental retardation.

Theoretical Formulations

One individual who contributed significantly to the theoretical consideration of cognitive development is Jean Piaget. We have already noted that his work, reviewed in previous chapters, has more recently come under heavy criticism (Flavell, 1982, 1985). Piaget's theoretical formulations remain worthy of discussion, however, particularly in the context of cognitive development. Unlike most theorists, Piaget was primarily interested in the functions and structures of intelligent activity rather than the content of intelligence per se. He outlined stages of intelligence development that change both quantitatively and qualitatively throughout the developmental period. It was Piaget's contention that, although different children progress through various stages at different rates, the sequence is always the same. Piaget's developmental stages are marked by the most recently emerging capability of the child. It is important to remember, however, that behaviors and processes preceding a given stage continue to occur and may be more intense and frequent than the newly emerging function.

Piaget's formulations provide an interesting framework from which to view cognitive development in children with mental retardation. It is speculated that these children, particularly those who are only mildly handicapped, do progress through Piaget's developmental stages, although their pace is somewhat slower than normal children's. The progression is demonstrable even though most individuals with retardation do not seem to develop spontaneously beyond Piaget's first two periods, sensorimotor and concrete operations. Thus children with mental retardation often have cognitive structures more typical of chronologically younger children.

From Piaget's perspective a child's cognitive capacities unfold naturally, although the influence of the environment is substantial. Through adaptation to the environment the child shapes the exact nature of structures that unfold. A child's readiness to develop the next sequence of intellectual structures is governed largely by neurological capacity or readiness, whereas the stimulus for actual progression into the next stage comes from the environment. This view of cognitive development appears to have important implications for teaching children with mental retardation, since education should present an environment that stimulates development of maximum potential. For Piaget, conceptualization of an idea precedes verbalization. In other words, children must experience and understand a phenomenon actively in the real world before they are able to put the event into words and demonstrate mastery of the problem. Children who have opportunities to encounter life experiences appropriate to their stage of cognitive development can be assisted in growth and development of cognitive potential through appropriate environmental stimulation (Sharav & Shlomo, 1986). As we continue sorting out the interactions between system maturation and the environment, we may find that developing cognitive abilities can be a more central focus of the teaching process than in the past (McCall, 1987).

Cognitive development in individuals with mental retardation has been of particular interest to behavioral scientists for many years. In 1944 Inhelder, for example, proposed a system of classifying people with retardation according to cognitive development. Inhelder believed that severely retarded individuals are fixated at the level of sensorimotor intelligence. If so, such individuals simply repeat over and over again the innate behaviors that are observed at birth with very little knowledge about the objects with which they interact. Those who advance further within the sensorimotor stage are more closely oriented to the world around them, recognize familiar objects, and demonstrate intentionality in their behavior. They may be able to use trial-and-error experimentation with objects in their environment to produce a novel effect. Assimilation and accommodation may be clearly differentiated, and the individual may actively seek new accommodational experiences. A limited ability to use symbols to represent events that are not directly in the individual's perceptual field is also a possibility, as well as the capacity to manipulate and combine these images or symbols. Such abilities may permit the use of rudimentary language and a beginning level of thinking and anticipation of events in the environment. Thus even though such individuals may be severely handicapped when compared to those of normal intelligence and similar chronological age, they possess certain remarkable capacities that provide potential for interacting with the environment and for learning.

Inhelder's classification scheme viewed people with moderate retardation as incapable of progressing beyond the preoperational intuitive subperiod. Such an individual could behave like a normal child who is about four to seven years old. The individual's functions might include the ability to grasp mentally a series of distinct and spatiotemporally separate events in succession. Inhelder would envision individuals with moderate retardation as being aware of their own thought processes and able to distinguish truth from fantasy. At this level the cognitive system can transcend time, space, and reality, and thus the capacity to think of past, present, and future exists at least to a limited degree. People who are moderately retarded are generally unable to conceptualize any other point of view from their own and remain basically egocentric. Their conceptualization of the symbols used to represent reality remains concrete, and they depend heavily on perceptual experiences to provide mental representation of events. Their attention typically focuses on the most immediate, interesting, and compelling attribute of an event, and they have a very limited ability to transfer attention voluntarily to another dimension of the situation. Similarly, persons with moderate retardation usually cannot mentally reverse an operation or an event in order to examine its components. They also exhibit a very limited capacity to reason logically. In general, people functioning at this level of development show many signs of ability to think and function much like an older child, for example, using language with reasonable effectiveness, getting along socially, adapting, and solving some problems (Strain, 1985). Their abilities are quite limited, however. Inhelder's and Piaget's descriptions have contributed to our understanding of cognitive difficulties that individuals in this particular stage of development encounter. The child who is chronologically of preschool age and who exhibits some of the linguistic or cognitive behaviors typical of this developmental stage is tolerated well by society. The cognitive "mistakes" of such a child are seen as amusing or as something that time will correct. The adult with retardation, however, who functions at the preoperational subperiod has similar cognitive traits but is tolerated to a much lesser degree. Such a person is expected to function at a much more advanced cognitive level, and the person's limitations frequently become distressing to others. More often than not, the abilities that have been developed or can be developed are overlooked.

From Inhelder's perspective the individual with mild retardation may be able to progress beyond the level of concrete operations, and those who previously were classified as borderline retarded may be able to use simpler forms of formal operations when they reach adulthood. A person functioning at this level is able to move beyond what is expected of the normal preschool-age child, to use well-organized cognitive systems that permit more effective coping with the environment. One significant development is overcoming the tendency to stumble into perplexity and contradiction in thought—a characteristic of the preschool child. Cognitive operations develop whereby the individual can engage in an advanced level of logic, establishing concepts and events of reality more systematically.

Implications for Professional Intervention

The specialist in early childhood education is perhaps the professional most intimately concerned with the cognitive development of the preschool child, whether that child has retardation or is of normal intelligence. The primary goal of early childhood education is to provide an environment that stimulates maximum social and cognitive development. We have already examined the important implications of early environment for the development of optimal intellectual functioning later in life. As children progress beyond the age of two, environmental stimulation appears to play a different role in their development. During the first two years, general stimulation in a wide variety of areas seems to affect individuals' ultimate level of functioning. For example, such factors as parental behavioral style and attitude, particularly the mother's, are strongly related to cognitive development (Berry & Gunn, 1984; Crockenberg, 1983; Mahoney, Finger, & Powell, 1985; McConachie & Mitchell, 1985; Rosenberg, Robinson, & Beckman, 1986). But as the child enters the preschool period at three, four, and five years of age, general sensory stimulation does not produce the same benefits. Instead, more specific experiences with particular and focused stimulation become influential in the child's progress. As expressed in Piaget's notions, conceptualization grows out of reality experiences, and the child develops the capacity to represent events symbolically both in thought and language. The objective of the early childhood education specialist is to provide specific tangible experiences that are consistent with the child's cognitive capacity and that stimulate development of cognitive structures. The initial challenge for the educational specialist working with a preschooler who has mental retardation is to understand the child's level of cognitive development. If, for example, the child is functioning at the sensorimotor stage but has potential for development into the preoperational thought period, the specialist may direct efforts toward preparing the child for preoperational thinking. The child may be given experiences with a variety of spatial problems, such as physical activities that provide a contrast between objects in the environment and the child, and a recognition of how these objects can be manipulated and experienced in a consistent, predictable manner. Through such techniques the education specialist may build a program for the young child that facilitates progression into the next cognitive stage of development. Early intervention programs are important to the developmental progression of young children with mental retardation (Casto & Mastropieri, 1986; Peterson, 1987).

PSYCHOSOCIAL DEVELOPMENT

Core Concept	*Developmental problems in social and emotional functioning can have a serious impact on a young child's ability to adapt and chances to succeed.*

The overall growth and development of a young child involves many different components. Each component is essential to the whole with respect to development, and each is interrelated in complex ways. Psychosocial development is a vital process for all young children regardless of intellectual capacity. The development of social and emotional functioning has pervasive effects on children's intellectual functioning: when children have a serious problem in psychosocial development, they are unlikely to be able to fulfill their intellectual potential. Thus the development of psychosocial functioning is of central concern. In what follows we explore several theoretical positions that have particular implications for development in the preschool period. We stress the implications of each theory for the potential intellectual functioning of children with normal intelligence as well as for preschool-aged children with mental retardation.

Theoretical Formulations

Theories of psychosocial development are somewhat different from those in other behavioral domains. In many cases the topics under discussion are extremely abstract, less specific with respect to behavioral definitions, and more difficult to measure (Peterson, 1987). But this does not detract from the importance of considering them; few would deny that these abstract concepts represent some behavioral reality.

Development of Trust, Autonomy, and Initiative
Erik H. Erikson viewed child development primarily from a psychoanalytical perspective. Erikson (1968) hypothesized that infancy is the time of the child's first social achievement—basic trust. To the extent that his or her parents provide nurturance, familiarity, security, and continuity of experience, an infant can develop a basic sense of trust in both the immediate environment and the people in it. An infant's behavior reflects constant testing, experimenting, and exploring of the world in order to discover its predictability or the extent to which it can be trusted. Erikson believed that when an adequate mothering relationship is not present, an infant develops a sense of mistrust of the environment and the people in it. He also contended that such an experience is irreversible and influences the evolution of all subsequent stages. Clearly all infants experience trust and mistrust to some degree; it is the predominance of one over another that is critical for successful completion of this first stage.

Development of autonomy and initiative are involved in Erikson's depiction of emotional development during early childhood. Initially children undergo a struggle to attain autonomy and a sense of self and of separateness. As part of this process, they must overcome the hazards of doubt and shame. They learn to exercise control over the processes of having and letting go. The family environment offers restraint and freedom in an appropriate balance to permit young children to experiment without becoming the victims of indiscriminate use of the abilities to hold on and to let go. As this process evolves, children begin to develop a sense of autonomy, which is important in further development of independent functioning.

Erikson also conceived of a second stage in early childhood, which begins at about the end of the third year. This stage involves the struggle to gain a sense of initiative and to overcome the perils of guilt. The difference between this and the establishment of autonomy is likened to the difference between knowing oneself and knowing one's potential. Now children develop a sense of conscience, which is the regulatory or control function of the personality. If this function is overdeveloped, they may become too inhibited and even self-destructive, with a diminished capacity for creativity and initiative. As with all developmental processes, the desirable outcome is dominance of the positive task.

Development of Attachment

Attachment behavior is yet another important emotional component of personality with great implications for future development. Infancy is a crucial period for the emergence of this behavior (Peterson, 1987; Thoman, 1987). As attachment evolves, the reciprocal behaviors of the mother and other significant individuals are often caretaking behaviors. The infant's behavior reflects efforts to maintain proximity to the mother first and then to other members of the family who, in turn, reciprocate the expressed needs for proximity. There are many specific ways in which an older infant maintains proximity, although five basic patterns emerge: sucking, clinging, following, crying, and smiling. Some of these behaviors are evident at birth but are manifested as self-directed attachment behavior at about the age of four months. As development progresses, an infant exhibits sophisticated goal-directed systems of behavior to maintain proximity to the mother. These systems of behavior usually become apparent between nine and 18 months.

Visual and tactile contact are crucial for the development of attachment behavior. The nature of visual and tactile interactions provides an important indication of the adequacy of attachment formation. Using the mother as a base of security from which to operate, the infant explores the larger world but maintains visual contact during the process. Tactile contact is periodically reestablished, and then exploration continues. When the child becomes frightened, distressed, or uncomfortable for any reason, he or she tries to stay close to the mother by such stratagems as clinging and following. When a serious threat of separation occurs, intense anxiety, anger, and violent distress result. These feelings and behaviors remain strong throughout infancy and are highly apparent throughout early childhood, although they begin to lessen in intensity.

Environmental Antecedents to Self-Esteem

Interest in developing a better understanding of the influence of environmental factors on emotional and social development has been great. In this area theories typically have not been oriented toward child development, although their logical implications for infants and young children are clear (Guralnick & Bennett, 1987). Early theorists have suggested that individuals need a psychological atmosphere of unconditional positive regard in order to develop to their full potential (e.g., Rogers, 1951). This type of atmosphere must come from the significant others in the environment and involves total and unconditional acceptance of the feelings and values of the young child. It does not, however, mean that others must always agree with the child; they must only accept the feelings and values as real to the child. Evaluative comparison, rejecting judgments, lack of trust, and harsh punishment lead to the development of underlying doubts of worthiness and competence on the part of the child and may block the development of self-esteem, acceptance, and assurance.

The role of parents and other family members in early development of self-esteem is extremely important. Children whose families give them the feeling that they mean a lot to their parents tend to develop high levels of self-esteem. Parental attention and concern, as well as restrictions on behavior, can convey such feelings. In this type of familial environment the children are made aware of their successes, and they experience frequent success in their efforts toward development and learning. But children in these families are also made aware of situations in which they have not succeeded and are encouraged to develop the behavioral changes needed to achieve success and approval. High self-esteem seems to be related to a high level of stimulation, activity, and vigor in the family. Typically there is a high level of communication among members of the family, including differences of opinion, dissent, and disagreement, leading to the development of mutual knowledge and respect.

Implications for Intellectual Functioning

Many of the factors of major concern in psychosocial development are also important components of intellectual functioning. For example, the role of early stimulation is immediately apparent in both psychosocial and intellectual domains. Personality theorists focus on the crucial relationship of the infant or young child with at least one significant adult who provides the necessary care and love for the child. The child receives this adult's attention and affection primarily through the sensory channels that are so critical in the development of intellectual functioning. Thus it appears that there must be a significant interaction or interdependence between the development of psychosocial and intellectual functions, although the precise nature of this relationship is not yet known. Children who are victims of potential restriction of intellectual development through environmental deprivation are also likely to exhibit signs of attenuated emotional development. Such concomitant developmental inadequacies may be evident simply because of missing elements in the vital stimulation of sensory modalities. A child who is unable to develop adequate emotional security, self-esteem, or social relationships with family members and peers is also likely to be inhibited in intellectual performance. Whether the inhibiting influence becomes permanent or significant is probably a result of interaction among a number of as yet nebulous factors. But supporting optimal psychological development in early life probably has a favorable influence on the child's ability to function intellectually.

There is relatively little understanding of specific psychosocial development in the infant or preschooler with mental retardation. These children seem to show developmental lags in the psychosocial features examined, since they remain dependent and relatively immature in social interactions for a prolonged period. It is not clear, however, whether this developmental lag arises from the intimately related neurological bases for both areas of development or whether there is an environmentally generated psychosocial delay arising from lack of interaction with significant adults. Evidence suggests that sociometric status ratings by preschoolers' nonhandicapped peers is related to their prosocial behavior (Strain, 1985). It seems reasonable to assume that the young child with mental retardation might exhibit a psychosocial delay similar to Piaget's cognitive ones. All efforts possible should be made to sustain an optimal level of psychosocial development for the child with mental retardation.

Professional Intervention

Psychosocial development is no less important for the child with mental retardation than for the child of normal intelligence. Professionals working with children who have retardation must be as concerned with this area of development as they are with cognitive domains (Slavenas, 1985). Such a child may be particularly at risk in terms of adverse environmental influences on emotional development because of unfavorable parental reactions. The family may need assistance from mental-health specialists (psychologist, psychiatrist, psychiatric social worker) to facilitate the maintenance of optimal mental health and development for all family members. Both parents and child may have glaring needs. Professionals may provide short-term assistance and intervention during periods of crisis, such as at the time of the child's birth, when the diagnosis of mental retardation is confirmed, or during periods of intense physical, social, or emotional stress in the family. Long-term assistance or intervention may be needed if the family experiences unusual or prolonged stress leading to disorganization of the family unit. It may be difficult for the family to accept such assistance since it threatens the emotional integrity of the family unit and the individual members. Accepting assistance often means recognizing a need that is most difficult to acknowledge and, for many families, represents a weakness or failure that they shun. Friends, health-care professionals, and educators should be alert to signs of need for mental-health intervention and should help the family accept such assistance.

In many cases mental retardation is not apparent at birth. Under such circumstances the family often becomes aware of the child's handicap during the first months or years of life. It is not uncommon for the family to experience particular stress and crisis as members seek to allay their fears, restore their hopes for the normal, healthy baby they thought they had, and reach some level of resolution concerning the reality of the situation. The longer the family has lived with the belief that the child is healthy and normal, the more difficult the adjustment. Chapters 9 and 13 discuss further the difficult emotional problems that families of retarded children experience.

NEW ISSUES AND FUTURE DIRECTIONS

A discussion of infancy and early childhood would be incomplete without some attention to the effectiveness of early intervention programs aimed at enhancing children's development. This is particularly true for children with mental retardation and other children who are at risk for handicap or developmental delay. Interpretation of early intervention outcomes, however, is not an easy task. The expectations placed on such widespread undertakings as Head Start were in retrospect probably unrealistic. But this does not mean that such programs or other early stimulation approaches are ineffective. Overall analyses of the influence of early intervention suggests substantial gains for both at-risk and handicapped youngsters (Casto & Mastropieri, 1986; Casto & White, 1985). Interpretations of individual studies must be viewed cautiously, and broad, sweeping generalizations about effects from such limited evidence are suspect (Guralnick & Bennett, 1987). Still, enthusiasm about the worth of early intervention remains high among those most knowledgeable about early childhood development (e.g., Caldwell, 1987). We anticipate that early intervention programs will flourish in the future even as more caution is exercised with respect to expectations.

Parents have become increasingly active partners in early intervention promoting the development of handicapped and at-risk children. They have moved from an ancillary role to more central involvement in collaborative planning and implementation of many aspects of intervention with their children. Comprehensive planning now includes the development of an individualized family service plan (IFSP), which considers the child's needs in the context of overall family needs and dynamics (Hardman, Drew, Egan, & Wolf, 1990). In the future treatment and other interventions for young children with mental retardation will more centrally involve parents and other family members.

Future directions and issues for the young child with mental retardation also include important contributions from the medical field. Medical technology for this group of youngsters, like others, is developing at a dramatic pace. Medical management of these children continues to require attention to their higher incidence of chronic health problems—seizures, congenital abnormalities, and susceptibility to infectious diseases. Research and development efforts in drug therapy, nutrition, and surgery (for example, repair of birth defects, shunt implantations, and so on) will continue to have a significant impact on infants and young children with mental retardation. Some medical treatments are unconventional in the sense that they are either experimental or raise ethical questions and controversy. One such procedure involves facial surgery with Down syndrome children for cosmetic purposes and also to improve oral function (aiding speech). The appearance normalization aspect of this technique has raised questions on the part of some who believe it unnecessary. Perhaps even more unconventional is the application of cell therapy with Down syndrome children. This procedure involves the injection of fresh fetal lamb brain tissue into the young child. Proponents claim dramatic alteration of developmental characteristics; others note that evidence for such change is not available and urge caution because of potentially serious allergic reactions (Pruess & Fewell, 1985). While such procedures may seem so unusual as to stretch our imagination, it is important to remember that altering genetic material was similarly unthinkable only a few years ago.

CORE QUESTIONS

1. How does the brain develop during infancy and early childhood?
2. How can one trace the development of myelinization from a behavioral standpoint in very young children?

3. How does the early development of sensory organs influence a young child's learning?
4. How might environmental deprivation of stimuli affect the cognitive development of young children and result in mental retardation?
5. How are parents potentially important in early childhood intervention programs?
6. How do Chomsky, Lenneberg, and Skinner differ in their theories of language development?
7. How is early sensory stimulation important for both emotional and intellectual development?
8. How do parents and other family members influence the development of self-esteem? How can they create an environment that promotes realistic views of self-worth for a young child?
9. How does Inhelder's view of mental retardation limit the development of moderately retarded individuals?
10. How would Piaget see the cognitive developmental progress of individuals with and without mental retardation as the same?

ROUND TABLE DISCUSSION

Human development during infancy and early childhood is extremely important. Much that occurs at this stage of life provides a foundation for many later skills and abilities. Physiological systems are developing, and they interact with aspects of cognition, language, and social development in a complex fashion that ultimately comes together to present an individual's sum potential.

In your study group or on your own, examine how physiological growth and development relate to language, cognition, and social competence. Explore the role of the environment during this time, including aspects of parental interaction and behavior. Examine how parents can be important interveners and also how they might contribute to mental retardation in a child. Describe how you might discuss early childhood development with potential parents in order to facilitate their lives as parents and field-based developmental specialists.

REFERENCES

Affleck, G., Tennen, H., & Gershman, K. (1985). Cognitive adaptations to high-risk infants: The search for mastery, meaning, and protection from future harm. *American Journal of Mental Deficiency, 89,* 653–656.

Allen, D. A., Affleck, G., McGrade, B. J., & McQueeney, M. (1984). Factors in the effectiveness of early childhood intervention for low socioeconomic status families. *Education and Training of the Mentally Retarded, 19,* 254–260.

American Academy of Pediatrics (1971). *Standards of child health care. Council on Pediatric Practice.* Evanston, IL: Author.

Berger, J., & Cunningham, C. C. (1986). Aspects of early social smiling by infants with Down's syndrome. *Child Care, Health and Development, 12,* 13–24.

Berry, P., & Gunn, P. (1984). Maternal influence on the task behaviour of young Down's syndrome children. *Journal of Mental Deficiency Research, 28,* 269–274.

Bruder, M. B. (1987). Parent-to-parent teaching. *American Journal of Mental Deficiency, 91,* 435–438.

Bryant, D. M., & Ramey, C. T. (1987). An analysis of the effectiveness of early intervention programs for environmentally at-risk children. In M. J. Guralnick & F. C. Bennett (Eds.), *The effectiveness of early intervention for at-risk and handicapped children* (pp. 33–78). Orlando, FL: Academic.

Burns, K. A., Deddish, R. B., Burns, W. J., & Hatcher, R. P. (1983). Use of oscillating waterbeds and rhythmic sounds for premature infant stimulation. *Developmental Psychology, 19,* 746–751.

Cahalane, S. F. (1989). Screening for genetic disease. In G. B. Reed, A. E. Claireaux, & A. D. Bain (Eds.), *Diseases of the fetus and newborn: Pathology, radiology and genetics* (pp. 599–614). St. Louis: C.V. Mosby.

Caldwell, B. M. (1987). Sustaining intervention effects: Putting malleability to the test. In J. J. Gallagher & C. T. Ramey (Eds.), *The malleability of children* (pp. 115–125). Baltimore: Paul H. Brookes.

Cardoso-Martins, C., Mervis, C. B., & Mervis, C. A. (1985). Early vocabulary by children with Down syndrome. *American Journal of Mental Deficiency, 90,* 177–184.

Casto, G., & Mastropieri, M. A. (1986). The efficacy of early intervention programs: A meta-analysis. *Exceptional Children, 52,* 417–424.

Casto, G., & White, K. (1985). The efficacy of early intervention programs with environmentally at-risk infants. In M. Frank (Ed.), *Infant intervention programs: Truths and untruths* (pp. 37–50). New York: Haworth.

Chomsky, N. (1957). *Syntactic structures.* The Hague: Mouton.

Crockenberg, S. (1983). Early mother and infant antecedents of Bayley Scale performance at 21 months. *Developmental Psychology, 19,* 727–730.

Erikson, E. H. (1968). *Identity, youth and crisis.* New York: W.W. Norton.

Flavell, J. H. (1982). Structures, stages, and sequences in cognitive development. In W. A. Collins (Ed.), *The concept of development: The Minnesota symposia on child psychology* (Vol. XV). Hillsdale, NJ: Lawrence Erlbaum.

Flavell, J. H. (1985). *Cognitive development.* Englewood Cliffs, NJ: Prentice-Hall.

Garber, H., & Heber, R. F. (1977). The Milwaukee Project: Indications of the effectiveness of early intervention in preventing mental retardation. In P. Mittler (Ed.), *Research to practice in mental retardation: Care and intervention* (Vol. 1, pp. 119–127). Baltimore: University Park Press.

Gesell, A. (1941). *Wolf child and human child.* New York: Harper & Brothers.

Goldberg, S., Marcovitch, S., MacGregor, D., & Lojkasek, M. (1986). Family responses to developmentally delayed preschoolers: Etiology and the father's role. *American Journal of Mental Deficiency, 90,* 610–617.

Greenberg, D., Uzgiris, I. C., & Hunt, J. McV. (1968). Hastening the development of the blink response with looking. *Journal of General Psychology, 113,* 167–176.

Gregory, R. L., & Wallace, J. G. (1963). Recovery from early blindness. *Experimental Psychology Monograph* (Whole No. 2).

Guralnick, M. J., & Bennett, F. C. (1987). Early intervention for at-risk and handicapped children: Current and future perspectives. In M. J. Guralnick & F. C. Bennett (Eds.), *The effectiveness of early intervention for at-risk and handicapped children* (pp. 365–382). Orlando, FL: Academic.

Guralnick, M. J., & Bricker, D. (1987). The effectiveness of early intervention for children with cognitive and general developmental delays. In M. J. Guralnick & F. C. Bennett (Eds.), *The effectiveness of early intervention for at-risk and handicapped children* (pp. 115–173). Orlando, FL: Academic.

Hardman, M. L., Drew, C. J., Egan, M. W., & Wolf, B. (1990). *Human exceptionality: Society, school, and family* (3rd ed.). Boston: Allyn & Bacon.

Hass, W. A., & Hass, S. K. (1972). Syntactic structure and language development in retardates. In R. L. Schiefelbusch (Ed.), *Language of the mentally retarded* (pp. 321–342). Baltimore: University Park Press.

Hebb, D. O. (1949). *The organization of behavior.* New York: John Wiley & Sons.

Heber, R. F., Dever, R. B., & Conry, J. (1968). The influence of environmental and genetic variables on intellectual development. In H. J. Prehm, L. A. Hamerlynck, & J. E. Crosson (Eds.), *Behavioral research in mental retardation* (pp. 1–23). Eugene: University of Oregon Press.

Heber, R. F., & Garber, H. (1971). An experiment in prevention of cultural-familial mental retardation. In D. A. Primrose (Ed.), *Proceedings of the Second Congress of the International Association for the Scientific Study of Mental Deficiency* (pp. 31–35). Warsaw: Polish Medical Publishers.

Heber, R. F., Garber, H., Harrington, S., Hoffman, C., & Falendar, C. (1972). *Rehabilitation of families at risk for mental retardation: Progress report.* Madison: University of Wisconsin Press.

Inhelder, B. (1944). *Le diagnostic du raisonnement chez les débiles mentaux.* Neuchâtel, Switzerland: Delachaux et Niestle.

Kaiser, A. P., Alpert, C. L., & Warren, S. (1987). Teaching functional language: Strategies for language intervention. In M. E. Snell (Ed.), *Systematic instruction of persons with severe handicaps* (pp. 247–272). Columbus, OH: Charles E. Merrill.

Lenneberg, E. H. (1969). On explaining language. *Science, 164,* 635–643.

Levine, M. D., & Jordan, N. C. (1987). Neurodevelopmental dysfunctions: Their cumulative interactions and effects in middle childhood. In J. J. Gallagher & C. T. Ramey (Eds.), *The malleability of children* (pp. 141–154). Baltimore: Paul H. Brookes.

London, I. A. (1960). Russian report on the post-operative newly seeing. *American Journal of Psychology, 73,* 478–482.

Mahoney, G., Finger, I., & Powell, A. (1985). Relationship of maternal behavioral style to the development of organically impaired mentally retarded infants. *American Journal of Mental Deficiency, 90,* 296–302.

Mason, M. K. (1942). Learning to speak after six and one-half years of silence. *Journal of Speech Disorders, 7,* 295–304.

McCall, R. B. (1987). Developmental function, individual differences, and the plasticity of intelligence. In J. J. Gallagher & C. T. Ramey (Eds.), *The malleability of children* (pp. 25–35). Baltimore: Paul H. Brookes.

McConachie, H., & Mitchell, D. R. (1985). Parents teaching their young mentally handicapped children. *Journal of Child Psychology and Psychiatry and Allied Disciplines, 26,* 389–405.

McConkey, R., & Martin, H. (1983). Mothers' play with toys: A longitudinal study with Down's syndrome infants. *Child Care, Health and Development, 9,* 215–226.

Murdock, J. Y., & Hartmann, B. (1984). *Communication and language intervention program (CLIP) for the moderately to severely impaired.* Springfield, IL: Charles C. Thomas.

Ottinger, D. R., Blatchley, M. E., & Dennenberg, V. (1969). *Stimulation of human neonates and visual attentiveness.* Paper presented at the meeting of the American Psychological Association, Washington, DC.

Pennington, B. F., van Doorninck, W. J., McCabe, L. L., & McCabe, E. R. B. (1985). Neuropsychological deficits in early treated phenylketonuric children. *American Journal of Mental Deficiency, 89,* 467–474.

Peterson, N. L. (1987). *Early intervention for handicapped and at-risk children.* Denver: Love Publishing.

Pruess, J. B., & Fewell, R. R. (1985). Cell therapy and the treatment of Down syndrome: A review of research. *Trisomy 21, a*(1), 3–8.

Ramey, C. T., & Campbell, F. A. (1987). The Carolina Abecedarian project: An educational experiment concerning human malleability. In J. J. Gallagher & C. T. Ramey (Eds.), *The malleability of children* (pp. 127–139). Baltimore: Paul H. Brookes.

Rogers, C. R. (1951). *Client-centered therapy: Its current practice, implications and theory.* Boston: Houghton Mifflin.

Rondal, J. A. (1988). Language development in Down's syndrome: A life-span perspective. *International Journal of Behavioral Development, 11,* 21–36.

Rosenberg, S. A., Robinson, C. C., & Beckman, P. (1986). Measures of parent-infant interaction: An overview. *Topics in Early Childhood Special Education, 6*(2), 32–43.

Scarr, S., & Arnett, J. (1987). Malleability: Lessons from intervention and family studies. In J. J. Gallagher & C. T. Ramey (Eds.), *The malleability of children* (pp. 71–84). Baltimore: Paul H. Brookes.

Sharav, T., & Shlomo, L. (1986). Stimulation of infants with Down syndrome: Long-term effects. *Mental Retardation, 24,* 81–86.

Skeels, H. M., & Dye, H. B. (1939). A study of the effects of differential stimulation. *Proceedings of the American Association on Mental Deficiency, 44,* 114–136.

Skinner, B. F. (1957). *Verbal behavior.* New York: Appleton-Century-Crofts.

Slater, M. A. (1986). Modification of mother-child interaction processes in families with children at-risk for mental retardation. *American Journal of Mental Deficiency, 91,* 257–267.

Slavenas, R. (1985). Classroom assessment of socialization. *Early Child Development and Care, 20,* 325–332.

Smith, L., & von Tetzchner, S. (1986). Communicative, sensorimotor, and language skills of young children with Down syndrome. *American Journal of Mental Deficiency, 91,* 57–66.

Snyder, M. L. (1988). Clinical assessment of sensorimotor knowledge in nonverbal, severely retarded clients. *Topics in Language Disorders, 8*(4), 1–22.

Strickland, S. R. (1971). Can slum children learn? *American Education, 7*(6), 3–7.

Strain, P. S. (1985). Social and nonsocial determinants of acceptability in handicapped preschool children. *Topics in Early Childhood Special Education, 4*(4), 47–58.

Thoman, E. B. (1987). Self-regulation of stimulation by prematures with a breathing blue bear. In J. J. Gallagher & C. T. Ramey (Eds.), *The malleability of children* (pp. 51–69). Baltimore: Paul H. Brookes.

White, B. L. (1967). *An experimental approach to the effects of experience on early human behavior.* Paper presented at the meeting of the Minnesota Symposium on Child Psychology, Minneapolis.

PART THREE

The Retarded Child During the School Years

CHAPTER NINE

The Elementary-School Age Child with Mental Retardation

■ Problems associated with mental retardation become a reality for children during the school years.

■ For children with moderate to profound mental retardation, deficits in intellectual and social functioning are evident before the school years.

■ Piaget described the intellectual development of the child in terms of stages or periods of intellectual growth.

■ The memory capabilities of children with mental retardation are deficient in comparison with their nonretarded peers'.

■ Distributed practice in a learning situation enhances the learning performance of children with mental retardation.

■ Children with mental retardation are able to grasp concrete concepts in a learning situation much better than abstract concepts.

■ Children with mental retardation develop learning sets at a slower rate than their nonretarded peers.

■ Most children with mental retardation benefit from instruction in the basic academic tool subjects.

■ Adaptive behavior deficiencies in school settings are associated with coping behavior, social skills, language development, emotional development, self-care, and applied cognitive and academic skills.

■ A child's problems in school-related settings are often compounded by inadequate social development.

■ Individuals with mental retardation are able to participate and be actively involved in their own local communities.

■ The more severe the mental retardation, the greater the probability that the child will exhibit physical problems.

■ Several environmental factors can contribute to health problems for children with mental retardation.

■ The national mandate for the education of handicapped children clearly indicates placement in the least restrictive environment.

■ Regular class placement with support services includes both the consulting teacher and resource room models.

■ Students with mental retardation may be educated in either part-time or full-time special education classrooms in the regular school building.

■ Special schools, although administratively convenient, do not provide critical opportunities for interaction between children with mental retardation and their nonretarded peers.

■ For students with mental retardation, learning in the school setting is a continual process of adaptation.

■ Instruction in academic areas may include both a foundation and/or functional approach to learning.

- Adaptive skills are necessary to decrease an individual's dependence on others and increase opportunities for school and community participation.

- Culturally different children with mental retardation need an educational experience that focuses on learning how to learn.

- In the future, educational reform efforts that focus on individualization in the schools and the effectiveness of social integration will benefit students with mental retardation.

Core Concept	*Problems associated with mental retardation become a reality for children during the school years.*

The beginning of elementary school is generally an exciting time for both children and their parents. It is a time to make new friends and begin associations. And even for the nonretarded child, the beginning of school is filled with uncertainty as well as anticipation. For children with mental retardation and their families, this may be the beginning of their difficulties with mental retardation. For many parents the problems of mental retardation first become a reality when their child enters school. Using the AAMR classification system (Grossman, 1983), the six-year-old child with mild mental retardation may have a developmental lag of only about one year. This maturational lag may have been so slight during early childhood that it was viewed as insignificant or not even noticed by the parents and family physician. This often happens when there are no physical or health problems. The child's difficulties surface when he or she is confronted with the academic and social demands of the school environment, and may become compounded if there is not proper educational assessment. A teacher may attribute difficulties to immaturity and not refer the child for specialized services during early primary grades.

Core Concept	*For children with moderate to profound mental retardation, deficits in intellectual and social functioning are evident before the school years.*

Whereas deficits associated with mild mental retardation may not be apparent by the time the child enters school, problems characterizing moderate, severe, and profound retardation are clearly evident. The term *education* takes on an entirely different meaning for these children. Before the legislative mandates of the 1970s, many children with moderate to profound retardation were excluded from public education programs because they were unable to meet the system's academic or social requirements. A different set of values has emerged for the 1990s, and it establishes a new goal for public education: raising the functioning level of the child to the next highest developmental level regardless of the severity of the disorder. For children with severe mental retardation the emphasis is not on academic learning, but on the development of skills that increase independence within the school, home, and community (for example, self-help skills, mobility, and communication). In this chapter we use the term *school-age child* to refer to a child in first through seventh or eighth grade.

Intellectual development, learning, personality, emotional development, motivational problems, and physical health characteristics of children with mental retardation and related theories are discussed in this chapter. In most instances these characteristics and theories are not limited to school-age children with mental retardation, but may follow the individual throughout life. We have elected to present these characteristics in this chapter, however, since it is often at the beginning of the school program that many of them initially manifest themselves to the professional working with the individual with mental retardation.

COGNITIVE DEVELOPMENT

Core Concept	*Piaget described the intellectual development of the child in terms of stages or periods of intellectual growth.*

To gain some understanding of the cognitive development of the school-age child, we briefly return to the theory of Jean Piaget. Piaget referred to the span from two to seven years as the period of preoperational thought and the span from seven to 11 years as the period of concrete operations. A few of the younger school-age children are completing the preoperational thought period; most function in the concrete operations period.

During the preoperations subperiod, perceptions are the child's dominant mental activity. At about the age of seven years, the child begins to move into a period in which perceptions are dominated by intellectual operations, the dominant mental activity of the concrete operations period. The ability to order and relate experiences to an organized whole begins to develop. Rather than being bound to irreversibility, as before, the child begins to develop mobility in thought processes and can reverse some mental operations and return to the starting point.

By four years old, the child is less self-centered and more able to take into account another person's point of view. Instead of centering on a one-dimensional property of a situation, the child is able to focus on several properties in sequence and move quickly from one to another.

This phase is termed concrete because the child's mental operations still depend on the ability to perceive concretely what has happened. No mental experimentation can take place without prior perception. The basic ability from which concrete operations develop is the ability mentally to form ordering structures, which Piaget called groupings and lattices. Lattices are a special form of groupings in which the focus is on the connection between two or more objects and the objects that are connected. Using lattices, the child can develop a classification hierarchy system in which he or she can understand that all humans are animals, but not all animals are human.

Children begin to be able to conserve number around the age of seven years, to conserve quantity (substance, amount of space occupied by an object) around ages seven or eight years, and to conserve weight around nine years of age.

During the preoperational period the child's egocentrism is evident in conversations with other children. During this developmental period conversations with other children the same age consist of collective monologues. Each child pursues a private, personal conversation regardless of what the other child says. During the concrete operational period, however, these children begin to take into account the other child's point of view and incorporate these views into their own conversations. Thus more meaningful communication emerges, and the children carry on dialogue, each responding to what the other has just said (Piaget, 1969).

This youngster is clearly progressing academically although more slowly than her peers who do not have mental retardation.

Children with mental retardation move through the same states of development as their nonretarded peers, but at a slower rate (Inhelder, 1968; Woodward, 1979). School-age children with mild mental retardation are slower in progressing from the preoperational stage into concrete operations, with delays as long as three to four years. Moderately retarded children may fixate at the preoperational level and not reach even the most basic stages of concrete operations until later adolescence. Children who are severely and profoundly retarded may fixate at the sensorimotor and preoperational stages and never reach the more advanced periods.

LEARNING CHARACTERISTICS

When we compare children with mental retardation to their nonretarded age-mates, we find that these children perform more poorly on tasks of learning and retention. Research on learning and mental retardation has increased dramatically since the early 1950s, but our understanding of how these individuals learn still needs considerable expansion.

In this section we discuss the learning characteristics of children with mental retardation. In addition, our attention is directed not only to the pertinent research in this area but also to some of its implications for classroom practice.

Memory

Core Concept	*The memory capabilities of children with mental retardation are deficient in comparison with their nonretarded peers'.*

The greater the severity of intellectual deficit, the greater the deficits in memory. Memory problems in children with mental retardation have been attributed to several factors. Some researchers have suggested that these deficits are associated with an inability to focus on relevant stimuli in a learning situation (Agran, Salzberg, & Stow-itchek, 1987; Mercer & Snell, 1977; Payne, Polloway, Smith, & Payne, 1981). Others postulate that children with mental retardation may be deficient in the development of learning sets (Borkowski & Day, 1987; Hallahan & Reeve, 1980). Frank and Rabinovitch (1974) stated that these children have inefficient rehearsal strategies that interfere with memory. Hardman and Drew (1975) suggested that children with mental retardation are unable to benefit from incidental learning cues in their environment. Additionally, these children may not be able to transfer knowledge effectively to new tasks or situations (Agran et al., 1987; Mercer & Snell, 1977; Payne et al., 1981; Stephens, 1972).

Literature on the memory of learned material strongly indicates that ability is related to type of retention task. The short-term memory of individuals with mental retardation, that is, the ability to recall material over a period of seconds or minutes, has long been a topic of interest. Early work in the area drew a somewhat confusing picture. Some evidence suggested that the short-term memory performance of children with mental retardation is no different from that of nonretarded individuals (Drew &

Prehm, 1970; Logan, Prehm, & Drew, 1968), whereas other researchers obtained results that indicate inferior performance by people with mental retardation (Borkowski, Peck, & Damberg, 1983; Brown, 1974; Butterfield, Wambold, & Belmont, 1973; Ellis, 1970). Probably the most programmatic research on short-term memory has been conducted in the laboratories at the University of Alabama. This work has fairly consistently indicated difficulties in short-term memory for individuals with mental retardation across the various levels of severity (Ellis, 1970). Zeaman and House (1979) have suggested that a high level of distractibility by external and irrelevant stimuli is also associated with short-term memory difficulties that people with mental retardation have. The child with mental retardation may take longer to understand the nature of a task than nonretarded age-mates. Several authors have suggested procedures that could be used in the classroom to compensate for these deficiencies (Clinton & Evans, 1972; Fisher & Zeaman, 1973; Mercer & Snell, 1977; Smith, 1968). The following procedures are among those that enhance short-term memory skills in children with mental retardation:

1. Reduce extraneous environmental stimuli, which tend to distract students and increase stimulus value of the task.
2. Present each component of stimuli clearly and with equivalent stimulus value initially.
3. Begin with simpler tasks, moving to the more complex.
4. Avoid irrelevant materials within the learning task.
5. Label stimuli.
6. Minimize reinforcement to avoid interference from anticipation of reward.
7. Provide practice in short-term memory activities.
8. Integrate practice material with new subject fields, making use of the child's successful experiences.
9. Dramatize skills involving short-term memory, making them methodologically central to the program.

Studies of long-term memory in persons with mental retardation are even less conclusive than those on short-term memory. Several researchers have obtained results suggesting that, on long-term memory tasks, retarded and nonretarded subjects do not perform differently (Cantor & Ryan, 1962; Jensen & Rohwer, 1963). Ellis (1963, 1970) has consistently contended that long-term memory is equal between retarded and nonretarded persons, although his attention to this area has been secondary to his major research on short-term memory. Other research has indicated that long-term memory performance is inferior for persons with mental retardation (Drew & Prehm, 1970; Logan et al., 1968).

As is evident from the preceding discussion, a substantial portion of the memory research with children who are retarded has been couched in terms of short-term and long-term memory. Much of the current thinking in cognitive psychology has moved away from a simple view focusing on memory time interval to an information-processing model. Linton (1980) described information processing in the following manner:

These (current) theories focus on the successive processing steps that information entering an organism undergoes. As you read the words on this page, for example, you are acting as an information processor. Words are perceived and attended to, patterns are recognized, meanings are accessed/retrieved, and some material is stored. Throughout such normal processing, information must be stored, sometimes only for a few moments (so that further processing can occur) and sometimes relatively permanently. (pp. 105–106)

Bray (1979) reviewed research on individuals with mental retardation in the context of an information-processing framework. He found that much of the cognitive research in mental retardation was conceptualized from an information-processing perspective even though early investigators lacked a formal model.

Distribution of Practice

Core Concept	*Distributed practice in a learning situation enhances the learning performance of children with mental retardation.*

Whereas many individuals appear to be able to function well by using massed practice, such as cramming for examinations, distributed practice, compared with mass practice, enhances the learning performance of children with mental retardation more than it does for normal individuals (Madsen, 1963). The teacher should give the child who is retarded short but frequent practice sessions on day-to-day tasks. The teacher should also allow for practice in a variety of situations and contexts and for the meaningful introduction of overlearning. This should result not only in an increased rate of acquisition but also should ensure a greater degree of retention.

Learning Concrete and Abstract Concepts

Core Concept	*Children with mental retardation are able to grasp concrete concepts in a learning situation much better than abstract concepts.*

The more concrete the material, the more apt the child with mental retardation is to learn. The teacher or parent may be advised to teach nothing with inanimate objects if the real, living object is available. Likewise it might be said that we should teach nothing indoors if we can teach the same thing outdoors. The child with mental retardation will grasp concepts more readily if the real object is present rather than a picture of the object. Instead of reading and looking at pictures of firefighters and their equipment, the child with mental retardation may learn more and faster on a field trip to a fire station.

Learning Sets and Transfer of Training

Core Concept	*Children with mental retardation develop learning sets at a slower rate than their nonretarded peers.*

Learning set and transfer of training appear to be interrelated in a person's ability to solve problems. Whereas *learning set* refers to an individual's ability to learn how to learn, *transfer* is generally regarded as the ability to apply learned responses and experiences from previous problems to new problems with similar components. Children with mental retardation develop learning sets at a slower rate than nonretarded children of comparable chronological age (Agran et al., 1987; Payne et al., 1981). The formation of learning sets can, however, be facilitated in the classroom. Payne et al. (1981) offered the following suggestions:

1. Prevent the development of failure sets that interfere with learning by providing for success experiences.
2. Present content to be learned in easy-to-hard progressions.
3. Present factual and conceptual information in sequence.
4. Assist the child in developing rules and generalizations (mediation strategies) to transfer learned information to new experiences.
5. Reinforce correct responses to stress successful experiences. (p. 29)

Although transfer of training is an essential component in human learning, there is a paucity of research in this area for our purposes. The evidence that does exist suggests that for the child who is mildly retarded the ability to transfer is not significantly impaired (Evans & Bilsky, 1979), but children who are moderately to profoundly retarded exhibit deficiencies in this area. The following are some suggestions for working with the child with mental retardation who is deficient in the development of generalization skills:

1. Age seems to make a difference in the ability to transfer learning for both retarded and nonretarded individuals. Younger children transfer learning with greater ease than do older children.
2. The individual with mental retardation can transfer learning best when both the initial task and the transfer task are very similar. Transfer is most effective if a considerable number of the operations involved in the first task can be performed as a unit in the transfer task.
3. Meaningfulness is extremely important to the person's ability to transfer. A more meaningful task is both easier to learn initially and easier to transfer to a second setting.
4. Individuals with mental retardation seem to be able to transfer learning more effectively if instructions are general rather than detailed and specific. This seems to

be an opposite trend to that found with nonretarded children who perform better if more detail is involved.

The above suggestions have several implications for working in an educational setting with the child who is mentally retarded. Initially it appears that transfer of training ought to be an important consideration in planning a child's early learning, but it is often left until quite late in the curriculum (for example, vocational training). It seems that transfer of learning by children who are retarded is most effective if the initial learning problem is a simulation of the transfer task. This is an important point when one is planning the activities and designing the materials to be used in educating children with mental retardation.

Since meaningfulness is so important to both effective learning and transfer of material, this area must receive particular attention from the person working with children who are mentally retarded. Often the meaning of a given activity is not readily evident. Children may then encounter more difficulty than would be the case if they were aware of how the task would help them. The teacher and others working with the children who are mentally retarded may find both learning and transfer facilitated if they make special efforts to show children how the task will be relevant to their later performance, to their lives, or even to current interests. This must be done carefully, however, to avoid too long and detailed explanations. If verbal instructions become too detailed or elaborate, the child with mental retardation encounters greater difficulty in transferring learning. The person working with the child who is mentally retarded must be clinically sensitive to finding the most effective level of detail.

Educational Achievement

Core Concept	*Most children with mental retardation benefit from instruction in the basic academic tool subjects.*

Children who are mildly retarded require an extremely systematic instructional program that accounts for differences in the rate of learning, but they may achieve as high as fourth- or fifth-grade level in reading and arithmetic. In a review of the literature on reading and mental retardation, Westling (1986) reported that "reading is generally considered the weakest area of learning, especially reading comprehension. Comparatively, students who are mildly retarded tend to do better on reading words than on understanding what they have read" (p. 127).

A significant relationship appears to exist between measured IQ and reading achievement (Carter, 1975). This seems to suggest that reading instruction be limited to higher-functioning children with mental retardation. A growing body of research, however, indicates that individuals with mental retardation can be taught to read at least a protective, or survival, vocabulary (Browder & Snell, 1987).

Children with mental retardation are also deficient in arithmetic skills, but the performance of children who are mildly retarded on computation tasks is more consistent with their mental age (Whorton & Algozzine, 1978). Frank and McFarland (1980) indicated that arithmetic skills are most efficiently taught through the use of money concepts. The immediate practical application motivates the student. Regardless of the approach used, arithmetic instruction must be concrete and practical to compensate for the child's deficiencies in reasoning ability.

ADAPTIVE BEHAVIOR

Core Concept	*Adaptive behavior deficiencies in school settings are associated with coping behavior, social skills, language development, emotional development, self-care, and applied cognitive and academic skills.*

For educational purposes, adaptive behavior for the school-age child is defined as the ability to apply the basic academic skills learned in school to daily activities. A child must also develop appropriate reasoning, judgment, and social skills that promote the development of positive interpersonal relationships (Polloway, Epstein, Patton, Cullinan, & Luebke, 1986). The State of Iowa Department of Public Instruction (1981) provided some excellent examples of in-school adaptive behavior deficiencies that may be associated with mental retardation:

1. *Lack of school coping behaviors* related to attention to learning tasks, organizational skills, questioning behavior, following directions, maintaining school supplies, and monitoring time use.
2. *Poor social skills* as related to working cooperatively with peers, social perceptions, response to social cues, use of socially acceptable language, and acceptable response to teacher.
3. *Poor language skills* as related to the ability to understand directions, communicate needs, express ideas, listen attentively, and voice modulation.
4. *Poor emotional development* related to avoidance of school work and social experiences as exemplified by tardiness, chronic complaints of illness, sustained or frequent idleness, aggressiveness under stress, classroom disruption, and social withdrawal.
5. *Poor self-care skills* related to personal hygiene, dress, maintaining personal belongings, and mobility in and about the school.
6. *Limited success in applied cognitive skills* related to initiating age appropriate tasks, solving non-academic problems, drawing conclusions from experience, and planning activities.
7. *Delayed academic development* related to ability to form letters, blend letter sounds, recall content from reading and listening, make mathematical computations, and repeat information in a logical sequence. (pp. 15–16)

Maintaining personal belongings is an important part of adaptive behavior.

Each of these areas contributes to a child's adaptation or eventual maladaptation within the school setting. In the following section we further examine the area of emotional development.

PERSONALITY AND EMOTIONAL DEVELOPMENT

Core Concept	*A child's problems in school-related settings are often compounded by inadequate social development.*

When children with mental retardation enter school, they are confronted with an environment that often tends to magnify their intellectual differences. This situation is compounded for children with mental retardation who may be unaware that they are different before the beginning of school. Intellectually inadequate and academically unsophisticated, many of these children fail to adjust to the academic world. Their academic problems are compounded by their social development, which is commensurate with their mental age but not with their chronological age. Thus many find rejection on two fronts; from the teacher frustrated with their academic limitations and from their normal peers frustrated with their social inadequacies. Failing in their efforts and rejected, children with mental retardation are more susceptible to emotional problems.

Most professionals agree that there is a higher incidence of emotional problems in persons who are retarded than in the general population (Epstein, Cullinan, & Polloway, 1986; Epstein, Polloway, Patton, & Foley, 1989; Polloway, Payne, Patton, & Payne, 1985). As many as two in five of these people may have emotional or personality deviations, compared with about half that proportion in the nonretarded population. It appears, however, that the majority of individuals with mental retardation who have emotional difficulties suffer from milder, transient problems (Beier, 1964; Menolascino & Egger, 1978).

Maladaptive behaviors may also be characteristic of children who are moderately and severely retarded. These behaviors include head rolling, body rocking, twirling, teeth grinding, and inappropriate vocalizations. Garrard and Richmond (1975) reported that some children who are severely retarded may also engage in self-injurious acts, including self-biting, head banging, and face slapping.

Several explanations have been offered for the greater frequency of emotional problems among children with mental retardation. These children may be subject to greater stress, frustration, and conflicts as a result of their intellectual deficiencies. Some of the most frequently mentioned problems appear to be related to either rejection or overprotection. Many parents consider their children extensions of themselves. When a child falls short of parental expectations, as happens with retardation, the situation may be too ego-damaging for the parents to cope. When a child with mental retardation is born into a family with intellectually limited parents, there may be little if any reaction. If, however, the child is born into other situations, parents may meet their feelings of frustration and failure by rejecting the child or have such strong feelings of guilt that they become overprotective.

Children with mental retardation often become dependent on other individuals for survival. They may have little control over their environment, and consequently they may have difficulty in finding and preserving their identity and integrity. Many children become frustrated and choose to resist. In doing so, they create problems for themselves and others. Sensing futility, they may become passive and submissive. The feelings of shame and guilt associated with consistent failures are often coupled with frustration and hopelessness.

The individual's emotional adjustment may to a great extent be a function of the public attitude toward children with mental retardation. It is well documented that nonretarded children hold negative attitudes toward their peers with retardation (Siperstein & Bak, 1985). In a questionnaire about attitudes toward children with mental retardation that Gottlieb and Corman (1975) administered to 430 adults, some revealing attitudes came out. A large majority of the respondents (88%) expressed an accepting attitude toward children with mental retardation, agreeing that parents should allow their normal children to play with a child who is mentally retarded. This acceptance was not, however, accompanied by equally strong support for integrated educational placement. Only 37% agreed that children with mental retardation would learn more if they were integrated into regular classes. Older respondents, parents of school-age children, and people with no previous contact with retarded persons tended to favor segregation of these children in the community. Peterson (1975) investigated the attitudes of nonretarded children toward their peers with mild retardation and found that subjects who had contact with children who are mildly retarded had more favorable attitudes toward them. Older subjects had more favorable attitudes toward younger subjects, and subjects whose parents had attained higher levels of education had more negative attitudes. These studies suggest that the development of more positive attitudes is essential for acceptance of children with mental retardation and for the development of the child's self-concept. Two investigations (Gresham, 1982; Siperstein & Bak, 1985) suggested that the social behavior of handicapped children could be improved if they were directly taught social skills prior to as well as during integration into the regular classroom.

Motivational Problems

Core Concept	*Individuals with mental retardation are able to participate and be actively involved in their own local communities.*

Individuals with normal intelligence excel in nearly all dimensions of human behavior when compared with children who are mentally retarded. But there is remarkable evidence of these individuals' ability to achieve. When motivated and producing at optimal levels, many people with mental retardation are able to be competitively employed and become useful and integral parts of society.

With the goal of useful integrated functioning in mind, many parents and professionals have sought to bring about maximum realization of potential for individuals who are mentally retarded. Maslow (1954) emphasized the natural and sequential development of the individual through basic stages of needs until he or she progresses to higher levels of motives and organization. The eventual goal for the individual is self-actualization, which reflects the developmental stage of maximum potential. Limited numbers of individuals are thought to have reached self-actualization. Such people as Albert Schweitzer, humanitarian, physician, theologian, and accomplished musician, and Leonardo da Vinci, artist and inventor, are sometimes mentioned as possible examples of self-actualization.

Maslow (1954) conceived of five levels of needs arranged in a sequence from lowest to highest:

1. Physiological needs, for example, to satisfy hunger and thirst
2. Safety needs, for example, to maintain security, order, and stability
3. Belonging and love needs, for example, to receive affection and identification
4. Esteem needs, for example, to experience prestige, success, and self-respect
5. Self-actualization needs

The prepotency of needs has important implications for parents and professionals (such as the special education teacher or rehabilitation counselor) who work with persons who are retarded. School-age children with mental retardation may have very real physiological needs. Some may come to school with severe nutritional deficiencies varying from improper diet to insufficient intake. They come hungry because of lack of food, tired because of lack of sleep and rest, cold because of lack of adequate clothing, or in physical discomfort because of lack of medical or dental attention. The observant teacher can identify these problems and make sure that proper attention is given to them. A bowl of milk and cereal before the start of school may be sufficient to turn the child's mind away from a growling stomach to a mathematics lesson. Likewise, providing for a child's clothing and medical and dental needs can change his or her perceptions of what is immediately important.

The professional can provide for many of the safety needs of a child who is mentally retarded. A teacher who notices that a child has been physically abused should report it immediately to the proper authorities. Whereas some schools may be justly criticized for their rigidity, others may offer the order and stability that are lacking in the homes of some children. The security of knowing that for five days a week he or she can expect a warm meal at noon and a certain amount of order in the day can be vital to the life and development of a child.

Nearly every child wants to be identified in a special way. Except in unusual circumstances, most children need affection and a sense of belonging to a group or an individual. For children with mental retardation who are lacking in social skills, this need can be difficult to fulfill. The special education teacher can in many instances facilitate group acceptance. Even if this does not happen immediately, teachers can provide a sense of belonging if they can accept the child as he or she is, as an individual worthy of concern and affection.

The child with mental retardation may not be able to progress beyond the needs to belong and to be loved. Prestige, success, and self-respect, which fulfill the need for esteem, may be formidable goals for these individuals. If the parent and professional look hard enough, somewhere buried amid all the disabilities of the most lacking child in the classroom is hidden some ability to do something as well as if not better than the rest of the children in the class. Capitalizing on this ability and drawing attention to it can bring the respect of peers in the classroom. Even if this cannot be achieved, the self-respect that comes with worthy accomplishment may suffice to meet this basic need.

Once the first four basic needs have been met, individuals with mental retardation can look toward the final goal—self-actualization. Although they may never be able to match the accomplishments of their nondisabled peers, individuals with mental retardation can find considerable satisfaction and contentment in being the best at whatever they can do, in being well liked by their peers, and in contributing to a better life for themselves and their families.

PHYSICAL AND HEALTH CHARACTERISTICS

Physical Differences

Core Concept	*The more severe the mental retardation, the greater the probability that the child will exhibit physical problems.*

The vast majority of children with mental retardation do not differ from nonretarded children in their physical appearance. There is, however, a positive correlation between severity of intellectual deficit and degree of physical anomaly (Hardman & Drew, 1977; Westling, 1986). With more severe mental retardation, there is a greater probability that the child will exhibit physical problems. Among children who are mildly retarded, there may be no noticeable differences because the retardation is not usually associated with genetic factors. For more severely affected children, physical differences are more evident and can sometimes be traced to biomedical conditions (for example, Down syndrome, hydrocephaly).

Motor development of children with mental retardation may be significantly below the norms for nonretarded children. Rarick and Dobbins (1972) indicated that these differences are not as evident if the comparison is limited to mildly retarded and nonretarded children. But Bruininks (1974) reviewed studies on motor performance of children with mild retardation and concluded that the children were inferior on measures like equilibrium, locomotion, and manual dexterity. A study by Bruininks (1977) confirmed that physiological development and severity of retardation are associated. Bruininks found that nonretarded children were superior to both mildly and moderately retarded children on motor-skill proficiency, whereas the performance of children who are moderately retarded was inferior to that of the group with milder retardation. Bunker (1977) indicated that moderately and severely retarded children exhibit significant delays in several areas of motor-skill development, including general body awareness, mobility, development of spatial concepts, awareness of body postures, control of body actions, body image, and self-help skills.

Two investigations conducted in the 1960s suggested that individuals with mental retardation are generally deficient in height and weight compared to nonretarded children (Fishler, Share, & Koch, 1964; Mossier, Grossman, & Dingman, 1965). Research studies have also shown a higher prevalence of vision and hearing impairments among children who are mentally retarded (Bensberg & Siegelman, 1976; Lloyd, 1970). Speech problems as well are more prevalent among children with mental retardation (Fawcus & Fawcus, 1974; MacMillan, 1982). In a study by Epstein et al. (1989) of over 100 students' individualized education programs (IEPs), speech and language problems were identified as the most frequent secondary handicap to mental retardation. The most common speech problems are articulation, voice, and stuttering problems (Hardman, Drew, Egan, & Wolf, 1990). Fink (1981), in a survey of Oregon service providers, reported severe speech delays in nearly 90% of 1,700 children with mental retardation. Most children with severe and profound retardation have multiple handicaps, exhibiting deficits in nearly every aspect of cognitive and physical development.

Health Differences

Core Concept	*Several environmental factors can contribute to health problems for children with mental retardation.*

There is a positive correlation between low socioeconomic status and mental retardation, particularly mild mental retardation. This means that children with mental retardation may be subjected to living conditions that contribute to their deficiencies, for example, poor nutrition, inadequate sanitation, and greater susceptibility to infections. Many families from low socioeconomic backgrounds must often depend on government-supported medical care. For others, health services may be minimal or nonexistent. During the school years, these conditions result in more illness and absences from school.

Health and sanitation problems are often difficult to overcome. Children with mental retardation may exist in a way of life that is acceptable to their particular subculture. They may feel little if any need to change their life style. Refinements in health-delivery services to make medical and nursing services more readily accessible are necessary. This should include not only services to expectant mothers and the ill but also preventive medicine and educational services by both public-health and social-service workers. The remediation of inferior and substandard housing, which promotes health hazards, needs priority as a consideration and is one of the more popular and publicized social issues. Unfortunately, the needs of a minority population and social conscience supported by adequate funding do not often coincide. Professionals must therefore teach these children to protect themselves from potential hazards and to become resourceful enough to find the best medical services available.

ALTERNATIVES FOR EDUCATIONAL PLACEMENT

Core Concept	*The national mandate for the education of handicapped children clearly indicates placement in the least restrictive environment.*

Special education for children with mental retardation has historically meant segregated education. Before the 1960s, most special education services were available only in self-contained classrooms that completely segregated the child with retardation from nonretarded peers. Additionally, these special education services were available primarily to the child with mild retardation who was defined as "educable," a term implying that, although the child was retarded, he or she could still benefit from some of the traditional academic curriculum taught in the public schools. Children functioning at lower levels (as determined by IQ tests) were generally excluded from public schools because they required "training" in such areas as self-help, language development, gross-motor skills, or academic readiness. The needs of children labeled "trainable" were not within the purview of the public education curriculum. For more severely retarded children, exclusion from the public schools was nearly universal. These children needed habilitation, not education. Children with severe and profound retardation were often labeled "custodial," implying their minimal functioning level and need to be watched over.

The passage of the Education for All Handicapped Children Act (Public Law 94-142) in 1975 was the culmination of years of litigation dealing with discrimination against handicapped children in this nation's schools. This law mandates that handicapped children must be educated in the least restrictive environment (LRE). The LRE concept requires that all handicapped children receive their education with nonhandicapped children to the maximum extent. In order to meet this mandate, federal law requires that a continuum of services be made available, ranging from placement in regular classrooms with support services to homebound and hospital programs. Figure 9–1 presents educational service options for students with handicaps.

Levels I through IV of the continuum involve integration, or "mainstreaming," of children with mental retardation in a regular education classroom with their nonretarded age-mates for at least some part of the school day. Some advocates and professionals have emphasized the full integration of students who are moderately and severely retarded into regular education classrooms.

Properly placed students with mental retardation in socially integrated situations profit from such experiences (Brinker, 1985; Stainback & Stainback, 1985). McEvoy, Nordquist, and Cunningham (1984) emphasized, however, that if integration is to be successful, regular classroom teachers may require extensive training and experience in assessing the behavioral characteristics of children with mental retardation.

We now turn our attention to some of the alternative placements available to children with mental retardation in our public schools. In the next section we discuss regular classroom placement with support services, the special education classroom in the regular school, and the special day school for students with mental retardation.

Regular Class Placement with Support Services

Core Concept	*Regular class placement with support services includes both the consulting teacher and resource room models.*

As depicted in Figure 9–1, placement at level II means that the student remains in the regular classroom with support services. The regular classroom teacher is responsible for any adaptation that may be necessary for the student's success in this environment. Consequently, this teacher must have the skills to develop and adapt curricula to meet individual needs.

Since regular teachers are an integral part of a successful educational experience for the child with mental retardation, it is important that they receive expanded university preparation in the education of handicapped children. The National Council for the Accreditation of Teacher Education (NCATE) and the National Advisory Council on Education Professions Development support this position. Necessary skills for the regular classroom teacher include an understanding of how a handicapping condition can affect the ability to learn academic skills or to adapt in social situations. The teacher must also be able to recognize a learning or behavior problem and seek out appropriate resources within the school that will facilitate the implementation of an appropriate individualized program. School districts also have a responsibility to the teacher and the child. Appropriate resources and consultative personnel must be available to assist the regular classroom teacher, and time must be set aside for planning and coordinating activities for the child.

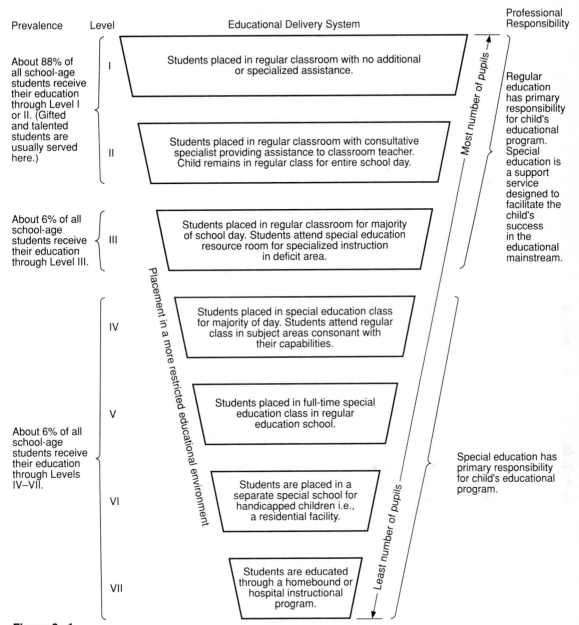

Figure 9-1

Educational service options for exceptional students

From *Human Exceptionality: Society, School, and Family* (3rd ed.) (p. 45) by M. L. Hardman, C. J. Drew, M. W. Egan, and B. Wolf, 1990, Boston: Allyn & Bacon. Copyright 1990 by Allyn & Bacon, Inc. Reprinted by permission.

The Consulting Teacher

The consulting teacher, sometimes referred to as a curriculum specialist, itinerant teacher, or master teacher, provides assistance to the regular classroom teacher or the child while the child remains in the regular classroom. This specialist may help a teacher to identify the child's specific problem areas and recommend appropriate assessment techniques and educational strategies. Reynolds and Birch (1988) suggested that an effective consultant has several positive characteristics. These are presented in Figure 9–2. Regular classroom teachers are trained and supported in their own backyard, so to speak, with emphasis on adapting the classroom environment to the needs of the child with mental retardation. If the child requires more support than a consultant can give, however, a more restricted setting such as a resource room may be necessary (Reynolds & Birch, 1982, 1988).

The consultant can also assist the regular class teacher in the implementation of a cooperative learning program between students with mental retardation and their nondisabled peers. Nondisabled student or peer tutors support teachers in delivering a more individualized approach to instruction. Mercer and Mercer (1989) suggested that peer tutors may help improve the retarded students' academic skills, promote cooperation between students, and develop self-esteem for the stigmatized children.

A student placed at level III in the cascade of services remains in the regular classroom most of the school day and goes to a special education resource room for a portion of his or her instructional programming. This service model still requires collaboration between regular classroom teachers and other consulting professionals.

---

1. Has state-of-the-art knowledge in the problem areas in which consultation is needed, has a reputation for the ability to diagnose and outline alternatives for treatment (instruction), and has built up experience and uses it well.
2. Makes sure all potential clients know in general how the process of consultation works. Offers services in a way that minimizes anxiety and does not stigmatize the recipient.
3. Is honest, spontaneous, courageous, and open to all facts, and makes no exclusions.
4. Is genuinely positive and authentic in expectations of constructive motives about people's competencies and is able to build mutually trusting relationships.
5. Is sensitive and responsive to others and has good knowledge of social dynamics.

6. Is interested in learning with others and communicating about processes of learning through consultation experiences.
7. Has a knack for being concrete and specific about approaches to problems, yet is also able to structure problems in broader theoretical terms.
8. Lacks the need for "professional distance"; prefers coequal relationships even though he or she is much more experienced than most others in the area of consultation. Finds rewards in successful performance by other persons, particularly by consultees or clients. Is noncompetitive and mature. Other people notice the maturity and feel comfortable with the consultant.
9. Has good research abilities and is able to access resources efficiently.

Figure 9–2

Characteristics of an effective consultant

From *Adaptive Mainstreaming* (pp. 124–125) by Maynard C. Reynolds and Jack W. Birch, 1988, New York: Longman. Copyright © 1988 by Longman Publishing Group. Reprinted by permission of Longman Publishing Group.

Services may range from assisting a teacher in the use of tests or modification of curriculum to direct instruction with students in the regular classroom. The regular education teacher must be able to participate as a member of a multidisciplinary team involved in the planning of appropriate educational services for the child. This team may include special educators, communication specialists, occupational or physical therapists, school psychologists, social workers, physical education specialists, and the child's parents.

The Resource Room

The resource room also reflects a philosophy of sharing of responsibility between regular education and special education for children with retardation. The resource room represents another effort to integrate children as much as possible into regular education and still offer them special education support services when needed. This approach allows the child to remain with nonretarded age-mates for the majority of the school day while removing a great deal of the stigma associated with separate full-day special education classrooms.

In the resource room program, children with mental retardation are assigned to a regular education teacher in the elementary grades and to a regular education homeroom teacher in the upper grades. These children are primarily in regular education and will participate in as many regularly scheduled activities as possible. Assignments, possibly with modifications, approximate the other children's. The two teachers arrange times for the children in resource programs to meet with the special education resource teacher.

The resource room teacher maintains a room within the school building and is a regular member of the school faculty. The special education teacher's function is essentially twofold. The first responsibility is to provide instructional support services to the handicapped child. These services can include orientation to the school for new students, tutorial services, counseling, and training of instructional aides if needed. A second major function for the resource room teacher is to serve as a liaison between the regular classroom teacher and the child. The resource room teacher is responsible for facilitating understanding between regular class teachers and the child, aiding regular class teachers in understanding the needs and nature of children who are retarded, and supporting the child academically and in areas of personal and social adjustment.

The Special Education Classroom in the Regular School

Core Concept	*Students with mental retardation may be educated in either part-time or full-time special education classrooms in the regular school building.*

Part-Time Special Class

The part-time special class (Level IV) involves the sharing of responsibility for the child by both regular and special education teachers. The major difference between a part-time special class and a resource room rests in the area of primary responsibility. In the resource room the child with mental retardation is primarily a student in the regular classroom with support services from special education. In the part-time special class the students are assigned to a special education teacher and class and remain in the same room with the same teacher for a large portion of the day. During the remainder of the day these students are integrated into as many regular education activities as possible. In most instances the child remains in the special classroom for academic subjects. Integrated classes are typically less academically oriented and include music, shop, home economics, physical education, and art. If the part-time special class functions as planned, a student has the advantage of a nonthreatening academic setting along with integration into the social mainstream. Note that in some school districts, programs referred to as resource rooms actually function as part-time special classes as we have described them.

Full-Time Special Class

A traditional approach to providing educational services to children who are mildly retarded is the full-time special class (Level V) in the regular education school. This approach has also been used more recently for children with both moderate and severe retardation. The full-time special class has been criticized because it totally segregates students from their nonretarded age-mates (Skrtic, 1986; Stainback & Stainback, 1984; Wang, Reynolds, & Wahlberg, 1986). This approach has, however, had its share of supporters. Some research in the 1950s indicated that social adjustment for children with mental retardation in full-time special education classrooms may exceed that of children with mental retardation in regular education classes, although academic performance between the two groups does not differ (Cassidy & Stanton, 1959). There are indications that children with mental retardation in special classes have less fear of failure than peers in regular classrooms (Jordan & deCharms, 1959). It has also been suggested that a child in a special class has a greater opportunity to excel and become a "star" (Baldwin, 1958). Proponents also argue that the self-contained class has a teacher who is thoroughly prepared and fully understands the needs and nature of children with mental retardation.

The Special School

Core Concept	*Special schools, although administratively convenient, do not provide critical opportunities for interaction between children with mental retardation and their nonretarded peers.*

Many classes for children who are moderately and severely retarded are located in special schools exclusively for handicapped children. Proponents of this arrangement argue that special schools provide services for large numbers of children with mental retardation and therefore offer greater homogeneity in grouping and programming for children. They also support this type of arrangement because it allows teachers to specialize in their teaching areas. For example, one teacher might specialize in art for children with mental retardation, another in physical education, and a third in music.

In smaller programs with only one or two teachers, these individuals may have to teach everything from art and home economics to academic subjects.

Special schools also allow for centralization of supplies, equipment, and special facilities for children with mental retardation. Smaller, isolated programs may not be able to justify the purchase of expensive equipment used only occasionally, but the special school can justify expenditures based on more frequent use by a larger number of classes.

Results of research studies on their efficacy do not support the arguments of the proponents of special schools (McDonnell & Hardman, 1988). Several authors (Brinker, 1985; Stainback & Stainback, 1985; Wehman & Hill, 1982; Wilcox & Bellamy, 1982) contend that, regardless of the severity of their handicapping condition, children with mental retardation do benefit from placement in a regular education facility where "opportunities for integration with nonhandicapped peers are systematically planned and implemented (Hardman et al., 1990, pp. 119–120). Several studies have indicated that educational outcomes for students are significantly improved in an integrated setting (Pumpian et al., 1980; Schutz, Williams, Iverson, & Duncan, 1984; Ziegler & Hambleton, 1976). Additionally, in appropriately implemented integrated services, there have been no substantiated detrimental outcomes for students with severe handicaps. (Guralnick, 1981; Schutz et al., 1984; Stainback & Stainback, 1981). Systematically planned interactions between severely handicapped and nonhandicapped peers yield improved attitudes and interaction patterns (Schutz et al., 1984; Stainback & Stainback, 1981; Voeltz, 1982).

The courts have also affirmed the application of the least restrictive environment clause of Public Law 94-142 to students with severe handicaps (*Armstrong v. Kline*, 1980; *Campbell v. Talladega County Board of Education*, 1981; *Fialkowski v. Shapp*, 1975; *Roncker v. Walters*, 1983). Specifically, severely handicapped students are to be educated to the maximum extent possible with their nonhandicapped peers, which includes attending regular schools, unless extenuating individual circumstances preclude this as an appropriate placement decision (Rostetter, Kowalski, & Hunter, 1984).

Critics argue that although administratively convenient to operate, special schools deprive children who are retarded of many of their basic rights. First, these schools are quickly identified as being different and exclusively for children with mental retardation. With a stigma attached to such schools, both the children and their parents may suffer. Critics also argue that the real world of society is not naturally segregated, and special schools remove children from the mainstream of society and education, depriving them of valuable experiences with nonretarded peers.

It should be noted that physical proximity (locating a class for severely retarded children in a regular education school) does not necessarily lead to integration. Integration requires a systematic effort on the part of all school personnel. What level of integration is possible for students who are severely retarded? Stainback and Stainback (1982) suggested that these students can be integrated for several kinds of activities, including the following:

Homeroom, art, music, recess, Thanksgiving and birthday parties, show and tell times, and rest periods. Nonhandicapped students could be encouraged to visit the special education classroom to work as tutors or simply to spend a little time with a severely retarded friend. In addition, teachers can facilitate interactions between nonhandicapped and severely retarded students in the school cafeteria, at assembly programs, in the hallways, and at the bus loading and unloading zones. (p. 88)

These authors also reported that prospective elementary education teachers who had the opportunity to interact with children who were severely retarded were not as fearful of or intimidated by their presence.

INSTRUCTIONAL APPROACHES

Core Concept	*For students with mental retardation, learning in the school setting is a continual process of adaptation.*

Students with mental retardation can and will learn if provided an appropriate instructional program and a teaching process oriented to their individual needs. The IEP includes an assessment of the child's current level of educational performance, statement of prioritized annual goals, short-term objectives, specification of educational services necessary to accomplish goals and objectives, and time lines for the implementation of services. The specific course of study, based on annual goals, is a critical factor in the implementation of an appropriate educational program. The selection of curricula for learners who are retarded has, however, been a problem for educators because of the students' heterogeneous needs. Since they do not learn as quickly or as effectively as their nonretarded age-mates, the traditional approach to teaching basic academic skills may not be appropriate for these students. For students who are moderately and severely retarded, academic skills like reading, writing, and arithmetic may not be a priority. Given the limited instructional time available in the schools, the course of study for these children may necessarily be oriented more toward adaptive living skills. In the following section we discuss some instructional approaches for children with mental retardation that emphasize the acquisition of both academic and adaptive skills.

Teaching Academic Skills

Core Concept	*Instruction in academic areas may include both a foundation and/or functional approach to learning.*

The primary instructional approach in the public schools emphasizes learning of foundation skills in the basic academic areas. For example, reading is learned as a set of sequenced skills that can be divided into three phases: (1) the development of readiness skills (left-to-right sequencing, visual and auditory discrimination skills, and memory

Table 9–1
A functional reading vocabulary

Go	Up	Dynamite	School
Slow down	Down	Explosives	School bus
Stop	Men	Fire	No trespassing
Off	Women	Fire escape	Private property
On	Exit	Poison	Men working
Cold	Entrance	Wet paint	Yield
Hot	Danger	Police	Railroad crossing
In	Be careful	Keep off	Boys
Out	Caution	Watch for children	Girls

skills), (2) word recognition or decoding skills (breaking the code and correctly identifying the abstract symbols in sequence), and (3) reading comprehension (giving symbols meaning). Each step in the process is a prerequisite for the next, and the whole forms a framework for higher levels of functioning. The learner who is retarded, however, may not efficiently acquire the necessary prerequisites within the time frame the schools prescribe. Many children with mental retardation just need more time to learn the skills for an instructional approach to be effective. Others may better invest their time and energy in such areas as self-care, mobility, or communication.

Another approach to learning academic skills is often termed functional and is consistent with an adaptive learning curriculum. In this approach the basic academic tools are taught only in the context of daily living activities. A functional life program in the area of reading focuses primarily on those words that facilitate adaptation in the child's environment (see Table 9–1). Functional mathematics skill development may relate more to environmental needs like telling time or spending money. Whatever the academic area, a functional approach pairs the skill being taught with an environmental cue. Browder and Snell (1987) stressed that when attempting to functionalize learned skills, the teacher must use instructional materials that are realistic. Traditional materials—workbooks, basal readers, flashcards, and so on—are not practical because the student is unable to relate the materials to his or her world.

The curricular approaches discussed above are not necessarily mutually exclusive. A foundation approach can incorporate many functional elements to reduce the abstract nature of the academic subjects and facilitate efficient learning for the student with mental retardation.

Teaching Adaptive Skills

Core Concept	*Adaptive skills are necessary to decrease an individual's dependence on others and increase opportunities for school and community participation.*

The public schools, which excluded many children with mental retardation for the better part of this century, now face the challenge of providing an educational experience that is consistent with the developmental needs of these children. Educational programming has been expanded to include the learning of adaptive skills necessary to decrease an individual's dependence on others and increase opportunities for school and community participation. The teaching of adaptive skills to children with mental retardation is based on the premise that if these skills are not taught through formal instruction, they will not be learned. For children who are not mentally retarded, teaching these skills is unnecessary because the children acquire them through daily experiences.

Adaptive skill content areas for school-age retarded children include motor, self-care, social, communication, and functional academic skills. The development of gross- and fine-motor skills is a prerequisite to successful learning in other adaptive areas. Gross-motor skills development relates to general mobility—balance and locomotor patterns. This includes neck and head control, rolling, body righting, sitting, creeping, crawling, standing, walking, running, jumping, and skipping. Fine-motor training includes learning to reach, grasp, and manipulate objects. For the child to develop motor skills, he or she must be able to fix on an object visually and track a moving target (Mori & Masters, 1980). The coordination of fine-motor skills and visual tracking (eye-hand coordination) is both a prerequisite to object-control skills that are required in vocational situations and a basis for learning leisure-time activities.

Self-care skills are essential to the child's independence at home and at school. The primary self-care areas are feeding, dressing, and personal hygiene. Feeding skills include learning to finger feed, use proper utensils, drink from a cup, and serve food. An example of a sequence for teaching feeding skills is the analysis by Barnard and Powell (1972) of the 18 steps for proper use of a spoon.

1. Orients to food by looking at it.
2. Looks at spoon.
3. Reaches for spoon.
4. Touches spoon.
5. Grasps spoon.
6. Lifts spoon.
7. Delivers spoon to bowl.
8. Lowers spoon into food.
9. Scoops food into spoon.
10. Lifts spoon.
11. Delivers spoon to mouth.
12. Opens mouth.
13. Inserts spoon into mouth.
14. Moves tongue and mouth to receive food.
15. Closes lips, removes spoon.
16. Chews food.
17. Swallows food.
18. Returns spoon to bowl. [pp. 97–98]

Dressing skills involve learning to button, zip, buckle, lace, and tie. Figure 9–3 is a test of dressing skill development. Personal hygiene skills include toileting, face and hand washing, bathing, brushing teeth, and shampooing and combing hair.

Instruction in social skills applies many of the self-care areas to the development of positive interpersonal relationships. Social-skill training stresses appropriate physical appearance, etiquette, use of leisure time, and sexual behavior. Communication is closely related to social-skill development because without communication there is no social interaction. The communication may be verbal or manual (for example, sign language or language boards), but most important is that some form of communication be present.

EDUCATING THE CULTURALLY DIFFERENT CHILD WITH MENTAL RETARDATION

Core Concept	*Culturally different children with mental retardation need an educational experience that focuses on learning how to learn.*

Because there are disproportionately large numbers of ethnic minority children in some classes for children who are mentally retarded (Chinn & Kamp, 1982; Willig & Greenberg, 1986), there is a critical demand for teachers who are sensitive to the needs of this population. Bessant-Byrd (1981) indicated that teachers must develop an understanding of the philosophy of various cultures and be able to use classroom materials that are characteristic of differing life styles. To meet the educational needs of the culturally diverse child with retardation, the teacher needs to focus on learning how to learn in addition to memorizing facts and acquiring basic skills. These children may have linguistic limitations both in their native dialect or language and in Standard English. Thus reading material should be primarily experience-oriented so that the child can draw from his or her own perceptions and experiences.

Chinn and McCormick (1986) have suggested four topics that should be considered in curriculum development for the culturally different child, including "(1) teaching values that support cultural diversity and individual uniqueness; (2) encouraging and accepting the qualitative expansion of existing ethnic values; (3) supporting exploration in alternative and emerging life styles; and (4) encouraging multiculturalism, multilingualism, and multidialectism" (p. 99). Since about one million minority children and youth drop out of school every year, the curriculum must convince these students that school is a positive social institution in which they are valued by teachers and agemates. Ethnic studies should focus on the use and meaning of societal labels and the image of culturally diverse people portrayed through the media. The curriculum for the culturally different child with mental retardation who is also living in poverty should include instruction on available resources for food assistance and medical care. Given the limited financial resources of the child's family, effective money management and consumer skills must also be emphasized. Finally, classroom teachers must believe in

Child's name: Date: Pretest of dressing skills	Independent	Verbal assistance	Physical assistance	Description of method child uses to complete the test
Undressing trousers, skirt 1. Pushes garment from waist to ankles 2. Pushes garment off one leg 3. Pushes garment off other leg				
Dressing trousers, skirt 1. Lays trousers in front of self with front side up 2. Inserts one foot into waist opening 3. Inserts other foot into waist opening 4. Pulls garment up to waist				
Undressing socks 1. Pushes sock down off heel 2. Pulls toe of sock pulling sock off foot				
Dressing socks 1. Positions sock correctly with heel-side down 2. Holds sock open at top 3. Inserts toes into sock 4. Pulls sock over heel 5. Pulls sock up				
Undressing cardigan 1. Takes dominant arm out of sleeve 2. Gets coat off back 3. Pulls other arm from sleeve				
Dressing cardigan flip-over method 1. Lays garment on table or floor in front of self 2. Gets dominant arm into sleeve 3. Other arm into sleeve 4. Positions coat on back				
Undressing polo shirt 1. Takes dominant arm out of sleeve 2. Pulls garment over head 3. Pulls other arm from sleeve				
Dressing polo shirt 1. Lays garment in front of self 2. Opens bottom of garment and puts arm into sleeves 3. Pulls garment over head 4. Pulls garment down to waist				
Undressing shoes 1. Loosens laces 2. Pulls shoe off heel 3. Pulls front of shoe to pull shoe off of toes				
Dressing shoes 1. Prepares shoe by loosening laces and pulling tongue out of shoe out of the way 2. Inserts toe into shoe 3. Pushes shoe on over heel				

Figure 9–3

Pretest of dressing skills

From *Occupational therapy for mentally retarded children* (p. 95) by M. Copeland, L. Ford, and N. Solon, 1976, Baltimore: University Park Press. Copyright 1976 by University Park Press. Reprinted by permission.

and communicate the basic tenet that people in this society exist in a pluralistic culture that values the intrinsic worth of every individual.

NEW ISSUES AND FUTURE DIRECTIONS

Core Concept	*In the future, educational reform efforts that focus on individualization in the schools and the effectiveness of social integration will benefit students with mental retardation.*

School Reform and Students with Mental Retardation

As we move through an era of reform and restructuring in our nation's schools, several emerging issues will directly affect the lives of students with mental retardation. For example, will future school reform movements focus exclusively on improving academic achievement for college-bound students, or will these efforts be more directed to improvements at the school building level with an orientation to individualized instruction and fostering of full participation for all students in a community setting? Obviously, reform efforts that focus only on improving academic achievement fail to acknowledge diversity and will inevitably result in the wholesale exclusion of students with mental retardation from the process. School-based reform initiatives will, however, be more responsive to the needs of students with mental retardation, since the change process accommodates individual student need while recognizing that there must be a common vision of excellence for all students in our nation's schools. Reform that deals with individual variability should take into account the needs of each student and match these needs against the demands of life in a community setting. For students with mental retardation, the curriculum needs to be broadened beyond academic performance to participation and access within their family setting, neighborhood, and community at large. This curriculum may include skills for self-help, independent living, adaptive behavior, recreation, and employment preparation (Hardman, McDonnell, & McDonnell, 1989). As described by Resnick (1987), school is a place to prepare people for life, as well as an environment in which one can engage in reflection and reasoning.

Teacher Education Reform and the Education of Students with Mental Retardation

University teacher education is critical to the success of effective educational programs for students with mental retardation. Over the past two decades these programs have begun to expand their curricula to include more functional, community-based, and social integration instruction. In the future, university teacher education programs in special education will have to concentrate efforts on ways to facilitate collaboration with regular education colleagues, and school administrators will have to address the needs of all students more adequately—including those with mental retardation. These programs will also need to assist potential teachers in special education to organize and use schools' resources more effectively (peer tutors, paraprofessionals, etc.) to meet the needs of students with mental retardation. Additionally, teacher education candidates from both elementary and secondary teacher programs, as well as potential school administrators, will require strategies that facilitate the success of students with mental retardation in an integrated public school setting. These strategies could include (1) functioning as a member of a multidisciplinary team; (2) supporting students with mental retardation to function in the social network of the school, and (3) developing effective pedagogy for students in a regular education setting.

The Social Integration of Students with Mental Retardation

As discussed earlier in this chapter, the issue of social integration in the public schools for all students with mental retardation continues to be hotly debated. Although the principle of normalization and the least restrictive environment clause of Public Law 94–142 indicate a strong preference for having every student with mental retardation participate in settings that are as close as possible to those available to nondisabled students, there are still professionals and parents who openly advocate socially segregated programs. As a recent report by the National Council on Disability (1989) stated, "A highly emotional discussion is taking place about the role of separate schools and the unique instructional needs of students with specific disabilities." (p. 31). In order to understand and meet the needs of students with mental retardation better in the least restrictive setting, in the future this debate must move from the realm of emotions to that of realities. Comparative studies across environments and functioning levels are needed before we can draw conclusions about what role, if any, segregated educational environments for students with mental retardation should play.

CORE QUESTIONS

1. Discuss Piaget's stages of development as they relate to children with mental retardation.
2. How do the memory capabilities of children who are retarded compare with those of their nonretarded peers?
3. Compare mass and distributed practice in relationship to the learning performance of children with mental retardation.
4. Discuss several suggestions for working with retarded children who are unable to transfer learning from one situation to another adequately.
5. What are some examples of in-school adaptive behavior deficiencies that children with mental retardation may exhibit?
6. Discuss possible explanations for the higher frequency of emotional problems in children who are mentally retarded.
7. Describe the cascade of educational services for children with mental retardation.
8. Why are segregated educational environments criticized for failing to meet the educational needs of children with mental retardation?
9. Describe adaptive skill content areas that children with mental retardation need instruction in.

10. Why is it important for students with mental retardation that school reform efforts concentrate more on school-based issues than on a top-down approach to declining academic achievement?

ROUND TABLE DISCUSSION

This chapter has discussed several aspects of the education of children with mental retardation in both integrated and segregated environments. It has also emphasized the need to provide for systematic and planned opportunities for interaction between retarded and nonretarded children if integration is to be successful.

In your study group or on your own, discuss the rationale for integrating children with mental retardation into both regular school and regular classroom environments. Given support for the integration of children who are retarded in the regular school, discuss ideas for planning appropriate interactions between retarded and nonretarded children both in and out of school.

REFERENCES

Agran, M., Salzberg, C. L., & Stowitchek, J. (1987). An analysis of the effects of a social skills training program using self-instructions on the acquisition and generalization of two social behaviors in a work setting. *Journal of the Association for Persons with Severe Handicaps, 12*(2), 131–139.

Armstrong v. Kline, 476 F. Supp. 583 (E.D. Pa. 1979), *aff'd* 78-0172 (3rd cir. July 15, 1980).

Baldwin, W. D. (1958). The social position of the educable mentally retarded in the regular grades in the public schools. *Exceptional Children, 25,* 106–108.

Barnard, K. E., and Powell, M. L. (1972). *Teaching the mentally retarded child: A family care approach.* St. Louis: C.V. Mosby.

Beier, D. C. (1964). Behavioral disturbances in the mentally retarded. In H. A. Stevens and R. Heber (Eds.), *Mental Retardation* (pp. 454–482). Chicago: University of Chicago Press.

Bensberg, G., and Siegelman, C. (1976). Definitions and prevalence. In L. Lloyd (Ed.), *Communication, assessment, and intervention strategies.* Baltimore: University Park Press.

Bessant-Byrd, H. (1981). Competencies for educating culturally different exceptional children. In J. N. Nazzaro (Ed.), *Culturally diverse exceptional children in school.* Reston, VA: ERIC Clearinghouse on Handicapped and Gifted Children.

Borkowski, J., & Day, J. (1987). *Cognition in special children: Comparative approaches to retardation, learning disabilities and giftedness.* Norwood, NJ: Ablex.

Borkowski, J. G., Peck, V. A., & Damberg, P. R. (1983). Attention, memory, and cognition. In J. L. Matson & J. A. Mulich (Eds.), *Handbook of mental retardation* (pp. 479–497). New York: Pergamon.

Bray, N. W. (1979). Strategy production in the retarded. In N. R. Ellis (Ed.), *Handbook of mental deficiency: Psychological theory and research* (2nd ed.) (pp. 699–726). Hillsdale, NJ: Lawrence Erlbaum.

Brinker, R. P. (1985). Interactions between severely mentally retarded students and other students in integrated and segregated public school settings. *American Journal of Mental Deficiency, 89*(6), 587–594.

Browder, D. M., & Snell, M. E. (1987). Functional academics. In M. E. Snell (Ed.), *Systematic instruction of persons with severe handicaps* (pp. 436–468), Columbus: Charles E. Merrill.

Brown, A. L. (1974). The role of strategic behavior in retardate memory. In N. R. Ellis (Ed.), *International review of research in mental retardation*. (Vol. 7). New York: Academic.

Bruininks, R. H. (1974). Physical and motor development of retarded persons. In N. R. Ellis (Ed.), *International review of research in mental retardation* (Vol. 7). New York: Academic.

Bruininks, R. H. (1977). *Manual for Bruininks-Ostertsky Test of Motor Proficiency.* Circle Pines, MN: American Guidance Service.

Bunker, L. K. (1977). Motor skills. In M. E. Snell (Ed.), *Systematic instruction of the moderately and severely handicapped.* Columbus: Charles E. Merrill.

Butterfield, E. C., Wambold, C., & Belmont, J. M. (1973). On the theory and practice of improving short-term memory. *American Journal of Mental Deficiency, 77,* 654–669.

Campbell v. Talladega Board of Education. U.S. District Court (1981).

Cantor, G. N., & Ryan, T. J. (1962). Retention of verbal paired-associates in normals and retardates. *American Journal of Mental Deficiency, 66,* 861–865.

Carter, J. L. (1975). Intelligence and reading achievement of EMR in three educational settings. *Mental Retardation, 13*(5), 26–27.

Cassidy, V. M., & Stanton, J. E. (1959). *An investigation of factors involved in educational placement of mentally retarded children: A study of differences between children in special and regular classes in Ohio* (Project No. 043). U.S. Office of Education Cooperative Research Program, Columbus: Ohio State University.

Chinn, P. C., & Kamp, S. H. (1982). Cultural diversity and exceptionality. In N. G. Haring (Ed.), *Exceptional children and youth* (3rd ed.). Columbus: Charles E. Merrill.

Chinn, P. C., & McCormick, L. (1986). Cultural diversity and exceptionality. In N. G. Haring & L. McCormick (Eds.), *Exceptional children and youth* (pp. 95–117). Columbus OH: Charles E. Merrill.

Clinton, L., & Evans, R. A. (1972). Single alternation discrimination learning in retarded adolescents as a function of within-trials variability. *American Journal of Mental Deficiency, 76,* 434–439.

Copeland, M., Ford, L., & Solon, N. (1976). *Occupational therapy for mentally retarded children.* Baltimore: University Park Press.

Drew, C. J., & Prehm, H. J. (1970). Retention in retarded and nonretarded children as a function of direction of recall and material associative strength. *American Journal of Mental Deficiency, 75,* 349–353.

Ellis, N. R. (1963). The stimulus trace and behavioral inadequacy. In N. R. Ellis (Ed.), *Handbook of mental deficiency* (pp. 134–158). New York: McGraw-Hill.

Ellis, N. R. (1970). Memory processes in retardates and normals. In N. R. Ellis (Ed.), *International review of research in mental retardation* (Vol. 4, pp. 1–32). New York: Academic.

Epstein, M. H., Cullinan, D., & Polloway, E. A. (1986). Patterns of maladjustment among mentally retarded children and youth. *American Journal of Mental Deficiency, 91,* 127–134.

Epstein, M. H., Polloway, E. A., Patton, J. R., & Foley, R. (1989). Mild mental retardation: Student characteristics and services. *Education and Training in Mental Retardation, 24*(1), 7–16.

Evans, R. A., and Bilsky, L. H. (1979). Clustering and categorical list retention in the mentally retarded. In N. R. Ellis (Ed.), *Handbook of mental deficiency: Psychological theory and research* (2nd ed.). Hillsdale, NJ: Lawrence Erlbaum.

Fawcus, M., & Fawcus, R. (1974). Disorders of communication. In A. M. Clarke & A. D. B. Clarke (Eds.), *Mental deficiency.* New York: Free Press.

Fialkowski v. Sharp, 405 F. Supp 946 (E.D. Pa. 1975).

Fink, W. (1981). *The distribution of clients and their behavioral characteristics in programs for the mentally retarded and other developmentally disabled throughout Oregon.* Eugene: Oregon Mental Health Division.

Fisher, M. A., & Zeaman, D. (1973). An attention-retention theory of retardate discrimination learning. In N. R. Ellis (Ed.), *International review of research in mental retardation* (Vol. 6). New York: Academic.

Fishler, K., Share, J., & Koch, R. (1964). Adaptation of Gesell Developmental Scales for evaluation of development in children with Down's syndrome (Mongolism). *American Journal of Mental Deficiency, 68,* 642–646.

Frank, A. R., & McFarland, T. D. (1980). Teaching coin skills to EMR children: A curriculum study. *Education and Training of the Mentally Retarded, 15,* 270–278.

Frank, H. S., & Rabinovitch, M. S. (1974). Auditory short-term memory: Developmental changes in rehearsal. *Child Development, 45,* 397–407.

Garrard, S. D., & Richmond, J. C. (1975). Mental retardation. I. Nature and manifestations. In M. F. Reiser (Ed.), *American handbook of psychiatry* (2nd ed.). New York: Basic Books.

Gottlieb, J., & Corman, L. (1975). Public attitudes toward mentally retarded children. *American Journal of Mental Deficiency, 80*(1), 72–80.

Gresham, F. M. (1982). Misguided mainstreaming: The case for social skills training with handicapped children. *Exceptional Children, 48,* 422–433.

Grossman, H. J. (Ed.). (1983). *Classification in mental retardation.* Washington, DC: American Association on Mental Deficiency.

Guralnick, M. J. (1981). Programmatic factors affecting child-child social interactions in mainstreamed preschool programs. *Exceptional Education Quarterly, 1*(4), 71–91.

Hallahan, D. P., & Reeve, R. E. (1980). Selective attention and distractibility. In B. K. Keogh (Ed.), *Advances in special education: Vol. 1. Basic constructs and theoretical orientations.* Greenwich, CT: JAI.

Hardman, M. L., & Drew, C. J. (1975). Incidental learning in the mentally retarded: A review. *Education and Training of the Mentally Retarded, 10*(1), 3–9.

Hardman, M. L., & Drew, C. J. (1977). The physically handicapped retarded: A review. *Mental Retardation, 15*(5), 43–48.

Hardman, M. L., Drew, C. J., Egan, M. W., & Wolf, B. (1990). *Human exceptionality: Society, school, and family* (3rd ed.). Boston: Allyn & Bacon.

Hardman, M. L., McDonnell, J., & McDonnell, A. (1989). The inclusive neighborhood school. Salt Lake City: Department of Special Education, University of Utah.

Inhelder, B. (1968). *The diagnosis of reasoning in the mentally retarded.* New York: John Day.

Jensen, A. R., & Rohwer, W. D., Jr. (1963). The effect of verbal mediation on the learning and retention of paired associates by retarded adults. *American Journal of Mental Deficiency, 68,* 80–84.

Jordan, T. E., & deCharms, R. (1959). The achievement motive in normal and mentally retarded children. *American Journal of Mental Deficiency, 64,* 80–84.

Linton, M. (1980). Information processing and developmental memory: An overview. In R. L. Ault (Ed.), *Developmental perspectives.* Santa Monica: Goodyear.

Lloyd, L. L. (1970). Audiologic aspects of mental retardation. In N. R. Ellis (Ed.), *International review of research in mental retardation* (Vol. 4). New York: Academic.

Logan, D. R., Prehm, H. J., & Drew, C. J. (1968). Effects of unidirectional training on bidirectional recall in retarded and non-retarded subjects. *American Journal of Mental Deficiency, 73,* 493–495.

MacMillan, D. L. (1982). *Mental retardation in school and society.* Boston: Little, Brown.

Madsen, M. C. (1963). Distribution of practice and level of intelligence. *Psychological Reports, 13,* 39.

Maslow, A. H. (1954). *Motivation and personality.* New York: Harper & Brothers.

McDonnell, A., & Hardman, M. L. (1988). A synthesis of "best practice" guidelines for early childhood services. *Journal of the Division for Early Childhood, 12*(4), 328–341.

McEvoy, M. A., Nordquist, V. M., & Cunningham, J. L. (1984) Regular- and special-education teachers' judgments about mentally retarded children in an integrated setting. *American Journal of Mental Deficiency, 89*(2), 167–173.

Menolascino, F. J., & Egger, M. L. (1978). *Medical dimensions in mental retardation.* Lincoln: University of Nebraska Press.

Mercer, C. D., & Mercer, A. R. (1989). *Teaching students with learning problems* (3rd ed.). Columbus: Charles E. Merrill.

Mercer, C. D., & Snell, M. E. (1977). *Learning theory research in mental retardation: Implications for teaching.* Columbus, OH: Charles E. Merrill.

Mori, A. A., & Masters, L. F. (1980). *Teaching the severely mentally retarded.* Rockville, MD: Aspen.

Mossier, H. D., Grossman, H. J., & Dingman, H. F. (1965). Physical growth in mental defectives. *Pediatrics, 36,* 465–519.

National Council on Disability (1989). *The education of students with disabilities: Where do we stand?* Washington, DC: Author.

Payne, J. S., Polloway, E. A., Smith, J. E., & Payne, R. A. (1981). *Strategies for teaching the mentally retarded* (2nd ed.). Columbus: Charles E. Merrill.

Peterson, G. (1975). Factors related to the attitudes of nonretarded children toward their EMR peers. *American Journal of Mental Deficiency, 79,* 412–416.

Piaget, J. (1969). *The theory of stages in cognitive development.* New York: McGraw-Hill.

Polloway, E. A., Epstein, M. H., Patton, J. R., Cullinan, D., & Luebke, J. (1986). Demographic, social, and behavioral characteristics of students with educable mental retardation. *Education and Training of the Mentally Retarded, 21,* 27–34.

Polloway, E. A., Payne, J. S., Patton, J. R., & Payne, R. A. (1985). *Strategies for teaching retarded and special needs learners.* Columbus: Charles E. Merrill.

Pumpian, I., Baumgart, D., Shiraga, B., Ford, A., Nisbet, J., Loomis, R., & Brown, L. (1980). Vocational training programs for severely handicapped students in the Madison Metropolitan School District. In L. Brown, M. Falvey, I. Pumpian, D. Baumgart, J. Nisbet, A. Ford,

J. Schroeder, & R. Loomis (Eds.), *Curricular strategies for teaching severely handicapped students functional skills in school and nonschool environments.* Madison: University of Wisconsin—Madison and Madison Metropolitan School District.

Rarick, G. L., & Dobbins, D. A. (1972). *Basic components in the motor performance of educable mentally retarded children: Implications for curriculum development.* Washington, DC: U.S. Office of Education.

Resnick, L. B. (1987). Learning in school and out. *Educational Researcher, 16*(9), 13–20.

Reynolds, M. C., & Birch, J. W. (1982). *Teaching exceptional children in all America's schools.* Reston, VA: Council for Exceptional Children.

Reynolds, M. C., & Birch, J. W. (1988). *Adaptive mainstreaming.* New York: Longman.

Roncker v. Walters, 700 F.2d 1058 (6th cir. 1983).

Rostetter, D., Kowalski, R., & Hunter, D. (1984). Implementing the integration principle of PL 94-142. In N. Certo, N. Haring, & R. York (Eds.), *Public school integration of severely handicapped students: Rational issues and progressive alternatives* (pp. 293–320). Baltimore: Paul H. Brookes.

Schutz, R. P., Williams, W., Iverson, G. S., & Duncan, D. (1984). Social integration of severely handicapped students. In N. Certo, N. Haring, & R. York (Eds.), *Public school integration of severely handicapped students: Rational issues and progressive alternatives* (pp. 15–42). Baltimore: Paul H. Brookes.

Siperstein, G. N., & Bak, J. J. (1985). Effects of social behavior on children's attitudes toward their mildly and moderately mentally retarded peers. *American Journal of Mental Deficiency, 90*(3), 319–327.

Skrtic, T. (1986). The crisis in special education knowledge: A perspective. *Focus on Exceptional Children, 17*(7), 1–16.

Smith, R. (1968). *Clinical teaching: Methods of instruction for the retarded.* New York: McGraw-Hill.

Stainback, S., & Stainback, W. (1981). A review of research on interactions between severely handicapped and nonhandicapped students. *Journal of the Association for the Severely Handicapped, 6,* 23–29.

Stainback, S., & Stainback, W. (1982). Influencing the attitudes of regular class teachers about the education of severely retarded students. *Education and Training of the Mentally Retarded, 17*(2), 88–92.

Stainback, W., & Stainback, S. (1984). A rationale for the merger of special and regular education. *Exceptional Children, 51,* 102–111.

Stainback, S., & Stainback, W. (1985). *Integration of students with severe handicaps into regular schools.* Reston, VA: Council for Exceptional Children.

State of Iowa Department of Public Instruction. (1981). *Assessment, documentation and programming for adaptive behavior: An Iowa Task Force Report.* Des Moines: Author.

Stephens, W. E. (1972). Equivalence formation by retarded and nonretarded children at different mental ages. *American Journal of Mental Deficiency, 77,* 311–313.

Voeltz, L. M. (1982). Effects of structured interactions with severely handicapped peers on children's attitudes. *American Journal on Mental Deficiency, 86,* 380–390.

Wang, M. C., Reynolds, M. C., & Wahlberg, H. J. (1986). Rethinking special education. *Educational Leadership, 44*(1), 26–31.

Wehman, P., & Hill, J. W. (1982). Preparing severely handicapped youth for less restrictive environments. *Journal of the Association for the Severely Handicapped, 7*(1), 33–39.

Westling, D. (1986). *Introduction to mental retardation.* Englewood Cliffs, NJ: Prentice-Hall.

Whorton, J. E., and Algozzine, R. F. A. (1978). Comparison of intellectual, achievement, and adaptive behavior levels for students who are mildly retarded. *Mental Retardation, 16,* 320–321.

Wilcox, B., & Bellamy, T. (1982). *Design of high school programs for severely handicapped students.* Baltimore: Paul H. Brookes.

Willig, A. C., & Greenberg, H. F. (1986). *Bilingualism and learning disabilities: Policy and practice for teachers and administrators.* New York: American Library.

Woodward, W. M. (1979). Piaget's theory and the study of mental retardation. In N. R. Ellis (Ed.), *Handbook of mental deficiency: Psychological theory and research* (2nd ed.). Hillsdale, NJ: Lawrence Erlbaum.

Zeaman, D., & House, B. J. (1979). A review of attention theory. In N. R. Ellis (Ed.), *Handbook of mental deficiency: Psychological theory and research* (2nd ed.). Hillsdale, NJ: Lawrence Erlbaum.

Ziegler, S. & Hambleton, D. (1976). Integration of young TMR children into regular elementary school. *Exceptional Children, 42*(8), 459–461.

CHAPTER TEN

The Adolescent with Mental Retardation and the Transitional Years

■ Components of an effective high school program for adolescents with mental retardation include: (1) a comprehensive curriculum that focuses on vocational preparation, (2) the teaching of adaptive skills, and (3) instruction in functional academics when appropriate.

■ Work is important not only for monetary rewards but *also* for personal identity and status.

■ Two important pieces of legislation that have had significant impact on vocational training for adolescents with mental retardation are the Vocational Rehabilitation Act and the Education for All Handicapped Children Act.

■ Work-study programs provide the student with integrated work and classroom experiences.

■ Career education focuses on preparation for life and personal social skills in addition to instruction in occupational skills.

■ Work experience is a method of training in which the student may participate in occupational activities in the community under actual working conditions.

■ In a community-referenced training approach, the demands of the work setting and the functioning level of the individual determine goals and objectives.

■ Socialization training includes the development of positive interpersonal relationships with family and peers as well as the acquisition of behaviors appropriate in a variety of community settings.

■ Some adolescents with mental retardation lack the financial resources or the skills and sophistication needed to maintain good personal appearance.

■ For individuals with retardation, the greatest value of recreation and leisure activities may be their contributions to emotional, psychological, and affective development.

■ The purpose of teaching academic tool subjects to adolescents with mental retardation is to enhance opportunities for independence in their classroom, family unit, and community.

■ Although effective educational and adult service models can provide greater opportunities for retarded individuals in community settings, no significant long-term changes will result without transition planning.

■ Effective transition planning is ongoing and begins with goals and objectives established from the time the student enters school.

■ The needs of adults with mental retardation are diverse and vary with the severity of the condition and the demands of the environment.

■ The purposes of transition planning are to establish a working relationship between parents and adult service agencies, identify resources for employment and community participation, access services before graduation, and locate systems that will help maintain needed services.

■ Parents must have the opportunity to learn as much as possible about adult service systems before their son or daughter leaves school.

■ The successful transition of the adult with mental retardation to life in an integrated community setting begins with integration during the school years.

Adolescence is a period of transition that encompasses the personal, social, and educational life of the individual. Adolescents are suspended between childhood and adulthood for several years, attempting to free themselves from the child's role but not yet ready to assume an adult's responsibilities. They work toward emancipation from the primary family unit while developing social and educational characteristics that gain them greater acceptance in society. For adolescents with mental retardation, educational goals during this period are directed toward employment opportunities and preparation for life as an adult.

The challenges of adolescence are obviously intensified for the individual with mental retardation. Many adolescents with retardation have the same physical attributes as their nonretarded peers but lack the capacity to cope with the demands of their environment or their own desires for emancipation from childhood. Adolescents with moderate or severe retardation, whose physical and cognitive differences may be readily apparent, focus on achieving as much social and occupational independence as possible.

In this chapter we consider the educational and vocational programs that public schools offer adolescents with retardation. Our discussion concentrates on expected outcomes of secondary education programs for students with mental retardation as well as analyzing the components of an effective high school experience. During the adolescent years, educational programs for individuals with mental retardation primarily focus on the skills necessary to make the transition from school to adult life successfully. For individuals with mild retardation, greater emphasis on applying academic tools like reading and arithmetic to vocational and functional needs begins during the junior high years. For children who are moderately or severely retarded, many of these skill areas are a central focus of the curriculum from the time they enter school.

EXPECTED OUTCOMES OF SECONDARY EDUCATION PROGRAMS

Core Concept	*Components of an effective high school program for adolescents with mental retardation include: (1) a comprehensive curriculum that focuses on vocational preparation, (2) the teaching of adaptive skills, and (3) instruction in functional academics when appropriate.*

A critical measure of the effectiveness of any educational program is the success of its graduates. Although 1990 marked the fifteenth anniversary of the passage of Public Law 94–142, the educational opportunities afforded by this landmark legislation have not yet led to full participation of special education graduates in the social and economic mainstream of their local communities (Hasazi, Johnson, Hasazi, Gordon, & Hull, 1989; National Council on Disability, 1989; Wagner, 1989). Several follow-up studies of special education graduates suggested that these handicapped adults were unable to participate fully in community activities, had little or no social life outside the family unit or primary caregivers, and were isolated from both handicapped and nonhandicapped peers (National Council on Disability, 1989). The vast majority of these adults were not employed (Brodsky, 1983; Hasazi, Gordon, & Roe, 1984; Hasazi et al., 1989; Mithaug, Horiuchi, & Fanning, 1985; Wagner, 1989; Wehman, Kregel, & Seyfarth, 1985).

In fact, Harris and Associates (1989) reported that the unemployment rate for people with disabilities was approximately 66% for adults between the ages of 16 and 64, more than 13 times higher than the overall unemployment rate of 5%. Other authors (Bellamy, Rhodes, Borbeau, & Mank, 1982; Bruininks & Lakin, 1985; Buckley & Bellamy, 1985; Whitehead, 1981) reported that service programs available to students with severe handicaps, including those with mental retardation, were not successful in producing meaningful outcomes or in moving individuals to less restrictive living or vocational options.

Since special education graduates are not fully accessing community services and programs, we need to identify what should be expected of high school programs. Goals are independence from primary caregivers, access to services and activities within the local community, and involvement in the economic life of the community (McDonnell, Hardman, & Hightower, 1989; McDonnell, Wilcox, & Hardman, in press; Wilcox & Bellamy, 1982). To be effective, a secondary program for students with mental retardation must be directed toward meeting each of these goals. Components of an effective high school program include a comprehensive curriculum that focuses on vocational preparation, the teaching of adaptive skills, and instruction in functional academics where appropriate. Secondary education programs should also incorporate integration with nonretarded peers, consistent parental involvement, and the implementation of systematic transition planning (Hardman & McDonnell, 1987; McDonnell et al., in press; Wilcox & Bellamy, 1982).

VOCATIONAL PREPARATION

Core Concept	*Work is important not only for monetary rewards but also for personal identity and status.*

The individual with mental retardation is often characterized as one who consumes services rather than one who contributes to the community. A consumer of services is dependent upon the charity of others. Employment assists in removing this image and placing the individual in the role of contributor. Work is important as a means to earn wages, and through wages we can obtain material goods that contribute to our quality of life. Work also confers personal identity and status.

From colonial days to the twentieth century, the pervasive belief in this country has always been that individuals should have the opportunity to seek their own livelihoods. This belief, however, has not applied equally to all. For persons with mental retardation, access to vocational training and employment has been negligible throughout most of this country's history. Even today many persons with mental retardation are unemployed or underemployed in spite of the dramatic increases in vocational research and development of the 1980s (Bellamy, Rhodes, & Albin, 1985; Moon, Goodall, & Wehman, 1985; Revell, Wehman, & Arnold, 1985). There are many explanations for this problem, some of which are recounted by the National Council on Disability (1989):

Vocational preparation for mentally retarded individuals often involves complex settings and circumstances.

Traditionally, many high schools have focused their employment preparation programs on a general assessment of student interests and strengths, and the teaching of vocational readiness skills in a classroom setting. This approach places high schools in a passive role in preparing students for employment. The instruction focuses more on general preparation for employment rather than training for a specific job(s). (p. 42)

In this section we examine the issues surrounding vocational preparation for persons with mental retardation, reviewing various approaches to vocational training including work-study, career education, work experience, and community-referenced training. Our discussion begins with the legislative mandates that have played such a vital role in the development of vocational services for citizens with retardation.

Legislative Mandates for Vocational Training

Core Concept	*Two important pieces of legislation that have had significant impact on vocational training for adolescents with mental retardation are the Vocational Rehabilitation Act and the Education for All Handicapped Children Act.*

Federal legislation has given broad support to comprehensive vocational preparation that is accessible to all persons with mental retardation. Two pieces of legislation are particularly important: the Vocational Rehabilitation Act and the Education for All Handicapped Children Act. These two laws have had a significant impact on the development and quality of vocational services to individuals with mental retardation.

Persons with mental retardation have been eligible for vocational services under the Barden-LaFollet Act ever since 1943, but few received any services until the 1960s. The Vocational Rehabilitation Act of 1973 (Public Law 93–112) greatly enhanced access to vocational rehabilitation services. The act established vocational training as a mandatory service for all qualified handicapped persons. Section 504 of this act contains basic civil-rights legislation for the handicapped, which makes it illegal to discriminate against handicapped individuals in access to vocational training and employment. Subsection 84.11 of the Federal Regulations for Section 504 states, "No qualified handicapped person shall, on the basis of handicap, be subjected to discrimination in employment under any program or activity to which this part applies" (*Federal Register,* 1977). Discrimination is prohibited in:

1. Recruitment, advertising, and processing of applications
2. Hiring, alterations in job status, rehiring
3. Rates of pay and other forms of compensation
4. Job assignments and classifications, lines of progression, and seniority
5. Leaves of absence and sick leave
6. Fringe benefits
7. Selection and financial support for training, conferences, and other job-related activities
8. Employer-approved activities, including social and recreational programs

The passage of this law did not mean that long-established negative attitudes toward handicapped persons suddenly disappeared. It was, however, a first step toward opening new vocational doors for handicapped people in general and for persons with retardation specifically. Career and vocational education for individuals with retardation became more important than ever. Section 503 of the same act emphasizes the regulations for affirmative action to employ handicapped people. If individuals with retardation are properly educated and can perform competitively for jobs, the federal government stands behind these individuals both in promoting affirmative action in their employment and in prohibiting any discrimination in their hiring. It is critical to reemphasize here that persons with retardation need to be educated and trained as competent employees. Although laws facilitate employment of the handicapped, they do not oblige an employer to employ or retain those who cannot demonstrate competence.

In addition to reaffirming the civil rights of persons with a handicap, the law has several other objectives (Meers, 1980):

■ To promote expanded employment opportunities for the handicapped in all areas of business and industry

- To establish state plans for the purpose of providing vocational rehabilitation services to meet the needs of the handicapped
- To conduct evaluations of the potential rehabilitation of handicapped clients and to expand services to them as well as to those who have not received any or received inadequate rehabilitation services
- To increase the number and competence of rehabilitation personnel through retraining and upgrading experiences (p. 33)

Current provisions of the Rehabilitation Act mandate services on a priority basis, with the most severely handicapped as the highest priority. Research studies published in the 1970s, however, indicated that many of these people continued to be excluded from vocational rehabilitation services (Bellamy, Horner, & Inman, 1979; Halpern, 1974; Sowers, Thompson, & Connis, 1979). In 1986 Congress passed new amendments to the Vocational Rehabilitation Act (Rehabilitation Act Amendments of 1986, Public Law 95–506) that strengthened the mandate to serve the most severely handicapped individuals. The amendments include provisions for supported employment, a new dimension in employment models for persons with mental retardation. Supported employment as defined in Public Law 95–506 means:

> competitive work in integrated work settings for individuals with severe handicaps for whom competitive employment has not traditionally occurred, or for individuals for whom competitive employment has been interrupted or intermittent as a result of a severe disability, and who because of their handicap, need on-going support services to perform such work. (Section 103)

(See Chapter 11 for a more detailed explanation of supported employment.)

The Education for All Handicapped Children Act of 1975 (Public Law 94–142) requires that all individuals with handicapping conditions who are between the ages of three and 22 years receive a free and appropriate education, including a vocational education. The provisions of this act are the basis for current vocational training for youths with mental retardation. Several investigations in the 1970s and 80s substantiated the need for appropriate training programs for adolescents with more severe retardation (Gold, 1974; Martin, Flexer, & Newbery, 1979; Wehman, Hill, Goodall, Cleveland, Brooke, & Pentecost, 1982; Wehman & Kregel, 1985).

Work-Study Programs

Core Concept	*Work-study programs provide the student with integrated work and classroom experiences.*

In a work-study program the responsibility for the student's program is usually shared by a special education teacher and a vocational rehabilitation counselor. The student spends a portion of the day in the classroom setting increasing tool subject skills that facilitate independent adult living (budgeting, transportation, interpersonal relation-ships, and so on). During the remainder of the day the student leaves the campus and receives training in an on-the-job training facility somewhere in the community (cler-ical, food service, custodial, auto repair, and so on). These facilities may range from sheltered to competitive employment settings. The kind of placement depends on the student's aptitude, ability, and readiness. The actual amount of time spent in each component of a work-study program varies considerably from one program to the next. At the end of three or four years, most schools grant a high school diploma. The student is then released from school and placed in some form of gainful employment.

During the 1970s several investigators attempted to determine the efficacy of work-study programs (see Brimer & Rouse, 1978; Chaffin, Davidson, Regan, & Spellman, 1971; Halpern, 1973, 1974). These investigations yielded inconsistent findings about

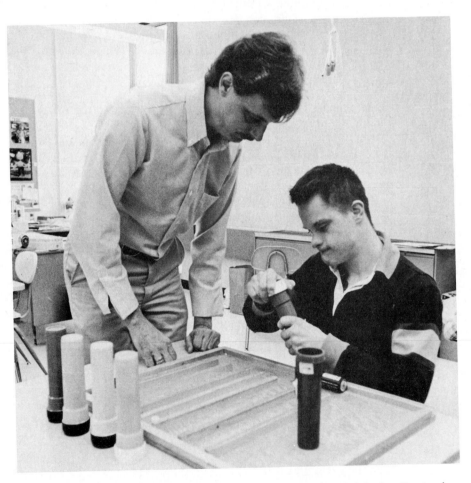

Work-study programs are often a shared responsibility between the special education teacher and a vocational rehabilitation counselor.

the efficacy of work-study programs. In a review of the literature on work-study programs, Peck, Apolloni, and Cooke (1981) indicated that "the selection of potential candidates for work-study . . . has been systematically biased toward serving those with the greatest prospects for gainful occupation. Such a sampling bias would greatly threaten the validity of studies that have compared served and unserved populations of students" (p. 13). Another important variable that always needs to be considered in such studies but cannot always be assessed accurately is the competence of the professionals working in various capacities during the training period. Training and educational programs for adolescents with mental retardation that are sound in their curriculum can be effective only if the professionals employed are competent. Students are very much affected by the teachers and the quality of vocational preparation even before the work experience begins. Vocational rehabilitation counselors also have a primary role in the development of student competencies. The employers providing the work training are likewise an integral part of the rehabilitation process. Finally, parents' attitudes may affect their children's performance. Preparation of students for effective and competitive functioning in an adult society can be facilitated by a concerted team effort, including work experience in the real world.

Regardless of program biases, the curriculum for adolescents with mild to moderate mental retardation at the high school level appears to have moved in recent years in the direction of work-study or some type of experience in an actual work setting. When students reach a vocational level class, they usually become eligible for assistance through vocational rehabilitation. If the individual meets eligibility requirements, a number of services become available that can enhance his or her chances of becoming vocationally competent. To be eligible for vocational rehabilitation services in most states an individual must (1) have a disability, (2) have a disability that represents a vocational handicap, or (3) represent reasonable feasibility for rehabilitation.

In the past, rehabilitation counselors working under rigid case closure quotas were hesitant to certify and accept as clients those students with mental retardation who were considered difficult to rehabilitate. In most states, quotas for rehabilitation counselors working with retarded persons have now either been eliminated or modified to realistic levels. In many instances the counselors come into the public schools and work closely with the special education teacher. The basic responsibilities of the vocational rehabilitation counselor working with mentally retarded students are given in the following list.

1. Certify all trainees for vocational rehabilitation services
2. Consult with school officials on training arrangements within participating school districts
3. Provide vocational rehabilitation services for individual trainees when extended services are needed (for example, psychotherapy or surgery)
4. Evaluate public school records pertaining to individuals referred for rehabilitation services
5. Initiate and conduct joint conferences with the work-study teachers
6. Approve all job training; evaluate training facilities, make training arrangements and agreements, and consult with the trainee and work-study teacher

7. Approve all expenditures for client services
8. Approve all individual vocational rehabilitation plans for clients accepted for vocational rehabilitation services
9. Maintain individual case records of the vocational rehabilitation clients

In addition to providing these services, vocational rehabilitation counselors can instigate other traditional rehabilitation services, such as the fitting of prosthetic devices, the provision of corrective surgery, and the payment of training fees. Rehabilitation counselors can also provide another important service by issuing subminimum wage exemption certificates when necessary. Many employers who are interested in hiring individuals with disabilities are hesitant to do so when the worker's production level does not meet the criterion set for other employees and minimum wage restrictions are nevertheless imposed. Under such circumstances, the vocational rehabilitation counselor can issue a subminimum wage exemption certificate that allows the employer to pay according to productivity.

Career Education

Core Concept	*Career education focuses on preparation for life and personal social skills in addition to instruction in occupational skills.*

Brolin (1982) contended that although the work-study programs instituted in the 1960s were a marked improvement over exclusively academically oriented curricula, they were still not enough to assure community adjustment for the adult with mental retardation. There is a need for a broadened concept, such as that offered through **career education.** Patton, Beirne-Smith, and Payne (1990) differentiated career education from the more familiar term *vocational education:*

> Vocational educators attempt to prepare students to enter the job market as competent, employable wage earners. . . . Vocational education focuses on the high school student who will soon be seeking full-time employment. Career educators, on the other hand, see preparing students for participation in adult life as their mission, and career education's emphasis extends from the elementary grades through secondary school and beyond. Vocational education is actually a subcategory of career education. (p. 347)

Both Brolin (1986) and Clark (1979) developed models of career education. Brolin's model consists of several competencies, experiences, and stages that are clustered into three curriculum areas: daily living skills, personal-social skills, and occupational guidance and preparation. The students learn competencies across these areas during four career education stages: career awareness, exploration, preparation, and placement/follow-up.

Clark (1979) developed a school-based career education model for students with disabilities that begins at the elementary-school level and continues into the adult years (see Figure 10–1). His model consists of four elements: (1) values, attitudes, and habits, (2) human relationships, (3) occupational information, and (4) acquisition of job and daily living skills. Career education is a total educational concept that systematically coordinates all school, family, and community components, thus facilitating the individual's potential for economic, social, and personal fulfillment.

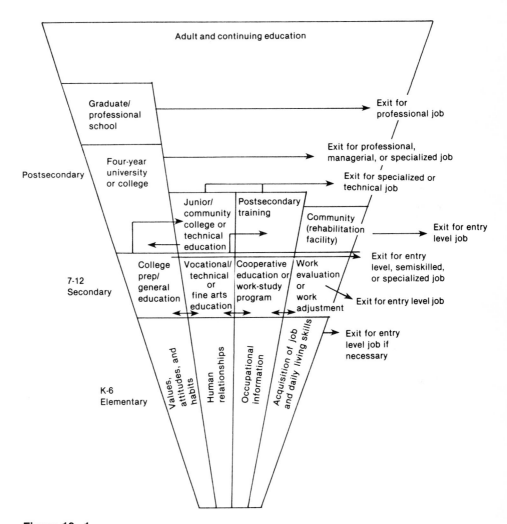

Figure 10–1

A school-based curriculum model for handicapped students

From *Career Education for the Handicapped Child in the Elementary Classroom* by G. M. Clark, 1979, Denver: Love Publishing. Copyright 1979 by Love Publishing Co. Reprinted by permission.

Work Experience

<table>
<tr>
<td>

*Core
Concept*

</td>
<td>

Work experience is a method of training in which the student may participate in occupational activities in the community under actual working conditions.

</td>
</tr>
</table>

Work experiences vary according to the philosophy of each particular program. Some programs begin work experiences in the school setting and eventually ease the student into community settings; others may have the student work in the community immediately. The difficulty and the type of assignment are usually dependent on the needs and the nature of each student. Before placements are made, each student's ability and interests are carefully evaluated. During the years spent in the vocational level class, the student may have an opportunity to work in a variety of settings to maximize exposure to different types of vocational experiences and possibly allow the student to find the permanent placement he or she would like at the completion of school. The primary purpose of the work experience, however, is not to develop specific vocational skills, but to enable the student to develop the work habits and interpersonal skills necessary to get and keep any job. If in the course of training specific skills are acquired, these naturally could be helpful in obtaining specific jobs at the end of school. But specific competencies must not be emphasized at the expense of the affective dimensions of vocational behavior.

The professional focusing on adolescents with retardation in work-experience programs frequently encounters problems that may hinder and even preclude the development of effective programming. As discussed in earlier chapters, the majority of persons with mental retardation come from families of lower SES. Work-related motivational problems sometimes develop when the student's family has existed for a number of years, if not generations, on public assistance. Difficulties can arise when the student in training or his parents realize that employment following school may be relatively low-paying. When remuneration is low, there may be little incentive to work unless work values have been emphasized. Too frequently individuals with disabilities are vocationally stereotyped. Individuals with mental retardation are often ushered into entry-level jobs only, becoming dishwashers or janitors. Although these occupations may be personally satisfying and rewarding to some individuals, they too frequently represent a general lack of consideration for personal interest and aptitude. The limitations of each individual must be considered, but training programs and vocational placements that consider only administrative convenience are inexcusable.

Another problem affecting work experiences is the sometimes inappropriate self-concept some people with mental retardation have about their abilities. Some individuals set vocational goals that cannot be realized. This problem becomes aggravated if the parents have inappropriate expectations for their children. Often these vocational expectations include educational requirements beyond the capabilities of these students. Whether these students are fantasizing or really believe that they possess greater capabilities than they have, problems do develop when they consider the work they have been assigned to be demeaning. In such situations parents, teachers, and counselors must help these individuals realize their limitations, as well as their potential, while not jeopardizing self-concept. The task then is to help the student exchange unrealistic vocational choices for those that are realistic and still satisfying. The student aspiring to become a nurse may be led into a nurse's aide position, while the aspiring pilot is led into a position in the airline industry loading baggage or maintaining aircraft. Effort should be directed toward finding acceptable alternatives without the loss of personal dignity.

Community-Referenced Training

Core Concept	*In a community-referenced training approach, the demands of the work setting and the functioning level of the individual determine goals and objectives.*

The community-referenced approach to vocational training, although similar to work-experience programs in many ways, has some very notable differences. The idea that individuals with mental retardation must get ready prior to going into community work settings is not acceptable in this approach. Vocational instruction focuses directly on the activities to be accomplished in the community work setting rather than on the development of skills in the classroom. Consequently, goals and objectives develop from the demands of the work setting considered in conjunction with the functioning level of the individual. Research has clearly indicated that individuals with retardation, including those moderately and severely affected, can work in community employment settings with adequate training and support (Bellamy et al., 1985; Mank, Rhodes, & Bellamy, 1986; Vogelsberg, 1986; Wehman, 1986; Wehman et al., 1982; Wehman & Kregel, 1985).

Effectively preparing adolescents for community work settings requires a comprehensive vocational program in the high school. The critical characteristics of a vocational program based on a community-referenced approach to instruction include:

1. A vocational curriculum that reflects the job opportunities available in the local community
2. A vocational training program that takes place at actual job sites
3. Training designed to sample the individual's performance across a variety of economically viable alternatives
4. Ongoing opportunities for students to interact with nonhandicapped peers in the work setting
5. Vocational training that culminates in specific job training and placement
6. Job placement linked to comprehensive transition planning, which focuses on establishing interagency agreements that support the individual's full participation in the community

Figure 10–2 diagrams the components of a community-referenced vocational preparation approach.

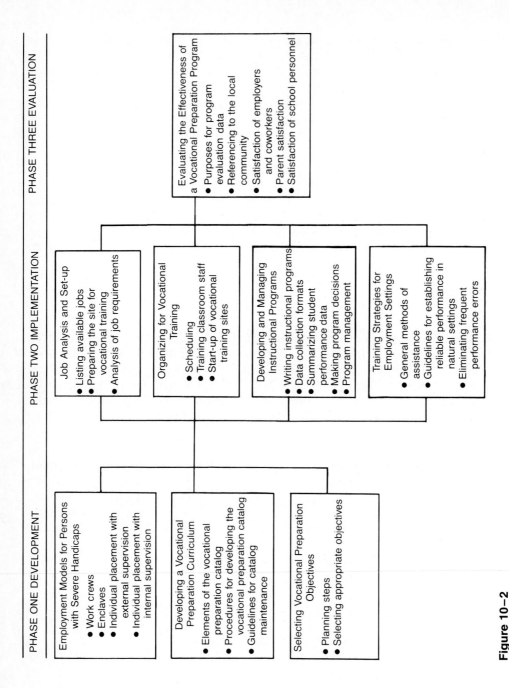

PHASE ONE DEVELOPMENT PHASE TWO IMPLEMENTATION PHASE THREE EVALUATION

Employment Models for Persons with Severe Handicaps
● Work crews
● Enclaves
● Individual placement with external supervision
● Individual placement with internal supervision

Developing a Vocational Preparation Curriculum
● Elements of the vocational preparation catalog
● Procedures for developing the vocational preparation catalog
● Guidelines for catalog maintenance

Selecting Vocational Preparation Objectives
● Planning steps
● Selecting appropriate objectives

Job Analysis and Set-up
● Listing available jobs
● Preparing the site for vocational training
● Analysis of job requirements

Organizing for Vocational Training
● Scheduling
● Training classroom staff
● Start-up of vocational training sites

Developing and Managing Instructional Programs
● Writing instructional programs
● Data collection formats
● Summarizing student performance data
● Making program decisions
● Program management

Training Strategies for Employment Settings
● General methods of assistance
● Guidelines for establishing reliable performance in natural settings
● Eliminating frequent performance errors

Evaluating the Effectiveness of a Vocational Preparation Program
● Purposes for program evaluation data
● Referencing to the local community
● Satisfaction of employers and coworkers
● Parent satisfaction
● Satisfaction of school personnel

Figure 10–2

Components of a community-referenced vocational preparation program

Adapted from *The Utah Community-Based Vocational Preparation Manual* by J. McDonnell, J. Hightower, and M. L. Hardman, 1987, Salt Lake City: University of Utah, Department of Special Education.

TEACHING ADAPTIVE SKILLS

Socialization

Core Concept	*Socialization training includes the development of positive interpersonal relationships with family and peers as well as the acquisition of behaviors appropriate in a variety of community settings.*

Adaptive skills teaching generally falls into three categories: socialization, personal appearance, and recreation and leisure time. Socialization training includes developing positive interpersonal relationships with family and peers as well as acquiring behaviors appropriate in a variety of community settings. It is important for adolescents with mental retardation to become aware of their strengths and limitations as they interact with adults and age-mates in a social context.

One of the greatest needs in the area of socialization for adolescents with retardation is access to social outlets. Because adolescents with mental retardation lack the social sophistication most children learn through observation, many of them are unable to plan and successfully carry out social activity. Their social problems include several facets, such as transportation, planning parties, asking for and accepting dates, behavior on dates, and financing social activities.

Transportation is a problem for many teenagers. Some are unable to drive because they are not old enough or because they lack access to an automobile. If the adolescent is unable to drive because of age or inability to pass driver's training, parents and teachers can offer instruction in the use of public transportation. The ability to use public transportation may be important not only for social but also for vocational reasons. If public transportation is not available, then parents, the schools, or volunteers must provide transportation. For those young people able to profit from it, driver's education should be made available in the public schools. Driver's education is a debatable issue for the adolescent with mental retardation. It can be argued that only the most capable students with mental retardation should be encouraged to drive. These would include those who possess the coordination and ability to think critically in emergencies.

Since the adolescent with retardation may not be able to take the initiative in planning social activities, the responsibility to provide social activities rests with volunteer groups, local associations for persons with retardation, and parents. Many social functions can be planned at school with the aid of the teacher. If a university is nearby, special education and recreation therapy majors might be available to assist in planning and supervising functions.

Learning of proper social behavior and personal interaction skills should begin early in the home and continue throughout the school years. Most adolescents with mental retardation are eager to learn, as they would like to be as much like their normal peers as possible. They would prefer to avoid any behavioral patterns that draw attention to their limitations.

Adolescents who are eager to show their affection for others of the opposite sex may lack the skills to do so in socially acceptable ways. They may try to emulate what they have seen on the television or movie screen or what they have heard their peers discussing. Unfortunately, many are unable to distinguish reality from fantasy and are unable to read their environment to determine what is really acceptable and what is not. Both parents and professionals should help the individual learn acceptable behavioral patterns that are pleasing to others.

Personal Appearance

Core Concept	*Some adolescents with retardation lack the financial resources or the skills and sophistication needed to maintain good personal appearance.*

By the time children reach adolescence, they usually have become acutely aware of their personal appearance in relationship to sex-role expectations. At this time many adolescents develop heterosexual interests and are concerned with making positive impressions on the opposite sex. Adolescents typically conform to peer opinions, activities, and appearances. Girls become increasingly aware and interested in the use of cosmetics and more fashionable hairstyles and clothing. They are also concerned with their height and weight. Boys are also concerned with their clothing, hairstyles, and physical attributes.

Some adolescents with mental retardation lack the financial resources or the skills and sophistication needed to maintain good personal appearance. While most adolescents learn to fix their hair, use cosmetics, and coordinate clothing styles from peers or siblings, retarded adolescents frequently have little if any help. They may be unable to learn from observing the examples set by others and experimenting on their own.

The onset of puberty brings about many changes in the adolescent. These changes include physiologic and behavioral differences, of which the most noticeable is the attainment of sexual function. When these physical changes begin to occur, estrogen, progesterone, and testosterone production levels also increase. These hormones are essential for secondary sex characteristics (such as broadening of the shoulders and increased muscle mass in boys and widening of the hips in girls). Changes occur in reproductive systems and in distribution of body hair and adipose tissue. When and how fast these changes happen varies: girls' puberty changes generally begin between the ages of 10 and 14 years; boys' adolescent developmental changes tend to occur later, between 12 and 16 years.

The beginning of reproductive capabilities is evident with the beginning of menstruation for girls and seminal emission for boys. Menstruation is usually irregular and not accompanied by ovulation for several months. Likewise, boys' mature sexual capabilities may not occur for several months after the first indications of development.

Unless adolescents with retardation are prepared for the great physiological changes brought about by puberty, they may come as traumatic experiences. The adolescent girl with retardation who has not been prepared for menstruation may find

Personal appearance becomes important for the mentally retarded youngster during adolescence.

her initial experience frightening and may be too embarrassed to seek help. Who is responsible for providing sex education is a hotly debated issue. Whereas some individuals believe that sex education belongs in the school, others consider sex education primarily if not exclusively the responsibility of the parents (Kempton, 1983). Rauh, Johnson, and Burket (1973) contended that, after school tax levies, sex education is probably the most controversial subject confronting American public schools today. Several school districts that have developed sophisticated, sequential sex education programs have given them up because of public pressure.

It would be fine if either the school, the home, or the church would assume sole responsibility for sex education. Unfortunately, in many instances no one is willing to do so. Teachers are hesitant to offer sex education without authorization. Peers are the only constant source of information about sex, but adolescents' ideas are often distorted or highly inaccurate. This problem is certainly not unique to those with retardation, but it is more acute for them, because they are often less able to locate accurate information. The nonretarded adolescent can seek and find information in a library. The adolescent with mental retardation may not be able to read or comprehend the written information, even if it is made available.

Parents tend to have difficulty discussing their child's sexual maturation with their pediatrician. Even though they may recognize the need for information to deal effectively with their child, they are reluctant to ask questions. Not until the natural course of physical development forces the issue of sex education into the open do many parents of individuals with mental retardation seek counsel (Fischer & Krajicek, 1974).

Kempton (1983) suggested that retarded children's general attitude toward accepting themselves as sexual beings tends to reflect the attitude of adults important to them. If the adults are comfortable with all facets of themselves, the children will also be comfortable. Fisher and Krajicek (1974) suggest that the common advice that adults should answer only those specific questions the child asks about sex is not generally applicable to children with retardation. Some of these children have verbal skills inadequate to pose questions, so adults must take the initiative in sex education. Success in dealing with sex education depends greatly on adults' willingness to give the child permission to ask questions or to wonder about sexual matters. Cultural implications that sex is something dirty and should not be discussed tend to restrict adequate parent-child interactions. Although our Puritan heritage has imposed inhibitions that influence society's official attitude, some points of view in our culture are diametrically opposed to one another with regard to sexual permissiveness. There is little doubt that sexual activity among adolescents is on the increase. Related to the increase of sexual activity among adolescents is an increasing incidence of sexually transmitted diseases. Adolescents, including those with retardation, will continue to engage in sexual activity with or without the approval of society. Unless they receive adequate sex education, both unwanted pregnancies and sexually transmitted diseases are inevitable. While school boards, parents, and the public argue over who should take responsibility for sex education, many adolescents with mental retardation remain in ignorance, victims of our indecision.

In addition to changes in sexual function, puberty may also bring about cosmetic changes like acne. Acne frequently causes emotional scarring far more significant and permanent than any physical scars (Reisner, 1973). Nonretarded adolescents have the advantage of being able to read and ask questions. Some go to a dermatologist to help protect their appearance. The adolescent with retardation may have difficulty in locating necessary help. Many lack the financial resources to receive treatment from a dermatologist. Unable to groom themselves adequately and maintain an acceptable cosmetic appearance, retarded adolescents may find social acceptance nearly impossible.

Unfortunately, some parents of children with retardation make the assumption that the retarded child's intellectual limitations render physical appearance of little consequence. Yet most children with retardation strive constantly to be as much like their normal peers as possible. They want nothing to draw attention to the fact that they are different. Being less well groomed first draws attention, then hinders or even precludes social acceptance. Parents and teachers must be aware that looks usually have a bearing on self-concept, and programs and curricula must include attention to appearance in the education of adolescents.

Parents may lack ability or desire to teach children with retardation adequate grooming skills. In such situations responsibility falls on the schools. How the students are taught may take several different forms. Positive discussions in a class are a possible means. Guest speakers from clothing stores can usually be brought into the schools, or the teacher can take students to stores for a demonstration. People in cosmetic sales are usually very cooperative and often teach and demonstrate the use of cosmetics for the girls. If a dermatologist is not available, then the school nurse should be able to provide the necessary information about skin care and treatment of acne problems. Beauty colleges that train cosmetologists are frequently willing to provide their services to teach students with retardation how to shampoo and take care of their hair.

Even if students are able to learn how to groom themselves properly, money problems at times present an obstacle to individuals with mental retardation. Many come from lower SES families whose resources are insufficient to purchase the necessary clothing and supplies. There are several alternatives for approaching this problem. First, the students can learn to make their own clothing. Even the boys can learn how to sew in order to repair and make clothing. This can be taught either by the teacher or through a cooperative arrangement with the school home economics program. Learning to sew makes a wider choice of clothing styles available and develops a leisure activity at the same time. Other benefits also derive from making one's own clothing, for example, the pride that comes from creating and making something of value. There is also the benefit of learning to measure and to follow directions, which sewing requires.

Recreation and Leisure

Core Concept	*For individuals with retardation, the greatest value of recreation and leisure activities may be their contributions to emotional, psychological, and affective development.*

Recreation and leisure activities are also essential components of the adolescent's social world. The adolescent may spend anywhere from 30 to 40 hours a week in school or at work. By the year 2000, however, working adults may be spending much less than the traditional 40 hours at their jobs. Obviously there will be a real need to develop expanded recreation and leisure activities for all of society. For individuals with disabilities, including those with mental retardation, the opportunities for recreation and leisure in a community setting vary considerably according to age and severity of condition. For many adults with disabilities, television may be their only consistent leisure-time experience (Hardman, Drew, Egan, & Wolf, 1990). Yet involvement in a recreational activity may be one of the few times these individuals view themselves as successful. Today the picture for physical education and recreation for retarded adolescents is encouraging. Some agencies and communities are initiating new programs specifically for persons with mental retardation. Many colleges and universities have developed special or adaptive physical education, recreation, and therapeutic recreation programs that prepare individuals to work with handicapped persons. Other programs, such as the Special Olympics, sponsored by the Joseph P. Kennedy, Jr., Foundation, have provided for athletic competition for children and adults with mental retardation. Recently Special Olympics expanded into a Unified Sports Program that involves both nondisabled and retarded individuals in integrated team sports.

Although the development of structured leisure-time programs for adolescents with mental retardation is encouraging, much remains to be done. It is disconcerting to realize that most free-time activities for adolescents with mental retardation are napping and watching television. Yet training procedures like those used in therapeutic recreation for the development of leisure-time skills can be effective. The goal of therapeutic recreation is to assist individuals with mental retardation to take advantage of leisure-time opportunities as a means to enhance their independence in the community (Hardman et al., 1990).

TEACHING ACADEMIC SKILLS

Core Concept	*The purpose of teaching academic tool subjects to adolescents with mental retardation is to enhance opportunities for independence in their classroom, family unit, and community.*

The objectives of an academic skills program for adolescents with mental retardation, regardless of the severity of the individual's retardation, are primarily functional—directly oriented to daily living activities, leisure time, and vocational preparation. The means to achieve these objectives differ across severity levels. For the adolescent with mild mental retardation, academics may be a higher priority than for the student who is more severely retarded. This is because the mildly retarded adolescent may be able to assimilate functional academic skills better into his or her daily living and vocational activities. Because adolescents with moderate and severe retardation have a diminished capacity for applying academic tools to daily living, it is necessary to emphasize adaptive skill training for these students.

A functional academic program includes instruction in reading, language, and arithmetic. A functional reading program focuses on reading for protection and information. A protective (sometimes referred to as survival) vocabulary teaches the student to read building signs (push/pull, men/women, entrance/exit), street signs (walk/don't walk, stop, caution, railroad crossing), and other common environmental safety words (keep out, danger, poison, hazard, do not enter). An informational reading program teaches functional skills related to vocational proficiency (components of a job application form, reading classified ads) and the use of maps, telephone directories, and catalogs. Browder and Snell (1987), in a recent review of the literature, indicated that research has found that students with moderate to severe mental retardation can be taught to read a protective or survival vocabulary.

In a survey of professionals in career education, Schilit and Caldwell (1980) compiled a list of career/vocational words as an aid for teachers in more effectively preparing

Teaching academic skills to students with mental retardation is one of many areas where computer technology may be effectively used.

retarded adolescents to enter the working world (see Figure 10–3). A reading program more oriented toward leisure-time activities helps the student get the most out of television, magazines, and newspapers (for example, movie listings).

Functional language programs focus on the use of expressive and receptive skills. Instruction in expressive language includes effective oral skills in carrying on a conversation, talking on the telephone, and responding to questions. Some degree of writing proficiency may also be necessary to enhance community and vocational independence. These skills range from the basic ability to write one's name to the more

1. Rules	35. Employee	69. License
2. Boss	36. Layoff	70. Poison
3. Emergency	37. Take-home pay	71. Office
4. Danger	38. Unemployed	72. Power
5. Job	39. Cost	73. Qualifications
6. Social Security	40. Deduction	74. Earn
7. First-aid	41. Fired	75. Transportation
8. Help wanted	42. Closed	76. Withholding
9. Safety	43. Part-time	77. Vote
10. Warning	44. Correct	78. Break
11. Signature	45. Foreman	79. Cooperation
12. Time	46. Time-and-a-half	80. Dependable
13. Attendance	47. Worker	81. Money
14. Absent	48. Buy	82. Physical
15. Telephone	49. Raise	83. Hazardous
16. Bill	50. On-the-job	84. Net income
17. Hired	51. Entrance	85. Strike
18. Overtime	52. Responsible	86. Owner
19. Punch in	53. Hospital	87. Repair
20. Directions	54. Hourly rate	88. Alarm
21. Paycheck	55. Schedule	89. Gross income
22. Wages	56. Instructions	90. Manager
23. Appointment	57. Save	91. Reference
24. Income tax	58. Union	92. Uniform
25. Interview	59. Credit	93. Hard-hat
26. Supervisor	60. Elevator	94. Authority
27. Vacation	61. Punctuality	95. Training
28. Apply	62. Rights	96. Holiday
29. Full-time	63. Hours	97. Late
30. Income	64. Payroll	98. Personal
31. Quit	65. Attitude	99. Tools
32. Check	66. Reliable	100. Area
33. Careful	67. Work	
34. Dangerous	68. Caution	

Figure 10-3

One hundred essential career/vocational words

From "A Word List of Essential Career/Vocational Words for Mentally Retarded Students" by J. Schilit and M. L. Caldwell, 1980, *Education and Training of the Mentally Retarded, 15*(2), pp. 113–117. Copyright 1980 by the Council for Exceptional Children. Reprinted by permission.

complex task of filling out a job application form. Receptive skills are also needed for daily conversations and job interviews. Good oral skills are useless if the individual cannot also listen to and understand what others say.

The intended outcomes for a functional arithmetic program are generally basic management of personal finances, consumer skills, and telling time. A personal finance program instructs the adolescent in several areas, including budgeting money, establishing and using credit, taxes, insurance, and wages. Consumer skills include identifying coins and bills of all denominations, making change, and reading bus or train schedules and timetables.

TRANSITION PLANNING

Core Concept

Although effective educational and adult service models can provide greater opportunities for retarded individuals in community settings, no significant long-term changes will result without transition planning.

Each year approximately 60,000 adolescents with mental retardation leave school and face life as adults in their local communities. The transition from school to adult life is not easy. Many adults with retardation find that they cannot get services critical for success in the community (Brodsky, 1983; Hasazi et al., 1985, 1989). These individuals may face long waiting lists for vocational and housing services (McDonnell, Wilcox, & Boles, 1985). Transition planning must facilitate the coordination and expansion of services within the community for each adult with retardation (Schalock, 1985; Wehman, Kregel, & Barcus, 1985). Professionals and parents have come to the realization that a systematic transition planning process must begin during the school years and carry over into adulthood.

Federal and state initiatives for transition planning were begun in 1983 and focused on the development of new programs to facilitate transition from school to adult life. The critical components of transition planning were identified as: (1) effective high school programs that prepare students to work and live in the community; (2) a broad range of adult service programs that can meet the various support needs of individuals with handicaps in employment and community settings; and (3) comprehensive and cooperative transition planning between educational and community service agencies in order to develop needed services for graduation (Will, 1984). The remainder of this section focuses on a process designed to address the critical components of transition planning and facilitate coordination and expansion of services within the community for each individual with retardation.

Coordinating Transition Planning

Core Concept

Effective transition planning is ongoing and begins with goals and objectives established from the time the student enters school.

The foundation for a formal transition planning process is laid in high school. High schools must organize their programs and activities to produce outcomes that facilitate success for the individual during the adult years. These outcomes for the adult with retardation include being able to function as independently as possible in daily life. The individual should also be involved in the economic life of the community, both in paid and unpaid work. The handicapped adult should be able to participate in social and leisure activities that are part of community life. The school's role in the transition process includes assessing individual needs, developing transition plans for each student, coordinating transition planning with adult service agencies, and participating with parents in the planning process (Hardman et al., 1990; Hardman & McDonnell, 1987; McDonnell & Hardman, 1985; McDonnell et al., in press).

Determining Individual Need

Core Concept	*The needs of adults with mental retardation are diverse and vary with the severity of the condition and the demands of the environment.*

For many adults with mild mental retardation, assistance may be unnecessary following school. Others may need a short-term support system. For adults with moderate to severe retardation, the assistance necessary to ensure appropriate access to community services may have to be long-term and intense. An effective transition planning system must take into account both the short- and long-term service needs of the individual. McDonnell et al. (in press) stated that, in order to identify the level of support an individual will require, parents and school must look at the individual's performance during high school in a variety of areas (self-care, work, residential living, recreation and leisure time). Assessment in self-care includes activities like grocery shopping, using public transportation, crossing streets, maintaining a schedule, and so forth.

Developing a Transition Plan

Core Concept	*The purposes of transition planning are to establish a working relationship between parents and adult service agencies, identify resources for employment and community participation, access services before graduation, and locate systems that will help maintain needed services.*

Approximately two years before the student leaves school, work should begin on a formal transition plan. The plan serves several purposes: (1) establishment of a formal working relationship between parents and postschool case managers and adult service providers, (2) identification of the services and resources that will ensure meaningful employment and community participation, (3) access to services before graduation, and (4) identification of systems that will facilitate the maintenance of needed services (McDonnell et al., in press). In order to address each purpose, parents and professionals must work together to review potential services that are now or should be made available as the student leaves school. They identify activities that will facilitate access to these services and establish time lines and responsibilities for completion.

The components of the transition plan outlined by McDonnell et al. (in press) are:

1. *Vocational placement or program.*   Specify the type of placement or program most appropriate for the student. Determine how the resources between school and

postschool service programs will be coordinated to ensure that appropriate jobs are identified and the student trained for them.

2. *Residential placement.*   Determine which residential alternative is the most appropriate for the student. If the family feels it is in the best interest of the adult with retardation to remain home for some time after leaving school, then appropriate family support services need to be in place. If the individual is to move into a residential placement immediately following school, then alternative living arrangements must be made.

3. *Leisure alternatives.*   Identify the leisure activities most important to the student. Activities should be planned to ensure that the student has the necessary resources or skills to participate in the activities regardless of where he or she chooses to live after leaving school. Resources or skills include financing the activity, finding transportation, locating a peer to accompany the student, and so on.

4. *Income and medical support.*   Balance the potential array of service alternatives with the individual's supplemental security income program. Ensure that needed cash awards or medical benefits are not jeopardized by other services.

5. *Transportation.*   Determine specific transportation needs for vocational, residential, and leisure alternatives. Identify alternatives for each activity, method of financing transport, and strategies to coordinate transportation between school and adult service providers.

6. *Long-term support and care.*   Identify the need for guardianship and/or specific trusts or wills. Specific services or agencies need to assist parents in drawing up these legal documents. Figure 10–4 presents a format for the development of a written transition plan.

Involving Parents in Transition Planning

Core Concept	*Parents must have the opportunity to learn as much as possible about adult service systems before their son or daughter leaves school.*

Parent education during their child's high school years should include the characteristics of adult service agencies, criteria for evaluating adult service programs, and potential as well as current service alternatives for the adult with mental retardation. School districts need to offer ongoing educational programs for parents to acquaint them with the issues involved in the transition from school to adult life. Every school district should develop and use a transition planning guide to help parents complete critical planning activities (McDonnell & Hardman, 1985).

Integration with Nonretarded Peers

Core Concept	*The successful transition of the adult with mental retardation to life in an integrated community setting begins with integration during the school years.*

Student: _____ Bob Robins _____   Meeting Date: _____ 10/15/85 _____
                                       Graduation Date: _____ 6/7/87 _____

Participants:
       Parent(s) _____ Mrs. Robins _____
       School _____ William B. _____
       DSH Case Manager _____ Susan L. _____
       DVR Case Manager _____ N/A _____

Planning Area: Vocational Services	Responsible Person	Time lines
Transition Goal		
Bob will initiate work training in Wasatch Work Crew Program	William B.	12/15/85
Support Activities		
1. Complete application process	Mrs. Robins Susan L.	11/1/85
2. Obtain UTA bus pass	Mrs. Robins	11/1/85
3. Teach bus route to Wasatch business office	William B.	11/14/85
4. Establish planning meeting with Wasatch WCP director	Susan L.	1/10/86

Figure 10–4

High school transition plan for a severely handicapped student

From "Planning the Transition of Severely Handicapped Youth from School to Adult Services: A Framework for High School Programs" by J. McDonnell and M. L. Hardman, 1985, *Education and Training of the Mentally Retarded, 20,* 275–286. Copyright 1985 by the Council for Exceptional Children. Reprinted by permission.

Integration is an affirmation of the importance of the learning and performance opportunities provided by social interaction with normal peers. During the high school transition years, the integration of mentally retarded students with their nonretarded peers may take place in several contexts. First, it may occur in the regular classroom. The student with mental retardation may participate in a variety of academic or nonacademic classes (physical education, shop, art, music). Second, the student with retardation, although receiving much formal educational experience within a self-contained special education classroom, still participates in "normal" school activities (school assemblies, lunch, hall interaction). Such a student may also have the chance to interact with nonretarded students in the special education classroom through such programs as peer tutoring. Nonretarded peer tutors volunteer to assist mentally retarded students as part of their high school educational experience. Peer tutors may assist the student in any context within the classroom, such as vocational, adaptive learning, or recreation and leisure activities. In a review of best practice indicators for

1. A number of current and future age-appropriate integrated school and community environments have been identified for each individual learner	YES	NO
2. Ecological analyses are used to identify barriers and facilitators to participation in identified school and community environments	YES	NO
3. A plan for increasing participation in identified age-appropriate school and community environments should be reflected in the IEP	YES	NO
4. Learners with severe handicaps have opportunities to interact with age-appropriate peers and other community members within identified school and community environments	YES	NO
5. The learner's educator or related services personnel functions as a trainer/advocate to age-appropriate non-handicapped peers, other teachers, and community members	YES	NO

OVERALL BEST PRACTICE SCORE: SOCIAL INTEGRATION

NOT IMPLEMENTED		PARTIALLY IMPLEMENTED		TOTALLY IMPLEMENTED
1	2	3	4	5

The LEA has a written policy statement addressing social integration of learners with severe handicaps	YES	NO

Figure 10–5
Best practice indicators for social integration

From *Best Educational Practices '86: Educating Learners with Severe Handicaps* (p. 5) by W. Fox, J. Thousand, W. Williams, T. Fox, P. Towne, R. Reid, C. Conn-Powers, and L. Calcagni, 1986, Burlington: University of Vermont, Center for Developmental Disabilities. Copyright 1986 by W. Fox. Reprinted by permission.

educating learners with severe handicaps, Fox et al. (1986) suggested that the handicapped student must have access to the same environments as nonhandicapped peers. "A primary goal of social integration should be to increase the *number* of integrated community and school environments in which learners . . . can participate" (p. 4). Figure 10–5 highlights best practice indicators for social integration.

NEW ISSUES AND FUTURE DIRECTIONS

Planning for the Future During the High School Years

For adolescents with mental retardation, the effective high school experience of the future will be one that is comprehensive in its approach and involves a transition planning process oriented to individual needs, preferences, and environments. A recent

Harris poll (Harris & Associates, 1989), however, indicated that the majority of students with disabilities age 17 and over were not involved in transition planning as a component of their high school program. The poll also found that less than half these students had received any job counseling during high school, and of those who did, their parents did not consider it to be effective.

As we move into the 1990s, the schools need to develop transition planning that is outcome-driven, focusing directly on providing access to natural environments to teach and apply different skills. In the past, many high schools have focused more on getting the student ready by teaching vocational skills in the classroom rather than in an actual job. This places schools in a passive role instead of engaging professionals in actively preparing and placing students in jobs. A recent study on the employment status of students with disabilities after they leave high school emphasized the need for the schools' active involvement in job preparation. Hasazi et al. (1989) found that graduates with disabilities who had secured a job placement before leaving school were more likely to stay employed.

To facilitate employment preparation at the high school level in future years, it will also be necessary for family and adult service providers to be integrally involved in transition planning. The schools cannot do this task alone. Coordination of family, schools, and adult service agencies should concentrate on identifying specific roles and responsibilities for all participants in the student's transition plan.

CORE QUESTIONS

1. What are three components of an effective high school program for adolescents with mental retardation?
2. What basic civil rights were established under Section 504 of the Vocational Rehabilitation Act?
3. Distinguish between work-study, career education, and work-experience programs.
4. Identify the components of a community-referenced vocational preparation program.
5. Discuss the barriers to socialization facing the retarded adolescent.
6. What difficulties face the retarded adolescent in attempting to maintain an appropriate personal appearance?
7. What is the value of recreation and leisure activities?
8. Discuss the objectives of a functional academics program for an adolescent with mental retardation.
9. Discuss the school's role in the transition planning process.
10. Why is integration with nonhandicapped peers an important aspect of a quality educational experience for adolescents with mental retardation?

ROUND TABLE DISCUSSION

Adolescence is accurately described as a period of transition from childhood to adult life. In recent years professionals have come to the realization that educational programs for adolescents with mental retardation must focus more on performance required for successful adjustment to community life as adults and less on academics. This chapter discusses a process for transition planning that focuses on matching the individual's functional capabilities with the demands that will be placed on him or her as an adult.

In your study group or on your own, design a transition plan for a student with mental retardation. Take into account the individual's capabilities in relation to preparation for employment, residential living, and access to recreation and leisure-time experiences. You may choose to use the components of the transition planning process as discussed on pages 294–295 as a guideline for the development of your plan.

REFERENCES

Bellamy, G. T., Horner, R. H., & Inman, D. P. (1979). *Vocational rehabilitation of severely retarded adults: A direct service technology.* Baltimore: University Park Press.

Bellamy, G. T., Rhodes, L. E., & Albin, J. M. (1985). *Supported employment.* Unpublished manuscript, University of Oregon, Eugene, OR.

Bellamy, G. T., Rhodes, L. E., Borbeau, P., & Mank, D. M. (1982). *Mental retardation services in sheltered workshops and day activity programs: Consumer outcomes and policy alternatives.* Unpublished manuscript, University of Oregon, Specialized Training Program, Eugene, Oregon.

Brimer, R., & Rouse, S. (1978). Post-school adjustment: A follow-up of a cooperative program for the educable mentally retarded. *Journal for Special Educators of the Mentally Retarded, 14,* 131–137.

Brodsky, M. (1983). *Post high school experiences of graduates with severe handicaps.* Unpublished doctoral dissertation, University of Oregon, Eugene, Oregon.

Brolin, D. E. (1982). *Vocational preparation of persons with handicaps* (2nd ed.). Columbus, OH: Charles E. Merrill.

Brolin, D. E. (1986). *Life-centered career education: A competency-based approach* (rev. ed.). Reston, VA: Council for Exceptional Children.

Bruininks, R. H., & Lakin, K. C. (1985). *Living and learning in the least restrictive environment.* Baltimore: Paul H. Brookes.

Buckley, J., & Bellamy, G. T. (1985). *A national survey of day and vocational programs for adults with severe disabilities: A 1984 profile.* Unpublished manuscript, University of Oregon, Specialized Training Program, Eugene, OR.

Chaffin, J., Davidson, R., Regan, C., & Spellman, C. (1971). Two follow-up studies of former mentally retarded students from the Kansas work study project. *Exceptional Children, 37,* 733–738.

Clark, G. M. (1979). *Career education for the handicapped child in the elementary classroom.* Denver: Love Publishing. *Federal Register.* (1977, May 4).

Fischer, H. L., & Krajicek, M. J. (1974). Sexual development of the moderately retarded child. *Clinical Pediatrics, 13*(1), 79–83.

Fox, W., Thousand, J., Williams, W., Fox, T., Towne, P., Reid, R., Conn-Powers, C., & Calcagni, L. (1986). *Best educational practices '86: Educating learners with severe handicaps.* Monograph Series. University of Vermont, Center for Developmental Disabilities, Burlington.

Gold, M. W. (1974). Redundant cue removal in skill training for the mentally retarded. *Education and Training of the Mentally Retarded, 9*(1), 5–8.

Halpern, A. S. (1973). General unemployment and vocational opportunities for EMR individuals. *American Journal of Mental Deficiency, 78,* 123–127.

Halpern, A. S. (1974). Work-study programs for the mentally retarded: An overview. In P. L. Browning (Ed.), *Mental retardation: Rehabilitation and counseling.* Springfield, IL: Charles C. Thomas.

Hardman, M. L., Drew, C. J., Egan, M. W., & Wolf, B. (1990). *Human exceptionality* (3rd ed.). Boston: Allyn & Bacon.

Hardman, M. L., & McDonnell, J. (1987). Implementing federal transition initiatives for youths with severe handicaps: The Utah Community-based Transition Project. *Exceptional Children, 53*(6), 493–498.

Harris, L., & Associates. (1989). *International Center for the Disabled survey III: Employing disabled Americans.* New York: Author.

Hasazi, S. B., Gordon, L. R., & Roe, C. A. (1984). Factors associated with the employment status of handicapped youth exiting high school from 1975 to 1983. *Exceptional Children, 51,* 455–469.

Hasazi, S. B., Johnson, R. E., Hasazi, J., Gordon, L. R., & Hull, M. (1989). Employment of youth with and without handicaps following school: Outcomes and correlates. *Journal of Special Education, 23,* 243–255.

Kempton, W. (1983, April). Teaching retarded children about sex. *PTA Today,* 28–30.

Mank, D. M., Rhodes, L. E., & Bellamy, G. T. (1986). Four supported employment alternatives. In W. E. Kiernan & J. A. Stark (Eds.), *Pathways to employment for adults with developmental disabilities* (pp. 139–154). Baltimore: Paul H. Brookes.

Martin, A., Flexer, R., & Newbery, J. (1979). The development of a work ethic in the severely retarded. In G. T. Bellamy, G. O'Conner, and O. Karan (Eds.), *Vocational rehabilitation of severely handicapped persons.* Baltimore: University Park Press.

McDonnell, J., & Hardman, M. L. (1985). Planning the transition of severely handicapped youth from school to adult services: A framework for high school programs. *Education and Training of the Mentally Retarded, 20*(4), 275–286.

McDonnell, J., Hardman, M. L., & Hightower, J. (1989). Employment preparation for high school students with severe handicaps. *Mental Retardation, 27*(6), 396–404.

McDonnell, J., Hightower, J., & Hardman, M. L. (1987). *The Utah community-based vocational preparation manual.* Salt Lake City: University of Utah, Department of Special Education.

McDonnell, J., Wilcox, B., Boles, S. M. (1985). *Do we know enough to plan for transition? A national survey of state agencies responsible for services to persons with severe handicaps.* Unpublished manuscript. University of Oregon, Eugene, OR.

McDonnell, J., Wilcox, B., & Hardman, M. L. (in press). *Secondary programs for students with developmental disabilities.* Boston: Allyn & Bacon.

Meers, G. D. (1980). *Handbook of special vocational needs education.* Rockville, MD: Aspen.

Mithaug, D. E., Horiuchi, C. N., & Fanning, P. N. (1985). A report on the Colorado statewide follow-up survey of special education students. *Exceptional Children, 51*(5), 397–404.

Moon, S., Goodall, P., & Wehman, P. (1985). *Critical issues related to supported competitive employment.* Richmond: Rehabilitation and Training Center, Virginia Commonwealth University.

National Council on Disability. (1989). *The education of students with disabilities: Where do we stand?* Washington, DC: Author.

Patton, J. R., Beirne-Smith, M., & Payne, J. (1990). *Mental retardation* (3rd ed.). Columbus: Charles E. Merrill.

Peck, C. A., Apolloni, T., & Cooke, T. P. (1981). Rehabilitation services for Americans with mental retardation: A summary of accomplishments in research and development. In E. L. Pan, T. E. Backer, & C. L. Vash (Eds.), *Annual review of rehabilitation* (Vol. 2). New York: Springer.

Rauh, J. L., Johnson, L. B., & Burket, R. L. (1973). The reproductive adolescent. *Pediatric Clinics of North America, 20,* 1005–1020.

Reisner, R. M. (1973). Acne vulgaris. *Pediatrics Clinics of North America, 20,* 851–864.

Revell, W. G., Wehman, P., & Arnold, S. (1985). A supported work approach to competitive employment of individuals with moderate and severe handicaps. In P. Wehman & J. W. Hill (Eds.), *Competitive employment for persons with mental retardation: From research to practice* (pp. 46–64). Richmond: Rehabilitation Research and Training Center, School of Education, Virginia Commonwealth University.

Schalock, R. L. (1985). Comprehensive community services: A plea for interagency collaboration. In R. H. Bruininks & K. C. Lakin (Eds.), *Living and learning in the least restrictive environment* (pp. 37–64). Baltimore: Paul H. Brookes.

Schilit, J., & Caldwell, M. L. (1980). A word list of essential career/vocational words for mentally retarded students. *Education and Training of the Mentally Retarded, 15*(2), 113–117.

Sowers, J., Thompson, L., & Connis, R. (1979). The food service vocational training program: A model for training and placement of the mentally retarded. In G. T. Bellamy, G. O'Conner, & O. Karan (Eds.), *Vocational rehabilitation of severely handicapped persons.* Baltimore: University Park Press.

Vogelsberg, R. T. (1986). Competitive employment in Vermont. In F. R. Rusch (Ed.), *Competitive employment issues and strategies* (pp. 35–50). Baltimore: Paul H. Brookes.

Wagner, M. (1989). *The transition experience of youths with disabilities: A report from the national longitudinal transition study.* Menlo Park, CA: SRI.

Wehman, P. (1986). Competitive employment in Virginia. In F. R. Rusch (Ed.), *Competitive employment issues and strategies* (pp. 23–34). Baltimore: Paul H. Brookes.

Wehman, P., Hill, M., Goodall, P., Cleveland, P., Brooke, V., Pentecost, J. (1982). Job placement and follow-up of moderately and severely handicapped individuals after three years. *Journal of the Association for the Severely Handicapped, 7,* 5–16.

Wehman, P., & Kregel, J. (1985). A supported work approach to competitive employment of individuals with severe handicaps. In P. Wehman & J. W. Hill (Eds.), *Competitive employment for persons with mental retardation: From research to practice* (pp. 20–45). Richmond: Rehabilitation Research and Training Center, Virginia Commonwealth University.

Wehman, P., Kregel, J., & Barcus, J. M. (1985). From school to work: A vocational transition model for handicapped students. In P. Wehman & J. W. Hill (Eds.), *Competitive employment for persons with moderate and severe mental retardation: From research to practice* (pp. 169–198). Richmond: Rehabilitation Research and Training Center, Virginia Commonwealth University.

Wehman, P., Kregel, J., & Seyfarth, J. (1985). Transition from school to work for individuals with severe disabilities: A follow-up study. In P. Wehman & J. W. Hill (Eds.), *Competitive employment for persons with mental retardation: From research to practice* (pp. 247–264). Richmond: Rehabilitation Research and Training Center, Virginia Commonwealth University.

Whitehead, C. (1981). *Final report: Training and employment services for handicapped individuals in sheltered workshops.* Washington, DC: Office of Social Services Policy, Office of the Assistant Secretary for Planning and Evaluation, U.S. Department of Health and Human Services.

Wilcox, B., & Bellamy, G. T. (1982). *Design of high school programs for severely handicapped students.* Baltimore: Paul H. Brookes.

Will, M. (1984). *OSERS program for the transition of youth with disabilities: Bridges from school to working life.* Washington DC: Office of Special Education and Rehabilitative Services.

PART FOUR

The Adult with Mental Retardation

CHAPTER ELEVEN

The Adult with Mental Retardation

■ Successful adjustment of the adult with mental retardation to community living depends on vocational opportunities, adequate housing, medical services, recreation and leisure time, and access to public transportation and buildings.

■ Small community residential models for adults with mental retardation include group homes, semi-independent apartments, and foster care.

■ Adults with mental retardation often do not participate in such civic activities as voting.

■ The treatment of persons with mental retardation by law enforcement officials and the judicial system varies from one community to another.

■ Leisure-time and recreation activities are an important source of pleasure and relaxation for the adult with mental retardation.

■ Many individuals with mental retardation desire and value marriage and sexual intimacy.

■ Adults with mental retardation are capable of self-sufficiency and social adaptation within the community.

■ For individuals with mental retardation, institutional living is widely viewed as detrimental to intellectual, psychological, and physical development.

■ There are three service alternatives for competitive employment for persons with mental retardation: (1) employment with no support services, (2) employment with time-limited support services, and (3) employment with ongoing support services.

■ The purpose of a sheltered workshop is to prepare the person with mental retardation for competitive employment or provide a terminal sheltered job.

The study of the entire life cycle of individuals with mental retardation is a relatively new phenomenon. Until recently professionals devoted most of their attention to development during childhood, because it progresses rapidly, is easily categorized, and is clearly significant for later life. Thus, while adulthood normally constitutes most of an individual's life, it has been slow to get the attention it deserves (Bellamy & Horner, 1987; Hardman, Drew, Egan, & Wolf, 1990).

Adulthood generally marks a time of transition from relative dependence to increasing independence and responsibility for one's life. Various professions disagree about just when adulthood begins. From a legal standpoint an individual becomes an adult upon reaching a specific age. Legal age for adulthood varies from 18 years in some states to 21 years in others. Thus the law instantaneously transforms adolescents into adults on a specified birthday. A person may also be transformed from adolescent to adult or vice versa by crossing state lines.

Many public school officials have tended to view either the completion of a high school program or the exclusion from school because of age (often 21 years) as the point at which the school's responsibility ends. Presumably by this time the individual will have reached some semblance of adulthood. Professionals in the health sciences tend to equate specific levels of physical development with adulthood. This criterion might preclude those with certain physiological deviancies regardless of intellectual or social competence. Adding to the frustrating lack of uniformity in criteria is a behavioral science view emphasizing that an adult must show specific behavioral patterns.

Adults with mental retardation are a paradox. They have achieved adulthood because they have lived long enough to deserve the distinction. But some of these adults are unable to be completely independent. They lack the intellectual skills to meet typical high school graduation requirements and may lack behavioral characteristics considered essential for adequate adult functioning.

Many individuals who are mildly or moderately retarded endure the frustrations of childhood and adolescence with the hope and expectation that adulthood will bring emancipation from the many problems associated with school. While academic pressures and some intellectual demands tend to relax on completion of school, other demands and pressures find their way into the life of an adult with retardation. What does society expect of an adult? Adults work, earn money, and buy the necessities of life and as many of the pleasures they want or can afford. An adult socializes, often marries, has children, and tries to live as productively and happily as possible. The adult with retardation may be unable to find or hold a job. If jobs are available, wages may be so low that even the necessities of life may be out of reach. What if the adults with retardation have no one to socialize with, no one to love or be loved by? What if they must become dependent on parents for mere existence, and the parents become too old to help or die? There are many such "what ifs" for adults with retardation, who may just exchange the frustrations of earlier life for new and sometimes harsher ones.

Little research focuses on the adult with retardation (Hardman et al., 1990). Most studies concern retarded children in the educational system, since the deficiencies of persons with mental retardation are most glaring when they are in school. Not until 1973 did the Association for Retarded Children change its name to the Association for Retarded Citizens. Although this association has long campaigned for the rights of all with retardation, the name change was indicative of a growing recognition of the need to emphasize programming at all stages of life. We support the emphasis on children and youth, but we are concerned about the lack of emphasis on appropriate opportunities, programs, and services for adults with mental retardation. The individual will be an adult three times as long as he or she is a child or an adolescent, if average life expectancy is reached. Therefore, it seems only appropriate for us to devote more time to the needs and nature of adults with mental retardation.

COMMUNITY LIVING

Core Concept	*Successful adjustment of the adult with mental retardation to community living depends on vocational opportunities, adequate housing, medical services, recreation and leisure time, and access to public transportation and buildings.*

The availability of appropriate services within the community creates a better opportunity for the individual with mental retardation to achieve what has become commonly referred to as "normalization." The principle of normalization was first articulated by Nirje (1969) and Bank-Mikkelsen (1969), and it was expanded and advocated in the United States by Wolfensberger (1972). Normalization means "making available to the mentally retarded patterns and conditions of everyday life which are as close as possible to the norms and patterns of mainstream society" (Nirje, 1969, p. 181). Normalization does not mean just providing a normative situation, like a home in the community. Without support services, the individual with retardation may not be able to meet the demands of the community. Nirje (1970) stated that:

> normalization will not make a subnormal normal, but will make life conditions of the mentally subnormal as close as possible, bearing in mind the degree of his handicap, his competence and maturity as well as the need for training activities and availability of services. . . . The awareness that mostly only relative independence and integration can be attained (is) implied and stressed by the words "as close as possible." (p. 63)

Wolfensberger (1983) suggested a rethinking of the term *normalization* and introduced the concept of "social role valorization"—giving value to the individual with mental retardation. He stated that "the most explicit and highest goal of normalization must be the creation, support, and defense of valued social roles for people who are at risk of social devaluation" (p. 234). We must attempt to attain socially valued roles and life conditions for people whom society now devalues. Strategies to accomplish this goal would enhance the individual's social image or perceived value in the eyes of others and enhance individual competence within society.

The principle of normalization or social role valorization has brought with it a strong emphasis on deinstitutionalization, the process of returning those residing in large centers for persons with mental retardation to community and home environments. The principle does not apply, however, only to individuals moving from an institution to a less restrictive setting, but also to people already living in the community, for whom a more "normal" life style is a worthy goal.

Parents or guardians of the person with mental retardation and administrators often make the decisions about residential living (McDonnell, Wilcox, & Hardman, 1991). Often the individual has no opportunity to voice opinions or preferences in the decision-making process. This has been based on the premise that the individual with mental retardation is incompetent to participate in these decisions.

There are many areas of everyday living that most individuals take for granted, such as shopping, crossing streets, making daily purchases, and getting transportation. Yet unless people with mental retardation receive systematic instruction in these areas, a number of problems can develop. For example, a group of young adults with mental retardation living in a community-based home had not had any instruction about using traffic lights to cross streets and were walking against red lights. Not until the trainers in the group home recognized the problem did the residents get appropriate training.

In the following sections, we address various aspects of life in the community. These include residential alternatives, community participation, marriage and sexuality, and adjustment to community life.

Community-Based Residential Living

Core Concept	*Small community residential models for adults with mental retardation include group homes, semi-independent apartments, and foster care.*

As we move into the 1990s, the vast majority of people with mental retardation, along with their families and professionals, are advocating nationwide expansion of small, community-based residences located in residential neighborhoods and staffed by trained support personnel. Residents in these settings would use existing services in the community for education, work, health care, and recreation. Other alternatives might also be appropriate, such as living with a local family, foster care, or adoption.

As is true for people without disabilities, community services for people with mental retardation should promote personal autonomy, social integration, and choice of life style. Many professionals have advocated residential settings that provide training in community living. These programs emphasize activities that develop skills for independent functioning in daily activities.

Several systems for classifying community residential programs have been developed over the years (Baker, Seltzer, & Seltzer, 1977; Campbell & Bailey, 1984; McDonnell et al., 1991; Schalock, 1986). Table 11–1 presents a summary of current program models, as described by Hill and Lakin (1986). In this chapter we discuss three widely used residential models for adults with mental retardation living in the community: group homes, semi-independent apartments, and foster care.

Group Homes

There is considerable variation in organization and many alternatives within the group home model. **Small group homes** are usually a community residence with up to four persons living in a single dwelling. **Large group homes** may have as many as eight to 12 residents. Trained house parents or professionals staff these homes; they often have an assistant to serve as a relief person when they are off duty. In some instances a house director works on a full- or half-time basis to handle administrative matters. Many group homes are now employing shift workers who are on duty for four to seven days at a time as a team. Small group homes are usually integrated in residential neighborhoods. The homes emphasize programs that provide daily living experiences as similar as possible to those of nonretarded individuals. Day placements for work skill training are typical of these programs.

State funds supplemented by fees paid by the residents usually finance these homes. As might be expected, a fairly high percentage meet with some opposition from the community, especially neighbors. Baker et al. (1977) found in their study of group homes that 19% of the residents in the study returned to institutions or hospitals, 24% went on to live in an apartment, 26.5% returned to their families, and 5% were placed in foster homes. The rest stayed in group homes. In some instances these homes become an individual's permanent residence; in others they serve as an intermediate

Table 11–1
Community residential models

Original Definition	Proposed Definition
Residential facility Any living quarters which provided 24-hour, 7-days-a-week responsibility for room, board, and supervision of mentally retarded people as of (date), with the exception of: (a) single family homes providing services to a relative; (b) nursing homes, boarding homes, and foster homes that are not formally state licensed or contracted as mental retardation service providers; and (c) independent living programs which have no staff residing in the same facility.	(No definition)
Program models A home or apartment owned or rented by a family, with one or more retarded people living as family members (e.g., foster homes)	A residence owned or rented by a family as their own home, with one or more mentally retarded people living as family members (e.g., foster homes)
A residence with staff who provide care, supervision, and training of one or more mentally retarded people (e.g., group residence)	A residence with staff who provide care, supervision, and training of one or more mentally retarded people (e.g., group residence)
A residence consisting of semi-independent units or apartments with staff living in a separate unit in the same building (e.g., supervised apartments)	A residence consisting of semi-independent units or apartments with staff living in a separate unit in the same building (e.g., semi-independent living program)
A residence which provides sleeping rooms and meals, but no regular care or supervision of residents (e.g., boarding home)	A residence with staff which provides sleeping rooms, meals, and supervision, but no formal training or help with dressing, bathing, etc. (e.g., board & supervision facility)
A residence in which staff provide help with dressing, bathing, or other personal care, but no formal training of residents (e.g., personal care home)	A residence with staff who provide help with dressing, bathing, or other personal care, but no formal training of residents (e.g., personal care facility)
A nursing home (e.g., ICF or SNF)	A facility that provides daily nursing care with primary emphasis on residents' health care needs (e.g., nursing home)

From "Classification of Residential Facilities for Individuals with Mental Retardation" by B. K. Hill and K. C. Lakin, 1986, *Mental Retardation 24*(2), p. 109. Copyright 1986 by the American Association on Mental Deficiencies. Reprinted by permission.

step to a more normalized situation. Group decisions about daily administrative issues may lead to better operations than decisions made individually.

The availability of group homes was the subject of a survey conducted by Janicki, Mayeda, and Epple (1983). They found that in the 1970s there was a dramatic increase in the availability of group homes in the United States. The survey indicated that in 1980 there were more than 5,700 group homes in this country, an increase of over 900% since 1973. Janicki et al. also reported that approximately 23,500 persons were living in group homes for persons with mental retardation, a growth rate of 183%. These authors concluded, however, that although there had been considerable expansion in the development of group homes, "There still appears to be an outstanding need for more group home beds nationally" (p. 50). A survey of adult service agencies across the United States corroborated this conclusion (McDonnell, Wilcox, & Boles, 1986). These agencies reported long waiting lists for both employment and residential services.

In a study of 132 group homes, Baker et al. (1977) found that 21% of the residents were engaged in competitive employment, 51% in sheltered workshops or educational programs, and 16% in day activity centers. The mean age of these residents was 29 years, with 35% of the group listed as mildly retarded, 48% as moderately retarded, 13% as severely retarded, and the remaining 4% handicapped, nonretarded individuals.

Semi-independent Apartments

The **semi-independent apartment** represents the least supervised and least restrictive of all supervised residential models.

Several variations on the semi-independent apartment have developed over the years:

1. *Apartment clusters.* Comprised of several apartments fairly close together. They function to some extent as a unit and are supervised by a resident staff member who lives in one of the apartment units.
2. *Single co-residence apartment.* Single apartments in which an adult staff member (usually a college student) shares an apartment with two or three roommates who are mentally retarded.
3. *Single apartment.* An apartment occupied by two or more retarded adults whom a nonresident staff member assists. This is the most independent kind of living arrangement in the model.

These three variations provide different degrees of independence, and individuals living in this type of residential model may be less seriously retarded than those living in other residential models. Most residents are responsible for or contribute to apartment maintenance, meal preparation, and transportation to place of employment.

Foster Family Care

The purpose of **foster family care** is to provide a surrogate family for the individual. One goal of foster family care is to integrate the individual into the family setting, with the assumption that within the normal family environment and with the foster family's understanding, he or she will learn behavior acceptable to the family and, if feasible, will work. One problem of this model is that a person with mental retardation living in a surrogate family may assume a dependent, childlike role and become overprotected. In general these placements offer residents adequate productive daytime activities and opportunities to manage their physical environment, both fundamental components of normalization. Those who operate the foster homes generally receive a per capita fee from the state. These settings accommodate from one to six adults. Activities and quality of care are to some extent at the discretion of the operator. If the operator's goal is to make a profit, they may spend very little on their foster residents to increase profits.

One other setting that some consider to be a community residential alternative is the sheltered village. **Sheltered villages** for adults with mental retardation are usually located in rural areas; they are secluded and spread over several buildings. Although rules, activities, and relative freedom within each sheltered village vary, they do have one common characteristic: in this setting the individual with mental retardation is

Community participation for adults with mental retardation may include many activities undertaken by nonretarded individuals.

isolated from the outside community. The rationale is that residents are better off in isolation than being exposed to the potential failures, frustrations, and demands of the outside world. Many of these facilities are private, and a number are church supported. Of the community models we have discussed, the sheltered village conflicts most with the principle of normalization.

Community Participation

Core Concept	*Adults with mental retardation often do not participate in such civic activities as voting.*

Exercising the Right to Vote

Participation in social and civic activities like voting is difficult and often confusing for many adults with mental retardation. For example, in a survey on voting practices of adults with mental retardation, Edgerton (1967) found no adults with mental retardation who had ever voted. Gozali (1971) investigated 68 mildly retarded individuals' knowledge about and participation in democratic political processes. The subjects ranged in chronological age from 21 to 28 years and in IQ from 68 to 82. All had attended special education programs. Each individual was asked 60 questions relating to citizenship. Gozali found that most did poorly on the test, and none had even registered to vote.

Core Concept	*The treatment of persons with mental retardation by law enforcement officials and the judicial system varies from one community to another.*

The Mentally Retarded Offender

Throughout the years various studies have found a disproportionately high number of individuals with mental retardation involved in delinquent or criminal activity (Kvaraceus, 1945; McAfee & Gural, 1988; Peterson & Smith, 1960). Studies suggest that approximately 10% of the prison population meets the AAMR definition of mental retardation (DeSilva, 1980; Reichard, Spencer, & Spooner, 1980). These data are consistent with an earlier study conducted by Allen (1969) in which he polled correctional institutions from across the United States. His surveys revealed that the percentage of persons with mental retardation (using 70 IQ as a cutoff) in correctional institutions was three times as high as their percentage in the general population. In other words, approximately 9% of the inmate population had IQs of 70 or below, as compared with 3% in the general population.

Subsequent studies by Allen (1970) and Marsh, Friel, and Eissler (1975) also found that individuals with mental retardation who came into contact with the criminal justice system were often poor, black, and undereducated. Marsh et al. indicated that in over 90% of criminal cases involving people with mental retardation, the defendant pleaded guilty. These authors recommended that further research be undertaken to examine judicial alternatives that would more effectively meet the needs of people with mental retardation than prison does. The results of Allen's (1970) study suggest that in our system all are *not* equal before the law. Persons with mental retardation can seldom afford private defense lawyers and therefore must make do with court-appointed attorneys. The worth of such legal defense is debatable, given that both studies found the entire trial process a formality.

The results just mentioned agree with those Schilit (1979) found. In a survey of police officers, lawyers, and judges, Schilit found that 91% of these people did not have any formal training in mental retardation and consistently underestimated the functional capabilities of individuals with mental retardation. In fact, McAfee and Gural (1988) found that arresting officers were able to recognize individuals as being mentally retarded fewer than three times in 10. From this information we can draw several inferences about the criminal justice system:

1. The mentally retarded person who comes into contact with the criminal justice system is at a definite disadvantage due to the criminal justice system's unfamiliarity and uncertainty in dealing with mentally retarded individuals.
2. Preservice and inservice education for criminal justice system personnel is needed on the topic of mental retardation and the mentally retarded offender.
3. Mentally retarded individuals need to be trained about the criminal justice system and what to do if they come into contact with the criminal justice system.
4. There is a need for community agencies to begin dealing with this area of concern, that is, the mentally retarded offender and the criminal justice system.
5. The criminal justice system might need to reorganize itself to establish a system within itself to handle mentally retarded offenders. (Schilit, 1979, p. 22)

In some communities law enforcement officers are sympathetic to the person with mental retardation, whereas in others such a person may be viewed as a nuisance. Persons with mental retardation, who often lack financial resources and advocates may suffer greatly in our judicial system. We need to develop a system in which these individuals can receive adequate legal help when they are in difficulty. The American Civil Liberties Union has long served as an advocate for oppressed groups. This group, along with protection and advocacy systems for developmentally disabled persons in every state, local associations for citizens with retardation, and local bar associations, can serve as an effective advocate for people with retardation. Most persons who are mentally retarded have demonstrated positive capabilities in the social system. A concerted effort will increase the number of responsible individuals with retardation and decrease the number imprisoned.

| Core Concept | *Leisure-time and recreation activities are an important source of pleasure and relaxation for the adult with mental retardation.* |

Leisure Time and Recreation

Many adults who are mentally retarded have busy and active work schedules. For these individuals leisure-time and recreational activities provide a much-needed change from daily work schedules. Other adults with mental retardation have little if any work or regular daily activity. These individuals need recreational activities as a means to achieve more satisfaction and independence in their lives. However, as Schleien, Kiernan, and Wehman (1981) pointed out, "Remarkably few studies have investigated the leisure skill behaviors of mentally retarded adults living in community based residences" (p. 13).

Shannon (1985) found that adults with retardation spend significant amounts of time alone at home. Typical activities included watching television, listening to music, and looking at books and magazines. An earlier study (Stanfield, 1973) indicated that walking idly around the neighborhood was a frequent activity of many. Stanfield reported that 44% of his subjects were uninvolved in postschool or rehabilitation programs. This meant that a large number of subjects had almost no structured daily activity. Stanfield quotes one mother as saying: "At first it wasn't too bad. He enjoyed his vacation as he called it—and then he began to ask when school would start again. I don't have the time it takes —and I don't always know what to do for him." Stanfield concluded that the vast majority of adults with mental retardation had no social or recreational life apart from that of the immediate family.

Many forms of recreation and leisure are being recognized as relevant for retarded individuals.

Adults with retardation are too often left with lonely, inactive lives when meaningful leisure activities should be an integral part of their lives (Fain, 1986). Peck, Appoloni, and Cooke (1981) believed that successful training in leisure time could come about through the incorporation of systematic assessment, highly structured training procedures, and rigorous evaluation components. The adult with retardation is fully entitled to the pleasures of well-planned recreational activities. Efforts in this direction by recreation therapists, churches, schools, and family can help make life more meaningful for these adults.

Marriage and Sexuality

Core Concept	*Many individuals with mental retardation desire and value marriage and sexual intimacy.*

Adults with retardation place a high value on marriage and consider it a very desirable state to achieve (Edgerton & Bercovici, 1976). In interviewing a number of former hospital patients, Edgerton and Bercovici found that the desire to marry, particularly to someone not from the institution, was of paramount importance. One adult with retardation said that every woman wanted to marry a man not associated with the hospital. The speaker indicated that she had done everything to improve her chances— "speaking properly," buying nice clothing, and going to nice places. She avoided "hospital guys" (males released from the institution from which she herself had been released). She stated, "When I finally married an outside guy, I knew my troubles were over." A man indicated that the men from his group of former institutional subjects, including himself, had remained single because of their inability to meet nonretarded women. He further stated that the only women available to the men released from the institution were "hospital girls" or prostitutes.

Heshusius (1982) reviewed the literature for perceptions on marriage and sexuality of persons labeled mentally retarded, sorting the statements according to common elements. These generalized statements reflected a desire for and enjoyment of sexual contact as well as a fear of sexual intimacy. Many of those with retardation felt that sexual intimacy belonged with marriage. There was also some ignorance of basic facts about sexual relations. Heshusius stressed the need for more sensitivity on the part of society to a retarded person's need for sexual intimacy.

It seems clear from the available literature that mentally retarded persons do desire and value marriage and sexual intimacy. As a group, however, they are apparently not as successful as nonretarded peers in finding mates; this may result partly from their desire to marry normal individuals, or at least individuals who have had no previous association with an institution. This particular desire dovetails with the overall desire to live as normal a life as possible.

Sex education is a major concern, but it is often deliberately ignored in spite of the fact that individuals with retardation can learn new social/sexual skills (Abramson, Parker, & Weisberg, 1988; Foxx, McMorrow, Storey, & Rogers, 1984). As adults in the community, these persons are free in many instances to conduct their personal lives as they choose, and the results of their interpersonal relationships may depend on the instruction and training that they receive in sex education. As discussed by Timmers, DuCharme, and Jacob (1981), the sexual behavior of people with mental retardation is learned and will be directly affected by environmental factors. Abramson et al. (1988) suggested that people with mental retardation be guaranteed sex education and training. "This training must be designed to facilitate informed consent, sexual hygiene, and—when desired—conscientious contraception" (p. 332).

Another issue concerning sexuality and mentally retarded persons is the practice of sterilization. In past years sterilization was viewed as a means of eliminating or curtailing mental retardation, preventing individuals with retardation from having unwanted children, or preventing them from having children because of their alleged incompetence. In 1927 Justice Oliver Wendell Holmes issued his famous opinion for the Supreme Court, which upheld a state compulsory sterilization law. He stated that "three generations of imbeciles are enough" (*Buck v. Bell,* 1927). Following the Holmes opinion, there was a marked increase in the practice of sterilization. As many as 8,000 people were legally sterilized without their permission in the state of Virginia between the 1920s and the 1970s (Smith, 1989).

The prime targets for compulsory sterilization appear to have been individuals with mental retardation who are in the process of being released from institutions (Burt, 1973; Edgerton, 1969). In Edgerton's study of former patients at Pacific State Hospital, he found that 44 of the 48 subjects had undergone "eugenic" sterilization. During the period of their institutionalization, sterilization was considered a prerequisite to release. Form letters were sent to parents or guardians to gain consent for the procedure. These letters strongly implied that sterilization could permit parole and would be in the best interest of the individual. Unless there was strong objection, the surgery was routinely performed.

By 1935 mentally retarded persons constituted 44% of those sterilized in this country; by 1946 the percentage had increased to 69%. The rate of sterilization had increased through 1937 but leveled off by 1942 because of the shortage of medical personnel during the war years (Goldstein, 1964). Gamble (1951) reported that by 1951, 26,000 retarded individuals had been rendered parolable from institutions by sterilization.

The concern of discriminatory sterilization laws should not be limited exclusively to the institutional group. The question of whether or not society has the right to impose sterilization on any individual with retardation has great relevance for parents, professionals, and the individuals themselves. Prominent jurists like Burt (1973) and Allen (1969) considered involuntary sterilization of persons with mental retardation a violation of the individual's basic rights. It is interesting to note that two of the four unsterilized subjects in Edgerton's study were successful mothers with children of normal intelligence.

Primary issues are Who decides who must be sterilized? and What criterion is used to determine the decision? Should we sterilize all individuals with retardation, both in institutions and in the community? What are the criteria for determining sufficient retardation to warrant compulsory sterilization? Should we sterilize all individuals at the moderate level or below? Should we use a cutoff of 70 or 75 IQ, which would include all persons with mild retardation as well? Perhaps the strongest advocates of sterilization could justify using 100 IQ as a minimum criterion for the right of having children, since 100 IQ represents mean or average IQ. Obviously the setting of arbitrary criteria can be both unfair and potentially dangerous to the civil rights of every individual.

Research on Adjustment to Community Living

Core Concept	*Adults with mental retardation are capable of self-sufficiency and social adaptation within the community.*

The 1980s was an era of expansion in community living alternatives for persons with mental retardation. We have made significant advances in our knowledge of factors affecting community adjustment (Bruininks & Lakin, 1985; Peck et al., 1981; Eyman & Borthwick, 1980; Hasazi, Johnson, Gordon, & Hull, 1989; Hitzing, 1980; Tessler & Manderscheid, 1982). Much remains to be done, however, to use the information available effectively and to identify more specifically those variables that are associated with success in community programs. Follow-up studies of individuals with retardation date back to 1919. Fernald (1919) studied individuals discharged from an institution over a 25-year period and found considerable variability in their adjustment to community life. In the 1930s and 1940s, several studies compared the community adjustment of individuals with retardation with control groups of nonretarded individuals. These include studies by Fairbanks (1931), Baller (1936), and Kennedy (1948). Fairbanks and Kennedy conducted their studies during periods when economic conditions were generally favorable, as were general employment conditions. Baller's study was conducted in the middle of the Depression. When economic conditions are poor, individuals with retardation are among those most severely affected. Employers may consider them the most dispensable of their employees, so they are often the first to be laid off. This is particularly evident in Baller's study—only 20% of the subjects with retardation were gainfully employed as opposed to 50% of the control group (normal subjects). In Fairbanks' and Kennedy's studies, however, the retarded compared very favorably with the controls with respect to gainful employment. In all three studies, the marital status of the retarded person appeared to be somewhat comparable with the control subject. Home ownership, as reported by Fairbanks and Kennedy, also appeared comparable. These studies suggest that the majority of persons with retardation were able to make acceptable adjustments to community life. They were employed in semiskilled and unskilled jobs. Economic conditions and the type of community may have had some effect on their ability to adjust. Follow-up studies of the subjects suggest that even in later years, community adjustment of these individuals can be considered successful (Baller, Charles, & Miller, 1966; Kennedy, 1966). Another study in the 1960s (Edgerton, 1967) examined the posthospital lives of a number of individuals released from Pacific State Hospital, a California residential institution. The subjects of Edgerton's study were individuals with mild retardation who had received the benefit of vocational rehabilitation training programs both in the hospital and in the community. These individuals were considered among the more intellectually, socially, and emotionally capable in the institution. As a group, Edgerton found the subjects generally living comfortably, with most of them married and enjoying various leisure activities. By and large their existence was rather inconspicuous. Edgerton suggested that one of the greatest problems faced by this group was the stigma of the label of mental retardation. These individuals could not and would not accept the "fact" that they were or had ever been mentally retarded. To do so would have humiliated them and devalued their feelings of self-worth. Thus, much of their effort went to convince others, as well as themselves, that they were normal individuals. Many attributed their relative incompetence to the years spent in the institution, locked up and deprived of the knowledge and experience society requires for competent living and functioning.

In a follow-up to the 1967 study, Edgerton and Bercovici (1976) examined the lives of many of the same individuals several years later to determine what effect the passage of time had had on their community adaptation. They managed to locate 30 of the original 48 subjects. In this follow-up, the subjects expressed far less concern for passing as "normal," and stigma was less evident. Additionally, Edgerton and Bercovici found that "normal" benefactors played a smaller role. Overall, dependence on benefactors lessened over time. This may have been the result of less need for benefactors or a lessening availability of them. Edgerton and Bercovici concluded that the reduction in stigma may have helped decrease the need for benefactors, and the additional years of experience in community living may have reduced the need for assistance. While Edgerton and Bercovici rated the life circumstances for the total group as slightly worse compared with their status in the earlier study (1967), in general the subjects considered their circumstances happier. Their happiness was not necessarily a function of vocational success. Rather, happiness may have been more a function of being normal, and in periods of high unemployment, many normal people may not be working.

A second follow-up to Edgerton's 1967 study was conducted in 1982 (Edgerton, Bollinger, & Herr, 1984). This follow-up study focused on the personal and social resources of 15 persons with mild retardation originally studied in 1960 and 1961. These authors found still less dependence on others than reported in the previous investigations. These subjects, now ranging between 47 and 68 years of age, were described as more hopeful, confident, and independent by the investigators.

In the 1970s, several studies (Bellamy, O'Conner, & Karan, 1979; Close, 1975; Gold, 1973) demonstrated that under carefully controlled conditions even severely and profoundly retarded persons are capable of self-sufficiency and social adaptation within a community setting. More recent investigations (Bruininks, Meyers, Sigford, & Lakin, 1981; Conroy & Bradley, 1985; Eyman & Borthwick, 1980; O'Neill, Brown, Gordon, & Schonhorn, 1985) have focused on the feasibility of small community living situations for people with moderate and severe mental retardation. Over a five-year period, Conroy & Bradley (1985) monitored the transfer of mentally retarded residents from a large institution in Pennsylvania to small community living programs. They found that while the individual lived in the institution there was only minimal developmental growth, compared to substantial growth during the period of community living. Eyman and Borthwick (1980) compared the adaptive behavior of severely and profoundly retarded persons residing in an institution with the behavior of those living in a community setting. They reported that more than 80% of those with severe and profound retardation residing in an institution exhibited maladaptive behavior, compared to less than half of those living in community settings.

INSTITUTIONAL LIVING

Core Concept	*For individuals with mental retardation, institutional living is widely viewed as detrimental to intellectual, psychological, and physical development.*

Institutions for persons with mental retardation go under many different labels, for example, school, hospital, colony. These are some characteristics of an institution: (1) all aspects of life go on in the same place and under the same single authority; (2) activities are carried on in the immediate company of others, all of whom are treated alike and required to do the same thing together; (3) a system of explicit formal rulings and a body of officials govern tightly scheduled activities; (4) social mobility is grossly restricted; (5) work is defined as treatment, punishment, or rehabilitation; and (6) a system of rewards and punishments takes in the individual's total life situation (Goffman, 1975).

The deinstitutionalization movement in the United States came about because many institutions for the mentally retarded had become dehumanizing warehouses with no adequate treatment programs (Balla, 1976; Blatt, Ozolins, & McNally, 1979; *Homeward Bound v. Hissom Memorial Center*, 1988; "Staff report," 1985; *Wyatt v. Stickney*, 1972; Zigler, 1973). For persons with mental retardation, institutional living is widely viewed as a detriment to intellectual, psychological, and physical development.

Menolascino, McGee, and Casey (1982) suggested that there is an abundance of information and research data available indicating the following:

> (1) Prolonged institutionalization has destructive developmental consequences . . . (2) appropriate community-based residential settings are generally more beneficial than institutional placements . . . and (3) mentally retarded individuals with a wide spectrum of disabilities—including the severely and profoundly retarded—can be successfully served in community-based settings. (p. 65)

The most harmful aspect of institutional living is the emphasis on a restrictive regimen, with no attempt to personalize programs or living conditions to the needs of the residents (Hardman et al., 1990).

The legal and moral debate regarding what is a good or bad institution or whether there is a need for any large residential facility for persons with mental retardation continues. Some institutions for the mentally retarded have attempted in recent years to provide a more family-like environment for the retarded person instead of restricted dormitory living conditions. Changes include efforts to provide private or semi-private bedrooms, family dining facilities, individual clothing and hairstyles, and private possessions.

Neither parents nor professionals have agreed on criteria for determining whether the institution is an appropriate living and learning environment for any person with mental retardation (for example, the profoundly retarded). We can say, however, that the accomplishments of institutions in the past 90 years add up to very little. The institution of the twentieth century has been more concerned with social management than with the physical and psychological growth of the person with mental retardation. Across the United States these large public facilities continue to lose about 6,000 residents per year. They are being replaced by smaller, community-based programs (Haney, 1988; Hill, Lakin, & Bruininks, 1984).

COMPETITIVE EMPLOYMENT

Core Concept	*There are three service alternatives for competitive employment for persons with mental retardation: (1) employment with no support services, (2) employment with time-limited support services, and (3) employment with ongoing support services.*

From childhood on up we all fantasize about vocational choices. Fantasy may follow a person through life; aspirations, however, tend to fit actual abilities better as the individual matures. Since an individual's life style and ultimate personal satisfaction are often related to vocational satisfaction, counselors attempt to direct and aid students in finding acceptable vocational choices.

People with mental retardation are no different from others with respect to having vocational aspirations, but because of their intellectual limitations they may find it more difficult to obtain jobs that fulfill their aspirations. These difficulties and limitations may be caused not only by their own limitations but also by lack of imagination and creativity and by the stereotyping tendencies of professionals.

Sustained competitive employment for persons with mental retardation is a laudable societal goal. Employment is important for many reasons beyond monetary rewards, including adult identity, social contacts, integration with peers, and the perception of contributing to society. Yet research on adults with mental retardation clearly indicates that these people are underemployed (Hasazi et al., 1989; Wehman, Kregel, Shafer, & Hill, 1986). The U.S. Commission on Civil Rights (1983) indicated that disabled individuals have unemployment rates between 50% and 75%. A poll conducted in 1986 found that:

1. Two-thirds of disabled people between the ages of 16 and 64 were not working;
2. 66% of those not working, and of working age, indicated they would like a job;
3. A comparison of working and nonworking disabled individuals revealed that working individuals were more satisfied with life, had more money, and were less likely to blame their disability for preventing them from reaching their potential as a person. (International Center for the Disabled, 1986)

A report by the Organization for Economic Cooperation and Development (OECD, 1986) suggested that the common denominator around the world is "the lack of flexibility of systems which on occasion discourage the search for employment. A further feature of many [countries] is that benefits cease when employment is found, but are not easily obtained again if the individual is unemployed" (p. 18).

In December 1986 the OECD sponsored a conference of member nations to address public policy and practices that promoted the successful transition of students with disabilities into adult life, specifically the world of work. One significant conclusion of the conference was that social policy results in a far from coherent set of practices related to transition. Different agencies within countries (education, labor, health) are operating at cross-purposes. "Where education and labor departments might be pursuing the objectives of maximizing autonomy and economic self-sufficiency, social security agencies might be providing pensions and services on the basis of an individual's total economic dependency" (OECD, 1986, p. 16). For the individual with mental retardation, the messages are indeed mixed. One government entity communicates that people with mental retardation should strive to be contributing members of society, while another supports their dependence. The OECD concluded that the proper role of governments may be to stimulate opportunities for people with disabilities in both private and public sectors. This would include legislation and policy development, a mandated process for interagency coordination, strategies to change public attitudes, and the dissemination of information regarding effective model programs that enhance community living and participation. The high unemployment rates of people with mental retardation seem to be attributable to several factors. First, traditional employment models have been oriented to either no training for the individual after leaving school or short-term training programs with the expectation that the individual will need no ongoing support while on the job. Another factor associated with underemployment is related to an emphasis on sheltered or protected work settings where the individual is placed for training, but does not earn significant wages. The average annual wage in sheltered work settings and work activity centers is about $400 (Whitehead & Rhodes, 1985). The individual with mental retardation may remain in such settings for most, if not all, of the adult years.

There are, however, some good reasons to be optimistic about competitive employment for people with mental retardation. We are now seeing great emphasis put on improvement of employment services. Research knowledge is expanding, and there is more emphasis on employment with both state and national policymakers (Ferguson & Ferguson, 1986; Stark & Kiernan, 1986). The concept of competitive employment for persons with mental retardation has changed dramatically in recent years (Hill et al., 1985; O'Neill & Stern, 1985; Vogelsberg, 1985; Will, 1985). Competitive employment can now be described in terms of three service alternatives: (1) employment with no support services, (2) employment with time-limited support services, and (3) employment with ongoing support services.

Employment with No Support Services

The adult with mental retardation may be able to locate and maintain a community job with no additional support services from public or private agencies. The individual finds a job independently either through contacts made during school vocational preparation programs or through such sources as a job service, want ads, family, friends, and so forth. For the person with mild retardation, competitive employment without support is possible if adequate vocational training and experience are available during the school years (Brolin, DuRand, Kromer, & Muller, 1975). A major concern of professionals preparing individuals with mental retardation for competitive employment is identification of characteristics related to vocational success. If these characteristics can be identified, vocational training programs and early educational programs can be developed to emphasize the positive characteristics that tend to enhance vocational success.

Employment with Time-Limited Training and Support Services

After the individual with mental retardation finishes school, he or she may have access to several services on a short-term basis, including vocational rehabilitation, vocational education, and on-the job training. As Will (1985) wrote, "Access to such time-limited services is generally restricted to individuals thought capable of making it on their own after services are completed." Vocational rehabilitation services are the best known of all time-limited employment services. To qualify for vocational rehabilitation, the individual must have an employment-related disability. The expectation is that the individual will be independently employed following rehabilitation training. After the individual completes the training, rehabilitation services terminate, unless the individual fails on the job and has to be retrained.

In examining the reasons for occupational failure among adults with retardation it becomes evident that few people lose their jobs because of actual inability to perform the tasks they have been assigned. Rather, failure has tended to be related more to personality and an inability to adjust to the job situation.

Hill et al. (1985) found that lack of academic skills did not preclude job placement or retention. Of their 155 mentally retarded clients in community jobs, the majority had very limited mathematics or reading skills, and half could not tell time.

Employment with Ongoing Support Services:
The Supported Employment Model

Supported employment is defined as work in an integrated setting for individuals with severe handicaps (including those with mental retardation) who will probably need continuous support services and for whom competitive employment has traditionally not been possible. As defined in the legislation (1986 amendments to the Vocational Rehabilitation Act and the Developmental Disabilities Act of 1984), supported employment placements must meet the following criteria: (1) the job must provide between 20 and 40 hours of work weekly and be consistent with the individual's stamina; (2) the individual must earn a wage either at or above minimum wage, or a wage commensurate with production level and based upon the prevailing wage rate for the job; (3) fringe benefits should be similar to those provided for nondisabled workers performing the same type of work; (4) employment must be community-based and provide the individual with regular opportunities for integration with nondisabled workers or with the public as a regular part of working; work should take place in settings where no more than eight persons with disabilities work together. Based on the above criteria, the U.S. government established multimillion dollar programs to fund states to initiate supported employment services through cooperative interagency services (education, vocational rehabilitation, developmental disabilities). State dollars to match federal funds or stand alone are being allocated for supported employment services in nearly every state in the Union.

In a relatively short time supported employment has become a viable alternative for rehabilitation training and employment of individuals with severe handicaps. Research on the effectiveness of supported employment services has documented the success of this employment delivery system (Bellamy, Horner, & Inman, 1979; Kiernan & Stark, 1986; Wehman et al., 1986). While the efficacy of supported employment services has been well documented by research and demonstration, there is a growing fear that the rapid expansion of this employment service-delivery system in the United States will result in failure to safeguard the essential elements of the concept. Bellamy, Rhodes, Mank, & Albin (1988) reported that supported employment services are expanding at a rate that makes it extremely difficult to monitor the quality indicators that are at the foundation of long-term success for people with more severe disabilities. As expansion continues, the need for trained personnel in administrative positions is more acute. Vogelsberg (1987) has identified several areas that require immediate attention to maintain the integrity of supported employment services. These include: (1) procedures to assure that future programs do not repeat previous difficulties; (2) accountability in regard to quality of life, budget, and resource utilization; (3) understanding of expansion, conversion, downsizing, reducing administrative levels, and recognition of the importance of direct contact personnel; (4) policies and procedures regarding interagency cooperation; and (5) refinement of strategies for employment retention, job mobility, and fringe benefits. Bellamy et al. (1988) have suggested that the field must move into a phase of policy implementation in providing supported employment services.

Bellamy and Horner (1987) highlighted four critical features of supported employment. First, remuneration for the individual is a program goal. Wages are a primary index of employment success. Noble and Conley (1986) compared the wages earned in supported employment with those of more conventional day programs. They reported that individuals in supported work placements earned significantly higher wages. Clients in integrated employment also worked more hours than persons in sheltered employment and work activity centers. Finally, client earnings were not correlated with severity of disability.

Although earnings are primary to the success of supported employment, they are not the sole indicator of quality. Bellamy and Horner's second critical feature is that work should take place in socially integrated settings rather than segregated facilities. Job placement in an integrated setting allows the individual to learn appropriate social and vocational skills side by side with nondisabled peers and apply the skills in the environment. The nondisabled employer and coworkers also learn about the potential of the disabled individual as a reliable employee and friend.

The third feature is that support on the job is continuous, based on individual need, and not time-limited. Time-limited services like vocational rehabilitation or vocational education have traditionally been restricted to disabled individuals who are supposed to need no support after reception of services. These time-limited services, then, terminate after the individual enters the work force. Unlike time-limited services, continuous services are made available as needed. Support does not end with placement in an employment setting or after a specified time for follow-up. Services are provided on the job and consist of whatever support is necessary to maintain employment. Continuous services include job development, job placement, ongoing postemployment training, skill maintenance and generalization, and follow-up services. The amount and type of continuous service are related to individual need, job demand, and the organizational structure of the supported employment program (McDonnell, Nofs, & Hardman, 1986).

The fourth feature is that supported employment is for people with mental retardation who have not usually been served in vocational programs. "There is . . . the clear possibility that supported employment may become the nation's first zero-reject employment program" (Bellamy & Horner, p. 498). Historically, adult services for people with more severe mental retardation could only be described as prevocational or nonvocational with a focus on "getting people ready" or lifelong custodial care. As indicated by Brown et al. (1979), however, traditional models of preparing people for work in sheltered settings have not been effective.

Supported Employment Within the Framework of Community Living

It is important for supported employment to be viewed in the larger context of supported living. Taylor (1987) described the state of the art for community living as "family supports to enable children with severe disabilities to live at home, the recruitment and support of adoptive and foster families for children who cannot remain at home, and the development of supportive living arrangements for adults with a range of disabilities" (p. 32). Supported living is an opportunity for people with mental retardation to live in a home wherever they want and with whomever they choose while receiving all the support needed. Supported employment fits within the framework of a supported life network for people with mental retardation. Services are defined by individual preference and need rather than by availability of facilities. The goals for the individual within a supported life network include increased independence, community integration, and productivity. Services must reflect these individualized goals, which will result in an improvement in the quality of life for the person with a disability. Services that focus directly on increasing independence promote higher adaptive behavior levels and greater opportunities for choice in residence, recreation, and employment. Services that support community integration will result in greater access to and participation in the community, including generic community services and programs like restaurants, swimming pools, theaters, parks, and so forth. Services that focus on increasing the individual's productivity move the individual from consumer to contributor through identity in the work force, wages to spend in the community, and taxpayer status. Supported employment is a service that increases productivity. It is defined as wage-generating work with an emphasis on continuous support determined as much as possible by the individual and congruent with other aspects of the person's supported living network. People with mental retardation can live and work successfully in as many different situations as nondisabled individuals. Work and living options are constrained only by inadequate support (Bellamy & Horner, 1987).

Structural Features of Supported Employment

The development of supported employment services as the basic structure of a vocational service system for individuals with mental retardation has several implications: (1) the evaluation of the employment program based upon client outcomes, (2) elimination of the continuum of employment alternatives based on the "getting people ready" philosophy of vocational services, and (3) the development of training and advocacy services that are directly linked to employment success (McDonnell et al., 1986).

The success of an employment service may be evaluated in several ways. For example, in the vocational rehabilitation system, success is determined by closure of an individual's file, based on completion of training and job placement and maintenance for a specified length of time. Other means of evaluation relate more to the process of establishing a vocational service than to client outcomes. Process questions may include: Is the client eligible for the vocational service? Is there an individualized work plan in place? Is the work plan consistent with a standardized vocational assessment of the individual? Does the plan contain goals and objectives? These questions are concerned with ensuring that a standardized process is in place that is consistent across all programs.

Although supported employment does not ignore process questions, its primary focus is on results for the client. Does the vocational service provide good employment outcomes for the individual served? Measures for success are meaningful wages and benefits, access to generic services and resources, contact with nondisabled peers, and job security. "The implication is that programs and providers are accountable to their clients and state agencies for achieving these outcomes" (McDonnell et al., 1986, p. 3). Where more conventional vocational services emphasize a broader rehabilitation function, supported employment focuses on work and wages. Since employment outcomes are the key variables in the evaluation process, programs must become more effective in identifying, developing, and maintaining work opportunities.

The traditional philosophy of "getting people ready" (the flow-through model) for jobs is not consistent with the supported employment concept. The basis for supported employment is that individual support needs determine program placement. Individual functioning level and performance demands in a given work environment are matched. And supported employment, as mentioned earlier, takes into account the job's compatibility with the individual's life needs, as well as consideration for family values and constraints. The underlying principle of supported employment is not to move people to less restricted job placements as a result of training, but to provide the necessary resources to support individuals in their current work site.

The purpose of supported employment is to achieve community-integrated employment success for the individual with a severe disability. Therefore, all training programs and advocacy efforts must be directed toward this goal. Developing skills for various job tasks is only one component of a supported employment training program. As indicated by McDonnell et al. (1986), program training objectives might include riding the mass transit systems, grooming, self-monitoring, and evaluation of work performance. These objectives facilitate the individual's participation in the social network of the business.

Supported Employment Models

Three basic models of supported employment are currently recognized: individual placement, the community work crew, and the enclave. Each model differs in terms of intensity of long-term support, training, support structure, organizational strategy and business base, number of workers per site, and levels of integration (see Table 11–2).

In the individual placement model, a job coach gives intensive one-on-one training to each person aimed at successful performance of specific job tasks and nonwork behaviors around the job setting. Initial training is usually continuous throughout the work day, but may be eventually faded to no more than an hour a day or less. The job coach may be responsible for as many as eight employees at sites throughout a community. Training and assistance may also be available through coworkers willing to support the individual in completion of job tasks or act as friends in the workplace. The type of work available in individual placements varies from entry-level custodial or food services jobs to jobs in high-technology industries.

A community work crew usually consists of five or six individuals (maximum of eight) with disabilities who are supervised by a crew supervisor. Work crews generally perform service jobs (custodial, food service, and so on) that are contracted with two or more businesses, industries, or private individuals. Training and support from the crew supervisor may be continuous and long-term, focusing on completion of the service task and fostering community-integration activities. Work crews are usually mobile, moving from site to site in the performance of their contract. Under such circumstances integration with nondisabled individuals may be difficult to achieve. There must be systematic efforts to create opportunities for social interaction between work crew members and nondisabled people.

In the enclave model, two to eight individuals with disabilities work in an industrial or business setting alongside nondisabled people. The enclave is usually supervised by a single nondisabled person trained in the requirements of a single host company or industry. Job support is usually continuous and long-term; training focuses on production tasks, appropriate nonwork behaviors in the job environment, and community integration. Jobs include manufacturing and small-item assembly. Kiernan and Stark (1986) indicated that the level of social integration is high in enclaves, with opportunities for integration in the work area, during breaks, and at lunch. It is possible, however, for enclaves to be physically isolated within a business operating on different work, break, and lunch hours. Conscious efforts are sometimes necessary to integrate enclaves with the nondisabled work force.

All three supported employment models give training in specific job skills at the work site. On-the-job training involves job analysis, development of systematic training programs, and the use of effective training strategies (McDonnell et al., 1986). The primary difference between the models in relationship to on-the-job training is the number of individuals being trained at a time. For example, in the individual placement model, training is always one on one. In a work crew, any number of individuals may be trained together.

The Efficacy of Supported Employment

During the past decade there has been considerable research into the vocational potential of individuals with mental retardation. Research and demonstration programs

Table 11−2

Comparison of three supported employment models

	Supported jobs	Enclave	Mobile Crew
Organizational strategy and business base	■ Nonprofit support to individuals and employers ■ Varied types of jobs	■ Nonprofit support to host company ■ Target manufacturing companies	■ Nonprofit ■ Crews operate from a van ■ Rural ■ Service contracts
Number of workers per job site	1 per job	6−8	5 per crew
Cost	Not yet known, expected to be similar to day programs	Less than half the cost of other day programs	Same as traditional day programs
Intensity of support	Low. Continuous initially, scaling to no more than 1 hour a day after several months	Medium. Continuous and long term	Medium. Continuous and long term
Training	Individual training for up to 4 months on: ■ job tasks ■ nonwork behaviors in and around job setting	Individual training on: ■ production tasks ■ nonwork behaviors in job setting	Individual training on: ■ service tasks ■ community integration activities
Supervisor	Two or three supervisors for 12 employees in separate businesses	■ One supervisor for 6−8 employees in host company ■ Host company assigns model employee as backup to supervisor	■ One supervisor for five employees ■ Continuous presence of one supervisor on service jobs for all five employees
Integration	High. Daily and continuous integration in individual job sites	High. Daily and nearly continuous integration with nonhandicapped peers, in work area, breaks, and lunchtimes	Medium. Breaks and lunch occur in community settings; work performed in community settings, but interaction with nonhandicapped persons is low

Adapted from *Pathways to Employment for Adults with Developmental Disabilities* (p. 149), ed. W. E. Kiernan and J. A. Stark, 1986, Baltimore: Paul H. Brookes. Copyright 1986 by Paul H. Brookes Publishing Co. Adapted by permission.

have indicated that with comprehensive vocational training these individuals can take their place in a community work force. It is important that training programs begin while the student is still in school so that valuable time is not lost. Effective high school programs should lead to greater independence and increased participation in the community, goals whose success is influenced by the opportunity to work.

The functional skills individuals with mental retardation need to work and live successfully in a community setting should be taught both in the behavior's natural setting and in the schools (Brown et al., 1979; Coon, Vogelsberg, & Williams, 1981; Gaylord-Ross & Holvoet, 1985; Horner, Jones, & Williams, 1985; Hupp & Mervis, 1981; Snell & Browder, 1987). A functional skill is one that has immediate use for the individual. For an individual with mental retardation to learn how to cross a street safely, shop in a grocery store, play a video game, or eat in a local restaurant, it is most effective to teach the skills in the setting where the behavior takes place. It would be naïve to assume that a behavior learned in a classroom will transfer to a setting outside the school. A growing body of research suggests that training in more natural surroundings is important if the skill is to remain useful. This training should involve (1) using many different people to teach the skill; (2) teaching the skill in a variety of settings in the community; and (3) using varied materials that will interest the learner and match performance demands.

Consider the individual with mental retardation who is learning to shop in a grocery store. Each grocery store has different characteristics—variations in size, arrangement, or locale. To determine situations where the behavior being taught is appropriate, one must first establish an instructional universe. For grocery shopping, possible instructional universes range from the corner grocery store, to every grocery store in the city where the student lives. Once the instructional universe is defined (for example, grocery stores within walking distance), teaching examples are selected, sequenced, and implemented within it. Skills will have been successfully taught when, following instructions that use examples of appropriate situations, the student can perform across all appropriate situations.

Frequent and age-appropriate interactions between individuals with mental retardation and their nondisabled peers enhance opportunities for successful participation in the community during the adult years (Brinker & Thorpe, 1984; Brown et al., 1983; Gaylord-Ross, Harry, Breen, & Pitts-Conway, 1982; Soder, 1980; Voeltz, 1980). Research indicates that integrated settings not only increase social interaction and change the attitudes of people without disabilities, but also facilitate the individual's rate of learning critical life skills. Instruction for adults with mental retardation should focus on the skills that are most relevant for independent functioning in an integrated community environment (Bates, 1980; Beebe & Karan, 1986; Brown et al., 1983; Horner, McDonnell, & Bellamy, 1986; Horner, Sprague, & Wilcox, 1982; McDonnell & Hardman, 1985; Snell & Browder, 1986; Wilcox & Bellamy, 1982). If individuals with mental retardation are to participate fully in the community, they must perform competently at different activities and in different environments.

Individuals with mental retardation can work successfully in community employment settings with adequate training and long-term support. At the same or less public expense these individuals can be competitively employed instead of attending segregated day-care centers (Bellamy & Horner, 1987; Hill et al., 1987; Hill, Wehman, Banks, & Metzler, 1987; Revell, 1987; Rusch & Mithaug, 1980; Sowers, Thompson, & Connis, 1979; Vogelsberg & Williams, 1983; Wehman & Kregel, 1985).

Since the passage of the Education for All Handicapped Children Act, research and demonstration programs have clearly made improvements in vocational training and placement of persons with mental retardation. Supported employment is successfully being used to place and maintain individuals with mental retardation in jobs in the community. Research findings indicate that ongoing training and assistance in the job setting is more effective than vocational services in segregated settings.

Several investigators have reported successful community job placements, on-the-job training, and follow-up of individuals with mental retardation under the supported employment model. In Utah, Vermont, Virginia, and Washington, supported employment programs have withstood the test of time and replication. One state reported placing more than 150 individuals in community work settings over a six-year period; by far the majority were still on the job, and average earnings were above minimum wage.

The components of an effective community employment program include (1) placement in a job that is consistent with the abilities and interests of the individual; (2) on-the-job training that includes direct instruction by a trained professional and enables the individual to perform all skills the job calls for; (3) continuous assessment and monitoring of the individual's job performance; and (4) availability of systematic follow-up services to ensure the individual's skill retention years after the initial placement. Most persons with mental retardation can work in competitive employment situations. However, "some ongoing support for retraining, contingency management, or crisis intervention is typically needed—support that is seldom available in the truly competitive work setting" (Bellamy & Horner, 1987, p. 495). This ongoing assistance is embedded in the concept of supported employment.

Core Concept	*The purpose of a sheltered workshop is to prepare the person with mental retardation for competitive employment or provide a terminal sheltered job.*

SHELTERED EMPLOYMENT

Sheltered employment provides both occupational training and remuneration for persons with mental retardation. Payne and Patton (1981) described several common characteristics of sheltered workshops:

1. Clients/employees usually work on contractual jobs.
2. These contract jobs are usually of short duration; therefore, a staff person is needed to bring in new jobs.
3. Most tasks are broken into small steps.

4. Jobs usually proceed in an assembly line fashion; one part is added at each step of the process until a final product is completed.
5. The facility may or may not provide vocational assessment and training for persons outside of the center. (p. 278)

Some sheltered workshops operate exclusively for clients with mental retardation; others serve a wider variety of handicapped individuals, such as those with visual impairments, cerebral palsy, or emotional disturbances. Some are operated by national programs like Goodwill Industries of America, Inc., which has more than 100 centers, and Jewish Vocational Service agencies, with more than 20 locations. Other workshops are community based and may be supported by the United Fund, religious groups, private endowments, or, more recently, public schools.

Typically, sheltered workshops restore or repair clothing or household articles, then sell them. Items come from collections or strategically located depositories. Other workshop revenue comes from contracts with various businesses or industries.

Workshop clients are usually compensated on a piecework basis at a rate comparable to that of other workers in that industry. Thus, if the typical industry worker is paid $4 for 10 units of work an hour, the workshop client should be paid $2 for five units. Some workers are relatively productive and may earn more than $10 per day. Others are less capable and may earn less than a dollar per day. Whitehead (1981) stated that "Department of Labor compliance investigations have regularly revealed underpayments of wages to workshop clients" (p. 7).

Over the years the sheltered workshop model has been criticized. Questions have been raised about the value of such placements for individuals who earn little. From a purely economic standpoint the justification for maintaining services for these individuals is questionable. Their wages are so low as to be of next to no value even to themselves, and their productivity is so low that their contribution to the employment field may also be considered nearly negligible.

Gold (1973) criticized the lack of consistent, remunerative work and challenging tasks in sheltered workshops. Workshops have also been criticized for not having systematic procedures to evaluate the production capabilities of clients and for failure to provide vocational tasks consistent with their clients' range of capabilities.

In many respects the sheltered workshop contradicts any focus on community living and gainful employment. Industry employs workers to turn out a product. In the sheltered workshop, the product is often the means to produce workers. And for many workers the sheltered setting becomes the permanent work setting. Bellamy and Horner (1987) summed up the need for change: "Segregation in large sheltered facilities appears quite unnecessary when current procedures for developing work and work supported behaviors are used" (p. 496).

The U.S. Government Accounting Office reported that "handicapped persons employed in sheltered workshops have not received adequate reevaluations of their capabilities for competitive employment" (Smith, 1985, p. 7). Day habilitation and work activity centers are intended to provide programming that will prepare the person for more advanced work, preferably in a competitive employment situation. The results, at least for people with mental retardation, have not reflected the stated philosophy.

Current rates of progress in day activity and work activity programs suggest that people with mental retardation will spend the better part of their adult lives being "prepared" for competitive employment. As Wieck (1988) summed it up, "The effects of existing sheltered and day programs resulted in large numbers of people earning small wages, working in segregated sites, experiencing unemployment, and not moving through the continuum" (p. 221). People with severe handicaps have been traditionally placed in sheltered vocational preparation settings not because they are incapable of work, but because policymakers and disability professionals have been more oriented to "serving" these individuals than creating opportunities for employment.

NEW ISSUES AND FUTURE DIRECTIONS

Historically, human-service programs for adults with mental retardation have primarily focused on protection and care. The objective of such programs was to protect the individual from society, and society from the individual. This philosophy resulted in services that isolated the individual in large institutions and offered physical care in place of preparation for life in a heterogeneous world. With the international movement of the past two decades to educate students with disabilities in the public school system, new goals have become clear: (1) employment, useful work and valued activity; (2) personal autonomy, independence, and adult status; (3) social interaction, community participation, leisure, and recreation; and (4) roles within the family.

It is time for society to recognize that expectations for adults with mental retardation are no different from those for people without disabilities. A common set of indicators applies to both disabled and nondisabled people. As described in an international conference held in 1986 for government officials from around the world,

- There should be only one comprehensive social policy. Policies for those with disabilities should not be separate from other policies;
- Integration in the education system cannot be discussed separately from general policies for primary and secondary education;
- There is need for coherent objectives for services so that pensions/benefits and other provisions enhance autonomy and competence;
- Young people with disabilities have the same human rights as others and thus have a right to adult status. (OECD, 1986)

Although the characteristics of a "quality life" are certainly individual and personal, indicators seem to be widely accepted in western society. These are:

All people are empowered to make their own choices about adult living, including selecting friends, where they will live, and what jobs they will hold. Empowerment has three aspects: control of the environment, involvement in community life, and social relationships. Quality of life can be assessed by the answers to such questions as "Do you have a key to the house in which you live?" (controlling the environment); "Do you earn enough money to pay for your basic needs, including housing and food?" (involvement in the community); and "Do you have the opportunity of interacting with friends and neighbors?" (social relationships).

Each person is valued as an individual capable of personal growth and development. As such, everyone is treated with dignity, and has the opportunity to participate in all aspects of community life. Participation in community life includes access to adequate housing, opportunities to exercise citizenship (for example, voting), access to medical and social services as needed, and access to recreation and personal services (parks, theaters, grocery stores, restaurants, public transportation).

Each person has the opportunity to participate in the economic life of the community. Work is important for reasons beyond its monetary rewards—social interaction, personal identity, contribution to the community, and so on. Work removes the individual from being viewed solely as a consumer of service. Important personal needs include adequate and fair compensation, safe and healthy environments, development of human capacities, growth and security, social integration, constitutionalism (the rights of the worker and how these rights can be protected), the total life space (the balanced role of work in one's life), and social relevance (when organizations act in socially irresponsible ways, employees see their work and careers as less valuable) (Hackman & Suttle, 1977). Several indicators of a "quality of work life" for nondisabled adults have been identified by assessing the degree of employer satisfaction with the work process. These indicators include: (1) adequate and fair compensation, (2) safe and healthy environments, (3) development of human capacities, (4) growth and security, (5) social integration, (6) affirmation and protection of worker rights, and (7) a balance between work and personal life (Hackman & Suttle, 1977). Given the above indicators, the question is whether or not there should be separate standards of quality for persons with mental retardation. In fact, quality indicators do differ for the more conventional models of employment preparation for people with mental retardation (day habilitation, sheltered workshops, work activity centers). Sheltered workshops are designed as protected places for long-term employment, and people with mental retardation may be placed in these settings with little or no reassessment of their competitive employment potential. Supported employment differs significantly from conventional work programs. The goals for people with mental retardation in a supported employment program are the same as those for nondisabled people. What income does the job provide? What kind of life style does the income allow? How attractive is the work life (coworkers, challenge, safety, status)? How good is job security?

CORE QUESTIONS

1. Define and discuss the principle of normalization.
2. Describe three widely used community residential models for adults with mental retardation.
3. Discuss some of the reasons why a disproportionately higher number of adults with mental retardation are charged with delinquent or criminal behavior.
4. Why is sex education especially important for persons with mental retardation?

5. Summarize the research on the adjustment of persons with mental retardation to community living.
6. Why is institutionalization considered detrimental to the intellectual, psychological, and physical growth of the individual?
7. Discuss some of the reasons for high unemployment among persons with mental retardation.
8. Define and discuss the concept of supported employment.
9. What are some of the criticisms of sheltered employment?

ROUND TABLE DISCUSSION

The principle of normalization emphasizes that the person with mental retardation should have the same opportunities and access to services as nonhandicapped individuals. It is much more than just the opportunity to live or work in the community because it means providing the support services necessary to assist the individual in successfully meeting the demands of adult life.

In your study group or on your own, discuss the range of activities and services that must be available for an adult with mental retardation to live and work successfully in the community. How would you ensure that these services are available?

REFERENCES

Abramson, P. R., Parker, T., & Weisberg, S. R. (1988). Sexual expression of mentally retarded people: Educational and legal implications. *American Journal of Mental Retardation, 93*(3), 328–334.

Allen, R. C. (1969). *The retarded citizen: Victim of mental and legal deficiency.* Unpublished paper. (Available from Institute of Law, Psychiatry, and Criminology, Washington, DC: George Washington University). Portions of this paper published in *Legal rights of the disadvantaged,* 1969, Washington, DC: U.S. Department of Health, Education and Welfare.

Allen, R. C. (1970). The law and the mentally retarded. In F. J. Menolascino (Ed.), *Psychiatric approaches to mental retardation.* New York: Basic Books.

Baker, B. L., Seltzer, G. B., & Seltzer, M. M. (1977). *As close as possible: Community residences for retarded adults.* Boston: Little, Brown.

Balla, D. (1976). Relationship of institution size to quality of care: A review of the literature. *American Journal of Mental Deficiency, 81,* 117–124.

Baller, W. R. (1936). A study of the present social status of a group of adults who, when they were in elementary schools, were classified as mentally deficient. *Genetic Psychology Monographs, 18,* 165–244.

Baller, W., Charles, C., & Miller, E. (1966). *Mid-life attainment of the mentally retarded: A longitudinal study.* Lincoln: University of Nebraska Press.

Bank-Mikkelsen, N. E. (1969). A metropolitan area in Denmark: Copenhagen. In R. B. Kugel & W. Wolfensberger (Eds.), *Changing patterns in residential services for the mentally retarded* (pp. 227–254). Washington, DC: President's Committee on Mental Retardation.

Bates, P. (1980). The effectiveness of interpersonal skills training in the social skill acquisition of moderately and severely retarded adults. *Journal of Applied Behavior Analysis, 13,* 237–248.

Beebe, P. D., & Karan, O. C. (1986). A methodology for a community-based vocational program for adults. In R. H. Horner, L. Meyer, and H. D. Fredericks (Eds.), *Educating the learner with severe handicaps: Exemplary service strategies* (pp. 3–28). Baltimore: Paul H. Brookes.

Bellamy, G. T., & Horner, R. H. (1987). Beyond high school: Residential and employment options after graduation. In M. E. Snell (Ed.), *Systematic instruction of persons with severe handicaps* (3rd ed.) (pp. 491–510). Columbus, OH: Charles E. Merrill.

Bellamy, G. T., Horner, R. H., & Inman, D. (1979). *Vocational habilitation of severely retarded adults: A direct service technology.* Baltimore: Paul H. Brookes.

Bellamy, G. T., O'Conner, G., & Karan, O. (1979). *Vocational rehabilitation of severely handicapped persons: Contemporary service strategies.* Baltimore: University Park Press.

Bellamy, G. T., Rhodes, L., Mank, D., & Albin, J. (1988). *Supported employment and community implementation guide.* Baltimore: Paul H. Brookes.

Blatt, B., Ozolins, A., & McNally, J. (1979). *The family papers: A return to purgatory.* New York: Longman.

Brinker, R. P., & Thorpe, M. E. (1984). *Evaluation of severely handicapped students in regular education and community settings.* Princeton: Educational Testing Service.

Brolin, D., DuRand, R., Kromer, K., & Muller, P. (1975). Postschool adjustment of educable retarded students. *Education and Training of the Mentally Retarded, 10,* 144–148.

Brown, L., Branston, M. B., Hamre-Nietupski, A., Pumpian, I., Certo, N., & Gruenewald, L. (1979). A strategy for developing chronological age-appropriate and functional curricular content for severely handicapped adolescents and young adults. *Journal of Special Education, 13,* 81–90.

Brown, L., Nisbet, J., Ford, A., Sweet, M., Shiraga, B., York, J., & Loomis, R. (1983). The critical need for non-school instruction in educational programs for severely handicapped students. *Journal of the Association for the Severely Handicapped, 8,* 71–77.

Bruininks, R. H., & Lakin, K. C. (1985). *Living and learning in the least restrictive environment.* Baltimore: Paul H. Brookes.

Bruininks, R. H., Meyers, C. E., Sigford, B. B., & Lakin, K. C. (Eds.). (1981). *Deinstitutionalization and community adjustment of mentally retarded people* (AAMD Monograph No. 4). Washington, DC: American Association on Mental Deficiency.

Buck v. Bell, 274 U.S. 200 (1927).

Burt, R. A. (1973). Legal restrictions on sexual and familial relations of mental retardates—old laws, new guises. In F. F. de la Cruz and G. D. LaVeck (Eds.), *Human sexuality and the mentally retarded.* New York: Brunner/Mazel.

Campbell, V. A., & Bailey, C. J. (1984). Comparison of methods for classifying community residential settings for mentally retarded individuals. *American Journal of Mental Deficiency, 89,* 44–49.

Close, D. W. (1975, May). *Normalization through skill training: A group study.* Paper presented at the annual convention of the American Association on Mental Deficiency, Portland, OR.

Conroy, J. W., & Bradley, V. J. (1985). *The Pennhurst longitudinal study: A report of five years of research and analysis.* Philadelphia: Temple University Developmental Disabilities Center.

Coon, M. E., Vogelsberg, T., & Williams, W. (1981). Effects of classroom public transportation instruction on generalization to the natural environment. *Journal of the Association for the Severely Handicapped, 6*(2), 46–53.

DeSilva, B. (1980, August). Offender: A problem—a program. *Corrections Magazine, 6,* 25–33.

Edgerton, R. B. (1967). *The cloak of competence.* Berkeley: University of California Press.

Edgerton, R. B., & Bercovici, S. M. (1976). The cloak of competence years later. *American Journal of Mental Deficiency, 80,* 485–497.

Edgerton, R. B., Bollinger, M., & Herr, B. (1984). The cloak of competence: After two decades. *American Journal of Mental Deficiency, 88*(4), 345–351.

Eyman, R. K., & Borthwick, S. A. (1980). Patterns of care for mentally retarded persons. *Mental Retardation, 18,* 63–66.

Fain, G. S. (1986). Leisure: A moral imperative. *Mental Retardation, 24*(5), 261–283.

Fairbanks, R. F. (1931). The subnormal child: Seventeen years later. *Mental Hygiene, 17,* 177–208.

Ferguson, D. L., & Ferguson, P. M. (1986). The new victors: A progressive policy analysis of work reform for people with very severe handicaps. *Mental Retardation, 24*(6), 331–338.

Fernald, W. E. (1919). After-care study of the patients discharged from Waverly for a period of twenty-five years. *Ungraded, 5,* 25–31.

Foxx, R. M., McMorrow, M. J., Storey, K., & Rogers, B. M. (1984). Teaching social/sexual skills to mentally retarded adults. *American Journal of Mental Deficiency, 89*(1), 9–15.

Gamble, C. J. (1951). The prevention of mental deficiency by sterilization. *American Journal of Mental Deficiency, 56,* 192–197.

Gaylord-Ross, R., Harry, T., Breen, C., & Pitts-Conway, V. (1982). *The social integration of autistic and severely handicapped students.* San Francisco: San Francisco State University.

Gaylord-Ross, R. J., & Holvoet, J. F. (1985). *Strategies for educating students with severe handicaps.* Boston: Little, Brown.

Goffman, E. (1975). Characteristics of total institutions. In S. Dinitz, R. R. Dynes, & A. C. Clarke (Eds.), *Deviance: Studies in definition, management, and treatment* (p. 410). New York: Oxford University Press.

Gold, M. W. (1973). Research on the vocational rehabilitation of the retarded: The present, the future. In N. R. Ellis (Ed.), *International review of research in mental retardation* (Vol. 6). New York: Academic Press.

Goldstein, H. (1964). Social and occupational adjustment. In R. Heber & H. Stevens (Eds.), *Mental retardation.* Chicago: University of Chicago Press.

Gozali, J. (1971). Citizenship and voting behavior of mildly retarded adults: A pilot study. *American Journal of Mental Deficiency, 75,* 641.

Hackman, J. R., & Suttle, J. L. (1977). *Improving life at work: Behavioral science approaches to organizational change.* Santa Monica: Goodyear.

Haney, J. I. (1988). Toward successful community residential placements for individuals with mental retardation. In I. W. Heal, J. I. Haney, & A. R. Novak Amado (Eds.), *Integration of developmentally disabled individuals into the community* (2nd ed.) (pp. 125–168). Baltimore: Paul H. Brookes.

Hardman, M. L., Drew, C. J., Egan, M. W., & Wolf, B. (1990). *Human exceptionality: Society, school, and family* (3rd ed.). Boston: Allyn & Bacon.

Hasazi, S. B., Johnson, R. E., Gordon, L. R. & Hull, M. (1989). A statewide follow-up survey of high school exiters: A comparison of former students with and without handicaps. *Journal of Special Education, 23,* 243–255.

Heshusius, L. (1982). Sexuality, intimacy, and persons we label mentally retarded: What they think—what we think. *Mental Retardation, 20*(4), 164–168.

Hill, B. K., & Lakin, K. C. (1986). Classification of residential facilities for individuals with mental retardation. *Mental Retardation, 24*(2), 107–115.

Hill, B. K., Lakin, K. C., & Bruininks, R. H. (1984). Trends in residential services for people who are mentally retarded. *Journal of the Association for Persons with Severe Handicaps, 9*(4), 243–250.

Hill, J. W., Hill, M. L., Wehman, P., Banks, P. D., Pendleton, P., & Britt, C. (1985). Demographic analyses related to successful job retention for competitively employed persons who are mentally retarded. In S. Moon, P. Goodall, & P. Wehman (Eds.), *Critical issues related to supported competitive employment* (pp. 30–56). Richmond: Rehabilitation Research and Training Center, Virginia Commonwealth University.

Hill, M. L., Banks, P. D., Handrich, R. R., Wehman, P. H., Hill, J. W., & Shafer, M. S. (1987). Benefit-cost analysis of supported competitive employment for persons with mental retardation. In P. Wehman, J. Kregel, M. S. Shafer, & M. L. Hill (Eds.), *Competitive employment for persons with mental retardation: From research to practice* (pp. 112–143). Richmond: Rehabilitation Research and Training Center, Virginia Commonwealth University.

Hill, M. L., Wehman, P. H., Banks, P. D., & Metzler, H. M. D. (1987). Employment outcomes of people with moderate and severe disabilities provided supported competitive employment after eight years. In P. Wehman, J. Kregel, M. S. Shafer, & M. L. Hill (Eds.), *Competitive employment for persons with mental retardation: From research to practice* (pp. 144–164). Richmond: Rehabilitation Research and Training Center, Virginia Commonwealth University.

Hitzing, W. (1980). ENCOR and beyond. In T. Apolloni, J. Cappuccilli, & T. P. Cooke (Eds.), *Achievements in residential services for persons with disabilities: Toward excellence.* Baltimore: University Park Press.

Homeward Bound v. The Hissom Memorial Center. U.S. District Court (1988).

Horner, R. H., Jones, D. N., & Williams, J. A. (1985). A functional approach to teaching generalized street cross. *Journal of the Association for Persons with Severe Handicaps, 10*(2), 71–78.

Horner, R. H., McDonnell, J., and Bellamy, G. T. (1986). Teaching generalized skills: General case instruction in simulation and community settings. In R. H. Horner, L. Meyer, and H. D. Fredericks (Eds.), *Educating learners with severe handicaps: Exemplary service strategies.* (pp. 289–314). Baltimore: Paul H. Brookes.

Horner, R. H., Sprague, J., & Wilcox, B. (1982). Constructing general case programs for community activities. In B. Wilcox & G. T. Bellamy (Eds.), *Design of high school programs for severely handicapped students* (pp. 61–98). Baltimore: Paul H. Brookes.

Hupp, S. C., & Mervis, C. B. (1981). Development of generalized concepts by severely handicapped students. *Journal of the Association for the Severely Handicapped, 6*(1), 14–21.

International Center for the Disabled. (1986). *The ICD survey of disabled Americans: Bringing disabled Americans into the mainstream.* New York: Author.

Janicki, M. P., Mayeda, T., & Epple, W. A. (1983). Availability of group homes for persons with mental retardation in the United States. *Mental Retardation, 21*(2), 45–51.

Kennedy, R. A. (1966). *A Connecticut community revised: A study of the social adjustment of a group of mentally deficient adults in 1948 and 1960.* Hartford: Connecticut State Department of Health, Office of Mental Retardation.

Kennedy, R. J. R. (1948). *The social adjustment of morons in a Connecticut city.* Willport, CT: Commission to Survey Resources in Connecticut.

Kiernan, W. E., & Stark, J. A. (1986). *Pathways to employment for adults with developmental disabilities.* Baltimore: Paul H. Brookes.

Kvaraceus, W. C. (1945). *Juvenile delinquency and the school.* Yonkers, NY: World.

Mank, D. M., Rhodes, L. E., & Bellamy, G. T. (1986). In W. E. Kiernan & J. A. Stark (Eds.), *Pathways to employment for adults with developmental disabilities* (pp. 139–153). Baltimore: Paul H. Brookes.

Marsh, R. L., Friel, C. M., & Eissler, V. (1975). The adult MR in the criminal justice system. *Mental Retardation, 13,* 21–25.

McAfee, J. K., & Gural, M. (1988). Individuals with mental retardation and the criminal justice system: The view from the states' attorneys general. *Mental Retardation, 26,* 5–12.

McDonnell, J. J., & Hardman, M. L. (1985). Planning the transition of severely handicapped youth from school to adult services: A framework for high school programs. *Education and Training of the Mentally Retarded, 20*(4), 275–286.

McDonnell, J., Nofs, D., & Hardman, M. L. (1986). *The Utah supported employment training manual.* Salt Lake City: Department of Special Education, University of Utah.

McDonnell, J., Wilcox, B., & Boles, S. (1986). Do we know enough to plan for transition? A national survey of state agencies responsible for services to persons with severe handicaps. *Journal of the Association for Persons with Severe Handicaps, 11,* 53–60.

McDonnell, J., Wilcox, B., & Hardman, M. L. (1991). *Secondary programs for students with mental retardation.* Boston: Allyn & Bacon.

Menolascino, F. J., McGee, J. J., & Casey, K. (1982). Affirmation of the rights of institutionalized retarded citizens (Implications of *Youngberg v. Romeo*). *TASH Journal, 8,* 63–71.

Nirje, B. (1969). The normalization principle and its human management implications. In R. B. Kugel & W. Wolfensberger (Eds.), *Changing patterns in residential services for the mentally retarded* (pp. 179–195). Washington, DC: President's Committee on Mental Retardation.

Nirje, B. (1970). The normalization principle and its human management implications. *Journal of Mental Subnormality, 16,* 62–70.

Noble, J., & Conley, R. (1986, November). *Accumulating evidence on the benefits and costs of supported and transitional work for persons with severe disabilities.* Paper presented at the annual meeting of the Association for Persons with Severe Handicaps, San Francisco.

O'Neill, J., Brown, M., Gordon, W., & Schonhorn, R. (1985). The impact of deinstitutionalization on activities and skills of severely/profoundly retarded multiply handicapped adults. *Applied Research in Mental Retardation, 6,* 361–371.

O'Neill, C., & Stern, J. (1985). State-wide systems change in employment services for individuals with developmental disabilities in the state of Washington. In S. Moon, P. Goodall, & P. Wehman (Eds.), *Critical issues related to supported competitive employment* (pp. 213–229). Richmond: Rehabilitation Research and Training Center, Virginia Commonwealth University.

Organization for Economic Cooperation and Development. (1986). *Young people with handicaps: The road to adulthood.* Paris: Author.

Payne, J. S., & Patton, J. R. (1981). *Mental retardation.* Columbus: Charles E. Merrill.

Peck, C. A., Apolloni, T., & Cooke, T. P. (1981). Rehabilitation services for Americans with mental retardation: A summary of accomplishments in research and development. In E. L. Pan, T. E. Backer, & C. L. Vash (Eds.), *Annual review of rehabilitation* (Vol. 2). New York: Springer.

Peterson, L., & Smith, L. L. (1960). A comparison of post school adjustment of educable mentally retarded adults with that of adults of normal intelligence. *Exceptional Children, 26,* 404–408.

Reichard, C. L., Spencer, J., & Spooner, F. (1980). The mentally retarded defendant-offender. *Journal of Special Education, 14,* 113–119.

Revell, G. (1987). An agency perspective on employment for the citizen who is mentally retarded. In S. Moon, P. Goodall, & P. Wehman (Eds.), *Critical issues in supported employment* (pp. 183–197). Richmond: Rehabilitation Research and Training Center, Virginia Commonwealth University.

Rusch, F. R., Mithaug, D. (1980). *Vocational training of mentally retarded adults.* Champaign, IL: Research Press.

Schalock, R. (1986). *Transitions from school to work.* Washington, DC: National Association of Rehabilitation Facilities.

Schilit, J. (1979). The mentally retarded offender and criminal justice personnel. *Exceptional Children, 46,* 16–22.

Schleien, S. J., Kiernan, J., & Wehman, P. (1981). Evaluation of an age-appropriate leisure skills program for moderately retarded adults. *Education and Training of the Mentally Retarded, 16*(1), 13–19.

Shannon, G. (1985). *Characteristics influencing current recreational patterns of persons with mental retardation.* Unpublished doctoral dissertation, Brandeis University, Waltham, MA.

Smith, J. D. (1989). *The sterilization of Carrie Buck.* New York: New Horizons.

Smith, M. (1985). *Sheltered workshops for handicapped persons: Background information, current issues and legislation.* Washington, DC: Congressional Research Services, U.S. Library of Congress.

Snell, M. E., & Browder, D. M. (1987). Domestic and community skills. In M. E. Snell (Ed.), *Systematic instruction of persons with severe handicaps* (3rd ed.) (pp. 390–434). Columbus, OH: Charles E. Merrill.

Soder, M. (1980). *Research and development concerning integration of handicapped pupils into the ordinary schools.* Stockholm: National Swedish Board of Education.

Sowers, J., Thompson, L., & Connis, R. (1979). The food service vocational training program: A model for training and placement of the mentally retarded. In G. T. Bellamy, G. O'Conner, & O. C. Karan (Eds.), *Vocational rehabilitation of severely handicapped persons.* Baltimore: University Park Press.

Staff report on the institutionalized mentally disabled. (1985). Washington, DC: U.S. Senate Subcommittee on the Handicapped, Committee on Labor and Human Resources.

Stanfield, J. S. (1973). Graduation: What happens to the retarded child when he grows up? *Exceptional Children, 39,* 548–552.

Stark, J. A., & Kiernan, W. E. (1986). Symposium overview: Employment for people with mental retardation. *Mental Retardation, 24*(6), 329–330.

Sutter, P. (1980). Environmental variables related to community placement failure in mentally retarded adults. *Mental Retardation, 18*(4), 189–191.

Taylor, S. (1987). Continuum traps. In S. Taylor, D. Biklen, & J. Knoll (Eds.), *Community integration for people with severe disabilities.* New York: Teacher's College Press.

Tessler, R. C., & Manderscheid, R. W. (1982). Factors affecting adjustment to community living. *Hospital and Community Psychiatry, 33*(3), 203–207.

Timmers, R. L., DuCharme, P., & Jacob, G. (1981). Sexual knowledge, attitudes and behaviors of developmentally disabled living in a normalized apartment setting. *Sexuality and Disability, 4,* 27–39.

U.S. Commission on Civil Rights. (1983). *Accommodating the spectrum of disabilities.* Washington, DC: Author.

Voeltz, L. M. (1980). Children's attitudes toward handicapped persons. *American Journal of Mental Deficiency, 84,* 455–464.

Vogelsberg, R. T. (1985). Competitive employment programs for individuals with mental retardation in rural areas. In S. Moon, P. Goodall, & P. Wehman (Eds.), *Critical issues related to supported competitive employment* (pp. 57–81). Richmond: Rehabilitation Research and Training Center, Virginia Commonwealth University.

Vogelsberg, R. T. (1987). *Supported employment data system.* Unpublished manuscript, Temple University, Philadelphia.

Vogelsberg, T., & Williams, W. W. (1983). *Vocational services in Vermont.* Unpublished manuscript, University of Vermont, Burlington.

Wehman, P., & Kregel, J. (1985). A supported employment approach to competitive employment of individuals with moderate and severe handicaps. *Journal of the Association for Persons with Severe Handicaps, 10*(1), 3–11.

Wehman, P., Kregel, J., Shafer, M. S., & Hill, M. L. (1986). *Competitive employment for persons with mental retardation: From research to practice.* Richmond: Virginia Commonwealth University.

Whitehead, C. W. (1981, March). *Training and employment services for handicapped individuals in sheltered workshops: Final report.* Washington, DC: U. S. Department of Health and Human Services.

Whitehead, C., & Rhodes, S. (1985). *Guidelines for evaluation, reviewing, and enhancing employment related services for people with developmental disabilities.* Washington, DC: National Association of Developmental Disabilities Councils.

Wieck, C. (1988). The transition to productive employment. In B. L. Ludlow, A. P. Turnbull, & R. Luckasson (Eds.), *Transitions to adult life for people with mental retardation: Principles and practices* (pp. 215–231). Baltimore: Paul H. Brookes.

Wilcox, B., & Bellamy, G. T. (1982). *Design of high school programs for severely handicapped students* (pp. 1–60). Baltimore: Paul H. Brookes.

Will, M. (1985). OSERS programming for the transition of youth with disabilities: Bridges from school to working life. In S. Moon, P. Goodall, & P. Wehman (Eds.), *Critical issues related to supported competitive employment* (pp. 12–29). Richmond: Rehabilitation Research and Training Center, Virginia Commonwealth University.

Wolfensberger, W. (1969). Will there always be an institution? II. The impact of the new service models—Residential alternatives to institutions. *Mental Retardation, 9*(6), 31–38.

Wolfensberger, W. (1972). *Normalization: The principle of normalization in human services.* Toronto: National Institute on Mental Retardation.

Wolfensberger, W. (1983). Social role valorization: Proposed new term for the principle of normalization. *Mental Retardation, 21*(6), 234–239.

Wyatt v. Stickney, 344 F. Supp. 387; 344 F. Supp. 373 (M.D. Ala. 1972).

Zigler, E. (1973). The retarded child as a whole person. In D. K. Routh (Ed.), *The experimental psychology of mental retardation.* Chicago: Aldine.

CHAPTER TWELVE
The Older Person with Mental Retardation

Core Concepts

Research on Aging and Retardation

  Methodological Problems / Identifying the Older Person with Mental
  Retardation

Characteristics of the Older Person with Mental Retardation

  Mental Functioning / Social and Personal Functioning

Programming and Future Research

New Issues and Future Directions

Core Questions

Round Table Discussion

References

■ Problems in research methodology have contributed to the relative lack of information on elderly individuals with mental retardation. Some problems relate to aging research generally; others arise specifically from mental retardation.

■ Identifying the elderly with mental retardation has been difficult because of disagreement on who is old and problems in actually finding such individuals.

■ Age-related changes in mental functioning of older people with mental retardation are of great interest and are often compared to changes in nonretarded peers.

■ The social and personal functioning of elderly people with mental retardation provides some extremely interesting areas of study. Evidence is currently confusing and may in some ways challenge the normalization principle.

■ Service programs and living arrangements for elderly people with mental retardation also raise interesting questions about normalization.

Study of elderly people with mental retardation continues the progression through the developmental cycle. In some ways the content of this chapter extends the material in Chapter 11, although the focus is altered to suit the group. Distinguishing between the aged and adults is not as simple as it may appear. There is, however, legitimate reason to give special attention to the latter part of adulthood—the final phase of the life cycle. Interest in aging and geriatrics has grown dramatically in the past few years. In part this may be because society can afford to be increasingly humanitarian. Another reason is the visible presence of an increasing number of older persons. As medical sophistication has progressed and survival needs have been satisfied, the longevity of the general population has increased.

Aging: What does it mean? Who is an old person? Certainly these are questions most people can answer. An old person is perhaps one's grandmother or grandfather. An old person may be one who is retired. But a child's definition of an old person is very different from a 45-year-old's. For the most part, people's perceptions of age involve specific examples from personal experience, or individual conceptualizations. One does not have to probe very far to see that answers vary a great deal. It follows that the conceptual basis from which a behavioral scientist operates must also vary. If aging is considered from a physiological viewpoint, it looks very different from its appearance from a cultural standpoint. Different individuals and characteristics emerge from the different definitions. The problem is further compounded by different attitudes and philosophies.

This chapter focuses on the aging of the mentally retarded population. We have emphasized throughout this volume that people with mental retardation represent one part of the complete spectrum of humanity. Although they are different from the nonretarded in some respects, they are similar in many others. To ignore this is to be blinded by either attitude or lack of information. The process of aging must be given attention for the elderly with retardation as well as for the population in general. The major emphasis of both research and service for those who have retardation has fixed on childhood. One has only to scan the literature that has accumulated over the years to note that even attention to retardation in adolescents declines dramatically. Retarded children do, however, grow up, and they grow old and die.

RESEARCH ON AGING AND RETARDATION

Compared to many areas of behavioral science, there has been relatively little study of aging in populations with mental retardation (Cotten, Sison, & Starr, 1981). In fact, the information available is so limited that it was characterized in earlier editions of this book as nearly nonexistent. With rare exceptions (e.g., Kaplan, 1943), no interest in this area has been evident until recently. Although there is still an urgent need for additional study, aging is gaining priority (Janicki & MacEachron, 1984; Janicki & Wisniewski, 1985; Seltzer & Seltzer, 1985).

Our introductory statement drew attention to the lack of clarity about who the retarded elderly are. Some of the reasons for this lack of clarity that were alluded to receive additional attention in this section. We review research in an attempt to explore how the mentally retarded elderly are both like and unlike their nonretarded peers. Since we have limited research data on older people with retardation, we sometimes use the nonretarded population as a reference group.

Methodological Problems

Core Concept	*Problems in research methodology have contributed to the relative lack of information on elderly individuals with mental retardation. Some problems relate to aging research generally; others arise specifically from mental retardation.*

A number of factors contribute to the paucity of research in the area of aging and mental retardation. Some involve lack of interest and an uncaring attitude toward the population (Dybwad, 1985), although recently these have changed for the better. Others involve the methodological problems of conducting research on aging in general and with the mentally retarded population specifically (Seltzer, 1985a).

Some of the methodological problems encountered in investigations on aging involve fundamental difficulties in research design. These difficulties, reviewed in depth by Schaie and Gribbin (1975), represent very serious impediments to increasing our knowledge of aging. We must consider these design problems before we can interpret existing data on the elderly and on the process of growing old.

Two of the most common approaches to studying aging are the cross-sectional design and the longitudinal design. Cross-sectional studies sample subjects from several age levels (say, ages 40 to 49, 50 to 59, 60 to 69, and 70 to 79) and compare certain measures between groups. Longitudinal studies select a single group of subjects and follow it through the years to compare behaviors at different ages. Each approach compares attributes at different ages to determine how the aging process affects them. Although on the surface these approaches appear suited to their purpose, problems have arisen that make reliable interpretation of data difficult.

The cross-sectional design is by far the more convenient procedure since all subjects are assessed at approximately the same time. A sample of subjects at each level is selected, and the investigator records the desired data. Data are then compared between age levels to see whether any differences between groups result. The problem is that the investigator can incorrectly attribute differences to aging. Although observed differences may be caused by age differences, there also may be other explanations. Differences between the group that is 40 and the group that is 70 years old, for example, could be the result of sociocultural change over the 30 years that have passed since the older group was 40. It is quite likely (and observations of the past quarter century would confirm) that many social and cultural changes have occurred in such a period of time. People with mental retardation also may be affected by the enormous changes in treatment over the years. Differences between groups may be from aging, different sociocultural influences, different treatments, or combinations of all three.

Longitudinal investigations are not plagued by the problem of sociocultural change in the same fashion as cross-sectional studies. Since the same sample is followed through a period of years (even a life span) generation gap differences are not as potent. It cannot be denied, however, that a given person changes behaviors in response to altered sociocultural influences. A more serious difficulty is the problem of sample attrition over the period of the study. Because subjects are inevitably lost during the investigation, the sample available at age 70 years is likely to be quite different from the initial sample at 40 years. Thus differences might result because the composition of the sample has changed rather than from the effects of age. This has been called "experimental mortality" and is an inherent design problem of longitudinal studies (Drew & Hardman, 1985).

An additional difficulty of longitudinal studies is that the researcher may die before the investigation is over. This has frequently led to the use of retrospective studies that do not take direct measurement at earlier ages but rely on reports based on the memory of the subjects and others close to them. Such studies are rife with problems of reliability and accuracy.

These methodological problems are serious threats to the soundness of research on the effects of aging. They do not, however, imply that the study of aging is impossible or should not be undertaken. We have wanted to alert the reader about problems in reading and interpreting research on the elderly. Obviously, there are times when research results need to be interpreted cautiously in order not to generalize beyond the data or make unsound inferences based on preliminary findings.

Identifying the Older Person with Mental Retardation

Core Concept	*Identifying the elderly with mental retardation has been difficult because of disagreement on who is old and problems in actually finding such individuals.*

Investigators studying the aging process in mental retardation face even more difficulties than those who study aging in general. Since little research has focused specifically on this population, there is little information to use as a point of departure. Great progress has been made recently in research on the elderly with mental retardation, but there are still difficulties in identifying, detecting, and diagnosing these individuals (Foelker & Luke, 1989).

Faced with this situation, researchers are forced to address some fundamental questions as they begin. One of the basic questions immediately raised was mentioned earlier: Who is an old person with retardation? Among mentally retarded people age ranges for the elderly have varied considerably and have been arbitrary. Both 40 and 55 years have appeared in the literature—hardly ages that would be considered old among nonretarded people. Dickerson, Hamilton, Huber, and Segal (1974) speculated that a mentally retarded person who lives to 45 or 50 years of age is probably considered old. Dickerson et al. indicated, however, that persons with mental retardation may be subject to double or triple jeopardy with regard to the normal loss pattern associated with advancing age. This does not mean that the aging process (physiologically) is necessarily more rapid in the population with mental retardation. Dickerson et al. made it clear that part of their speculation was based on such factors as where the person resides and what minimal services are available for the elderly handicapped. Agreement about who is old among people with retardation remains a problem for researchers (Seltzer, 1985b).

We have suggested that identification of the retarded elderly is not so simple a task as it might appear. A related question pertains to the size of the population. Although there is not a great deal of literature on this topic, it has had some attention (e.g., Foelker & Luke, 1989). Estimates vary widely with the nature of the population studied, the age used as a lower limit, and the procedures employed for calculating prevalence. Tymchuck (1979) estimated the size of this population using a 2% prevalence figure and the 1970 census, and came up with a figure of 1.2 million retarded people over 45 years of age in this country. More current estimates indicate that there are between 200,000 and 460,000 elderly retarded people (Jacobson, Sutton, & Janicki, 1985; Seltzer, 1985b).

Some writers have focused on institutionalized populations. For example, Payne (1967) found that 18.2% of the institutionalized population sampled (17 institutions in 13 western states) was over 40. Kriger (1975), however, found only a very small number of retarded persons older than 40 in institutions. A search of Ohio records produced only 110 names of elderly institutionalized persons with retardation (only 75 of these individuals could actually be found). These figures are particularly striking because estimates said more than 38,000 should have existed, based on percentage projections.

Results like Kriger's raise some extremely interesting questions about aging and mental retardation. Where are the retarded elderly? Perhaps the use of population percentage projections is inappropriate for this group, although no particular logic explains why. It does seem, however, that the state of Ohio (or any other state, for that matter) must have more retarded individuals over 40 than were found. Are they hidden or invisible because of a lack of services, and therefore not on anyone's records? Do they have a shorter life span? Have they adapted to the point that they are no longer evident as being retarded? These types of questions are central to the study of aging in the mentally retarded. Definitive answers have yet to be found.

CHARACTERISTICS OF THE OLDER PERSON WITH MENTAL RETARDATION

It is not surprising that a complete picture of the elderly with retardation is lacking. Problems encountered in the study of aging generally are compounded by additional complications specific to the population with mental retardation. Interest in this area is growing, however, and some evidence is available about the characteristics of this population.

Mental Functioning

Core Concept	*Age-related changes in mental functioning of older people with mental retardation are of great interest and are often compared to changes in nonretarded peers.*

Decline in mental functioning is a characteristic typically associated with aging. Most people would agree that older people they know are frequently less mentally alert and often not as generally capable as younger individuals. People often compare the present functioning of an older person with recollections of their functioning when younger. Although there are many unanswered questions about this perception, it is a widely held view in our culture. This perspective appears to have influenced research on aging, which often seems to presume that aging erodes cognitive ability. Decline in mental functioning *may* occur as age increases, but when such a perspective unduly influences scientific investigation the knowledge base may be biased (Labouvie-Vief, 1977). We must exercise caution in interpreting results. One question related to our particular focus concerns the influence of aging on older people with retardation. Do such people experience a further decline in mental functioning as they age? Does the rate of mental decline occur in fashion similar to that for nonretarded peers (if, in fact, it occurs at all)? Precise answers to these questions remain elusive even with more attention being paid to older retarded populations (Janicki & Jacobson, 1986).

Certain common beliefs about decline in mental functioning have influenced the field of mental retardation. These views generally presume not only a general decline of intelligence with age, but also a more rapid decline in the mentally retarded population. However, solid research evidence on the general nature of intellectual change as a function of age is unclear (e.g., Horn & Donaldson, 1976). Furthermore, some research does not support the idea of a more rapid decline of mental function among people with mental retardation (Goodman, 1977a, 1977b).

Other researchers have focused specifically on the mental functioning of individuals with mental retardation and have included other subjects in their samples as well (Bell & Zubek, 1960; Fisher & Zeaman, 1970; Kaplan, 1943). In most cases results were mixed, although there is some support for a decline in measured intelligence. Bell and Zubek, for example, conducted a cross-sectional study using subjects from 15 to 64 years of age. They reported that full-scale IQs seemed to hold rather well between 20 and 45 but declined thereafter. Kaplan's early investigation (1943) used a different design and assessed measured intelligence of retarded individuals over 45 years of age.

Subjects in his study had been tested previously, and the earlier test scores were compared with the retest performances to determine the degree of change. An average of nearly 15 years had elapsed between testings. Although some decline in measured intelligence was noted, results did not suggest that the subjects' rate of decline was much different from what might be expected of nonretarded counterparts. In fact, certain specific performance areas showed an improved functioning over earlier assessments (for example, vocabulary performance in males).

Fisher and Zeaman (1970) studied the mental functioning of over 1100 institutionalized subjects with retardation. They found that higher-level subjects continued to grow in mental age until their late 30s, while growth for lower-level subjects tapered off earlier. These researchers also found that mental age for subjects at all levels showed a tendency to decline after 60 years of age. Measured intelligence (IQ) dropped substantially between 5 and 16 years of age despite growth in mental age. Between 16 and 60, however, IQ was relatively stable.

Research results indicate a mixture of findings, a situation that is not surprising given the limited attention to the area. In part these varying data may be the result of different research designs and samples. The evidence does point to a decline in mental functioning as people with mental retardation grow old—at least in terms of measured intelligence. It is not at all clear how such a decline compares with performance by nonretarded peers, although it may not be substantially greater (Janicki & Jacobson, 1986). It is also unclear how specific areas of functioning that are a part of the global measured intelligence vary with age.

One must be cautious in interpreting these results. Situational factors, such as the testing itself, can substantially alter an individual's performance. They may cause enhanced or diminished performance depending on the individual and the situation. This type of influence has long been recognized by investigators in the field of gerontology (e.g., Botwinick, 1969; Fisher, 1973; Furry & Baltes, 1973; Lair & Moon, 1972). One factor that may well result in declining test scores is the increased cautiousness that is observed in older people in general. Botwinick's results in particular highlighted "risk avoidance" or greater cautiousness in the elderly (1969).

Such a characteristic as increased cautiousness stands out most prominently in tasks with a time limit. Cautiousness also comes into play in situations that have the potential to produce anxiety, such as the presence of a nonroutine authority figure (the psychometrician). Both of these conditions often exist in a testing situation. If older people with retardation exhibit the same increased cautiousness as older people in general (and there is no reason to expect that they would not), the timed responses required by testing will have a substantial negative influence on their scores. They simply may fail to respond within the allotted time.

The presence of a psychometrician may create some special concern for the elderly person with retardation. Kaplan (1943) suggested that a mental test is an important occurrence in the life of such a person (recall that nearly all of the data available on these people involved institutionalized populations). He specifically stated that this provided strong motivation for these older patients to do well, because doing poorly might result in negative consequences. A good performance could have favorable results (such as institutional parole or release). Although Kaplan's logic is appealing, more recent studies make this line of reasoning dubious.

Part of the investigation by Dickerson et al. (1974) involved interviews with older mentally retarded patients. Many of these individuals had resided in the institution for an extended period (20 to 60 years). Most patients did not view parole or release favorably. In large part they were happy in the institution and tended to make such comments as, "I like it here," "All of my friends are here," "I'd be afraid to go—there is so much crime," and "I'm safe here" (Dickerson et al., 1974, p. 8). These investigators further reported that some subjects were reluctant to be interviewed because they were afraid that would mean they would have to live elsewhere. One can certainly argue that these patients' desire to remain in the institution might be based on the wrong reasons, but their reactions were indisputable—they tended to feel comfortable in the institution and did not wish to move elsewhere, whether from fear of the unknown or for other reasons. Such reactions are at variance with Kaplan's (1943) interpretation and might encourage poorer test performance.

Other factors may also contribute to the apparent decline in mental functioning by older people with retardation. It should be noted, however, that these points are largely speculative since research on these topics comes mainly from the general field of gerontology rather than mental retardation. For example, age deficits are typically evident on tasks that are paced (Kinsbourne, 1973; Taub, 1972), tasks that require a constant switching of attention (Craik, 1971), and tasks that involve free recall rather than recognition (Harwood & Naylor, 1969). Although these findings do not come from studies of subjects with retardation, it is probable that similar studies done with this population would produce similar results. The tasks noted are very reminiscent of the activities included in an intelligence test.

Age deficits have also been found with tasks that require a change of learning set (Traxler & Britton, 1970). This is another area that has not been extensively investigated with older retarded subjects. The literature does, however, suggest that subjects with retardation (undifferentiated by age) are particularly susceptible to a formation of sets that diminishes their ability to transfer learning to other situations (Drew & Espeseth, 1968). In view of these findings, it is reasonable to expect that older people with retardation would be more likely to form sets than both younger retarded and older nonretarded individuals. This, of course, is speculative, since specific investigation of the topic remains to be undertaken.

Research on the mental functioning of aged people with retardation has been limited in both depth and scope. This is probably more a reflection of the limited research on this group than of a lack of interest in mental functioning. We anticipate increased activity on this topic in the future.

Social and Personal Functioning

Core Concept	*The social and personal functioning of elderly people with mental retardation provides some extremely interesting areas of study. Evidence is currently confusing and may in some ways challenge the normalization principle.*

It is evident from the interviews conducted by Dickerson et al. (1974) that the people in their sample, for the most part, did not want to live outside the institution. Their reasons for wishing to remain varied considerably in terms of specifics, as suggested by their remarks noted earlier. Most probably they had very little information about life outside the institution; after all, the average length of institutionalization was 38 years. The institution had become their home, and they seemed to view the outside world as a place of uncertainty and a place to be feared. Their remarks reflect feelings of security in their institutional placement.

An additional theme also seems to emerge, however. These older patients made repeated reference about being happy and about their friends. One older gentleman even made note of having been very active with "his ladies" (age unreported, although he had been in the institution for 57 years). This raises some very interesting questions about the quality of life that the elderly with mental retardation have. What are their social and personal lives like? As stated before, information on this topic is limited, although there have been some reports that provide a glimpse of life for the mentally retarded population at this stage of the life cycle.

Talkington and Chiovaro (1969) reported on a pilot project supported by Title III of the Older Americans Act and focused on programming for the special needs of the elderly person with retardation. The project included more than 100 older institutionalized individuals ranging in age from 50 to 72. The description of these individuals at the beginning of the project differs from the impressions of Dickerson et al. (1974). Talkington and Chiovaro characterized their subjects as being mostly inactive, showing behavioral patterns that suggested senility and "regressive trends in self care" (p. 29). They also noted that these older patients showed a general lack of interest and characteristic feelings of worthlessness. Although the investigators reported that their project made substantial progress, the description of their subjects before the program is not a very favorable one. Most of the patients in the project had been forgotten by their families; the families of some were nonexistent because of death and moves to other locations. Such findings place the all-important family support networks on shaky ground (Seltzer, 1985b). It is promising to see that social agency networks are increasingly serving elderly people with mental retardation (Seltzer, Krauss, Litchfield, & Modlish, 1989). But such assistance cannot replace family support.

Silverstein, Herbs, Nasuta, and White (1986) found a generally low level of adaptive behavior functioning in institutionalized Down syndrome subjects as a function of aging. Recent research, however, suggests an improvement in adaptive behavior for older adults with mental retardation following deinstitutionalization (Fine, Tangeman, & Woodard, 1990). A general increase in socially related behavioral expression took place after subjects moved from a large institution to small, community-based facilities.

Despite their differences, there are similarities in the findings of Dickerson et al. (1974) and Talkington and Chiovaro (1969). Dickerson et al. also reported that several of their subjects no longer had close relatives who were alive or active in visiting the institution. One of their subjects, a female, had lived in the institution for 52 years. During the interview this woman reported that her brother had brought her to the institution when she was initially placed (an arrangement made by her mother). Since that time she had not seen her brother or her mother. This particular patient, however, was atypical in the Dickerson study—she was the one woman in the sample who desired to live outside the institution.

Clearly, a comprehensive picture of the social and personal functioning of the retarded elderly is not available at this time. Many dimensions of this topic remain unexplored. The literature that exists presents somewhat unexpected results in terms of the general ideas laypeople have about growing old. Although they may not have had an old age that most of us would choose, aged mentally retarded people do not seem to view their lot in life as miserable. Many in the Dickerson et al. study seemed satisfied. This is only one source of data, but it does raise some interesting questions for future research.

PROGRAMMING AND FUTURE RESEARCH

Core Concept	*Service programs and living arrangements for elderly people with mental retardation also raise interesting questions about normalization.*

Programming for older people with retardation has received even less attention than research on aging and retardation generally. Janicki, Ackerman, and Jacobson (1985) found that state service plans for developmental disabilities gave little consideration to these people. There has, however, been general concern for educating, placing, and treating individuals with retardation as nearly normally as possible. This popular notion has emerged from the least restrictive alternative and normalization concepts and has kindled an interest in community living arrangements for adults with retardation. The positive outcomes of such placements (Fine et al., 1990) prompt further interest in these types of arrangements. Research suggests that a large proportion of older people with retardation who now live in restricted and institutional situations do not need to (Edgerton, 1989). Future programming plans must increasingly anticipate changes in this population as health care continues to improve (Sison & Cotten, 1989).

Community living arrangements have raised much controversy from time to time. Often objections come from neighborhood residents who are fearful for the physical well-being of their families or believe the value of their property will be reduced by the proximity of facilities for people with retardation. These arguments have been the most prominent in objections to community living placements. We must, however, also consider an issue that surfaces only occasionally, but that relates specifically to the elderly person with retardation—the well-being of the individual. The evidence available is confusing, particularly if one supports the normalization principle.

Research cited earlier (e.g., Dickerson et al., 1974) suggested that older people with retardation are largely comfortable in residential settings and may even fear being placed in the larger community. Some evidence also indicates that aged mildly and moderately retarded individuals in state residential facilities (intermediate care facilities providing 24-hour supervised residential living) "fared better on almost all measures (medical status, medication consumption, and behavior problems)" than their nonretarded counterparts (Cotten et al., 1981, p. 363). Further, the subjects in this study

In future years it is likely that retarded elderly persons will be more integrated into community living and interacting with the general public.

were no different from their nonretarded peers in terms of adaptive behavior, although they tended to function more poorly with respect to communication skills.

We must interpret this evidence with care, since a number of factors are involved. First of all, the research is very limited, and a great deal more investigation is essential. Second, we must consider the amount of time that the individuals in these studies had spent in residential living placements. The Dickerson et al. (1974) study examined subjects who had spent an average of 38 years in institutions. Cotten et al. (1981) studied retarded subjects with an average of nearly 20 years of institutionalization but nonretarded subjects with an average of only 1.5 years. The retarded subjects were naturally more accustomed to such living arrangements than the nonretarded subjects. The many years of residential living may well have influenced findings in the Dickerson et al. (1974) study. In this case, familiarity may have bred comfort and security.

Meyers, Borthwick, and Eyman (1985) studied the place of residence of nearly 60,000 mentally retarded individuals in California by age, ethnicity, and level of retardation. These investigators found that a decreasing proportion of subjects who were either older or more severely retarded lived in their natural homes. Of particular interest in this investigation was the finding that, although the Caucasian group represented the largest part of their sample, this group was the lowest with regard to living in their natural homes. Both Latino and black clients were much more likely to be living at home, perhaps because of sociocultural differences.

Our accumulated evidence on living arrangements for the retarded elderly, although growing, still remains sparse. The general picture can, however, be interpreted cautiously, and projections can be presented. Our data suggest that some older people with retardation are doing satisfactorily in residential settings and that many of them may wish to remain there. We must ask ourselves how these data fit with the principle of normalization. Actually they fit very well if one considers the *individual* and the past experiences he or she has had. For elderly subjects with retardation, residential living may represent much or most of their past. These individuals may be most comfortable in a residential setting, whether it is a nursing home for the elderly or a similar setting specifically designed for people with retardation. Thus normalization placement might be best viewed on an individual, case-by-case basis. Imposing external requirements from some theoretical perspective does not necessarily serve the individual best. If the least restrictive environment approach is effectively in place for individuals with retardation who are now youngsters, normalization that is sensitive to both individual needs and the theoretical principle may be much more similar when this generation becomes elderly.

Other programming for older mentally retarded individuals has also been largely ignored. For example, such support services as specialized counseling and social, medical, and legal services for this population are insufficient. Such services often need to be different because of the unique problems of the older person with retardation. The process of planning and effectively delivering services to older citizens with mental retardation differs substantially from that for nonretarded populations (Hawkins & Eklund, 1989, 1990).

Massive research is necessary for a better understanding of the retarded elderly. The empirical knowledge based on this population is extremely thin. We do not have a firm grasp on how many aged people with retardation there are, or where they are in general. Such information, plus a clear definition of what old means in this group, is fundamental to further research. It is difficult to describe characteristics and to prescribe programming coherently unless these basic questions are answered.

Investigation of the aged mentally retarded population is obviously a rich area of study for beginning researchers in mental retardation. It represents an area of specialization that promises an exciting career. In order to promote this important area of study, however, it is necessary to initiate research training programs focusing on the topic. Future researchers in this area will have to study both mental retardation and gerontology, then synthesize the two for use with the elderly with retardation. The research needed is unlikely to come from either mental retardation or gerontology singly.

Who are the retarded elderly, and what are their characteristics? These were general questions with which we began this chapter, and in large part they remain unanswered. The final part of the life cycle of the individual with mental retardation has had very little examination in comparison to earlier phases. We still cannot answer the question whether or not people with retardation tend to age more rapidly than their nonretarded peers. In some cases they do seem to become prematurely old. Certainly people of the ages under discussion in this chapter (45 to 55) are not considered old in the general population. If, in fact, this population does age more quickly, it is not at all clear whether it results from factors related to mental retardation or to environmental factors that may be associated with mental retardation, such as poor health care.

It is interesting to note that people with mental retardation seem not to experience middle age to any marked degree. They tend to behave and are often thought of as being in an extended childhood and adolescent phase for a large part of their lives. We do not know whether this is because of their historic residential placement and consequent (lack of) expectations. Again, the need for research with comparable groups that have not been institutionalized is evident. Although the topic of the adult with mental retardation has been receiving greater attention in recent years, adulthood is shortened by the conception that 45 or 50 is old. Once again the question is: Is this a function of mental retardation, the sociocultural environment, or both? Certainly the types of services available to people with mental retardation greatly affect this phenomenon. The literature on this population suggests that aged retarded individuals have in the past tended to spend most of life in institutions. Many who are discharged are placed in nursing homes—facilities that society characteristically reserves for the elderly. This very pattern of placement seems largely to eliminate middle age from the life of the individual with retardation.

When older mentally retarded people are placed in nursing homes, they tend to be grouped with patients who are senile. Dickerson et al. (1974) suggested that this is one phenomenon that contributes to the invisibility of elderly people with retardation. No one distinguishes their behaviors from those of elderly patients in general, so they lose their diagnosis of mental retardation. Obviously one must question whether or not such programming practices are appropriate for and in the best interests of these individuals. If they are (a matter not yet determined), is it advisable to relabel these people with a term that carries such negative connotations? As we have said again and again, mental retardation is a complex problem that involves an interaction of many forces and influences. It is a problem that society has at least partially created, and society must address it. The life of the aged individual with retardation continues to reflect these interacting variables.

NEW ISSUES AND FUTURE DIRECTIONS

The preceding section poses a number of questions, several of which began the chapter and remain unanswered. The literature available on the latter part of the life span has grown tremendously in recent years. However, the future of services to the retarded

THE BILL OF RIGHTS FOR THE ELDERLY PERSON WITH MENTAL RETARDATION

1. The right to an adequate standard of living, economic security, and protective work.
2. The right to humane services designed to help them reach their fullest potential.
3. The right to live as independently as they are able in the community of their choice, in as normal a manner as possible.
4. The right to an array of services that is generally available to other elderly groups.
5. The right to choose to retire. In addition, the opportunity to retire "to something," rather than just "from something."
6. The right to participate as a member of the community, having reciprocal interdependency.
7. The right to be considered a person and not merely "elderly" or "retarded."
8. The right to protected, personal well-being, and to a qualified guardian, when required.
9. The right to be involved in setting one's goals and making one's decisions. The right to fail if necessary.
10. The right to a positive future, and having enough involvement with life to prevent a preoccupation with death.
11. The right to be romantic, not asexual.
12. The right to sufficient activity and attention to permit continued integrity of self, individual identity, and purpose.
13. The right to an interesting environment and life style, with availability of sufficient mobility to provide a variety of surroundings.
14. The right to live and die with dignity.

Source: From "The Elderly Mentally Retarded Developmentally Disabled Population: A Challenge for the Service Delivery System" by P. D. Cotten and C. L. Spirrison, in S. J. Brody and G. E. Ruff (Eds.), *Aging and Rehabilitation* (pp. 159–187), 1986, New York: Springer. Copyright 1986 by Springer-Verlag New York, Inc. Reprinted by permission.

elderly depends heavily on consolidating our knowledge of this population. For example, a very important issue that remains unclear relates to prevalence. We are still operating with estimates that show great variability, too much to be able to argue convincingly for specialized services. This is particularly true when the cost of such services competes for funding with those for the geriatric population in general—a group that is also growing substantially.

Other issues pertain to ethical concerns particularly relevant to this age group. Howell (1988) discusses dilemmas that recur with older retarded individuals and illustrate some of the similarities and differences between this group and the general population of elderly people. One dilemma of particular note is competence to refuse recommended treatment—an issue that is not uncommon for elderly people in general. The difference with older people who are retarded, however, is that they may be considered incompetent by reason of mental ability irrespective of age. Does this factor really make such individuals less competent to refuse treatment? This is a question that remains unanswered but one that faces care providers in a very real way when they are working with a Mildred or a Charles. These are no longer hypothetical issues when real people are involved.

The future of services for retarded elderly people is uncharted territory. Balancing real life with the hypothetical ideal presents many challenges for people working with this population. It is important to think carefully as we enter these unknown areas, to draw upon the desirable as we develop service plans that will work within the constraints of society's ability to provide. Cotten and Spirrison (1986) articulated many elements of a desirable quality of life for the retarded elderly in the form of a bill of rights. These are presented on page 356.

CORE QUESTIONS

1. How have the general methodological problems encountered in conducting gerontological research contributed to problems in investigation of the mentally retarded elderly?
2. Why have aged people with retardation been characterized by some as an "invisible" group?
3. What effect does invisibility have on social services for the elderly with retardation?
4. How does disagreement about who is old contribute to research difficulties on elderly retarded people?
5. The general perception of older people is that they have a reduced level of mental functioning. Does this perception hold for older individuals with retardation?
6. Do people with mental retardation decline in mental functioning more rapidly than nonretarded people?
7. What factors other than reduced mental functioning may enter the picture in terms of mental performance for older populations?
8. What is life like for older institutionalized retarded individuals from a social and personal standpoint? Do they like their life, or are they generally unhappy?
9. If we, nonretarded professionals, subscribe to the normalization principle, how may some of our views run counter to the desires of older retarded citizens who are currently in institutions? Who is right, and what factors need consideration in answering this question?
10. Why do some people object to community-based living arrangements for older individuals with mental retardation?
11. How do age and ethnicity relate to living placement for people with mental retardation?

ROUND TABLE DISCUSSION

The notions of mainstreaming and normalization have been much in evidence throughout this volume at many different stages of the life cycle. In some ways these principles represent an imposition of what one group (mental retardation professionals) believes is best upon another group (people with mental retardation). When we reach the level of old age these considerations take on other facets, such as what people want or what makes them happy.

In your study group or on your own, examine the principles of mainstreaming and normalization with regard to the mentally retarded elderly. Consider why the notions seem more complicated by the fact that many older retarded people have been institutionalized for many years. How might this influence their perceptions of satisfaction? How might such results be different 20 or 30 years from now? How do these matters influence the manner in which you might plan services for elderly retarded people over the next decade?

REFERENCES

Bell, A., & Zubek, J. P. (1960). The effect of age on the intellectual performance of mental defectives. *Journal of Gerontology, 15*, 285–295.

Botwinick, J. (1969). Disinclination to venture response versus cautiousness in responding: Age differences. *Journal of Genetic Psychology, 119*, 241–249.

Cotten, P. D., Sison, G. F. P., Jr., & Starr, S. (1981). Comparing elderly mentally retarded and non–mentally retarded individuals: Who are they? What are their needs? *Gerontologist, 21*, 359–365.

Cotten, P. D., & Spirrison, C. L. (1986). The elderly mentally retarded developmentally disabled population: A challenge for the service delivery system. In S. J. Brody & G. E. Ruff (Eds.), *Aging and rehabilitation* (pp. 159–187). New York: Springer.

Craik, F. I. (1971). Age differences in recognition memory. *Quarterly Journal of Experimental Psychology, 23*, 316–323.

Dickerson, M., Hamilton, J., Huber, R., & Segal, R. (1974). *The aged mentally retarded: The invisible client—a challenge to the community.* Paper presented at the annual meeting of the American Association on Mental Deficiency, Toronto.

Drew, C. J., & Hardman, M. L. (1985). *Designing and conducting behavioral research.* New York: Pergamon.

Drew, C. J., & Espeseth, V. K. (1968). Transfer of training in the mentally retarded: A review. *Exceptional Children, 35*, 129–132.

Dybwad, G. (1985). Thoughts on aging among persons with disabilities. In M. P. Janicki & H. M. Wisniewski (Eds.), *Aging and developmental disabilities: Issues and approaches* (pp. xi–xii). Baltimore: Paul H. Brookes.

Edgerton, R. B. (1989). Retarded people of adult years. *Psychiatric Annals, 19*, 205–209.

Fine, M. A., Tangeman, P. J., & Woodard, J. (1990). Changes in adaptive behavior of older adults with mental retardation following deinstitutionalization. *American Journal on Mental Retardation, 94*, 661–668.

Fisher, J. (1973). Competence, effectiveness, intellectual functioning, and aging. *Gerontologist, 13*, 62–68.

Fisher, M. A., & Zeaman, D. (1970). Growth and decline of retardate intelligence. In N. R. Ellis (Ed.), *International review of research in mental retardation* (Vol. 4, pp. 151–191). New York: Academic.

Foelker, G. A., & Luke, E. A. (1989). Mental health issues for the aging mentally retarded population. *Journal of Applied Gerontology, 8,* 242–250.

Furry, C. S., & Baltes, P. B. (1973). The effect of age differences in ability-extraneous performance variables on the assessment of intelligence in children, adults, and the elderly. *Journal of Gerontology, 28,* 73–80.

Goodman, J. F. (1977a). IQ decline in mentally retarded adults: A matter of fact or methodological flaw. *Journal of Mental Deficiency Research, 21,* 199–203.

Goodman, J. F. (1977b). Aging and intelligence in young retarded adults: A cross-sectional study of fluid abilities in three samples. *Psychological Reports, 41,* 255–263.

Harwood, E., & Naylor, G. F. K. (1969). Recall and recognition in elderly and young subjects. *Australian Journal of Psychology, 21,* 251–257.

Hawkins, B. A., & Eklund, S. J. (1989). Aging and developmental disabilities: Interagency planning for an emerging population. *Journal of Applied Gerontology, 8,* 168–174.

Hawkins, B. A., & Eklund, S. J. (1990). Planning processes and outcomes for an aging population with developmental disabilities. *Mental Retardation, 28,* 35–40.

Horn, J. L., & Donaldson, G. (1976). On the myth of intellectual decline in adulthood. *American Psychologist, 31,* 701–719.

Howell, M. C. (1988). Ethical dilemmas encountered in the care of those who are disabled and also old. *Educational Gerontology, 14,* 439–449.

Jacobson, J. W., Sutton, M. S., & Janicki, M. P. (1985). Demography and characteristics of aging and aged mentally retarded persons. In M. P. Janicki & H. M. Wisniewski (Eds.), *Aging and developmental disabilities: Issues and approaches* (pp. 115–142). Baltimore: Paul H. Brookes.

Janicki, M. P., Ackerman, L., & Jacobson, J. W. (1985). State developmental disabilities/aging plans and planning for an older developmentally disabled population. *Mental Retardation, 23,* 297–301.

Janicki, M. P., & Jacobson, J. W. (1986). Generational trends in sensory, physical, and behavioral abilities among older mentally retarded persons. *American Journal of Mental Deficiency, 90,* 490–500.

Janicki, M. P., & MacEachron, A. E. (1984). Residential, health, and social service needs of elderly developmentally disabled persons. *Gerontologist, 21,* 128–137.

Janicki, M. P., & Wisniewski, H. M. (1985). Some comments on growing older and being developmentally disabled. In M. P. Janicki & H. M. Wisniewski (Eds.), *Aging and developmental disabilities: Issues and approaches* (pp. 1–5). Baltimore: Paul H. Brookes.

Kaplan, O. (1943). Mental decline in older morons. *American Journal of Mental Deficiency, 47,* 277–285.

Kinsbourne, M. (1973). Age effects on letter span related to rate and sequential dependency. *Journal of Gerontology, 28,* 317–319.

Kriger, S. F. (1975). On aging and mental retardation. In J. C. Hamilton & R. M. Segal (Eds.), *Proceedings of a consultation-conference on the gerontological aspects of mental retardation.* Ann Arbor: University of Michigan.

Labouvie-Vief, G. (1977). Adult cognitive development: In search of alternative interpretations. *Merrill-Palmer Quarterly, 23,* 227–263.

Lair, C. V., & Moon, W. H. (1972). The effects of praise and reproof on the performance of middle aged and older subjects. *Aging and Human Development, 3,* 279–284.

Meyers, C. E., Borthwick, S. A., & Eyman, R. K. (1985). Place of residence by age, ethnicity, and level of retardation of the mentally retarded/developmentally disabled population of California. *American Journal of Mental Deficiency, 90,* 266–270.

Payne, D. (1967). *1,500,000 bits of information: Some implications for action.* Boulder, CO: Western Interstate Commission for Higher Education.

Schaie, K. W., & Gribbin, K. (1975). Adult development and aging. *Annual Review of Psychology, 26,* 65–96.

Seltzer, M. M. (1985a). Research in social aspects of aging and developmental disabilities. In M. P. Janicki & H. M. Wisniewski (Eds.), *Aging and developmental disabilities: Issues and approaches* (pp. 161–173). Baltimore: Paul H. Brookes.

Seltzer, M. M. (1985b). Informal supports for aging mentally retarded persons. *American Journal of Mental Deficiency, 90,* 259–265.

Seltzer, M. M., & Seltzer, G. B. (1985). The elderly mentally retarded: A group in need of service. *The Journal of Gerontological Social Work, 8,* 99–119.

Seltzer, M. M., Krauss, M. W., Litchfield, L. C., & Modlish, N. J. (1989). Utilization of aging network services by elderly persons with mental retardation. *Gerontologist, 29,* 234–238.

Silverstein, A. B., Herbs, D., Nasuta, R., & White, J. F. (1986). Effects of age on the adaptive behavior of institutionalized individuals with Down syndrome. *American Journal of Mental Deficiency, 90,* 659–662.

Sison, G. F., & Cotten, P. D. (1989). The elderly mentally retarded person: Current perspectives and future directions. *Journal of Applied Gerontology, 8,* 151–167.

Talkington, L., & Chiovaro, S. (1969). An approach to programming for aged MR. *Mental Retardation, 7* (1), 29–30.

Taub, H. A. (1972). A comparison of young adult and old groups on various digit span tasks. *Developmental Psychology, 6,* 60–65.

Traxler, A. J., & Britton, J. H. (1970). Age differences in retroaction as a function of anticipation interval and transfer paradigm. *Proceedings of the 78th Annual Convention of the American Psychological Association,* 683–684.

Tymchuck, A. J. (1979). The mentally retarded in later life. In O. J. Kaplan (Ed.), *Psychopathology of aging* (pp. 197–209). New York: Academic.

PART FIVE

Family, Social, and Legal Issues

CHAPTER THIRTEEN

Mental Retardation and the Family

- Parents of children with mental retardation progress through stages ranging from awareness to acceptance.

- Denial is a common parental reaction, especially during the initial stage of adjustment.

- Parents may project blame for the child with mental retardation on the people they believe are responsible for their suffering.

- Common fears of parents are associated with having other children, loss of friends, a lifetime of care, and impact on the family unit.

- When parents of children with mental retardation are unable to blame someone else, they may blame themselves.

- When parents begin to realize what has happened, they may react with grief or mourning.

- Parents may choose to isolate themselves because of their feelings of shame and guilt.

- Parents may show rejection through strong underexpectations of achievement, unrealistic goals, escape, and reaction formation.

- The final step in adjustment is acceptance of the child's disability, the child, and oneself.

- Parents of children with mental retardation must have their needs and feelings recognized and understood by each other, friends, family, and professionals.

- Parents' search for a cause is generally in two directions: theological or medical.

- When parents have accepted their child's condition, they usually seek out a cure.

- Organizations such as the Association for Retarded Citizens and the Association for Persons with Severe Handicaps can provide valuable information and services to parents.

- Families with a child who is mentally retarded must be able to maintain typical functioning as nearly as possible.

- One of parents' greatest concerns is what the future will hold for the child when they are no longer able or available to provide care.

- Individuals with mental retardation need to feel accepted.

- Every child with mental retardation, no matter how severely disabled, has the ability to grow and develop.

- The effect a child with mental retardation has on siblings is receiving increasing attention from professionals.

- Siblings who are not disabled often become neglected members of the family.

- The parent/professional partnership needs to be reinforced and expanded as we move through the 1990s.

The family is the oldest and most enduring of all human institutions. It has survived empires, wars, famine, plague, depression, recession, and the constant changes of social values. The family is based on both an emotional and a hereditary bond between parents and children. The primary family unit consists of parents and their children, and the extended unit includes grandparents and more distant relatives. Family systems exist for various reasons, including the need for security, belonging, and love. The family provides a socially acceptable vehicle for bringing children into the world. Many individuals see children as an extension of themselves; others perceive their children as a means to attain some degree of immortality. Unfortunately, the conception of some children is unplanned, and the children are unwanted.

A child may have a positive or negative effect on the relationship between husband and wife. The child may draw the parents closer together with a commitment toward a common goal. But the child's presence may also result in discord and conflict. Either way, the arrival of a child usually represents a dramatic change in life style for a couple. Financial problems may plague new parents. Recreational and social activities have to be curtailed or modified. Travel over long distances may become difficult because of expense, inconvenience, and sometimes the uncooperative behavior of the child. Entertainment may become a problem because of the expense or difficulty of obtaining baby-sitters.

Couples with children may find that their childless friends do not understand the needs and nature of children and parenthood. This may result in a change in friendship patterns, marking an end to a relatively independent and carefree life style. Housing needs may change significantly. The small apartment that once seemed most adequate suddenly becomes confining. The comfortable and socially convenient "adults only" apartment complex must be vacated for one that is less to their tastes. A two-seater sports car may no longer be practical, since the space needed for the child and the child's belongings dictates a larger, more practical, but less enjoyable mode of transportation.

The list of complications, inconveniences, expenses, and changes in life styles brought on by a new child is endless. Many of these negative aspects of parenthood are often overshadowed by the sheer joy and pleasure that the child brings to the new parents. The displeasures of diaper changing and the sleepless nights caused by the infant's crying tend to fade away with the first smile, the first step, and the first spoken word. With these first accomplishments, parents begin to envision the fruition of their dreams and hopes of parenthood—healthy, bright, capable, beautiful children doing all the things that the parents did or wished they could have done.

The parents of children with mental retardation may find few of the joys that compensate for the frustrations and inconveniences of having a child (Turnbull & Turnbull, 1985; Volpe & Koenigsberger, 1981). Delayed maturation may preclude the child's exhibiting skills associated with normal development. Developmental delays impede the ability of children with mental retardation to smile at their parents, mimic voices, or take their first steps at the same times as nondisabled infants. Dreams and hopes for the child's future are often shattered. The child may threaten the parents' self-esteem, feelings of self-worth, and dignity. Many individuals view the procreation of healthy children as one of the main purposes of existence. The birth of a child with a mental disability may cause parents to view themselves as failures in what they consider one of their fundamental purposes in life. For some parents, feelings of failure and loss of self-worth are temporary. For others, these emotions may last a lifetime. What can be said with certainty is that "the process of adjustment for parents is continuous and distinctly individual" (Hardman, Drew, Egan, & Wolf, 1990, p. 460).

No response, reaction, or feeling can be considered typical, mature, good, or bad. Parental reaction to the growth and development of a child with mental retardation is unpredictable. Reactions are based on emotions, and for the parents, the magnitude of their feelings and reactions is as great as they perceive the problem to be.

In this chapter we address the impact of the child with mental retardation on the family. The needs of the child, the parents, and the siblings are discussed in the context of the needs of the family unit and of its relationship with professionals.

THE IMPACT OF THE CHILD WITH MENTAL RETARDATION ON THE FAMILY

Core Concept	*Parents of children with mental retardation progress through stages ranging from awareness to acceptance.*

A child with mental retardation has a profound impact on the family. If the condition is not readily apparent at birth, it becomes evident only with the passage of time. There are conditions associated with mental retardation, however, that are easily recognizable from the outset.

Stages from Awareness to Acceptance

One of the first authors to suggest that parents of retarded children move through a series of stages was Rosen (1955). He enumerated five stages through which parents of children with mental retardation progress from the time they first become aware of a problem until they accept the child. Rosen's five stages are referred to throughout this chapter: (1) awareness of a general problem in the child's growth and development; (2) recognition that the basic problem is mental retardation; (3) search for a cause for the retardation; (4) search for a cure; and (5) acceptance of the child.

It is important to emphasize that while some parents go through distinct periods of adjustment, others cope without passing through any set sequence of stages. As Blacher (1984) pointed out: "The question of whether sequential stages of parental adjustment to a handicapped child are clinically and scientifically derived fact, or an artifact of researchers' attempts to perpetuate ideas from the literature, remains to be determined" (p. 67).

The severity of the retardation is always an important variable in this adjustment process. A child who is mildly retarded may not have any physically distinguishing characteristics that suggest mental retardation. Many parents are unaware that the child is retarded until academic failure occurs in the public schools. The degree of impact, frustration, or disappointment, however, does not necessarily correlate directly with the degree of deficiency. Parents of children who are severely retarded may find it easier to acknowledge problems than others whose children are only mildly affected. The child's disability is obvious to the parents of children who are severely retarded, and acknowledgment (not necessarily acceptance) generally comes quickly.

The religious background of the parents may affect their attitude toward mental retardation. Etiology and age of onset are also important factors. Physical traumata that may permanently impair a child who has developed normally may be more debilitating to the parents than congenital retardation.

The family's socioeconomic and intellectual status also has an impact on their reception of a child with mental retardation. Some families at lower socioeconomic levels place less emphasis on cognitive development and skills and, at times, more emphasis on the development of physical attributes. This is particularly true when members of the family work primarily in occupations that are physically rather than cognitively demanding. But in a situation in which a family places great emphasis on cognitive development and members of the family work primarily in professional settings requiring a higher level of education, reactions may be quite different. A child with mental retardation born into a family in which education and white-collar jobs are held in high regard may be a greater threat and disappointment to the family.

For the parents of children who are severely retarded, awareness and recognition of the basic problem may come simultaneously. Parents of children with mild mental retardation become aware of the problem only gradually, as the child fails to develop or progress as anticipated. Problems may be more obvious to parents with other children who have developed normally.

For many parents, although inconsistent growth and developmental patterns may be indicated, the actual problem does not manifest itself until the child is in school, fails academically, and is evaluated and declared retarded by the school psychologist. When the parents are informed that their child is retarded, they may acknowledge the condition and recognize it for what it is, or they may resort to a variety of defense mechanisms to aid in coping. The initial impact, which Blacher (1984) referred to as "emotional disorganization," has several forms. It may result in some sort of a transient stress disorder for the parents, or it may have a permanently debilitating effect on the entire family unit. Featherstone (1980) wrote that the advent of a child who is disabled may attack the foundations of a marriage by inciting powerful emotions in both parents, including feelings of shared failure. Other authors (Cleveland, 1980; Lamb, 1983) indicated that fathers and mothers may react very differently to the child. The mother may take on the role of physical protector and guardian of the child's needs, while the father is more reserved in his role. He may cope by withdrawing and internalizing his feelings.

The presence of a child with mental retardation need not create a family crisis. How the event is defined by the family determines whether or not a real crisis exists. There are few families, however, in which the stigma of mental retardation that our society imposes will not cause the event to be interpreted as a crisis. The professional can help the family cope by examining its resources, including role structure, emotional stability, and previous experiences with stress.

Parental Reactions

Core Concept	*Denial is a common parental reaction, especially during the initial stage of adjustment.*

Denial

Denial provides self-protection against painful realities. Parents may minimize the degree of disability or simply deny that any problem exists. They close their minds to their child's limitations or explain their child's limitations by implying laziness, indifference, or lack of motivation. Denial can be both useless and destructive. It is useless because refusal to accept the reality of a child's disability cannot make the problems disappear. It is destructive because it impedes the child's own acceptance of limitations and may prevent necessary education and therapy.

Denial symptoms are both frustrating and exasperating to the professional. The parent(s) may refuse to recognize the conditions for what they are; consequently, treatment is frequently delayed and sometimes never provided. Federal law requires parental consent before placement of a child in special education, so the child with mental retardation whose parents deny that the problem exists will be excluded from any special education programs. Denial may also deprive the child of necessary medical treatment, which only adds to the frustration of professionals endeavoring to help the family.

Although denial strains the relationship between parents and professionals, professionals should always be aware of the extreme emotional stress placed on the family and realize that, for the time being, this reaction may be the only one possible for the parents. With time, patience, and continued support, professionals may eventually help parents face the reality of their situation. Eventually, parents may realize that the birth of a child with retardation need neither stigmatize their lives nor cast any doubts on their integrity as adequate parents or human beings.

Core Concept	*Parents may project blame for the child with mental retardation on the people they believe are responsible for their suffering.*

Projection of Blame

Another common parental reaction is projection of blame. Targets are individuals, frequently physicians, whom the parents associate with considerable frustration and agony. For example, blame is often directed at the allegedly incompetent obstetrician as follows:

> If only the doctors had taken better care of my wife (or me) before the baby was born, they would have known something was going wrong and could have prevented it.

If only the doctor had not taken so long to get to the hospital, help would have been there early enough to keep something from happening.

If they'd had enough sense not to use so much anesthesia.

The other allegedly incompetent physician is the pediatrician who did not properly attend to the child immediately after birth or failed to treat an illness or injury adequately. Usually this blame is not justified, since the mental retardation is not directly correlated with incompetent medical care. Parental hostility may be more frequently justified by inadequate and sometimes even improper counseling on the part of the physician. Although skilled in the medical aspects of their practice, physicians are often ill-equipped to counsel parents because they know little about the resources available for the care and treatment of children with mental retardation. As suggested by Hardman and Drew (1980), it is important for physicians to "be knowledgeable about community resources that are available, including other parents, educators, clergy, family counselors, etc. The parents may choose not to consult these individuals, but at the very least they should be informed of their availability" (p. 166).

When retardation is evident and can be diagnosed at birth, it is usually the responsibility of the attending physician to inform the parents. Some may see the task of telling parents that their child is retarded as difficult, and physicians have been criticized for not assuming this professional responsibility in a sensitive, caring manner. The manner in which the physician counsels the parents may have a profound and long-lasting impact. As Hardman et al. (1990) wrote, "They cannot prevent the shock felt by parents as they learn of the child's impairment, but they can lessen its impact. They can also provide parents with perspective and direction as they attempt to adjust their lives and make room for the child" (p. 481).

Other professionals subject to parental criticism are school personnel who may have the primary responsibility of informing parents that their children have been evaluated and diagnosed as mentally retarded. Even if the counseling is carried out as professionally as can be expected by school personnel, frustrated parents may still use these individuals as scapegoats, projecting blame on them. Individuals in the school setting most likely to receive the brunt of the projected blame from parents are former teachers. Parents may place the blame for the child's retardation on previous teachers for their supposed failure to teach the child. Once again, this blame may be without justification. At times, however, frustration and anger toward professionals may be warranted because of failure to meet the needs of parent or child.

Core Concept	*Common fears of parents are associated with having other children, loss of friends, a lifetime of care, and impact on the family unit.*

Fear

The unknown can make every person anxious at one time or another. Anxiety in turn may generate fear. Parents of children who are mentally retarded face so many unknowns that fear is a natural and common reaction. Some of these fears may seem completely absurd to the professional. Yet they are very real to the parents and must be acknowledged, heard with sensitivity, and responded to appropriately. Until parents have satisfactory information, the fears will persist. Unfortunately, answers to all parents' questions are usually not available, and anxiety may persist. Common parental questions are:

> What caused this disability, and if we choose to have other children, will they be retarded, too?
>
> How will our friends and relatives feel about us and the child?
>
> Will we always have to take care of the child, or are self-care and independence possible some day?
>
> What will this do to our family?
>
> Who will take care of the child when we are no longer able?

Parents may lack knowledge and experience and need something on which to base their hopes or a means to control their fears.

Core Concept	*When parents of children with mental retardation are unable to blame someone else, they may blame themselves.*

Guilt

Human nature generally dictates that blame for wrong be assigned somewhere. When parents of children with mental retardation are unable to blame someone else, they blame themselves. They begin to look for and often find something in their lives or their behavior that may be responsible for why this happened. When they look hard enough, a seemingly logical reason appears, and they feel guilt.

Guilt is insidious and debilitating. Assuming blame does not eliminate the disability, and intense feelings of guilt can erode parents' positive self-concept. Guilty parents are difficult to work with, and their negative emotions are extremely difficult to dispel. Professionals working with parents who are experiencing feelings of guilt can help them channel their energies into more productive activities.

Core Concept	*When parents begin to realize what has happened, they may react with grief or mourning.*

Mourning or Grief

Grief is a natural reaction to situations that bring extreme pain and disappointment. We all grieve when we lose something that we cherish or value. The birth of a child with mental retardation represents the loss of a dream—hope for a healthy son or daughter.

Peterson (1987) suggested that parents of an atypical infant experience recurrent sorrow and frequent feelings of inadequacy that persist over time. Wikler, Wasow, and Hatfield (1981) found that the grief process may not be time-bound. These authors reported that some parents of children with mental retardation experience chronic sorrow and may not reach eventual adjustment.

The birth of a child who is retarded represents the loss of the parents' positive self-image. To the parents the event may seem more like a death. In some instances parents may react to the birth of such a child with death wishes. Hart (1970) cited a father's reaction shortly after the birth of a child with Down syndrome. The father stated that he felt as if he were in mourning and should be dressed in black. Other parents either consciously or unconsciously wish for the death of their child with retardation. It is not uncommon for parents to harbor death wishes toward a child, particularly when the child becomes burdensome and they wish to end their ordeal. Hart said that some parents institutionalize a child who is diagnosed as retarded immediately after birth, announce that the child was stillborn, and even place an obituary notice in the newspaper. Some parents, preoccupied with thoughts of "when the child dies" or "if the child should die," unconsciously wish for the child's death. Many parents would deny their death wishes if confronted, as they are unable to acknowledge these hidden wishes on the conscious level. Other parents, however, are consciously aware of their death wishes and may or may not be willing to express these feelings publicly. More recently, however, a growing number of individuals have been willing to risk public censure by refusing to grant permission for surgery or medical treatment that would prolong the life of their child. Although such decisions raise many moral and ethical questions, only these parents know the true extent of the emotional, financial, and physical hardships they have had to endure. Judeo-Christian ethic tends to place a high value on human life. The difficult issue of who holds the responsibility for life-and-death decisions has yet to be resolved.

Core Concept	*Parents may choose to isolate themselves because of their feelings of shame and guilt.*

Withdrawal

There are times when we want and need to be alone. We can be alone physically or have others around us and still feel isolated. We may choose to shut others out of our thoughts, giving us a kind of freedom—freedom to think by ourselves, rest, meditate, and do things in our private world. Solitude can be therapeutic.

Although therapeutic in many instances, withdrawal is also potentially damaging. Parents may withdraw from friends, relatives, professional workers, or activities that may facilitate the healing process. By withdrawing, parents can construct a protective barrier or space and silence against outside pain, if not against the hurt inside. Staying away from social functions protects against "nosy" questions about the children and the family. By keeping away from restaurants and other public places the family avoids critical eyes staring at the child who is different.

Core Concept	*Parents may show rejection through strong underexpectations of achievement, unrealistic goals, escape, and reaction formation.*

Rejection

Parental rejection has such a negative connotation that anyone who has been described as rejecting is frequently stereotyped and prejudged, not only as an incompetent parent, but as a person devoid of basic humanity. In the everyday dynamics between parents and children, there are many instances in which the child's behavioral patterns exceed the parents' tolerance level. Thus, if even typical children can elicit negative reactions from their parents, it is easy to understand how a child who is mentally retarded can frequently cause such reactions. It is possible for this rejection to go to extremes. There are four common ways in which parental rejection is expressed:

1. *Strong underexpectations of achievement.* Parents so devalue the child that they minimize or ignore any positive attributes. The child often becomes aware of these parental attitudes, begins to have feelings of self-worthlessness, and behaves accordingly. We thus have what is often referred to as a self-fulfilling prophecy.
2. *Setting unrealistic goals.* Parents sometimes set goals so unrealistically high that they are unattainable. When the child fails to reach these goals, parents justify their negative feelings and attitudes on the basis of limited performance.
3. *Escape.* Another form of rejection may include desertion or running away. It may be quite open and obvious, as when a parent leaves the family and moves out of the home. Other types of desertion are more subtle—the parent is so occupied with various responsibilities that there is little, if any, time to be at home with the family. This could take the form of "demanding special projects at the office" or perhaps the requirements of "various responsibilities at the church." Other parents place the child in a distant school or institution when comparable facilities are available nearby. It is important to emphasize here that placement of a child in an institution is not necessarily equated with parental rejection.
4. *Reaction formation.* When parents deny negative feelings and publicly present completely opposite images, this may be classified as reaction formation. The parents' negative feelings run contrary to their conscious values, and they cannot accept themselves as anything but kind, loving, warm people. For example, parents who resent their child with mental retardation may frequently tell friends and relatives how much they love their child.

Many parents are in an untenable position when dealing with professionals. If they express honest feelings of not liking their child, they are condemned as rejecting parents. If they profess genuine love for their child who is retarded, they may be suspected of manifesting a reaction formation.

Core Concept	*The final step in adjustment is acceptance of the child's disability, the child, and oneself.*

Acceptance

Acceptance is the final step in the long, difficult road to adjustment for the parent. Acceptance can develop in three areas: (1) acceptance that the child has a disability, (2) acceptance of the child as an individual, and (3) parents' acceptance of themselves. Acceptance of

Parental acceptance of a child with mental retardation facilitates a healthy interaction between parent and child and promotes the child's development in many ways.

the child is a major and critical step in the healing and growing process. This step means recognizing that the child is an individual with feelings, wants, and needs like all other children (Blacher, 1984). The child has the potential to enjoy life and provide enjoyment to others. As each child with mental retardation grows into adolescence and adulthood, realistic and attainable goals can be set. The attainment of these goals can bring satisfaction, pride, and pleasure to both parents and child.

The process of reaching self-acceptance is a long and difficult one for the parents. It is filled with pain, frustration, self-doubt, and ego-shattering experiences. Featherstone (1980) pointed out that although some parents may never reach full acceptance, they do experience positive feelings as they attempt to move in that direction. In spite of all the hurts and debilitating experiences, the parents can emerge with a firm conviction that the child is an individual worthy of respect. The child's integrity as a member of the human race has not been diminished; instead, it has been enhanced. The family has not only endured a major crisis; its members have grown into stronger, wiser, and more compassionate human beings.

THE NEEDS OF PARENTS

Parents of children who are mentally retarded exhibit the same range of behavior as parents of more typical children. Most are well-adjusted, but some may have varying social and intellectual deficiencies. Parents of children who are mentally retarded, however, differ from most parents in that services historically provided to more typical children are often denied to families with a retarded child (Hardman et al., 1990; Payne & Patton, 1981). In the following section we examine some needs that often go unmet.

Communication

Core Concept	*Parents of children with mental retardation must have their needs and feelings recognized and understood by each other, friends, family, and professionals.*

It is important for parents to know they have the support of those who care about them. For professionals working with families, support implies recognition of each family member's individual needs (Patton, Beirne-Smith, & Payne, 1990). One of parents' critical needs is to receive accurate information from professionals. Information should be presented in terms that parents can understand, rather than in what is often meaningless jargon. Parents often feel ambivalent when receiving information from professionals. Most parents want the truth in order to deal with their problems effectively. But they may have considerable difficulty dealing with the truth if it is too painful.

Unfortunately, in many cases both parents and professionals may not have the communication skills necessary for positive interaction (Sawyer & Sawyer, 1981; Winton, 1988). Too many professionals talk down to parents. They sometimes believe that parents lack sufficient experience or background to understand the information presented. This can result in an interaction that is confusing and disappointing to all parties concerned (Hardman et al., 1990). Occasionally, professionals even withhold pertinent information. Barash and Maury (1985) asked 33 parents of children with Down syndrome how they were informed about their child's condition. They found that there was considerable variation from professional to professional in accuracy of information presented, when and how parents were told, and nature of future guidance. Professionals must remember that parents have the right to question information or decisions made by professionals that are inconsistent with family values (Henley & Spicknall, 1982).

Parents are often concerned about the child's future development. They want to know how and when the child will develop and what the prognosis is for the future. Gayton (1975) wrote that many professionals take a "Don't worry about it now" attitude and label the parents overanxious if they persist. He warned that if the professional does not give parents reliable information or direct them to responsible sources, they may search on their own. In this search, they may find outdated material containing many misconceptions about their child's condition. Parents must have accurate information as early as possible to alleviate their anxiety and give them the feeling that they are doing something to help.

Understanding the Causes of Mental Retardation

Core Concept	*Parents' search for a cause is generally in two directions: theological or medical.*

When a child is first diagnosed and the parents recognize and acknowledge the condition, they may immediately attempt to find the cause of the condition. Most often this search leads them in one of two directions—a theological explanation or a medical explanation.

Religious Counseling and Theological Explanation

In times of crisis, people frequently turn to religion for comfort, security, and sanction. Some seek assurance that they are not to blame; others seek some help in picking up the "broken pieces of their life." Wolfensberger and Kurtz (1969), however, found that in studies conducted during the 1960s even religious parents of children with retardation found little guidance and comfort from their spiritual leaders. It remains a problem in the 1990s, given the still widespread interpretation that mental retardation is primarily a medical problem. Clergy must have more current training and information if we are to overcome the misconceptions associated with the condition.

Mental retardation within a family unit may precipitate a theological crisis. The advent of a child who is retarded can either weaken or strengthen religious beliefs, and the particular faith of the parents may affect their response to the event. Religious orientation may be directly related to degree of acceptance.

Family acceptance of mental retardation may be a function of religious affiliation. Catholics consider redemption a continual process, so humanity continually experiences suffering for its sins. This is not to imply that the advent of a particular child results from the sins of the parents, but rather is an expiation for all humankind. Methodists believe that the child with a disability is a function of nature missing its mark. Mormons believe that individuals with mental retardation are part of the divine plan—their premortal existence was as whole spirits, and their presence on earth is merely temporal and for a short time in comparison to eternity. They contend that when such children leave their earthly existence, they again assume a more perfect existence. Rabbis tend to assign no particular theological explanation: the event occurred.

Explanations within specific denominations or religious groups may vary according to the theological interpretation of each religious leader. We wish to show here only that there are divergent theological views. Considering these divergent views, one can perhaps understand why parental reactions differ with religious affiliation. Those who have no theological explanation may find acceptance far more difficult than those who are convinced that the child is part of a divine plan. Some devout parents view the child with mental retardation as a religious responsibility. Some even look on themselves as martyrs, ready to accept the responsibility as a God-given cross to be borne patiently and submissively (Kravaceus & Hayes, 1969).

As stated earlier in this chapter, clergy have tended to view mental retardation as more a medical than a religious issue. Whether or not this position is correct makes little difference to the need for sound religious counseling for the family. Religious leaders need to have a better grasp of the problems involved in counseling parents of children with a disability. A greater amount of time could profitably be spent during divinity school training in the area of pastoral counseling as it relates to addressing these problems. It is also important for religious leaders to conceptualize clearly the theological implications in their own minds. There is a distinct need to formulate a plan for counseling parents in light of the theological implications. Through this plan the church may assist parents better to deal with feelings of anxiety and guilt. If religious institutions are to reflect the social conscience of society, they must undertake affirmative action to educate congregations about children with mental retardation and to provide effective programs for them.

Medical Explanations

For many parents, it is the physician who first delivers the news that the child is mentally retarded. In some cases, for example, Down syndrome or physical trauma, diagnosis is made at birth. In others, parents learn of the child's condition during the early childhood years or after formal schooling begins. Regardless of when the information is transmitted, medical counseling must be done with great skill to alleviate or minimize the parents' guilt feelings.

Physicians have been widely criticized for the way they inform parents. Wolraich (1982) indicated that "parents have been unhappy not only about how they are told, but also with what they were told about their child's condition" (p. 324). Generally, parents want a medical opinion on the nature of the child's condition, the prognosis for the child, and the possibility of having a second child who is mentally retarded. Any pregnancy involves some degree of risk. The odds, the risks, and the possible consequences should be clearly articulated by the professional. After the information is given, the decision whether or not to have another child is rightfully that of the parents.

To provide comprehensive medical counseling and services to persons with mental retardation and their families, several considerations must be addressed:

1. The physician in community practice (general practitioner, pediatrician, and so on) must receive more medical training in the medical, psychological, and educational aspects of exceptional populations.
2. Physicians must be more willing to treat disabled patients for common illnesses when the treatment is irrelevant to the patient's disability.
3. Physicians need not become specialists in specific disability areas but must have enough knowledge to refer the patient to an appropriate specialist when necessary.
4. Physicians must not expand their counseling role beyond medical matters but must be aware of and willing to refer the patient to other community resources. [Hardman et al, 1990].

Searching for a Cure

Core Concept	*When parents have accepted their child's condition, they usually seek out a cure.*

Once parents acknowledge that their child is mentally retarded, they may immediately invest their energy in finding a cure. Unfortunately, in the majority of cases prospects for a complete cure are remote. When retardation is a function of emotional problems or environmental deprivation, some remediation techniques may be prescribed (for example, psychotherapy and environmental enrichment). If treatment begins early enough, some positive results are possible.

In certain conditions, such as galactosemia or phenylketonuria, dietary controls can minimize the damage. Physical therapy and speech therapy can improve functional level. In many instances the prescribed treatments may improve both intellectual and functional levels. Seldom, however, is it possible to move these children out of the ranges of mental retardation into what we could classify as a normal range of intelligence.

Where financial resources permit, parents may take the child from one professional to another hoping to receive the diagnosis they want to hear. During this process it is necessary for professionals to help protect these parents from unscrupulous individuals who willingly provide programs of remediation at great expense, though often with few, if any, positive results. When parents seek sanctions for questionable treatment programs, the most prudent approach is to refer them to professionals who are well-known for the reliability of their judgments or to organizations like the American Association on Mental Retardation and the Association for Retarded Citizens.

Searching for Help

Core Concept	*Organizations such as the Association for Retarded Citizens and the Association for Persons with Severe Handicaps can provide valuable information and services to parents.*

Twenty-five years ago, a few parents of retarded people looked around and saw . . . nothing. They were suffering from the deep hurt that society has always handed out free to anybody who is "different." And they were different all right. They had the audacity to give birth to children who were not perfect. The citizenry was indifferent or the citizenry was offended and frightened. I imagine that many of these parents would have preferred to curl up and die rather than attempt to change a whole country. But that was the catch, they couldn't die either. If they died no one could be depended upon to care for these inconvenient retarded people. . . . So the Association for Retarded Citizens was born. (Isbell, 1979, p. 170)

Many parents are in a state of confusion and find that professionals are often unable to give advice or refer them to other resources beyond their own area of expertise. The physician is able to provide basic medical information; the school is a resource on educational matters. Each is limited, however, in its ability to provide information about other resources. One of the most comprehensive sources of information for families with a child who has retardation is the Association for Retarded Citizens (ARC). The membership of this organization comprises anyone interested in promoting the welfare of persons with mental retardation; the majority of the membership, however, consists of families with persons who are mentally retarded. The ARC serves two very useful functions for parents. First, it helps them become aware that they are far from being the only ones in the world with their seemingly unique problem. In the group they find other parents who have experienced the same type of frustration they are presently experiencing and who can share with them the various methods they have used to cope. These more experienced parents and the ARC professional staff can also give advice about various services available for the child.

If the community is so small that there is no local organization, parents can contact the office of the state Association for Retarded Citizens to obtain the necessary information and the location of the nearest local affiliate. Parents may write directly to the Association for Retarded Citizens (2501 Avenue J, Arlington, Texas 76011), from which a considerable amount of helpful literature is available.

Another helpful organization is the Association for Persons with Severe Handicaps (TASH) (7010 Roosevelt Way N.E., Seattle, Washington 98115; telephone (206) 523–8446). TASH members include people with disabilities, professionals, families, and others committed to enhancing the quality of life for people with severe and profound intellectual disabilities. TASH works on behalf of people with severe disabilities to create more opportunities for them to learn in integrated educational environments and actively participate in community life.

The community may have other resources to assist parents besides TASH and ARC. For example, some communities have organized **pilot parent programs** that assist parents who have recently given birth to a disabled child or learned of their child's disability. Pilot parents are a local group of parents helping other families with children who are disabled.

On the national scene there are several federally funded advocacy programs for persons with a disability. These include the Disability Rights Education and Defense Fund, which was established to advance the civil rights of individuals with a disability through guiding and monitoring national public policy. The Developmental Disabilities and Bill of Rights Act of 1975 (Public Law 94-103) established a protection and advocacy system in every state for persons with a developmental disability. State protection and advocacy systems are authorized to pursue legal and administrative remedies to protect the rights of persons with developmental disabilities who are receiving education and treatment in a given state. *Closer Look* (The National Information Center for the Handicapped) has provided special education and habilitation information to thousands of parents across the country. These services include practical guides to finding services; parents' information packets that include a description of community resources; civil rights information; and access to reports that update parents on events concerning people who are disabled. In 1986 *The Exceptional Parent,* a magazine for families, published a resource guide for parents (Directory of Community Resources, 1986). The directory included information about recreation, religious organizations, resources for the traveler with a disability, and architectural barriers.

Maintenance of Family Functioning

Core Concept	*Families with a child who is mentally retarded must be able to maintain typical functioning as nearly as possible.*

Many problems can hinder maintaining the family unit. First, parents may be so guilt-ridden for having a child who is retarded that they believe they must dedicate every moment of their lives to the child's welfare. These intense feelings of obligation may interfere with the parents' daily interactions with each other, with their children who are not disabled, and with their friends and relatives. Second, the additional financial burden of the child with retardation may reduce normal expenditures for recreation and other activities, as well as for basic necessities. Third, the problems of care may be so acute that the parents are either unwilling or unable to find someone to look after the child while they engage in even minimal recreational or social activities.

The problems just listed are not uncommon. Parents may need assistance to dissipate or at least minimize their guilt feelings. They must be helped to realize that the presence of a child with retardation need not destroy family relations. At times, however, parents are so intensely engrossed with care for the child that they become oblivious to the needs of other family members, including their own. The burdens of the child with a disability make social and recreational enjoyment much more difficult to attain.

When the financial burdens created by the birth of the retarded child become so great that they interfere with recreational and social activities, parents should be directed toward the many types of activities available at minimal or no cost. Various resources, including local social-services agencies or ARC, can make respite care available for the child. Respite care provides temporary relief for families with a child living at home. The family can either leave the child with trained personnel in a community living setting for short periods of time or have someone come to the home and care for the child. This allows the parents to leave the child for short periods of time knowing he or she is receiving good care. In a survey of 339 families, Upshur (1982) reported that the most common reason for day or evening care is the "need for relief time; the most common for overnight care is recreation or vacation" (p. 5). Parents may also be willing to share responsibilities with other parents who may be more in tune with the routine and needs of the child who is mentally retarded.

The ability of the family to maintain some degree of socialization may be partly a function of how well their extended family and neighbors accept the child. Studies conducted in the 1960s found that the wife's side of the family tended to be more accepting and supportive (Barsch, 1968; Farber, 1968). Successful integration within the extended family and with neighbors may well be a function of teaching these groups, as well as the immediate family, to accept the child. Although the advent of a retarded child creates many additional burdens and problems, life within the family unit must continue in a way that provides optimal opportunity to develop and maintain sound mental health for everyone.

Bennett (1986) advised parents about a balanced approach to rearing a child with disabilities.

- Get the best expert advice you can and use it.
- Develop realistic and specific goals for your child for both the present and the future.
- Don't continually "second guess" yourself or your mate.
- Spend a reasonable amount of time and effort working with your child.
- Reach out to other parents. [pp. 50–52]

Planning for the Future

Core Concept	*One of parents' greatest concerns is what the future will hold for the child when they are no longer able or available to provide care.*

A child with mental retardation usually lives at home and attends public school until about age 22. At this age the individual may not function socially and intellectually as an adult, but the schools' responsibility ends. If employment, residential, medical, and recreational services are available, some direct support may continue.

Parental concerns often focus on where and how the child's needs ultimately will be met. The thought of forcing a child who has spent many years in the community and family setting into an institution is extremely difficult for parents. Parents often want to make necessary arrangements for continued support and focus on other matters through carefully planned provisions like trusts for their grown child with retardation.

Parents who are interested in setting up a trust for their child can usually locate an attorney to help them.

THE NEEDS OF THE CHILD WITH MENTAL RETARDATION

Children with mental retardation are more like their nondisabled peers than they are different. They have all the same basic needs as their age-mates.

Core Concept	*Individuals with mental retardation need to feel accepted.*

Acceptance is a basic need of all human beings. Children with mental retardation are no different in this from anyone else. They need to be accepted as worthy individuals. Loss of self-esteem, feelings of inadequacy, and depression can make it difficult for parents to love a child. Physical stigmata or lack of normal responsiveness may also delay the parents' attachment. The effects on the child are insidious, and many children who are mentally retarded desperately seek someone with whom they can identify. With the integration of children with mental retardation into classes and schools with typical children, acceptance is even more crucial. By carefully educating a child's classmates and teachers about the child, fears of the unknown may be dispelled, leaving the way open for acceptance. The professional can and should be someone who exudes warmth and acceptance. By finding and capitalizing on the positive attributes of the child, the professional can assist the parents in realizing the child's worth and can guide them toward acceptance.

Core Concept	*Every child with mental retardation, no matter how severely disabled, has the ability to grow and develop.*

Parents and professionals are responsible for providing the fertile environment and the proper atmosphere for the child to grow and develop. Unless parents give these children a wide variety of experiences, their learning and adjustment may be greatly curtailed. Parents may be easily embarrassed and hypersensitive to what others may think of their child's public behavior. Unless children with mental retardation have the opportunity to visit malls, ride buses, and eat in restaurants, they will be deprived of important experiences that all children should have for maximum social development.

A second important variable that affects adjustment is a balance of control within the child's environment. The child who is dependent solely on family members may develop an attitude of helplessness and a loss of self-identity. It is often far easier for a parent to dress a child who is retarded, for example, than it is to teach the child to dress. Teaching may be a long and painful experience. When the child has learned to dress without help, however, another level of independence has been achieved, and self-esteem has probably improved. The other extreme is equally insidious. A child who completely controls and dominates the environment by overwhelming a too patronizing family with unreasonable demands also fails to make an acceptable environmental adjustment. As the child learns to interact, participate, and accept responsibilities successfully in the family, these experiences can be transferred into the educational setting, peer group relationships, and other social contacts.

THE NEEDS OF SIBLINGS

Core Concept	*The effect a child with mental retardation has on siblings is receiving increasing attention from professionals.*

As the sibling of a mentally retarded child, I felt cheated because my brother was not the same as other kids. I was waiting for the day he would wake up and be like me, a day that will never come. So many times he pleaded for the affection he desperately needed and so many times I turned my back and ignored his appeal. I did not understand. (Dubinsky, 1986, p. 54)

Literature in the field of mental retardation has focused a great deal of attention on the effect a child with mental retardation has on parents; the child's effect on siblings, however, has in the past been ignored or relegated to secondary importance. In more recent years, considerable attention has focused on this important subject. Researchers have become increasingly aware that the birth of a child with mental retardation has consequences for the development of other children in the family.

The literature has addressed itself to the following questions:

How does the child with mental retardation affect the development and adjustment of siblings who are not disabled?

What are the attitudes of these siblings toward the child with mental retardation?

What factors influence these attitudes?

What are the fears and concerns of the siblings? How can negative effects be avoided or minimized?

As a child grows older and abilities become more apparent, there is occasional readjustment of roles and expectations. Regardless of birth order, the child with mental retardation eventually becomes the youngest child socially. At times, siblings are under pressure to assume more responsibility and act older. In a study of children with mental retardation and their siblings, Farber (1968) found that the siblings' relationship with their mother was adversely affected by the retarded child's high degree of dependency. Younger nondisabled and retarded children tend to be treated on a more equal basis, but as they grow older the nondisabled siblings assume a superordinate position. Farber found that siblings who as young children had limited interaction with their retarded brother or sister were less affected than those who had interacted freely. Schild (1976) suggested that one of the potential problems faced by siblings is their parents' unrealistically high expectations for them. The parents try in this way to compensate for the deficiencies of the child with mental retardation.

Siblings want to know and understand the condition of their brother or sister who is disabled. They need to know how to act and react as family members. They need their questions answered. Open communication with siblings enhances the positive side of their relationship with their brother or sister. Lamb (1980) reviewed several books that may help children accept siblings with disabilities. These stories help children understand the joys and frustrations of being the sibling of a child with a disability. Sometimes parents relate to nondisabled children with good intentions, but use poor techniques. They do what they think is best, but it may not have a positive outcome or be in the best interest of the family unit. If parents can communicate what they are doing and why they are doing it, however, the unpleasantness of the situation may at least be understandable to the nondisabled children.

Siblings must also deal with peer reaction like teasing and ridicule. These problems usually come at an age when the sibling lacks the maturity and understanding of the situation to resolve them effectively. Parents may compound siblings' frustration and confusion by refusing to discuss the problems of mental retardation (Grossman, 1972). Many parents are so overwhelmed by the burden of dealing with their own problems and identity with respect to their child with mental retardation that they are ill-equipped to recognize the needs of their other children. Often they are unable to recognize or help them with the many stresses and traumata created by the presence of a child with mental retardation.

| Core Concept | *Siblings who are not disabled often become neglected members of the family.* |

Siblings of children with mental retardation are neglected for a number of reasons. First, parents are often taken up with the responsibilities of caring for the child with mental retardation. Parents neglect their nondisabled children at times because their guilt forces them to devote all their time to the child who is disabled. Parents may neglect their nondisabled children because they are attempting to escape from the entire family, which has become a threat to their self-esteem. They may even neglect a nondisabled child because they have come to believe that they are unfit as parents. Some children suffer because their parents are incompetent as parents and would not have given them adequate attention in any case. These children are often in desperate need of attention. If they are unable to get the attention they need at home, they try to attract it in socially unacceptable ways at home, at school, and in the community.

Resentment is a common reaction on the part of siblings. Although the reaction is typical, many parents and children who hold these feelings of resentment do not realize that such feelings are to be expected. It is important that parents and siblings be assisted in dealing with these feelings in an emotionally constructive manner.

Hunter, Schucman, and Friedlander (1972) wrote that a nondisabled child may develop feelings of anger toward the sibling with retardation. Nondisabled children may become angry because of the lack of personal attention to them and the apparent favoritism shown toward the child with the disability. Resentment may develop because the disability prevents the family from going on certain types of outings; because treatment, therapy, special schooling, and so on, place financial constraints on the family; and because the nondisabled child may have to assume unpleasant responsibilities like baby-sitting. The child may even wish for the other child's death, or at least that the sibling with retardation would just go away (Gordon, 1975; Grossman, 1972).

The sibling may have guilt feelings, sometimes because of negative feelings toward the child with mental retardation. Guilt feelings may even be present because the sibling was fortunate enough to be normal and the other child disabled.

Nondisabled children may also feel fear. When they are younger, siblings may be fearful that they too may become retarded. As they get older, they may be afraid that they too may have children with disabilities. And they may be fearful that some day, when the parents are no longer able to provide care, they will have to assume responsibility for their sibling (Grossman, 1972).

Siblings are often ashamed and embarrassed. They may be embarrassed to be seen in public with their sibling, embarrassed to tell their friends, embarrassed to bring their friends home or to have a date pick them up at their home. It is understandable that a teenager may be reluctant to be picked up at the house by a friend if the sibling with retardation is ill-mannered and exhibits unpredictable behavior.

Wentworth (1974) wrote that embarrassment is perhaps the second most prevalent emotional reaction that siblings experience. She went on to say that the degree of embarrassment may be a function of the age both of the child who is disabled and of the nondisabled peer. A younger child with a disability seems like a helpless person who needs to be mothered. It may be easier for nondisabled children and their peers to accept the child at this age. As children become older, less attractive, and more difficult to control, they can be a much greater source of embarrassment. Older children, particularly in their adolescent years, become more cognizant of and easily influenced by peer approval. Since teenagers are often cruel in their remarks, siblings can become increasingly embarrassed as tactless remarks are made about a brother or sister with a disability.

In summary, siblings' needs are often overlooked. Careful guidance by parents and professional workers can lead to a healthy adjustment to the problems created by the presence of a child with mental retardation.

NEW ISSUES AND FUTURE DIRECTIONS

Core Concept	*The parent/professional partnership needs to be reinforced and expanded as we move into the 1990s.*

The field of mental retardation continues to experience dynamic change as we move closer to the new century. Educational, medical, and social services are expanding with

Parents can be important partners in intervention programs such as infant stimulation.

new and innovative approaches. Such developments as integrated education, fetal surgery, and supported employment are bringing about significant positive outcomes in the lives of people with mental retardation and their families. One issue, however, has remained unchanged over the years: the necessity to reinforce and expand the parent/ professional partnership in meeting the individual needs of people with mental retardation. No one issue has received more lip service without achieving results indicating that such a partnership is truly valued among both professionals and parents. In the field of education, for example, active participation by parents in educational decision making continues to be infrequent in spite of the mandate for parental involvement in Public Law 94-142. A recent survey (*Serving Handicapped Children,* 1988) found that less than half of the parents of students with disabilities attend their child's IEP meeting each year. Harris and Associates (1989) reported that 27% of the parents they surveyed do not contribute to the development of objectives on the IEP. Twain (1987) found that IEP goals nominated by parents were consistently ranked lower than teacher-nominated goals. An earlier study (Goldstein, Strickland, Turnbull, & Curry, 1980), found that parent input in the IEP process is not as highly valued as the law intended. These researchers observed that during IEP meetings teachers talked almost twice as much as parents. What is worse is that in 36% of the conferences observed, parents spoke less than twice during the whole process.

It is surprising, given what we know about the importance of this partnership, that the relationship between parents and professionals continues to be strained at best. As we move through the 1990s, it is clearly time to reevaluate the nature of the parent/professional partnership and move beyond rhetoric. Specific activities need to be explored that will maximize positive relationships. Three specific areas where positive parent/ professional relationships are critical are (1) developing individualized education and adult service programs; (2) keeping parents informed about educational and community services; and (3) supporting organized parent advocacy (McDonnell, Wilcox, & Hardman, 1991). Organized parent advocacy moves beyond advancing personal interests to supporting change for a larger constituency of individuals, such as all people with mental retardation. The history of mental retardation is replete with examples of parent advocacy. Nearly all significant changes in services to people with retardation have occurred as a result of it. As such, it is imperative for professionals to continue to support and participate in this effort. As suggested by McDonnell et al. (1991), parent advocacy now and in the future is absolutely necessary if we are to bring about services focusing on individual need and implement rapid systems change.

CORE QUESTIONS

1. Discuss the stages in parents' adjustment to a child with mental retardation.
2. Discuss the common parental reactions to a child with mental retardation that we have addressed in this chapter.
3. In searching for a cause, parents often seek either theological or medical explanations. Compare and contrast these two concepts.

4. What are some organizations that may benefit parents of children with mental retardation?
5. What are three problems that may hinder family functioning?
6. What are some basic needs of children with mental retardation?
7. What are some basic needs of siblings?
8. In what three areas is parent/professional collaboration essential?

ROUND TABLE DISCUSSION

In this chapter, you have learned about stages that parents progress through in dealing with a retarded child. These stages include awareness of the problem, recognition of the problem, searching for a cause, searching for a cure, and acceptance of the child. Review the discussion of these stages from pages 366–374 of the text.

In your study group, organize a role-playing activity. Beginning with awareness and moving through acceptance, assign individuals to role-play the reactions and feelings of parents at each stage as they face the challenges of raising a child who is retarded.

REFERENCES

Barash, A., & Maury, E. (1985). Giving the news about a child's disability. *Exceptional Parent, 15*(4), 32.

Barsch, R. H. (1968). *The parent of the handicapped child.* Springfield, IL: Charles C. Thomas.

Bennett, C. (1986). Parenting a special child: How difficult is it? *Exceptional Parent, 16*(4), 50–52.

Blacher, J. (1984). Sequential stages of parental adjustment to the birth of a child with handicaps: Fact or artifact? *Mental Retardation, 22*(2), 55–68.

Cleveland, M. (1980). Family adaptation to traumatic spinal cord injury: Response to crisis. *Family Therapy, 29*(4), 558–565.

Directory of community resources. (1986). *Exceptional Parent, 16*(1), 33.

Dubinsky, P. (1986). My special brother. *Exceptional Parent, 16*(3), 54.

Farber, N. W. (1968). *The retarded child.* New York: Crown.

Featherstone, H. (1980). *A difference in the family: Living with a disabled child.* New York: Penguin.

Gayton, W. F. (1975). Management problems for mentally retarded children and their families. *Pediatric Clinics of North America, 22*(3), 561–570.

Goldstein, S., Strickland, B., Turnbull, A., & Curry, L. (1980). An observational analysis of the IEP conference. *Exceptional Children, 46*, 278–286.

Gordon, S. (1975). *Living fully.* New York: John Day.

Grossman, F. K. (1972). *Brothers and sisters of retarded children.* Syracuse, NY: Syracuse University.

Hardman, M. L., & Drew, C. J. (1980). Parent consent and the practice of withholding treatment from the severely defective newborn. *Mental Retardation, 18*(4), 165–169.

Hardman, M. L., Drew, C. J., Egan, M. W., & Wolf, B. (1990). *Human exceptionality: Society, school, and family* (3rd ed). Newton, MA: Allyn & Bacon.

Harris, L., and Associates. (1989). *The ICD survey III: A report card on special education.* New York: Author.

Hart, N. W. (1970). Frequently expressed feelings and reactions of parents toward their retarded children. In N. R. Bernstein (Ed.), *Diminished people.* Boston: Little, Brown.

Henley, C., & Spicknall, H. (1982). Solving school-related problems. *The Exceptional Parent, 12*(4), 21–26.

Hunter, M. H., Schucman, H., & Friedlander, G. (1972). *The retarded child from birth to five: A multidisciplinary program for the child and family.* New York: John Day.

Isbell, L. (1979). Yes! In T. Dougan, L. Isbell, & P. Vyas (Eds.), *We have been there.* Salt Lake City: Dougan, Isbell, & Vyas Associates.

Kravaceus, W. C., & Hayes, E. N. (1969). *If your child is handicapped.* Boston: Porter Sargent.

Lamb, C. B. (1980). Fostering acceptance of a disabled sibling through books. *Exceptional Parent, 10*(1), 12–13.

Lamb, M. E. (1983). Fathers of exceptional children. In M. Seligman (Ed.), *The family with a handicapped child: Understanding and treatment.* New York: Grune and Stratton.

McDonnell, J., Wilcox, B., & Hardman, M. L. (1991). *Secondary programs for students with developmental disabilities.* Boston: Allyn & Bacon.

Patton, J. R., Beirne-Smith, M., & Payne, J. S. (1990). *Mental retardation* (3rd ed.). Columbus: Charles E. Merrill.

Peterson, N. L. (1987). *Early intervention for handicapped and at-risk children: An introduction to early-childhood special education.* Denver: Love Publishing.

Rosen, L. (1955). Selected aspects in the development of the mother's understanding of her mentally retarded child. *American Journal of Mental Deficiency, 59,* 522.

Sawyer, H. W., & Sawyer, S. H. (1981). A teacher-parent communication training approach. *Exceptional Children, 47*(4), 305–306.

Schild, S. (1976). The family of the retarded child. In R. Koch & J. C. Dobson (Eds.), *The mentally retarded child and his family* (rev. ed.). New York: Brunner/Mazel.

Serving handicapped children: A special report. (1988). Princeton, NJ: Robert Wood Johnson Foundation.

Turnbull, A. P., & Turnbull, H. R. (1985). *Parents speak out.* Columbus: Charles E. Merrill.

Twain, K. (1987). *Parental participation in IEP conferences.* Unpublished master's thesis, University of Oregon, Eugene, OR.

Upshur, C. C. (1982). Respite care for mentally retarded and other disabled populations: Program models and family needs. *Mental Retardation, 20*(1), 2–6.

Volpe, J. J., & Koenigsberger, R. (1981). Neurologic disorders. In G. B. Avery (Ed.), *Neonatology, pathophysiology, and management of the newborn* (2nd ed.). Philadelphia: J.B. Lippincott.

Wentworth, E. H. (1974). *Listen to your heart: A message to parents of handicapped children.* Boston: Houghton Mifflin.

Wikler, L., Wasow, M., & Hatfield, E. (1981). Chronic sorrow revised: Parent vs. professional depiction of the adjustment of parents of mentally retarded children. *American Journal of Orthopsychiatry, 51*(1), 63–70.

Winton, P. J. (1988). Effective communication between parents and professionals. In D. B. Bailey & R. J. Simeonsson (Eds.), *Family assessment in early intervention* (pp. 207–228). Columbus: Charles E. Merrill.

Wolfensberger, W., & Kurtz, R. A. (1969). Religious and pastoral counseling. In W. Wolfensberger & R. A. Kurtz (Eds.), *Management of the family of the mentally retarded.* Chicago: Follett.

Wolraich, M. L. (1982). Communication between physicians and parents of handicapped children. *Exceptional Children, 48*(4), 324–329.

CHAPTER FOURTEEN
Social and Ethical Issues

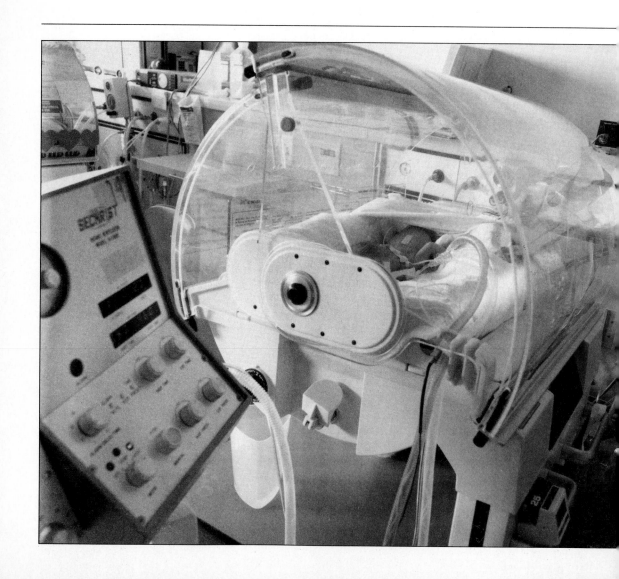

- The complex social and ethical issues relating to mental retardation are often reduced to questions of individual versus societal rights.
- During the prenatal period ethical questions usually focus on prevention, by minimizing the probability that individuals with mental retardation will be born.
- During the early years of life ethical issues pertaining to mental retardation are particularly troubling to many because they often deal with the life or death of a child with mental retardation.
- Social and ethical issues during the school years often relate both to society's responsibility and to the level of effort required to meet the educational and other treatment needs of the child with mental retardation.
- The social and ethical issues of the adult years once again pit the interests of society against the individual's rights. They often relate to adult functions like marriage and reproduction.
- Research and professional ethics in mental retardation involve a wide variety of issues where individual rights must be balanced against the need for scientific information and the complexities of appropriate treatment.

It has become increasingly obvious as we have proceeded through this volume that mental retardation is an extremely complex phenomenon. There are few, if any, simple answers; philosophies vary, and viewpoints and value systems often conflict. It seems only appropriate that one of the concluding chapters in this book should examine what is perhaps the most turbulent of all areas: social and ethical issues related to mental retardation.

Social issues and considerations are central to the problem of mental retardation and have been throughout history. As noted in earlier chapters, attitudes toward and treatment of retarded individuals have always reflected the prevailing philosophies of human existence and human worth. These philosophies are the source of ethics, the rules that guide or govern conduct and define what is good or bad.

Many of the issues discussed in this chapter have recurred in the philosophies and prevailing actions of societies throughout history. During certain periods some practices were unquestioned because they were accepted as being in harmony with the best interests of the human species and civilized society. Contemporary civilization has, however, publicly deplored such practices as euthanasia, or mercy killing, and has described their perpetrators as inhumane and barbaric. At the same time that this public representation has been put forth, many loudly denounced actions have quietly continued. Only in the last 15 to 20 years have public statements and examinations of these practices been forthcoming, breaking what Duff and Campbell termed a "public and professional silence on a major social taboo" (1973, p. 894). Although these authors were specifically discussing the withholding of care from defective infants, others have described a variety of treatment conditions and practices (Horan & Mall, 1977). As public awareness has increased, many people have been shocked not only by the actions and conditions that exist, but also by the realization that we are in many ways a hypocritical society (Lusthaus, 1985). It is now our task to progress from shock to serious examination of our fundamental values concerning what is right and important in this society and to determine the most effective means to achieve the desired outcomes. We must balance these considerations with our ability and willingness to pay. This chapter is one attempt at such examination.

BACKGROUND

Core Concept	*The complex social and ethical issues relating to mental retardation are often reduced to questions of individual versus societal rights.*

Any discussion of social and ethical issues requires some exploration of the philosophical foundations of society. Our daily activities seldom include any conscious consideration of philosophy, and in many quarters it has become fashionable to express indifference or even unfavorable attitudes about its place in contemporary civilization. Regardless of how we define philosophy, each of us operates on the basis of some set of guiding principles, whether explicit or implicit, that form a general code of ethics governing our behavior. And any reasonably consistent ethical code derives from a philosophy of life.

Two philosophic positions are important in an examination of social and ethical issues related to mental retardation. These philosophies—utilitarianism and formalism—represent polarized viewpoints of the rights and worth of individuals in society. Utilitarianism holds that an individual's rights are limited to those granted by the larger society. Formalism rests on the notion that it is the individual who has basic rights and that those rights cannot be abrogated or curtailed by society—the individual's rights supersede society's. Neither philosophy is workable in its pure form in a complex society. Adherence to strict utilitarianism leads to a tendency for the group with the greatest power to continue in power, and often expand that power by substantially limiting the rights of those with less power. Pure formalism is also problematic. As the rights of some are maintained, the rights of others diminish. Where on the continuum between these two extremes can we operate comfortably? This is an enormously difficult question, but one that we must seriously address if we are to ensure individual rights without unduly taxing society in general (Boggs, 1986).

One of the topics we discuss in this chapter, euthanasia, is defined in Webster's New Collegiate Dictionary as "the act or practice of killing or permitting the death of hopelessly sick or injured individuals . . . for reasons of mercy." This topic, although not unknown to most people, was brought dramatically into the public eye by the case of Karen Ann Quinlan, a 22-year-old New Jersey woman whose life was being maintained by means of an artificial support system. For nearly a full year from the time of her admission to the hospital in April 1975, she remained comatose, her life apparently wholly sustained by a respirator and tubal feeding. At the time of the New Jersey Supreme Court decision in March 1976, it was the opinion of all individuals involved that there were no medical procedures available to facilitate her recovery and that termination of artificial support would result in almost immediate death. This case entered the courts because of a disagreement between Karen's family and the attending medical personnel. After much agony and soul-searching, her parents had requested that the life-support system be terminated. Her physicians refused to take this action. To make a complex case even more difficult, after cessation of life support, Karen Quinlan continued to survive in a comatose state. She died in June 1985, more than 10 years after she was initially admitted to the hospital. Although that closed her story in one sense, the repercussions and issues raised by this case will continue for a very long time.

How often treatment is withheld and patients are allowed to die is not well documented on a general basis, although some investigations have been conducted with specific populations (Duff & Campbell, 1973). The regular occurrence of decisions "not to resuscitate," however, is commonly known among hospital personnel. The practice is sufficiently common that most hospitals use some type of "Code 90" sticker to indicate that the patient is to receive no intensive care or resuscitation (Fletcher, 1973).

The general topic of euthanasia warrants a great deal of attention. More directly related to our present area of inquiry, however, is the practice of euthanasia with mentally retarded individuals. Attention to this issue (at least in terms of published material) has focused most heavily on euthanasia with newborns who are or appear to be retarded at birth. This type of action usually involves a request on the part of the parents to withhold some routine surgical or medical treatment needed for the infant to survive. If the physician agrees, the newborn usually dies.

The practice of life management is far more widespread than most of us realize, but it is not typically open for public discussion. More than a decade ago, Robertson characterized it as "common practice for parents to request, and for physicians to agree, not to treat" infants who are defective at birth (1975, p. 214). Duff and Campbell (1973) investigated the background of 299 consecutive deaths that were recorded in a special-care nursery and found that 43 of them involved withholding of treatment. This figure represents over 14% of the sample studied. Other cases have come to light since Duff and Campbell published their findings. Robertson characterized the withholding of treatment from handicapped infants as a procedure that "is rapidly gaining status as 'good medical practice' " (1975, p. 214). It is also an issue that was seldom discussed openly in the past (Duff & Campbell, 1973; Hardman & Drew, 1980). Euthanasia and withholding of treatment are topics that are now more openly debated, although they remain highly controversial (Heifetz, 1989; Hollander, 1989).

One's initial reaction to the topic of euthanasia may be straightforward—that it is a barbaric practice and should not be permitted. Unfortunately, it is not quite that simple. The issue is rife with complexities from many different perspectives, as we discuss more fully later in this chapter.

One factor that influences social and ethical problems was mentioned obliquely in our references to formalist philosophy. Pure formalism inevitably curtails the rights of some individuals or segments of society as it emphasizes the rights of others. This dilemma has been termed the "competing equities" issue, and it presents some perplexing problems for contemporary society, particularly in the area of handicapped citizens' rights. For example, the competing equities issue enters into the euthanasia controversy. Some contend vigorously that it makes little sense to expend the extraordinary resources necessary to maintain life support for a terminally ill patient when resources are so badly needed by others. Another part of this same contention involves the sentiment that valuable resources like expensive equipment and medical talent should be deployed to generate the greatest benefit to society. People with this viewpoint, which sounds a lot like utilitarianism, would make big cuts in the resources available for citizens who are terminally ill, aged, or mentally retarded.

The competing equities issue also comes into play with philosophical viewpoints that are not so clearly utilitarian. For example, formalism is very much in evidence as some call for maximal effort to maintain life support for infants who are severely handicapped at birth. This position is often based on the infants' right to life, which from the formalist viewpoint cannot be abridged in any fashion by anyone. Competing equities are evident as one considers the potential conflict between the rights of the infant and the rights of the parents. Some have argued that the psychological, social, and economic burdens imposed by the care of a child with mental retardation are so extreme that parents should have the right to choose another alternative, particularly when extraordinary life-support measures are involved. Thus the rights of parents and the rights of handicapped infants present potentially conflicting situations without easy answers (Hardman & Drew, 1980).

It is evident from this brief overview that we intend to address a wide variety of social and ethical issues in this chapter. The issues present complexities and controversies that defy simple solution. It is not the purpose of this chapter to present answers or to assume that one position is better than another. In most cases the proponents on both sides are not only earnest in their viewpoints but also are well-armed with legitimate arguments to support their opinions.

THE LIFE CYCLE: ISSUES AND ETHICS

Although many ethical issues are not limited to a given age group, there are patterns that relate to different stages of the life cycle. The rest of this chapter is therefore organized in the same life-cycle format as the book. Discussions focus on prenatal ethics and issues and those particularly relevant to early childhood, the school years, and adulthood. Certain issues, such as competing equities, transcend life-cycle stages and are examined as appropriate throughout the chapter.

Prenatal Issues and Ethics

Core Concept	*During the prenatal period ethical questions usually focus on prevention, by minimizing the probability that individuals with mental retardation will be born.*

The prenatal period presents some uniquely difficult ethical questions. Since we are referring to the time before a child is born, we are addressing the task of prevention of mental retardation. The concept of preventing retardation historically has had very favorable connotations and continues to sound like an extremely laudable goal. Some have questioned the philosophical basis for this position (Hauerwas, 1986) and some of the means to this end have been controversial, to say the least. They strike at the very core of morality and therefore become prominent as social and ethical issues.

Genetic Screening and Counseling

Previous chapters have taken note of disorders associated with inherited conditions or predispositions. Some of these are conditions in which the probability of occurrence increases because of family origin (such as Tay-Sachs disease). Others become more probable because of the age or condition of the parent(s) (such as Down syndrome). Many professionals believe that genetic screening and counseling should be routine when such high-risk situations exist (Narayanan, Madhu Rao, Subbakrishna, & Sridhara Rama Rao, 1987; Nielsen, 1987). Although this is logical from the perspective of preventing mental retardation, various segments of the population object to this proposal. Some view genetic screening and counseling as interference in individual rights and freedom to mate and reproduce by choice. These objections strike par-particularly sensitive chords when they relate to conditions (for example, sickle cell anemia and Tay-Sachs disease) associated with ethnic or family origins. It is understandable how such procedures could be viewed as discriminatory and aimed at reducing the reproduction of certain ethnic groups. Such an interpretation, however, goes far beyond the purpose typically defined and associated with genetic screening and counseling.

Genetic screening involves research that examines a population in search of certain genetic makeups that relate to disease or may cause some disease or defect in offspring. Since our present discussion focuses on the prenatal period, our immediate concern relates to the genetic causes of disease or defect.

After genetic screening comes genetic counseling for the parents or potential parents. Genetic counseling includes providing information about the condition, the frequency with which it occurs (if possible, translated into the probability of occurrence in the situation at hand), and what behavioral and physical characteristics might be expected if it does occur. All of these areas should be dealt with, including various reproductive options. The genetic counselor must also be prepared to answer all questions openly and completely for the parents to become informed about the problem they face (Harper, 1981).

The fundamental purpose of screening and counseling is to ensure that parents or potential parents are thoroughly informed about the genetic disorder under consideration. It is not the counselor's task to make a decision for them. If the information provision and discussion approach is adhered to, the argument of discrimination and interference with individual rights is largely disarmed. It would seem that parents are even better prepared to exercise their rights if they are fully aware of the potential outcomes and options. As with most emotionally charged issues, however, this point of view does not prevent some from continuing to put forth arguments against genetic screening and counseling.

Genetic counseling is an important resource for some couples as they consider starting a family.

Prenatal Assessment

The prenatal development period presents other difficult ethical questions in addition to those already discussed. An immediate problem is assessment and resulting actions. From the discussion in Chapter 6 you know that many techniques currently available permit prenatal assessment of fetal status. Among them are amniocentesis, chorion biopsy, fetoscopy, and ultrasonography (e.g., Cadkin, Ginsberg, Pergament, & Verlinski, 1984). In this area, as in genetic screening, significant strides in technological developments in prenatal fetal assessment can also present certain dilemmas (Perone, Carpenter, & Robertson, 1984; Zaner, 1986).

In Chapter 6 we took the position that evaluation should not be conducted unless it has a purpose. This runs counter to the practice of evaluating because it is the popular thing to do. Earlier we were referring to assessment that must result in some action related to service delivery (such as educational programming). If we are to remain consistent, we must take the same position here about prenatal assessment. As you will see, however, intervention in this context is controversial.

Abortion

What types of action might result from prenatal assessment? If assessment indicates either that the fetus is or is likely to be defective, one alternative that might be considered is abortion.

Perhaps no single topic that has received public attention is as controversial as abortion. Some factions contend vigorously that abortion is murder. This notion is based on the view that human life exists, with all its pertinent rights and qualities, from the time of conception or shortly thereafter. On the other side of the issue is a substantial segment of the population that maintains, with equal vigor, that abortion should be an option for any woman under any circumstances. This viewpoint is based on the proposition that a woman has the right to be in control of her body and that being forced to continue an unwanted pregnancy violates that right.

As one approaches the abortion issue in relation to mental retardation, the perspectives alter. Some people hold fast to their blanket opposition to abortion, but their numbers are fewer when a handicapped fetus is at issue. Some who do not favor abortion in general by virtue of religious or personal philosophy are ready to accept it in the context of handicapping conditions. In many cases this shift in perspective is not limited to mental handicaps but applies to any handicapping condition.

Such shifts are not limited to the issue of abortion. In this chapter on social and ethical issues, we give evidence of similar phenomena in relation to other topics. Society does not, for the most part, reconcile apparent inconsistencies in philosophic position. In some ways this may be viewed as an indictment of society in general and of those who represent the inconsistent philosophies specifically. Such an indictment, however, serves little purpose. It is more important to realize that belief systems offer some latitude for interpretation in practice.

Many people hold certain beliefs about abortion in the context of mental retardation. These beliefs may be quite different from an individual's general posture relative to abortion. Abortion is one action that may be taken if prenatal assessment indicates that the developing fetus is defective. In all cases the parents' belief system should prevail in the decision of whether to abort. This may present some conflict with attending medical personnel whose personal value system is opposed to abortion. When such a situation occurs, the physician should inform parents of their right to seek the services of other medical personnel if they so desire.

The decision to abort a defective fetus obviously conflicts with the position that abortion should not be permitted under any circumstances. This opinion often arises from the belief that the fetus has a right to life that cannot be abridged by anyone for any reason. Those who are more inclined to abort a defective fetus often argue that the quality of life for the handicapped individual is likely to be so diminished that no one would choose to live under such circumstances. This, of course, puts them in the position of deciding what the fetus would or would not choose (a point the opposing faction is quick to emphasize). A further point of contention involves the effect of a handicapped child on the parents and siblings. In many cases the immediate and continuing financial, psychological, and social burdens are extreme and detrimental to the family. Those who favor abortion contend that parents should at least have the option to decide. The opposing view counters with the right of the unborn fetus to life regardless of the consequences for others.

This conflict is irreconcilable because the disagreement is so fundamental. We are faced with competing equities that probably cannot be resolved to the satisfaction of both sides. More important, the conflict presents a very difficult dilemma for parents.

Ethical Issues During the Early Years

Core Concept	*During the early years of life ethical issues pertaining to mental retardation are particularly troubling to many because they often deal with the life or death of a child with mental retardation.*

The ethical issues related to mental retardation during the early childhood years are as complex as the prenatal ones. Some of these were noted briefly in the introductory section to this chapter. In all cases the issues involve agonizing problems that have no easy or simple solutions. Here we are considering the period from birth to five years of age as the early years.

Each developmental period is critical to a child's overall growth process. The first two months after birth, the neonatal period, is our first focus for discussion. Chapter 6 indicated that many authorities view the first half of the neonatal period as the most dangerous in the total life span. Many of the developmental processes that were under way before birth remain incomplete and are continuing at an extremely rapid rate. The infant is now without the protective environment provided by the mother's womb. Until a more complete arsenal of defenses develops, the baby is highly vulnerable to hazardous influences.

Life Management Issues
The first few hours after birth and the first month of extrauterine life also represent a prime setting for one of the most controversial ethical issues relating to the life of a handicapped infant. During this period the chances are greatest for withholding treatment from infants who are diagnosed as defective. This practice is often termed euthanasia, although there are some important distinctions between euthanasia and the decision "not to prolong life."

Ethical Issues
It is not surprising that there are some important parallels between the ethical reasoning applied to abortion and that pertaining to decisions about postnatal survival of an infant. To be philosophically consistent, one must use the same arguments and posture for abortion and euthanasia. Sometimes, although not always, this is the case.

The diametrically opposed viewpoints described previously for abortion continue for issues of postnatal survival. Ramsey (1973), for example, held that abortion should not be an option even when prenatal assessment indicates that the fetus is severely defective or diseased. In his view, any argument used to justify abortion could be used to support infanticide. Ramsey's argument was not based on the position that we would commit a given act. He was essentially saying that there is no distinct moral difference between infanticide and abortion; if we would not practice the former, then we should not practice the latter. Similar consistency is evident on the opposite side of the issue, perhaps best expressed by Joseph Fletcher (1973). He not only maintained that it is appropriate but suggested a moral obligation to abort a defective fetus. Fletcher said that the same reasoning holds for the practice of euthanasia with defective infants.

As would be expected, many philosophical positions fall between these two points of view. John Fletcher (1975), for example, supported an approach that emphasizes parental participation in life-and-death decisions both in the prenatal and postnatal situations. He accepted abortion of a seriously defective fetus, but not euthanasia of defective newborns. It was his belief that there are important moral differences between abortion and euthanasia.

Fletcher discussed three differences. His first point was that a newborn infant has a separate physical existence from the mother, which was not the case on a prenatal basis. Because of this, the infant has become a patient with independent rights to care and support. The essence of Fletcher's point was that the newborn has an independent status, and can and should be considered separately from the mother. The fetus does not have independent status, so (he maintains) the status of the fetus should not be considered separately. Fletcher's second point related closely to his first. Since the newborn is separate physically from the mother, he or she is now much more accessible. Fletcher argued that this places a greater obligation on the physician to heal and relieve suffering. Fletcher's third point rounded out what he saw as the morally relevant differences between abortion and euthanasia. In this context, he noted a major difference in parental acceptance and loyalty to the unborn fetus when compared with the newborn. It was his contention that parental loyalty is much stronger to the newborn than to the fetus.

Fletcher's position accepted abortion but viewed euthanasia with disfavor. He noted two further points against euthanasia that are frequently discussed and debated. The first is the obvious danger of euthanasia when practiced by unprincipled individuals. The second involved the danger of changing society's attitude toward infants from one of great caring to one of accepted selective euthanasia.

We should mention that, throughout the discussion of John Fletcher's point of view, the term *euthanasia* has been used. This is because he was very careful to use that term when examining the rationale for his position. For Fletcher and many others interested in this area, the term *euthanasia* has very specific connotations.

In many situations with seriously defective infants, the decision is more whether to prolong life than whether to perform actual euthanasia. These two concepts have different meanings that may be very important from legal and moral standpoints. Euthanasia suggests mercy killing, or the beneficent termination of a life that might otherwise continue. According to George Fletcher (1968), failure to prolong life, however, means not "artificially lengthening a life that would otherwise end" (p. 119). These differences, though subtle, clearly become part of the controversy.

Legal Issues

From a legal standpoint the distinction between euthanasia and the decision not to prolong life is the difference between acts and omissions. Euthanasia, as just described, involves the act of terminating a life that would continue if the act were not committed. Not to prolong life, on the other hand, involves omission: the physician, by failing to act, permits death to occur. Fletcher (1968) noted that the act of terminating life is first-degree murder in the eyes of the law, regardless of motive. The legal view of omitting action depends on the relationship of the physician to the other person. If the individual is a patient who has a reasonable expectation that the physician will provide treatment, failure to do so is legally no different from acting to terminate a life. If the individual is not a patient, the physician is not legally bound to intercede in the same fashion. Fletcher also pointed out that "there is a significant gap between the law in theory and the law in practice" (1968, p. 120). He cited only one case in which a physician was brought to trial for an act of euthanasia. The physician was acquitted even though he admitted performing the act and his nurse testified to it. With regard to acts of omission the gap between theory and practice seems even greater. Fletcher noted that no cases can be found in which a physician has been found either criminally or civilly liable for deciding not to prolong life.

The absence of case law pertaining to acts of omission seems particularly significant when viewed in the context of a defective newborn. Since there is usually an attending physician during and after birth, establishment of the infant's patient status is automatic. As mentioned previously, if the physician omits life-saving action for a patient who has a reasonable expectation of treatment, the law views this no differently from an act to terminate life. In practice, however, society has chosen to look the other way when decisions not to prolong life are made. This is particularly true in the case of a defective newborn. Even John Fletcher modified his position on postnatal practice under such circumstances. He stated that "allowing the infant to die by withholding support while relieving pain is a decision, in my view, that can be ethically justified for reasons of mercy to the infant and relief of meaningless suffering of the parents and medical team" (1975, p. 77). He was careful to qualify this position, however, by using such terms as "cases of terribly damaged newborns for whom death is the desirable outcome when therapy either is not available or will only prolong the ordeal" (p. 77). Thus he remained more reluctant than some to permit postnatal management of life even for handicapped infants. This is not the case with many physicians and ethicists dealing with this issue.

The preceding discussion clearly illustrates a discrepancy between legal theory and case law having to do with postnatal life management. Should the theory be changed? If society has tacitly decided that selective euthanasia and decisions not to prolong life are acceptable, then one might wonder why formal statements (law) do not support the decision. As might be expected, this issue has been raised.

The study by Duff and Campbell (1973) was of particular importance because it provided at least a limited public data base showing how often treatment is withheld from handicapped infants. After examining their data and the ethical ramifications, Duff and Campbell turned to the legal issues in their final statements. They took a strong position: if withholding treatment from severely handicapped infants is a "violation of the law, we believe the law should be changed" (1973, p. 894). There has been considerable debate about the legislation of voluntary euthanasia. The idea of changing the law has received attention from both sides. The logic in favor of changing the law is perhaps deceptively simple when it is presented, as we have done, in relation to acceptable behavior. There are, however, some persuasive arguments against such change.

One of the arguments against changing the laws is the extreme difficulty of developing legal standards that can be effectively put into practice. One might expect that legislation removing criminal liability for decisions to withhold treatment would be very narrow in its definitions. Those that are most reluctant to speak to these issues use terms such as "terribly diseased," "tragically deformed," and "hideously damaged." But even if legislation with very strict and narrow criteria were developed, application of legal standards by society and the development of case law has a way of continuously expanding jurisdiction. There is great difficulty in distinguishing between the clear cases and those that are less clear. For example, Robertson (1975) suggested that treatment might be withheld from "profoundly retarded, nonambulatory hydrocephalics who are blind and deaf" (p. 267). To this Burt (1976) responded by asking, "What about those only blind? only deaf? and so on" (p. 439). This illustrates the difficulty of defining workable legal standards. Regardless of the care with which definitions are prepared, there will always be the next hard case that does not quite fit the description and requires professional judgment.

Burt also presented other persuasive points to argue against changing the laws. One of his points involved the change in attitude that frequently occurs when court arguments are made over actions specifically authorized by legislation. Litigation relating to acts specifically addressed by legislation often involves arguments presented in a cool, rational, and dispassionate fashion. Burt clearly believed that the dispensing of life or death is an issue that we cannot afford to treat in a dispassionate manner. His concern was that explicit authority, such as that which might be found in legislation, would place life-and-death decisions for defective newborns in a context in which either choice could be made with equal ease. Burt believed that this should not be the case and that death decisions should be reached reluctantly, and he contended that the current state of affairs promotes that reluctance as a result of the mere existence of potential criminal liability.

The description of Burt's arguments might suggest that he was firmly opposed to the withholding of treatment. This is not the case. It should be emphasized that he was in opposition to changing the law and thereby specifically authorizing such action. With the following statements, he placed this position squarely in the arena of social and ethical issues:

> I am not suggesting that existing values must change or that no self-respecting physician would ever or should ever withhold treatment from a newborn. Rather, I am suggesting that if we are evolving toward new values in this matter, we must do so gradually, hesitantly, and looking backward to what we have been, as often as we look forward to imagine what we will become. (p. 446)

Burt's arguments warrant serious consideration regardless of whether one agrees with him or not. One does not have to search very far into the past to discover topics and issues that have experienced an expansion of what is allowed. Topics like abortion and euthanasia are discussed, examined, and practiced in ways that would have been viewed as clearly beyond the realm of possibility 30 years ago. In some cases technological advances have occurred that seem subtly to have governed philosophical changes. In other areas it is not altogether clear what has fostered change, but we still find ethical decisions being considered that would previously have been thought wholly impossible (e.g., Hollander, 1989). Perhaps no other issue gives so much pause as postnatal life management.

Life Management Decisions

As we look both backward and forward in examining our values, several immediate questions arise in relation to life management. How are life management decisions made? Who makes such decisions, and under what circumstances? For whom are these decisions made? We have offered some examination of the last question. In most cases those who debate the issues of life management are discussing infants who are extremely damaged or defective at birth. But "extremely" and its ilk are adverbs that may be broadly defined and are subject to differing interpretations.

The Johns Hopkins Case   In at least one case that received considerable publicity, there could be substantial debate about how severely handicapped the infant was. This case occurred at Johns Hopkins Hospital with a two-day-old full-term male infant who had facial characteristics and other features suggesting Down syndrome. No cardiac abnormalities were evident, but the infant began vomiting a greenish substance shortly after birth. X-ray examination indicated duodenal atresia (a congenital absence or closure of a portion of the duodenum).

It is important to discuss duodenal atresia momentarily to place this case in perspective. Diamond (1977) reviewed the case and examined the issues involved in medical intervention through surgical correction of the intestinal obstruction. He indicated that the problem could be corrected with a survival rate of 98%, and that mortality was higher for newborns with acute appendicitis. Diamond thought that the ethics and value structure that would require performance of this nearly risk-free operation on a nonhandicapped infant did not pertain in the case of a handicapped infant.

The intestinal obstruction could be surgically corrected with negligible risk. The infant reportedly had no additional complicating factors other than the clinical impression of Down syndrome. Is Down syndrome an example of an extremely handicapping condition? This may be a debatable issue. Some would answer with an unqualified affirmative. Others might note the potential intellectual range of Down syndrome children and would disagree. The answer is not clear-cut, although one factor that may come into play occasionally is that Down syndrome is visually evident. The decision in the Johns Hopkins case was to withhold treatment. Following discussion with the parents, surgical correction of the duodenal atresia was not performed, and all feeding and fluids were discontinued. Fifteen days later the infant died of starvation and dehydration.

There are many ethical issues raised by the Johns Hopkins case. One can certainly question the humaneness of permitting an infant to starve to death over a 15-day period. This is a particularly difficult question, since the decision not to operate made it impossible for the infant to receive food and fluids in a normal manner. But the issue concerning the degree of handicap represented by Down syndrome is equally provocative for our question regarding on whom life management decisions will focus. It is questionable whether Down syndrome can be described as an extreme, a terrible, or a tragic handicap. Some Down syndrome children reach a level of intellectual functioning classified as moderate or even mild mental retardation.

The possibility that mildly or moderately retarded infants are vulnerable to negative life management decisions raises serious concerns. This is particularly true in the context of earlier discussions about proposals to enact legislation authorizing selective life management. We noted before that application of legal standards by society and the development of case law expand legal jurisdiction. Even in the absence of legal authorization, advancing technology frequently seems to desensitize society to encroachment on value structures. These tendencies should be carefully considered as we develop new values in life management. Will future life management decisions include the mildly handicapped? This may already be the case for visible handicaps like Down syndrome. Will future life management include the election of a particular sex on the part of parents? Perhaps only beautiful infants will receive favorable decisions. These suggestions are clearly repugnant; but some accept many practices that society once thought were wildly impossible. We wish to emphasize that we are not taking a position on life management practices. Instead we intend to provoke the most serious examination possible of the social and ethical issues related to such treatment alternatives with mentally retarded individuals.

Decisions: Who and How?

The earlier questions posed included how life management decisions are made, who makes such decisions, and under what circumstances. In part these issues are related to the discussion just presented. Certain other points, however, warrant at least brief attention.

Neither the how nor the why question can be answered simply. A physician's patients, when they are adults and mentally competent, have the right to be fully informed about proposed medical treatment. It is generally agreed that such patients then have the legal right to accept or reject that treatment and, in fact, to reject any treatment. When the patient is a minor, however, or not judged to be mentally competent, the decision process is vastly altered. In the case of handicapped infants, parents have the right to informed consent but do not have sole decision-making prerogatives. Shaw (1977) argued that when physicians or society disagrees with the parents' decision, it is subject to review. His statement concerning review by physicians and society specifically addressed situations when the parents' decision involves the rejection of treatment. It is clear from published reports that this is the case in public decision making. It is patently unacceptable for medical personnel to reverse a parental decision to prolong life publicly. Off the record, however, medical personnel do report cases in which unilateral (but not public) decisions are made to withhold treatment in certain circumstances.

Consent

The act of consent is not simple. Although *informed consent* is a term in popular usage, it is a misnomer. The AAMR believed the problems of consent were so important that it commissioned a special task force to examine the complexities of this topic. This effort resulted in publication of the AAMR *Consent Handbook* (Turnbull, 1977), which examined consent in detail and from the standpoints of both definition and application.

Although consent has specific meanings in a variety of contexts, the ramifications of consent often result in legal interpretations. This is certainly so in the current discussion. The *Consent Handbook* defined consent principally as a legal concept. Three elements of consent must be considered: capacity, information, and voluntariness. For the most part these three elements must be present for effective consent. It is also important to realize that consent is seldom, if ever, permanent and may be withdrawn at almost any time. Generally the act of withdrawing consent must also include the three elements of capacity, information, and voluntariness.

The elements of consent are of particular importance in the context of our discussion of life management decisions with handicapped infants. The *Consent Handbook* defined the first element—capacity—in terms of three factors: the person's age, the person's competence, and the particular situation. An infant does not have the legal or logical capacity to consent specifically on at least two of these factors. A person under the age of majority (generally 18 years) is legally incompetent to make certain decisions. Likewise, it is clear that an infant does not have the developed mental competence to understand and give consent. Thus in terms of capacity the parents, legal guardians, or other persons acting on behalf of the parents have the authority to consent for an infant. The issues involved in decision making generally for and by mentally retarded persons are complex (Drane, 1985; Gaylin & Macklin, 1982).

The second element of consent—information—also must receive careful consideration. The *Consent Handbook* discussed this element as follows:

> The focus is on "what" information is given and "how" it is given since it must be effectively communicated (given and received) to be acted upon. The concern is with the fullness and effectiveness of the disclosure: is it designed to be fully understood, and is it fully understood? The burden of satisfying these two tests rests on the professional. (p. 8)

The last sentence of this quotation is particularly important in life management decisions with handicapped newborns. Clearly the giving or withholding of consent rests primarily with the parents, but in a sense such decisions are the joint responsibility of parents and medical personnel. For effective information to be present, the physician must see that the information about the infant's condition is designed to be fully understood, and that it is fully understood.

The third element of consent—voluntariness— also has great relevance. Although voluntariness may appear to be a simple concept, subtle influences in the process of giving or withholding consent make it far from simple. The *Consent Handbook* noted that the consenting individual must be "so situated as to be able to exercise free power of choice without the intervention of any element of force, fraud, deceit, duress, overreaching or other ulterior form of constraint or coercion" (p. 10). This places even greater responsibilities on the physician. Information must be complete and without explicit or implicit inclusion of personal judgment. This may be particularly difficult, since physicians are typically viewed as authority figures by the lay public, and they certainly are not without their own feelings or beliefs in such situations. It may also be that parents are highly vulnerable to persuasion immediately after the birth of a handicapped infant (Hardman & Drew, 1980).

Life management through euthanasia or withholding of treatment from handicapped infants may be one of the most complex social and ethical issues related to mental retardation. The preceding discussion has illustrated the agonies these decisions involve and the stress that social values are under in such situations. Perhaps nowhere is the concept of competing equities so evident. The rights of the infant and the rights of the parents may be in direct conflict, depending on the values and attitudes of the parents. Such conflict is not news to those who work with retarded children and their families. What may be new or unique is the stark realization that the decisions being made involve a degree of gravity that is totally unfamiliar to most of us—the actual dispensing of life or death.

Other Issues

The neonatal period and the remaining portion of the early years also represent a high-risk time for other actions involving an infant with mental retardation. Some of these actions also come under consideration as we examine social and ethical issues. If a child is definitely identified as being mentally retarded during this period of time, it is likely that a visible clinical syndrome is evident (Down syndrome) or that the handicap is in the moderate to severe or profound range. More often than not, a mildly retarded child without physical evidence of a problem is not diagnosed with any degree of certainty until formal schooling begins. Parents of children with mild retardation may have some concerns about developmental delays, but these are often private concerns that remain in the back of their minds and are not discussed or are rationalized and denied. Parents of children who are diagnosed as mentally retarded during their early years, however, must address the issues of care and early education on a more immediate basis, which often raises ethical considerations that are emotionally laden and cause extraordinary stress.

Institutionalization Decisions

The type of care and where such care is going to occur frequently surface as considerations with children who are diagnosed as retarded during their early years. One issue that often arises with such children is whether or not they should be institutionalized. This is always an agonizing choice for parents and frequently is made doubly difficult by the type and amount of information on which they can base their decision. The discussion in Chapter 6 indicated that prediction of a child's ultimate level of functioning is extremely difficult during the very early periods of life. Although predictive accuracy improves as the child grows older, assessment procedures that are useful during infancy are quite unreliable in terms of later functioning. Additionally, parents of very young retarded children are often interacting with medical personnel as their primary source of information. Historically physicians have had too little training to meet this challenge effectively, although significant efforts have recently been made in many medical schools to include such preparation. Physicians' assessments of children have consequently been subject to considerable error, particularly when there is also a physical handicap or defect present (Hardman & Drew, 1977). For example, research by Pearson and Menefee (1965) indicated that pediatricians consistently underestimated the level of intellectual functioning of these children, resulting in a tendency to recommend institutionalization more frequently.

Many social and ethical issues are involved in this situation. One immediate consideration pertains to the inclination to recommend or at least favor institutionalization based on estimates of the degree of handicap by medical personnel. The general concern relates as much as anything to the magnitude of consistent error in estimates by pediatricians. Pearson and Menefee (1965) found that approximately two-thirds of the assessments were close to one full standard deviation away from administered standardized test scores. This, coupled with their report that pediatricians consistently misjudged and underestimated the level of functioning, heightens the concern even further. Such data present a rather uncertain basis for the decision to institutionalize.

Recent efforts have been evident to improve the preparation of physicians for working with all handicapped individuals and their families (Johnston, 1987). We have observed significant leadership by some medical personnel responsible for preparation programs, which are excellent and appear to be having a substantial impact. Some pediatricians in teaching hospitals have become extremely knowledgeable about education of handicapped individuals and have done a great deal to foster an interdisciplinary team effort with special education and psychology. The fact remains, however, that many medical personnel currently in practice were trained before this concern arose. Their level of knowledge and the nature of their approach to handicapped children may reflect the type of findings reported earlier.

Placement of a young child with retardation in an institution once again raises the issue of consent and the three elements that must be present for consent to be effective. Remember that effective consent must include capacity, information, and voluntariness. Parents' consent for institutionalization of the child must have these three elements to be legitimate. The element of information raises particular concern. The parents may be interacting with medical or other professional personnel who are not properly equipped to provide complete and appropriate data for decision making. Professionals who have provided inadequate information or advice in terms of a child's placement have seldom suffered the consequences in the past. Their immunity, however, may be disappearing as parents and advocates for individuals with retardation bring suits to alter decisions previously made from inadequate information or advice. Malpractice might be an appropriate concept for professions other than medicine.

Institutional Conditions
No decision for treatment or placement of a child with retardation should be made casually or without full consideration of its ramifications. This is particularly the case when the decision involves possible placement of a child in a residential institution. Such a decision involves perhaps the most restrictive placement possible and represents

a dramatic removal of an individual from the societal mainstream. Although this type of placement is appropriate in certain situations, when inappropriate it can be very detrimental.

Residential institutions historically have had a very poor image as treatment and habilitation agencies for individuals with retardation. Some of this poor image may be undeserved or have extenuating circumstances. But conditions in institutions have often been less than desirable; in some cases institutions have been deplorable, dehumanizing warehouses that have very negative effects on residents' psychological development (Hardman, Drew, Egan, & Wolf, 1990). A judiciary subcommittee of the United States Senate conducted five days of hearings during the summer of 1977 while considering legislation on the civil rights of institutionalized persons. The hearings resulted in more than 1100 pages of testimony and exhibits by individuals involved with mentally retarded people either as professionals or as other interested parties. These pages include graphic descriptions of institutional problems and conditions, most of them unfavorable.

The desirability of institutional placement may thus be questioned on arguments of unacceptable conditions alone (although the restrictiveness of placement raises additional questions). The assignment of any human being to live in some of the subhuman conditions that have existed raises serious issues of societal values. Fortunately, as noted earlier, others have raised and continue to raise such questions in a number of public

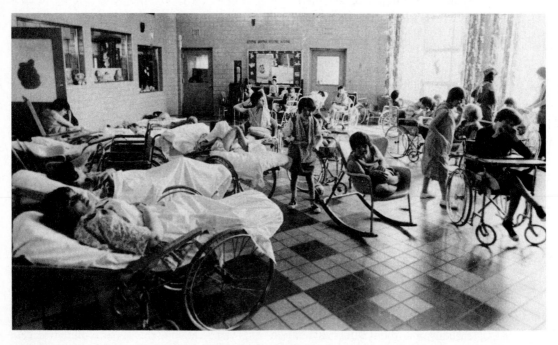

Institutions have not had a favorable reputation regarding living conditions for those with mental retardation, and such placement involves many questions.

forums, and dramatic changes are under way. Some of these changes have been initiated by institutional personnel themselves; others have emerged as a result of efforts by advocates for citizens with retardation. In general, very young children are less often committed to institutions. This is a favorable move in view of the assessment difficulties. It also reduces the likelihood that institutionalization will occur on the basis of inadequate information and increases the probability that other treatment alternatives will receive more serious consideration. Although changes for the better are under way, it is important for society to continue examining its value structure vis-à-vis services for those with mental retardation. Was it by intent or by neglect that deplorable institutional conditions were allowed to evolve? Do such conditions reflect society's implicit philosophical position on the value of human life or a statement of belief that retarded individuals are somehow "less human"? These questions are much like those posed earlier; they have no single or simple answers.

A final note is in order relative to institutional placement in general and to the particular context of the early years. The issue of competing equities once again makes its presence felt. Here, as before, the competing equities question may place the handicapped child at the opposite pole from the parents and the rest of the family. On the one hand is the child's right to live and develop in the best environment possible. On the other hand is the impact on the family. What effect does the child's presence (and the presence of a handicap) have on the parents and any nonretarded siblings who may be a part of the family? In many cases the impact is unknown at the outset, and reports have varied all the way from favorable to destructive. One factor is a constant in this consideration: the impact is not minimal.

Ethical Issues During the School Years

Core Concept	*Social and ethical issues during the school years often relate both to society's responsibility and to the level of effort required to meet the educational and other treatment needs of the child with mental retardation.*

In part, social and ethical issues that surface during the school years are similar to some discussed earlier in the chapter. Competing equities, consent, and placement issues are not limited to a particular age level. They can be observed in nearly all areas of service delivery to handicapped individuals. The manner in which these issues emerge, however, alters considerably with different phases of the life cycle.

Placement Issues
The placement of mentally retarded children in educational settings raises a variety of issues, including philosophical questions as well as practical questions of implementation. Earlier sections of this book have examined educational programming for children and youth with mental retardation. From these discussions it is clear that one placement alternative involves what some have called pull-out programs. Such programs remove a child with retardation from the educational mainstream and provide almost

the complete educational experience away from the child's nonhandicapped peers. Examples of this type of placement include self-contained special education classes, special schools, and residential institutions. Earlier sections have noted that such placements exist as alternatives but should be viewed as existing on a continuum with others that involve specialized programming for the child within the educational mainstream. This view is not one that has prevailed historically.

Special classes and other pull-out programs for children with mental retardation have a long history. The first public school special classes in the United States were organized in 1896. Enrollment in such programs increased at a steady rate until recently. By 1922 there were more than 23,000 children enrolled in special classes, and by 1958 this number had increased to more than 196,000 (Mackie & Robbins, 1960). The increase in special classes for retarded children was based on the belief that such placement was more beneficial than the regular classroom. Both the data and the logic supporting this as the sole approach to educating handicapped children have been seriously questioned in recent years. According to current thinking, handicapped individuals should be treated and educated as closely as possible to the mainstream of society (Hardman et al., 1990).

Much of the current approach to the education of handicapped children has been captured in Public Law 94–142, which is discussed in Chapter 15. Public Law 94–142 is an extremely complex piece of legislation that raises many questions and issues. One of these relates specifically to the placement of handicapped children in the least restrictive appropriate educational environment. This concept is very different from the logic that supported pull-out programs as the primary means for educating children with mental retardation. It emphasizes a continuum of service alternatives and requires that education agencies develop procedures to assure that handicapped children are educated with nonhandicapped children to the degree appropriate. The least-restrictive-placement concept thus emphasizes that special classes, separate schooling, or other removal of handicapped children from the regular educational environment should be alternatives of choice only when the child's handicap is such that satisfactory education cannot be accomplished in regular classes, even with the use of supplementary aids and services. The least-restriction principle raises many issues. We examine these in chapters on the school years and legal issues. Additionally, the least-restriction principle has raised several questions and issues that warrant attention in the context of social and ethical domains.

Least-Restriction Principle

One of the issues raised by the least-restriction principle represents a somewhat fluid combination of competing equities and the formalism-utilitarianism philosophical conflict. As stated earlier, pure formalism presents a dilemma because, as the rights of some are made more distinct, they impinge on others. This dilemma is nearly definitional in the way it relates to competing equities. Education of children with mental retardation in least restrictive placements may create some of these exact problems. For example, least restrictive placement means that a substantial number of mildly retarded children have their primary placement in regular classrooms. Even with supplementary aids and ancillary services, these children require additional in-class attention that the teacher is often not accustomed to providing, and they may demand skills that the teacher does not have. Many teachers face this prospect with great anxiety.

In parts of the country, teacher expectations about least restrictive placements have emerged in contract negotiations between school districts and teachers' bargaining organizations (unions and professional associations). For example, in some areas teacher organizations have taken the stand that class size must be reduced by three nonhandicapped children for each handicapped child placed in the regular classroom. This raises an immediate question of where those three nonhandicapped children will go. If a regular class had three handicapped children enrolled, it would result in the displacement of nine nonhandicapped children. Such an arrangement could easily result in a significant increase in the number of classrooms, and even schools, in a district. This instantly gives rise to the issue of cost and also the possibility of increased busing. When these matters are considered, the competing equities problem emerges very significantly. Taxpayers are already less than enthusiastic about how much of their income goes to public education. Parents of nonhandicapped children have legitimate reasons for irritation as they are asked to pay more while their children are shifted from class to class (or are bused).

But this is only one instance of the competing equities issue in the schooling of children with mental retardation. The dilemma rests squarely on the philosophical questions raised by formalism in our complex society. When we make more distinct the legitimate rights to an appropriate education for some, this very act may impinge on the rights of others. The social value question at stake is at once simple and complex: Who sacrifices? Is it a matter of requiring that all be equally disadvantaged or all equally advantaged? Or do we turn to a utilitarian philosophy in which an individual has only those rights granted by society at large (the privileged)? It may be possible for society to ensure an appropriate education for all handicapped children without significantly imposing a disadvantage on nonhandicapped children. This cannot, however, be accomplished without a cost, and society must determine whether it is willing to pay that cost. The least-restriction principle places a strain on societal values, for the question cannot go unanswered. And our social structure is not accustomed to addressing such difficult questions in an orderly manner.

Appropriate Education Issues

The language of Public Law 94–142 raises many questions related to the school years. But one particular piece of the language is strikingly provocative. The term *appropriate* was mentioned in the discussion of least restriction: least restrictive appropriate placement. This term is found in several parts of the legislation and connotes a qualitative description of the educational programming. Placement and educational program should be appropriate for the nature and degree of the handicap.

That part of the legislation dealing with appropriate education may be problematic from at least two standpoints. The first relates to the term. *Appropriate*, like many adjectives, is a general term subject to a wide variety of definitions. Although this is characteristic of legislative language, the range of implemental or operational outcomes is as varied as the number of individuals responsible for implementation. This brings us to the second problem. Public Law 94–142 is a revolutionary piece of legislation. Some have suggested that it is so revolutionary that it may wither and die because of our inability to make the changes required on a mass basis. Consequently, professionals have been so engaged in responding to the law's major and obvious principles that the term *appropriate* has been largely ignored. This presents a significant dilemma because appropriateness of the educational or treatment program was the raison d'être for the legislation. In fact, appropriate education is a fundamental assumption that underlies the public's support for education in general. Some responses to the concepts of Public Law 94–142 have seemed to ignore appropriateness to such an extent as to raise ethical questions. One of these involves a "paper compliance," in which efforts are concentrated more on making a child's program look appropriate on paper than on ensuring the actual appropriateness of the program. Although such situations existed in the past, they have become increasingly common with the advent of the federal legislation.

Paper compliance detracts from the effectiveness of educational programming, the fundamental purpose of the legislation. It also brings into question the professional ethics of those who ensure it. Initial reaction to this type of compliance may be much like that suggested in the context of life management—that it is unethical and should not be permitted. Whereas most of us would agree in principle, this problem, like those we have discussed previously, is not susceptible to a simple solution.

Although one cannot excuse paper compliance, it is not difficult to understand some of the reasons why it happens. First of all, the public schools are not generally well equipped to implement Public Law 94–142 on a widespread basis. Chapter 15 outlines in detail the major principles of the law. It is a massive piece of legislation, which, if interpreted and implemented as intended, means immense changes in most school districts. In many cases these changes require personnel and skills that are not currently available. Some of these resources might not be available by the time that compliance is required, even if the schools had the money to buy them. From the perspective of those who are charged with the responsibility of implementation, the task often seems overwhelming. Once again, while we may not excuse or condone paper compliance, it is not difficult to see how it can happen.

Additional factors add to the complex issue of providing "appropriate" educational programming as defined in Public Law 94–142. The law is a prescriptive piece of federal legislation that, from many educators' viewpoint, is being imposed on them by outsiders. This outside imposition has at least two sources from the perspective of many who are required to comply. First of all, many regular elementary and secondary educators view the law as being imposed on them by special education. This has not exactly met with favorable reaction since one segment of the profession (and a smaller one at that) is dictating what appropriate education is to another, larger, segment of the profession. The outside imposition perspective also becomes evident because this is a federal law that in part dictates how education will be conducted at the state and local levels. This raises the immediate question of whether or not the law is a case of federal intervention in states' rights. Appropriate education, least restrictive placement, competing equities, and states' rights are merely samples of the issues that complicate value questions related to the school years. Although the context has changed, the philosophical and operational differences are no more easily resolved than they were in the early years.

Ethical concerns have also arisen about specific procedures used in the education and treatment of handicapped children. Behavioral principles have long been employed to achieve educational progress with mentally retarded children. In some cases, application of these principles has involved the use of punishment or aversive consequences to change inappropriate behavior. Such techniques have received considerable attention as being both unethical and unnecessary (Butterfield, 1990; LaVigna & Donnellan, 1986; Mulick, 1990). Aversive treatment procedures create a number of difficulties, including potential legal and ethical problems. Additionally, such procedures are seen as restrictive in the sense that they are intrusive and do not represent contingencies that exist in the mainstream environment. This often makes it difficult for the handicapped person to generalize behavior learned to more natural settings where, for example, a time-out room does not exist. Thus there are also questions about generalization of instruction, further highlighting the questionable propriety of aversive techniques (Donnellan, LaVigna, Negri-Shoultz, & Fassbender, 1988).

Consent

The introductory comments to this section stated that consent is also a relevant issue for the school years. Parents must be actively involved in the decision process that results in changing the educational program for their child. In terms of our specific focus—the child with mental retardation—this process includes consent for assessment or diagnosis as well as any programming changes that might occur as a result of such assessment.

Consent in the context of the school years involves the same basic principles that we discussed previously with regard to life management decisions. To be effective, parental consent for all action, including assessment and programming, must include the three elements of capacity, information, and voluntariness. As before, consent is seldom if ever permanent and may be withdrawn at nearly any time. The educator who is attempting to obtain consent carries a heavy burden—just as the medical professional did earlier—in terms of ensuring that the three elements of consent are present.

One element of consent that is altered somewhat in the context of the school years is capacity. For the most part, capacity to consent for the mentally retarded child remains with the parents, as before. From a strictly legal standpoint, the capacity to consent does not rest with a child because of age (under the age of majority) and lack of mental competence to understand the nature and consequences of consent. Good practice, however, would suggest that a blanket assumption of incapacity throughout the school years is inappropriate. Specifically, older individuals with retardation (adolescents or young adults) who are functioning at a nearly normal level may be quite capable of participating in the consent process. Depending on the situation and the individual, they may be able to give consent directly or concurrently with a third party, such as the parents. Inclusion of a third party in consent is likely if the information is complex or the individual less able. As before, the process of obtaining effective consent involves the exercise of considerable judgment. There are few set rules that one can follow to relieve the need for exercising solid professional judgment. The burden of obtaining effective consent rests heavily with the professional, a situation that may create a certain amount of discomfort but that must prevail if the rights of individuals with retardation are to be adequately protected.

Ethical Issues During Adulthood

Core Concept	*The social and ethical issues of the adult years once again pit the interests of society against the individual's rights. They often relate to adult functions like marriage and reproduction.*

The social and ethical issues that surface during adulthood ring familiar. Many of the principles, philosophical differences, and agonizing social questions remain relatively constant. As before, however, the stage of the life cycle alters the issues considerably. Here we focus on those social and ethical issues that we hope will promote the most serious questioning on the part of the reader.

The emergence of certain social and ethical issues during the adult years is not surprising. Questions of marriage, reproduction, and sterilization become considerations during this part of the life cycle. As with most of the issues discussed in this chapter, these topics are highly controversial.

Sterilization Issues

Although life management decisions are complex, the issues surrounding sterilization of individuals with retardation are no less perplexing. Controversy about sterilization has a very long history, and legal authority for it varies throughout the country.

Arguments for and Against Sterilization   One of the ways to approach the topic of sterilization is to examine how and why mentally retarded individuals receive different consideration from their nonretarded peers (Kunjukrishnan & Varan, 1989). Both the historical controversy and the legal authority to sterilize people with mental retardation (see Chapter 15) clearly indicate different consideration. For example, although voluntary sterilization of nonretarded citizens is mostly viewed as an individual prerogative (a means of birth control), involuntary sterilization laws pertaining generally to nonretarded citizens are unheard of. A variety of justifications have been advanced for sterilization of those with mental retardation. Krishef (1972, p. 36) summarized these arguments as those that hold sterilization to be "(1) in the best interest of society and the state, (2) in the best interest of the retarded individuals, and (3) in the best interest of the unborn children."

Many people express strong opposition to sterilization of individuals with mental retardation. Arguments on this side of the issue are varied and include (1) concern about the potential misuse of legal authority to sterilize, (2) some evidence that some of the prosterilization arguments noted before do not consistently hold true, and (3) concern about the rights of the individual and the manner in which the process is undertaken. Each of these areas presents serious societal and legal issues that warrant examination.

The first prosterilization argument held that sterilization of mentally retarded individuals was in the best interest of society and the state. This is a particularly difficult premise, depending on how one views the support for it. This proposition may also exemplify, perhaps more clearly than any other issue, how the best interest of the state may come into conflict with rights of an individual. One very important basis for the "benefit to society and state" argument involves a reduction in the numbers of individuals with retardation. As such it is another approach to the prevention of mental retardation. Proponents of this position point to the fact that such a reduction would decrease the number of citizens requiring extra services from society and would lessen the cost burden for such care on the state and the taxpayers. This argument is utilitarian; such savings, if they were to occur, could be redirected to those societal needs that might ultimately result in greater productive return to the general public.

One question that is immediately raised concerns the degree to which such a practice would actually result in reduced incidence of mental retardation. The answer is anything but obvious. If sterilization is viewed as preventing only the transmission of inferior or damaged genetic material, the reduction in incidence is quite minimal. Mental retardation that can be directly attributed to genetic causation represents a very small proportion of all cases. Furthermore, those individuals whose mental retardation can be attributed to genetic causes are more likely to be functioning at lower levels, some in the severe to profound range. For a number of reasons one can make the case that such individuals are less likely to engage in procreation to begin with. The difficulty with this entire line of reasoning becomes evident when one views the broad perspective of mental retardation. First of all, earlier sections of this volume have examined the nature vs. nurture controversy in considerable detail for effects on development of intelligence (and mental retardation causation). It is clear from these earlier discussions that determination of environmental influences cannot be accomplished with great precision. It is also evident that the environment does have a significant role in causing mental retardation, particularly in the milder range of handicap. Therefore sterilization is not solely focusing on the transmission of inferior genetic material.

Thus the question remains, To what degree would a massive sterilization program reduce the incidence of mental retardation? Although the answer remains speculative, some data are available. Bass (1967) made reference to a Danish program that involves genetic counseling and voluntary sterilization of people with retardation. This program, directly aimed at preventing reproduction by retarded individuals, had been in operation for 25 years at the time of Bass's research in 1967. Results suggested that the incidence of mental retardation was reduced by "approximately 50% a generation" (p. 45). Bass also cited the work of Reed and Reed (1965), who suggested that a similar reduction in incidence might be expected if voluntary sterilization were to become widely accepted in the United States.

Although limited, this study does suggest that a rather substantial reduction in incidence might be expected if sterilization of mentally retarded individuals were conducted systematically. This might appear to lend support to the "best interest of society" argument. It is evident, however, that our complex and diverse society is not willing to accept such a practice in a single-minded fashion. The reasons for this are as varied as our culture.

One very strong influence is our apparent unwillingness to overrule the rights of individuals in favor of the rights of the larger society in any blanket fashion. One of the individual rights that seems to loom large in this regard is the right of procreation. As early as 1921 the importance of this individual right was noted in a legal interpretation of the Constitution. At this time the Michigan attorney general issued an opinion, based on the Constitution, that held that the right to have and retain the power of procreation was second only to the right to life itself. It is generally accepted that such a fundamental individual right can be abrogated only on a voluntary basis by the individual involved. One must then ask the question, How did compulsory sterilization laws come to exist in certain states? Obviously, in these situations the state deemed that its interests superseded the rights of people with mental retardation.

Consent Issues

Even voluntary sterilization of mentally retarded individuals presents some complex questions both conceptually and with regard to implementation. The moment we move into a voluntary status with respect to sterilization we once again face the question of consent. The concept of consent in the context of sterilization however, presents some interesting implementation problems that we have not encountered earlier.

The element of capacity was discussed earlier with particular focus on the person's age and competence. As mentioned previously, a person under the age of majority is legally incompetent to make certain decisions. Since our main focus in this section is the adult years, age is not a consideration with regard to capacity. Competence does, however, become an issue. The basic question is whether or not a retarded adult has the mental competence to understand sterilization and its implications. This question is unanswerable in a general sense. It would seem most logical to consider each case individually, depending on the person's level of functioning. But some would disagree vigorously. A decision concerning sterilization has been described as being so extraordinarily important and complex that many individuals of normal intelligence are perhaps not competent to comprehend its implications fully (Baron, 1976). Whereas this may be true for only some nonretarded individuals, it does seriously raise the competence issue when a person with mental retardation is involved. This in no way suggests, however, that the opinion of the retarded person being considered for sterilization should be ignored.

The natural people to turn to for assistance in obtaining consent would seem to be the parents or legal guardians of the individual. This has been the case in our earlier discussions of other procedures requiring consent. It is assumed that they will consider such decisions with the best interests of their ward being the first and foremost concern. This may not, however, be a sound assumption with respect to sterilization. In fact, Murdock (1974) suggested that "parents or guardians often have interests that conflict with those of the retarded child. The parents of a retarded child may have understandable fears that the grandchild will also be retarded. Moreover, parents may perceive a danger of their retarded child proving to be an unfit parent, and might wish to avoid the risk of shouldering responsibilities of grandchildren" (p. 917). If such a situation does exist it is clear that parental input in the consent process may not be motivated solely by consideration of the candidate's best interest.

There has been a noticeable tendency for the courts to intervene and review parental decisions regarding consent for sterilization. The court wishes to ensure that the individual's best interests are protected and are the sole determining factor influencing the sterilization decision. This presents a difficult dilemma, one that makes the consent process extremely complicated. Court intervention itself is complicated. To assure objectivity the court must hear information and arguments on both sides. This requires that advocates for both sides be present in court and be equally informed and articulate. It further requires that the arguments on both sides include all relevant information and that information that is presented be limited to the issues pertaining to the best interests of the individual. Presentation of information or arguments relating to either the state's or the parents' interests is not relevant.

This brief discussion represents only the tip of the iceberg in terms of the complex issues related to consent for sterilization. Although we began our examination with a focus on the element of capacity, the elements of information and voluntariness quickly became intertwined in the considerations. Our discussion demonstrates how issues can become extremely complicated as attempts are made to protect individual rights. It also raises other social questions that are not easily answered: Do the parents' rights and interests have no value? What about the interests of the state? The concept of competing equities becomes evident in situations in which the rights and interests of all parties are not in harmony. These are familiar questions, reminiscent of the extreme philosophical differences presented at the beginning of the chapter.

Marriage Issues

The issues pertaining to the marriage of adults with mental retardation are closely related to sterilization, and the two are often considered together. Marriage issues are perhaps not as legally complicated, since an irreversible medical procedure is not involved. Possibly the overriding issues or questions in this area concern the existence of laws restricting marriage for individuals with retardation. As indicated in other chapters, many states have laws restricting the right to marry for those classified as mentally retarded. One has to ask why these laws exist. Are these laws aimed at the protection of the individual or are they basically for the protection of society?

We present this question in order to examine the issue. For some, the evidence is so compelling that objective examination of this issue is tantamount to ignoring how such laws came into existence. Wolfensberger (1975) discussed restrictive marriage laws as a part of society's need to prevent procreation by people with mental retardation. Credence for the perception certainly arises from the widespread negative attitudes toward sexual expression and marriage among mentally retarded people (Chapman & Pitceathly, 1985; Pitceathly & Chapman, 1985). If not credence, certainly interest is added to this examination by the wording of early legislation cited by Wolfensberger (1975). He cited an 1895 bill passed by the Connecticut House of Representatives. It reads as follows:

> Every man who shall carnally know any female under the age of forty-five years who is epileptic, imbecile, feeble-minded, or a pauper, shall be imprisoned in the State prison not less than three years. Every man who is epileptic who shall carnally know any female under

the age of forty-five years, and every female under the age of forty-five years who shall consent to be carnally known by any man who is epileptic, imbecile, or feeble-minded, shall be imprisoned in the State prison not less than three years. (p. 40)

It should also be noted that a law to prohibit the marriage of mentally ill and mentally retarded people was proposed at the national level in 1897 and received a great deal of support. One could interpret the above wording from either perspective (that is, individual or societal protection) since specific mention of intent is absent. But there is little real question about intent. The historical commentary seems to have been captured by Wilmarth in 1902. His focus was on the "abatement of this evil" and a search for ways to accomplish it (Wolfensberger, 1975, p. 40).

It does seem that society's interests have been paramount, at least historically. One must raise the question of whether or not this is still the case. Some of these old laws remain on the books. What about current legislation? Are current laws and efforts merely more carefully disguised attempts to protect the best interests of society, or are they really aimed at achieving some balance between the rights of individuals and the rights of our larger culture? There are strong arguments on both sides.

The questions and issues discussed throughout this chapter are not pleasant topics. We might wish to avoid them if possible. They are, however, social and ethical questions of great importance. These are issues that test the strength of societal fabric. We cannot ignore what seems to be the fundamental question: Are individuals with mental retardation considered subhuman, or at least less deserving of the rights of the rest of humanity?

RESEARCH AND PROFESSIONAL ETHICS IN MENTAL RETARDATION

Core Concept	*Research and professional ethics in mental retardation involve a wide variety of issues where individual rights must be balanced against the need for scientific information and the complexities of appropriate treatment.*

The field of mental retardation has a special link to ethics, as is evident from our foregoing discussion. People who are mentally retarded are in a high-risk category with respect to ethical vulnerability. They are among those who need special consideration and protection. This places great responsibility on professionals working in the field as researchers and care providers.

To learn more about mental retardation it is necessary to conduct research on individuals within that population. This often raises concern because by virtue of investigating those with mental retardation we are in some ways invading their privacy and subjecting them to risk even though we might have the most honorable of intentions. In order to discover more effective methods of teaching, placing, medicating, and otherwise treating these individuals it is necessary to study them and learn about their characteristics. We cannot avoid conducting research with mentally retarded people in order to protect them. In fact, some have held that it would be unethical *not* to conduct such research (e.g., Drew & Hardman, 1985).

Conducting research with mentally retarded individuals while simultaneously protecting their rights as individuals requires constant vigilance. A careful balance must be struck between the behavioral scientist's need to invade and the individual subject's rights. For the population we are discussing special care must be taken in the areas of consent, privacy, and harm. Likewise, issues of deception (explicit lying to subjects as well as omitting details about the study) remain controversial in mental retardation, as they do in all behavioral science (Baumrind, 1985; Fisher, 1986; Trice, 1986). Certain medications and other treatments inherently pose some risk, and inappropriate applications may be harmful. All of these considerations make research on mental retardation challenging. Such safeguards as institutional review boards (sometimes known as human subjects committees) used by universities and other agencies to monitor research are vital to protecting subjects and maintaining a balance between the needs of scientists and subjects' rights. Likewise, many professional associations and societies have ethics committees and codes of ethics to guide their members (Drew & Turnbull, 1987).

Research is not the only area where professional ethics comes into play in the field of mental retardation. Schools, treatment centers, and other care provision agencies must also be careful to administer the most effective treatment possible efficiently, while simultaneously remaining conscious of the rights of people with mental retardation. In some cases, the treatment administered may involve some risk, as is the case with some medications. Once again people with mental retardation are at risk and are more vulnerable than the population in general. It is vital that professionals be adequately trained and qualified to administer the treatment being employed. Occasionally (we hope rarely), this does not happen because of personnel shortages, lack of knowledge, or carelessness. As before, it is essential that agencies and professional associations remain vigilant to ensure the well-being of people with mental retardation (Turnbull, 1986).

NEW ISSUES AND FUTURE DIRECTIONS

This volume, through all of its editions, has been based on the concept of human development. At this point in the text, you the reader are well aware that the life span in our interpretation begins at conception and terminates with death. These two boundaries of the life span—the very first and the very last phases—are stages where the future will witness the most dramatic ethical developments.

Chapters 6 and 7 examined the beginning of the life span, both in terms of normal development and for causation of mental retardation at this early stage. In many respects, this phase of the life cycle already presents society with extremely controversial ethical questions. At this phase we spoke of abortion, euthanasia, and withholding of treatment. Terminating pregnancy has been a known and practiced procedure for a very long time. Abortion, however, remains a volatile, controversial social question that continues to appear in the news and in the courts. It will continue to do so in the future as society remains uncertain where it stands.

Euthanasia and withholding of treatment will continue and become more acceptable as topics of public conversation. These issues were not openly discussed a few years ago, as Duff and Campbell's (1973) comment that such topics represented a "public taboo" shows. Even more recently, publication of papers by two of the current authors on these topics resulted in telephone calls criticizing them for discussing such issues publicly (Hardman & Drew, 1978, 1980). These topics will continue to be important ethical issues in the future, and our observations suggest that they will appear more openly in the literature (see Heifetz, 1989; Hollander, 1989; Wolfensberger, 1989).

Advances in medical technology are already presenting us with new and perhaps equally controversial topics for the first part of the life cycle. We are rapidly developing the capability to determine certain aspects of a person's genetic makeup through genetic engineering. This holds great potential for the prevention of those types of mental retardation that have known genetic causes. It also, however, presents a serious question that will emerge in the next wave of public awareness on such topics. To what degree is society ready to have some people determine the genetic makeup of others? This would certainly represent a kind of ultimate control. Genetic engineering will clearly raise new ethical issues.

The last phase of the life cycle will also present challenging issues in the future for workers in mental retardation. More than ever before, people who are mentally retarded are surviving to old age and becoming part of our growing elderly population. Questions about how society will care for these people are now being raised as ethical dilemmas (Howell, 1988). The issues of quality of life and dying with dignity will surface more publicly and test society's ability to understand the complete cycle of human development.

The future ethical issues in mental retardation will be many. We have only touched on some of the more controversial points. Those mentioned, at both ends of the life cycle, are truly life-and-death issues.

CORE QUESTIONS

1. How do utilitarianism and formalism relate to individual and societal rights in dealing with mental retardation?
2. How do genetic counseling and abortion relate to prevention of mental retardation?
3. Duff and Campbell (1973) have taken the position that if nontreatment of certain infants is in violation of the law, then the law should be changed. How does this position fit with formalist philosophy, and how does it fit with utilitarianist philosophy? What are your views, and why do you believe as you do?
4. It appears that selective nontreatment of defective infants is more common than the general public knows. Who should make these judgments, which are life-and-death decisions? On what basis(es) did you make your decision?
5. Special services for children with mental retardation often cost a great deal more than educational services for their nonretarded peers. To what degree do you think that parents of nonretarded children should be held responsible for the increased costs of educating mentally retarded children? On what basis do you believe as you do?

6. Sterilization of adults with mental retardation is often justified on the basis of the general welfare of society and the state. How might the best interests of the state and those of the individual be in conflict? Whose interests should prevail, and why?

7. How did early marriage laws related to people with mental retardation seem to place society's interests above those of the individual? Has this changed? Explain your reasoning in both cases.

8. How may scientific investigations aimed at improving the lot of those with mental retardation also be in conflict with their individual rights?

9. How does the interdisciplinary nature of the mental retardation field contribute to professional ethical difficulties?

ROUND TABLE DISCUSSION

Social and ethical issues related to mental retardation are complex and vary to some degree depending on the life cycle period being considered. In many ways, however, these questions can be reduced to the fundamental questions of individual versus societal rights embodied in utilitarianism and formalism. These perspectives are found in various forms throughout the study of mental retardation.

In your study group or on your own, examine mental retardation, considering both individual and societal interests. Think in terms of prevention of mental retardation, abortion, withholding of treatment, provision of service, sterilization, and research. Where do you stand philosophically? Does your position shift depending on age, topic, severity, or other basis(es)? Do you feel comfortable with your position(s)? Why?

REFERENCES

Baron, C. H. (1976). Voluntary sterilization of the mentally retarded. In A. Milunsky & G. J. Annas (Eds.), *Genetics and the law* (pp. 267–284). New York: Plenum.

Bass, M. S. (1967). Attitudes of parents of retarded children toward voluntary sterilization. *Eugenics Quarterly, 14,* 45–53.

Baumrind, D. (1985). Research using intentional deception: Ethical issues revisited. *American Psychologist, 40,* 165–174.

Boggs, E. M. (1986). Ethics in the middle of life. In P. R. Dokecki & R. M. Zaner (Eds.), *Ethics of dealing with persons with severe handicaps: Toward a research agenda* (pp. 1–15). Baltimore: Paul H. Brookes.

Burt, R. A. (1976). Authorizing death for anomalous newborns. In A. Milunsky & G. J. Annas (Eds.), *Genetics and the law* (pp. 435–450). New York: Plenum.

Butterfield, E. C. (1990). The compassion of distinguishing punishing behavioral treatment from aversive treatment. *American Journal on Mental Retardation, 95,* 137–142.

Cadkin, A. W., Ginsberg, N. A., Pergament, E., & Verlinski, Y. (1984). Chorionic villi sampling: A new technique for detection of genetic abnormalities in the first trimester. *Radiology, 151,* 159–162.

Chapman, J. W., & Pitceathly, A. S. (1985). Sexuality and mentally handicapped people: Issues of sex education, marriage, parenthood, and care staff attitudes. *Australia and New Zealand Journal of Developmental Disabilities, 11,* 227–235.

Diamond, E. F. (1977). The deformed child's right to life. In D. J. Horan & D. Mall (Eds.), *Death, dying, and euthanasia* (pp. 127–138). Washington, DC: University Publications of America.

Donnellan, A. M., LaVigna, G. W., Negri-Shoultz, N., & Fassbender, L. L. (1988). *Progress without punishment: Effective approaches for learners with behavior problems.* New York: Teachers College Press.

Drane, J. F. (1985). The many faces of competency. *Hastings Center Report, 15*(2), 17–26.

Drew, C. J., & Hardman, M. L. (1985). *Designing and conducting behavioral research.* New York: Pergamon.

Drew, C. J., & Turnbull, H. R., III. (1987). Whose ethics—whose code: An analysis of problems in interdisciplinary intervention. *Mental Retardation, 25,* 113–117.

Duff, R., & Campbell, A. (1973). Moral and ethical dilemmas in the special-care nursery. *New England Journal of Medicine, 289,* 890–894.

Fisher, K. (1986). Ethics in research: Having respect for the subject. *The APA Monitor, 17*(4), 1, 34–35.

Fletcher, G. P. (1968). Legal aspects of the decision not to prolong life. *Journal of the American Medical Association, 203,* 119–122.

Fletcher, J. (1973). Ethics and euthanasia. In R. H. Williams (Ed.), *To live and to die: When, why, and how* (pp. 113–122). New York: Springer.

Fletcher, J. (1975). Abortion, euthanasia, and care of defective newborns. *New England Journal of Medicine, 292,* 75–78.

Gaylin, W., & Macklin, R. (Eds.). (1982). *Who speaks for the child: The problems of proxy consent.* New York: Plenum.

Hardman, M. L., & Drew, C. J. (1977). The physically handicapped retarded individual: A review. *Mental Retardation, 15*(5), 43–48.

Hardman, M. L., & Drew, C. J. (1980). Parent consent and the practice of withholding treatment from the severely defective newborn. *Mental Retardation, 18,* 165–169.

Hardman, M. L., Drew, C. J., Egan, M. W., & Wolf, B. (1990). *Human exceptionality: Society, school, and family* (3rd ed.). Boston: Allyn & Bacon.

Harper, P. S. (1981). *Practical genetic counseling.* Baltimore: University Park Press.

Hauerwas, S. (1986). Suffering the retarded: Should we prevent retardation? In P. R. Dokecki & R. M. Zaner (Eds.), *Ethics of dealing with persons with severe handicaps: Toward a research agenda* (pp. 53–70). Baltimore: Paul H. Brookes.

Heifetz, L. J. (1989). From Munchausen to Cassandra: A critique of Hollander's "euthanasia and mental retardation." *Mental Retardation, 27,* 67–69.

Hollander, R. (1989). Euthanasia and mental retardation: Suggesting the unthinkable. *Mental Retardation, 27,* 53–61.

Horan, D. J., & Mall, D. (Eds.). (1977). *Death, dying, and euthanasia.* Washington, DC: University Publications of America.

Howell, M. C. (1988). Ethical dilemmas encountered in the care of those who are disabled and also old. *Educational Gerontology, 14,* 439–449.

Johnston, R. B. (1987). *Learning disabilities, medicine, and myth: A guide to understanding the child and the physician.* Boston: Little, Brown.

Krishef, C. H. (1972). State laws on marriage and sterilization of the mentally retarded. *Mental Retardation, 10*(3), 36–38.

Kunjukrishnan, R., & Varan, L. R. (1989). Interface between mental subnormality and law: A Review. *Psychiatric Journal of the University of Ottawa, 14,* 439–452.

LaVigna, G. W., & Donnellan, A. M. (1986). *Alternatives to punishment: Solving behavior problems with non-aversive strategies.* New York: Irvington.

Lusthaus, E. W. (1985). Involuntary euthanasia and current attempts to define persons with mental retardation as less than human. *Mental Retardation, 23,* 148–154.

Mackie, R. P., & Robbins, P. B. (1960). Exceptional children in local public schools. *School Life, 43,* 14–16.

Mulick, J. A. (1990). The ideology and science of punishment in mental retardation. *American Journal on Mental Retardation, 95,* 142–157.

Murdock, C. W. (1974). Sterilization of the retarded: A problem or a solution? *California Law Review, 62,* 917.

Narayanan, H. S., Madhu Rao, P., Subbakrishna, D. K., & Sridhara Rama Rao, B. S. (1987). Observation of mentally retarded cases with special reference to consanguinity. *NIMHANS, 5,* 121–123.

Nielsen, K. B. (1987). Fragile x syndrome: A new cause of mental retardation. *Skolepsykologi, 24,* 366–370.

Pearson, P. H., & Menefee, A. R. (1965). Medical and social management of the mentally retarded. *General Practitioner, 31,* 78–91.

Perone, N., Carpenter, R. J., & Robertson, J. A. (1984). Legal liability in the use of ultrasound by office-based obstetricians. *American Journal of Obstetrics and Gynecology, 150,* 801–804.

Pitceathly, A. S., & Chapman, J. W. (1985). Sexuality, marriage and parenthood of mentally retarded people. *International Journal for the Advancement of Counseling, 8,* 173–181.

Ramsey, P. (1973). Abortion. *Thomist, 37,* 174–226.

Reed, E. W., & Reed, S. C. (1965). *Mental retardation: A family study.* Philadelphia: W.B. Saunders.

Robertson, J. A. (1975). Involuntary euthanasia of defective newborns: A legal analysis. *Stanford Law Review, 27,* 213–269.

Shaw, A. (1977). Dilemmas of "informed consent" in children. In D. J. Horan & D. Mall (Eds.), *Death, dying, and euthanasia* (pp. 75–90). Washington, DC: University Publications of America.

Trice, A. D. (1986). Ethical variables? *American Psychologist, 41,* 482–483.

Turnbull, H. R., III. (Ed.). (1977). *Consent handbook.* Washington, DC: American Association on Mental Deficiency.

Turnbull, H. R., III. (1986). Public policy and professional behavior. *Mental Retardation, 24,* 265–275.

Wolfensberger, W. (1975). *The origin and nature of our institutional models.* Syracuse, NY: Human Policy.

Wolfensberger, W. (1989). The killing thought in the eugenic era and today: A commentary on Hollander's essay. *Mental Retardation, 27,* 63–65.

Zaner, R. M. (1986). Soundings from uncertain places: Difficult pregnancies and imperiled infants. In P. R. Dokecki & R. M. Zaner (Eds.), *Ethics of dealing with persons with severe handicaps: Toward a research agenda* (pp. 71–92). Baltimore: Paul H. Brookes.

CHAPTER FIFTEEN
Legal and Legislative Issues

<table>
<tr><td>

*Core
Concepts*

</td><td>

- The influence of legal and legislative activities has had a profound effect on the delivery of services for all disabled persons.
- The Constitution and the Bill of Rights do not specify whether education is a right or a privilege.
- Litigation over the past thirty years has had a direct impact on all aspects of special education programs and service-delivery models.
- *Brown v. Board of Education of Topeka* (1954) was the first time that education was unequivocally determined to be a right that was to be available to all persons on equal terms.
- Current legislation requires that all children be provided a free and appropriate education in the least restrictive setting.
- Legal and legislative activities have had both a positive and a negative impact on special education programs.

</td></tr>
</table>

Although our field's involvement in legal and legislative actions is relatively recent, there is little being proposed that is truly new. The primary change represents a belated recognition by society that exceptional persons have not been dealt with fairly and that "the right to be human, based upon principles of equality, is applicable to all individuals" (Drew, Hardman, & Bluhm, 1977, p. 101).

<table>
<tr><td>

*Core
Concept*

</td><td>

The influence of legal and legislative activities has had a profound effect on the delivery of services for all disabled persons.

</td></tr>
</table>

If a democratic society is to remain viable, there needs to be a direct correspondence between the laws of that society and the equal application of those laws to all citizens. The fact that this has not always been the case is apparent to anyone with even a cursory understanding of history. The question, however, is not whether a nation has fairly applied its laws, but whether it has ensured open access to the laws for redress of grievances, both for individuals and groups. Recent legislative and legal activity is evidence that the rights of the exceptional person have been recognized and responded to in a manner that has far-reaching implications for *all* people. But those concerned with the well-being of all citizens know that nothing is truly secure in a changing world. This is particularly true of the most fragile of all societal priorities—human rights. There are still people who think one group or another is of little consequence or importance. History should have taught us that such attitudes eventually undermine the rights and freedoms of everyone. A long-delayed beginning has been made, but there must be a continued and vigilant involvement by all persons concerned for humanity.

This chapter examines some of the historical antecedents that have influenced recent legislation and court decisions, provides a review of current legislation, and identifies some of the legal issues concerning education that will be of continuing concern.

HISTORICAL ANTECEDENTS

Core Concept	*The Constitution and the Bill of Rights do not specify whether education is a right or a privilege.*

All constitutional concerns about education come under the framework of promoting health, morals, comfort, and general welfare. The purposes of education have been many and varied; they have been influenced by many factors, such as the prevailing philosophies of the times, economics, and changing political inclinations. There has been a general agreement that schools are responsible for preparing students to take their place in society. The New Hampshire Supreme Court in *Fogg v. Board of Education* (1912) indicated that the purpose of school was the education of citizens for societal needs and that school was more a duty than a right.

Rulings like *Fogg* laid the groundwork for later court decisions that further delineated the states' responsibility toward all citizens in regard to education. Public education functions as an arm of the state and provides for the education of future citizens. Such delegation of power places education squarely in the center of the political process and all of its related pressures. This is evident both from our history and from recent laws that have been enacted by federal and state legislatures. Schools are both a social institution and a governmental agency and are thereby affected by society's awareness of needs as expressed by changing political climates.

Core Concept	*Litigation over the past thirty years has had a direct impact on all aspects of special education programs and service-delivery models.*

There has been a fairly long history of actions by the federal government that relate to handicapped people. Some factors that have directly influenced the current state of affairs need to be mentioned. Since World War II, there has been a decided change in the legislative and legal involvement in special education generally and for people with mental retardation in particular. This involvement has included a variety of individuals and groups and has been influenced by many factors, including: (1) the impact of barbaric practices toward minorities in Nazi Germany; (2) the many maimed and crippled soldiers returning from World War II, the Korean conflict, and the Vietnam War; (3) economic prosperity; (4) a national recognition that disability does not mean lack of worth to either the community or the individual; (5) the involvement of parent groups; and (6) significant advances in medical and social sciences. Additional impetus has come from the highly visible accomplishments of individuals disabled in some way, for example, Helen Keller and President Franklin D. Roosevelt. The exposure and acceptance of mental retardation has been aided by public knowledge about the presence of the condition in families of public figures. We know, for example, about President Kennedy's sister, Senator Hubert Humphrey's granddaughter, and Senator S. I. Hayakawa's son, all of whom have mental retardation. All of these influences have interacted to heighten public awareness of handicapping conditions.

LITIGATION

Litigation regarding students' education has a very long history in the United States. For the most part, the outcomes of court cases have reflected prevailing societal philosophies. In the mid-20th century, a philosophical shift was under way that had an important impact on education for handicapped people. Two legal cases during this time are of particular importance: *Beattie v. State Board of Education, City of Antigo,* (1950) and *State Board of Education v. in Re: Petty* (1950). Although neither of these cases involved persons with mental retardation, they are important as precedents.

The first case, *Beattie v. State Board of Education, City of Antigo,* concerned a boy with cerebral palsy who was excluded from a public school class because of his condition, which,

The courts have been very important in shaping services for those with mental retardation.

it was argued, caused a depressing effect on classmates and teachers. The public schools had recommended placement in a school for deaf and speech-defective children and refused his enrollment in the regular school program. The boy rejected such placement and was supported in his decision by his parents. An appeal was made to the local school superintendent, who asked for a ruling from the state superintendent of public instruction for Wisconsin. After no firm direction was given by the state superintendent, the school refused to allow the boy to enroll in the public school. The critically important factor in this case was the action of the jury in the municipal court of Antigo, Wisconsin. The jury ruled in favor of reinstating the boy in the public school. This decision signaled a change in that the rights of a student took precedence over the traditional view favoring segregation of "defective" children. Although this decision was overruled on appeal to the Wisconsin Supreme Court, an important dissenting opinion was written. It was based on two reasons that later became significant: (1) that the school board should yield to public opinion as represented by the municipal court jury, and (2) that the boy's physical appearance and related behaviors (cerebral palsy) did not have a harmful effect or infringe on other children's right to an education.

The second case (*State Board of Education v. in Re: Petty* [1950]) occurred in Iowa. In this case an argument almost diametrically opposed to that of *Beattie* was heard. The school board sought permission from the parents to place their child in a school that would best meet his educational needs. The court decision directed the parents to place the boy, who was deaf, in the state school for the deaf. The parents refused and instead placed him in a rural school near where they lived. An appeal was presented before the Iowa Supreme Court based on the parents' contention that the lower court had not shown that the boy could not be educated in the public rural school. After expert testimony the Iowa Supreme Court unanimously ruled that the boy would have to be enrolled in the school for the deaf. This case is important in that it established a handicapped child's right to an appropriate education.

Core Concept	Brown v. Board of Education of Topeka *(1954) was the first time that education was unequivocally determined to be a right that was to be available to all persons on equal terms.*

A dramatic sequence of events in 1954 had far-reaching effects on education. In *Brown v. Board of Education of Topeka* (1954), the issue was segregation and "equal opportunity." The U.S. Supreme Court, in reaching its decision, stated:

> Today education is perhaps the most important function of state and local governments. Compulsory school attendance laws and the great expenditure for education both demonstrate our recognition of the importance of education to our democratic society. . . . In these days, it is doubtful that any child may reasonably be expected to succeed in life if he is denied the opportunity of an education. Such an opportunity, where the State has undertaken to provide it, is a right which must be made available to all on equal terms. . . . We conclude that in the field of public education the doctrine of "separate but equal" has no place. Separate educational facilities are inherently unequal. Therefore, we hold that the plaintiffs and others similarly situated for whom actions have been brought are, by reason of the

segregation complained of, deprived of the equal protection of the laws guaranteed by the Fourteenth Amendment. (p. 492)

Brown has had a profound effect on special education. Its importance rests primarily with the fact that the decision stated unequivocally that education is a "right" that must be "available to all on equal terms." This decision removes any argument that education is a privilege and in effect opened the doors to all children for a free and appropriate public education. Subsequent legislation, such as Public Laws 93-380, 94-142, and 101-336 (discussed in a later section), has supported the rights of handicapped people by protecting them against discrimination solely on the basis of handicapping condition. This legislative activity has emphasized such areas as access to public facilities, procedural due process, least restrictive placement, free and appropriate education, and nondiscriminatory evaluation.

Over the years many court cases have involved special education either directly or indirectly. These cases have focused on matters relating to architectural barriers, classification, commitment to institutions, criminal law, custody, education, employment, guardianship, intelligence testing, limitation of treatment, sterilization, voting, and zoning. The status of court cases in these areas has been reported at various times in journals like *Mental Retardation and the Law, Exceptional Children,* and *Education of the Handicapped Law Review.*

In 1967, in *Hobson v. Hansen,* Judge J. Skelly Wright ruled that placing children in different tracks based on performance tests during their early school years violated the equal-protection clause of the Constitution. In reviewing this case Judge Wright found that there was a disproportionate number of blacks in special education relative to their prevalence in the community. He stated:

The evidence shows that the method by which track assignments are made depends essentially on standardized aptitude tests which, although given on a system-wide basis, are completely inappropriate for use with a large segment of the student body. Because these tests are primarily standardized on and are relevant to a white middle class group of students, they produce inaccurate and misleading test scores when given to lower class and Negro children. As a result, rather than being classified according to ability to learn, these students are in reality being classified according to their socioeconomic and psychological factors which have nothing to do with innate ability. (p. 514)

On appeal, in *Smuck v. Hobson* (1969), the appellate court supported Judge Wright's ruling abolishing tracking in District of Columbia public schools.

One of the first cases involving classes for youngsters with mental retardation was heard in the Superior Court of Orange County, California (*Arreola v. Board of Education,* 1968). Suit was brought on behalf of 11 Mexican-American children. It sought to prohibit special education classes for those who were educably mentally retarded unless the following three conditions were met: (1) a hearing was held before placement (due process), (2) intelligence tests allowed for cultural differences, and (3) the curriculum was educationally sound and retesting was periodically scheduled. The judge ruled in favor of the plaintiffs.

Beginning in 1970 a number of other cases were contested in the courts that involved classes for students with mental retardation. In *Spangler v. Pasadena Board of Education* (1970), the U.S. District Court for the Southern District of California found that the Pasadena schools had several problems including: (1) a racial imbalance in both faculties and student bodies; (2) use of intelligence tests that were both inaccurate and unfair; and (3) increased segregation by a disproportionate number of black students' being assigned to "slow" classes. A case filed in the Massachusetts federal District Court in the same year (*Stewart v. Phillips,* 1971) also related to testing and minority students. In this case, for the first time, monetary damages were included in the grievance of the plaintiffs, who were poor and black. It was alleged that pupils had been irreparably harmed when they had been placed in classes for mentally retarded children based on a single IQ score from a discriminatory test.

The U.S. District Court for the Northern District of California concluded that nine Mexican-American children had been denied equal educational opportunity in *Diana v. State Board of Education.* The plaintiffs maintained that they had been placed in classes for educable mentally retarded children on the basis of culturally biased intelligence tests. Since the children were from homes in which Spanish was spoken, it was argued that discrimination had occurred because the children were tested in English and tests had been standardized on children whose first language was English. Certain conditions were agreed upon for future direction in special education decisions: (1) if the home language was other than English, the child must be tested in both English and the home language; (2) testing was to be restricted to tests or test sections that did not include "unfair" verbal questions; (3) children whose primary language was not English and who had already been placed in classes for mentally retarded youngsters must be retested; (4) all school districts had to provide both information about retesting and a plan to assist children to return to the regular program; (5) IQ tests were to be revised and normed for Mexican-American children; and (6) if a significant difference existed between the percentage of Mexican-American pupils in classes for children with retardation and in the school as a whole, a written explanation for this difference must be provided.

Covarrubias v. San Diego Unified School District (1971) was a related and essentially a follow-up case. This case was filed on behalf of 17 minority students enrolled in classes for educable mentally retarded children in the San Diego school district. The basis for the case was also denial of equal education because of the cultural bias of intelligence tests. In this case monetary damages were requested, as they had been in *Stewart v. Phillips* (1971). The rationale for this request was that the school district had deprived the students of equal protection under the law. It was further requested that special education classes be discontinued until testing approaches could be altered to account for cultural influences.

During 1970 the Association of Black Psychologists asked the San Francisco school board to impose a moratorium on both intelligence and ability testing of black children. The basis for their request was the inappropriate design, construction, and standardization of certain tests used with black children. This issue was brought to the courts in *Larry P. v. Riles* (1972). In this case, a class action suit, the plaintiffs contended that the tests used were discriminatory when used to place and maintain minority children in classes for students with mental retardation. This case was filed on behalf of six black elementary school–aged children in San Francisco. The plaintiffs argued that the children were not mentally retarded but were victims of tests that failed to account for their ethnic background. The lawyers requested that the public schools be required to do the following: (1) assess black children with tests that would take into account their cultural background; (2) prevent placement of black children in special classes on the basis of inappropriate tests; (3) direct San Francisco public schools to reevaluate all black children presently enrolled in classes for children with mental retardation using nondiscriminatory tests; (4) remove any record of the plaintiffs' ever having been in classes for mentally retarded children; (5) require the schools to ensure that the distribution of blacks in special education classes for children with retardation be proportional to the number of black children in the total population; and (6) declare that the assignment of black children on the basis of discriminatory tests was a violation of the Fourteenth Amendment to the Constitution.

In 1972, a preliminary injunction was issued in *Larry P.,* stating that black children could not be placed in classes for youngsters who were educably mentally retarded on the basis of IQ tests as traditionally administered. This preliminary injunction supported the six points made by the plaintiffs. In 1979, on appeal of *Larry P.,* the court ruled in favor of the plaintiffs. The court held that the defendants had placed a disproportionate number of black children in classes for educably mentally retarded youngsters.

In a case related to *Larry P. v. Riles,* IQ test items were not found to be discriminatory against black children. In *Parents in Action on Special Education (PASE) v. Hannon* (1980), the judge concluded that he differed with Judge Peckham of the *Larry P.* case because the tests had not been adequately analyzed. The court also found that only one Stanford-Binet test item and eight test items on the WISC and WISC-R were biased against black children. It was argued that these few test items did not make the tests unfair or have a significant effect on the child's score.

Three of the more important cases concerned with providing free and appropriate education for handicapped youngsters have been *Pennsylvania Association for Retarded Children (PARC) v. Commonwealth of Pennsylvania* (1972), *Mills v. Board of Education of the District of Columbia* (1972), and *Battle v. Commonwealth of Pennsylvania* (1980). Referring to the precedent set in *Brown* (1954), the courts in the first two cases ruled that when a state has assumed the responsibility to provide public education, it must make it available to all on equal terms. In *PARC* the court ruled that Pennsylvania had a constitutional duty to provide a free public education to all retarded children in the Commonwealth. Further, the court reasoned that because all children with mental retardation can benefit from educational and training programs, there was no rationale for exclusion of such children from the educational system. This case has caused a number of similar class action suits, which collectively led Congress to enact Public Law 93-380, the Education Amendments of 1974.

In *Mills v. Board of Education of the District of Columbia* (1972) the court ruled that the board of education had the obligation to provide specialized education that would benefit the child. The court further held that to deny educational opportunity to handicapped children is a violation of due process of law. Therefore, it is illegal to suspend, expel, or reassign children without prior hearing or periodic review.

The issue of extending the school year for some handicapped children was addressed in *Battle v. Commonwealth of Pennsylvania* (1980). It was argued that pupils who were either severely or profoundly impaired or severely emotionally disturbed often required a longer school year because of the learning regression that occurs during summer vacations. The court ruled that the school year could be extended based on the free and appropriate education provision of the Education of the Handicapped Act when required on an individualized education plan (IEP). In *Georgia Association for Retarded Citizens v. McDaniel* (1981) the issue of an extended school year again came up. The court ruled in favor of an extended school year, if justified. The case was appealed to the U.S. Supreme Court, which refused to hear arguments, leaving the lower court's decision standing.

Other cases related to education that have been landmark court actions include: *Wyatt v. Stickney* (1972), *Jackson v. Indiana* (1972), *Souder v. Brennan* (1973), and *Wyatt v. Aderholt* (1974). In *Wyatt v. Stickney* (1972) it was established that the mentally ill had the right to treatment in the least restrictive environment. This includes the right to (1) an individualized treatment program, (2) an environment that is psychologically and physically humane, (3) qualified and adequate staff, and (4) programs offered in the least restrictive way possible. The case that ensured due process in institutional commitment was *Jackson v. Indiana* (1972). The court ruled that committing a person to an agency (such as a state institution or a mental hospital) until recovery could, in effect, be a life sentence without recourse to appeal. Such action was considered a denial of both equal protection and due process. It was the court's decision that persons not competent to stand trial must either be released or be civilly committed. In a related case it was ruled that people in state institutions could not be subjected to involuntary servitude (*Souder v. Brennan* [1973]). It was required that work records of patient-laborers in state institutions be kept and that their rights be explained to them.

Since the mid-1960s there has been a series of cases establishing the right to treatment for those who are mentally ill and mentally retarded in state institutions. One such case, *Pennhurst State School v. Halderman* (1981), eventually reached the U.S. Supreme Court. In this case, the trial court judge had found that people with mental retardation had a constitutional right to appropriate treatment in the setting that least restricted personal freedom. The judge ordered the state school for those with mental retardation to be closed, arguing that it was too restrictive a setting for minimally adequate treatment. On appeal, the court found that the substantive rights of people with mental retardation were enforceable and that Pennhurst State School had violated those rights. The U.S. Supreme Court (1981) reversed the court of appeals' decision. In so doing the Supreme Court interpreted Public Law 94-103, the Developmentally Disabled Assistance and Bill of Rights Act of 1974, as a funding bill rather than an act requiring enforcement of the provisions of the Fourteenth Amendment. Further, the Court stated that they found nothing in the act (P.L. 94-103) that required states to provide funding for federally mandated programs such as appropriate treatment in the least restrictive environment for individuals with mental retardation.

The public schools have also been involved in litigation because of claims that proper services were not being provided. In *Hendrick Hudson District Board of Education v. Rowley* (1982), the issue was whether a severely hearing-impaired child should be provided with a sign-language interpreter in academic classes. Her IEP stipulated that she be enrolled in the regular program, be provided a hearing aid, given speech therapy, and receive additional instruction from a tutor of the deaf. Her parents argued that she also needed a sign-language interpreter. School officials maintained that such an interpreter was not required because she was making satisfactory social and academic progress. The U.S. Supreme Court decided that a free and appropriate education was being provided by the personalized program that had been developed along with necessary supplementary services. Further, the court reasoned that a law cannot and does not guarantee that schools maximize the potential of handicapped children, but only that they make public education available to all.

The case of *Irving Independent School District v. Tatro* (1984) concerned an eight-year-old girl with spina bifida. She needed a catheter replaced every three to four hours in order to be able to stay in school. The public schools contended that such a procedure was a medical service and was not required under Public Law 94-142. The U.S. Supreme Court agreed to hear the case and decided that replacement of the catheter could be done by a school nurse or a trained layperson; it was not a medical service per se. The court contended that to do otherwise would deny the child access to an education in the least restrictive setting.

Smith v. Robinson (1984) was a case that questioned whether parents could be reimbursed for attorney's fees in a successful law suit. The Supreme Court upheld a lower court ruling that Congress had intended that Public Law 94-142 be the only law to protect the rights of handicapped individuals. Since it did not provide for attorney's fees, parents could not use other laws to gain payment of attorney's fees. It should be noted that the Congress reacted to this ruling by passing Public Law 99-372, the Handicapped Children's Protection Act of 1986, which is discussed in the section on legislation.

The U.S. Supreme Court also heard *Burlington School Committee of the Town of Burlington v. Department of Education of the Commonwealth of Massachusetts* (1985). This case questioned whether public schools were obligated to pay for private schooling for a pupil whose parents placed the child in a private facility while the case was still under review. The court ruled in favor of the parents, indicating that to do otherwise would be in violation of a free appropriate public education for the child and would lessen the parents' right to participate in developing an IEP. However, parents who unilaterally place their child in a separate program may be reimbursed for the expense only if the private educational program is subsequently approved through appeal (Goldberg, 1986). For a follow-up on subsequent court cases related to payment of attorney's fees the reader is directed to Yell and Espin (1990).

FEDERAL LEGISLATION

As a result of the court cases reviewed in the preceding section, Congress has enacted a number of laws that are having a tremendous impact on education. In this section we review major legislation passed by Congress, particularly two major public laws that are of particular importance to special education, Public Laws 93-380 and 94-142.

Legislation, 1965–1973

Our review of federal legislation beginning with 1965 does not suggest that legislation passed before that date is unimportant. Indeed, laws passed before 1965 have had significant effects on educational provisions for handicapped youngsters and on the establishment of vocational rehabilitation programs. With respect to mental retardation, certainly Public Laws 85-926 (1958) and 88-164 (1963) were indications of increased federal involvement in these areas. However, it was not until the early 1960s that legislation that had profound impact nationally was enacted at the federal level.

Federal aid to education became a fact of life beginning in the mid-1960s with Public Law 89-10, the Elementary and Secondary Education Act (ESEA) of 1965. This statute represented, for the first time, a commitment by the federal government to improve public school education in the United States. It included assistance to local public schools for meeting the needs of children designated as "educationally deprived." A companion bill enacted in 1965, Public Law 89-313, amended a section (Title I) of Public Law 89-10 and provided for support of children in state-operated (or state-supported) schools serving handicapped individuals, which had not been included for funding purposes under the original act.

ESEA was amended again in 1967 in Public Law 89-750. A section (Title VI) of the act made funds available to states in order to expand programs and better meet the needs of handicapped children. Also under this amendment, the National Advisory Committee on Handicapped Children was instituted to advise the commissioner of education. During this period Congress established the Bureau of Education for the Handicapped (BEH) as the office responsible for administering all educational programs for those with handicaps.

In 1967 ESEA was amended yet again to provide more programs for handicapped individuals (see P.L. 90-247). It was recognized that , despite passage of ESEA, a number of handicapped students were still being excluded. Therefore, the amendments in Public Law 90-247 specifically designated funds for those with handicaps and for assisting state education agencies to expand their programs for handicapped youngsters. In the Vocational Education Amendment of 1968 (P.L. 90-576), Congress required that at least 10% of each state's vocational education funds coming from the federal government be allocated for handicapped individuals.

Experimental preschools and early education programs for handicapped children were highlighted in 1968 with the passage of Public Law 90-538, the Handicapped Children's Early Education Assistance Act. Also in 1969, Public Law 91-60 was passed, establishing a National Center on Educational Media and Materials for the Handicapped. A direct precursor to Public Laws 93-380 and 94-142 was Public Law 91-230 (1970), particularly the amendment creating the Education of the Handicapped Act (EHA) (1971). Part B of EHA provided grants to states to assist their initiation, expansion, and improvement of programs for the education of handicapped children.

Public Law 91-517 (1970), the Developmental Disabilities Services and Facilities Construction Act, was oriented toward the broader area of developmental problems and away from traditional special education categories. This act was for the purpose of assisting the states to provide necessary community services and to construct facilities to carry out state plans. In addition, Public Law 93-112, the Rehabilitation Amendments of 1973, extended and recodified the Vocational Rehabilitation Act Amendments first passed in 1943 (P.L. 78-113). In the 1973 amendments Congress included a section that prohibits discrimination on the basis of mental or physical disability (Section 504). This law affects every federally assisted program or activity in the United States. Major features of this law include:

1. Requiring state rehabilitation agencies to give priority to individuals with the most severe handicaps and to expand and improve services to these individuals
2. Instituting written rehabilitation programs for clients
3. Authorizing states to develop a Consolidated Rehabilitation Developmental Disabilities Plan
4. Studying the role of sheltered workshops for rehabilitation and employment of handicapped individuals
5. Studying the coordination of programs for handicapped people
6. Forbidding discrimination against qualified handicapped persons in federally assisted programs
7. Establishing a federal Interagency Committee on Handicapped Employees
8. Providing a client assistance program
9. Developing an interagency board to assure compliance with the Architectural Barriers Act of 1968 (P.L. 90-480)

The final regulations for this law were in effect June 3, 1977. By July 5, 1977, all institutions receiving financial assistance from the Department of Health, Education and Welfare (HEW) were required to return an assurance of compliance with regard to this law. During the balance of 1977 all agencies submitted data testifying that (1) existing facilities would be accessible to handicapped people, (2) agencies that receive funds from HEW and that employ 15 or more persons did not discriminate on the basis of handicap, and (3) any structural changes required in existing facilities would be identified and a plan developed to ensure completion of such changes. During 1978 it was required that all agencies receiving HEW funds were to evaluate themselves as to their accommodation, with respect to both programs and accessibility, for handicapped individuals. Also, all public schools were required to provide a free, appropriate education for all qualified handicapped children by September 1, 1978.

Legislation, 1974–1990

This section reviews the public laws that have had and will continue to have a significant impact on education and our society in the coming years. The laws have historical references stemming from the needs identified in programs, legislation, and court decisions.

Public Law 93-380: Education Amendments of 1974
Public Law 93-380 extended and amended the Elementary and Secondary Education Act of 1965 (P.L. 89-10), its subsequent amendments, the Education of the Handicapped Act

(P.L. 91-230), and a number of other education statutes emanating from Congress. This public law had significant implications for those with handicaps. It included provisions for significantly increased funding to assist states in meeting the right to education requirements imposed by courts and legislatures. It also required states to develop plans for implementing educational opportunities for all handicapped children, including procedural safeguards to prevent discrimination in identification, evaluation, and placement of handicapped youngsters, and the retention of handicapped students in regular classrooms whenever possible. Additionally, Public Law 93-380 included sections on aid to state-supported schools; this provision allowed handicapped children in an appropriate program to be counted as one-and-a-half children for budget purposes and permitted up to 20% of funding for adult education to be used for educational programs for institutionalized persons.

Public Law 93-383, Housing and Community Development Act of 1974
In Public Law 93-383 the 93rd Congress revised all major housing legislation. Several aspects of this law had an impact on handicapped people. It included provisions assuring that handicapped individuals, along with elderly people, received financial assistance from the Department of Housing and Urban Development (HUD) in leasing and/or purchasing adequate housing. HUD was also authorized to award grants for special demonstration projects that designed housing for persons with special needs.

Public Law 93-156, Rehabilitation Act Amendments of 1974
This legislation authorized the president to call a White House conference to investigate the problems of handicapped citizens and to propose administrative and legislative recommendations for handling these problems. This law also included several amendments to the rehabilitation legislation, such as providing a broader definition of the word *handicapped*. The definitional emphasis changed from a focus on handicaps related to employment or vocational objectives to a view of functional limitations in one or more of a person's main life activities. The law also required that vocational rehabilitation clients have the opportunity to be involved in decisions affecting their programs. Finally, the requirements for written rehabilitation plans were refined.

Public Law 93-647, Social Service Amendments of 1974
Public Law 93-647 involved a complete revision of federal and state social services program agreements. The following goals were set forth relative to handicapped people: (1) economic self-support to prevent, reduce, or eliminate dependency; (2) self-sufficiency to reduce and prevent dependency; (3) prevention of abuse, neglect, or exploitation of both children and adults unable to protect themselves; (4) provision of community-based, home-based, or other less intensive and more natural care of individuals to prevent inappropriate institutional care; and (5) referral, admission, and other services to institutionalized persons when other types of care are not feasible or appropriate.

The law also specified requirements for state submission of plans to HEW that included: (1) fair hearing restrictions of client information, (2) identification of responsible state agencies, and (3) other factors that would ensure proper care of persons being served by vocational rehabilitation programs. Lack of state compliance could result in termination or withholding of a percentage of federal funds.

Public Law 94-103, Developmentally Disabled Assistance and Bill of Rights Act of 1974

This act significantly amended early legislation by (1) broadening the term *developmental disabilities;* (2) extending formula grant supports to states and grants to university-affiliated centers; and (3) requiring grant recipients to take affirmative action in employing and promoting qualified handicapped persons. The act also specified actions to be taken in protecting the rights of persons with developmental disabilities.

Core Concept	*Current legislation requires that all children be provided a free and appropriate education in the least restrictive setting.*

Public Law 94-142, Education for All Handicapped Children Act of 1975

The enactment of this law represented a culmination of legal and legislative activities by both parents and professionals. In many ways it is a continuation of what Dimond (1973) called "the quiet revolution," which had its beginnings in the civil rights movement of the 1950s. Public Law 94-142 did not represent a totally new concept relative to requirements or the involvement of the federal government in determining rights to education. In fact, this legislation included much of what had been in the Education Amendments of 1974 (P.L. 93-380) and in Section 504 of the Rehabilitation Amendments of 1973 (P.L. 93-112). Public Law 94-142 builds on previous actions and underscores the notion that education is a *right* for handicapped people.

Public Law 94-142 was signed by President Ford on November 28, 1975, after it received overwhelming congressional support (Senate vote 87 to 7; House vote 404 to 7). The Education for All Handicapped Children Act has four major purposes.

1. *Full education opportunities.*   The goal is to provide all handicapped children with a free and appropriate education. Priorities are given to children not being served and to children who are severely handicapped.
2. *Procedural safeguards.*   The act specifies policies and procedures for safeguarding the due process rights of parents and children. Similarly, educational agencies are protected by the same procedural safeguards. These safeguards include:
   a. The right to be fully informed and included in all decisions about identification, evaluation, educational planning and programming, and program evaluation
   b. The assurance that placement decisions will not be based on biased or discriminatory data
   c. The assurance that educational placement will be in the least restrictive setting, with nonhandicapped children whenever and wherever possible
   d. The right to access to and control over all educational records, with assurance of the confidentiality of such information

e. The right to appeal decisions made by the schools regarding any facet of the child's educational program

f. The right to obtain an independent evaluation of the child

g. The child's right to be represented by surrogate parents for those children who are wards of the state or whose parents or guardians are unknown or not available

h. The right to an impartial hearing regarding program disputes between the parents or child and the school

3. *Appropriate education.*   To ensure that each eligible handicapped child receives an appropriate education, the law requires that an individualized education program (IEP) be developed. The criteria for eligibility apply to children who meet the statutory definition and who are in need of special education or related services. The definition in Section 4 of the Act includes children who are mentally retarded, hard of hearing, deaf, orthopedically impaired, other health impaired, speech impaired, visually impaired, severely emotionally disturbed, and children with specific learning disabilities who are in need of special education and related services. Not all children who are disabled, however, need or require special education, since some can successfully attend school without additional assistance. An IEP is not required for these children.

The IEP is one of the most critical components of Public Law 94-142. It is a plan of action and a statement of goals for the child, developed by the school in conjunction with the parents of the child. It is not a contract, although school districts are legally responsible for ensuring that special educational services are provided. The IEP is not a day-by-day instructional map, but a plan that delineates needed special educational services that are appropriate for the child.

4. *State assistance.*   To implement Public Law 94-142, the federal government will provide supplementary monies, guidelines, and technical assistance to state and local educational agencies. The purpose of this assistance is to ensure that an equal educational opportunity is provided for all handicapped children needing services. Subsidies under Public Law 94-142 are based on the excess cost of educating children in special education and providing related services.

During the 1977–1978 school year, all states in compliance with the law received assistance based on the number of children (aged three through 21 years) receiving services. Additional allocations were possible for service provisions for preschool handicapped children. A ceiling on the number of handicapped children (aged five through 17 years) was set at 12% for each state. Federal financial assistance to the states is based on a payment formula that specifies a gradually increasing percentage. The formula was derived from the national average expenditure per child multiplied by the number of handicapped children in each state who receive special education and related services that are publicly augmented.

Public Law 95-602, the Rehabilitation Comprehensive Services and Developmental Disabilities Act Amendments of 1978

This act changed the criteria to be used in defining a developmental disability. No longer would a categorical disability (like mental retardation) suffice. Henceforth, the chronic nature and severity were used along with three or more functional limitations (for example, capacity for independent living, economic self-sufficiency, learning, mobility, self-care, self-direction, and receptive and expressive language) in defining disability. In addition, the law required that states select priorities to be emphasized in providing services (case management, child development, and so on). Grant funds were to be tied to the service-delivery pattern chosen by each state.

Public Law 97-35, Omnibus Budget Reconciliation Act of 1981

This act reduced federal funding for domestic programs and emphasized defense spending. The effect was to hold special education (and other related areas) funding levels constant from 1981 through 1984. The act also discontinued financial support for many services needed by persons who were mentally retarded. For example, home services, respite care, habilitation services, and so forth, were no longer supported by federal funds. Those states requesting waivers had to show that such care was less expensive than what could be provided in an institution.

Public Law 99-372, Handicapped Children's Protection Act of 1986

This act came in response to the dissenting opinion of three Supreme Court Justices in *Smith v. Robinson* (1984). There are three major parts to this law: (1) allowing courts to award reasonable attorney's fees to parents (or guardians) of a handicapped child if the parents' suit is successful; (2) allowing parents to utilize previous laws (Section 504 of the Rehabilitation Act and Section 1988 of the Civil Rights Act) in protecting the rights of handicapped children; and (3) allowing for payment of fees in cases that occurred prior to *Smith v. Robinson* (1984).

Public Law 99-457, Education of the Handicapped Amendments of 1986

This legislation extended the provisions contained in the 1975 Education of the Handicapped Act (P.L. 94-142). Additionally, these amendments provide full service programs for infants and toddlers (birth through two years of age) and for preschool handicapped children (three to five years of age).

Public Law 101-336, Americans with Disabilities Act of 1990

This act is being acclaimed as an historic breakthrough for persons with disabilities. It is comparable to Public Law 94-142 in its importance and impact in extending federal civil rights protection to Americans with disabilities, including AIDS. Handicapped people now have the same rights against discrimination in jobs, accommodations, transportation, and services that have been previously extended to minorities, women, and the elderly.

There are four parts to the law as passed by Congress and signed by President Bush:

1. *Employment.*   Beginning on July 26, 1992, employers, employment agencies, labor organizations, or joint labor management committees may not discriminate against any qualified individual with a disability with respect to any term, condition, or privilege of employment. Employers having 15 or more employees may not discriminate against qualified individuals with disabilities. Until that date only employers

with 25 or more employees are affected. In addition, employers must make reasonable accommodations for disabled applicants or employees. Private clubs and religious organizations are not affected by this provision.

2. *Public accommodations.* Public accommodations must not discriminate on the basis of disability as of July 26, 1992. This includes all public facilities—restaurants, theaters, hotels, libraries, child-care centers, and so on. Alterations to public places must be made to ensure that they are accessible to the disabled. This includes the removal of physical barriers in existing facilities and ensuring that bathrooms, telephones, drinking fountains, and other amenities are accessible to handicapped individuals if the cost is not unreasonable. New construction of office buildings must be made accessible. Elevators are not required for buildings three stories or less or smaller than 3,000 square feet per floor unless the building is a shopping center or the professional office of a health-care provider.

3. *Transportation.* Any buses or public rail vehicles ordered after August 26, 1990 must be accessible to handicapped people. If a disabled person cannot use a scheduled bus route, that person must be provided special transportation services. By July 26, 1995, all rail systems are to have one car per train that is accessible by handicapped individuals. Any new bus stations must be accessible, and renovations to existing stations must ensure handicapped access. Renovations are to include accessibility to needed facilities (bathroom, telephones, drinking fountains) as long as the costs are not out of line with the overall costs of the renovations. For public rail systems their "key stations" must be accessible by July 26, 1993, unless an extension is granted. Amtrak stations must be accessible by July 26, 2010.

   Privately owned buses and van companies must order handicapped-accessible vehicles after July 26, 1996 (a year later for small companies). Like public companies, private facilities must be made accessible to handicapped individuals.

4. *Operations of state and local governments.* Discrimination against qualified handicapped persons by state and local governments will not be allowed. In addition, all government facilities must be accessible to handicapped people as required by section 504 of the Rehabilitation Amendments (1973).

5. *Telecommunications relay services.* Companies providing telephone service to the public must provide telephone relay services to persons using telecommunications equipment for the deaf (TDDs) or similar equipment.

NEW ISSUES AND FUTURE DIRECTIONS

In earlier editions of this book we described advances made on behalf of people with disabilities and pointed out that the legal consequences had many far-reaching implications for our society. The involvement of the legal profession and legislative bodies with education was highlighted as an example of a multidisciplinary interaction that had been used to end discrimination toward handicapped people. As we know, the treatment of persons with mental retardation has been exclusionary and has denied them their rights as citizens. The actions of the federal government in passing landmark legislation (such as P.L. 94-142 and P.L. 101-336) has gone a long way to provide the same rights to those with handicaps that other citizens enjoy.

Core Concept	*Legal and legislative activities have had both a positive and a negative impact on special education programs.*

However, the passing of laws and various court actions are only one part of the solution. Prasse (1988) discusses the overall effect of litigation on special education. He recognizes the contributions that the courts have made in addressing problems in education, but states that there has been a resulting price, both monetarily and psychologically. Prasse lists three negative aspects of litigation: (1) lack of educational expertise in the judiciary, (2) cost of litigation, and (3) length of litigation. Further, the legal process, involving lay judges and juries, does not always appreciate that answers to scientific questions are not readily available.

MacMillan, Hendrick, and Watkins (1988) have questioned the overall impact of past court cases (like *Diana* and *Larry P.*) and of Public Law 94-142 on children who are lower achievers. They believe that the law has given the appearance of redressing past problems, but that educators are still unsuccessful in teaching many children from low socioeconomic areas, whatever the label. Additionally, the press for excellence in our public schools has been directed toward children with average and particularly above average academic ability, and the effect on lower functioning children is not yet known. MacMillan et al. (1988) state that successful educational programs for children of families with lower socioeconomic status are as far off today as they were before all the litigation and the enactment of Public Law 94-142. In a similar vein Taylor (1990) discusses the impact of the *Larry P.* decision on intelligence testing and overrepresentation of minorities in special education programs. He maintains that we should focus on the discriminatory use of intelligence test scores rather than looking for bias in intelligence tests per se. Taylor maintains that the act of declassifying a student who is labeled mildly mentally retarded may at times be more harmful than beneficial by depriving the child of the most appropriate education programs. Finally, although the legal requirement of quotas may be sound statistically, it may be detrimental to educational programming.

The press for a redress of grievances and problems of the past has brought education, particularly special education, into the legal arena. In so doing the field may have become more reactive than proactive. The *Tenth Annual Report to Congress* has been reviewed by Gerber and Levine-Donnerstein (1989) among others (Greenburg, 1989; Wyche, 1989). Gerber and Levine-Donnerstein question the document's value—other than as a reporting device—in that it fails to put forward important educational questions. They believe that the report does a good job of reporting statistical changes and trends in special education, but fails to provide a direction for the future.

It is apparent that the enactment of legislation and the results of litigation are not going to provide all the answers. They do play an important role, but, as we have seen, their impact is both positive and negative. Education still faces the problem of developing and providing effective programs for all children. In the important task of pursuing legal and legislative changes we have made many advances, and it would appear that the time is here to come together as a field, pursue those positive consequences of legal and legislative decisions, and identify our agenda for the future. As a field we appear to be in a state of ferment, with many proposals about our purpose and the ways and means to implement educational programs for children with handicaps. We see this as potentially a very positive development in that thoughtful, reasoned, and at times heated dialogue reflects the dynamism of the field. There is a need for an acceptance of our mission of understanding the educational and emotional needs of handicapped people. Rather than being a field which emphasizes only the humanitarian aspect of providing educational programs and services, as important as that is, we should be emphasizing research on learning, thinking, and study of effective programs. The scholarly study of mental retardation has many implications for education as a whole. We need to draw from our experience and reemphasize this important fact as we strive to provide better lives for all handicapped persons.

CORE QUESTIONS

1. What were some of the factors influencing the change in attitude toward those with mental retardation since World War II?
2. What was the importance of *Beattie v. State Board of Education* (1950) and *State Board of Education v. in Re: Petty* (1950) in relation to persons with mental retardation?
3. What is the importance of *Brown v. Board of Education of Topeka* (1954) for providing programs for disabled persons?
4. Review the litigation described in this chapter. Identify and briefly discuss the primary rulings in these cases and their implications for special education.
5. What did Dimond (1973) mean by the "quiet revolution?"
6. Identify and briefly describe the four major purposes of the Education for All Handicapped Children Act.
7. Briefly discuss the importance of the Americans with Disabilities Act of 1990.
8. What are some of the major problems and opportunities facing special education in the years to come?

ROUND TABLE DISCUSSION

Review the chapter and the references regarding the major impact that the legal system and federal legislation have had on the field. Then identify some of the implications they have for both scholarly investigation and the study of effective programming.

REFERENCES

Arreola v. Board of Education, 160-577, Superior Court, Orange County, Cal. (1968).

Battle v. Commonwealth of Pennsylvania, 629 F. 2d 269 (3rd Cir. 1980).

Beattie v. State Board of Education, City of Antigo, 169 Wisc. 231, 172 N.W. 153 (1950).

Brown v. Board of Education of Topeka, 347 U.S. 483, 74 S. Ct. 686 (1954).

Burlington School Committee of the Town of Burlington v. Department of Education of the Commonwealth of Massachusetts, 53 L.W. 4509 (1985).

Covarrubias v. San Diego Unified School District, 7-394, Tex. Rptr. (1971).

Diana v. State Board of Education, C-70-37 R.F.P., (N.D. Cal. 1970, 1973).

Dimond, D. (1973). The constitutional right to education: The quiet revolution. *Hastings Law Journal, 24,* 1087–1127.

Drew, C. J., Hardman, M. L., & Bluhm, H. P. (1977). *Mental Retardation: Social and educational perspectives.* St. Louis: C.V. Mosby.

Fogg v. Board of Education, 82 Atl. 173 (1912).

Georgia Association for Retarded Citizens v. McDaniel, 511 F. Supp. 1263 (N.D. Ga. 1981).

Gerber, M. M., & Levine-Donnerstein, D. (1989). Educating all children: Ten years later. *Exceptional Children, 56,* 17–27.

Goldberg, S. S. (1986). Reimbursing parents for unilateral placements in private special education schools. *Exceptional Children, 52,* 390–394.

Greenburg, D. (1989). *The Tenth Annual Report of Congress:* One more ride on the merry-go-round? *Exceptional Children, 56,* 10–13.

Hendrick Hudson District Board of Education v. Rowley, 73 L.Ed. 2d 690 (1982).

Hobson v. Hansen, 269 F. Supp. 401 (D.D.C. 1967, *aff'd sub norm).*

Irving Independent School District v. Tatro, 104 S. Ct. (1984).

Jackson v. Indiana, 406 U.S. 715 (1972).

Larry P. v. Riles, 343 F. Supp. 1306 (N.D. Cal. 1972), 502 F. 2d 963 (N.D. Cal. 1979).

MacMillan, D. L., Hendrick, I. G., & Watkins, A. V. (1988). Impact of *Diana, Larry P.,* and P. L. 94-142 on minority students. *Exceptional Children, 54,* 426–432.

Mills v. Board of Education of the District of Columbia, 348 F. Supp. 866 (D.D.C. 1972).

Parents in Action on Special Education (PASE) v. Hannon, U.S. District Court, N.D. Ill., No. 74 (3586) (1980).

Pennhurst State School v. Halderman, Civil Action Nos. 79-1404. 79-1489, 79-1414, 79-1415, 79-1489, U.S. Third Circuit Court of Appeals (1981).

Pennsylvania Association for Retarded Children (PARC) v. Commonwealth of Pennsylvania, 343 F. Supp. 279 (E.D. Pa. 1972).

Prasse, D. P. (1988). Legal influence and educational policy in special education. *Exceptional Children, 54,* 302–308.

Smith v. Robinson, 104 S. Ct. 3457 (1984).

Smuck v. Hobson, 408 F. 2d 175 (1969).

Souder v. Brennan, 367 F. Supp. 808 (D.D.C. 1973).

Spangler v. Pasadena Board of Education, 311 F. Supp. 501 (C.D. Cal. 1970).

State Board of Education v. in Re: Petty, 241 Iowa 506, 41 N.W. 672 (1950).

Stewart v. Phillips, 70-1199-F (D. Mass. 1971).

Taylor, R. L. (1990). The *Larry P.* decision a decade later: Problems and future directions. *Mental Retardation, 28* iii–vi.

Wyatt v. Aderholt, 368 F. Supp. 1382, 1383 (M.D. Ala. 1974).

Wyatt v. Stickney, 344 F. Supp. 387, 344 F. Supp. 373 (M.D. Ala. 1972).

Wyche, L. G., Jr. (1989). The *Tenth Annual Report to Congress:* Taking a significant step in the right direction. *Exceptional Children, 56,* 14–16.

Yell, M. L., & Espin, C. A. (1990). The Handicapped Children's Protection Act of 1986: Time to pay the piper? *Exceptional Children, 56,* 396–407.

APPENDIX

International Definitions and Classifications

The material on definition and classification presented in this text pertains largely to terms used in the United States. It is useful for students of mental retardation to be aware of other approaches to this phenomenon and to have an idea of how they compare. This appendix provides an overview of perspectives used in other countries and a comparative picture of how they relate to those used in the United States. Readers should be aware that in many cases limited information is available from other nations. The countries discussed here were selected because of divergent perspectives (from those of the United States) or information available.

SOVIET UNION

Descriptions of scientific philosophies and methods used in one country by scientists of another country are often subject to misinterpretation. Whether because of inadequate information, bias, or some other factor, inaccuracies do occur and often serve to deter communication as well as to promote discord. It is our opinion that this type of difficulty may have been operative as some have interpreted the approach to mental retardation taken by the Soviet Union.

Historically most general perceptions of the Soviet approach to mental retardation have suggested that the only mental subnormality acknowledged there is related to central nervous system damage. Indicative of this perspective is Scheerenberger's (1964) discussion, which stated that in the Soviet Union "mental retardation is dependent upon the occurrence, or suspected occurrence, of brain injury." Although providing more latitude than many interpretations, Scheerenberger's treatment is somewhat out of harmony with the impression conveyed by some of the most notable Russian scientists (Luria, 1963; Vygotsky, 1978). The early perception that mental retardation in the Soviet Union is viewed only as neurologically caused does not fit with recent literature (e.g., Gindis, 1988; Holowinsky, 1990).

Both Gindis (1988) and Holowinsky (1990) discuss mental retardation in the Soviet Union with at least some attention to cultural and sociological elements. Holowinsky notes that "in the Soviet Union, individuals with mental retardation are either described as *umstvenno otstaly*, which is a generic term directly translatable as intellectually backward, or as *oligophrenics*, which implies neurological insult" (1990, p. 211). *Umstvenno otstaly* seems to be similar to U.S. terminology of mild mental retardation for which etiology is often unknown or speculative. Oligophrenia, on the other hand, more often refers to more severe deficits for which an etiology of neurological damage can be confirmed. Russian literature suggests that oligophrenia is studied in terms of heredity (e.g., Portnov, Marincheva, & Gorbachevskaya, 1985). Although the terminology and conceptual approach are different from what most of us are accustomed to, the outcomes are similar to some classification literature that has emerged in the United States. Pevzner (1973) suggests that oligophrenia could be viewed in terms of five types, including those associated with (1) frontal lobe maldevelopment, (2) psychopathological behavior, (3) a variety of visual-motor and auditory defects, (4) perceptual impairments and cortical defects, and (5) diffuse maldevelopment of cortical hemispheres without substantial neurological implications. Although these specific classifications are somewhat different from many categorization approaches, they are similar to the types of classification involved in parts of the AAMR medical categories (Grossman, 1983). Clearly the parameters of classification differ, however.

ARGENTINA

The concept of mental retardation generally used in Argentina involves central nervous system impairment with biological etiology. Environmental influences are usually not thought to be involved in causing mental retardation. The primary classification scheme is a symptom severity model, with measured intelligence as the criterion measure. The term *mentally weak* has been commonly used for generic reference to mental retardation. This term is also used in combination with the category labeled teachables, characterized by an IQ range of 50 to 70. Measured IQs ranging from 25 to 50 are associated with a category termed imbeciles or trainables, and IQs of 0 to 25 fall into the lowest category which is designated idiot or custodial. This approach employs multiple classification parameters in an interactive fashion. Clearly a symptom severity parameter is evident for measured intelligence. Labels seem to mix parameters. The labels teachable, trainable, and custodial seem similar to those used with an educability expectation parameter. Corresponding terms such as imbecile and idiot appear in early literature on mental retardation in the United States, but their use has been discontinued for the most part. These labels were just that, *labels*. They did not serve as adjectives on any symptom severity continuum (such as mild, moderate, and severe). These labels also did not describe syndromes or etiology in any specific sense. The use of such terms in Argentina probably represents a classification scheme in transition.

AUSTRALIA

Symptom severity has also been the general approach to classification of mental retardation in Australia, with an emphasis on a clinical or medical model rather than a social systems or normalization approach (Cocks, 1985). Australians primarily employ the AAMR classification scheme, so both measured intelligence and social adaptability serve as criteria. In line with the AAMR approach, Australians carefully consider developmental history in diagnosis. Categories in terms of IQ ranges are usually from 55 to 79 for mildly handicapped or slow learners; approximately 30 to 50 for moderately handicapped, intellectually limited, or trainable, and below 30 for severely retarded people. This approach basically uses two classification parameters, symptom severity and educability expectation.

Research on mental retardation in Australia mirrors many of the concerns evident in the United States. There is considerable concern about providing services (Parmenter, 1988), mainstreaming issues (Brewer & Smith, 1989), teaching transition skills to severely handicapped adolescents (Horsfall & Maggs, 1986), and parent-related matters (Baxter, 1989a, 1989b). Research is also concerned with autism and mental retardation (Attwood, Frith, & Hermelin, 1988; Roberts, 1989) and prevention of mental retardation (Hayes, Elkins, Fraser, & Bowling, 1986). These are topics that ring very familiar and parallel much of the work being done in the United States.

FRANCE

Interest in mental retardation problems in France has been evident since as early as the 13th century although, as in other countries, viewpoints have varied over the years (Mahendra, 1985). France essentially defines mental retardation with the intelligence test. In one way this is not surprising, since it was Binet's task to identify children with learning problems when he developed his intelligence assessment instrument. Lafon and Chabanier (1966) suggested that there was considerable diversity of approach within the French professional community working in the area of mental retardation. From a research framework they noted two primary philosophical camps: (1) the psychological (psychometrics, social psychology, and sociology as techniques) and (2) the organic (focusing on a search for organic etiology).

Lafon and Chabanier (1966) outlined a classification scheme that seems to represent a synthesis of several frameworks, including clinical, educational, and measurement concerns:

1. A threshold or marginal category, important but particularly difficult to define, including children who are not defective but are unable to attain the average level of their classmates. These are children with a limited intelligence representing the lowest level of normal intelligence. They are characterized by a certain slowness in performing their school work and they have serious difficulties in conceptualization. As a rule they are at the bottom of their class. Their IQ lies between 80 and 100. They are only unadapted within the academic framework, which distorts the current educational structure.
2. Persons with a mild mental deficiency (IQ 65 or above), capable of an independent life and adjustment to a working community.
3. Persons in whom a mild mental deficiency is complicated by associated disorders. These children are not, strictly speaking, intellectually inferior to those of group 2, but the "extra burden" they carry makes their social adjustment more difficult.

4. Moderate mental deficiency (minimum IQ 50). Comparative independence and adaptation to simple work is possible after rehabilitation, but these cases usually require special care throughout their lifetime.
5. Severe mental deficiency (IQ 30 to 50). This "semieducable" group is capable of some social adjustment in a sheltered environment.
6. Profound mental deficiency, "profoundly retarded" group (IQ less than 30). These cases are educable only very slightly or not at all, and their adaptation to group life is doubtful and risky. [p. 225]

GERMANY

There is no German word that translates directly as mental retardation. The term most commonly used in German is *Schwachsinn,* whose closest translation is feeblemindedness or mental deficiency. *Schwachsinn* implies both descriptive and etiological concepts. From a descriptive standpoint the symptom severity parameter uses IQ for the most part. (Three classification levels have often been found in the literature — moronity, imbecility, and idiocy.) Schmidt and Baltes (1971) noted that "there is a strong trend, however, primarily with respect to research efforts, to get away from a global IQ measure to a multivariate consideration of the pattern of intelligence" (p. 351). The German research literature has typically viewed etiology in terms of three categories of mental retardation: (1) psychogenic-reactive, (2) exogenous, and (3) endogenous. Psychogenic-reactive mental retardation includes such causation as psychological disorders (for example, neurosis) and sociocultural deprivation. Exogenous mental retardation represents a category in which there is demonstrated organic brain damage not resulting from heredity. The endogenous category involves no evidence of brain injury or other neurological pathology and searches for a familial history of retardation.

German research in mental retardation reflects a number of themes that are evident in current U.S. literature. There is concern about the social integration of mentally retarded individuals (Kurth & Nissler, 1988), the use of behavior modification (Muthny & Haag, 1987), parental coping behaviors (Hinze, 1988), and issues relating to mentally retarded offenders (Heinz & Mayrl, 1988). German research also reflects work in diagnostic assessment (Doering & Suhrweier, 1988), coping behaviors of retarded adults (Graser, Gillen, & Dahlinger, 1987), and medical research and treatment of syndromes (Fehlow & Tennstedt, 1986). Any of these topics would be likely to appear in the literature on mental retardation in the United States. Another topic that also appears in the German literature is somewhat different, involving what is called "intelligence training" with retarded children (Masendorf & Klauer, 1986, 1987). This research, while seeming to involve the training of intelligence on the surface, appears upon closer examination to reflect basic studies of cognition.

GREAT BRITAIN

From a legal framework there have been two main categories generally used in Great Britain, subnormality and severe subnormality (Simon, 1978). This terminology was a result of the Mental Health Act of 1959 and was legislatively defined in social and developmental terms. Subnormality was defined as follows (Stevens & Heber, 1968):

> A state of arrested or incomplete development of mind (not amounting to severe subnormality) which includes subnormality of intelligence and is of a nature or degree which requires or is susceptible to medical treatment or other special care or training. (p. 6)

Severe subnormality was defined as:

> A state of arrested or incomplete development of mind which includes subnormality of intelligence and is of such a nature or degree that the patient is incapable of living an independent life or of guarding himself against serious exploitation, or will be incapable when of age to do so. (p. 6)

The term *mental subnormality* is employed generically, irrespective of severity. The upper limit is not specifically delineated, but usage seems to focus on an upper measured IQ boundary of 70.

British scientists working in mental retardation occasionally use terminology that predates the 1959 Mental Health Act. Terms such as *mentally defective* and *mentally deficient*, as well as *feebleminded, imbecile,* and *idiot* can be found in the post-1959 British literature and were defined for research and clinical purposes aside from those involved in legislative definitions. Tizard (1965) stated:

> Interesting as the United States classification is, however, the traditional, and for many purposes still the most useful, way of classifying the mentally subnormal behaviourally is according to the severity of *grade* of the defect. Three main grades have been distinguished, namely (1) idiots, (2) imbeciles, and (3) feebleminded persons (British terminology) or morons (United States usage). (p. 8)

(Idiot and imbecile groups were frequently termed low-grade defectives, whereas the feebleminded or moron individuals were referred to as high-grade defectives.) Tizard was apparently combining the United States terminology of that time with another of a much earlier vintage, since symptom severity was being employed and the terminology he cited had been out of use for some time. The British terminology was linked to IQ level, with general ranges of 50 to 70 for the feebleminded, 20 to 50 for the imbecile, and below 20 for the idiot classification. While terminology remains substantially different in Great Britain, recent literature reflects some concerns similar to those found in the United States, for example, the rights of those with mental retardation (Hudson, 1988), neighborhood attitudes regarding group homes (Pittock & Potts, 1988), and integration issues (Danby & Cullen, 1988). Some of these concerns, such as educational mainstreaming, represent somewhat different conceptual frameworks because of fundamental differences in the social systems of the United States and Great Britain (Danby & Cullen, 1988).

SCANDINAVIA

Work with mentally retarded individuals in Scandinavian countries has had a tremendous impact on efforts in the United States during the past two decades. This influence has emerged more in terms of philosophy than definition or classification. Definition and classification issues in Scandinavia have been much less important than issues of treatment of mentally retarded people. One of the most important current concepts related to mental retardation is normalization, which refers to an existence that is as close to mainstream society as possible. The principle of normalization came from Scandinavia and was articulated in print by both Danish and Swedish professionals (Bank-Mikkelsen, 1969; Nirje, 1969). This notion has been an important contribution in mental retardation internationally, although little research on the principle has been conducted outside Scandinavia, and it has been subject to frequent misconceptions and resistance in some areas (Anstey & Gaskin, 1985; Nirje, 1985; Perrin & Nirje, 1985). Wolfensberger (1972) stated that "until about 1969, the term 'normalization' had never been heard by most workers in human service areas. Today, it is a captivating watchword standing for a whole new ideology of human management" (p. 27).

COMMENTS

As discussed earlier, several classification frameworks are used in the United States. The AAMR manual of terminology includes three parameters in an attempt to meet the diverse needs of professionals working in the field of mental retardation. The etiological classification scheme has been used by medical personnel and others primarily involved in diagnosis and treatment of clinical forms of retardation. The adaptive behavior and measured intelligence parameters are ostensibly used in combination for a variety of service purposes. Measured intelligence in the AAMR scheme is essentially a symptom severity approach similar to the educational classification of educable, trainable, and custodial (SMH) mental retardation. Although the educational approach involves statements of expected achievement, the primary classificatory technique is measured intelligence.

The variety of international approaches to mental retardation is highly apparent even from the cursory overview given here. Certain countries are rather firmly settled into a particular philosophical framework and are pushing forward in efforts aimed at progress within that framework. Others show much more variation—occasionally confusion—with respect to both definition and classification. Certain factors seem common to all. A developmental emphasis is present in the definition and classification systems of several countries, even those with highly divergent philosophical positions (the U.S.S.R., Great Britain, France). Similarly, the social adaptation factor is present as at least a partial international concern (for example, in the United States, Great Britain, France). Perhaps the most common factor cutting across international borders is that of symptom severity in terms of measured intelligence.

REFERENCES

Anstey, T. J., & Gaskin, M. (1985). Service providers' understanding of the concept of normalizaton. *Australia and New Zealand Journal of Developmental Disabilities, 11*, 91–95.

Attwood, A., Frith, U., & Hermelin, B. (1988). The understanding and use of interpersonal gestures by autistic and Down's syndrome children. *Journal of Autism and Developmental Disorders, 18*, 241–257.

Bank-Mikkelsen, N. E. (1969). A metropolitan area in Denmark: Copenhagen. In R. Kugel & W. Wolfensberger (Eds.), *Changing patterns in residential services for the mentally retarded* (pp. 227–254). Washington, DC: President's Committee on Mental Retardation.

Baxter, C. (1989a). Investigating stigma as stress in social interactions of parents. *Journal of Mental Deficiency Research, 33*, 455–466.

Baxter, C. (1989b). Parent-perceived attitudes of professionals: Implications for service providers. *Disability, Handicap, and Society, 4*, 259–269.

Brewer N., & Smith, J. M. (1989). Social acceptance of mentally retarded children in regular schools in relation to years mainstreamed. *Psychological Reports, 64*, 375–380.

Cocks, E. (1985). Roadblocks to appropriate services for persons with an intellectual disability in Australia. *Australia and New Zealand Journal of Developmental Disabilities, 11*, 75–82.

Danby, J., & Cullen, C. (1988). Integration and mainstreaming: A review of the efficacy of mainstreaming and integration for mentally handicapped pupils. *Educational Psychology, 8*, 177–195.

Doering, H., & Suhrweier, H. (1988). Results of a test of motor development conducted as a part of special education school admissions procedure. *Psychologie für die Praxis, 6*, 39–48.

Fehlow, P., & Tennstedt, A. (1986). Neurocutaneous syndrome with ventricular tumor. *Psychiatrie, Neurologie und medizinische Psychologie, 38*, 606–611.

Gindis, B. (1988). Children with mental retardation in the Soviet Union. *Mental Retardation, 26*, 381–384.

Graser, H., Gillen, K., & Dahlinger, K. (1987). Styles of coping with handicap in mentally retarded adults. *International Journal of Rehabilitation Research, 10*, 127–138.

Grossman, H. J. (1983). *Classification in mental retardation*. Washington, DC: American Association on Mental Deficiency.

Hayes, A., Elkins, J., Fraser, D., & Bowling, F. (1986). Galactosaemia: A preventable form of mental retardation. *Australia and New Zealand Journal of Developmental Disabilities, 12*, 235–241.

Heinz, G., & Mayrl, J. (1988). Treatment of mentally ill offenders in a day hospital: A new rehabilitation method. *Nervenarzt, 59*, 350–355.

Hinze, D. (1988). Mothers and fathers of handicapped children. *Frühforderung Interdisziplinar, 7*, 97–105.

Holowinsky, I. Z. (1990). Mental retardation research in the Soviet Union. *Mental Retardation, 28*, 211–218.

Horsfall, D., & Maggs, A. (1986). Cooking skills instruction with severely multiply handicapped adolescents. *Australia and New Zealand Journal of Developmental Disabilities, 12*, 177–186.

Hudson, B. (1988). Do people with a mental handicap have rights? *Disability, Handicap and Society, 3*, 227–237.

Kurth, E., & Nissler, R. (1988). Attitudes toward special education students and aspects of social integration in young adulthood: Studies in a rural district. *Psychiatrie, Neurologie und medizinische Psychologie, 40*, 102–109.

Lafon, R., & Chabanier, J. (1966). Research on mental deficiency during the last decade in France. In N. R. Ellis (Ed.), *International review of research in mental retardation* (Vol. 2, pp. 253–277). New York: Academic.

Luria, A. R. (1963). Psychological studies of mental deficiency in the Soviet Union. In N. R. Ellis (Ed.), *Handbook of mental deficiency: Psychological theory and research* (pp. 353–387). New York: McGraw-Hill.

Mahendra, B. (1985). Subnormality revisited in early 19th century France. *Journal of Mental Deficiency Research, 29*, 391–401.

Masendorf, F., & Klauer, K. J. (1986). Equality and difference as cognitive categories: An experimental study involving intelligence training of mentally retarded children. *Zeitschrift für Entwicklungspsychologie und pädagogische Psychologie, 18*, 46–55.

Masendorf, F., & Klauer, K. J. (1987). Intelligence training with retarded children: A cognitive process-oriented approach. *Psychologie in Erziehung und Unterricht, 34*, 14–19.

Muthny, F. A., & Haag, G. (1987). Behavior modificaton and therapy in rehabilitation. *International Journal of Rehabilitation Research, 10*, 195–200.

Nirje, B. (1969). The normalization principle and its human management implications. In R. Kugel & W. Wolfensberger (Eds.), *Changing patterns in residential services for the mentally retarded* (pp. 179–195). Washington, DC: President's Committee on Mental Retardation.

Nirje, B. (1985). The basis and logic of the normalization principle. *Australia and New Zealand Journal of Developmental Disabilities, 11*, 65–68.

Parmenter, T. R. (1988). An analysis of Australian mental health services for people with mental retardation. *Australia and New Zealand Journal of Developmental Disabilities, 14*, 9–13.

Perrin, B., & Nirje, B. (1985). Setting the record straight: A critique of some frequent misconceptions of the normalization principle. *Australia and New Zealand Journal of Developmental Disabilities, 11*, 69–74.

Pevzner, M. S. (Ed.). (1973). *Clinical-genetic research of oligophrenia.* Moscow: Pedagogika.

Pittock, F., & Potts, M. (1988). Neighbourhood attitudes to people with a mental handicap: A comparative study. *British Journal of Mental Subnormality, 34*, 35–46.

Portnov, V. A., Marincheva, G. S., & Gorbachevskaya, N. L. (1985). Familial craniometaphyseal dysplasia in combination with oligophrenia. *Zhurnal Nevropatologii i Psikhiatrii, 85*, 404–409.

Roberts, J. M. (1989). Echolalia and comprehension in autistic children. *Journal of Autism and Developmental Disorders, 19*, 271–281.

Scheerenberger, R. C. (1964). Mental retardation: Definition, classification, and prevalence. *Mental Retardation Abstracts, 1*, 432–441.

Schmidt, L. R., & Baltes, P. B. (1971). German theory and research on mental retardation: Emphasis on structure. In N. R. Ellis (Ed.), *International review of research in mental retardation* (Vol. 5, pp. 349–392). New York: Academic.

Simon, G. B. (1978). Services in the United Kingdom. In J. Wortis (Ed.), *Mental retardation and developmental disabilities* (Vol. 10, pp. 242–258). New York: Brunner/Mazel.

Stevens, H. A., & Heber, R. (1968). An international review of developments in mental retardation. *Mental Retardation, 6*, 4–23.

Tizard, J. (1965). Introduction. In A. M. Clarke & A. D. B. Clarke (Eds.), *Mental deficiency: The changing outlook* (rev. ed., pp. 3–22). New York: Free Press.

Vygotsky, L. S. (1978). *Mind in society: The development of higher psychological process.* Cambridge: Harvard University Press.

Wolfensberger, W. (1972). *The principle of normalization in human services.* Toronto National Institute on Mental Retardation.

LEGAL CASE CITATION INDEX

Italics indicate that an item is cited in the references.

AUTHOR INDEX

SUBJECT INDEX

465